THE COMMUNITY INTERPRETER®

An International Textbook

Marjory A. Bancroft, MA, Sofía García-Beyaert, MA, Katharine Allen, MA,
Giovanna Carriero-Contreras, Denis Socarrás-Estrada, MA

Published by Culture & Language Press,
a division of Cross-Cultural Communications, LLC.

For further information, contact the publisher.

Culture & Language Press
10015 Old Columbia Road, Suite B-215
Columbia, MD 21046
410-312-5599

www.cultureandlanguage.net
clp@cultureandlanguage.net

Suggested citation

To refer to the textbook as a whole please use the following format:
Bancroft, M.A., García-Beyaert, S., Allen, K., Carriero-Contreras, G., & Socarrás-Estrada, D. (2015). The Community Interpreter®: An International Textbook. (M. A. Bancroft, Ed.). Columbia, Maryland: Culture & Language Press.

When citing information from one of the chapters, please use the following format:
[Chapter author(s)]. (2015). [Chapter title]. In M. A. Bancroft (Ed.), The Community Interpreter®: An International Textbook (pp. [page range]). Columbia, Maryland: Culture & Language Press.

When citing information from the Ethics and Standards document, please use the following format:
García-Beyaert, S., Bancroft, M.A., Allen, K., Carriero-Contreras, G., & Socarrás-Estrada, D. (2015). Ethics and Standards for The Community Interpreter®: An International Training Tool. Columbia, Maryland: Culture & Language Press. Online access: www.thecommunityinterpreter.com

Dedication

For community interpreters, who give voice, dignity and humanity to so many individuals around the world.

To our families, who have supported us during our work—even when they missed us.

The Community Interpreter®
An International Textbook

Contents

PREFACE

How to use this textbook

Community interpreting is a young profession. In many countries around the world, it has developed at high speed. Today, there is an urgent need for clear guidance for trainers and instructors of community interpreters, and for interpreters themselves, who may lack access to quality training.

This textbook represents the first publication of its kind: a textbook designed for community interpreters who practice in different countries around the world. The book can be used:

- As a training manual to guide short programs.
- As a textbook for use in universities, colleges and other institutions of higher education.
- For self study.
- To support the development or delivery of online training programs for interpreters.

Together with a companion workbook, entitled *The Community Interpreter®: An International Workbook of Activities and Role Plays,* this textbook can be used to create and deliver an entry-level program for community interpreters in almost any country.

Each country, of course, has diverse professional practices: one textbook cannot claim to address the unique professional work environment of community interpreters in all nations. This book does, however, purport to tackle many of the most persistent challenges in the field and proposes practical, easy-to-implement strategies based on the highest professional standards. It also guides interpreters on how to develop problem-solving skills and use decision-making tools that they can apply almost anywhere.

Thus, the authors hope that interpreters and trainers in the field will find valuable tools, models, strategies, techniques and decision-making guidance in this book that will help them adapt its content to their local context. Every situation in community interpreting is unique. The best solution to each challenge will also be unique. This book is intended to focus on solutions that make sense in the local context while supporting, at each stage, the right of the participants in the interpreted encounter to have control of, and take responsibility for, their own communication, a concept referred to here as "communicative autonomy," which is a fundamental principle for this textbook.

A special note about legal interpreting and this textbook

Community interpreting supports the access of immigrants and refugees, indigenous populations and the Deaf and hard of hearing to basic and often vital community services. As a profession, it includes sub-specializations such as medical, educational, social services and faith-based interpreting. Whether or not legal interpreting is considered to be part of community interpreting is a controversial question.

In practice, both within and across countries, it is often unclear whether legal interpreting should be considered part of community interpreting. For example, in the United States legal interpreters base their conduct on ethics, standards, protocols, requirements, best practices and professional cultures that are quite different from those for community interpreters. Yet in Canada, legal interpreters are expected to follow the same national standards of practice for community interpreters that medical and social services interpreters follow (HIN, 2007).

As a result, this book addresses all the specializations of community interpreting listed above, including legal interpreting, with the caveat that legal interpreting is a special case where interpreters must first and always follow any accepted standards for legal or court interpreters that exist in their areas of practice.

Community interpreting ethics

Although young, this profession has grown at such speed that many questions have arisen about what constitutes appropriate conduct by community interpreters in the field. No international code of ethics yet exists for community interpreters. Thus, the five authors of this textbook have taken it upon themselves to craft a document listing what they consider to be key community interpreting ethics and standards of practice for training purposes. This document precedes the first chapter of the book, and the rest of the textbook builds on that foundation.

As a profession, community interpreting does not yet exist in many countries. Often, family members, friends and even children are pulled in to interpret whether in hospitals, government agencies, police stations, shelters for abused women or other services—even courtrooms. It will likely be some time before the world comes to understand the urgent need to rely on *professional community interpreters* for any area of community services where language barriers arise. This textbook, with the ethics and standards document it is based on, is one paving stone on the road to professionalization for the field at large.

How to contact the authors

The five authors of this book found it an extraordinary adventure to write this book. Although each chapter has a listed author or authors, all of us collaborated intensively as co-creators and co-editors. To a considerable degree, this textbook is a joint effort. The conceptual journey it entailed, unparalleled in our professional experience, surpassed anything imagined at the inception of the project.

We hope this textbook is of practical use for interpreters and those who educate, employ and support them. The authors remain available for questions, concerns or comments. Please call us, email us or write to us care of the publisher at:

Culture & Language Press
10015 Old Columbia Road, Suite B-215
Columbia, Maryland 21046
USA
clp@cultureandlanguage.net
+1 410-312-5599

ACKNOWLEDGMENTS

ACKNOWLEDGMENTS

We cannot possibly thank everyone who contributed to the growth and development of *The Community Interpreter*®. This textbook is only the visible artifact of a groundbreaking program. *We thank the many who came before us and those who showed us the path ahead.*

Pat Hatch is a pillar of support for interpreters and language access. For decades, she has blazed a trail of advocacy across the mid-Atlantic. Years ago at the Maryland Office of Refugees and Asylees, she was instrumental in planning the interpreter training project that inspired the creation of this program. Beyond a doubt, without Pat this book would not exist.

Our deep thanks, too, to Cynthia Roat, author of *Bridging the Gap: A Basic Training for Medical Interpreters* and an inspirational leader in the field.

Next, the groundbreaking work of the National Council on Interpreting in Health Care (NCIHC) built a solid foundation for not only medical but all community interpreting in the United States. In addition, the International Medical Interpreters Association (IMIA) has developed a wealth of materials that informed this book. InterpretAmerica helped to lay national and international groundwork for interpreting as a profession and raised the profile of community interpreting in the process; Professor Barry Olsen, co-president of InterpretAmerica, also made valuable contributions to Chapter 4, as did Jonathan Levy.

Thanks are also due to others whose work or support contributed to the many previous editions of *The Community Interpreter*® when it was a training manual. These individuals include Irfana Anwar, Zarita Araujo-Lane, Shiva Bidar-Sielaff, Pamela Bohrer Brown, Jean Bruggeman, Eric Candle, Rosa Carrillo, Paul Cushing, Hank Dallman, Esther Diaz, Bruce Downing, Lois Feuerle, Julia Puebla Fortier, Isabel Framer, Emily Frelick, Michelle Gallagher, Nora Goodfriend-Koven, Nataly Kelly, Dr. Robert Like, Ellen Little, Holly Mikkelson, Laura Pfeifer, James Plunkett, Barbara Rayes, Susan London Russell, Kinza Schuyler, Ana Stover and Mara Youdelman.

The authors would like to thank the kind contributions of colleagues who provided helpful feedback on previous versions of the "ethics and standards" document that appears at the beginning of this textbook, with special gratitude to Beverly Treumann, Julie Boéri, Maria Rosaria Buri, Ann Corsellis, Erik Hertog, and Stephen Lank.

To be honest, the five authors also want to thank one another: for everyone's patience and willingness to postpone our production schedule for family emergencies, and for combining love, honesty, openness and curmudgeonliness at all the right times. We are not perfect—which made the process even better. We held tight as a team despite inevitable disagreements and have not fractured but grown closer, like our own special family. What a gift!

Finally, our warmest thanks to the community interpreters around the world whose work inspired us. To you we dedicate the book for your professionalism, your passion and your joy in giving. The future of the field belongs to you.

ABOUT THE AUTHORS

Marjory A. Bancroft, MA

Marjory Bancroft is an international leader in community interpreting. A native of Canada residing in the United States, she has lived in eight countries and studied seven languages. Language and culture are the tapestry of her life.

Marjory holds a bachelor's degree in French linguistics and a master's degree in linguistics from Université Laval in Quebec City (the oldest francophone university in North America) and advanced language certificates from universities in Spain, Germany, and Jordan. In addition to her work interpreting and translating in Canada and the United States, she has taught translation, English and French in several countries: for immigrant schools in Montreal, Universitá Laval, Yarmouk University in Jordan, continuing education programs, public schools and the Canadian Embassy in Washington, District of Columbia (DC). For three years she managed a nonprofit language bank of 200 interpreters and translators.

In 2001 she founded Cross-Cultural Communications (CCC), the only national training agency for community interpreting and cultural competence. CCC offers *The Community Interpreter*®, the leading international program in community interpreting. CCC has 122 licensed trainers in 28 U.S. states, Washington, DC, and six other countries. Marjory is also the executive director of The Voice of Love, a national nonprofit agency that supports interpreting for survivors of torture, war trauma and sexual violence.

The author of numerous publications and training curricula, Marjory speaks and keynotes widely at conferences across the United States and abroad. A past board member of the National Council on Interpreting in Health Care, she sits on international committees and is the world project leader for a new international standard on requirements for interpreting services for the International Organization for Standardization (ISO).

Sofía García-Beyaert, MA

Sofía García-Beyaert is a practicing interpreter and a researcher in the field of public policy and cross-linguistic communication. Born to a Belgian mother and a Spanish father, Sofía grew up speaking Spanish and French and exposed to a variety of cultural subtleties. She blames such exposure for her insatiable interest in multiculturalism.

As a participant in an international triple qualification program, Sofía graduated with honors with a bachelor's degree in applied languages and a focus in legal and economic translation from the following institutions: Universidad de Granada (Spain), Université de Provence Aix-Marseille I (France) and Northumbria University (United Kingdom). At the Universidad de Granada, Sofía took further specialized training in conference interpreting in 2004–2005. She also holds a master's degree in social and political science from the Universitat Pompeu Fabra (Barcelona, Spain), 2005.

Since 2010, she has been an active member of the government-recognized research group of MIRAS (*Mediació i Interpretació: Recerca en l'Àmbit Social*), which belongs to the Universitat Autònoma de Barcelona (UAB), and received formal recognition for distinction in scientific quality from the Catalonian government. She has taught postgraduate and master's classes in community interpreting, and has developed curricula for such programs at the School of Translation and Interpreting Studies of the same university. The author of several academic publications, she has presented her work at international conferences. Sofía is currently completing her doctoral dissertation on the institutionalization of community interpreting at the UAB Institute of Government and Public Policy.

Katharine Allen, MA

Katharine Allen is the co-president of InterpretAmerica, which hosts annual international summits on interpreting and provides an international forum for advances in the field. She is also owner of Chatterbox, LLC. A native of the United States, she lives in California.

Katharine holds a bachelor's degree in community development from Brown University and a master's degree in translation and interpretation (MATI) from the Monterey Institute of International Studies (now the Middlebury Institute of International Studies, MIIS, at Monterey). A practicing interpreter and translator, she provides interpreter training, curriculum development and language access consulting services. She is an instructor for the Glendon College Masters of Conference Interpreting Program at York University, Toronto.

She has also taught medical interpreting train-the-facilitator workshops at MIIS and for professional interpreting associations. She is a co-developer of medical interpreting curricula for large healthcare organizations, programs for victim services interpreters, indigenous interpreters and military programs targeting global health and disaster relief efforts. Katharine publishes in the field and speaks and keynotes across the United States and internationally. She served on the board of the California Healthcare Interpreting Association from 2002 through 2009, including a two-year term as president.

Giovanna Carriero-Contreras

Giovanna Carriero-Contreras owns and directs Cesco Linguistic Services, a language company in Colorado. A native of Italy, she resides in the United States.

Giovanna graduated from the Instituto Orientale, Naples, Italy, in modern foreign languages and literature in 1992, and from the School of Translation and Interpretation in Geneva in 1997. A year later she began her career in the United States as an Italian translator with a Colorado-based company. Since then she has worked as translator, interpreter, tester and senior project manager, and has developed expertise in workers' compensation interpreting.

In 2004 Giovanna launched Cesco. An active interpreter and trainer, she has also developed innovative approaches to teaching interpreting modes and skills, note-taking and interpreting for workers' compensation. She served three years as co-chair of the board of the Colorado Association of Professional Interpreters. Currently she is a member of the U.S. delegation to the International Organization for Standardization (ISO) for interpreting standards. She is the mother of two sons in addition to three daughters from the Democratic Republic of Congo.

Denis Socarrás-Estrada, MA

Denis Socarrás-Estrada is a practicing conference and community interpreter who spent seven years as an instructor for the University of Alcalá master's program in public services (community) interpreting, where he also supervised many master's theses. He has also taught English language and literature in various institutions. A native of Cuba who spent a decade in Spain, he now resides in the United States.

Denis holds a bachelor's degree in teaching English as a foreign language from Cuba and a master's degree in intercultural communication, interpreting and translation in public services from Spain. He is currently completing a doctorate in modern languages, literature and translation at the University of Alcalá, Madrid, Spain. He has studied in five countries, and his research interest is in interpreting studies and training methodology for public services interpreting.

Denis is a member of the European Society for Translation Studies (EST) and the *Formación e Investigación en Interpretación y Traducción en los Servicios Públicos* (FITISPOS) group. An active educator and trainer of interpreters, he is concerned with research in the didactics of interpreter training, interpreter cognitive and emotional processes and interpreter performance. Denis publishes in the field and speaks widely at conferences.

GLOSSARY

Note

Unless otherwise stated, the definitions in this glossary were developed by the authors to provide clarity regarding how the terms are used within this textbook.

No definitions are included for the terms L1, L2 and L3 (first, second or third language, respectively) or A, B and C languages. While *A language* typically refers to one's native or most-proficient language, *B language* to one's second-most proficient language and *C language* to a language that is fairly well understood but not necessarily spoken fluently by an individual, there is no clear or consistent international usage of these terms.

Advocacy

Taking action or speaking up on behalf of a service user whose safety, health, well-being or human dignity is at risk, with the purpose of preventing harm.

Bias

A personal attitude or perspective that is not impartial and tends to favor one viewpoint or social group over another.

Note: Bias is often unconscious.

Bidirectional

Interpreting performed back and forth between one language and another, in either direction.

Bilingual

Possessing the ability to speak two languages at a defined level of fluency.

Note: How someone is determined to be fluent in two languages varies among and within geographic regions and interpreting specializations.

Chuchotage

A variation of simultaneous interpreting performed in a low voice (not whispering) for a public speaker and a small number of listeners.

Note: The word *chuchotage* is derived from the French *chuchoter,* which means "to whisper." This type of simultaneous interpreting is also known as whispered simultaneous (even though it is not whispered) or *susurrada* in Spanish.

Code of ethics

A set of directives that specifies the requirements or expectations intended to guide the conduct of practitioners of a profession.

Communicative autonomy

The capacity of each party in an encounter to be responsible for and in control of his or her own communication.

Note: This textbook takes as its most fundamental premise that community interpreting supports, or should support, the communicative autonomy of end users. Communicative autonomy also provides the underlying conceptual framework that shapes both the code of ethics and standards that appears prior to the first chapter and the textbook as a whole.

Community interpreter

A bilingual or multilingual individual who is deemed professionally qualified to interpret in community service settings.

Examples: A staff interpreter, freelance interpreter or bilingual staff member who has been trained to interpret and assessed for language proficiency and/or interpreting skills.

Community interpreting

A specialization of interpreting that facilitates access to community services for individuals who do not speak the language of service.

Consecutive mode (consecutive interpreting)

Understanding and reformulating a message in another language after the speaker or signer pauses.

Faith-based interpreting

Interpreting for a religious congregation, its leaders or its members as they carry out their religious practices and work.

Freelance interpreter

An interpreter who is not acting as an employee but as a self-employed independent contractor for interpreting assignments.

Note: Also known as a **contract interpreter** or **self-employed interpreter**. A freelance interpreter is an interpreting service provider (ISP), but an ISP can also be a multinational language company. Thus, all freelance interpreters are technically ISPs, but not all ISPs are freelance interpreters.

Healthcare interpreting

Interpreting for patients, their families and service providers in healthcare.

Note: Also known as medical interpreting.

Intercultural communication

The ability to communicate effectively across cultural differences.

Intercultural mediators

Individuals, who are usually bilingual and bicultural, tasked with assisting people of different cultural backgrounds to better understand each other's perspectives, typically with the goal of supporting effective delivery of community services.

Note: Also known as cultural mediators, intercultural mediators may or may not interpret, and may or may not receive professional training in (inter)cultural mediation and/or interpreting. This profession is most common in certain parts of Europe but also exists in other countries.

Interpreting

Rendering a spoken or signed message into another spoken or signed language, preserving the register and meaning of the source language content.

Note: This definition is derived from ISO, 2014, p. 1.

Interpreting service provider (ISP)

A person or entity that provides interpreting services.

Note: An ISP could be a freelance interpreter, a professional nonprofit interpreting service, a hospital department that provides interpreters, a small or large language company, a military service or defense contractor or a huge international corporation.

Intervening

The act of intervening: i.e., interrupting, an interpreted session.

Language access law

Legislation that requires or stipulates that the impact of discrimination in access to public services be reduced through the provision of competent language assistance.

Note: The term "language access law" is used primarily in the United States.

Language assistant

A person, such as a family member, friend or volunteer, who is asked to interpret or translate but has no professional qualifications in interpreting or translation.

Language law

Legislation that addresses the official use of language.

Language policy

Any official legislation, court decision or government policy that addresses the formal or legal use of one or more languages.

Note: Language policy can apply to a region, nation, state/province or locality. It can regulate or guide numerous activities, such as which languages must be taught in public schools.

Language service provider (LSP)

A person or entity that provides translation, interpreting, localization, language and/or any other language-related services.

Legal interpreting

Interpreting related to legal processes and proceedings, including but not limited to lawyer-client representation, prosecutor-victim/witness interviews, and law enforcement communications. (Framer, Bancroft, Feuerle, & Bruggeman, 2010, p. xi)

Mediation/strategic mediation

Any act or utterance of the interpreter that goes beyond interpreting and is intended to remove a barrier to communication or facilitate a service user's access to the service.

Note: The term *mediation* is a widely used term with many meanings, some of which are relevant for community interpreting. This term is therefore discussed in detail in Chapter 5, Section 5.2, of this textbook

Medical interpreting

Interpreting for patients, their families and service providers in healthcare.

Note: Also known as healthcare interpreting.

Mode

A technique for the delivery of interpreting.

Note: The three widely accepted modes are consecutive interpreting, simultaneous interpreting and sight translation.

Note-taking

A language-neutral, symbols-based, visual and spatial method used in consecutive interpreting to capture meaning using the minimum number of pen strokes possible.

Relay interpreting

Interpreting between two languages by means of a third language.[1]

Note 1: This definition is derived and adapted from a definition put out by the European Commission Directorate General for Interpreting

Note 2: At least two interpreters are necessary for relay interpreting. One interpreter relays the message into a shared language, while the second interpreter relays that message from the shared language into the third language. Relay interpreting can be unidirectional or bidirectional.

Remote interpreting

Interpreting that involves at least one interpreter who is not physically present with other parties to the session and who is interpreting using a remote (distant) platform.

Note: Remote interpreting usually involves interpreting via telephone or video. Sometimes all participants to the encounter are located in different places.

Service provider

A person providing a community service.

Examples: A doctor, teacher, social worker, lawyer or psychologist.

Service user

Someone who seeks or needs access to a community service.

Note: This textbook addresses and refers only to service users who do not speak the language of service, in particular migrants, Deaf consumers and indigenous residents.

Sight translation

Oral rendering of the meaning of a written text.

Simultaneous mode (simultaneous interpreting)

Understanding and reformulating a message in another language while the speaker or signer is still speaking.

Source language

The language from which one interprets.

[1] See http://ec.europa.eu/dgs/scic/what-is-conference-interpreting/relay/index_en.htm.

Speaker

Someone who speaks or signs in any language.

Standards of practice

A set of formal guidelines that offer practitioners of a profession clear strategies and courses of action to support professional conduct.

Stereotypes

Overgeneralizations about a social group that allow for no, or few, exceptions.

Summarization

Reformulating the primary content of a message in a shorter form.

Note: Summarization can be performed in the same language or in another language. For interpreters, summarization is not a widely accepted practice; it is usually considered a last resort.

Target language

The language into which one interprets.

Unidirectional

Interpreting from only one source language into one target language.

Unobtrusive

The quality of not drawing attention to oneself or one's presence.

Whispered simultaneous

See *Chuchotage.*

ETHICS AND STANDARDS for The Community Interpreter®
An International Training Tool

by Sofía García-Beyaert, Marjory A. Bancroft, Katharine Allen, Giovanna Carriero-Contreras, Denis Socarrás-Estrada

TABLE OF CONTENTS

Preface

Statement of Purpose

The purpose of this document is to support the education and training of community interpreters. It does so by providing structured and detailed guidelines for professional conduct in accordance with principles and values that underlie widely accepted practice in the field. The authors also wrote *The Community Interpreter®: An International Textbook,* in which this document serves as a training tool.

The contents of this document are based on a critical distillation and selection of principles and standards included in codes of ethics for interpreters around the world. The document also represents a contribution to the further evolution of professional practice. It tackles issues that have proven controversial or unclear and proposes new guiding concepts.

The concept of *communicative autonomy* is introduced in this document as a fundamental principle. Communicative autonomy is defined here as the capacity of each party in an encounter to be responsible for and in control of his or her own communication.

In modern medicine, "First do no harm" is a precept that guides its practitioners. The authors of this document propose that supporting communicative autonomy is a comparable fundamental precept that should underlie every aspect of the development and practice of community interpreting.

Definition of Community Interpreting

Community interpreting is defined here as interpreting that facilitates access to community services. Depending on how community services are provided from country to country, they can be delivered by publicly funded organizations, for-profit entities, nonprofit organizations or any combination of the three. Typical examples of community interpreting include medical, mental health, educational, social services and faith-based interpreting. Community interpreting may also encompass some of the interpreting conducted in conflict and disaster zones and interpreting for refugees.

Community interpreting may involve interviews or meetings. It can involve consecutive or simultaneous interpreting and/or sight translation. It might be performed for two speakers, several speakers or groups. Finally, community interpreting can take place during face-to-face encounters, or—increasingly—remotely (with the aid of technology—using telephonic, video and Voice over Internet Protocol platforms).

Community interpreting as a profession has many other names around the world, including public service interpreting, dialogue interpreting and liaison interpreting. Once an unregulated and informal activity performed primarily by untrained individuals (volunteers, family members, friends or untrained bilingual staff), community interpreting is rapidly professionalizing in many parts of the world.

Note: In this document, the term *service provider* refers to anyone involved in providing a community service. The term *service user* refers to the consumer who seeks to apply for or receive that service. While it is true that interpreters, too, are service providers, for clarity they are referred to in this document exclusively as *interpreters*.

Conceptual Framework and Structure

The communicative autonomy of service users and service providers is identified in this document as a fundamental principle for the profession of community interpreting. Communicative autonomy also provides the underlying conceptual framework that shapes this document. Either in a direct or an indirect way, every ethical principle, standard of practice and example in the document supports communicative autonomy.

Communicative autonomy

When service users and service providers encounter language barriers, they may need professional assistance to communicate. Yet having an intermediary—the interpreter—inserted into the process of giving and receiving messages has an inescapable impact on the communicative process. The professional community interpreter is trained to use a variety of strategies to keep that impact to a minimum, such as strategic positioning, the use of direct speech (first person), choosing which interpreting mode to use, refraining from side conversations and so on. These strategies help both service users and providers to be responsible for their own dialogue, despite the interpreter's presence. They support communicative autonomy.

> **DEFINITION**
>
> **Communicative autonomy**
>
> The capacity of each party in an encounter to be responsible for and in control of his or her own communication.

The ethics and standards outlined in this document align with these strategies and provide a framework that can help the interpreter strive for an unobtrusive presence. In this way, the parties can stay focused on communicating directly with each other and not with the interpreter.

Document structure

This document includes the *Community Interpreter's Pledge*, eight ethical principles, forty-one standards of practice and eighty-two examples.

The pledge serves a double purpose: it is a statement of commitment for the interpreter and serves as a summary of the document's key content. As a mnemonic tool, it may help interpreters grasp the essence of the document and the interconnection among its key ethical principles.

Each ethical principle is supported by several standards of practice. Each standard of practice provides specific guidance about how to observe and adhere to the ethical principles. Each standard is illustrated by examples of how Ana and Zere, two fictional interpreters, show ethical conduct in response to real-life situations by applying relevant standards. The solutions that Ana and Zere choose in each case are not the only acceptable solutions. Rather, they offer suggestions for practice that closely align with the principles and standards of this document.

Taken as a whole, the document provides both overarching guidelines and concrete examples. This format is intended to offer practical guidance for community interpreters around the world who encounter challenging situations and seek guidance about a reasonable course of action.

Special Considerations

Legal interpreting

The interpreting profession in some countries or regions views legal interpreting as falling under the umbrella of community interpreting, while in other countries legal interpreting (or at least court interpreting) is considered a separate specialization. In many countries, there is little discussion or consensus on the matter.

The reality today around the world is that community interpreters who lack specialized training in legal or court interpreting frequently work in legal settings (both in and outside the courtroom). This document therefore includes examples of community interpreters who work in legal settings to reflect that reality.

It should be noted, however, that the requirements for legal interpreting vary from country to country and may be derived from legislation, case law, statutes and/or other rules and requirements based in law that take precedence over any interpreting ethics and standards created by professional bodies or other organizations. Community interpreters who work in legal settings should familiarize themselves with the legal interpreting ethics of the regions where they practice and the settings where those specialized requirements may apply.

Summarization

The topic of summarization has been poorly examined in community interpreting and lacks established protocols and techniques. Many training programs forbid summarization and do not teach how to perform it. Yet most community interpreters—including highly qualified professionals—have to summarize in certain situations, such as fast-paced emergencies or when speakers are incoherent due to mental illness, dementia or the influence of drugs or alcohol.

This document accepts summarization as a professional technique, one that should be applied only when absolutely necessary. Summarization is therefore referred to in relevant standards.

Technology and ethical practice

The integration of new technologies into many aspects of daily and professional life is an inescapable reality. Technology is impacting the interpreting profession in many ways. Interpreting services increasingly include remote interpreting options, such as video remote interpreting, remote simultaneous interpreting, over-the-phone interpreting and even interpreting via mobile applications. In addition, interpreters now routinely obtain work and communicate with potential employers via email and online professional profiles. As professional practice moves onto remote platforms, so too does the need to have clear standards for how to abide by community interpreting ethics in the online environment.

Although technology is referred to in relevant standards of this document, community interpreter ethics and standards urgently need specialized supplementary guidance to help interpreters engage in ethical practice where technology is involved.

Disclaimers

The authors of this document come from Canada, Cuba, Italy, Spain and the United States. The views represented here seek to be inclusive of community interpreting as ideally practiced by professional interpreters in different countries, but they are informed by and reflect the cultural perspectives and worldviews of the authors.

The information provided here is not advice. It is provided as is, without any representations or warranties. If you have any specific questions about professional practice as reflected in this document or elsewhere, you should consult your local or national interpreters association or a lawyer.

Acknowledgment

The authors would like to thank the kind contributions of colleagues who provided helpful feedback on previous versions of this document; with special gratitude to Beverly Treumann, Julie Boéri, Ann Corsellis, Erik Hertog, Maria Rosaria Buri and Stephen Lank. Responsibility for the content of this document and for any errors in the resulting work remains the authors'.

The Community Interpreter's Pledge

A pledge is a commitment. The following pledge for community interpreters captures key ethical principles for the profession and involves a conscious intention to take action.

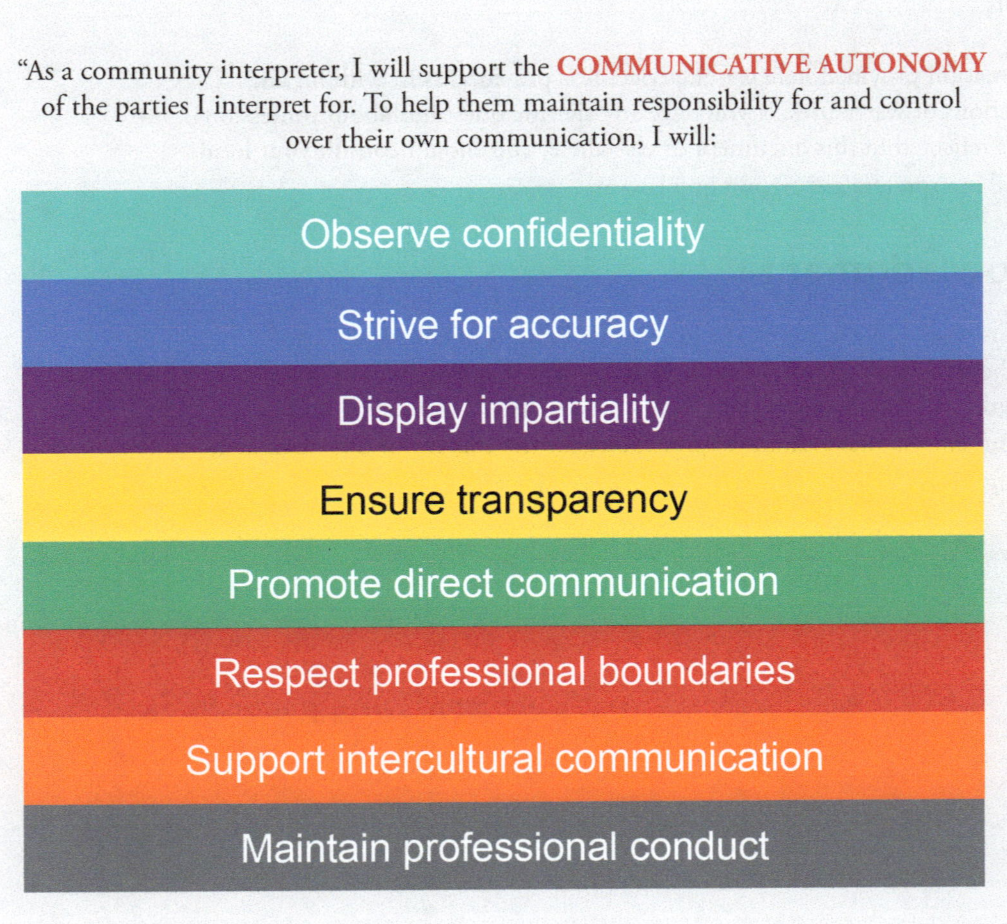

Ethical Principles and Standards of Practice

The Community Interpreter's Pledge above lists the eight ethical principles that this document addresses. For each ethical principle there is an explanation of the principle itself, a commentary section, a set of standards of practice that show how the community interpreter can adhere to and support each ethical principle, and two examples of situations showing how each standard could guide the interpreter's conduct in real life.

A Code of Ethics for *The Community Interpreter*®

Confidentiality

The community interpreter does not disclose private or proprietary information learned during the execution of his or her professional duties, except where disclosure is required by institutional regulations or by law.

Accuracy

The community interpreter strives to interpret every message without omissions, additions, distortions or any other changes to the original message.

Impartiality

The community interpreter refrains from allowing personal beliefs to manifest in his or her professional conduct, especially when rendering the content and tone of the message.

Transparency

The community interpreter interprets everything that is said to ensure that all messages expressed during the encounter are communicated to all parties.

Direct communication

The community interpreter initiates and actively supports practices that enable service users and providers to engage in direct communication.

Professional boundaries

The community interpreter should maintain professional boundaries, both during and outside the interpreted encounter.

Intercultural communication

The community interpreter intervenes to promote meaningful communication across cultural differences only when necessary for clear communication and without articulating the interpreter's beliefs or speculations about any of the parties' cultures.

Professional conduct

The community interpreter's conduct should reflect the highest standards of the profession by showing adherence to professional ethics and best practices.

CONFIDENTIALITY

Ethical principle

The community interpreter does not disclose private or proprietary information learned during the execution of his or her professional duties, except where disclosure is required by institutional regulations or by law.

Commentary

Many service professions require their practitioners to respect confidentiality, that is, the non-disclosure of private information learned while engaging in professional practice. The information not to be disclosed can relate to the identity of the service user, the business practices of the service provider's organizations and content shared during the service delivery.

While confidentiality is a fundamental right of service users in many countries, it is also a key condition for ensuring effective service provision. To be effective, most services require that a bond of trust be established between the service provider and the service user. For example, to foster a therapeutic alliance, therapists need to gain the trust of their patients. Lawyers also need their clients to trust them and not hide any relevant facts that can be crucial for a competent defense. Thus, confidentiality as a principle serves a public interest, because it is essential for the smooth functioning of community services.

Community interpreters also need to earn the trust of everyone involved in the delivery of a service. They, too, must observe confidentiality. Confidentiality is required both by the interpreting profession and by the setting and professional environment in which they interpret, such as a hospital or government agency. In many countries, confidentiality in the delivery of public services is also a legal requirement.

In some cases, public interest in disclosing information holds greater weight than public interest in the preservation of confidential information. These exceptions may be regulated and will vary from one region to another. However, in the absence of an official rule mandating disclosure, the community interpreter must observe confidentiality indefinitely.

Confidentiality is the only ethical principle that appears to be a universal requirement for the interpreting profession.

Standards

To observe **CONFIDENTIALITY** before, during and after the interpreted encounter:

1. The community interpreter should use professional discretion to avoid sharing personal information disclosed by participants, even when that information was disclosed at a public event.

Example 1: During a public school forum, a father discussed his struggles to support his child's learning after a painful divorce. As the interpreter at the event, Zere refrained from ever mentioning that story, despite the public setting where he learned of it.

Example 2: Ana interpreted for a birthing class, during which a wife and husband disclosed to the group that their house was in foreclosure in Ana's neighborhood. Ana told no one about the foreclosure.

2. The community interpreter should honor confidentiality indefinitely.

Example 1: Ana interpreted in a nursing home for an older woman who soon passed away. Ana revealed nothing about the woman to anyone, even after her death.

Example 2: Zere interpreted for an asylum seeker who lost his case and was deported to his homeland. Though Zere's friends wondered what had happened to this person, Zere never told anyone about the deportation.

3. The community interpreter should take additional steps to maintain confidentiality when information pertaining to an interpreted session is shared with other parties through the use of computers, electronic mail, facsimile machines, telephones, voicemail and other electronic technology.

Example 1: Zere often filed required reports about assignments through electronic means. He therefore set up strong password protection for his computer, phone and email to ensure service user privacy.

Example 2: Ana not only deleted assignment-related emails that included service users' names; she also made sure to immediately delete these messages from her email trash folder.

4. The community interpreter should not disclose private information, unless one of four conditions pertain:
(a) The service user has given explicit permission (preferably in writing) for disclosure of that information;
(b) A law, statute, legal requirement or workplace requirement compels the interpreter to disclose otherwise confidential information;
(c) The interpreter has signed an agency or inter-agency confidentiality agreement permitting the interpreter and a group of service providers to communicate information with one another about the service user; and/or
(d) The information disclosed is relevant for the service being provided and/or the service user's health, well-being or safety; it follows institutional regulations for the service being provided; and the interpreter discloses it only to a member of the treatment team or service team working with the same service user.

Example 1: After interpreting for a rape survivor and a therapist, Ana received a subpoena to testify in court about the session. A lawyer for the sexual assault center informed Ana that she was legally required to testify. Ana testified only after she made sure she understood why she was legally required to do so. (See condition (b) above.)

Example 2: A patient told Zere in private that he had a sexually transmitted infection but asked Zere not to tell the doctor about it. Zere had to share the diagnosis with the patient's doctor, because the diagnosis was vital for the patient's treatment plan. (See condition (d) above.)

5. The community interpreter should take the necessary steps to be informed about the terms and conditions for mandatory disclosure in his or her country and within the organization(s) where he or she interprets.

Example 1: Ana participated in a training session to better understand the complicated legal requirements governing confidentiality in healthcare in the country where she interpreted.

Example 2: After Zere moved to another region, he consulted an interpreter's association, websites and other interpreters about local confidentiality and reporting requirements. Soon after, he was able to correctly report a case of potential child abuse to the local government authority.

ACCURACY

Ethical principle

The community interpreter strives to interpret every message without omissions, additions, distortions or any other changes to the original message.

Commentary

Rendering a message inaccurately—however small the inaccuracy might seem—is equivalent to changing the message itself; to saying something different from the original. Changes in meaning due to inaccuracy can be subtle or extreme, but in either case a distorted message defeats the purpose of interpreting.

While accuracy is necessary for all interpreting, it is particularly important in community interpreting, where communicative autonomy is a fundamental principle. Most community interpreting involves interpreting a dialogic process: two or more individuals have a conversation where they build a shared understanding. The process of service provision is based on the exchange of messages and information, where details and nuances can impact decisions and courses of action. For that reason, accuracy in community interpreting is critical for effective service delivery and for the intended outcome of the communication process.

That said, even though accuracy is essential, the interpreter cannot always be sure to have achieved it. One reason for this paradox is that what the speaker means and what the listener understands are not always aligned. Interpreters cannot always control discrepancies between what is meant and what is understood (by them or by the parties). In addition, many concepts and expressions lack precise equivalents in other languages, yet the interpreter has to come up with linguistic solutions on the spot. As a result, interpreters can only strive for accuracy, yet the importance of that effort cannot be overstated.

Standards

To strive for ACCURACY before, during and after the interpreted encounter:

6. The community interpreter should interpret everything, including vulgar language and nonsensical statements.

Example 1: When a service user began to curse after hearing that his social welfare benefits were being terminated, Zere interpreted the curses in a comprehensible way without softening or changing the intended meaning.

Example 2: When the caseworker asked a mother why her children went hungry to school, the mother started changing the subject, interrupting herself every few words and discussing unrelated matters. As a result, her message was not coherent, yet Ana faithfully interpreted everything, rather than summarizing the coherent parts or creating her own clear version of the mother's words.

7. The community interpreter should make every effort to maintain the style, tone and register of the speaker.

Example 1: When an immigration representative used technical vocabulary that according to Ana might have been incomprehensible to the service user, Ana did not simplify the terms. Instead, she alerted both parties that these technical terms might cause misunderstandings.

Example 2: When a mother heard from a police officer that her son was murdered, she screamed and wept. Zere raised his voice and let it reflect the mother's distress without either shouting or crying himself.

8. The community interpreter should correct interpreting errors during or after the interpreted session, whether orally or in writing.

Example 1: After a medical appointment, Ana realized she had misinterpreted certain information about a blood disorder. She contacted the nurse, who immediately rectified this important error.

Example 2: While interpreting for an employee who was being fired, Zere realized he had omitted a whole sentence. Immediately he intervened to correct the omission.

9. The community interpreter should interpret in the mode that enables the greatest clarity and accuracy with the least distraction.

Example 1: During a session between a therapist and a torture survivor, Zere performed consecutive interpreting until the survivor became emotional and started speaking very quickly. Then Zere switched into simultaneous mode to avoid interrupting.

Example 2: After informing a father about his child's hearing test results, the teacher started a side conversation with the speech therapist. Ana switched to simultaneous interpreting but returned to consecutive interpreting when the teacher addressed the father again.

IMPARTIALITY

Ethical principle

The community interpreter refrains from allowing personal beliefs to manifest in his or her professional conduct, especially when rendering the content and tone of the message.

Commentary

Impartiality is a general principle of justice: non-judgmental treatment is needed for equity. Applying impartiality means avoiding taking sides based on personal preferences when making decisions (e.g., by judges) or reporting information (e.g., by journalists). Whether those preferences relate to personal vested interests or to personal feelings, the individual needs to acknowledge his or her own personal biases before being able to act impartially. An important guide to impartiality in general is to always bear in mind that the points of view and interests of all are equally important.

This last statement is particularly important for communicative autonomy. In community interpreting, the interpreter is always an intermediary. Precisely because the interpreter works as the middle person in the service delivery process, he or she should try to maintain the same attitude towards all participants. For the community interpreter, showing impartiality means not allying through one's behavior or conduct with any of the parties more than with any other. Impartiality also involves not displaying personal judgments about the attitude, beliefs or decisions of any of the parties.

In practice, impartiality in interpreting usually refers to transferring messages (through tone, body language, demeanor, etc.) in a manner that reveals none of the personal feelings or beliefs of the interpreter. But impartiality also applies to any professional decision made by the interpreter during or after an assignment.

No human being can distance themselves entirely from their feelings or internal bias, yet every interpreter can make a conscious effort to maintain respect for others and display a nonjudgmental attitude. In other words, community interpreters cannot be neutral in their feelings. Yet they can make every effort to be impartial in their behavior.

Standards

To show IMPARTIALITY before, during and after the interpreted encounter:

10. The community interpreter should refrain from taking sides during the interpreted session.

Example 1: A representative in social services showed insulting behavior towards a service user. Zere continued to interpret accurately and did not intervene to defend the service user or correct the provider during the interpreted session. (He did consider however reporting the incident once the interpreted session was over. See standard 15.)

Example 2: A doctor and nurse asked Ana to help convince a pregnant patient to have an amniocentesis, despite her religious objections. Ana politely refused but offered to interpret their concerns.

11. The community interpreter should avoid offering opinions or advice, even when requested to do so.

Example 1: During a medical appointment, a patient asked Ana, "Should I tell the doctor about the cornsilk tea?" Having stated in her introduction that she would interpret everything, Ana interpreted the question, and the doctor asked the patient about the tea.

Example 2: After the service user left, an attorney asked Zere, "Do you think my client was lying, or was that just his way of speaking?" Zere answered, "I don't know, but I'd be happy to interpret any questions you have for the client."

12. The community interpreter should, when interpreting, let his or her tone of voice, body language and demeanor reflect the speakers' feelings, not the interpreter's.

Example 1: A victim of domestic violence was speaking about her experience with an abuser. Ana's tone reflected the speaker's sadness, and it did not show her own reaction of distress.

Example 2: When interpreting for a young man in detention who was mistreated by a police officer, Zere did not show his anger or allow any personal feelings to influence his interpreting. (He did consider however reporting the incident once the interpreted session was over. See standard 15.)

13. The community interpreter should consider declining or withdrawing from an assignment if her or his faith, ethnic group, tribal, political or other affiliation may be perceived as unduly influencing her or his impartiality.

Example 1: Zere was asked to interpret for an individual whose tribal group was persecuted by Zere's ethnic group. Zere informed the service user and service provider of this fact and let the service user and provider decide whether Zere should be the interpreter for that assignment or not.

Example 2: During the session, Ana was accused by a service user of being prejudiced against that person's religion. Ana stated that she was ethically required to act impartially and she also offered to withdraw if her presence made the service user uncomfortable.

14. The community interpreter should declare all actual and potential conflicts of interest.

Example 1: Ana was asked to interpret for an assisted suicide. As an active supporter of an organization that opposed assisted suicide, Ana declared this conflict of interest to the interpreting agency and declined the assignment.

Example 2: On arriving at an attorney's office, Zere saw that he had already interpreted for the service user in several other settings. He disclosed the situation and let the attorney decide whether or not it constituted a conflict of interest.

15. The community interpreter, while avoiding taking sides during the interpreted session, may consider reporting a service provider who is breaking the law or violating his or her professional ethics to an appropriate supervisor or an institution of justice.

Example 1: A child-abuse investigator consensually recorded an interview with the father of the child but without warning him about the potential legal implications. After the encounter, Zere consulted a lawyer to learn if he should report such a situation and, if so, to whom.

Example 2: After a doctor forced a patient to sign a consent form for amputation surgery without explaining the benefits and risks of the procedure, Ana consulted the hospital ombudsman and her interpreting service to find out whether she should report the doctor before the surgery took place.

TRANSPARENCY

Ethical principle

The community interpreter interprets everything that is said to ensure that all messages expressed during the encounter are communicated to all parties.

Commentary

In the media, the corporate world and politics, the idea of transparency can be associated with the concept of accountability. In that context, transparency means operating in the public sphere, letting third parties have access to how companies and individuals make decisions, receive funding or present information. Corporations or political parties can be held accountable only if their actions are visible to others. Transparency is about visible processes.

In community interpreting, the interpreted encounter must be transparent so that everyone knows what is happening at any time. The interpreter has a clear obligation to accurately interpret everything that is stated by all parties. The interpreter should also interpret his or her own utterances whenever he or she has to intervene and speak as the interpreter.

In situations where third parties briefly become part of the interpreted encounter (for example, when a service provider consults a colleague by phone or when a new person briefly enters the room), what is said to and by these individuals should also be interpreted, or at least reported as accurately as possible.

Achieving transparency for the interpreter is relatively straightforward during dialogues where each participant takes turns and allows time for the interpreter to render the message fully. However, when the natural flow of the conversation is disrupted by conflict, when events move quickly or emergencies arise, maintaining transparency can be a challenge. In such cases, the interpreter may occasionally need to summarize or omit a portion of the utterances. In these cases, the principle of transparency is applied by letting the parties know that accurate interpreting was not possible at that time and that summarization took place instead.

Standards

To ensure TRANSPARENCY in interpreted encounters:

16. The community interpreter should interpret everything that is stated during the interpreted session wherever possible, including his or her own utterances.

Example 1: When the service provider called a colleague, Zere interpreted for the service user what he could hear, even though the call included some personal conversation between the service provider and the party on the other end of the phone line.

Example 2: During an appointment at a human-rights office, Ana shared her concern with the investigator that what she had interpreted about the plaintiff's next steps might not be clear. She immediately conveyed to the plaintiff exactly what she had told the investigator.

17. The community interpreter should make sure all parties know that everything that is stated will be interpreted.

Example 1: Ana always began her introduction by saying that she would interpret everything. Starting that way, even if she was cut off (which happened sometimes) she would be sure to have informed everyone of this basic aspect.

Example 2: Zere once interpreted by phone for a fire emergency. There was no time, at first, to state that he would interpret everything, but at the first opportunity he did so.

18. The community interpreter should inform the parties whenever he or she has had to summarize or omit part of the session.

Example 1: After a parent, a teenage child and a teacher began speaking all at once, Zere was obliged to summarize. As soon as possible, he informed all parties that summarization had taken place.

Example 2: Ana was interpreting at a child advocacy center when a small child who was being interviewed burst into tears. Ana interpreted what she could hear and then informed the investigator and everyone present that she had omitted the parts she couldn't understand.

19. The community interpreter, when intervening, should inform all parties that he or she is speaking as the interpreter.

Example 1: Zere made it a habit always to begin by saying, "As the interpreter, I…" whenever he intervened to request a clarification.

Example 2: Ana interpreted often in court, where a written record was made of the proceedings and interpreters were required to refer to themselves in the third person to avoid confusion. She maintained this habit outside the courtroom too as a clear way to mark the difference between interpreted messages and her own messages. For example, she said: "The interpreter requests a repetition."

DIRECT COMMUNICATION

Ethical principle

The community interpreter initiates and actively supports practices that enable service users and providers to engage in direct communication.

Commentary

The principle of direct communication is core to the interpreting profession. It addresses a real tension in interpreted exchanges: the role of the interpreter is to help overcome an existing barrier (the language barrier); yet, when working to overcome that barrier, the interpreter can easily become a barrier too. For example, many service users may feel more at ease with the interpreter than the service provider, because they share the same language and in many cases the same ethnicity and culture too. Some service providers, on the other hand, may see interpreters as "one of them," for interpreters are also professionals offering their services. It is thus very frequent for either party or all parties to view the interpreter as a confidant or ally and to engage in side conversations with the interpreter, both during and outside the session.

But an interpreter engaged in conversation is no longer interpreting. Rather, he or she is part of a new, separate conversation and cannot interpret at the same time. In order to support effective communication, the interpreter should foster the parties' interest in communicating with each other and not with the interpreter.

The interpreter needs to be aware of and, when necessary, actively deploy strategies to keep redirecting the service users and providers to engage directly with each other and, where possible, help them to forget the presence of the interpreter. An ideal encounter, often described by service users and providers, is when they simply cease to notice the interpreter and feel that they are communicating with each other without a barrier. This remarkable achievement represents the pinnacle of direct communication: striving for it should be the conscious goal of community interpreters.

Standards

To promote DIRECT COMMUNICATION in interpreted encounters:

20. The community interpreter should refrain from becoming an active participant in the communication and should intervene only when a major barrier to communication emerges.

Example 1: During a restaurant health inspection, Zere worried the owner did not understand the situation but waited to see if the misunderstanding would clear up. When it did, Zere was glad he had not intervened.

Example 2: A domestic-violence victim referred to her partner as her husband. Ana interpreted accurately, although she knew the victim was not married. When the victim's legal marital status became an issue for her case Ana then intervened to point out a possible miscommunication about whether "husband" meant "legal spouse," prompting the counselor to verify the victim's marital status.

21. The community interpreter should make every effort to ensure that all parties communicate directly with each other and not the interpreter.

Example 1: As part of her introduction, Ana always asked the service user and provider to speak to each other, not to her.

Example 2: Whenever a service provider looked at or talked to Zere, he would glance down at his notepad and point his hand in the direction of the service user.

22. The community interpreter should remain attentive to possible misunderstandings, including his or her own potential misunderstandings arising from misconceptions, biases or prejudices.

Example 1: During a parent-teacher meeting, Zere understood and interpreted for the teacher that the parents were refusing to take their daughter to after-school activities, when in fact they couldn't drive. Once Zere realized his misunderstanding, he clarified it at once.

Example 2: When a doctor used advanced medical terminology with a patient in worn-out clothing, Ana thought it would be necessary to request that the doctor use simpler language. Then the patient mentioned he was a retired doctor, and Ana realized her assumptions were mistaken.

23. The community interpreter should, whenever necessary, offer professional guidance on how to support direct communication.

Example 1: Ana sometimes made suggestions about the best positioning of chairs for the interpreted session.

Example 2: During a home visit, the caseworker kept asking Zere questions about the family instead of addressing the parents. After several attempts to redirect her, Zere intervened to explain why it was important to direct questions to the parents, not the interpreter.

PROFESSIONAL BOUNDARIES

Ethical principle

The community interpreter should maintain professional boundaries, both during and outside the interpreted encounter.

Commentary

Professional boundaries are a relevant concern for all those who work in the "helping and healing" professions, such as nurses, teachers and social workers. These professions require establishing some kind of rapport with service users. However, when a professional becomes personally involved with service users, negative outcomes are a common consequence, including occupational burnout.

Defining and respecting professional boundaries is also important for community interpreters, who are frequently expected to perform acts that exceed their scope of practice (that is, the range of tasks and duties that fall within the purview of the interpreter's professional responsibilities). For example, community interpreters are often asked to render personal services, such as driving a service user to the next appointment, or to perform a service provider's work, such as filling out forms or taking a patient history. As interpreters, they lack the service provider's training, credentials or experience and should engage only in the interpreting activities they were assigned to perform and for which they are trained.

Many community interpreters hold additional roles within the organization, because they are bilingual employees who interpret only part-time as one part of their job duties. It is acceptable for them to interpret on occasion in this way, if they have the requisite interpreter testing, training, skills and qualifications, but it is not feasible for them to interpret professionally *while* they execute other job responsibilities. In other words, a bilingual employee should not perform his or her primary job and interpret at the same time. Acting as a nurse, case manager or police detective *and* as an interpreter at the same time can lead to problems of accuracy, impartiality and role confusion. A nurse who interprets, for example, may have to touch the patient and reassure her, which will get in the way of the intense focus and complex cognitive skills required for interpreting.

Because community interpreting is still a young profession and widely misunderstood, it usually falls to the community interpreter to clarify his or her role and to decline requests that exceed the interpreter's scope of practice.

Standards

To respect PROFESSIONAL BOUNDARIES before, during and after the interpreted encounter:

24. The community interpreter should limit his or her assistance to facilitating communication and refrain from engaging in other types of assistance or support, even when requested to do so by the service user or provider.

Example 1: A service user asked Zere in private to help him negotiate with a creditor about an overdue bill. Instead, with the permission of the interpreter service that sent him to the assignment, Zere referred him to a charity that assisted immigrants.

Example 2: A receptionist asked Ana to fill out a patient health history form with the patient. Ana offered instead to sight translate the form in front of a qualified service provider so that patient and provider could fill it out.

25. The community interpreter, who simultaneously holds other professional or voluntary responsibilities should, during the interpreted session, limit his or her role to interpreting, even when requested to perform additional duties.

Example 1: Zere was a part-time refugee caseworker but never interpreted and acted as a caseworker in the same encounter.

Example 2: When requested to transport a patient Ana was interpreting for, Ana asked the nurse to bring in someone else to do that task, even though she had transported patients as a hospital volunteer in the past.

26. The community interpreter should, wherever feasible, avoid personal, business or romantic engagements with the service user.

Example 1: At a local market, Ana encountered a service user that she often interpreted for. After a polite greeting, with a smile and a warm voice, Ana left quickly to avoid engaging in overly personal conversation.

Example 2: Zere was invited to lunch by a service user that he had interpreted for and found attractive. Zere politely declined the invitation.

INTERCULTURAL COMMUNICATION

Ethical principle

The community interpreter intervenes to promote meaningful communication across cultural differences only when necessary for clear communication and without articulating the interpreter's beliefs or speculations about any of the parties' cultures.

Commentary

Intercultural communication refers to the ability to communicate across cultural differences. Understanding and respecting other cultures brings about new worldviews that are beneficial to all in multicultural societies.

Interpreters support intercultural communication through the act of accurately transferring messages across language differences. Their position as intermediaries is also crucial in detecting sources of misunderstanding caused by cultural differences. Community interpreters should promote communicative autonomy, even when cultural misunderstandings arise.

Service providers and users who experience cultural misunderstandings often think that an interpreter can remove such misunderstandings. Service providers who lack training in how to provide culturally responsive services often view the interpreter as a "cultural expert," while many service users expect the interpreter "to take care" of cultural misunderstandings. The reality is more complex.

Being an expert in any given culture is impossible: cultures are not fixed or tangible. On the contrary, cultures evolve and overlap both for geographical regions and individuals, so it is unreasonable to expect an interpreter to know everything about a certain culture at a given point in time as it relates to a specific individual.

In the presence of a cultural misunderstanding, the community interpreter might choose to intervene. The interpreter may point to a possible cultural difference that interferes with effective communication, but should avoid providing cultural explanations of his or her own. To promote intercultural communication, the community interpreter should let the parties explore each other's cultural views themselves.

It is worth noting that service systems have cultures too. These systems are culturally complex and often confusing. Interpreters may sometimes need to alert service providers to explain systemic cultural differences, rather than having interpreters tell service users "how things work here."
The interpreter's ability to support intercultural communication is thus based mainly on skills sets that involve maintaining an open-minded, respectful and proactive attitude; avoiding assumptions; assessing the probable cause of a cultural misunderstanding and being receptive to new perspectives and different communication styles.

Standards

To support INTERCULTURAL COMMUNICATION in interpreted encounters:

27. The community interpreter should point out cultural differences that service users or service providers have not identified themselves when they appear to be barriers to meaningful communication.

Example 1: An immigration representative was unaware that the client's cultural use of last names could jeopardize the case. Zere pointed out a possible misunderstanding about naming practices regarding paternal and maternal last names.

Example 2: Ana realized a patient might be resisting a particular date for surgery because it had cultural associations of death. She informed the doctor and patient that there might be a specific cultural meaning associated with the date.

28. The community interpreter should refrain from providing cultural explanations and instead direct parties to seek relevant cultural information from each other.

Example 1: Ana realized that a woman who had been raped by her abusive husband seemed to believe he had a right to forced conjugal sex. When Ana suggested to both parties that there might be different views about the rights of a husband to conjugal intercourse, the lawyer explored the client's beliefs about this subject.

Example 2: During an interview at school, Zere felt the mother was confused about the meaning of the term "progress report." Instead of explaining it, he pointed out this possible misunderstanding to both parties so that the teacher could explain.

29. The community interpreter should show respect for all parties while interpreting and when identifying and pointing out cultural differences and misunderstandings.

Example 1: Ana had to interpret for a group of abusive husbands who shared cultural opinions she found offensive. Ana showed respect by not allowing her own values to distort their statements.

Example 2: When Zere intervened to suggest that the service user clarify the cultural meaning of a religious belief, Zere was careful to do so with respect although the religion was not his own.

30. The community interpreter should never make statements about the service user or the service provider's cultural beliefs or intentions.

Example 1: A married woman grew upset over questions from a gynecologist. Zere felt he knew which questions offended her but simply pointed out a possible cultural misunderstanding about the types of sexual questions that some married women might find inappropriate.

Example 2: After a resident in a nursing home fastened a man's tie around her neck, a therapist asked Ana if there was a cultural explanation. Ana suspected there was but recommended that the therapist ask the resident directly.

31. The community interpreter should provide his or her explanation of a cultural difference or cultural misunderstanding only when such misunderstanding does not appear to be resolvable by the parties themselves and is likely to jeopardize a service user's health or safety, or to jeopardize public safety.

Example 1: Ana interpreted for a rape survivor who came from a country where the police could not be trusted, so she did not want her assault reported. Ana, concerned about public safety if the rapist remained free, privately alerted the victim advocate about different cultural beliefs regarding police.

Example 2: A patient refused critical blood tests without mentioning her cultural belief that her spirit could be harmed if blood was taken from her. Zere alerted both parties to a possible cultural misunderstanding about the consequences of blood drawing. When the doctor did not seek clarification about it, Zere advised both parties that the patient's refusal might relate to a belief about the potentially fatal consequences if blood was taken.

PROFESSIONAL CONDUCT

Ethical principle

The community interpreter's conduct should reflect the highest standards of the profession by showing adherence to professional ethics and best practices.

Commentary

The work environment often shapes professional conduct. Hospitals, schools, factories and farms are all examples of work settings in which both explicit and implicit rules govern professional activity to ensure safety and efficiency. There are also other rules, often designed by professional bodies, which address ethical and moral concerns, generally through codes of conduct. In part, because of all these rules, a professional culture emerges and evolves that leads to general expectations about appropriate behavior by professionals in that field.

Community interpreting is a young field of specialization. Too often, it is carried out by untrained volunteers or assistants. While some clear guidelines for professional conduct exist, they are not widely available or applied consistently. This situation contributes to general confusion about the role and practices of community interpreters. It also perpetuates a climate of low expectations.

When the role of the interpreter is not formalized, when expectations are unclear and standards are low, the impact on the profession and its ability to offer quality services can be huge. This problem has led to a low public opinion of community interpreters in many countries.

Sending a clear message about the value of professionalism in community interpreting is critical. Advocating for professional conduct is a shared responsibility of all interpreters.

Standards

To show PROFESSIONAL CONDUCT before, during and after the interpreted encounter:

32. The community interpreter should arrive at the interpreting assignment prepared and on time.

Example 1: When asked to interpret for a gay-rights discrimination complaint, Zere looked up websites and relevant terminology in both languages, watched a film about this type of discrimination and spoke to a senior interpreter for guidance.

Example 2: After accepting a new assignment, Ana researched how long it would take to arrive and left in advance to avoid rush-hour traffic.

33. The community interpreter should adopt a dress code appropriate for both professional interpreters and the setting where the assignment takes place.

Example 1: At one nonprofit legal service where Zere interpreted often, even lawyers frequently wore jeans, but Zere always wore professional clothing. However, in other settings, such as hospital operating rooms, he asked for guidance about required or recommended clothing.

Example 2: For home visits to new mothers in high-crime neighborhoods, Ana wore discreet, casual clothing in order not to draw attention to herself, but just before entering each home she added an attractive scarf to look more professional.

34. The community interpreter should display a respectful demeanor that balances professionalism and warmth for all parties present.

Example 1: Ana decided to make conscious efforts to show equal respect for both service users and providers in her posture, tone of voice and general conduct.

Example 2: Whenever he interpreted for torture survivors, refugees and others who had endured great suffering, Zere smiled during his introduction and displayed an open posture and respectful tone of voice to indicate that despite his professional boundaries he was a compassionate human being.

35. The community interpreter should make sure that the conditions of the working environment support quality interpreting and should politely request any necessary adaptations.

Example 1: In a refugee resettlement center, a family group kept interrupting each other, making it impossible for Zere to interpret accurately. He politely requested all parties to take turns speaking.

Example 2: During a Video Remote Interpreting (VRI) assignment, the sound quality was so poor that Ana (who was working from a different location than the nurse and patient) politely requested the nurse to move closer to the microphone to ensure clear audio signals.

36. The community interpreter should not be involved with personal matters during an assignment.

Example 1: When Zere's childcare provider was sick, Zere did not take his child to the interpreted session but instead made sure to have a family member available to care for the child.

Example 2: Ana's phone vibrated in her pocket during a session, but Ana refrained from checking for messages until after the assignment.

37. The community interpreter should accept only assignments for which he or she is qualified and should disclose all professional limitations when appropriate.

Example 1: At a hospice, Zere was asked by a chaplain to sight translate a prayer text that he did not understand well. Prior to the assignment, Zere checked online for a possible translation, which he could not find. Zere then disclosed his limitations and offered to withdraw.

Example 2: Ana declined all requests that involved local conferences and meetings until she had received adequate qualifications and experience in simultaneous interpreting.

38. The community interpreter should typically refrain from accepting gifts from service users or providers.

Example 1: A grateful service user brought Ana a bracelet. Ana graciously thanked her but suggested that the gift giver instead might wish to write a note of thanks or donate the gift to a charity.

Example 2: When Zere refused a gift and the service user grew culturally offended, Zere explained that if he accepted gifts, many other service users with little money might feel that they too should give him gifts. He also disclosed that he could lose interpreting assignments and violate his professional ethics if he accepted gifts.

39. The community interpreter should not seek new business opportunities for his or her own benefit while on assignment.

Example 1: Zere had business cards, but when on assignment for interpreting service providers, he never handed out his own business card to anyone.

Example 2: When Ana was sent by a language company to interpret for a driver's license exam and saw other people waiting there who probably needed an interpreter, she did not try to sell her services to them.

40. The community interpreter may accept a new business opportunity offered during an assignment only with formal approval from the first assigning organization.

Example 1: The service provider at an organization that served children with autism asked Ana to come back to interpret for the same family. Ana referred the requester to the nonprofit interpreting service that had sent her on the assignment.

Example 2: While on an interpreting assignment, Zere was asked to translate a document in a language for which he was a qualified translator. He referred the requester to the language company that sent him, which then gave Zere the assignment.

41. The community interpreter should engage in activities and initiatives that advance his or her professional development.

Example 1: To improve her performance and increase her knowledge of interpreting, Ana joined her local professional interpreters association, took several advanced training courses online and attended conferences. She also asked for advice and feedback from other interpreters.

Example 2: Once a week, Zere and another interpreter met and practiced together. Zere also set up a plan to learn 10 new English terms a day and take advanced training in simultaneous interpreting.

INTRODUCTION TO COMMUNITY INTERPRETING

by Katharine Allen and Marjory A. Bancroft

CHAPTER 1

LEARNING OBJECTIVES

After completing this chapter and its corresponding exercises, the learner will be able to:

OBJECTIVE 1.1	**The Profession of Community Interpreting** Discuss the profession of community interpreting and four driving forces that have shaped the field.
OBJECTIVE 1.2	**Interpreter Credentials** Analyze and compare interpreter credentials, including certificates and certification.
OBJECTIVE 1.3	**Ethics and Standards for Community Interpreters** Demonstrate an understanding of eight core ethical principles for community interpreters.
OBJECTIVE 1.4	**Application of Ethical Principles** Apply ethical principles for community interpreters to common communication barriers.
OBJECTIVE 1.5	**Applying Ethical Principles** Examine two techniques for resolving ethical challenges in community interpreting.
OBJECTIVE 1.6	**Reflective Practice** Explore the concept, meaning and application of "reflective practice" for community interpreters.

Introduction

Chapter 1 offers a broad overview of community interpreting as a profession, including medical, educational and social services interpreting. It explores the background and history of the profession and introduces topics that will be explored in-depth in later chapters. Some of the key forces that have moved the field forward and are addressed in this chapter include international migration, language and cultural barriers to accessing community services. Rapid globalization, language policies and laws and technological change have also had a huge impact on the field.

This chapter considers minimum competency requirements for community interpreters and the availability of adequate training around the world. It explores how community interpreting fits into the larger profession of interpreting. Finally, Chapter 1 also takes a detailed look at eight core ethical principles that have shaped the profession by giving it a foundation. The chapter closes with a focus on how reflective practice will help community interpreters drive the profession forward by allowing them to engage in professionalization even when they lack supervision or support.

1.1 The Profession of Community Interpreting

Overview

The gift of communication

The following true story provides an overview for this chapter and the book. It illustrates the need for the profession of community interpreting and how it differs from other interpreting specializations. It also highlights the deep need for qualified interpreters in this field.

The Gift of Communication

A True Story by the Lead Author of This Chapter

I enter the room as I have so many times before. The parents are there, the baby wrapped in blankets, cradled in his mother's arms. I have interpreted for so many families like this one, accompanying them as they wend their way through the system of programs for "early intervention services" for very young children. This case is not like the others. This family will be different, for all of us. By the end, I will have learned huge lessons about community interpreting.

María and Alejandro have been pulled suddenly into the nightmare of caring for a child with multiple and catastrophic disabilities. Their son Jorge, barely a month old, was revived after 15 minutes with no heartbeat. The resulting brain damage is severe and permanent. Jorge is alive and can breathe on his own, but little more.

The case is so complicated that the regional center takes the unusual step of appointing me as the primary interpreter for all the agencies involved in the infant's care. María and Alejandro are receiving help from 16 of the 18 agencies that work together to help their baby. Each agency marches to its own set of rules and regulations. Coordinating their services requires long phone calls and meetings, all of which I help arrange and for which I interpret.

Today we are in María and Alejandro's room, one of three bedrooms in a small, cramped apartment that houses 10 people: one family per bedroom, and the grandmother and a couple of cousins sleep in the living room. The queen bed takes up most of the room where we are standing. Medical equipment of all shapes and sizes lines the walls. Machines to

Learning Objective 1.1

After completing this section, you will be able to:

- Discuss the profession of community interpreting and four driving forces that have shaped the field.

help Jorge breathe, eat and take his medications sit next to special strollers and seats. A whole pharmacy of medications is neatly arranged on the dresser top, next to doilies and images of the Christ Child.

María sits on one side of the bed, I on the other. Jorge lies on a blanket in the middle while the physical therapist stretches and massages his rigid muscles. As the therapist works, Maria describes their latest visit from the home health nurse, who, despite my repeated efforts, did not engage an interpreter. Now María is full of questions and concerns because she didn't really understand the nurse. I pull out my cell phone and start making calls to see if I can track down the nurse.

That was just one meeting. Soon the appointments multiply. As the weeks slip by, hardly a day passes without a message for me about this case. The phone rings. It is Alejandro. Jorge has been admitted to a hospital five hours away. Can I inform his case coordinator and the other programs? The baby is spiking high fevers and is on a respirator. The family ends up staying there for three weeks. They must wear masks and gloves to see Jorge.

The whole time they are there, the hospital never successfully conveys to María and Alejandro that they need to wear the mask and gloves for <u>their</u> protection, not Jorge's. He has methicillin-resistant Staphylococcus aureus (MRSA): a dangerous, antibiotic-resistant staph infection. He comes home improved—but not cured. By the time the hospital informs the medical case coordinator in our area about the infection, we have all been exposed to MRSA, including two healthcare providers who are pregnant.

Like so many community interpreters, I work mostly alone, in isolation. At the time this story takes place, I do not know about professional associations, codes of ethics or standards of practice. I've had no in-depth training. I'm flying by the seat of my pants: in other words, trying to be professional but not sure what a professional interpreter is supposed to do in a case like this. I struggle every day, trying to prevent miscommunications, wanting the family to have full access to the care they need and have a right to while respecting professional boundaries.

The lessons I am learning about healthcare could fill a book. The sheer will, love, faith and indomitable strength of spirit showed by this couple as they fight for their son's life is an encyclopedia of love. But the deepest lesson comes unexpectedly.

We are in yet another doctor's office, someone new to the case. The doctor enters, goes straight to the parents, shakes their hands and starts speaking to them in fluent Spanish. María and Alejandro are stunned. Through all the long months of caring for their child, not a single doctor has been able to communicate with them in their own language. I move back to a corner. I watch tears roll down their faces. Their relief is so palpable it fills the room. As the meeting goes on, they relax. They ask the doctor everything they want to know. Their shoulders straighten. I can tell they leave the room feeling lighter. Better.

I walk out humbled by what I have witnessed. No matter how accurately we interpreters convey meaning and capture content, no matter how adeptly we negotiate culture and transmit tone and feeling, we achieve only a pale imitation of the power of direct communication between individuals who share a language.

This truth does not for an instant negate the critical role that we interpreters play. It only reinforces the need for a high level of training and skill to support the vital work we do. I know that for a time, I served as a lifeline to María and Alejandro. I gave them access to the world of care that they needed for their son.

I also know now that I needed training and guidance to do a better job that was not available in my small desert town in California. Later I moved my whole family hundreds of miles away, for two years, to get the training I needed. Yet I will never forget what María and Alejandro taught me.

Defining "community interpreting"

> **DEFINITION**
>
> **Community interpreting (ISO)**
>
> bidirectional interpreting that takes place in communicative settings (2.2.3) among speakers of different languages for the purpose of accessing community services (ISO, 2014, p. 1).

Where migrants travel, language barriers emerge. Migrants need to communicate with service providers in clinics, schools, police stations and human service agencies.

Jorge's story above can be multiplied across millions of families in communities around the world. It could take place in nearly any country where immigrants, refugees, indigenous peoples and the Deaf or hard-of-hearing need to access community services across language barriers. Today, the profession of community interpreting is a vital profession.

Yet even today, we lack a single, agreed-upon definition for community interpreting. That lack of a common understanding was noted 20 years ago (Mikkelson, 1996). It is still true today, and the confusion has had a direct impact on the field. Most recently, for example, the International Organization for Standardization (ISO) published the first international standard for community interpreting. It defined community interpreting as "bidirectional interpreting that takes place in communicative settings ... among speakers of different languages for the purpose of accessing community services." Yet not everyone would even agree that community interpreting is always bidirectional (working both into and out of their working languages).[2] Not knowing (or at least, agreeing on) what community interpreting *is* makes it difficult to train interpreters, support them and clarify their role. It is even harder to advocate for adequate payment for community interpreters without a broadly accepted understanding of the profession.

The need to professionalize is urgent. In the United States alone, data from the U.S. Census Bureau show that more than 25 million residents (about 9 percent) speak limited English (Pandya, McHugh, & Batalova, 2011, p. 1). In some countries, such as Canada, the numbers of immigrants are higher still, and countries around the world from the European Union (EU) nations to countries in Africa, Asia and Oceania (including Australia and New Zealand) are seeing a surge in residents who do not speak the national or official languages.

Overall, there is widespread acceptance that community interpreting helps immigrants, indigenous minorities, the Deaf and others to access community services. A great number of these residents have legal and/or ethical or human rights to many public services. But without a universal understanding of the community interpreting profession and its requirements, it is difficult for those residents to obtain quality access to such services.

There is also no clear consensus on the role of the community interpreter: for example, whether or not an interpreter should perform cultural mediation or advocate for service users, two topics that this textbook will clarify in Chapters 3 and 5, respectively. There are currently no national or international standards that require a minimum level of training or even language proficiency skill levels for community interpreters. Only one international standard (ISO, 2014) specifies any desired qualifications.

Finally, no national or international entity is currently responsible for overseeing or regulating the professional activity of community interpreters. Some countries are making strides: for example, the UK

[2] E.g., at many health education programs, public school events and other public meetings in community settings, the community interpreter for a public speaker works only from one language to the other, not in both directions.

has a public registry for interpreters holding a Diploma in Public Service Interpreting (DPSI). Public service interpreting is the name used in the UK for community interpreting.

In fact, the name of the profession itself causes confusion. Multiple names exist. Bancroft (2015, p. 218) gathered the following list:

- Public service interpreting (a term used primarily in Europe)
- Liaison interpreting
- Bilateral interpreting
- Dialogue interpreting
- Community-based interpreting
- Bidirectional interpreting
- Triangle interpreting
- Cultural interpreting
- Cultural (or intercultural) mediation
- Consecutive interpreting (even though "consecutive" is properly speaking an interpreting mode)
- Contact interpreting
- Face-to-face interpreting
- Triad interpreting
- Discourse interpreting
- Intra-social (or social) interpreting
- Language mediation

Even this list is incomplete. More recently the term *public service interpreting* seems to have gained a foothold in Europe, while *community interpreting* remains "the most widely accepted term in Canada" (HIN, 2007, p. 11) and in the United States. In addition ISO, following the participation of 29 member nations and much discussion, formally adopted the term *community interpreting*. In 2014, ISO published the first international standard for community interpreting (ISO, 2014). Critical Link International, the only international association that supports community interpreting, also uses that term. This international textbook therefore uses the term *community interpreting*.

What is community interpreting?

For decades, community interpreting has been casually assumed to be "medical, educational and social services interpreting." What about legal interpreting? Is it part of community interpreting? The answer is less clear.

Another rapidly growing area is faith-based interpreting (interpreting for religious congregations, their leaders or their members as they carry out their religious practices and work). Is it part of community interpreting? If an immigrant enters a bank and needs an interpreter to open an account, is this an example of business interpreting or community interpreting? Today, the realization is that community interpreting is not defined by its sub-specializations, such as medical interpreting, but by what it *accomplishes*.

This international textbook offers the following definition.

> **DEFINITION**
>
> **Community interpreting**
>
> A specialization of interpreting that facilitates access to community services for individuals who do not speak the language of service.

Defining "community interpreter"

Here is a definition provided by the authors for *community interpreter:*

> **DEFINITION**
>
> **Community interpreter**
>
> A bilingual or multilingual individual who is deemed professionally qualified to interpret in community service settings.
>
> **Examples:** A staff interpreter, freelance interpreter or bilingual staff member who has been trained to interpret and assessed for language proficiency and interpreting skills.

Anyone who does not meet this definition is not, for the purposes of this textbook, considered to be a community interpreter. A friend, family member or casual bystander asked to interpret in a school, health department or senior center, for example, may be considered a *language assistant* but should not be called an interpreter. The word *interpreter* should be reserved for professionally qualified individuals. ISO supports this concept by first defining what an interpreter is and then defining the community interpreter as follows[3]:

> ***Interpreter***
>
> *[A] language professional who conveys a message produced in a source language (2.4.5), be it spoken or signed, into a target language (2.4.6), spoken or signed, in real time and whose task is to convey every element of the message.*
>
> ***Community interpreter***
>
> *[An] interpreter (2.3.2) who facilitates communication, be it spoken or signed, in any communicative setting (2.3.3), be it private or public, between two or more speakers who do not share a common language, for the sole purpose of accessing community services (ISO, 2014, p. 3).*

[3] The numbers in parentheses in these ISO definitions refer to other definitions in the standard.

Community interpreting is distinct from other interpreting specializations, such as conference or business interpreting, in several key ways.

- Face-to-face community interpreting is usually performed by local interpreters for local residents.
- Community interpreters usually perform their assignments for public (government) and community/nonprofit organizations.
- Most of them work bidirectionally (both into and out of their working languages) on a daily basis.
- While usually fewer than 30 languages are required for conference interpreting, nearly any language could be needed in community interpreting. For example, in the United States, about 380 languages[4] are spoken.[5]
- The majority of community interpreters do not work in a booth but have direct contact with service users and providers, whether in person, by phone or by video.
- Community interpreters may be expected to serve as cultural liaisons to immigrant communities, or act as outreach workers and advocates (see Chapters 3 and 5).

In community settings, furthermore, participants in the encounter often have to navigate complex personal interactions. Take the example of an emergency phone call where a woman is screaming, "My husband is dying," and describes an emergency situation at top speed, where the husband has a severed artery and is bleeding to death in front of her while the dispatch operator remains calm and asks questions through the interpreter. These are complex, high-stakes situations.

In addition, it is important to recognize the professional diversity of community interpreters. A growing number of them may be trained, professional interpreters who work solely in community settings or also interpret for businesses, government officers, conferences and appeal courts.
There are various categories of interpreters as well, for example:

- Full-time staff interpreters earning a full-time salary and benefits, like retirement plans.
- Independent freelancers taking contract jobs from language companies, courts or nonprofit language services.
- Bilingual staff members whose primary job is not interpreting but who are asked or expected to interpret part-time or as needed (a task that may or may not be in their job description).
- Volunteers, in "language banks" or networks set up by hospitals, charities and even government agencies.

The qualifications of all these types of interpreters vary widely. The diversity of backgrounds and job descriptions for community interpreting has spurred an ongoing debate in many parts of the world about who is and who should not be considered a community interpreter. For example, many believe that community interpreting should be carried out exclusively by dedicated staff interpreters and freelance interpreters but not by volunteers or by bilingual employees whose primary job duties are other than interpreting volunteers. Others, however, including the U.S. National Council on Interpreting in Health Care, take no such position. In this view, the real question is whether an interpreter has the qualifications and skills required

[4]According to U.S. Census Bureau public data available at www.census.gov
[5]As a result, one language company has a contract with the U.S. immigration courts to provide services in more than 300 languages: http://www.prnewswire.com/news-releases/lionbridge-awarded-contract-by-united-states-department-of-justice-for-language-services-expects-contract-to-generate-100-million-over-6-years-62002642.html

to interpret at a professional level. Whoever meets that level of qualification should be considered competent to perform community interpreting. Whoever doesn't, should not. This second view is important because many interpreters for less common languages cannot realistically make a full-time professional living from interpreting. In addition, in some countries like the United States it is impossible, on a practical level, to stop bilingual staff from interpreting. Therefore by admitting the reality one can at least require that bilingual employees who interpret receive professional training and be tested to assure they have the competency to interpret.

The reality even today is that almost any bilingual individual might be asked to act as a language assistant in community services, including family, friends, small children and casual bystanders. Bilingual employees and volunteers also interpret every day in community settings, whether or not they are qualified to do so. This reality holds true in almost any country where community interpreting exists at all. It is even true in high-risk settings such as courts and hospitals.

Should Bilingual Staff Interpret in Healthcare Settings?

The National Council on Interpreting in Health Care (NCIHC) in the United States does not forbid (or endorse) the idea of bilingual employees interpreting in healthcare. Rather, NCIHC has preferred to focus on raising the bar of the profession so that *all* interpreters in healthcare meet the same standards, which include professional training, testing and, ideally, certification for all medical interpreters, whether or not they are freelance interpreters, staff interpreters or bilingual employees who interpret part-time—and who are also known as "dual role interpreters."

In most places around the world, including industrialized nations, community interpreting has yet to reach the level of professionalization where credentialing is required.

Where does community interpreting take place?

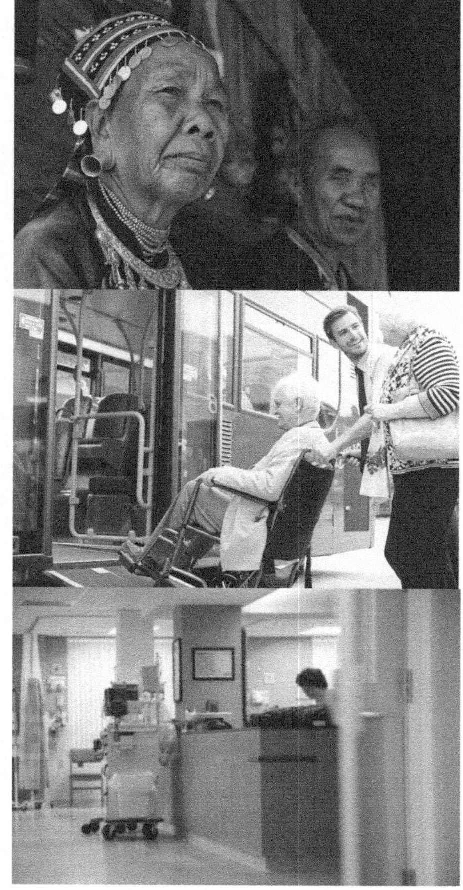

Community interpreting takes place almost anywhere that community services are offered. Such services typically include public services funded by tax dollars, those offered through nonprofit and charitable organizations, and certain for-profit services. Here are just a few examples:

- Hospitals, doctors' offices and outpatient clinics
- Social services
- Refugee and resettlement services
- Public housing
- Legal services[6] and law enforcement
- Gender-based violence/domestic violence and sexual assault agencies
- Community mental health centers
- Immigration advocacy agencies
- Elementary, secondary and university-level education
- Disability and rehabilitation services
- Job training programs
- Transportation services
- Libraries
- Multicultural events and festivals

Each of these environments has its rules and regulations, terminology, service expectations and logistical challenges. This diversity of settings has important implications. To be effective, many community interpreters must be competent to perform many different jobs. They must master specialized terminology and subject-matter knowledge. While every interpreting specialization has its complexities and challenges, community interpreting often requires interpreters to navigate a dizzying array of settings, interactions and topic areas.

Is Medical Interpreting Part of Community Interpreting?

The simple answer is yes: medical interpreting is indeed part of community interpreting because it facilitates access to a vital community service. Yet many medical interpreters do not know they are community interpreters! Why not?

The reason is that medical interpreting in many countries is professionalizing at a faster rate than other areas (or sub-specializations) of community interpreting. The reasons may be the high stakes of medical interpreting, where language barriers can make the difference between life and death.

However, always remember that medical interpreters are indeed community interpreters according to accepted practice and international standards (ISO, 2014).

[6]Note: Many individuals and organizations do not consider legal and/or court interpreting to be part of community interpreting. See ISO (2014, p. 13) for a discussion of this point, which Chapter 4 addresses in detail.

The origins of modern community interpreting

History of Modern Interpreting

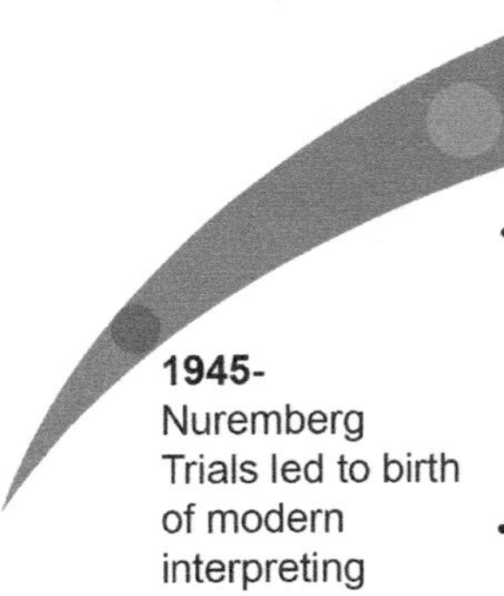

1945-
Nuremberg Trials led to birth of modern interpreting profession

1960s and 1970s-
- **Community interpreting** starts to professionalize in Australia, Sweden, Canada and the United States
- **Signed languages** get legal recognition in some countries.

1960s and 1970-
- Court interpreting becomes a recognized profession.
- Medical interpreting becomes a specialization within community interpreting.
- Legislation in several countries supports the growth of the profession.

The early years

http://unprofessionaltranslation.blogspot.com/2010/07/earliest-depiction-of-interpreter.html

No one knows when community interpreting began. While interpreting was known in ancient Egypt, it was probably most important for political delegations and merchants. Consider the earliest known image of an interpreter, which apparently dates back to 1330 BC.

> *Horemhab was an exceptionally clever man who rose from the rank of commoner to become general of the Egyptian army, and eventually pharaoh. At the period depicted, he was already regent to the boy pharaoh Tutankhamen and was in charge of foreign affairs. He is shown conveying the pharaoh's reply to a delegation of Syrian and Libyan vassals come to petition for protection from incursions by mountain people and Bedouin. He does so through one of the interpreters who were kept at court in Memphis for receiving delegations from outlying territories, and here we see the interpreter cleverly "animated" by the device of a double figure facing both ways, as though turning alternately towards speaker and listener.* (Harris, 2010)

In ancient times, interpreters around the world helped rich and poor alike to communicate with travelers, merchants, religious groups and others. For example, Christianity and Islam established charitable work and missions around the world that often provided trained interpreters.

Perhaps the most famous and striking example of community interpreting—and also business and military interpreting—occurred during the Spanish conquest of the Americas. Spain published standards of performance for interpreters for soldiers, explorers and missionaries who communicated with indigenous tribes—in 1548! The language uncannily echoes many modern requirements today. For example:

> *Interpreters had to be duly sworn to perform their task "well and faithfully," expressing the matter before them "clearly and frankly," "without hiding or adding anything," "without acting in favor of any of the parties," and "without deriving any profit from their task other than the pay due to them."* (Pöchhacker, 2004, p. 13)

Legislation included 14 laws intended to regulate interpreter conduct in the Spanish colonies in the Americas, for example:

- *Interpreters for the Indian languages shall have the necessary capacities and qualities.*
- *The interpreters shall not accept or ask for gifts.*
- *The interpreters shall not hold private meetings with Indian clients.*
- *The interpreters shall not act as advocates for the Indians.* (*Ibid.*)

The most famous interpreter of that era was the young woman of Mexican descent known as "la Malinche." As the interpreter for the famous explorer, Cortés, she was called a traitor by many of her compatriots, though today she is admired.

A profession is born

Community interpreting as a formal profession did not exist until the 20th century, when the modern interpreting profession was born. The League of Nations was founded in 1919 and began with only two official languages, French and English. (For comparison, today the European Union has 24 official languages.) In 1927, simultaneous interpreting may have been first performed professionally in Geneva, Switzerland, during the International Labor Conference. However it proved to be too costly and complicated to perform regularly until Andre Kaminker invented the first simultaneous interpreting equipment. This equipment was used at the famous Nuremberg Trials for World War II war criminals, which are widely considered to mark the birth of the interpreting profession.

After the Nuremberg events, conference interpreting quickly became an established and reputable interpreting profession around the world. Today, conference interpreting includes interpreting for high-level government, diplomatic and corporate meetings. It enjoys high prestige. Interpreters for the United Nations, the European Parliament, high-level government meetings and international conferences are all conference interpreters, and the International Association of Conference Interpreters (AIIC) has members in more than 90 countries.

Court interpreting soon became the second specialization to establish itself. The purpose of court interpreting is usually to support due process and equal access to justice. For example, the Austrian Code of Penal Procedure of 1803 required courts to provide interpreting services, and a 1975 law was passed in Austria on expert witnesses and court interpreters, the *Sachverständigen- und Dolmetschergesetz,* in collaboration with the Austrian Association of Court Interpreters. Then in 1978, a landmark law in the United States called the Court Interpreters Act (28 U.S.C. §1827) established the profession of court interpreting to put defendants who spoke limited English on an equal footing with those fluent in English.

An emerging profession: Community interpreting

What makes Community interpreting "different"

Community interpreting has a special niche among the interpreting professions. Unlike other specializations, it "weds issues of language and culture to concepts of social justice and equity" (Bancroft, 2015). In other words, community interpreting is not only about enabling access to a community service: it is embedded in broader movements that support global social justice and human rights and consider equal access to healthcare, education and basic human services a "civil" or "human" right.

The birth of Community interpreting

Modern-day community interpreting can be traced to the 1970s, when both the term and the profession itself took root. Australia faced increasing demand for interpreting services in community settings due to large waves of immigration after World War II. The largely English-speaking nation with many aboriginal languages was transformed into a nation of immigrants (Pöchhacker, 1999). Anti-discrimination laws were passed that mandated access to services such as healthcare, education and social services for aboriginal peoples, immigrants and other linguistic minorities (Moody, 2011, pp. 38-39).

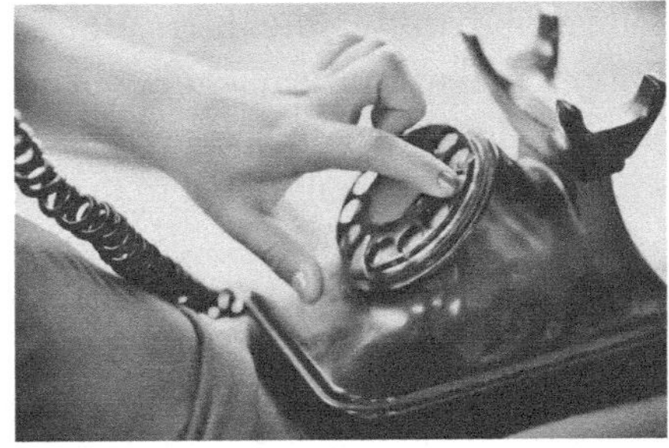

Formal testing and credentials for both spoken and sign language interpreters soon followed, and Australia's national Translating and Interpreting Service, founded in 1947, started its first emergency telephone interpreting service in 1973.[7] Later the National Accreditation Authority for Translators and Interpreters (NAATI) was established.

Community interpreting evolved at roughly the same time in Sweden (Wande, 1994; Niska, 2004) when local governments employed interpreters in community settings and established interpreter training programs; community interpreting itself may have begun in Sweden as early as 1968 (Hein, 2009). By the mid-1970s, interpreting for both spoken and signed languages was becoming common in medical, legal, educational and faith-based settings.

Australia and Sweden helped pave the way for other nations to follow in the 1980s and 1990s, especially in Europe, the United States and Canada. For example, the U.S. Registry of Interpreters for the Deaf established a sign language interpreting profession in the 1960s, and the U.S. Federal Court Interpreters Law passed in 1978. In a seminal event for the field, the first international conference on community interpreting was held by an organization called Critical Link (now Critical Link International) in Toronto, Canada, in 1995.

[7] See http://www.tisnational.gov.au/About-TIS-National/History-of-TIS-National

The expansion of community interpreting

As recently as 10 years ago, community interpreters in Asia, Latin America and the Middle East were rare, sparse or non-existent (Bancroft, 2005). A decade later, indications of professional growth in those regions have grown. The world has seen the birth of many professional associations, national and international meetings of interpreters and a rapid growth in research on community interpreting (Pöllabauer, 2012), as the collected papers of all Critical Link conferences to date attest in addition to research bibliographies (e.g., Vargas Urpi, 2012).

At the triennial Critical Link conference, the largest international forum for community interpreting, presentations come from researchers around the world. Projects like the Cairo Community Interpreter Project[8] and the Telephone Interpreting Services for South Africa,[9] the emergence of medical interpreting as a profession in Japan[10] testify to the rapid expansion of the field. The international chapters of the International Medical Interpreters Association include Brazil, South Korea, Costa Rica, Japan, South Africa, China, Egypt and Russia.[11] There is also a World Association of Sign Language Interpreters.[12]

In addition, throughout Africa's 53 nations, masters and PhD level programs for community interpreting exist, as they do in developing nations such as Canada, the United States and the European Union, particularly Spain. Professional associations for translators (which often include interpreters) exist in Israel, South Africa, Egypt and Morocco, for example.

---

[8] See http://www.aucegypt.edu/gapp/cmrs/ccip/Pages/default.aspx
[9] See http://www.aucegypt.edu/gapp/cmrs/ccip/Pages/default.aspx
[10] See, e.g., http://www.healthhokkaido.com/files/Articles_Oshimi/interpreters.cfm
[11] See http://www.imiaweb.org/about/internationalchapters.asp
[12] See www.wasli.org

One Conference: Many Worlds

During a 2012 international conference hosted in Belfast by the International Association of Translation and Intercultural Studies (IATIS), at which two of the authors presented, a surprising number of presentations addressed community interpreting around the world, including:

- Ad hoc interpreting for refugee applicants in the Korean Administrative Court: Dr. Jieun Lee
- Lay participation in criminal procedures and its implications to court interpreting in Japan. How court interpreting could be detrimental to guaranteeing fair trials: Prof. Makiko Mizuno Kinjo
- Revisiting health care interpreting in the Western Cape (South Africa): The linguistic and extra-linguistic reality: Dr. Harold Lesch
- Understanding and Redefining Different Capacities Required of Professional Interpreters in the Gaza Strip, Palestine: Dr. Mohammed El Haj Ahmed Islamic University of Gaza
- "Do nothing" to "Do no harm": Collaborative values in medical interpreting: Ms. Robyn Dean (Scotland)
- Creating a 'sense of community' amongst adult translators and interpreters studying online: Dr. Kim Wallmach (South Africa)
- Child language brokering in Italy: children's views on their experience as ad-hoc interpreters: Dr. Rachele Antonini and Dr. Ira Torresi
- Liaison Interpreting Research in Mainland China: Lihua Jiang
- Providing Virtual Training to Interpreting Students in Africa - Evaluation of a Pilot Project: Carmen Delgado Luchner and Manuela Motta ETI (Geneva)
- Language-related legislation in South Africa, the right to education in a language of one's choice, and the role of educational interpreting in giving effect to students' linguistic human rights: Johan Blaauw
- The Voice of Love Project: Interpreting for Survivors of Torture, Trauma and Sexual Violence: Marjory Bancroft.
- Constructing a code of ethics for South African Sign-Language interpreters – guiding principles, approach and practice: Mr. Johan Blaauw
- The interpreter as cultural and educational broker in the inclusive classroom: Dr. Jemina Napier, Della Goswell and Dr. Breda Carty (Australia)
- Interpreting for Korean overseas adoptees: Dr. Nam, Won Jun
- The Institutionalization of Community Interpreting as a Complex Matter of Recognition: Sofia Garcia-Beyaert (Spain)
- "Es mi companero de chabolo (He's my cellie)" The issue of trust in interpreting in prison settings: Dr. Aida Martinez-Gomez Gomez (United States)
- A comparison of South African Sign language interpreters: a corpus approach: Jennifer Wehrmeyer Unisa
- The variable identity of the educational interpreter: Johan Blaauw (South Africa)

The IATIS conference is a testament to the professionalization of community interpreting.

Medical interpreting

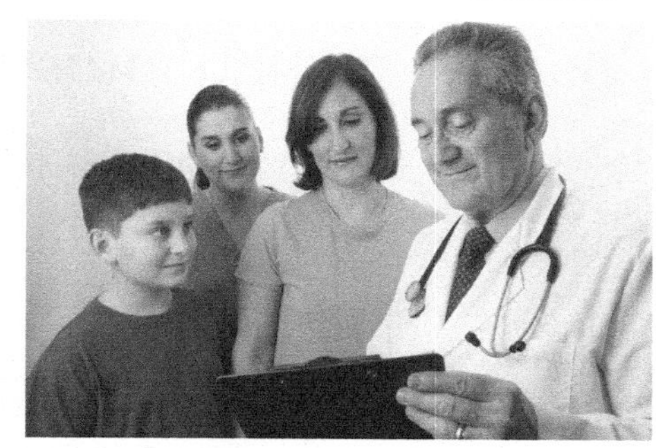

Medical interpreting has a particular history. In some countries, it is simply part of the evolution of the profession as a whole. In others, such as the United States and Japan, medical interpreting, also known as healthcare interpreting, has played a distinct role.

Medical interpreting in such countries started to professionalize earlier, and more rapidly, than any other area of community interpreting (excluding legal interpreting, which many do not consider to be part of community interpreting: see Chapter 4, Section 4.3). As a result, in the United States community interpreters follow national ethics, standards of practice, protocols and requirements for medical interpreting even when they perform social services, educational or faith-based interpreting because no other national ethics, standards and best practices exist.

This reality has led to a peculiar situation where many medical interpreters today do not realize, or acknowledge, that they are in fact community interpreters.

The need for indigenous interpreters

Africa is a continent of deep linguistic diversity, where the need for interpreters is less for immigrants than for indigenous citizens. For example, South Africa has 11 official languages, a language act dating to 2000 and an established interpreting profession. Yet community interpreting is still emerging, with interesting gains in educational and sign language interpreting.[13] Community interpreting across Africa informally takes place on a wide scale, but the professional infrastructure needs support. The same is true in parts of the Middle East and Asia, where interpreting for migrants is growing but interpreting for indigenous residents is often essential. For example, intraregional migration in Latin America has increased (OAS, 2011, p. 9), and so too the need for community interpreters for indigenous languages. Mexico has a national institute for indigenous languages (http://www.inali.gob.mx).

Interpreting for refugees, conflict zones and the "internally displaced"

Several organized efforts to train community interpreters have sprung up for international aid organizations that work with refugee or internally displaced populations (those who flee war, conflict or oppression in one part of their own country but remain, living like refugees, somewhere else within their borders). One example is Red T: an organization dedicated to "the protection of translators and interpreters in conflict zones and adversarial settings."[14] Another is InZone, a humanitarian interpreting project of the University of Geneva. Both train interpreters where conflict and natural disasters are occurring.[15] Both groups have been active in Africa and the Middle East. Regarding interpreting in Israel, see, for example, Morris, 1993; Schlesinger, 1994; and Schuster, 2013.

[13] Several papers on health care, educational and sign language interpreting in South Africa were presented at the fourth international conference of the International Association of Translation and Intercultural Studies (IATIS), 2012, in Belfast: http://www.iatis.org/index.php/4th-iatis-conference/itemlist/category/74-abstracts

[14] See http://red-t.org/

[15] See http://inzone.fti.unige.ch/

Driving forces

Four key driving forces

Today, diverse and powerful factors have led to the exponential growth of community interpreting. Four powerful trends have combined to help trigger the transformation. These driving forces are:

1. Global migration.
2. Language laws and policies.
3. Concerns for quality of care (especially in public services and healthcare).
4. The impact of technology and globalization.

Factors Driving Community Interpreting Today

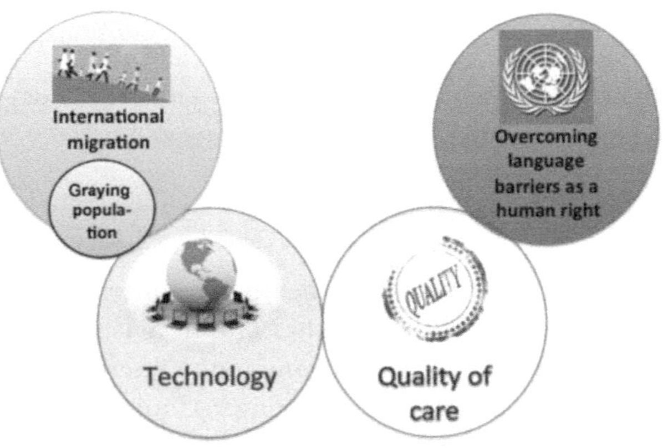

Global migration

A planet on the move

For as long as nations have existed, so has international migration. Yet never before has the planet seen such a broad and diverse group of nationalities, ethnicities, and language groups on the move. According to 2013 UN statistics, more people than ever before live away from their country of origin: 232 million people (3.2 percent of the world's population) have migrated from their home countries.[16] Europe and Asia receive the highest number of foreign born (143 million) but the United States has the largest absolute number (45 million).

Many factors drive international immigration, including war, hardship, human rights violations and the desire for a better life (Golash-Boza & Menjivar, 2012). Migrants seek new opportunities, employment or even a better climate. The economic reality, however, is simple: affluent nations (in part due to low birthrates) urgently need immigrant workers. Foreign-born labor fuels much of the world's economy.

[16] See http://esa.un.org/unmigration/documents/worldmigration/2013/Chapter1.pdf

What migration brings

Many foreign-born residents bring a wealth of assets to their new homes, including:

- The drive to succeed.
- Rich cultural perspectives.
- Language skills needed for globalization.
- Diverse educational and professional backgrounds.
- A strong work ethic.
- A streak of independence combined with fortitude and resilience.

Migrants also bring significant economic contributions. A 2009 UN fact sheet[17] shows that migration contributes to economic growth, improves trade and development, leads to immigrants sending money back to the "home countries" and fosters the transfer of skills and ideas. In short, migrants play an important role in world health and well-being, and migration is a brute economic necessity (Anderson, 2000). These immigration trends appear to be one primary factor in the exponential growth of community interpreting and its professionalization.

Language laws and policies

What are language laws and policies?

Another driving force is language policy and language legislation. Language laws are a broad category of legislation addressing the official use of language. Language policies can be formal legislation or guidelines. "Language policy" refers to any official legislation, court decision or government policy that addresses the formal or legal use of one or more languages.

Language policies or laws can apply to a region, nation, state/province or locality. They may regulate how organizations are run and which languages individuals or employees may speak in public services, commercial settings or workplaces. (Some language policies can even address other concerns, such as educational or national security priorities.) Language policies, especially when enacted into law, tend to promote, require or encourage the use of one or several languages. Sometimes they can be used to devalue certain peoples and even contribute to genocide.

The impact of language laws and policies

In summary, such policies and laws have been instrumental in helping to professionalize community interpreting in a number of countries because:

- Some language policies and laws promote a positive regard for language diversity.
- Some mandate the provision of interpreting services in the language of consumers in publicly funded services (or specific services, such as education, healthcare or court systems.
- Some policies or laws address the need for qualified interpreters in community services.

[17] GMG Fact-Sheet on Contribution of Migrants to Development: Trade, Investment and Development Linkages, 2009, p1. See http://www.globalmigrationgroup.org/sites/default/files/uploads/documents/UNCTAD_GMG_factsheet_trade_investment_development_May2010.pdf

Certain language policies and laws are general and broad, while others specify a specific service such as healthcare or education: for example, the WHO Declaration on the Promotion of Patients' Rights states (WHO, 1994, p. 10) states:

Information must be communicated to the patient in a way appropriate to the latter's capacity for understanding, minimizing the use of unfamiliar technical terminology. If the patient does not speak the common language, some form of interpreting should be available.

Language laws and access to services

Language policies and laws have emerged around the world for many reasons. They have become especially common in regions and nations with a large influx of immigrants. Such laws and policies have also emerged in countries with significant linguistic minorities and those with Deaf residents.

Matters such as renting an apartment, getting a vaccination or registering one's child at school can be nearly impossible without language assistance—much less preparing for a trial or undergoing a sexual-assault examination. Many services providers try to handle this type of challenge by asking children to interpret, writing notes to Deaf individuals or asking an untrained bilingual colleague (or someone waiting in the reception area) to interpret. As a result, many individuals and families are denied the service or receive poor quality of service. To proactively address the situation, the governments of many countries have protected the rights of linguistic minorities through language policies, including language access laws.

Language access laws

What are language access laws?

Language access can be defined as the use of language assistance to facilitate the ability of an individual who does not speak, read, write or understand the language of service well to obtain meaningful access to that service.

Language Access Law

Legislation that requires or stipulates that the impact of discrimination in access to public services be reduced through the provision of competent language assistance.

A *language access law* requires that the impact of discrimination in access to public services be reduced through the provision of competent language assistance. For example, bilingual employees could offer direct services in another language; the agency could provide professional interpreters; and/or important documents (such as consent forms or medical discharge instructions) could be translated.

This usage of the term "language access" derives from U.S. policies (see below), but the concept and term "access" in this context can be found elsewhere. For example, the following text comes from a 2011 bill for a proposed language act in South Africa[18] (which has not yet passed, despite prior efforts over many years): **2.** *The objects of this Act are— [...] to facilitate equitable access to the services and information of the national government.* In 2014, the European Network for Public Service Interpretation and Translation (ENPSIT) stated (ENPSIT, n.d., p. 2) that "ENPSIT supports the democratic right of equal access to public services."

Such laws can manifest themselves at different levels. For example, in the United States, these laws are passed at the federal, state and local levels. In the European Union, there may be directives at

[18] South African Languages Bill, 2011, http://www.pmg.org.za/files/bills/111104b23-11.pdf

the European Union level[19] and specific laws at the level of a state member. As a common denominator, such laws tend to address access to services in healthcare, social services, housing, transportation and schools, courts and/or education. Title VI of the U.S. Civil Rights Act of 1964 addresses *all* programs, services and entities that receive federal financial assistance.

The impact of language access laws

In general, where language access laws exist they tend to have a beneficial impact on the professionalization of community interpreting (Pöchhacker, 1999). By requiring or encouraging language assistance, such laws tend to:

- Increase requests for community interpreters.
- Require or encourage the provision of competent and qualified interpreters.
- Thereby increase opportunities for the training and education of community interpreters.
- Promote efforts to provide meaningful credentials (such as certification) for community interpreters.

Concerns for quality of care

Since roughly the mid-1850s, the concepts of customer service, quality assurance and quality of care have gradually been adopted throughout many private industries and public services (Chassin & O'Kane, 2010). The continued evolution and spread of the basic belief that individuals deserve to be treated with respect and receive a high quality of service has also helped to professionalize community interpreting. Much of the public and nonprofit service sector worldwide is striving to offer high-quality services with good customer care while interacting with a growing number of service users who do not speak the language of service. The focus on quality increases awareness of the need for qualified interpreters.

"Customer service" as a modern concept has its origins in the Industrial Revolution. By 1946, the International Organization for Standardization (ISO) established its first customer service standard with 65 attendees from 25 countries. That standard, updated in 2014, covers for-profit and nonprofit services and products and states:

> *ISO 10002:2004 provides guidance on the process of complaints handling related to products within an organization, including planning, design, operation,* maintenance *and improvement. The complaints-handling process described is suitable for use as one of the processes of an overall quality management system.*[20]

[19] C.f. Directive 2010/64/EU of the European Parliament.
[20] ISO 10002:2014. The quote comes from an abstract available at https://www.iso.org/obp/ui/#iso:std:iso:10002:ed-1:v1:en

"Quality of care" in the healthcare field can generally be defined as follows:

> *Quality (of care) is a measure of the ability of a doctor, hospital or health plan to provide services for individuals and populations that increase the likelihood of desired health outcomes and are consistent with current professional knowledge. Good quality healthcare means doing the right thing at the right time, in the right way, for the right person and getting the best possible results. According to the mantra for the quality improvement movement, care should be "safe, effective, patient-centered, timely, efficient and equitable."*
>
> *A review of research in the field further identifies two core elements to any definition of "quality of care." It should 1) provide care of high technical quality, and 2) "all patients wished to be treated in a humane and culturally appropriate manner and be invited to participate fully in deciding about their therapy."* (Book et al., 2000, p. 2)

While the concept of quality of care may have originated in healthcare, quality of service has become a deep concern in many areas of public and community service.

The impact of technology and globalization

Technology and community interpreting

A final factor helping to push community interpreting forward is technology. At an ever-increasing pace, technology has penetrated almost every aspect of human interaction and communication. Cow-herders in jungle villages today often have smartphones. Smartphones are small computers. A smartphone today holds more practical applications than thousands of gadgets could deliver when purchased in a technology store in the 1990s. While estimates vary, and reliable international estimates are not easy to obtain, it is possible that mobile phone "penetration" will reach up to 70 percent of the world population by 2017; it also seems likely that more than one-third of these phones may be smartphones. Community interpreting, though a young profession, must navigate these swift changes in technology.

Technology is increasing demand for interpreting over remote platforms

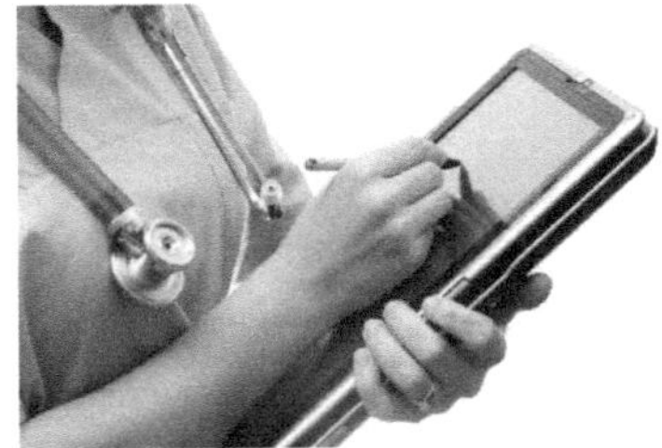

Mobile technology is a game-changer for international communication. When anyone can speak to anyone from anywhere to anywhere, the only communication barrier left is language. Growth trends confirm this point: the international Web conferencing market is expected to grow almost 10 percent between 2015 and 2020,[21] and the global telehealth and telemedicine market is projected to double that growth rate by 2019.

[21] See, e.g., http://www.futuremarketinsights.com/reports/details/web-conferencing-market#src=whatech

From the job perspective, these new technologies appear to increase the number of assignments for community interpreters. Interpreting and translation are two of the fastest-growing professions in the world. In the United States, for example, U.S. labor statistics show that the interpreting and translation profession is expected to grow by 46 percent between 2010 and 2020; globally, the language services industry is worth $42 billion (Pielmeier & DePalma, 2015). Much of that growth is pushed by increased demand for speedy multilingual communication.

To meet this demand, companies are racing to innovate new technologies and service platforms. The goal is to provide interpreter services anywhere, any time. New telephonic, video remote, and even app-based platforms are common. Interpreters are increasingly expected to master such technology if they want to find work.

Furthermore, many physical work settings are going all or partially virtual, such as healthcare and education. As the settings where interpreters traditionally work become virtual, the pressure for interpreters to adapt to new platforms increases. Even school districts, libraries, hospitals and social service programs are purchasing portable interpreting equipment for their interpreters.

Technology connects interpreters

Interpreters are no longer isolated from one another. Social media sites, listservs and services such as Facebook, Twitter and LinkedIn have led to an explosion of interpreting-oriented blogs and discussion forums. They allow community interpreters to stay connected to their native language resources, find training, download dictionaries and maintain their languages. Especially for interpreters in smaller language communities or isolated and rural areas, such resources can be critical. Sometimes the Internet is the only way to maintain contact with a professional community. Interpreters can practice with one another online, on their own initiative or as part of online training programs.

Online resources can also help community interpreters find enough work to make a living. For example, in some countries community interpreters who sign up with agencies and put up professional profiles on interpreting-related websites can receive electronic notifications of assignments. Typically, the first interpreter to respond gets the job.

Resources for interpreters

The interpreter today has access to vast resources online that a generation ago were out of reach. With a good Internet connection, interpreters have easy and quick access to multilingual dictionaries and glossaries, websites, books, videos and audio resources and vast databases of information, often at little to no cost and in seconds.

Online resources have also expanded the interpreter training available. Interpreters can learn about both face-to-face and online training programs on the Web. Online training for interpreters from webinars and workshops to master's-level academic programs can be accessed from an Internet connection, no matter where you live.

How technology challenges interpreters

On the down side, with change comes adaptation and hardship. In some countries, community interpreters have seen their hourly rates go down as more for-profit companies compete to provide affordable language services. Technology has fueled this competition. In addition, many face-to-face assignments are being replaced by telephone or video systems that require the interpreter to sit in an isolated room in an institution or call center all day long—or even all night—taking call after call instead of interacting in person. Few strong guidelines or laws exist to protect working conditions for these interpreters.

Mastering technology may be easier for younger interpreters entering the profession than for senior interpreters. Those who adapt to changing technology may have more professional success. Those who do not may suffer from a loss of work and income as well as professional status and recognition. As one participant of an InterpretAmerica forum stated (Bancroft, Olsen, & Allen, 2011, p. 35):

Interpreters will not be replaced by technology. They will be replaced by other interpreters who use technology.

Despite these challenges, technology remains a powerful driving force in the professionalization of the field.

Professionalization of community interpreting

In recent years, great progress has been made toward the professionalization of the field. Some nations, such as Australia and Great Britain, have established formal educational pathways, certification and control over wages and work conditions.

The United States and Canada have made significant contributions by creating national ethics and standards for community interpreter services (Canada: HIN, 2007) and medical interpreting (the United States: NCIHC, 2004 and 2005), as well as national standards for healthcare interpreter training (United States: NCIHC, 2011) and a growing number of training and education programs. Both nations, however, lack nationally recognized professional associations and education pathways specific to community interpreting, though Canada seems closer to this goal. Canada is also the birthplace of Critical Link International and is currently developing certification for community interpreters, beginning with a provincial interpreters association in Ontario.[22]

In most countries, however, community interpreters still lack access to professional resources, such as training programs, national codes of ethics and professional associations. In short, the professionalization of this field is a work in progress.

[22] Association of Translators and Interpreters of Ontario (ATIO). See http://www.atio.on.ca/membership/applications/comapp.php

Let's Practice

Learning Activity 1.1 (a): Defining Community Interpreting
Learning Activity 1.1 (b): The History of Community (and Medical) Interpreting

In *The Community Interpreter®: An International Workbook of Activities and Role Plays*

REVIEW OF SECTION 1.1

This section provided a brief overview of the history and the current state of community interpreting around the world. Whether you are already practicing as a community interpreter or just beginning your studies, it is important to remember the following key points:

- Community interpreting is a young profession.
- It is one of the oldest activities in the world, but its professional roots can be found in the 1970s in Australia, Sweden, and later Canada and the United States.
- Community interpreting takes place wherever community services are provided and service users do not speak the language of service. The list of settings is diverse.
- The primary purpose of community interpreting is to enhance or enable access to community services for those who do not speak the language of service.
- Community interpreting today is driven by many forces, including:
    - Global migration.
    - Language laws and policies.
    - Concerns for quality of care.
    - The impact of technology and globalization.

1.2 Interpreter Credentials

Overview

A credential is a form of evidence of a qualification. It shows one's ability, or authority, to carry out a certain job or task. Many credentials exist for community interpreters, but not all of them are equal. A number of so-called credentials are meaningless, because the organizations that issued them have not assessed the interpreter and/or have no authority to issue such credentials.

This section examines what you, as a community interpreter (or an aspiring interpreter), need to know about the credentials that may be available where you live, and which ones matter. Misrepresentation of interpreter credentials is a common practice that dilutes the profession. It also undermines respect for community interpreters and slows the professionalization of the field. Always correctly represent your credentials.

For example, let's say you pay an annual fee to join a professional interpreting association. That membership in the association is a *credential.* It attests that you support the profession and care enough about quality interpreting to join a professional association. The credential says little more. In other words, in most cases the association is not saying you are "a qualified, professional interpreter," or, "This is an interpreter you can trust." In most cases, the association can only state that the interpreter has paid dues and is in good standing.

If, on the other hand, the association requires *testing* or some widely respected process of assessing the candidate (the most famous example would be AIIC—the International Association of Conference Interpreters, the leading worldwide organization for conference interpreters), then—and only then—would that membership become a significant credential.

Similarly, a certificate is not always to be trusted. Interpreters can easily get certificates for attending conferences, orientations and short trainings of varying quality. Unless the organization that issues the certificate has credibility and it is conferred only upon the completion of a respected program, that certificate may not be a serious credential. A more respected credential for community interpreters would be *certification* or *licensure*, discussed in detail in this section.

Learning Objective 1.2

After completing this section, you will be able to:

- Analyze and compare interpreter credentials, including certificates and certification.

Basic qualifications

An overview of interpreting credentials

Most interpreters lack clearly recognized national credentials. Few countries have a single, comprehensive credentialing system. With the exception of a handful of nations, such as Australia and Sweden, certification or another national credential for general interpreting does not exist, far less for community interpreting. However, some countries such as the UK have national registries for general or community interpreting that help community interpreters to establish their credibility. In addition, a growing number of countries have certification programs for specializations, like court or medical interpreting. In some countries, full academic pathways up to master's and PhD programs are available for conference or community interpreting.

Types of credentials

General interpreting credentials may include:

- Training or education certificates.
- General degrees, such as bachelor of arts.
- Interpreting degrees.
- Proof of language proficiency.
- Membership in professional associations.
- Professional awards or honors.

These are a few examples of the most common credentials for this field.

General education

In an ideal world, all professional interpreters would hold a university degree. At this time, requiring community interpreters to hold a university degree appears impractical. Interpreters should meet the educational standards required in a particular region. For example, many conference interpreters are expected to hold a university degree and/or a degree or credential in conference interpreting. The relevant credential for general education is a diploma for secondary studies or a degree in any subject from any accredited institution of higher education.

Training

Training programs typically take place *outside* institutions of higher education. They often range in length from a few hours to a few days. They are rarely longer than 60–90 hours and usually much shorter. Such programs vary by sector and region. Regardless of years of experience, interpreters should meet the minimum local training standards required for a given specialization. A certificate for the successful completion of a quality training program in community, medical, legal or social services interpreting is a valuable credential.

The usual credential for completing a training program is a certificate, or in some cases a signed letter, which may attest to any or all the following:

- Attendance at the program.
- Successful completion of the program following a written exam.
- Successful completion of the program following an oral exam of interpreting skills.

Higher education programs for interpreting

Interpreter education programs typically take place *inside* institutions of higher education. A growing number of these programs are available for conference, court and community (including medical) interpreting. Such programs range in length from a short certificate- or one-semester program to a full degree program of three to five years and masters or PhD programs. Some interpreting programs are often combined with translation studies. Degree programs may offer one specialization or several. Signed language programs are often generalist programs. The usual credential for attending a higher education program is one or more of the following:

- A college or university transcript showing a certain number of credits earned.
- A certificate.
- A degree in interpreting.
- A degree in interpreting and translation.

Language proficiency certificates

Testing an interpreter for language proficiency should be performed using an externally validated test administered by qualified raters. The test should ideally be calibrated to a national or international scale with recognized proficiency levels, such as the Common European Framework of Reference for Languages (CEFR) or the Interagency Language Roundtable (ILR). The test should result in a score that is easily compared to scores for other candidates of that nation or region.

The usual credential would be a letter, certificate or other document attesting to the level of language proficiency on the relevant scale. However, if the test itself was not externally and rigorously validated, administered by qualified, professional raters/examiners and calibrated to a recognized, credible scale of language proficiency, then this credential may be of dubious value.

Certification

Certification of interpreters involves a rigorous evaluation of interpreter skills resulting in a meaningful credential. It is discussed below in detail. Certification may be awarded for general interpreting or for a specialization, such as medical or court interpreting.

Maintaining certification usually, but not always, involves certain requirements, such as obtaining a certain number of continuing education credits over a specific period of time.

A common certification credential would be a document attesting that the interpreter has been awarded the certification in a specified language pair. His or her name may also be listed in a publicly available registry of such interpreters, with the language pair noted.

Licensing

Interpreter licensing, or licensure, differs from certification. Certification is a credential that distinguishes one interpreter from another interpreter who has not obtained that certification, but licensure confers the legal ability to practice a profession. For example, in many countries, lawyers are prohibited from practicing law until they pass a bar exam. In other countries, lawyers may practice law after obtaining a law degree without passing such an exam.

Interpreter licensing exists but is not common at this time. Such licensing may be for general interpreting or a particular specialization. Licensure is discussed in more detail later in this section. The usual resulting credential is a license conferred by a government agency permitting the interpreter to practice that specialization in a specific geographic region.

Portfolio assessments

For languages or regions where interpreter skills tests may not be available, or even valid language proficiency tests for that interpreter's working languages, proof of credentials may involve reviewing an interpreter's portfolio. Such a portfolio could document the interpreter's general education, interpreter education or training and professional experience. It might also include letters of recommendation, awards or other documents attesting to experience and skill.

Which credentials do you need?

What type of proof of qualifications and skills should you have to perform community interpreting? Regardless of your level of experience, a consensus has emerged around the world regarding the ***minimum*** set of qualifications and skills that community interpreters should possess.

In December 2014, ISO published the first international standards for community interpreting. The seminal document[23] stated that organizations providing interpreter services should verify that the community interpreter can meet at least one of the following criteria (ISO, 2014, p. 8):

> *a) a recognized degree (e.g., BA or BSc) in interpreting from an institution of higher education or a recognized educational certificate in community interpreting;*
> *b) a recognized degree in any other field from an institution of higher education plus two years of continuous experience in community interpreting or a relevant certificate from a recognized institution;*
> *c) a certificate of competence in interpreting awarded by an appropriate government body or government-accredited body for this field, and proof of further qualifications or experience in community interpreting;*
> *d) five years of continuous experience in community interpreting in cases where a) to c) cannot reasonably be met.*

[23] Disclaimer: Two of the authors of this textbook participated in the creation of this ISO standard.

Within some countries, such as the United States, the profession increasingly recognizes that any community interpreter should demonstrate the following:

- Be 18 years or older.
- Hold a high school diploma or equivalent.
- Demonstrate bilingualism and literacy, preferably by showing proof of a validated language proficiency test.
- Hold a certificate for professional training in community or medical interpreting of at least 40 hours.

In most countries there is still some disagreement about whether a community interpreter should hold a university degree or only a secondary school diploma, and also about how much training an entry-level community interpreter should receive.

Basic interpreting skill requirements

In addition, community interpreters should be able to (ISO, 2014, p. 7):

- *interpret in consecutive and simultaneous mode, as appropriate;*
- *sight-translate written materials written in both working languages (when applicable);*
- *take notes during the interpreted assignment if necessary (e.g., consecutive mode);*
- *monitor his/her own performance;*
- *demonstrate active listening skills;*
- *demonstrate effective delivery skills;*
- *possess strong memory skills;*
- *identify and convey the appropriate registers;*
- *demonstrate ability and anticipation to intervene during the interaction;*
- *develop effective problem-solving strategies;*
- *develop and practice effective intervention skills, including transparency;*
- *respect/manage professional scopes of practice and professional boundaries of all participants in the interpreted communicative event;*
- *cultivate and address self-awareness of personal bias;*
- *strive to improve performance through self-training, attendance of further training courses (which should be documented) and life-long learning;*
- *observe applicable standards of practice and code of ethics in his/her work;*
- *be a good team player and interpreting partner (e.g., cases of relays or multiple languages);*
- *be familiar with cultures of the source and target languages; or live in the target culture;*
- *strive for professionalism at all times;*
- ***support client autonomy (e.g., refrain from giving advice)*** [emphasis added]*;*
- *use chuchotage.*

The authors of this textbook are not aware of accepted national standards for qualifications and skills for community interpreters. However, in 2011, U.S. national standards for ***healthcare interpreter training*** were published by the National Council on Interpreting in Health Care (NCIHC) about specific minimum qualifications and skills for healthcare interpreters (**www.ncihc.org**).

Certification

Defining Certification

One credential for interpreters in particular has caused confusion: certification. Below are four definitions of the term *certification*. The first comes from the leading international standards organization and the others are from two community interpreting specialists and a U.S. national multidisciplinary group that supports quality interpreting in healthcare.

certification

> *third-party attestation related to products, processes, systems or persons*
>
> ISO/IEC, 2004, definition 5.5

> *In the strictest sense, certification means that a particular certifying body is guaranteeing that the certified individual has the capacity to perform a particular set of skills up to an established criterion.... First, a certification is guarantee of the candidate's abilities, and second, the candidate's skills have been compared to an established standard. In most cases, certification includes testing, however certification can also include or be based on education and experience alone. A certification without concrete skills testing in a field like health care interpreting, however, would have little credibility.*
>
> Roat, 2006, p. 3.

> *Certification recognizes practitioners who have demonstrated professional competence, such as completing a course of study and/or passing an examination, but is generally not required. Consumers have access to this information so that they can make educated decisions regarding which practitioners (certified or non-certified) they select to perform a given activity. Certification does not restrict entry into the profession, unless laws are passed that require certification in a given area.*
>
> Kelly, 2008a, p. 25

> *Certification: A process by which a governmental or professional organization attests to or certifies that an individual is qualified to provide a particular service. Certification calls for formal assessment, using an instrument that has been tested for validity and reliability, so that the certifying body can be confident that the individuals it certifies hold the qualifications needed to do the job. Sometimes called qualification.*
>
> NCIHC, www.ncihc.org

Judging by these four definitions, it is clear that certification is a controversial and confusing topic for interpreters. This section will try to shed some light on it.

Certification vs. licensure

Certification should be clearly distinguished from licensing or licensure. Kelly (2008a, pp. 25-26) makes the distinctions clear, for example:

> *In contrast, certification is a statement of an individual's qualifications. Certification can be issued by non-governmental bodies* [... It is] *based on the premise that one has a right to engage in the work. It serves to give the consumer information about the practitioner, and, in some cases, can be combined with state laws to control entry into a profession, although to a lesser degree than licensure.*

Concept	Licensure	Certification
View of the Activity	Presumes that the work activity is a privilege.	Presumes that the activity is a right.
Purpose	To strictly control the activity and/or restrict entry into the profession, often in the interest of safety.	To inform and educate consumers about the qualifications of individual providers.
Function	Grants permission to perform an activity.	Confirms that one meets certain criteria.
Adoption by Practitioners	Mandatory in order to perform an activity.	Voluntary. Non-certified individuals are still allowed to practice.
Decision Making	The government is empowered to require licensed interpreters; reduces the power of consumer to choose providers who may not be qualified.	Enhances the power of the consumer to choose from among certified or non-certified providers.
Reprimands	If licensing law is violated, the violator is subject to fines, penalties and/or other forms of punishment.	Certification could be revoked, but the individual may still practice.

Table 1-A: Conceptual Differences Between Licensure and Certification

Types of certification

Interpreter certification can broadly be broken into three basic categories:

- Government certification or licensure.
- Professional certification (administered by a professional body).
- Program certificates (awarded, for example, following a screening, orientation, training or test.) This latter type of "certification" is *not* recognized by the profession.

1. Government certification can be offered at the national, regional or state/provincial level, depending on the country in question. In the United States, for example, only one state (Washington state) requires state credentialing for community interpreters in public healthcare and social service sectors. That credential is awarded based on a state exam available in eight language pairs that can confer both certification and licensure. Some local governments can also certify community interpreters, but because their exams have not been externally validated, certification by a local government agency does not appear to be recognized or accepted by professional interpreting associations.

2. Professional certification is an exam given either by an organization accredited to administer a certification test, or by a professional association (that should ideally also be accredited by a body specialized in certification).[24]

[24] E.g., the two national medical certification programs for U.S. interpreters, discussed below, are both accredited by the National Commission for Certifying Agencies (NCCA), the accrediting body of the Institute for Credentialing Excellence (ICE).

Certification for interpreters exists in several nations and can sometimes lead to government licensure. Australia and the UK both have national accreditation: in Australia, certification is intended for general interpreters and many community interpreters obtain it; in the UK, public service (community) interpreters have their own national exam for the Diploma in Public Service Interpreting, a national credential.

3. *Program certificates* are often confused with certification. Certificates for training can be given to interpreters who attend courses or orientations as short as one hour and as long as one to two years of study. This type of credential is not recognized by professionals as "real" certification.

Certificates vs. certification

A certificate of training *is* a credential. It is *not* recognized as certification by the profession of community interpreting. In some countries, to state that you are "certified" because you hold a program certificate could be considered misrepresentation of your credentials.

Certification should be performed by professional organizations or government entities using a validated examination that adheres to national or international standards for professional certification. It is unfortunate that some organizations (such as school systems, hospitals and language companies, among others) claim to "certify" interpreters, typically after a brief orientation. Such "certification" is meaningless. It also leads to widespread confusion. This dilution of credentials devalues the profession and supports a sadly wide perception that community interpreting is not a "real" profession.

Community interpreter certification in the United States A case in point

Accepted certification programs in the United States

Here is an example of how interpreter certification plays out across a large country: a snapshot of certification in the United States today for community interpreters. U.S. programs accepted as valid certification include (assuming English as the other working language):

- National Board for Certified Medical Interpreters (Spanish, Russian, Vietnamese, Mandarin, Korean and Cantonese).
- Certification Commission for Healthcare Interpreters (Spanish, Mandarin and Arabic)
- Federal court interpreter certification (Spanish only).
- State court interpreter certification (20 languages).
- National Association of Judiciary Interpreters and Translators (NAJIT) certification for judiciary interpreters and translators (Spanish).
- Washington state certification for medical and social services interpreters (Cambodian, Chinese-Cantonese, Chinese-Mandarin, Korean, Laotian, Russian, Spanish and Vietnamese).
- Registry of Interpreters for the Deaf (RID) national certification for English and American Sign Language (ASL) interpreters.[25]

[25] Interpreters who hold this certification may take a specialized legal interpreter certification exam as well. Those who interpret English-Spanish-ASL who hold national ASL certification may take a special exam in Texas to get a credential as a "trilingual" interpreter. RID offers other specialized certifications, including those for Certified Deaf Interpreters.

How U.S. interpreter certification programs work

Interpreter certification programs in the United States typically include a written application with requirements to submit supporting documents, followed by a written exam in English, then an oral exam to test interpreting skills. State courts in the United States may have other requirements, such as a two- or three-day orientation and even a language proficiency test prior to taking the exam. Most programs require testing in consecutive, simultaneous and sight translation modes. Some require proof of language proficiency, training and/or other credentials.

How programs compare

The most rigorous interpreter certification exams in the United States are for ***court interpreters***. Official pass rates for the U.S. federal court interpreter certification exam (Spanish-English only) hover between 4 and 5 percent. Results for the 20 languages of state court interpreter exams vary by year, state and language: anecdotally, it appears that the pass rate is about 15 percent. Pass rates for sign language certification exams administered by RID are less than 50 percent and for oral exams for the two national medical interpreter certification programs between 70 and 75 percent.

Medical interpreter certification

In the United States, healthcare is "big business." As a result, medical interpreting here is more professionalized than other specializations of community interpreting. In 2009 and 2010, two national medical interpreter certification programs were established. *The history behind these programs is worth special mention.*

The story of medical interpreter certification in the United States dates to the 1990s. At that time, many groups across the country expressed a strong interest in developing a program to certify medical interpreters. The Massachusetts Medical Interpreters Association (MMIA, which became the International Medical Interpreters Association, IMIA, in 2008) piloted certification tests in Massachusetts and California. Soon the push for national certification grew intense. After early conflicts about who should lead the way, a broad coalition of entities was established: in 2008, 15 organizations founded the National Coalition on Health Care Interpreter Certification (NCC) to develop a national certification program.

In January 2009, IMIA and Language Line University (the testing arm of the largest telephone interpreting company in the world) separated from the NCC and announced the creation of their own national medical interpreter certification program. They founded the National Board of Certification for Medical Interpreters (NBCMI) as the legal certifying entity; NBCMI later became part of IMIA.

The other organizations within NCC then founded the Certification Commission for Healthcare Interpreters (CCHI), which unveiled its own certification program in 2010. Today, both NBCMI and CCHI actively certify interpreters. The two certification exams are somewhat different. For example, one includes a test for translation and also tests for simultaneous interpreting; the other has a written test that is 75 percent based on medical terminology. Both organizations offer credentials to interpreters who pass the written exam in English but who do not speak a language for which oral certification is available. Both NBCMI (with exams in six language pairs) and CCHI (with three language pairs) plan to develop oral exams in other languages.

The community interpreting profession in the United States has learned a great deal from the two programs, and competition between them may have enhanced the quality of both. Many U.S. healthcare organizations now routinely require interpreter certification. By promoting national dialogue and education about certification, both NBCMI and CCHI have helped to clarify what certification is and why it matters for interpreters.

Let's Practice

Learning Activity 1.2: Interpreter Credentials and Certification

In *The Community Interpreter®: An International Workbook of Activities and Role Plays*

REVIEW OF SECTION 1.2

At present, no internationally accepted credentials distinguish professional community interpreters from unqualified bilingual individuals. This situation has led to confusion in the field. One goal would be to establish clear national or international standards, and pathways for education and credentialing, based on ISO (2014) standards. Formal credentialing programs like certification could then, in each country, help to raise quality in the field. At a minimum, the community interpreter should:

- Be 18 years or older.
- Hold a secondary school diploma or equivalent.
- Demonstrate bilingualism and literacy, preferably by showing proof of a validated language proficiency test.
- Hold a certificate for professional training in community or medical interpreting of at least 40 hours.

In addition, according to ISO international standards for community interpreting (ISO, 2014), the community interpreter would have at last one of the following:

a) a recognized degree (e.g., BA or BSc) in interpreting from an institution of higher education or a recognized educational certificate in community interpreting;
b) a recognized degree in any other field from an institution of higher education plus two years of continuous experience in community interpreting or a relevant certificate from a recognized institution;
c) a certificate of competence in interpreting awarded by an appropriate government body or government-accredited body for this field, and proof of further qualifications or experience in community interpreting;
d) five years of continuous experience in community interpreting in cases where a) to c) cannot reasonably be met.

It is also important to keep the following in mind:

- Credentialing for community interpreters varies widely across countries.
- Meaningful credentials for community interpreters raise standards in the field.
- In general, credentials are more commonly available for legal and/or medical interpreters than for community interpreters.
- The most respected credentials in community interpreting today are typically certification and licensure.

Inform yourself about the credentialing options in your area. Be aware that:

- Meaningful credentials typically require training and testing.
- *A certificate is not the same as certification.*
- You need to understand the differences between a training certificate, certification and licensure.

1.3 Ethics and Standards for Community Interpreters

Introducing eight core ethical principles

One day an African interpreter in mental health faced the following situation: the therapist asked the client, "Have you heard any voices?"

"Yes," said the client. "Shanto came in the form of a little bird and spoke to me. "

The interpreter knew that in the culture of the client, it is not uncommon for healthy, happy individuals to experience a god or spirit speaking to them in the form of an animal or a bird. But if the interpreter explained the situation, perhaps she would be wrong. If she didn't, perhaps the therapist would think the client was crazy and hearing voices. What should this interpreter do?

This section introduces eight core ethical principles that have shaped the profession of community interpreting.

While community interpreting has many national codes of ethics and standards of practice, this textbook relies on a document created by the authors (García-Beyaert, Bancroft, Allen, Carriero-Contreras, & Socarrás-Estrada, 2015) that appears at the beginning of this textbook called *Ethics and Standards for The Community Interpreter®: An International Training Tool.* For ease of discussion the authors will usually refer to that document throughout this textbook as the *Ethics and Standards* document. Its purpose is to provide guidance on generally accepted principles of conduct for community interpreters in most parts of the world. The full document is available online as a separate document at www.thecommunityinterpreter.com.

Learning Objective 1.3

After completing this section, you will be able to:

- Demonstrate an understanding of eight core ethical principles for community interpreters.

Purpose of creating a code of ethics for international use

The authors' purpose in creating the *Ethics and Standards* document is *not* to replace any national or regional ethics and standards for community interpreters, where such documents exist. Rather, the goal is to support the education and training of community interpreters.

The *Ethics and Standards* document provides guidelines for ethical conduct that reflect common principles, values and practice accepted in the field throughout most of the world, although some of the content is innovative and reflects the special contributions of its authors. However, if a code of ethics for community interpreters exists that applies to your country or region, refer to that document. For example, community interpreters in the United States should study and adhere to the *National Code of Ethics for Interpreters in Health Care* (www.ncihc.org); interpreters in Australia should refer to the AUSIT standards (www.ausit.org); and those in Canada have the HIN (2007) standards. However, the discussion in this chapter can benefit almost any community interpreter.

Why ethics are essential

Ethics are the bedrock of a profession. They help you navigate the most common ethical challenges you face in the field. Community interpreters work in settings that often lead to ethical challenges and dilemmas, in part due to the variety of situations you encounter and confusion about your role.

Community interpreting can be a profoundly rewarding profession on many levels, both personal and professional. Yet it is also filled with the unexpected. No book, workshop or university degree could possibly address every situation you will encounter in the field. In addition, no matter how much experience you gain, there will still be times when you ask yourself, "What am I supposed to *do*?" Interpreter training and education programs can help you only up to a point. Once you are working as an interpreter, ethics and their related standards will provide you with the guidance you will need to make wise decisions.

For example, during an assignment, after a particularly confusing exchange the service provider might turn to you and ask, "Why can't this woman just answer my question? Is she even listening?" To be accurate, you should interpret everything. But if you do, the service user will probably be insulted and the session could fall apart. This type of choice represents an ethical challenge. When these moments come, you will need practical strategies to help you to think and act quickly. Professional interpreter ethics and standards are your guide.

What is a profession?

Section 1.1 defined the profession of community interpreting as "a specialization of interpreting that facilitates access to community services for individuals who do not speak the language of service." To frame that discussion, it is important to step back and consider what a profession *is*. In other words, what makes a certain type of activity a hobby but another type of activity a formal profession?

Code of Ethics

A set of directives that specify the requirements or expectations intended to guide the conduct of practitioners of a profession.

First, in the absence of a code of ethics or conduct, it is hard to defend the idea that a given activity is a profession. From this point of view, community interpreting is not yet a profession in most countries. Yet professional ethics are critical for community interpreters. Certain professions require the trust of their stakeholders, including the helping and healing professions such as healthcare, law, teaching and social work. Because service providers can easily abuse the public trust, codes of ethics offer clear guidance to promote both trust and accountability.

Community interpreting is such a profession. If the interpreter changes the message, violates professional boundaries or undermines the service user's autonomy, he or she is breaking trust. Ethics lay down clear mandates for acceptable conduct so that interpreters can know what to do and can be held accountable for their professional conduct.

Ethics alone do not make a profession: ethics are necessary, but not sufficient. Holly Mikkelson, a respected leader in legal interpreting in the United States, wrote an influential paper on the formalization of community interpreting as a profession, identifying the stages that most professional activities go through on the path to full professionalization (Mikkelson, 1996). She suggests a rough consensus that many professionals share:

- Mastery of an accepted body of knowledge for practitioners.
- A defined period of academic preparation.
- A certification or licensure exam to prove competence.
- Familiarity with established codes of ethics and standards of conduct.
- Ongoing continuing education.
- Service to a higher public good.

In addition, the profession itself should ideally have:

- Established, accepted codes of ethics and professional standards or best practices.
- Professional associations that oversee and support practitioners.
- A body of members regulated by a professional or governmental entity.
- Exclusivity or monopoly (meaning that only credentialed practitioners can practice in the field) through licensure, for example.
- Legal recognition of the profession.

Clearly community interpreting has a long way yet to go.

Existing ethics and standards for community interpreting

What is a code of ethics?

What is a code of ethics?

A code of ethics is a set of directives that specifies the requirements or expectations intended to guide the conduct of those who practice a profession. In short, it tells the members of a profession what to do as they conduct their work. Ethical codes exist to promote professional behavior, make practice of that profession more consistent, prevent wrongdoing and engage public trust.

Think of a code of ethics as a set of rules. Rules can be (and have been) defined in many different ways, including:

- A prescribed guideline for conduct or behavior.
- A set of principles or regulations that govern conduct within a particular activity or sphere.
- A written order or direction.
- A regulating principle.
- A precept or practice.

> **DEFINITION**
>
> **Code of ethics**
>
> a set of principles or values that govern the conduct of members of a profession while they are engaged in the enactment of that profession
>
> (NCIHC, 2004, p. 6)

In this view, ethics can be thought of as the strictest rules or directives for the practitioners of a profession. They are principles or values expressed in the form of "should" statements: that is, statements that tell you to "do this" and "don't do that." Ethics are often binding. For example, if you violate a code of ethics for interpreters and someone reports you, you might lose your certification or be barred from interpreting in settings such as courts. Ethics also tend to be more rigid than other types of guidelines such as standards.

What is an ethical principle?

What is an ethical principle?

An ethical principle is a precept in a code of ethics that focuses on a particular professional concern. (In legal interpreting ethical codes, the word "canon" may be used instead.) For example, Bancroft (2005) examined 143 codes of ethics and standards of practice for interpreters around the world in five different interpreting specializations and sign language interpreting; she found that every single document included a precept about accuracy. "Accuracy" might, therefore, be a universal ethical principle for interpreters.

In other words, ethical principles are the requirements that distill the essence of professional expectations about a certain topic or concern. Disregarding these principles or precepts can have professional or legal consequences, at least in cases where an authoritative body oversees the code. For example, interpreters can be, and are, stripped of certification or lose licensure (and thus the ability to practice as an interpreter) for violating ethical principles. Such consequences have also been imposed on other professionals, such as lawyers, doctors and teachers.

Ethics may be strict, but they are not laws. Laws are more black and white than ethics: if you drive above a specified speed limit, such as 120 kilometers (75 miles) per hour, and you are caught on radar, you have violated the law and may receive a ticket if you are caught. Ethics are not as stringent or specific. Interpreters must be accurate, for example—but how, exactly, can accuracy be measured? In addition, many codes of ethics are created by bodies that have no authority to impose consequences. So while one can speak of ethics as being the strictest set of "rules" or "requirements" for a profession, often no entity enforces them.

What are standards of practice?

Standards of practice provide a set of formal guidelines that offer practitioners of a profession clear strategies and courses of action to support professional conduct. For purposes of this textbook, the authors consider codes of ethics as the strictest principles available to guide the professional conduct of members of a profession, while viewing standards of practice as the *guidelines* that help us navigate the inevitable gray areas.

> **DEFINITION**
>
> **Standards of practice**
>
> Standards of practice are a set of guidelines that define what an interpreter does in the performance of his or her role, that is, the tasks and skills the interpreter should be able to perform in the course of fulfilling the duties of the profession. Standards describe what is considered "best practice" by the profession and ensure a consistent quality of performance. For health care interpreters, the standards define the acceptable ways by which they can meet the core obligations of their profession–the accurate and complete transmission of messages between a patient and provider who do not speak the same language in order to support the patient-provider therapeutic relationship. (NCIHC, 2005, p. 1)

Much confusion exists about the differences between codes of ethics, codes of conduct, standards of practice, guidelines for practice and other documents. Sometimes, a code of ethics includes standards of practice, and these standards offer guidance about how to adhere to ethics. Standards often give more explicit strategies than a code of ethics. For example, an ethical principle might require you to be accurate. A standard of practice might offer you such details about how to do so, such as maintaining the register (level of formality) and preserving the tone, intent and spirit of the original message. In short:

- Ethics are the strictest *directives* (rules or requirements) about conduct within a profession, while standards of practice offer *guidelines* about how to behave.
- Ethics tell us *what* to do; standards tell us *how* to it.
- Ethics are usually more rigid than standards.
- Violating ethics may have consequences (such as losing one's job, certification or the right to practice a profession).
- Violating standards might have milder consequences—if any.

Interpreting ethics and standards around the world

If ethics are the roadmap, standards help us to reach the destination. However, in many cases and in many countries, there may be no clear separation between ethics and standards in a particular document. Ethics and standards can be presented together in a hybrid document (not always labeled as ethics and standards). Conversely, ethics and standards can be folded into professional codes of conduct or guidelines for practice. For an overview with examples, see Bancroft, 2005.

Furthermore, community interpreting has relatively few formal codes of ethics and standards of practice, which interferes with the ability of community interpreters to be taken seriously as professionals. It also makes it harder to clarify their role. Community interpreters in areas without developed ethics and standards of practice might have to study documents from others parts of the world and adapt them to their local settings (the best they can) or refer to the *Ethics and Standards* document at the beginning of this textbook. Because no international body has published a formal code of ethics or standards of practice for community interpreting, in many regions there is an "an ethical vacuum." ISO worked for several years with 29 nations to produce an international standard for community interpreting (ISO, 2014). However, despite efforts to include a code of ethics, the standard does not provide one: community interpreters are urged to adhere to local ethics and standards (ISO, 2014, p. 11).

Common Guidelines

Examples of Principles from Interpreter Codes of Ethics and Standards of Practice Around the World (Bancroft, 2005)		
Confidentiality	**Accuracy**	**Impartiality**
Maintain strict confidentiality.	Be complete/interpret everything.	Maintain impartiality/neutrality.
Disclose only with client agreement or by law.	Be accurate.	Give no advice/recommendations.
Waive confidentiality in public settings.	Make no additions or omissions.	Insert no opinions, even if asked.
Offer no identifying details.	Retain fidelity to message/meaning.	Do not show feelings in face, gestures.
Adhere to confidentiality indefinitely.	Convey spirit of message.	Allow no influence of personal beliefs.
Professional competence	Promptly disclose and rectify errors.	Decline or withdraw from assignments affecting impartiality.
Use first person.	Maintain language register.	Exert no influence on parties.
Accept no assignments if unqualified.	Interpret vulgar language, gestures.	Do not engage in side conversations.
If discovered incompetent, withdraw.	Interpret disturbing messages.	Do not give parties personal contact info.
Accurately represent qualifications.	Favor meaning over literal interpreting.	Do not drive client anywhere.
Prepare for assignments.	Interpret nonverbal cues.	Refrain from interpreting for known parties.
Consult dictionary as needed.	Interpreter interprets untruths.	Be unobtrusive/maintain low profile.
Confirm arrangements in advance.	Interpret insults to client.	Engage in no discrimination or prejudice.
Ask for pauses to manage flow.	Ask for clarification as needed.	Avoid stereotyping.
Ask parties to slow speech as needed.	Interpret within cultural context.	Make no referrals to third parties.
Maintain transparency.	**Professionalism**	**Compensation**
Adopt appropriate positioning.	Maintain high performance standards.	No additional fees.
Pre-Session	Honor integrity of self and profession.	No gifts, gratuities, benefits.
Hold pre-session with client, provider.	Be punctual or early.	May share gifts of food with colleagues.
Clarify interpreter roles.	Respect laws/legal requirements.	Charge fair, reasonable fees (if contractor).
Ask parties to speak to each other.	Be accountable for decision-making.	Pro bono services sometimes acceptable.
Ask parties to pause if needed.	Do not cancel without good cause.	Accept no assignments from clients.
State everything will be interpreted.	If canceling/delayed, notify promptly.	**Professional development**
Provide clear introduction.	Be polite, courteous and discreet.	Pursue professional development.
Interpreter Roles	Keep cell phones/audible beepers off.	Maintain contact with the language.
Be flexible: adapt to situation.	Bring/send no third parties to work.	Support development of colleagues.
Maintain appropriate positioning.	Remain until dismissed.	Incorporate research into practice.
May perform some advocacy.	Dress in appropriate attire.	**Professional solidarity**
May provide information & referral.	**Interpreter rights and well being**	Engage in professional solidarity/ support.
If in conflict over role, withdraw.	Protect safety of interpreter.	Make no malicious remarks re: colleagues.
Report any advocacy to supervisor.	Practice self care.	Assist and support beginners.
Check for understanding.	Take break if too tired to interpret well.	Express respect for colleagues.
Do not interfere with provider roles.	**Client rights**	Promote the dignity of the profession.
Refer client questions to provider.	Do not exploit client trust.	**Conflict of interest**
Do not answer client questions.	Respect gender needs/roles.	Avoid/declare conflict of interest.
Let provider explain forms.	Promote client self determination.	Withdraw if conflict of interest presents.
Do not practice dual roles.	Promote patient self-sufficiency.	Inform parties of conflict.

(Bancroft & Rubio-Fitzpatrick, 2011, p. 70, adapted from Bancroft, 2005)

Limitations of professional ethics

It is nearly impossible to adhere to a given code of ethics with consistency, because reality in the field trump ideals. It can also be hard to make challenging decisions on the spot, with no time to reflect. As a result, it is your responsibility as a community interpreter to think deeply about how to apply the *values* that underlie a code of ethics. You will need to connect them in your mind to the complex social realities you encounter in the session. While values vary by code of ethics, in general ethical documents for community interpreting are concerned with supporting the intended *outcome* of the encounter, *fidelity* to the message and the *autonomy* of the speakers.

Ethics are words on paper. Interpreting happens in real life. No words on paper can ever encompass the complexity of community interpreting. In addition, any code that addresses an international body of practitioners faces the additional challenge of being general enough to apply to all countries, yet specific enough to be useful. We will turn to a document that attempts to do just that, written by the authors of this textbook.

International ethics and standards for community interpreters

Communicative autonomy: a bedrock value

In the absence of an international code of ethics for community interpreters, the authors of this textbook spent two years developing a document that provides a code of ethics and standards of practice for community interpreters around the world. Its purpose is to support the education and training of community interpreters by providing guidelines for ethical conduct.

Ethics and Standards for The Community Interpreter®: An International Training Tool (García-Beyaert et al., 2015) provides a summary of eight key ethical principles and 41 standards of practice intended to guide interpreters in any part of the world. Its content is the product of two related and complementary efforts. On the one hand, the document reflects areas where substantial international consensus exists regarding the community interpreter's practice; on the other, it contributes to the further evolution of the field by defining ethical practice in areas that seem controversial or unclear. The document also seeks to provide clarity by introducing the concept of *communicative autonomy* as a bedrock value (García-Beyaert et al., 2015, p. 2):

> *The concept of* communicative autonomy *is introduced in this document as a fundamental principle. Communicative autonomy is defined here as the capacity of each party in an encounter to be responsible for and in control of his or her own communication.*
>
> *In modern medicine, "First do no harm" is a precept that guides its practitioners. The authors of this document propose that supporting communicative autonomy is a comparable fundamental precept that should underlie every aspect of the development and practice of community interpreting.*

Exploring communicative autonomy

Exploring communicative autonomy

There is no standard definition for "communicative autonomy." It is not a concept widely discussed in community interpreting. Yet this notion is so fundamental to the profession that it could be considered a de facto foundational concept. Without it, community interpreters will never achieve clarity, far less consensus, on such fundamental issues as how to support accuracy or the role of the interpreter. The authors have therefore chosen to highlight the importance of the concept and to define it as follows:

> **DEFINITION**
>
> **Communicative autonomy**
>
> The capacity of each party in an encounter to be responsible for and in control of his or her own communication.

Community interpreting facilitates communication between parties who do not share a common language and seek to obtain or provide services. Language and cultural differences can undermine communicative autonomy because the speakers[26] rely on an intermediary—the interpreter—who has an inescapable impact on the encounter. A professional interpreter is trained to use a variety of strategies to keep that impact to a minimum, including careful positioning, the use of direct speech (first person), choosing which interpreting mode to use, refraining from side conversations and so on. These strategies, discussed in Chapters 2 and 3, help service users and providers to be responsible for their own dialogue despite the interpreter's presence.

The document *Ethics and Standards for The Community Interpreter®: An International Training Tool* aligns itself with these concepts and provides a framework to help the interpreter promote clear, direct communication. When all goes well, services users and providers will stay focused on communicating directly with each other and not the interpreter.

A code of ethics for the community interpreter

Introduction to the code

Introduction to the code

The eight ethical principles contained in the *Ethics and Standards* document reflect the five authors' joint expertise working, teaching and conducting research in the field. Like many such documents, it is presented as a list with each principle followed by relevant standards of practice. Such an organizational strategy shows how standards support ethical practice. This part of Chapter 1 will examine the ethical principles. The standards of practice will be explored in Chapter 5 because they provide a framework for reviewing the whole textbook.

---

[26] The term "speakers" in this textbook includes individuals who are Deaf or hard of hearing and who communicate in signed language. While a signed language is not itself oral, on the basis of extensive scientific evidence it is widely considered by specialists, researchers and many lawmakers around the world to be authentic human speech and comparable in most significant ways to any spoken language. The authors fully endorse this perspective.

In what may be a unique recommendation, this *Ethics and Standards* document proposes that community interpreters should ideally commit to following their professional ethics in a formal pledge. A pledge is a commitment. It involves a conscious intention to take action. The pledge proposed here is a synopsis of the content of the *Ethics and Standards* document.

Special considerations

Eight ethical principles

The following principles are taken from the *Ethics and Standards* document under discussion. They are intended to provide a summary or overview of all eight principles. The next part then explores each ethical principle to provide deeper understanding.

In Section 1.4 you will learn how to *apply* each principle to common challenges in community interpreting. In Section 1.5 you will learn two specific techniques that can help you with ethical decision making. Here, you will focus first on getting a sound grasp of what each principle means.

THE COMMUNITY INTERPRETER'S PLEDGE

As a community interpreter, I will support the communicative autonomy of the parties I interpret for. To help them maintain responsibility for and control over their own communication, I will:

- Observe confidentiality
- Strive for accuracy
- Display impartiality
- Ensure transparency
- Promote direction communication
- Respect professional boundaries
- Support intercultural communication
- Maintain professional conduct

A Code of Ethics for *The Community Interpreter*®

Confidentiality

The community interpreter does not disclose private or proprietary information learned during the execution of his or her professional duties, except where disclosure is required by institutional regulations or by law.

Accuracy

The community interpreter strives to interpret every message without omissions, additions, distortions or any other changes to the original message.

Impartiality

The community interpreter refrains from allowing personal beliefs to manifest in his or her professional conduct, especially when rendering the content and tone of the message.

Transparency

The community interpreter interprets everything that is said to ensure that all messages expressed during the encounter are communicated to all parties.

Direct communication

The community interpreter initiates and actively supports practices that enable service users and providers to engage in direct communication.

Professional boundaries

The community interpreter should maintain professional boundaries, both during and outside the interpreted encounter.

Intercultural communication

The community interpreter intervenes to promote meaningful communication across cultural differences only when necessary for clear communication and without articulating the interpreter's beliefs or speculations about any of the parties' cultures.

Professional conduct

The community interpreter's conduct should reflect the highest standards of the profession by showing adherence to professional ethics and best practices.

Ethical principle: Confidentiality

The principle

The community interpreter does not disclose private or proprietary information learned during the execution of his or her professional duties, except where the disclosure is required by institutional regulations or by law.

Application of the principle

Service users

Confidentiality, an everyday concept in most social service organizations, might not be well understood by service users, who might (for example) understand "private" to mean "secret." The user may not be aware that "confidential" personal information is available to certain other employees within the organization. Conversely, other service users may be fearful to disclose certain information because they come from countries where service providers may report their information to the police or government. Some service users may believe that no information they disclose is truly private—so they withhold information from fear. Yet service providers cannot provide a service effectively without the bonds of trust that allow a service user to speak freely and openly.

Interpreters

Many interpreters also do not understand the concept of confidentiality. (A statement on returning home as casual as, "Hi, honey—guess who I interpreted for today?" is a clear violation of confidentiality. Yet not all community interpreters understand how serious such a violation is.)

In addition, it can be hard to maintain for interpreters who come from or work with small immigrant or cultural communities. Yet interpreters for less commonly spoken languages should take extra care to maintain confidentiality. It is easy to lose the trust of community members (and service providers).

Often it might seem harmless to mention interpreting for a service user, but that is not the case. Keep in mind that even a small amount of information divulged by an interpreter (e.g., "I interpreted for a pregnant woman today") could identify the service user in smaller cultural communities. One interpreter at a U.S. hospital shared information with a family member; word got out to the community, and the interpreter was reported for breaching confidentiality, which affected her career.

Conversely, sometimes interpreters may be *required* to break confidentiality. If there is a threat of homicide or suicide, interpreters in a number of countries might be expected to break confidentiality and notify the authorities, such as the police. Similarly, in some countries, regions or states the interpreter must break confidentiality if there is a suspicion of child abuse or the abuse of a vulnerable adult. (A vulnerable adult could be a fragile elder or someone with a major disability.) You might also have to break confidentiality if you receive a subpoena to testify in court, but in that case you would have to consult a lawyer to be sure. Study the confidentiality requirements for the geographic area and the service settings where you work.

Ethical principle: Accuracy

The principle

The community interpreter strives to interpret every message without omissions, additions, distortions or any other changes to the original message.

Application of the principle

Accuracy: the impossible dream

Accuracy can feel like an unattainable goal for interpreters. No matter how much training or experience an interpreter has, a fast or incoherent speaker, unexpected content, a technical term, joke or colloquial idiom can catch you by surprise. These challenges can make even the best interpreter feel inadequate. The saying that "you are only as good as your last interpreting assignment" is a truth that all interpreters find out the hard way.

The community interpreter faces steep challenges for accuracy. First, the sheer array of possible speakers, topics and physical environments as well as the often high number of daily assignments can challenge your ability to stay focused and capture the message. A single school environment, for example, may require interpreting in classrooms, multipurpose meeting rooms (often with poor acoustics), tight office spaces or school libraries. Hospitals can include emergency departments, operating rooms, outpatient clinics, intensive care units, neonatal care and more.

The number one rule for any interpreted interaction is *if you can't hear it, you can't interpret.* So you will need to be able to ask for proper sound conditions. Yet many community interpreters find that realistic solutions can be difficult. After all, you don't want to look like you're demanding or unreasonable. Some problems can't be fixed. Also, what can you do if the situation speeds out of control? Perhaps someone is drunk and incoherent, or five speakers burst out all at once (speaking at top speed, with deep emotion). You will need to make decisions about how to handle common challenges for accurate interpreting.

Supporting a beneficial outcome: additional challenges

In addition, your role is linked to the intended service outcome—which isn't always positive. Sometimes the starving family doesn't qualify for food assistance; the lawyer can't take the case; or the child in surgery dies. Even so, typically you are there to help a positive outcome happen. As a result, you might be expected to do more (even much more) than just interpret: you might have to monitor the conversation for understanding (except, typically, in courts) and usually you are expected to address misunderstandings that arise. (Note: you are not expected to *fix* the misunderstanding but rather to point out the potential source(s) of miscommunication. See Chapter 3 for details.)

These expectations can impose additional effort and cognitive strain. For example, many service users nod politely at the service provider whether they understand or not. The provider may assume their understanding and be wrong. If the interpreter notes a serious misunderstanding, he or she may intervene by saying something like, "Excuse me, as the interpreter I'm concerned that what I interpreted about the pre-surgical instructions wasn't clear." Most court and conference interpreters do not have this extra task of monitoring for understanding.

The need for more training and resources

Finally, while community interpreters often work in highly complex settings, the field is still professionalizing and often lacks adequate training, preparation, supervision and guidance for new interpreters. Community interpreters are usually undertrained, particularly in message transfer skills. They urgently need access to affordable, quality training to build their active-listening, analysis and delivery skills. Fewer still are the community interpreters who get trained in proper note-taking techniques for consecutive interpreting or memory skills, two core skill sets that allows one to interpret longer segments with greater accuracy. Training in simultaneous interpreting is also relatively scarce for community interpreters.

The "one-sentence" interpreter

This lack of adequate training and preparation for community interpreters is a chronic source of stress. One way that interpreters often compensate for inadequate listening and memory skills is by interrupting speakers after short statements (e.g., one sentence), a tactic that helps ensure more accurate interpreting but distorts the communication in other ways.

How Enhancing Memory and Note-Taking Skills Supports Accuracy in Medical Interpreting: One Example

Consider a series of brief exchanges between a doctor and patient when the doctor launches into a longer description of the treatment plan, which includes eight or nine steps. After the first few steps, the interpreter asks her to pause for accuracy. Once he has interpreted them and the doctor resumes her explanation, she misremembers what she said earlier and leaves out a couple of the next steps, leading to an accidental break in communication with potentially harmful consequences. Yet the conversation moves on without anyone noticing.

In short, it is hard work to be accurate. As a result, most community interpreters will need to make conscious efforts to engage in professional development to improve their accuracy. A short training program is never adequate to assure adequate message-transfer skills.

Ethical principle: Impartiality

The principle

The community interpreter refrains from allowing personal beliefs to manifest in his or her professional conduct, especially when rendering the content and tone of the message.

Application of the principle

Emotional intensity

You might on any given day be the voice for:

- A family being evicted from public housing.
- A mother who receives the diagnosis that her child has autism.
- A political refugee sharing his story of torture and persecution with a therapist.
- An immigrant who loses his request for asylum in a hearing.

Just as doctors, nurses, social workers and therapists must maintain their composure each time they face human tragedy (and joy), community interpreters must learn to set aside their feelings to a degree. However, while most other workers get special training on how to cope with intense, traumatic or frightening situations (such as interpreting when a baby dies in childbirth), community interpreters rarely receive such training (Bambáren-Call et al., 2012).

Problematic expectations

Another challenge to impartiality is ignorance about the interpreter's role. Service users and providers can routinely pressure you to take on what can be inappropriate additional roles or tasks. A father might turn to you and ask for your opinion about the service provider. A lawyer may ask you whether he or she thinks his client is lying. A nurse or social worker might leave you alone with the patient with a long history form you are expected to fill out. *You* might have a clear understanding about your role, but those you interpret for often have no concept of what professional interpreting is about—or what you must do to act impartially.

Conflicts of interest

Impartiality is also about avoiding conflicts of interest. Your impartiality can be challenged just by belonging to the same ethnic, linguistic or religious community as the service user—or a different one. Sidestepping conflicts of interest is important yet it can be a chronic challenge if the group you interpret for is very small, or you live in a rural area and find yourself interpreting for the same service users often. In addition, sometimes your tribal or religious affiliation may have engaged in war or genocide against the service user's social group.

Before you can hope to achieve impartiality, you must have a clear understanding of what it *is* and *how* to maintain it. All chapters of this book will offer you practical tools, strategies and perspectives to help you maintain impartiality. In the meantime, if you arrive and find that you know the service user, always:

1. Disclose the relationship (the conflict, or potential conflict, of interest).
2. Offer to withdraw.
3. If all parties ask you to stay, self-evaluate to see if you should or shouldn't stay and whether or not you could act impartially.

Ethical principle: Transparency

The principle

> *The community interpreter interprets everything that is said to ensure that all messages expressed during the encounter are communicated to all parties.*

Application of the principle

How to be transparent

To be transparent, community interpreters need to interpret *everything* stated during the session (to the extent possible) and also to be *clear* who is speaking at any given time—including you, the interpreter.

Often, community interpreters are asked to behave as if they were "invisible." This is impossible, of course: what is intended by this request is that interpreters should take a background role and remain neutral in their behavior and unobtrusive. But for true transparency, it must be very clear to everyone present exactly what the interpreter is doing at all times and whether s/he speaks and acts from a personal perspective or as the faithful voice of the service user or provider.

Accuracy, impartiality and transparency

Transparency is essential. It is required even in situations that might feel uncomfortable to you, such as interpreting angry messages, distressing diagnoses or other unpleasant content—including your own mistakes.

Ensuring transparency often requires a conscious commitment. Simply stating, "He's angry," or, "She's saying bad words," because you feel too uncomfortable to interpret obscenities is a violation of accuracy and impartiality that undermines transparency. Yet often community interpreters (especially those without adequate training) do not interpret every message or report their interventions. This lack of transparency is noticed. It generates countless complaints. In fact, this problem might be the single most common complaint against community interpreters.

What is the point of transparency?

Lack of transparency can also contribute to a mistrust of community interpreters because it undermines the integrity of the profession. The goal of interpreting is not to change the message to "help out" the service user. Rather, the goal is to put the service user and provider on equal footing, as if they spoke each other's language. The service provider and the service user need to know *everything* communicated during an encounter to make appropriate and timely decisions. Without transparency, no equal footing is possible.

Transparency: a confusing concept for many interpreters

Interpreters often think they are transparent when they are not—probably because they don't truly understand the idea of transparency. For example, the interpreter may intervene and say one thing to the service provider ("She doesn't understand you. Can you please talk in simpler language?") and quite another to the service user ("I just asked the provider to explain something.") The situation is not transparent, but no one seems aware of that problem—not even the interpreter.

The profession at large is in general (if not universal) agreement that crude idioms, insults and other strong language should be interpreted, not softened or omitted. Most untrained interpreters, however, typically fail to interpret crude language with accuracy and transparency. They honestly think that saying, "She said bad words," is enough. Furthermore, there may be cultural issues that leave the interpreter unable to imagine why he or she would ever be expected to interpret "the bad words." Finally, what if interpreting profound insults could escalate a potentially dangerous situation, like interpreting for a violent offender in detention when a police officer crudely insults the offender? It is easy to say, "Be transparent!" Interpreters need practical guidance to do so.

Transparency supports effective service delivery, facilitates accuracy and promotes direct communication. Community interpreters need to understand it well or they will be tempted to omit certain messages that could cause cultural or emotional tension.

Ethical principle: Direct communication

The principle

The community interpreter initiates and actively supports practices that enable service users and providers to engage in direct communication.

Application of the principle

Is the interpreter a co-participant?

The interpreter's presence is essential to the success of the encounter. You are often, therefore, perceived as another participant when in reality your role is just the opposite. The encounter is not about you. It is not *your* conversation. This perception that you are a co-participant makes supporting direct communication a challenge, since the other participants often expect you to answer their questions, give your opinion or guide their conversation.

Balancing direct communication with the need to intervene

When a misunderstanding arises, the community interpreter (unlike interpreters in court or conference settings) is encouraged to monitor the situation and intervene if a misunderstanding arises. Here is the paradox: the *point* of intervening is to support direct communication by redirecting the parties back to each other—yet doing so distracts the participants from each other and makes you appear to be a co-participant.

In real life this tension means that community interpreters are tugged in multiple directions. They're told to remain impartial and restrict their role as much as possible to facilitating communication and intervening only when absolutely necessary. On the other hand, depending on the country or code of ethics they are bound by (if one exists), they are often given permission to intervene "as needed."

"Identifying" vs. "explaining" a communication barrier

Community interpreters are often encouraged or expected to *explain* communication barriers. "Explaining" is not at all what this textbook advises community interpreters to do. Interpreters who "explain" barriers to understanding undermine both direct communication and communicative autonomy.

Instead, in the view of many practitioners and the authors, community interpreters can help the parties discuss issues that are causing a misunderstanding directly with each other. Interpreters can do this by *identifying* out loud the communication barrier (e.g., "The interpreter wants to point out a possible misunderstanding about what *embolism* means,") rather than explaining it (in other words, don't tell the patient, "The doctor is referring to a blood clot"—instead, let the doctor explain what she means by *embolism.*) Techniques for intervening, mediation and cultural mediation are taught in Chapter 3.

Still, even when it is brief and appropriate, the act of intervening by its very nature inserts the interpreter into the middle of the dialogue. It should be done as rarely as possible.

Strategies that support direct communication

Professional community interpreters have a variety of strategies and techniques that support direct communication, such as making a professional introduction, averting eye contact while interpreting, using direct speech (first person), careful positioning, knowing which mode to use or switch to, proper note-taking and effective mediation protocol and scripts, all of which will be explored in subsequent chapters. In the end, though, direct communication relies heavily on interpreter self-awareness and a deep understanding of how direct communication works. You will need to develop a state of mindfulness. Watch for the communication dynamics between the service provider and user. Note the role you play in facilitating direct connection.

Ethical principle: Professional boundaries

The principle

The community interpreter should maintain professional boundaries, both during and outside the interpreted encounter.

Application of the principle

Most community interpreters need clear, strong guidance to maintain professional boundaries. Many cope with shifting roles all day, every day, especially if they hold down another job position and only get "pulled in" to interpret from time to time. To maintain professional boundaries, you may have to educate both service providers and users about your role. If you have another professional role, you may have to alert everyone that you will *only* be interpreting during that encounter.

Avoiding personal engagement with the service user if you belong to the same small cultural community can be hard. Perhaps you attend the same church, temple or mosque, or you shop at the same markets as service users. Perhaps you are a refugee who interprets for other refugees (and provides other services to them as well). You might be expected to attend weddings, funerals or citizenship ceremonies. You can't be rude and just walk away when someone greets you, but should—if culturally possible—avoid long conversations and personal relationships. The author of this chapter interprets in a small town of 5,000 people. She knows that you, like her, might see the service users you interpret for at your children's school, sport events, weddings and restaurants. How to navigate role boundaries?

In addition, many medical interpreters are also medical assistants, nurses or front-line healthcare staff. They might provide direct clinical care to a prenatal patient, switch to the interpreter role when the doctor examines her, then switch back right afterward to the "main" job. Likewise, many social workers, counselors, case managers and school staff do their work, then switch into the interpreter role during a session. Adhering to standards that tell you to avoid being alone with service users or never to speak to them outside the session can be unrealistic. Yet doing so, especially for mental health and legal services, could be legally dangerous or risky for the service.

The rest of this textbook will provide you with many techniques and strategies to help you maintain professional boundaries.

Ethical principle: Intercultural communication

The principle

The community interpreter intervenes to promote meaningful communication across cultural differences only when necessary for clear communication and without articulating either the interpreter's beliefs or speculations about any of the parties' cultures.

Application of the principle

Training community interpreters about cultural mediation

Around the world, there are many beliefs about what you, as a community interpreter, should do if a cultural misunderstanding arises while you interpret. In some countries, professional educators in the field will:

- *Forbid* you to address cultural issues directly.
- *Recommend* that you intervene to resolve a perceived cultural misunderstanding.
- *Encourage* you to explain the cultural issues yourself.
- *Strictly advise* you to simply point out what might be causing a cultural misunderstanding without explaining it yourself in any detail (the practice this textbook advocates).

In fact, you could see all the beliefs and practices listed above enacted in one country. In other words, even within one country or region, interpreters often get different and contradictory messages about how to manage cultural miscommunications. This lack of a clear consensus has led to a certain amount of chaos and controversy in the field. We are still working as a profession to clarify the issues surrounding cultural mediation: what it is, and if or how it to perform it. See Chapter 3 for details.

In some countries, particularly in Europe and North America (Canada, the United States and Mexico), dual side-by-side professions have emerged: community interpreters and cultural (or intercultural) mediators. See, for example, Rudvin, 2006; and Martín and Phelan, 2010. Chapter 5, Section 5.2, explores this topic in detail.

Facilitating intercultural communication

Facilitating successful intercultural communication in community interpreting involves a set of practices that include:

- Identifying a serious cultural concern that may be causing a misunderstanding.
- Guiding providers and users to explain their cultural differences to each other.
- Avoiding:
    - Cultural judgments.
    - Broad statements about culture.
    - Cultural statements about the service user, provider or institution.

As a bilingual professional with high exposure to cultural differences, you are likely to have special insights. They can help you play a key role. How to use your cultural knowledge, experience and insights to support intercultural communication is critical. Two key concepts that underlie successful intercultural communication include:

1. The fact that the interpreter is not a cultural expert.
2. The idea that communicative autonomy is not only a desired outcome but an essential principle in community interpreting.

The community interpreter: a cultural expert?

Regardless of the code of ethics you follow or common beliefs about whether and how community interpreters should address cultural misunderstandings, community interpreters are expected by many service users and providers to act as cultural "experts." Yet doing so is dangerous: interpreters should avoid playing cultural expert at all costs and instead ideally support the autonomy of service users and providers.

Now, the statement that the interpreter is not a cultural expert may cause confusion among interpreters as well as service users and providers. It might even offend some interpreters. Such a statement, after all, appears to directly contradict the common goal of engaging interpreters who are "culturally competent" or "culturally responsive." In reality, looking at interpreters as cultural experts is the recipe for a cultural disaster. The reason is simple. There is only one expert on the service user, and it is not the interpreter. It is the service user. Chapter 3 explores this topic in detail.

Communicative autonomy and intercultural communication

The idea that communicative autonomy supports successful intercultural communication is simple. The more that community interpreters can resist their impulse to explain culture and instead help those present explain it to each other, the more they can promote direct communication. Direct communication supports communicative autonomy.

By allowing all parties to speak for themselves, the interpreter is helping to make sure that they are in control of their own communication. While doing so is always important, it is perhaps especially so when it comes to the complex area of cultural beliefs and values.

Ethical principle: Professional conduct

The principle

The community interpreter's conduct should reflect the highest standards of the profession by showing adherence to professional ethics and best practices.

Application of the principle

Professional conduct and the community interpreter

Professional conduct goes beyond the protocols you follow (such as using direct speech, being prepared to take notes and stating in your introduction that everything will be interpreted). Professional conduct also means you should adopt practices considered "professional" in that setting, for example, arriving promptly and engaging in ethical business practices.

Dress codes, workplace safety practices, wellness protocols, customer-service expectations and prohibitions against accepting gifts are often part of general workplace policies for staff interpreters and freelance interpreters alike. Some of these expectations are surprising for community interpreters new to the profession.

Infection Control Protocols, Water and Medical Interpreters

Infection control protocols in many hospitals in the United States prohibit healthcare staff from carrying their own water bottles between patient rooms. The intent is to prevent germs traveling and potentially spreading infection to providers and patients. Instead, providers are expected to use water fountains and water stations. This protocol can offend some freelance interpreters who don't understand why they may not bring their own water bottle for *their* protection. After all, an interpreter's voice is an important "instrument"—and water is sometimes necessary to protect it.

One standard for professional conduct that often surprises community interpreters encourages interpreters to advocate for their own working conditions (see e.g., NCIHC, 2005). You may feel that it is not your job to ask to move away from a room next door because of a crying baby or request a break if you have been interpreting nonstop for two hours. Yet the profession is young, and the public is still unaware what proper workplace conditions mean for professional interpreters. It will fall on your shoulders to speak up on your own behalf. By doing so, you will help other interpreters as well.

Professional conduct in the field

In part because community interpreting is a young profession, you will need to exhibit professionalism in your appearance, manners and behavior at all times. It is important to help others understand that you are there as a *working professional*, not a language assistant. To uphold professional conduct, you will also need to learn what other professionals in your country do or don't do that would be appropriate for community interpreters. Here are a few examples, but they can vary from country to country:

- Decline assignments for which you are not qualified.
- Prepare for assignments (time permitting).
- Correctly represent your qualifications.
- Arrive promptly: plan to arrive at least 15 minutes early to allow for delays.
- Dress in business suits or semi-formal business clothing: for example, avoid jeans, shorts, tops that expose the chest, open-toed shoes and other casual clothes.
- Maintain a courteous, warm demeanor.
- Avoid accepting gifts.

These are just a few examples of professional conduct that are important for community interpreters in many and perhaps most countries. The rest of this textbook will show you many ways to exhibit professional conduct in the field.

Let's Practice

Learning Activity 1.3 (a): Communicative Autonomy: Role-Play Demonstration
Learning Activity 1.3 (b): The Community Interpreter's Pledge
Learning Activity 1.3 (c): Ethical Principles: Mix and Match

In *The Community Interpreter®: An International Workbook of Activities and Role Plays*

REVIEW OF SECTION 1.3

This objective introduced you to the concept of professional ethics and discussed a document called *Ethics and Standards for The Community Interpreter®: An International Training Tool,* developed by the authors of this textbook. It represents a distillation of their professional experience and expertise. The document explores international consensus around ethical behavior for community interpreters and supports eight core ethical principles.

This *Ethics and Standards* document is based on the concept of *communicative autonomy,* a foundational principles that is defined as "the capacity of each party in an encounter to be responsible for and in control of his or her own communication." The document also proposes a professional pledge that community interpreters can commit to integrate these eight core ethical principles into their professional practice as follows:

> *As a community interpreter, I will support the communicative autonomy of the parties I interpret for. To help them maintain responsibility for and control over their own communication, I will:*

- *Observe confidentiality.*
- *Strive for accuracy.*
- *Display impartiality.*
- *Ensure transparency.*
- *Promote direct communication.*
- *Respect professional boundaries.*
- *Support intercultural communication.*
- *Maintain professional conduct.*

The eight ethical principles listed in this section represent an important set of directives to guide your practice. In a sense, they are the heart and soul of the profession. These basic requirements provide a clear structure to help you engage in professional practice. By following a code of ethics, you enhance your professionalism and raise the bar for the profession as a whole.

1.4 Application of Ethical Principles

Overview

Confronting ethical challenges

The previous section discussed how ethical principles can help guide your conduct in the field. However, as clear as that kind of information may sound on paper, it is still not always clear what you should *do* when faced with real-life ethical challenges. It is impossible to anticipate each and every problem that will arise and map out a solution ahead of time.

In addition, interpreters often navigate situations where more than one possible "correct" course of action is possible. For example, if you enter the social worker's office and see that the service user you will interpret for is the abuser of a woman for whom you interpreted several weeks before, what will you do? The answer here does not fall neatly under one ethical principle. Community interpreters understandably want to know what the "right" answer is to as many situations as possible, but often there is no "right" answer. Depending on the particular situation, there may be several possible "possible" answers that allow you to support your ethical principles—but may still have negative consequences. In short, knowing *what* to do is never enough. To put your ethical principles into practice, you need to develop *effective decision-making skills.*

How can you decide what to do?

Real life is not predictable. The best you can do in many cases is to know your code of ethics well and have a decent understanding of your own values. However, over the years professional interpreters have adopted a number of practical strategies to help guide you through delicate situations. This section together with the next one and Chapters 3 and 5 will help you to find an appropriate and ethical solution for almost any given situation. By trying out some of the recommended strategies, you can find out what works best for you in your local context. Always, however, keep in mind the foundational principle of communicative autonomy and support direct communication.

Over time, you will learn to evaluate difficult situations quickly and decide on the best course of action. It takes experience, practice and

Learning Objective 1.4

After completing this section, you will be able to:

- Apply ethical principles for community interpreters to common communication barriers.

conscious decision making. Of course, you will also make mistakes along the way and learn from them. Interpreters are human beings, like everyone else. Making mistakes is part of your professional life. The real question is how you learn from your mistakes to make better decisions.

Four common barriers to clear communication

This section shows you how to apply core ethical principles to common real-life challenges around four common barriers to communication:

1. Linguistic challenges
2. Role confusion
3. Cultural misunderstandings
4. Service system barriers

For example, a paralegal is helping a woman fill out paperwork for a protective order to keep her abuser away. The paralegal keeps speaking to the interpreter, saying things like, "Ask her how many children she has," and, "Ask her to describe what happened when her husband got violent." In this chapter, you will learn how to apply ethical principles to decide what to do, such as intervening to request that the provider speak directly to the service user. Once you've decided *what* to do, the next task is to decide *how* to do it. This section teaches the *what.* Chapter 3 teaches the *how*—in other words, how to manage communication barriers. Chapter 4 focuses on managing these concerns in *specific settings.* Chapter 5 explores in depth the *role* of the community interpreter and brings all the knowledge of the previous chapters together, revisiting ethics and using standards of practice as a framework to guide you within that larger picture.

All these chapters teach specific strategies for *how* to take action once you have decided what to do. For now, we will focus on the *decision-making process you need to develop.* The situations we address are real and will ethically challenge you in real life. The goal is to be prepared.

Four key ethical principles

All eight ethical principles discussed in this textbook are important. No one ethical principle is more important than another. However, this section will look at how to apply four of them in some detail because these four can be especially challenging to apply. The four principles are:

- Observe **confidentiality.**
- Strive for **accuracy.**
- Display **impartiality.**
- Respect **professional boundaries.**

These four have proven to be good "gateway principles," meaning that once you have a clear understanding what they mean and have practice applying them, the other principles will become clearer and easier to integrate into your practice. Furthermore, the remaining four ethical principles are addressed in later chapters of this book.

Ethics and decision making: half the job

As discussed earlier, community interpreting differs from other interpreting specializations in three key aspects. Community interpreters:

1. Are usually expected to facilitate understanding between service users and providers to support the goal of the best possible service outcome.
2. Work in incredibly diverse and often challenging service settings.
3. May be bilingual employees who have primary jobs with no connection to interpreting.

These complex realities have led to a situation where few seem clear about what community interpreters should (and should not) do in the scope of their professional duties. Ethics can help guide you through this type of confusion.

Conference and court interpreters have a limited number of physical settings to work in, and they also typically have a more clearly defined role and work in a more structured environment. Interpreting from a booth or in a courtroom limits interactions with service providers and users. In addition, these interpreters are much more likely to be full-time, professional interpreters. As a result, they tend to have a much clearer idea of their role compared to community interpreters.

This is not to diminish the complexity of their work or the professional skills required of court and conference interpreters. Still, community interpreters have to master professional-level interpreting skills *and* the ability to manage complex environments. As a community interpreter, you will need to regulate your emotions and remain inwardly calm when situations become volatile, stressful or dire. Your ability to make appropriate ethical decisions is as important as your ability to interpret. One might go so far as to say that while for some types of interpreters the work is message-transfer skills, for community interpreters these skills are only half the job—and the other half is effective decision making.

Ethics are your *decision-making roadmap.* While the settings you work in are diverse, they share common ethical challenges. We will now explore four categories of challenges.

Four barriers to communication

The four barriers

This section will examine four common communication barriers interpreters face and provide strategies to address these challenges effectively. The four barriers are:

1. Linguistic challenges
2. Role confusion
3. Cultural misunderstandings
4. Service system barriers

First, you will examine the four barriers; then you will look at how four ethical principles can help you navigate these barriers effectively.

1. Linguistic challenges

Problems with "the linguistic envelope"

Confusion about language is something that all interpreters experience, regardless of their area of specialization. Linguistic challenges refer to any misunderstanding related to the *language* of the message, or in the words of a famous researcher, the "linguistic envelope" (Gile, 2009, p. 94). Linguistic challenges can include the listening conditions and have a variety of causes, including:

- A term or phrase that the interpreter doesn't understand.
- Too much noise.
- The service provider speaks in a high register, using language too complicated for the service user to follow.
- The service user does not answer direct questions, or answers them in indirect ways that baffle the service provider.
- The service user sometimes answers directly in the service provider's language, distracting the interpreter.
- The service user or provider uses a term that has no linguistic or conceptual match in the other language (such as *nurse practitioner* in English, or *timbang* in Filipino—which refers, roughly speaking, to a concept of balance in health).

An example of linguistic confusion

In this example, a Punjabi-speaking father has been summoned to a disciplinary proceeding for his son, who faces expulsion from his school. The father speaks some of the provider's language (English) and sometimes jumps in to answer questions directly, cutting off the interpreter. Other times, he begins to answer in English, then gets stuck and looks to the interpreter for help.

What should you do? You have several options. You could pause to intervene and remind both parties that you are ethically bound to interpret everything said. You could intervene and inform the parties that the situation is leading to confusion and request they pause for you to finish interpreting. Or you could direct your request to the principal and ask that he instruct the father to wait for you to interpret everything before responding, repeating your remarks to the father to maintain transparency. These are only some options. The question of *how* to decide among your options is addressed in the next section and other chapters.

Language Confusion

Service providers often experience language confusion: they assume that the service user speaks the dominant language of the country that he or she comes from and request interpreters for the wrong language.

For example, many migrants from Latin America do not speak Spanish or Portuguese but one of many hundreds of indigenous languages. Helping speakers of indigenous or less-common languages identify their preferred language can be difficult. Finding the right interpreter is even harder.

Spanish-English interpreters in the United States report being asked to interpret for nearly any Latin American indigenous language. However, on arrival they are also sometimes asked to interpret Portuguese, Russian, Arabic or Chinese... Why this happens is a mystery to them!

2. Role confusion

What is "role confusion"?

In simple terms, role confusion is the lack of clarity that arises when you are asked to do something that goes beyond your scope or duties as an interpreter. *You* may know from your training that you should restrict your activities to interpreting and only intervene when absolutely necessary to address specific communication barriers. However, the *services users and providers* may expect you to do many other things (such as share your opinions, explain concepts, fill out forms or even run errands.). These requests can cause role confusion for everyone, including you: they also bring ethical conflicts into play, which you then have to decide how to manage.

Community interpreters vs. cultural mediators

To add to the confusion, in some countries "cultural mediators" (or intercultural mediators) perform community interpreting but are often expected to "help out" service users; in certain countries that role of "helping out" may even be formally defined. But community interpreters who are not professional cultural mediators may still be expected to perform such non-interpreting services, leading to role confusion. (This issue is discussed in detail in Chapter 5.)

Such contradictory or complex expectations may add to personal confusion about your role. Your role can depend in part on where you work, your job title and your job requirements. Find out what they are. Be clear about what is expected of you. Whether or not you should perform the non-interpreting tasks you are expected to perform will depend on what type of interpreter you are:

1. A professional interpreter (contract or staff)
2. A bilingual employee (who interprets only as needed).
3. A cultural (or intercultural) mediator.
4. A volunteer asked to interpret.

In short, investigate your job description and expectations about your role ahead of time. Whether you work for an interpreter service, a hospital interpreting department, a nonprofit language bank or a multinational language company, find out the policies for interpreters and ask questions. Inform yourself.

An example of role confusion

The service user asks you for guidance.

During or after the session the service user says, "You know how this hospital works—how can I get good physical therapy here?" or, "How can I find cheap housing?" If you are a freelance interpreter, you are not allowed to answer these questions directly (unless they are about the interpreting, e.g., "What did you say? I can't hear you."). Instead, you would interpret the questions or inform one party that the other party has questions. However, if you are a bilingual employee and your primary job includes providing information to patients or clients, your approach might differ.

Medical "Dual Role" Interpreters

You may be a bilingual employee in healthcare who interprets part-time, also known as a "dual role" interpreter. Here is a simple guideline to help you see the difference between interpreting and providing a bilingual service.

If only you and the service user(s) are present and you are providing a service directly in the other language, then you are acting as *a bilingual healthcare provider*—not as an interpreter.

If three or more persons are present and you are interpreting for at least two of them, then you are *the interpreter*. Think of this as the "rule of three"—there have to be at least three people present, even if by phone or video, or no interpreting can take place.

3. Cultural misunderstandings

Expectations about the community interpreter's responsibility to address culture

Cultural misunderstandings occur in every country. They are one of the most common challenges that community interpreters face in their work. Chapter 3 addresses this issue in detail. Depending on where you work as a community interpreter, you may be strictly prohibited from addressing cultural issues at all (e.g., Canada) or you may be expected to act as a cultural mediator and solve cultural problems as they arise (in parts of Europe, for example: however, it is important to understand that a cultural mediator is not a community interpreter—even if the cultural mediator sometimes interprets. See Chapter 5 for details.) The most common situation worldwide is that the community interpreter is expected both to interpret and to navigate cultural barriers as needed by explaining them—whether or not this is ever clearly stated to the interpreter.

The authors of this textbook promote an approach that falls somewhere between Canada's model, where no cultural intervention is allowed, and the model that allows interpreters to explain cultural barriers as needed. Explaining anyone's mindset, cultural beliefs or practices would violate the foundational principle of communicative autonomy: therefore, the authors of this textbook lay out the strong case that it is *not* the interpreter's job to act as a cultural expert.

In other words, you are not expected to be able to explain anyone's cultural behavior. It *is* your job, however, to be aware of your own cultural biases and be able to point possible cultural misunderstandings that could lead to a potentially negative service outcome.

Ethical principles can help you navigate common cultural misunderstandings. Many fall under several broad categories, for example:

- The service provider is ignorant of the cultural beliefs the service user has about what caused his or her problem.
- The parties are unfamiliar with each other's cultural etiquette, such as greeting customs, norms for eye contact or standards for polite behavior.
- The service user and provider are working with unrecognized cultural assumptions, e.g., different understandings of what constitutes acceptable child discipline, how newborn babies should be cared for or what a spouse is (in law vs. common-law practice).

Be Careful of Cultural Assumptions

A True Story from Medical Interpreting

In one U.S. hospital, mothers from a particular indigenous group in Mexico seemed not to care about their newborn babies and instead allowed family members to assume complete care for them while the mothers were in the hospital. The nurses worried about this problem. They even considered calling Child Protective Services to trigger an investigation and take the babies into foster care.

Finally, through an indigenous interpreter, the hospital reached out to local indigenous community leaders and learned that the family members were protecting the new mothers while their milk came in. It turned out that the mother was expected to rest and care for herself so that she could then take good care of her newborn.

An example of a cultural misunderstanding

In many cultures, nodding does not mean yes. Even saying, "Yes," does not always mean yes. It can mean, "I respect you," "I am paying attention to you," "You are important," or "I am listening," and *not*, "Yes, I understand," or "Yes, I agree with you." Furthermore, many cultures teach respect for authority; thus, it can be seen as rude to disagree with a service provider.

One option is to intervene and make a general statement that what is being interpreted does not seem clear (to get the service provider to check for understanding). Another is to intervene and suggest that there may be a misunderstanding about the service. But remember: It is not your job to fix the misunderstanding. It *is* your job to give the parties the opportunity to address it (that is, *if your local or national code of ethics permits such interventions*).

4. Service system barriers

The impact of service system barriers

Sometimes the service system gets in the way. Service users may come from a country where such service simply doesn't exist, leading to confusion. Providers may be prejudiced. Interpreters are often asked to perform roles that belong to the provider, for example, when a provider says, "Just explain this procedure yourself, you've heard me so often you can do it in your sleep." Often, the provider is in a rush and impatient with cultural issues.

Service system barriers can be challenging because they are embedded in the system itself. If communication is impeded because an institution has inherently racist or discriminatory policies and procedures, there is little the interpreter can do. If the service user has a fundamentally different understanding of the service, the interpreter can identify that gap to the provider, but the provider—not the interpreter—will need to explain "how things work here." When a service user gets a poor explanation of the service, the situation can be incredibly frustrating for interpreters. Rather than let the mother go home and put liquid antibiotic in the child's ear, or let a job trainee leave without any understanding of how to access jobs on a computer database, the interpreter may be tempted to "help out." Many do. But it is not their job and can lead to other problems. The interpreter is not the service provider and usually lacks the training, qualifications and experience to provide such information safely.

An example of a service system barrier

The patient is an indigenous woman from Guatemala who does not speak fluent Spanish. The hospital has limited access to interpreters who speak her native indigenous language, Quiche. She is in the intensive care unit because of a serious ulcer than could require surgery and undergoing tests that require her to fast. The patient is convinced that her illness is being caused by the fasting and is trying to leave. A Quiche interpreter is unavailable, so a Spanish-speaking interpreter is called to convince the patient to stay and receive the tests. The interpreter does not speak Quiche at all. This example is a common one today: Spanish interpreters are often called to interpret for speakers of indigenous languages because the system has decided a Spanish interpreter is better than no interpreter at all.

Let's Practice

Learning Activity 1.4 (a): Ethical Principles: Application
Learning Activity 1.4 (b): Ethical Principles: "Yes, No, Maybe"

In *The Community Interpreter®: An International Workbook of Activities and Role Plays*

REVIEW OF SECTION 1.4

This section showed you how to apply core ethical principles to real-life challenges. It centered on four key barriers to community services that can lead to ethical concerns for interpreters:

1. Linguistic challenges
2. Role confusion
3. Cultural misunderstandings
4. Service system barriers

Community interpreters, compared to other interpreters, must manage many complex settings, address frequent misunderstandings about scope of practice and learn how to apply the appropriate ethical principles even in challenging circumstances to maintain professional conduct and support communicative autonomy.

1.5 Ethical Principles in Action

Overview

The previous two sections focused on introducing eight ethical principles and describing common ethical challenges faced by community interpreters around the world. This section offers two practical techniques for assessing and resolving ethical challenges. Note that these are *general* techniques. Details about how to apply them are taught in Chapters 3 and 5.

Learning Objective 1.5

After completing this section, you will be able to:

- Examine two techniques for resolving ethical challenges in community interpreting.

The first step for resolving an ethical challenge is having a strong awareness of the ethical principles involved and how to apply them generally. Remember that if your country or region has a code of ethics, use that code. If not, the *Ethics and Standards* at the beginning of this textbook will be useful. Then in order to find appropriate solutions to your ethical challenges or dilemmas, you will need to evaluate the nature of the challenge and assess the options available to you. This section introduces you to two techniques for evaluating ethical challenges and solving them. They are:

1. The CHIA ethical decision-making process
2. The SAY NO model

A third valuable tool is the Strategic Mediation Model. However, it is a more complex tool and is taught in Chapter 3.

The CHIA ethical decision-making process

The CHIA ethical decision-making process

The California Healthcare Interpreting Association (CHIA) is one of the most influential interpreting associations in the United States. In 2002 it published a seminal document that included ethics and standards of practice for healthcare interpreters (CHIA, 2002). Part of that document included a set of guidelines: six easy steps for making ethical decisions. This ethical decision-making protocol is also available at www.chiaonline.org.

These guidelines are incredibly valuable for interpreters who must decide—both on ethical grounds and to support a beneficial outcome—whether or not to mediate. You have to make many decisions quickly on the job, both during and outside the interpreted encounter. But the decisions you make *while* you interpret are often the hardest because (a) there is so little time to think; and (b) interpreting involves higher-level cognitive skills that are already very complex (see Chapter 2). Cultural barriers often trigger the toughest and most complex decisions and these will be explored at length in Chapter 3. Furthermore, your unconscious bias will often make the decision for you unless you have a specific plan in place about how to make decisions. Making reflexive decisions may not be helpful: if you feel yourself intuitively responding in a certain way without knowing why, question yourself to find out *what* you feel and *why* you that way.

Here is a helpful tool to analyze your decision-making process and improve it. The CHIA guidelines for ethical decision making come in the form of six points (CHIA, 2002, pp. 55-60). Please note that this process is typically one that you carry out *in your mind* during the encounter:

1. Ask questions to determine whether there is a problem.
2. Identify and clearly state the problem, considering the ethical principles that may apply and ranking them in applicability.
3. Clarify personal values as they relate to the problem.
4. Consider alternative actions, including benefits and risks.
5. Decide to carry out the action chosen.
6. Evaluate the outcome and consider what might be done differently next time.

These steps may seem like a lot to think about while you are interpreting. Try to study them ahead of time. See if you can apply the six CHIA steps to some of the most common challenges that you encounter, but do so at a time and place where you can think the steps through. Remember: if you are caught by surprise during the session, it will be hard to think through all six steps at once. Plan ahead.

Consider the following scenario

Imagine that you regularly interpret for a family with a young child who is receiving early intervention services for developmental delays (in other words, the child is not developing "on schedule" and needs professional help). The family also receives food assistance, including vouchers to buy formula for the child. When the child turns one year old, the program will stop providing formula and provide vouchers for milk only.

At the next evaluation, after the child turns one, the mother is concerned about a new rash that has developed on the baby's hands and feet. Yet the provider doesn't seem concerned. The mother, increasingly frustrated at the provider's lack of attention, turns to ask you for direct advice about the rash. You have seen that kind of rash before and suspect it might be caused by a milk allergy and also know that food allergies can aggravate certain developmental delays. What should you do? Clearly, the problem here involves multiple ethical principles:

- **Professional boundaries:** The service user has asked you, the interpreter, to provide direct advice about a medical problem about which you have no formal training. It falls outside your role to do anything but continue to interpret the mother's concerns and possibly intervene to point to her distress. Yet the provider won't address her concern, and you are confident that your input could help the mother and child.

- **Impartiality:** Your ability to maintain an impartial attitude toward all parties is stretched by this scenario. You have had personal experience with the rash the service user is experiencing. You are sure this information could help the child. Furthermore, a child's health and well-being (and perhaps safety) is in jeopardy. You want to help.
- **Professional conduct:** You have interpreted for this family multiple times. You care about them and what happens to them. It would be easy to act in unprofessional ways, as if you were a friend and not the interpreter.
- **A note on advocacy:** Advocacy is an ethical principle included in some codes of ethics. In a situation like this one, you may debate whether to advocate: for example, you may choose to speak to the provider outside of the session, or alert a supervisor or other provider involved in the case.

This kind of ethical challenge is surprisingly common for community interpreters. They work with service providers in helping professions every day and absorb huge amounts of knowledge. Community interpreters form their own opinions and insights. This scenario highlights how helpless you can feel in an imperfect service system. Witnessing poor care and negative consequences can be emotionally wrenching.

Inside those systems, you might have limited avenues to help. Over time, your frustration can build. You can be tempted to find other ways to help service users. Some interpreters violate the ethical principles of accuracy, transparency, impartiality, direct communication, professional boundaries and professional conduct when they:

- Provide additional information and explanations about the service.
- Refer service users to other services and/or providers (with or without permission).
- Warn service users about incompetent providers.
- Provide personal information about the service users to "help out."

These types of actions put you, the interpreter, at risk of moving far away from ethical practice. It can also deprive the service users and providers of control over their own communication. It is not enough to know how to interpret. You will have to manage situations.

You will practice how to apply the CHIA ethical decision-making process step by step in Chapter 3. Here, the goal has been to focus on that decision-making process itself.

The SAY NO model

One of the best things that a community interpreter can ever learn to do is how to say no effectively. This is especially the case when someone asks you to do something that would violate your professional ethics. The CHIA ethical decision-making process gives you a step-by-step tool to evaluate an ethical challenge and decide which action to take. Sometimes however—and probably often—the best course of action is to decline the assignment or request.

In other words, you will need to say, "No." Now, it is often hard to decline a request from to a colleague, service provider or service user. Some interpreters have naturally strong boundaries and find it easy to say no. Many interpreters have such a hard time saying no that it seems almost impossible. Most of us fall somewhere in between. Some of us have cultural backgrounds that make it harder to say no, and many women (most interpreters are women) are raised to say *yes* rather than *no* to most requests.

Yet it is incredibly common for community interpreters to be asked to perform tasks that go beyond your competence or scope of duties, such as interpreting beyond your skill level, performing written translations (when you have no qualifications as a translator). Just saying, "No, I can't do that, it's not in my ethics," or, "I'm not qualified to do that," can be difficult to say and rarely has the effect you want. In fact, you may end up irritating or angering the people you say "no" to, even though you have good reasons.

Fortunately, there is a way to decline inappropriate requests and still provide a solution. The following three-step approach typically produces a more positive outcome for everyone:

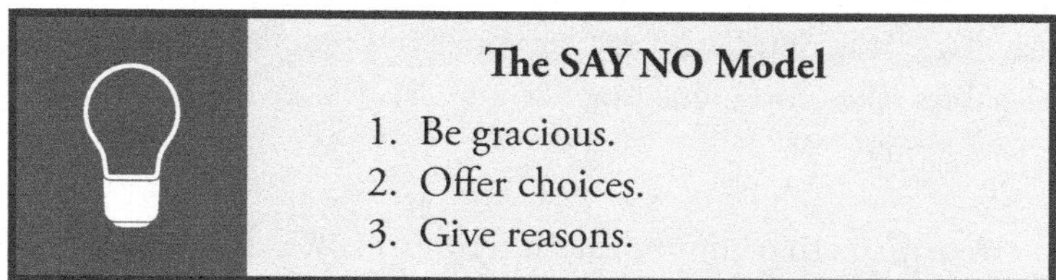

Let's take a common example. You have been asked to perform an assignment that exceeds your skill set, a family conference in a hospital intensive care unit, an assignment related to surgery for spinal bifida (a congenital defect of the spine that can cause paralysis of the lower limbs and also mental handicaps). What would you do?

1. Be *gracious.* E.g., smile and say warmly, "I would love to interpret for that special meeting—I know it's important for the family to have a qualified interpreter so everyone can understand what's going on."

2. Offer *choices.* "This would be a great assignment for Miranda. As a staff interpreter she's very familiar with the terminology. Or we can call our telephone interpreting vendor and ask for an interpreter trained in medical interpreting." **Note:** ***<u>It is critical that you offer at least two solutions when you say no</u>***. Offering choices gives the person options to focus on. It redirects attention toward problem solving and away from that feeling of being annoyed. The person no longer looks at *you* as a problem. Instead, the focus is on *solutions.*

3. Give *reasons.* "I'm afraid I'll make mistakes that could create misunderstandings for the family and hospital staff. The hospital might be liable for my mistakes. I've never interpreted for a family conference in intensive care before. This child has a lot of complicated medical and developmental issues that I don't know well."

Now, the order of these steps is very important. Do not change the order. You will find that almost instinctively you want to change the order by giving your *reasons* before the *choices*. Resist that temptation. ***The model will ONLY work well if you (a) follow the order of the three steps; and (b) offer at least two solutions (choices) in step 2.***

By the way, if you have any doubts, first try these three steps on anyone that you need to say "no" to, including children as young as one year old! If you try it first on family members, friends, colleagues or even supervisors, observe the difference between doing it this way and your usual way. You will most likely find that this model works better. Test it! (This way you will also find the key phrases that work best for you and be able to adapt them culturally.)

Also, when you have to decline a request, put yourself in the shoes of the person making that request. This person needs something from you. You won't do it. *You* seem to be the problem. But what does that person really need? How can you support the best possible outcome? By providing at least two solutions *before* you give reasons, this person will likely already be more relaxed because solutions has been identified. You will be remembered for your helpfulness in solving the problem and not for having caused one. Most important, the service user and provider are more likely to experience a positive service outcome when you conduct yourself as a professional.

This three-step technique is deceptively simple and actually requires practice to make the skill automatic. For example, we really mean it when we say you will want to provide your choices or solutions before giving your reasons to decline. People automatically tend to say "I can't do X, because of Y." It may feel odd at first when you practice this new model. Unlearning your mental habits takes conscious practice and can feel awkward. This is normal—but the effort *will pay off.*

The following examples are requests that community interpreters often must or should decline for ethical reasons. They can be helpful for practicing this new skill of saying, "no."

Request #1

Nurse: "Could you please translate these discharge instructions for the patient? Thanks."

Community interpreter: (following the three-step **SAY NO** model):

1. **Be gracious**: I would love to be able to translate these discharge instructions.
2. **Offer choices:** This is a job that Abdul is qualified to do. I know he's here today and he has been authorized by the hospital to do written translations into Arabic. If he is not available we could call the language services company he works with to see if they can find a qualified translator.
3. **Give reasons:** I've qualified to provide *oral* interpreting in English and Arabic, but I've never formally studied the written language. I'm afraid I could make mistakes that lead to the patient not following the instructions correctly. I don't want to do anything that would make you or me liable or harm the patient.

Request #2

Service user: (as she leaves the building with three young children in the pouring rain and sees the interpreter) "Oh, you were so kind when you interpreted for me today! We're all so tired. I need to get the kids home to give them dinner but I don't have any more bus passes. Do you think you could give me a lift into town?"

Community interpreter: (following the three-step SAY NO model):

1. **Be gracious:** I really wish I could give you ride home, I know that would make your life easier.
2. **Offer choices:** Let's go back inside. I think they still have some bus passes available. Or they may help you call someone who could pick you up.
3. **Give reasons:** I'm not allowed to drive clients in my car. If we got into an accident I could be personally liable for the medical and repair bills. I could also get into trouble at work if I took you home—I might even lose my job.

As with the CHIA ethical decision-making process, the **SAY NO** model offers you a strategy to help you maintain ethical conduct. Many service users and providers are unclear about the proper role of the interpreter. They will often ask you to step in and "help out" in ways that seem reasonable to them, but which give you an ethical "headache." Knowing how to say no professionally and proactively is a critical skill for community interpreters.

The Gift of Saying NO

Once you get used to immediately providing alternative solutions when you have to say no, you might find yourself using this technique in other areas of your life. One community interpreter reported that she successfully taught her children "how to say no" when their peers pressured them to do things they didn't feel comfortable doing at school. It worked like a charm!

Let's Practice

Learning Activity 1.5 (a): Decision-Making Protocols and Practice: The CHIA Tool

Learning Activity 1.5 (b): The SAY NO Model

In *The Community Interpreter®: An International Workbook of Activities and Role Plays*

REVIEW OF SECTION 1.5

This section introduced you to two techniques for assessing ethical challenges and resolving them:

- CHIA ethical decision-making process
- The SAY NO model

The remaining chapters in this textbook will show you how to apply those techniques. Ethical principles are broad, general statements. They put the foundation under your feet and give you the professional framework you need to guide your conduct. The two techniques provided in this section offer you concrete, specific strategies to help you apply, and abide by, your professional ethics.

1.6 Reflective Practice

Overview

"Reflective practice" is critical to your success. It will help you become a professional interpreter and maintain a high skill level. Reflective practice refers to the process of examining your work experiences critically to identify the lessons learned to improve your professional performance.

Does that process sound simple? It is, yet it is incredibly important. Many professions have integrated reflective practice into their training and continuing education programs.

The ability to analyze your performance to identify specific areas where you need improvement is essential if you want to enhance your skills. Getting feedback from your peers can be a second powerful tool for getting a better understanding of your strengths and weaknesses. Finally you can also learn from the experience of your colleagues. Focusing on these three skills sets, this section will give you the tools to help you assess and improve your own performance.

Learning Objective 1.6

After completing this section, you will be able to:

- Explore the concept, meaning and application of "reflective practice" for community interpreters.

Reflective practice and the community interpreter

Why reflective practice matters

Since the majority of community interpreters do not have a chance to pursue a university interpreting degree, or even a long training, many learn their skills on the job. Most are adult learners. Adults learn differently than children in a classroom setting. How adults learn, and how to teach them most effectively, can be distilled into several key points (Tusting & Barton, 2003; Bancroft, 2014). Most adults:

- Want knowledge related to their experience and real lives.
- Are more self-directed than children: they can learn on their own.
- Can reflect on their own learning process.
- Learn best by doing and from real-life experiences.

In addition, adult learners tend to reflect on their own experiences and view them from different perspectives.

Self-examination

How do we analyze our performance and give ourselves useful feedback? First, it is helpful to step back a moment and realize how we observe ourselves. Some of us are incredibly self-critical, while others prefer to see only our best points. When we give ourselves feedback on our professional performance, for example, by listening to a recording of our own interpreting, the key is to maintain *neutrality, objectivity and balance.* We are balanced when we do not feel either the desire to be perfect or disappointment at our mistakes but instead can focus on what we actually did and what to do better.

It is part of human nature to dislike criticizing our own performance, and especially when we do so during training programs: with others listening to our performance, we tend to want to justify our decisions. People drawn to language-related professions are often perfectionists.

In this context, "smart failure" is an interesting concept: making errors is necessary to develop skills. There are many ways to incorporate reflective learning into your practice. For the solo interpreter, getting into the habit of regularly recording yourself and listening to your interpreting is perhaps the single most accessible and effective strategy—but even better is recording yourself on video.

That said, not all of us like the sound of our own voice on a recording, much less watching ourselves on video. It can make us feel self-conscious and uncomfortable, which is why many of us avoid ever getting into this habit. Overcoming that obstacle is one of the simplest, most important steps you can take to support your interpreting practice. The rest of this section provides concrete guidelines for how to integrate reflective practice into your interpreting.

Constructive feedback

Why constructive feedback is essential

Interpreting is a skill that needs constant practice, refining, and learning. It also requires complex cognitive processes to function well. Interpreting is fundamentally a public-speaking and performance skill. If you cannot deliver your interpretation smoothly and intelligibly, it makes no difference if you are accurate, because no one will understand you clearly.

Community interpreters need concrete, specific strategies that allow them to observe all those cognitive processes as well as their public-speaking skills so they can improve them. These techniques can be of great service to you. Integrating reflective practice into your learning journey as an interpreter from the start will shorten the time it takes you to master the core skills and go further.

One of the best ways to achieve reflective practice for community interpreters is through *constructive feedback*. Learning proper constructive feedback techniques will allow you to evaluate your own performance and do the same for others. Knowing how to *receive* such feedback from others is just as important.

Feedback from yourself

It is vital for interpreters to become good critics of ourselves. Some of us will think we are much better than we are (at almost anything). Many of us can only see our flaws. Most of us know the truth is in between. When you listen to or watch your own performance, in some ways the feedback you give yourself is the most important feedback you will ever get. Write down what you did well—then analyze what could be better. (See the workbook for a detailed self-assessment form.)

The key is to be as objective as possible about ourselves. Try not to flinch when you hear mistakes or feel too proud about a well-interpreted turn of phrase. Instead, focus on the performance, not yourself. This advice sounds easy to follow, but it isn't: it is hard to apply in practice, because most of us dislike criticizing our performance and instead of focusing on how to improve it, we want to *explain and justify our mistakes.*

Remember: in reflective practice we are *here* to make mistakes—so that we can learn from them. Making mistakes (in this context) is a good thing. Mistakes help us learn what to do in the field. Better, in fact, that we learn in private so that we can perform well in public.

Feedback from others

When, where and how to get feedback from others can be difficult for working community interpreters. Academic programs regularly teach this practice: if you are in a study program, then following these guidelines may be easy. If you seek to improve your skills as a working community interpreter who has no contact with academic programs, you will need to be more proactive.

Be creative. Make your own opportunities for ongoing study and practice. Try to find a "study buddy" to meet once a week for practice and feedback. Attend interpreting conferences to meet other interpreters. Once you have a partner you enjoy working with, you are set. That is ideal.

However, you can engage in reflective practice on your own. Below are the guidelines to walk you through how to give yourself constructive feedback (a) without a partner; (b) with a partner; or (c) in small groups.

Constructive feedback guidelines

The following guidelines will help you set up practice sessions and provide constructive criticism to yourself and/or to fellow interpreters. If you practice with others, you need at least two people present, but not more than four.

Observe the interpreter

Before you can give feedback on interpreting, either to yourself or others, you first need to learn how to *observe* interpreting. Just as we are taught the core interpreting skills by breaking them down into their component parts of listening, analyzing and rendering, so too can we break down our observation into component parts to provide targeted feedback.

To observe your own performance, first you will need to record yourself as you interpret. (You can do so on audio alone or also visually. At first, however, you may want to focus on audio-only recordings.) Then you will play back the recording and listen to yourself, comparing yourself to the original text and your audio partner (the person speaking the role of a service provider and/or user). With the proliferation of smartphones and digital recording devices, obtaining the tools to record yourself with or without a live partner should, we hope, be easy.

If you are with a partner or small group, you have the added benefit of being able to visually observe their performances. When observing others as they interpret, first and foremost, **do NOT interrupt, help or allow the person interpreting to stop**. Do ***not*** let the interpreter "break frame" by pausing to explain an error or ask you for help. The struggle to find the right word or come up with a solution for a tricky phrase is a key part of developing your skills. *Let the interpreter struggle.*

In addition, in real-life interpreting when you make mistakes, no one is there to rescue you. You have to continue interpreting until there is an appropriate moment to intervene to request a clarification or explain an error. Getting into this practice of "thinking on your feet" in the safety of practice sessions where no one gets hurt by your mistakes is far better than learning how to do so on the job.

While observing others when they interpret, focus on the following areas and note anything that is particularly well done *first* before addressing any errors.

- *Accuracy and completeness*: Which parts of the dialogue were most accurate? Why? Were areas with slang, emotional content or technical vocabulary more accurate or less accurate than the rest? Was any content missed? Did anything inadvertently get added or changed? Did the interpreter capture the real meaning and the speaker's intention, tone and spirit? Were cultural nuances well conveyed?

- *Grammar*: Are the same general sentence structures used (e.g., complete sentences, fragments or garble)? Is the grammar correct? Does the grammar used reflect the original speaker? (For example, did the interpreter "clean up" the speaker's grammar mistakes or keep them? Did the interpreter change the grammar in any way?) Did the interpreter interpret direct speech?

- *Terminology*: Were all technical terms known? Did the interpreter paraphrase them instead of interpreting them? Is correct terminology a consistent problem? Was register respected or did the interpreter simplify any complex terms?

- *Delivery*: Was the rendition smooth and understandable? Were there many hesitations and backtrackings (starting a sentence over)? Did the interpreter use appropriate tone, volume and speed?

Giving feedback

- First rule: *Always let the interpreter speak first: let the interpreter report what he or she thought went well or what mistakes were made before you give feedback!* When you interpret, you often know where you made mistakes. You want a chance to tell your reviewers *before* they critique you to say what you know you did "wrong." If you give the interpreter the chance to self-evaluate first, he or she will feel more relaxed afterward and more able to focus on the good feedback that you provide. Interestingly, interpreters often know what they did badly, but they tend to underestimate what they've done well.
- *Make positive comments first.* Make sure to first mention *at least* one or two good things about your partner's performance. Never focus only, or right away, on negative points. Tell

the interpreter what he or she did particularly well, e.g., no content was missed, grammar and syntax were all correct, the delivery was smooth and easy to understand, the interpreter has a pleasant voice that reflected the speaker's intent, etc. Make note of any particularly clever or well-done solutions to interpreting challenges. "I really liked your use of such-and-such term to handle this phrase in the original." *Making positive comments before critical ones is necessary to allow the interpreter to "hear" the negative comments without being too defensive or wasting time justifying the mistakes.* Please note that we all tend to learn more by building on our strengths than focusing too much on our mistakes. We need a good balance of feedback.

- *Be specific.* Providing feedback that is too general makes it hard for the interpreter to learn from his or her mistakes. Give concrete examples:
    - Instead of: "I didn't like what you said here," you might say, "This section of the interpretation was in a lower register than the original."
    - Instead of: "your grammar was a bit shaky," you might say "these are the grammar issues I noted, [e.g., incorrect verb tense or saying *that* instead of *who*], but I still understood what you were saying."
    - Instead of: "you're really hard to understand," you might say, "sometimes you say things really softly, almost like you are mumbling: so maybe you can focus on speaking a bit louder next time."

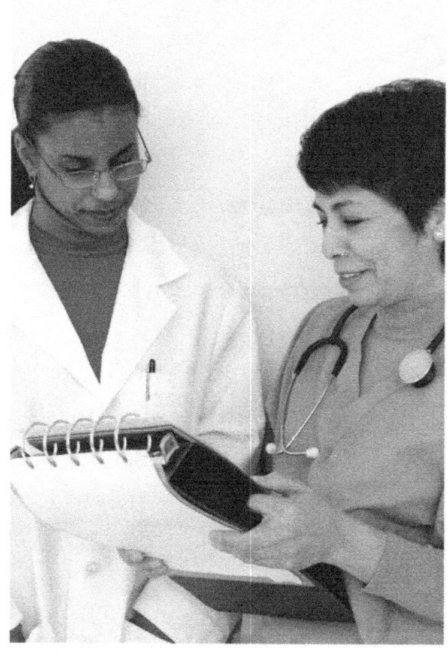

- *Be as neutral as possible when noting errors.* Instead of saying "you messed up here" you can say, "There was a mistake here."

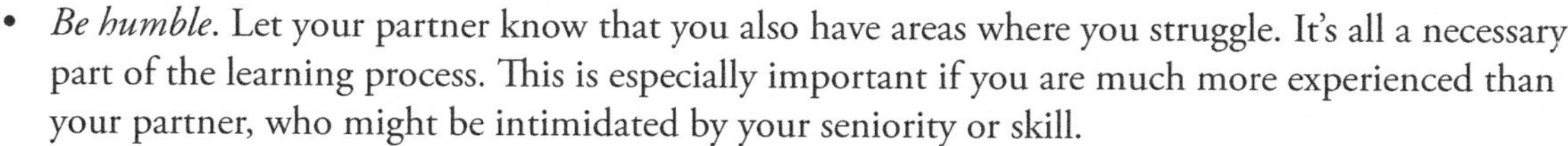

- *Be humble.* Let your partner know that you also have areas where you struggle. It's all a necessary part of the learning process. This is especially important if you are much more experienced than your partner, who might be intimidated by your seniority or skill.

- *Provide solutions.* If you have noted errors, explore how they could be handled next time. Brainstorm. Be creative. For example, think about what word choice would work better or point out specific resources or websites with helpful information.

- *Repetitive errors.* If your partner struggles with specific problems, such as delivery or numbers and addresses, point this out and then explore strategies for how he or she can try different approaches to overcome the problem.

- *Don't overwhelm your partner.* Especially in the beginning, when your partner might make frequent errors, focus on the feedback that seems most important; don't overwhelm him or her with too much criticism.

- *Check in*: Monitor your partner's response to your feedback. Is s/he receptive to the information? Have you hit a "sore nerve"—is your partner upset or reacting defensively?

Receiving feedback

Remember: getting feedback is an effective way to identify what you do well and what you need to improve. When you become a professional interpreter, this kind of feedback is hard to get. Getting feedback about your performance is a *positive* process that supports your learning. It is also interesting. It makes you think, grow and learn. Above all, it helps you to professionalize. For all these reasons, when you receive feedback:

- *Try not to respond defensively or apologetically.* Instead, focus on why you are there: to make mistakes and learn! Responding defensively takes up valuable time. Also, practice sessions are a safe place to make mistakes. Mistakes are essential: they allow you to acquire new skills. The process of making errors and identifying the most common ones will allow you to target your practice and improve your interpreting. Think back to a time when you acquired a new skill, such as riding a bike, driving a car or learning how to cook. Many times, doing things *wrong* is exactly what allows us to get it *right* next time.

- *Pay attention to patterns* or repeated feedback about how you struggle with specific areas or issues, and also areas in which you are doing well. This is how you will learn your own unique interpreting style and work to your strengths.

- *Be polite.* Don't interrupt the criticism with explanations or apologies. You will lose valuable time and won't "hear" the feedback as well. Just listen. Then say thank you afterward. This will encourage your partner to provide you with open and honest feedback. If you waste time justifying your mistakes, your partner may not give you accurate or objective information due to worrying about your feelings.

Additional tips for reflective practice

Chapter 2 provides many suggestions for practice and exercises to help you improve your skills. Meantime, when you engage in reflective practice, here are a few strategies to guide you.

Keep a journal

Many interpreters keep a journal to process their interpreting experiences. Write down how a particular assignment went to process what went well and what did not. It can also help to identify specific job tasks that we need to do better, whether related to preparing fully for each assignment, handling ethical challenges, providing customer service, or building glossaries and resources.

Set goals and objectives

Constructive feedback allows us to identify specific areas that we can then target for improvement. One concrete mechanism that allows you to measure progress is setting goals and objectives. *Write them down.* A huge body of research shows that writing down goals and objectives greatly increases the chances of success! For the goal, focus on writing general statements about *what* needs to be improved. Then for each objective state *how* and *when* that improvement will be achieved. Objectives should also have measurable outcomes.

- Sample goal: When I sight translate, I want to eliminate adding fillers.[27]
- Sample objective: I will record myself while sight translating the same consent form three times, then listen to the recording and note the number and location of fillers and repeat the process until I eliminate fillers from my sight translating.

Reflective practice for consecutive interpreting

Role plays are wonderful practice for consecutive interpreting. For written role-play materials, ideally two people will act out the role play while the third person interprets. If you have only two people, one person will need to read the dialogue for both parties. When it is your turn to interpret, *put the role-play sheet down!* The *interpreter* should not be reading the role-play text.

Even if this practice is being recorded (whether by audio or video) take notes while your partner is interpreting. Note specific things s/he is doing well or that s/he struggles with and any errors or terms s/he didn't know or omitted.

Reflective practice for sight translation

- Give the interpreter time to briefly review the text to make a note of any difficult terminology.
- Once the sight translation starts, encourage everyone who is practicing to *read the sentence **before*** they start speaking.
- Follow along with the text and mark with a pen or pencil any place the interpreter came up with a particularly good solution or where s/he struggled.
- Since delivery is particularly important for sight translation, note where the interpreter is backtracking (starting a sentence over again), using fillers or staying silent for extended periods and note the pace (too slow, too fast).

Reflective practice for simultaneous interpreting

Simultaneous mode can be trickier to observe and give feedback on because there are two sources of sound at the same time. If possible, you can follow along with the original speech and also listen to the interpretation. This will let you determine how much or how little of a lag the interpreter has, if s/he is missing content, or whether s/he is capturing the speaker's tone of voice.

Alternatively, you can listen to just the rendition and provide feedback on what you heard the interpreter say and how it felt to listen. If you have a written copy of the speech you can follow along, making notations with a pen or pencil.

Delivery is extremely important in simultaneous mode. Note whether the interpreting was smooth or choppy and whether the interpreter used lots of fillers, such as "um" or "eh," or long stretches of silence. An important feature of simultaneous, as you will see in Chapter 2, is the interpreter's "décalage" or lag time behind the speaker. Note whether the interpreter is keeping up well with the speaker, is too close to understand the meaning well before interpreting or falling too far behind the speaker to interpret effectively. Then work on strategies for improvement.

On your own, transcribe the speech as close to real-time as possible. I.e., type or write as quickly whatever you hear, as much as you can without pausing the audio recording. This can be a time-consuming exercise, but it helps to train your ear to listen carefully, it works your short-term memory and it helps your brain to practice doing two things at nearly the same time.

---

[27] Fillers are little words or sounds without meaning like uh, eh, er and hmm that indicate a speaker is thinking before continuing to speak. Interpreters for accuracy should interpret fillers but not add their own.

Creating glossaries

Capture the grammar and terminology advice you receive during feedback sessions. Note and research any terminology that you could not interpret during the practice session. Create an ongoing glossary of terms and difficult phrases and their solutions. You can do this online or on paper. See Chapter 4, Section 4.5, for more suggestions about developing glossaries.

Repeated content

Often we think there is less value to interpreting content that we have already heard, but repetition allows you to target specific problems. Then you can practice them over and over until the solutions feel automatic and easy.

How Repetitive Practice Can Help Medical Interpreters

Medical interpreting is one area where repetitive practice can help you—even if it seems you are just interpreting the same thing over and over.

For example, if you just can't remember those steps for how an electrocardiogram (EKG) is performed, repeatedly practice a role play about EKGs. The role play will help to anchor those steps in your mind. As a result, that information will be in your mind the next time you need it. You will be able to anticipate what the healthcare provider is going to say, and you will also find it much easier to remember and interpret what is said.

Let's Practice

Learning Activity 1.6 (a): Reflective Practice: Role-Play Demonstration
Learning Activity 1.6 (b): Reflective Practice: A Partner Exercise
Learning Activity 1.6 (c): Reflective Practice: Setting Goals and Objectives

In *The Community Interpreter®: An International Workbook of Activities and Role Plays*

REVIEW OF SECTION 1.6

This section, and its practice exercises in the workbook for this program, offer a solid introduction to reflective practice for the community interpreter. Integrating these practices will help you create a solid foundation for acquiring and improving your core interpreting skills. Such practice will serve you well throughout your entire career.

Reflective practice includes the following key elements:

- Observing yourself as you interpret, for example, by recording your interpreting and playing it back.
- Observing others while they interpret.
- Giving constructive feedback.
- Receiving constructive feedback.

Reflective learning is a core skill that all interpreters should master. Not only will it shorten the amount of time it can take you to acquire professional expertise: it will also provide you with a lifelong strategy for evaluating your performance and that of others in a proactive, thoughtful and intentional way.

CHAPTER 1 SUMMARY

This chapter introduced you to the profession of community interpreting. It is a young profession in rapid growth. While the practice itself has likely existed for millennia, professional community interpreting began in the 1970s in Australia and Sweden and expanded to Canada, Europe and the United States. Today it exists in all the inhabited continents. The profession has many names, including public service interpreting, but the most common name is community interpreting.

Medical, social services, educational and faith-based interpreting are all specializations within the larger umbrella of community interpreting. Legal interpreting is more disputed, particularly court interpreting (part of the broader field of legal interpreting). Historically, legal interpreting was long considered part of community interpreting, but today in many countries it is not clear whether legal interpreting is, or will continue to be, part of community interpreting.

As a result of the rapid growth of the profession, in particular for medical interpreting (where the stakes can be life and death), credentials and certification for community interpreters have become a focal topic in many countries. There seems to be agreement that community interpreters should be 18 years of age, hold a secondary diploma, receive professional training in interpreting and have a high level of language proficiency in both working languages. Certification programs exist, primarily for medical and court interpreters. Canada is exploring certification for community interpreters, the UK has a Diploma in Public Service Interpreting (DPSI) as well as a national registry for DPSI interpreters, and countries like Australia and Sweden (and the United States for sign language) have generalist certifications.

This chapter also explored in depth the basic ethical requirements for community interpreters. It defined ethics and standards of practice and explored what the authors consider to be eight key ethical principles for community interpreters: confidentiality, accuracy, impartiality, transparency, direct communication, professional boundaries, intercultural communication and professional conduct. One section addressed how ethical principles can help community interpreters navigate four common types of communication barriers:

1. Linguistic challenges
2. Role confusion
3. Cultural misunderstandings
4. Service system barriers

The following section explored two techniques to help community interpreters abide by their professional ethics: the CHIA ethical decision-making process and the SAY NO model.
The chapter concluded with a detailed exploration of reflective practice and why community interpreters should engage in it, including activities like self-recording one's own interpreting to enhance performance and identify areas for professional development.

INTERPRETING PROTOCOLS AND SKILLS

by Denis Socarrás-Estrada
with the special contribution of Katharine Allen (Section 2.6)

LEARNING OBJECTIVES

After completing this chapter and its corresponding exercises, the learner will be able to:

OBJECTIVE 2.1	**Stages of the Encounter** Identify and describe the three stages of a typical community interpreting assignment: pre-encounter, interpreted encounter and post-encounter.
OBJECTIVE 2.2	**Four Protocols for Community Interpreting** Discuss and practice four protocols for community interpreting: positioning, professional introductions, direct speech (first person) and turn-taking management.
OBJECTIVE 2.3	**Memory Skills** *(a)* Describe three memory processes: encoding, storage and retrieval. *(b)* Practice three cognitive strategies: mnemonics, chunking and imagery.
OBJECTIVE 2.4	**Message Transfer Skills** *(a)* Practice three cognitive processes: anticipating, multitasking and message analysis. *(b)* Explore two interpreting skills-building strategies: parroting (shadowing) and paraphrasing.
OBJECTIVE 2.5	**Modes, Summarization and Mode Switching** *(a)* Engage in three modes of interpreting: consecutive, simultaneous and sight translation. *(b)* Understand the rationale, skills and requirements for summarization. *(c)* Define, describe and practice mode-switching.
OBJECTIVE 2.6	**Note Taking for Consecutive Interpreting** *(a)* Understand the rationale, skills and requirements for consecutive note taking. *(b)* Practice three effective techniques for note taking: apply a simplified Rozan technique and develop symbol and abbreviation systems.

This chapter describes the main competences and competencies that you need to perform professional community interpreting. Competence and competency are so often confused that they are used interchangeably, even within our field. However, the authors make this distinction:

Competence: an innate or developed ability to perform a professional task (e.g., language proficiency)
Competency: a specific, acquired ability to perform a professional task (e.g. note-taking for consecutive interpreting).

To describe and help you practice the competencies and skills you need to master, this chapter will take into account a body of recent and robust research in the field of interpreting. The profile of professional interpreters described by Pöchhacker (2004, pp. 180–186) includes these competences:

- **Knowledge** (of languages and the world).
- **Cognitive skills** (analysis, attention and memory; [...] note-taking, whispered simultaneous interpreting, intercultural communication, turn-taking management and role performance").
- **Personality traits** (such as stress tolerance and intellectual curiosity).

Chapter 2 will address the skills and subskills related to interpreting in community services. Each section will include a theoretical and a practical part. The *theoretical* part defines the concepts, explains why the skill is necessary, provides direct examples of its application, and refers you to sound, up-to-date research that supports each concept. The *practical* part provides you with well-defined goals and suggestions supported by research about how to develop your skills. The workbook that accompanies this textbook contains many more exercises, activities and role plays to help you practice.

By studying this chapter, you will be able to develop, over time, the competencies and skills you need to perform as a seasoned professional. This set of competencies and skills is based on interdisciplinary research. Following the recommendations in this chapter can boost your performance level to the highest standards of the profession and help you to succeed. You will then support the profession itself and help it to achieve the prestige and reputation it deserves.

2.1 Stages of the Encounter

Overview

For practical purposes, a typical community interpreting assignment can be subdivided into three stages. The ***pre-encounter*** involves what interpreters do from the moment they have been assigned an interpreting task until they begin interpreting. The ***encounter*** takes place while the interpreter is interpreting for service provider(s) and service user(s). The ***post-encounter*** involves everything interpreters do after leaving the assignment.

This section explores what you need to know about each of these three stages, so that you are better prepared for a typical assignment in the field. Understanding these stages will help you plan ahead, reduce stress and keep you alert during the session. It will help you to understand how a careful analysis of the session can improve your performance.

Learning Objective 2.1

After completing this section, you will be able to:

- Identify and describe the three stages of a typical community interpreting assignment: pre-encounter, encounter and post-encounter.

The three stages

Three stages of the interpreted encounter

PRE-ENCOUNTER	• Preparation • Briefing
THE ENCOUNTER	• Professional introduction • Interpreting • Intervening / Mediating
POST-ENCOUNTER	• Debriefing • Analysis

Pre-encounter

Why planning matters

The main objective of the pre-encounter stage is to get ready for the assignment. You may need to discuss the encounter with your employer and/or a contracting party: in other words, the agency or person who requests you for the assignment. You may need to speak with the service provider in advance to learn details about the encounter.

Community interpreting is a socially, emotionally and physiologically demanding profession. It is also low in social support. Assignments can be complex. These are just some of the reasons why each assignment requires thorough and timely preparation to help you gather general and specific details—at least, when time permits. In addition, the sheer variety of service organizations, each with their own specialized terminology, jargon and context, often requires careful preparation of relevant terminology.

General preparation

First, you need to find out the following information:

- **Languages and regional dialectical variations:** Even major languages such as Arabic, Chinese, French, Portuguese and Spanish have regional variations. Make sure you ask the specific language variant needed to help determine if you are qualified for the assignment.
- **Date, time and length of the session:** Check your schedule before accepting the assignment, allowing a comfortable "cushion" of time between two assignments.
- **Location:** Make sure you have not only the address but also, if appropriate, the building name, floor, suite number (or name) and room number.
- **Contact person's details:** Ask for information about your contact person, including a phone number in case you are caught in a traffic delay or an emergency on your way to the assignment.
- **Type and topic of meeting:** You can ask about sensitive issues to be addressed.
- **Type of documents to be used and/or sight translated:** You can inquire if there are pamphlets, brochures or other information to help you to understand the service and its terminology.
- **Payment details:** These are affected by your employment status: see Chapter 4.

Plan for the Unforeseen!

You will need both a contact number for the period *before* the assignment and a contact number for the *date and time* of the assignment—especially on a weekend or evening. It is distressing to be stuck in traffic or to stand outside a locked door with no one to call.

Try to make sure your *interpreting toolkit* contains at least the following items:

- ID card and badge/name tag, if appropriate
- Pens and notepads (one pen is never enough)
- Dictionaries and glossaries (including electronic devices, smart phones and tablets, but verify first if electronic devices are permitted and, if appropriate, clarify that you intend to consult your device only to look up terms relevant to the assignment)
- Water and food (if permitted)
- Necessary items (eyeglasses, tissues, medications, etc.)
- Required documents (e.g., forms required by a hospital or interpreting service provider, such as proof of vaccinations)
- Pocket money (e.g., for parking, public transport or vending machines)

Specific preparation

For a successful performance, gather relevant information about the type of meeting, then research the topic. Prepare your dictionaries and glossaries, including specialized glossaries you have developed yourself for specific terminology and idioms. Look up websites of related institutions. Contact a colleague. See Chapter 4 for specific guidance on preparing terminology for an assignment.

How to prepare for a session when you don't have time to plan

Short-notice assignments are common in community interpreting. Preparing for assignments is ideal, but often not possible. It may be necessary to "activate" the basic elements of preparation. For example, if you know the session is a counseling session, a knee-surgery prep or a parent/student meeting, you can:

- Do a mental run-through to quickly analyze the setting.
    - Which professional and administrative protocols will you need to know?
    - What terminology might be needed?
    - Will the session require special protocols or dress codes?
- Evaluate your competence for that assignment.
- Check your emotional state to make sure you feel calm and sufficiently impartial to perform at a professional level—even you might see blood, witness an argument or interpret for the perpetrator of a crime.

Briefing

To be able to help two parties communicate and understand the setting, if possible, contact the service provider for a pre-encounter. Beforehand, ask the person who sent you to the assignment for any details available, but even if you receive that information it is still ideal to have a briefing—even a minute or two—with the service provider. This briefing, or pre-encounter, by phone or face to face, allows you to learn or share specific concerns about the encounter. It can save time and make the communication flow more smoothly.

Take into account that some service providers might have little to no experience working with interpreters. A briefing is a great opportunity to help them understand how professional interpreters work. Justify any request you make, for example, "I hear a lot of noise in this facility. I would need a quiet room for the session, or I might not be able to interpret accurately."

Of course, you probably will not have time to discuss most of the points above. This is why you will need to master the art of a short, professional interpreter introduction (see next page) to clarify your role.

Be Clear about Your Departure Time

If you have a tight schedule or time concerns, let your employer agency, organization, institution, supervisor, the service provider or the service user know about it *before* the assignment.

It would be ideal if you could stay as long as needed, but if you must leave by a certain time, *make sure you let all parties know this before the encounter begins.*

Encounter

Focus on interpreting

The encounter is the most important stage of the assignment. You are in the spotlight. The service provider and the service user both rely on you. Your main objective is to facilitate communication by managing the flow as unobtrusively as possible, rendering accurate messages, and being impartial.

Professional introduction

Your professional introduction is critical. It helps all parties to work effectively together. It introduces the service user and provider to how a professional interpreter works. For example, your introduction should always disclose that you will interpret *everything* stated during the encounter. In addition, your introduction can offer clear parameters for how the encounter will proceed. You can accomplish this in two languages in an introduction of fewer than 20 seconds!

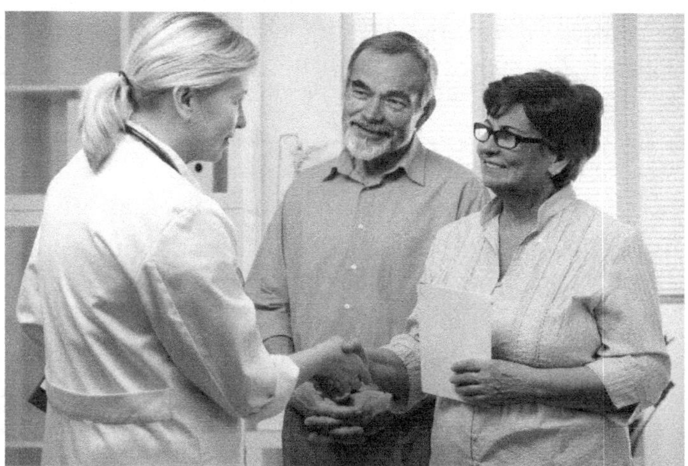

Keep in mind that not all service providers and users have worked with professional interpreters. You may ask them, if time allows, whether they have had any such experience. They might have even had encounters with untrained interpreters or family members who interpret. Their understanding of professional interpreting may be minimal. Knowing their past experience will influence how you work.

See Section 2.2 for how to perform a professional introduction.

Interpreting

During the encounter, take into account the following:

- Positioning (Section 2.2)
- Interpreting in first person (Section 2.2)
- Turn taking (Section 2.2)
- Accurate interpreting (Section 2.4)
- Intervention and strategic mediation (Chapter 3)
- Modes of interpreting: consecutive (usually the primary mode), simultaneous and sight translation (Section 2.5)
- Summarizing, which may be necessary but *only as a last resort* (Section 2.5)
- Note-taking (Section 2.6)
- Use of terminology resources, such as dictionaries and glossaries (Section 4.5)

Mediation

Often you will need to interrupt the speaker to alert everyone to a miscommunication or misunderstanding. The act of speaking in your own voice to address a communication concern is called mediation (or intervention, especially in the United States for medical interpreting). During the encounter you are doing only one of two things: interpreting or mediating. When you intervene to perform mediation, you are no longer interpreting. Because mediation is an important skill to master, Chapter 3 addresses it in depth.

A Common Concern: One Person Starts to Speak the Other Language

Problem: What do you do when one of the parties starts speaking in the other party's language?

Solution: In most cases, you could let that person speak in the other party's language (even if the communication seems very basic) if the dialogue flows smoothly. However, stay alert to chime in as soon as you notice a miscommunication. If the problem interferes with your ability to concentrate and interpret, you may need to request that each party speak only one language or inquire if your services are needed: exercise good judgment. Always speak in a calm, professional tone when intervening.

In a worst-case scenario, you could explain that you may have to leave the encounter because you cannot work effectively in those conditions.

The end of the assignment

Once the service provider and user have finished the interview, you may leave. If you must leave before the session ends, having let the parties know your departure time when you first arrived, remember to act with professional courtesy when you leave.

Post-encounter

When the interpreted session is over, the work is not done! In fact, some of your most important work begins the moment the session ends. After the session, do not speak with the service user. However, it might be both appropriate and helpful to follow up with the service provider. Where feasible and appropriate, you can also consider the following:

- **Debriefing the interpreter**: After a stressful session, you can benefit by expressing your thoughts and feelings with the service provider and getting specialized feedback (particularly in mental health).
- **Post-session provider questions**: The service provider might ask, "Do you think she understood what she needs to do?" "What was going on in there?" Be careful to clarify that you cannot read the service user's mind. You may clarify basic *communication* concerns (for example, "Her speech was a bit slurred"), but avoid speaking about the service user as a person (for example, never say he understood the consent form, seemed honest or had a certain belief). Focus your answers on the *communication*, not your opinions about the *person*.
- **Critical incidents**: If you witnessed a critical incident during the encounter, you may need to report it to the appropriate person. (See Section 5.3.)
- **Interpreter-service user exchange**: After the session, the service user might find you and ask for your advice. Try not to answer questions: bring the service user to an appropriate provider or the receptionist's desk and interpret the question or request. (If you are a *bilingual employee* acting called in as an interpreter, answer service user questions that you would normally answer in your regular job.)

  Special note #1: Keep in mind that for legal and mental health interpreting, *a freelance interpreter should almost never speak alone with the service user.* The legal or mental health consequences are too serious to risk.

  Special note #2: If you were *directly hired by the service user* to interpret, then of course you will need to answer the service user's questions, but do your best not to offer personal opinions.

Analysis

After every session, try to reflect on the session: what went well, what did not and why? This type of post analysis can enhance your competence and professional development:

- First, analyze your performance. Identify and write down positive aspects, areas for improvement, lessons learned and new terminology or protocol.

Build on Your Strengths

Keep in mind that most of us become competent by building on our strengths rather than focusing too much on our weaknesses. Start by identifying your *strengths* before you analyze your weaknesses.

- If you have been emotionally affected by the session, look for specialized support. Unmanaged emotional burdens can quickly turn into job stress, anxiety, burnout or vicarious trauma. (See Section 5.5.)

Stress and Memory

The human stress hormone cortisol has a negative impact on episodic long-term memory. It temporarily blocks memory retrieval (Wolf, 2009). Emotional burdens can also turn into cognitive problems, such as longer reaction time, verbal recall difficulties and memory losses, hesitations, incoherence, etc. These burdens can also interfere with your overall competence, health and wellbeing (Packard, 2009).

Let's Practice

Learning Activity 2.1 (a): Prepare for the Assignment
Learning Activity 2.1 (b): Debriefing Role Play

In *The Community Interpreter®: An International Workbook of Activities and Role Plays*

REVIEW OF SECTION 2.1

In this section, you explored the three stages of a typical community interpreting assignment. You learned what to do during each stage:

1. **Pre-encounter**
    - Preparation
    - Briefing
2. **Encounter**
    - Professional introduction
    - Interpreting
    - Intervening/Mediating
3. **Post-encounter**
    - Debriefing
    - Analysis

The knowledge you acquired here will help you prepare and perform. You can also analyze your performance in a dynamic cycle of professional development. Keep in mind:

- Because community interpreting is a socially, emotionally and physiologically demanding profession that is often low in social and institutional support, you need to prepare carefully for each assignment (if time permits).
- Gather as much information as you can about the assignment beforehand.
- If possible, try to meet the service provider before the encounter to gather details.
- Make a professional introduction to state how the session will proceed.
- Remember: you are there to facilitate meaningful communication through accurate and complete interpreting. Only intervene if a serious miscommunication arises.
- Try to monitor your performance and analyze it afterward.
- Look for specialized debriefing and support if you were emotionally affected.

2.2 Four Protocols for Community Interpreting

Overview

Community interpreters should follow standard protocols for the community service workplaces where assignments take place. However, there are also protocols specific to both general interpreting and community interpreting. In this section you will explore four of the most important protocols in the field: positioning, professional introductions, direct speech (first person) and turn-taking management. Following them will help you promote direct communication and enhance accuracy.

Remember that communicative autonomy is about letting the parties you interpret for remain responsible for and in control of their own communication. These protocols, if you execute them well, can help support communicative autonomy. This section will show you how and why these four protocols have such a big impact on direct communication.

Learning Objective 2.2

After completing this section, you will be able to:

- Discuss and practice four protocols for community interpreting: positioning, professional introductions, direct speech (first person) and turn-taking management.

The four protocols

Positioning

Positioning

The triad

Interpreting is a triadic interaction, that is, an interaction among three parties. In community interpreting, these parties are the service provider, the interpreter and the service user, e.g., doctor-interpreter-patient or teacher-interpreter-parent.

Sometimes, there may be more than three individuals present. For example, the interpreted session might include the service user and two family members, two providers (a doctor and a nurse) and more than one interpreter (a Spanish-English interpreter and a Spanish-Mixteco interpreter, or a sign language interpreter and a certified Deaf interpreter). However, there are mainly three *categories* of parties involved: service provider, service user and interpreter.

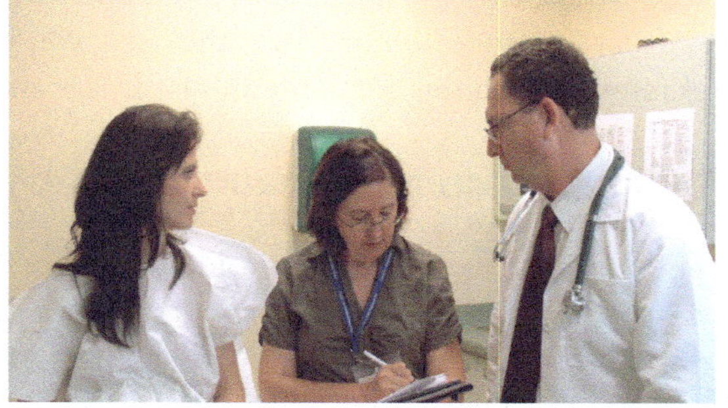

Sometimes the interpreter is not in the same room as the service user and/or provider—for example, the interpreter is working via phone or video (Chapter 4).

The unobtrusive interpreter

Although we speak about a triadic interaction, interpreters are not the center of the communication. You should ideally adopt an unobtrusive position, which means that while *the service provider and user are positioned to communicate directly with each other,* the interpreter is positioned so that he/she can monitor communication well without becoming the center of attention. By being unobtrusive you help the service user and provider establish a strong relationship and support both direct communication and communicative autonomy. Let's see why.

What "interpreter positioning" means

Positioning refers to choosing the appropriate place to stand or sit in relation to the service provider and user. The ***main objective*** of effective positioning is to promote direct communication between the parties.

Sign language interpreters must, of course, be much more visible than spoken language interpreters, because their signed language must be clearly visible to the service users. Their facial expressions and body languages are also instruments of communication. However, sign language interpreters are unobtrusive in other ways: for example, they typically do not wear colorful, attention-getting clothing or jewelry; they also keep their emotions well-hidden, reflecting instead those of all other parties to the session.

The interpreter's positions

Positioning for spoken vs. signed interpreting

This section addresses spoken interpreting. Sign language interpreting has specific protocols about positioning that are not relevant to the discussion below. The spoken interpreter's position will often depend primarily on the space where the encounter takes place. Although there is debate around the world over the issue, you will now examine positioning for common, basic scenarios.

Support communicative autonomy

The approach to take when considering where to stand or sit is to *adopt the position that will best support direct communication.* This goal is usually achieved by occupying an unobtrusive position that allows you to easily monitor the communication without entering the visual space of the service user and provider.

Power dynamics

Interpreters should take into account power dynamics, because service providers tend to hold more power than service users or interpreters. For example, service providers:

- Can be perceived as authority figures by the service user.
- Control the resources to some degree.
- Can act as gatekeepers to the service needed.
- Speak the societal language.
- Usually know the culture of the country, region and the service system (e.g., the healthcare system and biomedical culture) and the service institution.
- Often represent the majority population of the host country.

Meanwhile, service users represent a population that, historically, has experienced discrimination. They may have little knowledge of the service and limited control over the resources. This situation can be intimidating.

Four positions to consider

There are four *general* positions that community interpreters could adopt (although positioning choices vary widely around the world and within any specific country):

- ***An unobtrusive position out of all sight lines,*** *not too near either the service user or provider:* This is a position to adopt if other positions seem impractical or inappropriate. The goal is for everyone to hear you clearly (and for you to hear them)[28] without noticing your presence—if possible.
- ***Near the service provider***: This position, for example, standing just behind the provider, might reinforce the provider's power. It could make both parties think you support the provider more than the user, intimidating the service users. Also, the service user will probably look at you, not the provider. However, this position could detach you from a service user who is becoming dependent on you or wants to talk to you directly. It is useful when the service provider is demonstrating a practice.
- ***Near the service user***: This position, often preferred to be a little behind the user, can help balance the power dynamics. In some cases, this position might make both parties think you support the service user more than the provider. It could also make the service user speak to you more often. You would probably avoid this position in psychiatric inpatient facilities or detention settings (for health or safety reasons) or when working with survivors of rape or other violent crimes who might feel uncomfortable with someone behind them.
- ***The "isosceles triangle" position***: (A triangle with two sides of equal length.) This position keeps the service user and provider at the base of the triangle separated by a shorter distance than the one that separates them from the interpreter. It allows you a clear view of all parties' body language, including gestures and facial expressions. This arrangement can show your impartiality and promote direct communication. It could however make you the center of attention and seen as a co-participant.

[28]With the exception, of course, of sign language interpreters.

Viewpoints on positioning

Although no international consensus exists on positioning, it is still clear that *positioning makes a difference.* The wrong position, at the wrong time, can make the interpreter the center of attention. It can lead everyone to speak to you instead of each other. It can even help those present think you are a part of the conversation. Let's turn to how you can use effective positioning decisions to facilitate direct communication.

Positioning and Medical Interpreting

When deciding where to stand or sit, *keep health and safety issues in mind.* For example, if you work in healthcare settings, you might need to keep a safe distance mainly from patients with mental disorders and/or contagious diseases. You will need to consider privacy issues and might have to interpret from behind a curtain. Protocols in place, medical equipment, testing procedures and tiny exam rooms will all put constraints on your choice of position. Take into account that as you move from one setting to another, you could help spread diseases. In inpatient and hospital settings, you might need to keep a safe distance from detainees or violent offenders brought in by police officers.

Decision making and positioning

Interpreters cannot control all aspects of positioning. (For an excellent overview of this issue in medical interpreting, see NCIHC, 2003.) For example, during a sexual assault forensic exam or a gynecological exam, you might have to interpret from behind a curtain for patient privacy. So before the assignment and when you enter the room, be alert to find a position where you are not obtrusive and can best facilitate direct communication.

Avoid eye contact

One way to avoid attracting attention is to avoid direct eye contact while you interpret. When people need to communicate, they demand attention and feedback. If you do not look at them, they tend to look at anyone else who is paying attention to them. Don't worry if you find it uncomfortable to avoid eye contact when you interpret. This is a new habit to acquire, and you can learn it quickly. Try it.

When you are interpreting (i.e., after you have finished your introduction), simply stop eye contact. Start by focusing attention on your notepad to make it feel more natural to avoid eye contact if doing so feels rude, culturally odd or even disturbing. We do *not* recommend looking at the floor: on the contrary, as long as no one is looking at you, keep your head up and monitor the speaker's nonverbal communications, such as body language, gestures and facial expressions. If someone looks at you, just glance down at your notepad. Make eye contact only when you intervene, for example, to ask someone to pause; with that eye contact you acknowledge your presence and let everyone know you are speaking *as* the interpreter.

Other reasons to avoid eye contact

Social interaction. If you maintain eye contact while you interpret, you will almost certainly feel a natural desire to join the conversation. Even without realizing it you might show any of the six basic emotions (fear, sadness, anger, disgust, surprise and happiness), signs that let the other person know you are listening. If you don't give these types of signals, you might feel rude or uncomfortable, but doing so may distract you from interpreting. Also, eye contact with the parties might encourage them to speak to you.

Eye Contact Takes Your Attention

Interpreting involves a highly complex set of cognitive skills that lead to fatigue, and fatigue affects your accuracy. You will need to focus all your attention on interpreting. Anything like eye contact that distracts you can interfere with your accuracy and competence. Here are a few examples from the research literature about why that is the case.

- *Efficient processing of new sensory information involves a competition for attention that can disturb or impair your working memory.* (Awh, Vogel, & Oh, 2006)
- *Basic or "central attention" and verbal or object working memory can and do result in dual-task interference.* (Fougnie & Marois, 2009)
- *The human brain has limits on its ability to process a lot of data at once.* (Moscoso del Prado Martín, 2009)
- *Working memory capacity is jointly determined by attention control and memory abilities.* (Unsworth & Spillers, 2010)
- Lavie's Load Theory: *In conditions of high cognitive load, where most of the person's cognitive capacity is consumed with a difficult working memory task, for example, the person has few cognitive resources available to resist distraction by irrelevant information. The person can better disregard distracters in a low cognitive load condition to focus on relevant information.* (Weast & Neiman, 2010)

A professional introduction

Interpreters should introduce themselves to the service provider and user in typical encounters, excluding crises or cases where you have already recently interpreted for the same provider and/or service user. The main objective of your introduction is to communicate who you are, what you do and how you will do it. This introduction is a crucial step because community interpreting is still an emerging profession and unfamiliar to most people.

Your introduction should be brief, clear and concise: no more than 30 seconds, in both languages, but better if you can trim it down to 20 seconds—so practice. Use your smoothest tone and a smile to create rapport and gain trust. We suggest that in most cases, you introduce yourself first to service users, since they will be more comfortable and relieved knowing a professional interpreter is present. Then introduce yourself to the provider if you have not had a prior briefing. However, use your good judgment about whom to address first. For example, always address a lawyer first before speaking to a service user.

Use this moment to create professional rapport with the parties. This is the time when you speak as yourself, not serving as the voice of the service user or the provider. You can help to create trust and understanding about your role. Present your best smile, your warmest voice and your most sincere gaze while remaining clear, concise and to the point. In this way you will show both your professionalism and your humanity.

There are no international rules about what the community interpreter's introduction should include. The authors find the introduction should ideally include at least the following elements (again, time permitting):

- You will interpret *everything* stated by all parties during the session without adding, changing or omitting anything.
- You will maintain *confidentiality.*
- You will encourage the service provider and user *to speak to each other*, not to you.
- You will make a hand gesture [demonstrate the gesture] if you need *the parties to pause* to let you interpret.
- If you must depart at a certain time, say so.

Let's look at how this might sound in real life:

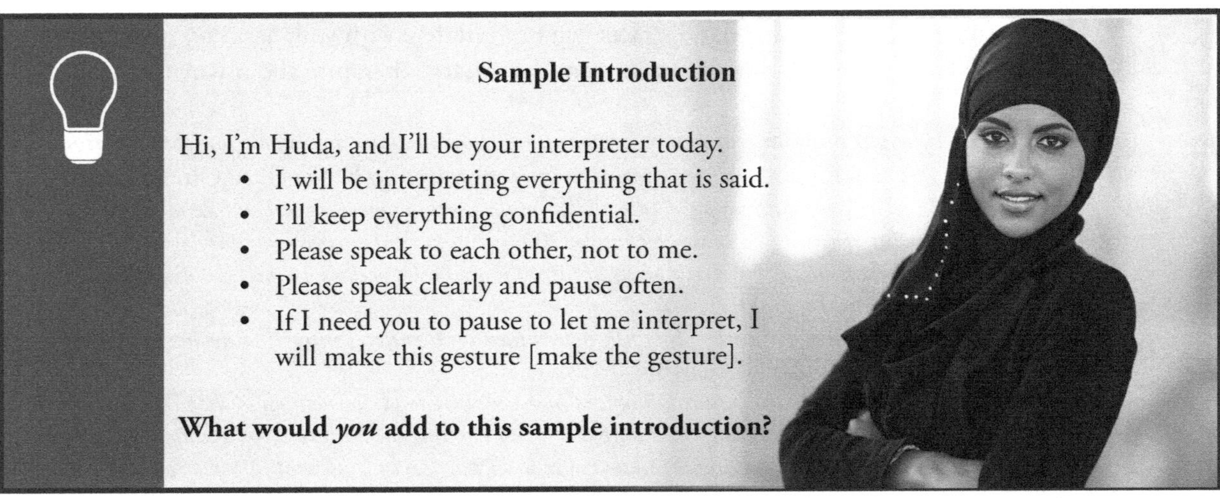

If the parties have never worked with a professional interpreter, and time permits, you may want to add some or all of the following details:

- You will ***use first person*** to interpret, for example, you could say, "If the user says '*I* felt dizzy,' I will say so and not, 'She said she felt dizzy.'"
- You will ***take notes*** only to ensure accuracy and destroy them after the session. If you need to keep case numbers or other notes, say so.
- You recommend ***they address questions to each other and not to you*** (except about the interpreting, e.g., "Interpreter, what did you say?").
- You may intervene to ***request clarification or repetitions***.
- You may ***encourage them to ask*** about anything you say that isn't clear.

The "Short" Introduction: Medical Interpeters, Take Note!

It is not always possible to include every element in the sample introduction given above due to time constraints. If so, make sure to include the fact that *everything* stated will be interpreted and also (for the patient) that you will respect confidentiality. Medical services (and others, like law enforcement, emergency calls and victim services) can be rushed and chaotic at times. Plan ahead for what you can say in the shortest time possible.

Direct speech: speaking in first person

Direct vs. indirect speech

Interpreters should use ***direct speech*** (first person) to interpret the messages into the second language (e.g., "I need to talk to you."). Interpreters may wish to use ***indirect speech*** or third person (e.g., "The interpreter requests a repetition.") when intervening to ask for repetition, clarification and/or addressing a linguistic or cultural barrier. Only court interpreters are obligated to refer to themselves in the third person. Community interpreters may *wish* to intervene that way or in another way, for example, "Excuse me, *as the interpreter*, may I request a repetition?" This choice is yours.

Why first person?

Compared to indirect speech, interpreting in direct speech (in first person):

- Is faster.
- Is easier than interpreting in third person.
- Is more accurate.
- Promotes direct communication.
- Doesn't result in as many interpreter additions or changes to the message.
- Has simpler sentence structures that are easier to remember.

Let's look at an example:

First person: "I have a terrible headache."
Third person: "***She says*** ***she has*** a terrible headache."
(***Addition***) (***Change***)

However, what often happens in real life interpretation is even longer, especially with those who have never been trained to interpret:

First person: "I have a terrible headache."
Third person: "***She says*** ***she's been having*** ***this*** terrible headache."
(***Addition***) (***Changes***) (***Change***)

The reasons that interpreters add more words when they interpret in third person are:

- Sentence structures in indirect speech tend to be more complex than direct speech.
- Because the interpreter is *reporting* on the speech, not *rendering* it, that indirectness leaves room to include the interpreter's sense of what the person is saying, resulting in additions that reflect the interpreter's "edits" of the message.

Interpreting in direct speech gives the speakers responsibility for their communication and helps to take you "out of the picture" in a clear way. It focuses you on the message content and not what you *think about* the message. First person is less intrusive than third person. In fact, it is often easy to tell untrained interpreters from trained ones, because most untrained interpreters tend to interpret in third person.

Why *not* third person?

If interpreters use third person to interpret, they can become the focus of attention. Where feasible, avoid it. Interpreting in third person usually or often:

- Is slower than first person.
- Makes communication between the service user and provider less direct.
- Takes longer to interpret.
- Is more cognitively difficult to interpret because it usually requires changes that lend themselves to unconscious additions and alterations.
- Involves changing the syntax (word order) in a way that leads to more complex sentence structures.
- Can sometimes generate confusion. ("He said that he asked him why he said all that." In this case, who is "he" and "him"?)

Exceptions to the direct speech "rule"

There are a few cases when the interpreter might need to interpret in indirect speech:

- The service user is a child, is elderly or is a mentally disabled person who gets confused by the use of first person.
- In an emergency situation you might have to summarize.
- You interpret for multiple parties, for example several family members.
- The content is so horrific (e.g., torture, rape or murder) that you feel the need to detach yourself briefly for self protection. *This is a controversial recommendation for legal interpreting. Do not switch to third person in legal interpreting. Also, always switch back to direct speech/first person as soon as possible.*

Note: To keep track of several parties in consecutive mode, you may need to switch to third person and/or use a gesture to indicate the speaker. Summarization as a "last resort" is discussed later in this chapter: it requires the disclosure (as soon as you are able) that you had to summarize.

Turn-taking skills or managing the flow

What "turn taking" means

In Europe and other parts of the world, professional interpreters tend to speak about "turn-taking skills," while in the United States you often hear the term, "managing the flow." Both terms address a basic concept: if people speak too fast, don't pause for you to interpret, speak over each other or otherwise create a flow of communication that you can't interpret, you will have to interrupt them to address that problem. For example, you might ask speakers to speak more slowly and pause more often.

Turn-taking management challenges

During the encounter, which usually takes place in consecutive mode (Section 2.5), you need to manage the turn taking and the flow for accuracy. Bear in mind the differences among cultures, genders and speech patterns. Some interpreters might find it socially rude to interrupt a speaker, especially an authority such as a police officer, doctor, teacher or attorney. Yet doing so to avoid summarizing is part of your job. Other challenges include emotional situations: perhaps five people are speaking all at once, or someone is shouting in anger. Be prepared.

How to engage in effective turn-taking management

Develop your memory skills

Since consecutive interpreting is the primary mode used in dialogue and community interpreting, acquire the skills to keep a balanced flow. You will typically need to enhance your memory skills to interpret longer segments without interrupting a thought (Section 2.3). However, building those skills takes time.

When should you ask the speakers to pause?

Ask speakers to pause when:

- Your memory capacity is full.
- Your note-taking skills are not developed enough to ensure accuracy.
- More than one speaker is speaking at once.
- A linguistic or cultural communication barrier arises.

What gesture should you use?

Every culture has gestures to indicate "stop," to interrupt a flow of conversation. Choose a culturally appropriate, professional gesture or act. For example, you could:

- Lean forward and make eye contact.
- Raise your hands to make a T-shape (like a "time-out" signal) with your hands.
- Raise your palm.
- Lift two fingers.
- Emit a low nasal or guttural noise, as if clearing your throat.
- Make a clear verbal request.

Remember, during your introduction you ideally had the chance to show the service provider and user the signal you will be using to request a pause.

What if they refuse to pause?

If someone does not pause when you make your signal, you will have to either take notes, switch to simultaneous mode—or even summarize, as a last resort. (See Section 2.5 for a discussion about modes and mode switching.) Cases when someone won't pause often enough, even after you request a pause, could include:

- An emotionally volatile person or situation.
- Emergencies and crises.
- Persons with mental disabilities.
- Small children, teens or the elderly.
- Speakers who are drunk or on drugs.
- Public events where the speaker talks too quickly, even after reminders.
- Interpreting for audio or video recordings.

"Train the speakers"

Once you've used your gesture a few times, you have effectively trained the parties to speak at an optimal pace. Soon they know roughly when to pause. After the first few minutes, it's common for everyone to get into a communicative flow that you can manage.

Interruption (Turn Taking) has a "Switch-Cost"

- The mind has to switch between tasks when we are interrupted.
- The speaker must pause, hold in mind where she left off, and resume when interpreting is done.
- *Being interrupted slows down our ability to resume where we left off.* (Carrier, 2009)

Let's Practice

Learning Activity 2.2 (a): Where Would You Sit or Stand?
Learning Activity 2.2 (b): A Professional Introduction
Learning Activity 2.2 (c): Turn-Taking Practice

In *The Community Interpreter®: An International Workbook of Activities and Role Plays*

REVIEW OF SECTION 2.2

In this section, you explored four important protocols for community interpreting:

- Positioning
- Professional introductions
- Direct speech (first person)
- Turn-taking management

Remember that:

- The main objective of effective positioning is to promote ***direct communication*** between the parties. Adopt an unobtrusive position to support direct communication. Avoid becoming the center of attention.
- Avoid eye contact while interpreting.
- The main objective of your introduction is to communicate who you are, what you do and how you will do it. Be brief and clear.
- Use direct speech (first person) to interpret. Use indirect speech (or third person) only when you intervene or in special circumstances.
- In consecutive mode, manage the turn taking or "flow" to get speakers to pause for you to interpret accurately.

2.3 Memory Skills

Overview

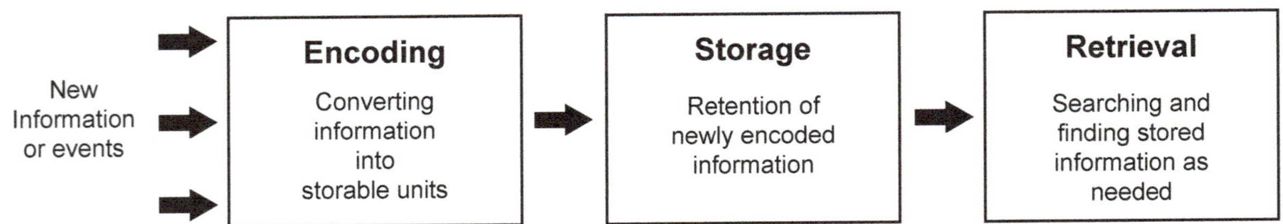

All three processes are essential for memory.

Memory is the mental capacity to **encode, store and retrieve** information. One of the interpreter's most valuable assets is memory. Everything we do as interpreters is based on or made possible by our memory. We use it to make many decisions per minute.

Your memory is critical for this work. If you develop strong memory skills, you will be able to interpret longer messages without interrupting the speakers. You will help them communicate more naturally, as if you were not there. You will be more accurate. You will support direct communication and communicative autonomy. In short, memory skills are among the most important skills of any interpreter.

If you ask people to pause often, they may forget what they planned to say, become distracted or grow irritated by your interruptions. They may have a low opinion of your professionalism and skills and not want you to come back. They may decide that community interpreters in general are not competent. In short, improving your memory skills is not an option or a luxury. It is a *requirement.*

Learning Objective 2.3

After completing this section, you will be able to:

Objective 2.3 (a)

- Describe three memory processes: encoding, storage and retrieval.
-

Objective 2.3 (b)

- Practice three cognitive strategies: mnemonics, chunking and imagery.

Memory processes

Encoding, storage and retrieval: that is memory process in a nutshell. Let's look at each of them.

Encoding is the process that allows the new information you learn to be converted into storable units. That way you can store and recall them later. ("Now, what did our trainer tell us about chunking?") To encode memories, we have to pay attention. If we daydream during an interpreting class—we don't encode the learning. Active listening is critical for accurate encoding. In medical interpreting, for example, the difference between interpreting "two pills four times a day" vs. "four pills twice a day" can result in misunderstandings, adverse reactions, lawsuits and even death.

Storage is the process of retention of newly encoded information so that you can retrieve later. The two main types of memory storage are: ***short-term memory*** (STM) and ***long-term memory*** (LTM). Long-term memory is, for instance, where your languages are stored. Obviously, interpreters need both kinds.

A more recent term for STM is ***working memory.*** **"The term 'working memory' evolved from the earlier concept of short-term memory (STM), and the two are still on occasion used interchangeably" (Baddely, 2012, p. 4).** This is memory that can help you understand, analyze, solve problems and make decisions—tasks that are all part of your job. Working memory is essential for professionals who make split-second decisions and perform under stress. However, long-term memory comes into play as well, for example:

- Memory about how syntax changes when you perform sight translation or switch to indirect speech/third person.
- Social memory about the context of the message, emotional cues and communication styles to help you understand when a speaker is being sarcastic.
- Cultural memories help you make sense of an idiom or a proverb so you can find the equivalent meaning in the target language.

Retrieval is the process of searching for and recalling stored information. Let's say you have just left your training class. You want to tell a friend about mnemonics and chunking. You "rummage" in your brain to remember what your trainer said. Perhaps you open your training workbook and glance at the relevant pages for a moment to refresh your memory. "Oh, now I remember!" you say. This is an example of retrieval.

Emotions and memory

Emotions affect every aspect of encoding, storage and retrieval. Excitement can motivate you in a training session to pay close attention so that you remember well. But anger and shouting by someone whom you interpret for can distract and derail you, which means you could have trouble recalling a message—even one you just heard. The impact of emotions on memory can be huge.

Strategies to enhance memory

Three cognitive strategies

As a community interpreter, you need to understand, store, recall and interpret a great deal of information. In fact, your brain may be so tired at night that it can't remember a single message you interpreted! To enhance your capacity, three of the most popular cognitive strategies for interpreter memory skills include:

- Mnemonics
- Chunking
- Imagery

Research supports them (Bower, 1970a, 1970b; Lindenberger, Kliegl, & Baltes, 1992). By learning and using these strategies, you will gradually find you can manage larger quantities of information, especially when you combine memory skills with note-taking skills (Section 2.6). By developing these two skill sets, you will be able to interpret greater chunks of information without interrupting the speakers nearly so often.

Mnemonics

Mnemonics are strategies that help us to use information we already know while we are encoding new information to help us retrieve that information later. Three of the most common mnemonic strategies are visualization, rhyme and acronyms.

Visualization can take many forms: for example, a story flashing before our eyes or symbols used in note-taking (such as a circle within a circle to show someone shouting).

Rhyme is often used today to help children remember, although historically rhyme has helped adults pass down knowledge over time. Many English-speaking children grow up saying this rhyme to help them remember how many days in a month)

Thirty days hath September,
April, June and November.
All the rest have 31,
Except February alone,
Which has 28 days clear,
And 29 in each leap year.

Acronyms are another way that many people, including interpreters, remember complex information. Here are a few examples.

Law (this acronym is used by a number of legal interpreters)

- Common law felonies: Mrs. Baker

M	=	Murder
R	=	Rape
S	=	Sodomy
B	=	Burglary
A	=	Arson
K	=	Kidnapping
E	=	Escape
R	=	Robbery

Medicine (used by some medical interpreters)

- ABC stands for airway, breathing and circulation (when doctors may have an unconscious or unresponsive patient):

A	=	Airway
B	=	Breathing
C	=	Circulation

- VINDICATE refers to a differential diagnostic procedure as a way for doctors to be sure they remember to consider all the possible pathological processes (many medical interpreters also study differential diagnosis):

V	=	Vascular
I	=	Inflammatory/Infectious
N	=	Neoplastic
D	=	Degenerative/Deficiency/Drugs
I	=	Idiopathic/Intoxication/Iatrogenic
C	=	Congenital
A	=	Autoimmune/Allergic/Anatomic
T	=	Traumatic
E	=	Endocrine/Environmental

Many interpreters use mnemonics to help them remember the ethical principles in the particular code of ethics they follow. Here is one created just for you, to help you remember the list of ethical principles at the beginning of this textbook. See if you can remember what they are by reading this sentence:

- Cats Are Incredibly Tame; Dogs Require Intense Pampering

(Note that mnemonic statements don't have to be *true*—just easy to remember!) Do you remember these ethical principles from the code of ethics at the beginning of this textbook? The capitalized letters in the mnemonic sentence above correspond to:

C	=	Confidentiality
A	=	Accuracy
I	=	Impartiality
T	=	Transparency
D	=	Direct Communication
R	=	Role Boundaries
I	=	Intercultural Communication
P	=	Professional Conduct

Chunking

Chunking is the process of taking information and breaking it into parts or "chunks" to help you recall the information. You divide a message into parts that have *meaning* (or to which you assign meaning). In other words, chunking is the process of organizing information into smaller, meaningful wholes. For example, you are a Canadian or U.S. interpreter who needs to interpret these numbers:

17735274668

This series looks like a meaningless string of numbers. But if you subdivide them in the following way, they will resemble a standard U.S. phone number: 1-773-527-4668, making the numbers more concrete and easier to remember by connecting them to phone numbers. In other words, you are *breaking up* and *reorganizing* the information to make it easier to remember—and interpret.

Let's take another example. You listen to someone speak the following paragraph out loud so that you can interpret it:

> The term chunking was coined by Miller (1956). He stated that the benefit of a chunking mechanism is that it mediates the amount of knowledge that one can process at a given time (Jones, 2012). For interpreters, this means that by mentally dividing the message into chunks, they understand it better and have already processed some of the meaning, which makes it easier to interpret. If chunking makes it easier to interpret, it may also reduce stress, allowing the interpreter to focus more on interpreting.

Now, which parts of that message naturally fell into "chunks" or pieces of meaning for you? Look at the printed paragraph. For you, maybe the first two sentences were one chunk of information, and the rest was another chunk. Or maybe there are several chunks of meaning. Sit down with the paragraph and make pencil marks where you think you sense a "chunk" of meaning: where would you put those marks? What are the main ideas?

The concept to grasp is that we don't process words. *We process meaning.* This is what we do all the time, naturally, as human beings who communicate. If you focus on words instead of chunks, you will drown in words. In fact, focusing on words when you interpret can make you "freeze" and miss information. Remember: the goal is to process meaning. Chunking enhances your retention. So rather than focusing on words:

- Break the message into manageable parts.
- Tease out *concepts.*
- Focus on key ideas.
- If you wish, think of a visualization or word that sums up that key idea.

Chunking by meaning, which is actually based on comprehension, increases the capacity of the short-term memory. (Zhang, 2012)

Imagery and visualization

Humans are visual creatures. We rely on visual cues and visual processes in every aspect of our lives (except those who are blind). Interpreting is no exception, and visualization can enhance both memory skills (including chunking) and note-taking.

Visualization is the ability to imagine pictures in our mind. Consider this example. You interpret in a school for a complicated playground story about a fight that could result in a student's expulsion. You need to understand *who did what to whom.* If you do visualize these events as a story, they may be easier to remember and interpret. In another example, the doctor recites a series of steps the patient needs to take to prepare for surgery. By creating a picture in your mind of each step, you can remember them better.

Visualization Is Not Always Helpful

Note that if you are interpreting traumatic content related (for example) to domestic violence, sexual assault, violent crime, torture or war trauma, you may wish to avoid visualizing as a memory technique. Visualizing atrocities can evoke intense emotional reactions in interpreters that interfere with cognitive processing and can reduce your accuracy. If visualizations come to your mind against your will, there are techniques that you can use to calm yourself. See Chapter 5.5 and Bancroft et al., *in press*, for details.

Let's Practice

Learning Activity 2.3 (a): Test Your Memory Skills!
Learning Activity 2.3 (b): Memory Skills Practice
Learning Activity 2.3 (c): Chunking

In *The Community Interpreter®: An International Workbook of Activities and Role Plays*

REVIEW OF SECTION 2.3

In this section, you studied three memory processes: encoding, storage and retrieval. You also explored three cognitive strategies: mnemonics, chunking and imagery.

Remember that:

- Memory is the mental capacity to encode, store and retrieve information.
- It is essential for interpreters to develop strong memory skills.
- Memory skills allow you to interpret longer messages without interrupting and distracting the speakers.
- Your emotions affect all memory processes.
- Chunking means dividing the message into smaller chunks of meaning to help you more effectively analyze, process and interpret.
- Try to visualize "who did what to whom" to help you remember and interpret longer messages.
- Practice memory strategies, such as mnemonics, chunking and imagery to improve your working memory capacity and interpreting capability.

2.4 Message Transfer Skills

Overview

Visualization is just one memory tool. If it doesn't work for you, try others.

Interpreting requires a great deal of mental, physical and emotional energy. It also involves a number of cognitive processes, such as:

- Attention (e.g., attentive listening to absorb messages and their meaning and catch subtle cues such as body language).
- Flexibility (to avoid errors, adapt to surprises, engage in multitasking, reformulate messages that seem unclear and manage the flow).
- Sensory storage (taking in environmental factors, including hearing or seeing the message).
- Working memory (to find the right terms, concepts and idioms) and long-term memory (for understanding the message, context, service systems, cultures, etc.).
- Problem solving (identifying communication barriers, assessing options and making decisions).
- Speed (your reaction time, efficient processing and conversion of meaning and the ability to deliver messages at an appropriate pace with sufficient clarity).

This section explores how you, the interpreter, can take current research about cognitive strategies and apply it to interpreting. Often, you may be unaware of just how much work is involved for your mind. This section will open your eyes to a new appreciation of the amazing brain you have—and the work you do each time you interpret.

Learning Objective 2.4

After completing this section, you will be able to:

Objective 2.4 (a)

- Practice three cognitive processes: anticipating, multitasking and message analysis.

Objective 2.4 (b)

- Explore two interpreting skills-building strategies: parroting (shadowing) and paraphrasing.

The interpreter's cognitive processes

> Humans draw inferences and make decisions under the constraints of limited knowledge, resources, and time.
>
> (Hoffrage & Reimer, 2004)

Decision-making is a complex process that requires the orchestration of multiple neural systems... [It] is believed to involve areas of the brain involved in emotion (e.g., amygdala...) and memory (e.g., hippocampus).

(Gupta, Koscik, Bechara, & Tranel, 2011)

As we mentioned in Chapter 1, about half your work as a community interpreter depends on your interpreting skills. The other half involves effective decision making. Both are important. In general, community interpreters need to work on enhancing accuracy by focusing on their message transfer skills. This section will introduce you to strategies that will enhance your accuracy.

Three message transfer skills

Anticipating

Why anticipation matters

You are interpreting for a patient who is talking about symptoms, such as a headache, earache and sore throat. You know from experience that the nurse is going to ask how long this problem has been going on. You are pretty sure that the patient, instead of giving a direct answer, will tell the nurse a story, discuss some family matter or say anything except a simple answer such as "three days," the kind of answer the nurse expects.

Knowing roughly what the nurse will say, and being emotionally prepared for her frustration, will help you to be more accurate. You will be ready to handle the verb tenses she might use. You know what the patient might answer, based on your past experience. That knowledge gives you time to plan a strategy. For example, when the patient goes on for three paragraphs instead of answering the question, will you:

- Simply interpret what the patient says? (Acceptable option.)
- Ask the patient to get to the point? (Unacceptable option.)
- Tell the nurse, "She doesn't really understand you." (Unacceptable option.)
- Explain to the patient, "In this healthcare system, you should give a direct answer to a direct question or providers can get annoyed." (Unacceptable option.)

If you are curious about why these options are labeled acceptable or unacceptable, see Chapter 3. Meantime, by planning mentally in advance, you can maintain accuracy and plan how to handle your own impatience or emotions.

How anticipating works

Anticipating as applied to interpreting means that you can foresee what is probably about to happen or be said (at least roughly), then plan for it. For linguistic accuracy, interpreters anticipate the word or phrase to come that will complete an expression or sentence, which helps you to interpret accurately in a way that is easy to understand. For decision making, if you know what is about to be said, you can plan whether or not to intervene and what kind of mediation to perform if you do. From a linguistic perspective, this technique is helpful when taking notes for consecutive interpreting (see Section 2.6) and also when using simultaneous mode. The ability to anticipate what will come next can be trained; it can also come from experience.

For example, a first-time encounter interpreting for magnetic resonance imaging (MRI) can be difficult to anticipate unless you have done excellent preparation, but after interpreting for a few MRI exams, you can anticipate much of what will be said from experience.

Anticipation benefits

Anticipating can help you to:

- Improve your focus.
- Respond in a timely manner.
- Calculate quickly.
- Make appropriate decisions.
- Multitask without errors.
- Remember concepts.
- Be more articulate and smooth in your delivery.

The last point is important. A number of providers complain they cannot easily understand interpreters. Some of this problem is due to interpreters' accents and foreign intonations, but often it is due to choppy or poor delivery. Smooth delivery nearly always makes it easier for service users and providers to understand you.

Easy patterns to be anticipated

Learn to anticipate the following patterns you might encounter daily:

- Common collocations (words often spoken or written together, e.g., "consent form")
- Grammar (the usual tenses, noun endings, syntax, etc.)
- Phrasal verbs (e.g., "fill out," "hand in," "turn away")
- Idioms (e.g., "He's feeling blue" can refer to someone who is sad or depressed)
- Dates (different order in different languages, which can be a problem when sight translating: in the Czech Republic, for example, 18.6 would mean June 18)
- Series of similar or related words (synonyms, etc.)
- Proper nouns (names of people, places or things, e.g., Memorial Hospital)

The Risks of Anticipation in Medical Interpreting

Interpreters should train and learn this skill, including medical interpreters. Many medical encounters follow set routines that become easy to learn over time, especially in such common specialties as pediatrics, prenatal and family medicine.

But be careful of overconfidence that could lead to mistakes and subsequent backtracking and self-corrections, which could affect the quality of your interpreting. Or you might not even notice your mistake, which could have serious medical consequences. Every medical case is unique, despite common patterns. Of course, the same can be true in other settings, but not always with such serious potential consequences.

Multitasking

What multitasking means

Multitasking is the ability to do several things at once. We all do it some of the time. Interpreters have to multitask whenever they interpret. You might need to take notes and interpret from them. In simultaneous interpreting, you listen *while* you interpret. You need to read body language to assess comprehension, detect possible misunderstandings and intervene appropriately to prevent miscommunication. In short, successful community interpreting requires both cognitive and emotional involvement—at the same time.

On the one hand, finding language equivalences in a target language means you have to assess possible meanings and registers while making the best choices in a millisecond. On the other hand, interpersonal interactions require your awareness of others' feelings in addition to your own self-awareness, empathy, personal detachment and emotional balance. This emotional and linguistic complexity helps to make community interpreting a rich and fascinating profession. Few community interpreters complain that they are bored!

The interpreter's multitasking checklist

Based on Gile's review of his Effort Models (Gile, 1999), enhanced by (Zhang, 2012), the box on the next page shows you a list of techniques that professional community interpreters use during any session, even if they are not intentionally aware of them. As you look at this list, think of the respect everyone should have for community interpreters!

Message analysis

Your miraculous brain

It is amazing what you and your brain do every time you interpret. You already have nearly all the skills you need to interpret. Now put them into play.

The steps in this section for message analysis may look complicated, yet they are simple. You already perform them every day. For example, any time you take a class and learn something new, hear a story or find out how to apply for a driver's license or cook a new recipe, you use your brain in the same ways that you will need to interpret.

The trick in interpreting is to make the process of understanding and acting on a message more *intentional* and *immediate*, because you have to perform the analysis on the spot.

THE COMMUNITY INTERPRETER'S CHECKLIST

Before the encounter

1. Get your pens, notepad and terminology resources ready. ☐
2. Analyze what the session is about to help you prepare and focus. ☐

At the beginning of the encounter

3. Scan the room to make a decision about which unobtrusive position to adopt. ☐
4. Smile and use body language to create rapport and show empathy. ☐
5. Use a calm, firm voice to help establish trust, credibility and professionalism. ☐
6. Give a professional introduction to establish clear parameters for the session. ☐
7. Listen to and analyze the service user's language and regionalisms. ☐
8. Discriminate other surrounding noise. ☐

While interpreting

9. Engage in active listening. ☐
10. Read body language (eye cues, hand gestures, leg positions, etc.). ☐
11. Use imagery to aid in retention. ☐
12. Replicate or take into account the speakers' tones, volumes and gestures. ☐
13. Reorganize and reformulate the message based on *meaning* (not the words). ☐
14. Remember to use direct speech (first person). ☐
15. Deliver the message in the target language in a clear, understandable voice. ☐
16. Become aware of, assess and do not act on your own biases. ☐
17. Avoid eye contact while interpreting. ☐
18. Take notes as needed; recognize and interpret from notes. ☐
19. Maintain objectivity, detachment and regard for safety. ☐
20. Maintain utmost accuracy. ☐
21. Engage in problem solving and decision making as needed. ☐
22. Switch to indirect speech (third person) if direct speech is problematic. ☐
23. Read body language and contextual cues (without making eye contact). ☐
24. Monitor your output. ☐
25. Intervene to correct yourself, if necessary. ☐
26. Manage turn taking. ☐
27. Maintain impartiality. ☐
28. Identify communication barriers. As needed, plan how to address them. ☐
29. Intervene only if the consequences of a miscommunication are serious. ☐
30. Switch back smoothly to interpreting after mediating. ☐
31. Maintain transparency: report even your own interventions. ☐
32. Avoid side conversations. ☐
33. Check a dictionary, glossary or other resource, if necessary. ☐
34. Switch modes as needed. ☐
35. Assess whether or not to perform a sight translation, if so requested. ☐
36. Change position as needed. ☐

After the session

37. Leave the room whenever the provider leaves. ☐
38. Avoid being alone with the service user, if possible. ☐
39. Debrief with the provider (if possible) if the session left an emotional impact. ☐
40. Practice self care strategies, as needed. ☐

The more you can identify strategies that help you analyze what you are hearing, the better you will be able to convert what you hear into the target language.

Four steps for basic message analysis

Your goal is to find words, concepts and structures that are *equivalents* of the original message in a target language. This section offers you a basic introduction to the concept of message analysis within the pragmatic framework of four steps:

- Listen to the message.
- Extract the meaning.
- Find equivalent target-language concepts to reformulate the message.
- Assess the rendered message.

An example of message analysis

Let's say a service user states, "I threw up the whole week long" to a therapist. You listen to the message and notice that "I threw up" (vomited) and "the whole week long" are two pieces of meaning that do not make literal sense put together in this context. You realize this problem is due to cultural linguistic meaning: in the patient's country and language, "I threw up" does not always refer to literal vomiting. It can mean, "I was so upset I couldn't eat, and every time I tried to, the food wouldn't go down because I was too stressed."

You then search for equivalents in English. You decide to say "all week" (very close to the original) but you convert "I threw up" into three possible reformulations:

1. "I was too stressed to eat."
2. "I was too stressed to keep food down."
3. "I was so stressed I couldn't swallow a bite."

Now you have to choose the rendition that feels *most accurate in this context.* You decide to deliver the message in an anxious tone of voice (to replicate the speaker's tone) by saying, "I was too stressed all week to eat."

Afterward, you evaluate the message for accuracy. If you change your mind about the option you chose, you can correct yourself by saying to both parties, "The interpreter should have said just now that the patient stated, 'I was so stressed all week I couldn't keep food down.'" Or, instead, you could intervene to suggest that the provider ask the patient to clarify the meaning of "I threw up all week long." Either strategy might work well, depending on the context and situation.

Step 1: Listen

It sounds so easy: "First, listen to the message." But this step is harder than it appears. Even for a simple sentence like, "You have no idea!" the interpreter must listen very actively and carefully to take into account the following:

Attention and focus

How often does our mind wander? All the time. Yes, that can happen while you interpret—with disastrous results. You might be tired. Perhaps you have a new baby. If you interpret traumatic content—for example, in psychiatric hospitals, prisons, war zones or refugee camps—you might find that your mind is wandering because you need to distance yourself from the content. For accuracy, you will still need to focus.

Context

Any aspect of the content could affect meaning. The environmental, social, professional, personal, cultural and even religious context can affect it. For example, the word *shahada* in Arabic has a rich cultural and religious meaning that could never be adequately rendered by a single word in a European language. Technically, *shahada* means something like *testimony*. In reality, a book could be written about its meaning.

Body language, gestures and tone of voice

It is not your job to interpret body language or gestures (and a legal interpreter should almost never do so) unless the result is a communication barrier. However, you will constantly need to assess the meaning inherent in body language, gestures and tone of voice to help you find adequate equivalent messages in the target language. For example, if a Spanish speaker in parts of Latin America says *pie* (which means *foot*) but points to his leg (because in certain countries, *pie* may often be used colloquially to refer to either *foot* or *leg*), seeing that gesture may affect your interpreting decisions.

In another example, if an Asian speaker is asked by a healthcare provider to assess her pain and says, "It's not too bad" in a quiet voice, but you can hear the acute pain in her voice through your cultural and social knowledge, you might choose to interpret the statement in a louder tone that reflects some of the pain you hear, because the provider could otherwise miss those nuances. Such nuances can be important for diagnoses and decisions about managing pain and prescribing medications (including dosages).

Long-term memory

As the interpreter, you bring a great deal of experience, knowledge and social awareness to the encounter. Use it to help you analyze the message. For example, when the service user says *brother*, does he mean a blood brother, a distant cousin or a friend? When the provider says, "Did you understand?" and the service user says, "Yes," with a nod, does that really mean the service user understands? Can you analyze the Greek or Latin roots and affixes (suffixes and prefixes) in medical terms such as *narcolepsy* in such a way that, even if the term is new to you, you can interpret the meaning of it accurately? Your long-term memory comes to your aid constantly as you interpret.

Intent

Is the speaker angry or upset? Did she intend to say something bigoted or unkind ("Do your people always act that way?") or was she just being insensitive? The meaning of a simple message, such as *Sure!* can be quite different, depending on whether the speaker is sarcastic, angry, sad or resigned. You, the interpreter, will have to decode the intent from the context, body language (including facial expressions), tone of voice and other factors. All of them affect how you understand and interpret the message.

Other aspects

Other aspects of language and communication that influence your understanding of a message include regionalisms, communication styles, the register, literal and figurative language, idiomatic meaning, power dynamics and cultural references.

Step 2: Extract the meaning

Whether the message is long or short, you may need to break it down into smaller parts or chunks of meaning in order to be able to accurately render it. Consider the sentence, "Although your PAP test was normal, since the colposcopy showed CIS, I'm recommending a cone biopsy be done to find out what's really going on." Here are a few examples of breaking that message down:

"Although your PAP test was normal..."	Do you know what a PAP test is? If not, find out (request a clarification, consult a dictionary or a device, etc.). What does "normal" mean here?
"...the colposcopy showed CIS..."	Here are two somewhat complex medical terms, one of which indicates cancer—CIS or carcinoma in situ, a diagnosis that the patient may or may not already know. Cancer is a "big" diagnosis, yet CIS is not as serious as most cancers.
"...so I'm recommending a cone biopsy be done to find out what's going on."	A doctor's recommendation is the beginning of a negotiation in much of Western medicine. This recommendation contains yet another medical term that the patient might or might not know.

Step 3: Find equivalent target-language concepts to reformulate the message

The medical terms

Let's return to the example above:

- Do the names for the three medical terms (PAP test, colposcopy and CIS) exist in the target language?
- If you left a country 20 years ago, perhaps they *do* exist there now.
- **Do you have a bilingual medical glossary resource to consult?**
- Would the patient understand these terms if you interpreted them literally or would the patient understand better if you (a) kept the English name for the terms, (b) requested a clarification from the doctor and/or (c) used both the English and the target-language term when you interpret? (Answer: we recommend option (c) if you have concerns about the patient's ability to understand.)
- If you know that CIS refers to cancer, but suspect the patient does not, how will that concern affect your interpretation?

Sentence structures

English often uses a passive sentence structure (e.g., "recommend that a cone biopsy be done"), a common structure in English, if not in most other languages. Common sentence structure equivalents are something to study and practice so that you don't waste time and mental energy reformulating them. The question of equivalent sentence structures to capture meaning can be particularly important in sight translation because written texts tend to have more complex sentence structures than speech.

Lose the words, find the meaning

Focusing on words will slow you down; focusing on chunks of meaning will speed you up. You are also less likely to panic and get "hung up" on the individual words.

Step 4: Assess the rendered message

You have made your decision. You rendered the message. Now what?

The part that comes next is natural, almost reflexive. As you listen to your own interpreting (at least, in consecutive mode), you are aware of what you render. Part of you scans the message for accuracy, which is your number one concern. If you make a mistake, a warning message flashes in your mind, perhaps unconsciously. You can do a better job if you monitor your interpreting consciously to assess whether your rendition and delivery:

- *Maintains the register.* If the original message was delivered in scholarly, formal, informal, colloquial or slangy phrasing, maintain the equivalent register.
- *Captures the diction.* Did your diction (word choice) include the right words and phrases to convey the same style of communication and the impact of a message?
- *Conveys the affect, intent and tone.* Your reformulated message should reveal the emotional expressivity of the speaker or signer.
- *Prioritizes the key components of the message.* Some languages put stress on key words or word order, diction, tone of voice, etc. to highlight important parts of a message.

If you assess the message (consciously or unconsciously) and realize you made a mistake, correct it. Also, be kind to yourself. You might think, "Oh, no, if I just had a little more time I *know* I could have said it better!" However, you don't have that time. Do your best. Practice at home. And be patient as you learn and grow professionally.

Two skills-building strategies

Parroting (shadowing) and paraphrasing

Component skills are part of the interpreting skill set but do not involve actual interpreting. Parroting/shadowing and paraphrasing are two of the most critical component skills for all interpreters. They play a foundational role in developing your interpreting skills. They help you activate your vocabulary and enhance your listening skills and comprehension. They can result in faster reaction time, more precise diction and effective multitasking.

So if you don't see how these practice activities can help you *interpret*, be patient. The effort will pay off.

Parroting/shadowing

The value of parroting/shadowing

Parroting, also known as *shadowing*, means repeating word for word in the same language what a speaker says. (*Shadowing* can also refer to a practice where a novice interpreter follows a professional interpreter at work to observe her or his performance. To avoid confusion, *shadowing* is not used with that meaning here.)

Parroting, or shadowing, is an effective training and practice strategy for interpreters. Although more useful for simultaneous interpreting skills, this technique also helps you for consecutive interpreting. It accelerates cognitive processes and improves your word choice. Parroting will help you develop the skills to listen, understand, speak and monitor yourself. It will increase your speed and enhance your diction, fluency and speaking rate (Jiahong, Liberman, & Cieri, 2006). It can reinforce the neural pathways—the connections inside your brain—that help you to quickly access the concepts, terms and sound productions stored in your long-term memory (Curlik & Shors, 2013).

How to parrot

A great warm-up

Parroting is a basic skill-building activity that will help you stretch or warm up for interpreting, because it requires active listening, simultaneous comprehension and speech production. You can do it in a three-stage process using two or all of your working languages (i.e., English-English, Spanish-Spanish, Italian-Italian). We recommend you start with the language in which you are most fluent. Parrot a recorded speech, a radio speaker, a television program or any other recording, but do not begin with a fast or complex talk. Start with slow speeches, so that you don't suffer attention fatigue or get frustrated or demotivated.

Instructions for parroting

When you begin parroting:

- Select a relatively slow recording of about 100–120 words per minute (wpm) about two minutes long.
- Parrot the whole recording in your strongest language.
- Do not interpret: be sure to repeat all words in the same language.
- Next, select a medium-paced recording (130–150 wpm), about two minutes, and start repeating words in the same language.
- Select a more rapid speech (more than 160 wpm) of about two minutes and repeat the words in the same language.

Once you have processed around 780–860 words for about six minutes, your stronger language should be well activated. Then repeat the three-stage process with your second-strongest language, then with any other working language(s).

What types of recordings?

When you start off, choose speeches that address your main interests and make sure they are *simple* speeches (generally avoid TED talks, politicians and economists!). You may find it fun to select speeches about people you know and your own culture, topics you have studied or your favorite hobbies, sports and leisure activities. When you get ready for an interpreting assignment, select recordings related to that topic.

Paraphrasing

How paraphrase practice helps you

Paraphrasing means saying the same thing in different words *in the same language*. You reformulate sentences but keep the basic meaning of the message (Christoffels & De Groot, 2004). Interpreters who engage in this activity for practice usually paraphrase by changing the word order, using synonyms and finding equivalent idioms.

Paraphrasing will help you develop the skills to process large numbers of "chunks of meaning." It will also help you to process, understand and render complex messages and complicated sentence structures. This technique, if you practice it long enough, will help you have access in a split second to a wider number of word choices when you interpret.

After all, interpreting almost by definition *is* paraphrasing: using different words to render the same meaning. As a result, paraphrasing in the same language helps you reduce your reaction time when you interpret and produce natural speech that is easy to understand.

How to paraphrase

Start off by reading lists of synonyms, phrasal verbs or idioms. Later you can ask someone to read you words or short phrases at random from the same list and paraphrase them.
This exercise will reinforce your working and long-term memory. You can also read a short paragraph and try to paraphrase it. Initially you can paraphrase words and short expressions without time pressure. Later, increase the level of difficulty by paraphrasing longer chunks of information faster. Next:

- Select a slow speech (100–120 wpm) of about two minutes in your strongest language and start restating the sentences in the same language, keeping the same meaning. Do so while the speaker is still speaking, if you can.
- Select a medium-paced speech, neither fast nor slow (130–150 wpm), also of two minutes in the same language, and do the same.
- Select a rapid speech (more than 160 wpm) of two minutes in that language and do the same.

Once you have processed around 780–860 words for about six minutes, proceed with your second most fluent language and then any other working languages. After you practice parroting and paraphrasing for close to half an hour, you should be ready to interpret.

Parroting will improve your working memory, mental flexibility and the ability to immediately grasp meaning and find an alternative way to express that message. You will also have set the foundation for similar mental processes using both languages.

Let's Practice

Learning Activity 2.4 (a): Anticipation
Learning Activity 2.4 (b): The Interpreter's Checklist
Learning Activity 2.4 (c): Parroting (Shadowing)
Learning Activity 2.4 (d): Paraphrasing

In *The Community Interpreter®: An International Workbook of Activities and Role Plays*

REVIEW OF SECTION 2.4

In this section you have practiced three cognitive processes: anticipating, multitasking and message analysis. You also explored two interpreting skills-building strategies: parroting (shadowing) and paraphrasing. Here are a few key points to remember:

- Anticipation is a helpful skill to produce quick, comprehensible messages and foresee situations based on your knowledge and experience and the context.
- Successful community interpreting requires both cognitive and emotional involvement. Finding language equivalences in a target language means assessing possible meanings while making best choices in a millisecond. Interpersonal interactions require your awareness of others' feelings in addition to your self-awareness.
- This section offered you a basic introduction to the concept of message analysis in four steps. The steps are:
    - Listen to the message.
    - Extract the meaning.
    - Find equivalent target-language concepts to reformulate the message.
    - Assess your rendered message.
- Parroting is a basic skill-building activity that will help you stretch or warm up for interpreting, because it requires active listening, simultaneous comprehension and production of speech.
- Paraphrase practice will help you develop the skills to understand, process and render complex messages and complicated sentence structures.

2.5 Modes, Summarization and Mode Switching

Overview

Modes of interpreting in community settings

Three modes—and summarization

The three modes

Now that you have worked on the primary component skills of interpreting, it is time to apply them to the task at hand: *interpreting. Interpreting* involves communicating an oral or signed message between speakers of different languages, from a source language into a target language. A mode is a technique for the delivery of interpreting. Whenever you interpret, you will have to select the correct mode for the work.

Some interpreting specialists argue that there are only two real modes, consecutive and simultaneous; they think that sight translation should be considered a "technique" and not a mode. However, in most parts of the world sight translation is considered a third mode, and it is widely used in community interpreting. In addition, many community interpreters summarize as a last resort, when none of the three modes is possible. In this sense, from a practical perspective summarization functions as a de facto mode. It is not accepted as a mode, because interpreters should almost never have to summarize, yet summarization is needed more often in community interpreting than in other specializations. This section will therefore examine all three modes and also summarization.

Learning Objective 2.5

After completing this section, you will be able to:

Objective 2.5 (a)
- Engage in three modes of interpreting: consecutive, simultaneous and sight translation.

Objective 2.5 (b)
- Understand the rationale, skills and requirements for summarization.

Objective 2.5 (c)
- Define, describe and practice mode-switching.

"Three modes [of interpreting] are now recognized by the interpreting profession . . . simultaneous interpreting, consecutive interpreting, and sight translation." (NAJIT, 2006)

- **Consecutive,** *the primary mode*
    - Short consecutive (interpreting about one minute or less)
    - Long consecutive (interpreting for more than one minute)
- **Simultaneous**
    - Interpreting while someone is still speaking, with a slight delay
    - Whisper interpreting or *chuchotage*: simultaneous interpreting in a low voice for one or two persons or a small group
- **Sight translation,** a hybrid of translation and interpreting
- **Summarization,** *a technique of last resort*

Public speaking techniques

All modes, even summarization, require effective public-speaking skills: being able to speak with confidence and clarity while reflecting the speaker's tone, spirit and intent. Aspects of effective speaking include:

- Pronunciation that is clear and easy to understand.
- Strong vocal production (use your full lung capacity to make your voice richer and stronger).
- Good breathing techniques to enhance your voice quality and delivery.

Breathe deeply and rhythmically from the abdomen, not the chest. This breathing technique has a calming and therapeutic effect because deeper breathing releases tension and promotes relaxation. Developing good breathing habits will help you protect your vocal cords as well, and it can promote rapid thinking.

Consecutive interpreting

Why use consecutive as your primary mode?

Consecutive interpreting, the most common mode of interpreting, involves understanding a message in the source language and reformulating and rendering it into the target language after the speaker has paused (speaker in this textbook also refers to signer). Community interpreters should work primarily in consecutive mode because it facilitates dynamic, direct communication in dialogue. Other advantages include:

- Most parties in community settings find consecutive less distracting than simultaneous interpreting.
- You can take notes, which will enhance your accuracy.
- The slower pace of consecutive allows you time to find precise equivalencies.
- You may have more time to assess whether or not to intervene.
- Consecutive interpreting is less exhausting than simultaneous, so you can perform it longer with more accuracy.
- Consecutive allows the participants more time to make decisions.

The chief disadvantage of consecutive over simultaneous interpreting is, of course, time: consecutive interpreting can take twice as long (or longer) compared to simultaneous.

It will however allow you easier opportunities to intervene to ask for clarification, repetition, or address any linguistic or cultural barriers that could potentially arise. You may be less likely to distract or confuse the speakers by speaking over them, and you give them time to process the interpreted utterances (and yourself time to assess your own accuracy).

Short vs. long consecutive

Transparency Is Important in *All* Modes

Regardless of the mode you interpret in, make sure to maintain transparency and let all parties know everything that you say if you intervene.

There are two main types of consecutive interpreting: short and long. No standard definition exists for either short or long consecutive. In general, short consecutive tends to be based on dialogue interpreting (question-and-answer) and conversation. Most community interpreting is bidirectional (going back and forth between both languages). Long consecutive is more common for public statements or discourse such as the opening remarks in a court trial; it is usually unidirectional (interpreting from only one source language into one target language).

There is no actual agreement on the cut-off between short and long consecutive, but here is a general idea of the difference:

- Short (interpreting approximately three to five brief statements or less than one minute of speech)
- Long (interpreting approximately six or more statements or more than one minute of speech)

Special remarks about long consecutive

In conferences and courtrooms, long consecutive is typically used when someone speaks in longer passages. The interpreter is expected to capture and deliver 3–5 minutes of speech. He or she might stand and interpret through a microphone, like a public speaker, in one direction, e.g., from Mandarin into French. The content shared is often abstract or technical and requires excellent note-taking skills. In courtrooms, however, when the defendant or witness is testifying or being questioned, long consecutive is usually bidirectional. The statements can be long, and the interpreter must capture them with precision. Long consecutive requires strong note-taking skills, and the delivery must closely match the tone and demeanor of the speaker. *Keep in mind that even in a medical appointment, one statement can easily exceed six sentences.*

Special remarks about short consecutive

In community settings, dialogue is the norm. Short dialogue consecutive tends to involve a back-and forth conversation with many short statements. The content is usually concrete. It can be technical, like a doctor explaining a disease or a psychologist reviewing the results of testing, but it is not abstract. The interpreter must interpret in and out of two languages. Registers vary widely. Delivery is conversational, not like a public speech. In dialogue interpreting, long, complex statements can come up at any time. Note-taking skills are essential for both long and short consecutive.

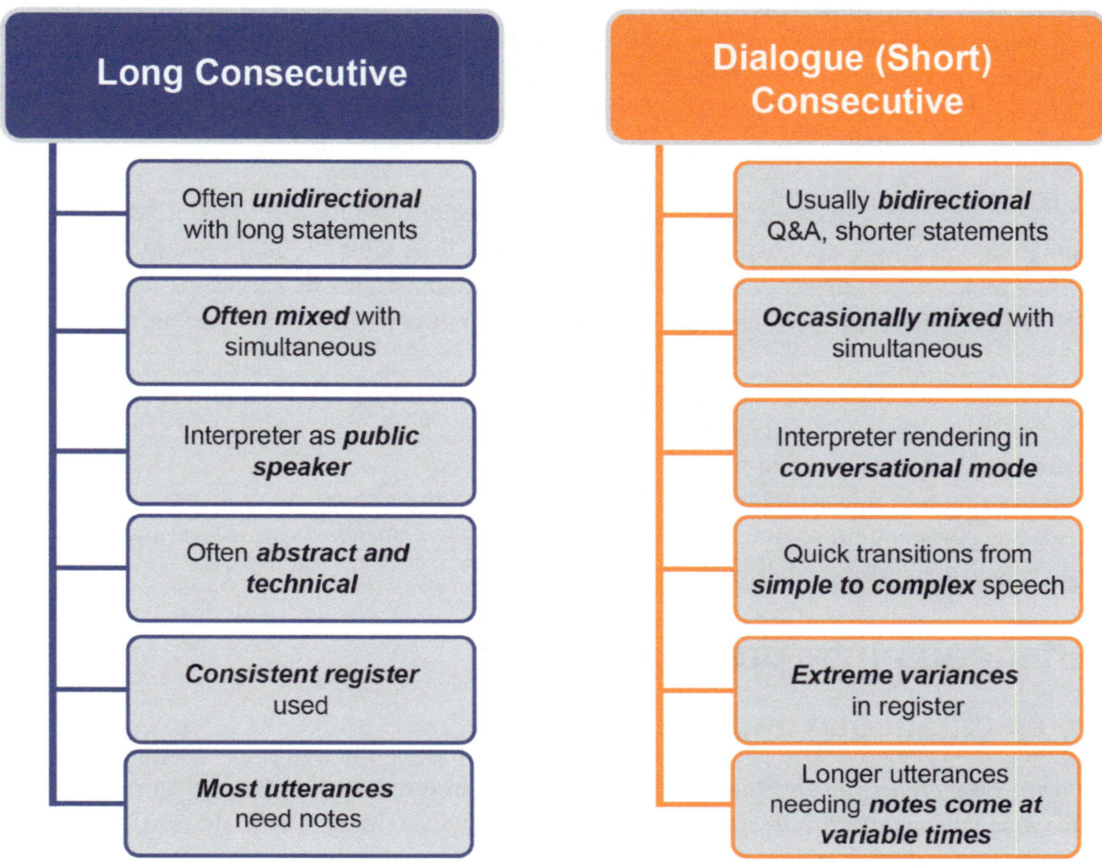

As a community interpreter, over time you will need to develop long consecutive skills, including note-taking, for the following reasons:

- Sometimes speakers get emotional and do not like (or refuse) to be interrupted.
- Providers often have detailed instructions or complex information to convey; they may lose the thread of their thoughts if you interrupt often.
- Interrupting can have other negative impacts: it could make a trauma survivor stop telling her story, offend, upset or intimidate a speaker or lead to someone forgetting to say something important.
- Speakers who are drunk or high on drugs, have dementia or mental illness or are very young may not be able or willing to pause and let you interpret.

How to perform consecutive interpreting

To perform effective consecutive interpreting:

- Listen and understand the message, including its nonverbal, contextual and sociocultural components.
- Remember the whole message.
- Take notes to support your memory as needed.
- Render the message in the target language, while maintaining the tone and emotional feeling of the source message.
- Manage the communication flow and turn taking.
- Identify and alert all parties about possible communication barriers.

In addition, you will need to learn how to:

- Manage your emotions (even basic feelings, such as fear, disgust, surprise, anger, sadness and happiness) so as not to show them while you interpret.
- Achieve a degree of self-awareness, self-regulation, social skills, empathy and motivation.
- Develop special skills when interpreting for vulnerable or traumatized individuals.

While all the above could be true for simultaneous interpreting, you will likely find the need to address those issues more intensively when you interpret consecutively. Here are a few additional points:

- More memory capacity can be needed in consecutive than in any other mode.
- Note-taking is usually necessary for effective and accurate consecutive interpreting. See Section 2.6.
- Turn-taking management (managing the flow) requires knowing when to interrupt the speakers and how to do so graciously and effectively.
- Sometimes you may need to switch to simultaneous mode.
- Monitoring for understanding requires attention, focus and awareness.
- Alerting parties about communication barriers will make demands on your tact, interpersonal skills, sensitivity and confidence.

Simultaneous interpreting

Where simultaneous mode is used

Simultaneous interpreting involves understanding a message in the source language, then rendering it into the target language with a *décalage* (a delay of a few seconds or up to a full statement), while the speaker/signer keeps talking/signing. It is the most common mode in conference interpreting and when a speaker gives a presentation to an audience.

Simultaneous can be used in all interpreting specializations. In community interpreting, it is the preferred mode for sessions that involve public speaking because it is more immediate, saves time and is less tiring for an audience.

Why simultaneous interpreting after 45 minutes requires a team of interpreters

Substantial research over the decades confirms that simultaneous interpreting makes such demands on the brain that the interpreter's accuracy degrades drastically after just 30 minutes (Moser-Mercer, Künzli, & Korac, 1998). You might not know it, but if you continue to interpret in simultaneous after 30 minutes, you will make many mistakes. After an hour, you could be performing like a drunk person and not even be aware of your mistakes! As a result, *all simultaneous interpreting assignments lasting longer than 45 minutes should be performed in teams of at least two interpreters trading roles about every 15 to 30 minutes* (so that one interpreter rests while the other interprets). An added advantage is that if one interpreter freezes due to forgetting a term, the other interpreter can often help.

However, community interpreters rarely work in teams, except perhaps for signed language. In conference interpreting there is a high level of awareness and usually the resources available to pay for a team of interpreters. In community interpreting, funding is scarce and people seem to believe that interpreting is easy. *Yet at a minimum, after two hours of even consecutive interpreting most interpreters need a break.*

If you are requested to perform a simultaneous interpreting assignment of longer than 45 minutes, you may need to formally request a "team interpreter." Otherwise, no one may assign you one. Be prepared to explain why you need another interpreter.

Where is simultaneous interpreting needed?

In community settings the need for simultaneous interpreting often arises for:

- Workshops or seminars (e.g., job training, refugee orientations, landlord-tenant information).
- Public government meetings.
- School-based services and events.
- Health education (e.g., birth classes, diabetes management seminars).
- Legal clinics (e.g., updates on immigration, disability laws or citizenship).
- Libraries (e.g., storytelling, orientations, public talks).
- Team meetings with multiple service users and providers in public forums.

How to perform in simultaneous mode

In order to perform simultaneous interpreting, you need to begin interpreting while the speaker is still speaking, with a very short delay or *décalage*. To process two languages simultaneously requires a high level of mastery of all registers, general and technical vocabulary, and a wide knowledge of regional variations. You will have no time to reflect: you will have to interpret on the spot. While this immediacy reduces pressure on your memory skills, it increases the demand for other cognitive skills. Developing these skills requires energy, specialized, intensive, long-term training and a great deal of practice.

Equipment for simultaneous interpreting

Technical requirements

When interpreters interpret for a large number of people, they might need to use technical equipment both to hear high-quality speech (or see signed language clearly) and to amplify the interpreter's voice or visually display signed-language interpreting. Such equipment could be placed in fixed or portable booths, but for most community interpreters (at least for spoken interpreting), the equipment will probably include headsets and a microphone and a transmitter.[29] Those who listen to the interpreting will typically be provided with an earpiece and a receiver whose volume they can adjust. Each receiver is set on a specific channel to which the interpreter's transmitter is also set. For events with multiple spoken languages, each interpreter will have a transmitter, and the receivers will be set to the channel for the appropriate interpreter.

Who pays for the equipment?

Portable simultaneous interpreting equipment has come down in cost in recent years. It is now affordable for many community services and even for interpreters. Such equipment might be found in schools, libraries and healthcare organizations. A number of companies provide it as a rental service.

[29] Many complex technologies exist to support effective communication among Deaf speakers and/or between Deaf and hearing speakers. These technologies are impossible to address in this brief section.

Should you buy simultaneous interpreting equipment?

Community interpreters do not usually need to buy and/or carry this equipment unless it is required for the assignment and agreed on ahead of time. In typical service settings, you tend to work in a limited space with one provider (or very few providers) and one service user (or very few users). One problem is a growing number of complaints that some interpreters bring this equipment and use it for simultaneous interpreting at appointments when consecutive is the preferred mode (perhaps mistakenly believing that it will make them look more professional). Such equipment can be disruptive.

Still, some freelance community interpreters may wish to purchase the equipment on their own or with a group of colleagues to be able to provide simultaneous interpreting. Often, service providers ask for simultaneous in whisper mode because their organizations have not invested in simultaneous equipment. They might appreciate a community interpreter having such equipment available for public events.

Verify that the equipment will be provided

You will need to notify the requester or language service ahead of time if simultaneous equipment is needed. Unless you provide it yourself, ask someone in the organization or the interpreting service to supply the equipment. Then make sure it arrives. You can't perform effective whisper interpreting for a large group.

Chuchotage (whispered simultaneous)

What is chuchotage?

Chuchotage is a French word that means "whispering." This term refers to simultaneous interpreting for a public speaker and a very small number of listeners by an interpreter who speaks in a low voice. It is also known as whisper interpreting, whispered simultaneous or *susurrada* in Spanish.

Chuchotage does not require the use of equipment or involve whispering. *Whispering for a long time can hurt or harm your vocal cords and make it impossible for you to interpret for a period of time.* Instead, place yourself near the small group and perform simultaneous interpreting in a low voice. Interpret *sotto voce* (Hall, Smith, & Wicaksono, 2011), which means speaking softly using normal speech, not whispering.

The difference, compared to regular simultaneous mode, is that you sit or stand close to an individual or a small group and use a low tone of voice instead of using technical equipment that allows listeners to be positioned far away from you. *Chuchotage* is not typically needed by signed language interpreters because they are signing when someone speaks, or speaking when someone signs. But it can be challenging for spoken language interpreters in community settings to hear the speaker over their own voice.

In community interpreting, whispered simultaneous is used most often for an organized community event with an audience, and in most countries the speaker rarely has interpreting equipment. Often, you may have trouble hearing the speaker. For this situation, firmly request that the speaker use a microphone or find a position for you and your listeners where you can hear as clearly as possible and quietly interpret.

The main challenges of chuchotage

The disadvantages of *chuchotage* are:

- It is effective only for a small number of individuals.
- It draws attention to those individuals and can make them feel separate or visible.
- Your interpreting can distract other participants.

Whispered simultaneous can also:

- Degrade interpreting quality.
- Bother some of the individuals you interpret for.
- Bother other people sitting or standing nearby.
- Affect or harm your voice.

Suggested guidelines for using chuchotage in community settings

Simultaneous interpreting, including *chuchotage*, is emerging as a common preference in community settings. That preference is often due to time constraints. Bear in mind that choosing the appropriate mode will support your main objective, which is to help ensure accurate, fluid communication.

Special concerns for chuchotage

Whispered simultaneous interpreting requires almost the same skills as regular simultaneous interpreting. The main difference is that you will have to lower the volume and avoid bothering your listeners and those nearby. Try to be as unobtrusive as possible.
For that purpose, please do not:

- Touch or sit/stand too close to the listeners.
- Wear strong perfume or cologne.
- Wear fashion paraphernalia (such as jewelry) that could produce annoying distracting sounds.
- Cough, sneeze, clear your voice or yawn near the listener's ear(s).

Do not whisper!

Because *chuchotage* means "whisper interpreting," many interpreters do whisper. As mentioned earlier, *if you whisper, you may strain or hurt your vocal cords, or even damage them.* Avoid whispering! Also, remember to sip water once in a while to care for your vocal cords when you perform *chuchotage* (often recommended for interpreting in general).

Sight translation

What is sight translation?

Sight translation (sometimes referred to as sight interpreting) means reading and understanding written content in the source language and rendering it into the target language. In short, sight translation involves orally translating a written text (or rendering it in signed language).

Community interpreters should be able at a minimum to sight translate *short* (1–2 pages) *and simple documents*. Sight translation is often used for documents like consent forms, eligibility assessments, intake forms, prescriptions, brochures about services, among others. You might also be asked to sight translate text messages or text on a computer screen or a portable electronic device, such as a tablet.

Which sight translations should you perform?

In some U.S. hospitals, medical interpreters are not permitted to perform sight translation. It is felt that the risk of patient errors and misunderstandings and the legal liability is too high. Unless you are a skilled, highly proficient professional interpreter, avoid sight translating long or complex documents. Even if you have the skills required, it is nearly always better to follow the guidelines below anyway, because so many service users cannot easily understand the complex, often legal language of official documents used in community services.

Using your best judgment, instead of sight translating the document you can *ask the service provider to explain it while you interpret the explanation*. Then the service user:

- Will understand the content and important points in the document more clearly.
- Be able to ask questions more easily.
- Perhaps feel less intimidated.
- Be more likely to become better informed and ready to make an appropriate decision, such as whether or not to sign the document.

There is no national or international rule about which documents a community interpreter should, or should not, sight translate. Try to assess (a) your skill level; and (b) the desired service outcome. To help you decide, the authors have developed the "CALL model."

The CALL model

Unless you are already a highly qualified interpreter working with a highly educated service user, use your best judgment and try to avoid sight translating documents that are:

C	=	Complex
A	=	Advanced
L	=	Legal
L	=	Long

In this context, these terms mean:

Complex: A text written in a high register, with long sentences, complicated syntax and/or abstract content that make the document difficult to render smoothly.

Advanced: A highly specialized or technical text with jargon and difficult terminology.

Legal: Any document that has to be signed, includes legal terminology or is clearly part of a legal process.

Long: Any document that exceeds one or two pages of text.

If you are asked to sight translate a document that meets one, or more, of the CALL criteria above, instead of accepting to sight translate it, consider asking the provider to explain the document and then interpret the explanation. There are many reasons for this recommendation. First, unless you have developed the appropriate skills, you could make serious mistakes. The service user might misunderstand or be misinformed and suffer consequences that could lead to liability for the service organization, the interpreting service that sent you, the provider and you.

Another important reason is that many of these documents should be *translated* (not sight translated) by the service institution to provide a good service. Finally, as mentioned, sight translating a long, high-register document might put the service outcome at risk if the service user does not understand your sight translation. An explanation by the provider is much easier to understand—and to interpret. Consider the CALL model, your skill levels and the outcome. Then make your decision. *When in doubt, do not sight translate.*

Sight Translation and Medical Interpreters

The stakes are high in medical interpreting. Sight translating a long, complex medical document that the patient then misunderstands is such a high-risk process that some U.S. hospitals forbid interpreters to sight translate.

In some cases, having the interpreter sight translate a text is a way of avoiding providing a quality service. For example, informed consent is not a consent form: it is a *process* whereby the health professional should explain, in lay language, the purpose, procedures, alternatives, risks and benefits involved in the healthcare intervention so that the patient can ask questions and make an informed decision. Sight translating a consent form is not an acceptable substitute for this process.

If you think you should not sight translate a document, ask the service provider to explain the document; then interpret the explanation in consecutive or whispered simultaneous mode.

The steps to perform sight translation

Each time you perform sight translation, be sure to follow these steps:

Before the sight translation

- Make sure that the provider remains present.
- Assess the text to see if you should sight translate it or not (using the CALL model).

During the sight translation

- Read the text from beginning to end.
- Identify any challenges, such as unfamiliar terms, complex syntax or high register.
- Ask for clarification as needed.
- Consult dictionaries, glossaries or electronic resources, if necessary.
- Render the text from beginning to end, keeping a natural reading flow.
- Do not stop-and-start, or start over.
- Do not simplify or change any parts of the text.

After the sight translation

- Self-assess the accuracy of your sight translation.
- Decide if you should continue to sight translate such texts.

Special techniques for sight translation

Marking a text

Parsing involves analyzing the words and phrases in a sentence in order to grasp its grammatical structure and meaning. For sight translation practice, read a whole sentence and parse it to mark any confusing words and difficult phrases *before* you start to sight translate it. You could do so by underlining the tricky phrases and writing a brief comment on top of them while learning and practicing. (When you work, you will likely not be able to mark up real documents.)

If you have a good memory, you could instead "mark" the sentence in your mind while doing the initial reading, and then remember the "mark" once you reach that point in the text. Otherwise, you may want to use tiny colored stickers (for example, miniature Post-it® notes). Marking a text this way might sound like a lot of work but it could help you to:

- Save time.
- Avoid pauses.
- Avoid fillers.
- Reduce mistakes.
- Prevent rereading and backtracking.
- Reduce self-corrections.
- Make your rendition more fluid, coherent and natural.

Remember to Remove Your Marks!

Once you have finished sight translating, make sure you remove all the "marks" (or sticky notes) without leaving any traces on the document before handing it back.

Special challenges for sight translation

Sight translation takes practice. Remember: you may have to scan the same sentence several times to come up with a rendition. Good delivery when you sight translate is perhaps even *more* important than for consecutive or simultaneous interpreting, or the listener(s) might not understand you. Because sight translation involves making a written text oral, and normally we do not speak using the same syntax as a text, sight translation can feel odd or uncomfortable at first, but you get used to it fairly quickly with practice.

Some challenges include the fact that most texts you sight translate have:

- Higher register than oral speech.
- More technical or advanced terminology.
- More complex sentence structures.
- Longer sentences.
- Often greater use of the passive voice (which is hard to interpret or sight translate).

Because you are used to interpreting spoken speech, you may not have a mental plan about how to translate formal sentence structures. You are likely to "trip over," stop and waste time thinking about a problem in sight translation. It can feel harder to find an equivalent meaning and move on. Long sentences can cause you to freeze, slow down or get confused. You may actually have to think consciously about grammar and sentence structures in ways that you almost never do for consecutive or simultaneous interpreting.

It is also very hard to sight translate into your weaker language(s). Sight translation requires a high level of literacy in both languages, but if you sight translate into your native or primary language, usually you are more at ease and fluid. In your weaker language, you may stumble and hesitate. This kind of delivery makes it harder for the listener(s) to understand you. Finally, you typically know fewer synonyms and alternative phrases in your second language than your primary or dominant language.

How to decline a sight translation request

Do you remember the three-step **SAY NO** model from Chapter 1? That model will serve you well if you decline to perform a sight translation.

Using the SAY NO model (Chapter 1) to decline a sight translation request:

- ***Be gracious*****:** e.g., "This is an important document, and I'm happy you have so much confidence in my ability to sight translate it."
- ***Offer choices*****:** e.g., "I think it would be much faster, safer and easier for the patient to understand if you explain the document while I interpret your explanation. Or perhaps you could summarize it or have it translated."
- ***Give reasons*****:** e.g.,
    - "This form is very long and has a lot of legal terminology. I'm not qualified to sight translate legal documents."
    - "I might make mistakes and miss important details. If the client misunderstands, you and the agency and I would be legally liable."
    - "I see a number of unfamiliar terms that I would need to look up."
    - "If you explain the form while I interpret, that will save a lot of time."

You don't have to give a lot of reasons: two or three may be enough.

Summarization

What is summarization?

Summarization involves listening/reading and understanding a message or document and then reformulating the essence of it in the target language. In community interpreting it is a last resort whenever consecutive, simultaneous or whispering are not appropriate for emergencies, crises or situations when speakers can't or won't pause.

Summarization has a nasty reputation. Many consider it the hallmark of an unqualified interpreter. Yet summarization in community interpreting is a critical skill.

When to perform summarization

From a functional perspective, summarization is, or acts like, a mode: a technique for delivering the interpreted message. In general, you should not perform summarization in legal interpreting. (See NAJIT, 2005). However, unlike consecutive or simultaneous, summarization should be used when situations spiral out of control and you cannot manage the flow. You are allowed to summarize only in extreme situations, such as:

- Emergencies (e.g., fires, hospital emergency departments, emergency dispatch calls, scenes of accidents, major police incidents).
- Crises (e.g., when several people start shouting or crying all at once, someone is too angry to pause or someone faints).
- Mental health (psychotic or out-of-control patients).
- Elderly (for those with dementia, or who are too confused to pause).
- Small children (who do not understand what interpreters do).
- Substance abuse (someone drunk or high who will not pause or speak coherently).
- Audio/video recordings (unless you are able to pause them).
- Public speakers who speak too quickly.

When to Summarize

Summarize in community settings **ONLY IF** the situation gets out of control and you have no other choice.

How to summarize

If a situation in consecutive interpreting veers out of control:

- Switch to simultaneous first.
- If simultaneous is not adequate, summarize.
- At the first opportunity, notify all parties that you had to summarize.

Summarization is a complex skill, as demanding as any interpreting mode. All the cognitive skills required for simultaneous interpreting are also required for summarization. You will need to maintain calm and exercise the following skills:

- The ability to withstand high-pressure situations and function at a high level.
- The competence to scan a situation and assess if, and for how long, to summarize.
- An aptitude for filtering out distracting noises, events and emergencies, while still assessing danger to focus on the linguistic messages.
- The ability to analyze the message and extract its meaning at top speed.
- The ability to prioritize segments or concepts that are important for listeners.
- Delivery skills that allow you to speak rapidly, yet clearly, without fillers and at a level volume, even in high-stakes situations.

Should you summarize or explain a document?

You should not ever summarize a document in almost all cases, except major emergencies. Unless you are a bilingual employee acting as interpreter and you have been trained and are qualified to perform the provider's job, you are not qualified to summarize a document. Summarizing involves deciding which parts of the document are relevant to the service user and which are not. That decision should be performed by a professional service provider. Never explain or summarize a document.

A few important points about summarization

Summarization can be performed either consecutively or simultaneously. You will need to make a judgment call about which to perform. How you maintain transparency when summarizing can play out differently between these two modes. In a dialogue setting, when you interpret consecutively you can be transparent with both parties that you are summarizing or just had to summarize. For simultaneous interpreting you can typically alert only the listeners, not the speaker.

Also, decide whether you are going to summarize in first or third person. Which approach is best? There is no official answer, but if you summarize in direct speech, you are more likely to maintain a direct, personal connection to the speaker. You focus more on the communication and can feel more like you are "in the skin" of the speaker. As a rough guideline, when you interpret for service delivery, try to summarize in direct speech and make clear you have just summarized. Indirect speech is more natural if you are summarizing a side conversation because, when you summarize in third person, you are removing yourself at least one degree from the direct communication process, reporting a conversation and not acting as a bridge; you may thus have a stronger tendency to "filter" the communication through your personal biases.

Mode switching

Mode switching and decision making

Even though consecutive interpreting is considered the primary mode in community interpreting, you may have to switch between modes often in a single session. It is important to know which mode to use and when to switch. For consecutive interpreting, either wait for speakers to pause or get them to pause by using a sign, gesture or speech cue. If the speaker still doesn't pause, you might have to shift to simultaneous.

If the service provider points to a computer screen and asks you to inform the service user what it says, you might have to switch to sight translation. But if the service user then interrupts your sight translation to ask the provider a question, suddenly you are back to consecutive interpreting. This decision-making process can be speedy and even stressful.

If you are interpreting consecutively when suddenly you have to switch to simultaneous, remember to render the last statement *before* diving into simultaneous. If you cannot perform well in simultaneous, make sure to have the speakers pause.

How to switch modes

Sometimes it is not always clear which mode to select. Settings vary. So do human needs. Consider the following criteria:

- Does the mode I plan to use facilitate direct communication?
- Will it help me be more accurate?
- Which mode will be easiest to understand?
- Do I have enough training to perform in simultaneous? Can I take notes? Am I strong or weak in sight translation?

Resort to simultaneous interpreting *whenever necessary*

Even when community interpreters work in consecutive mode, there are circumstances where switching to simultaneous can be necessary and helpful, for example:

- When asked to perform in simultaneous by the service provider.
- When people speak too quickly and won't pause for you to interpret.
- To interpret side conversations.
- To avoid interruption of an emotional outpouring that might feel insensitive to interrupt (e.g., a rape survivor recounting her assault).

In addition to being sensitive about when to switch modes, for simultaneous consider whether to perform at a normal volume or switch to *chuchotage*. For example, if a trauma survivor is speaking when you switch, you might prefer *chuchotage* so as not to distract him.

Examples of mode switching

When you decide which mode to use, consider these factors.

How many people are present?

For a dialogue between a service provider and one or two service providers, consecutive is the most common mode. For encounters with multiple service providers and/or family members, you may need to switch to whispered simultaneous (*chuchotage*) at times.

What is the purpose of the session?

Will there be a public presentation about landlord-tenant law or special education services? In that case, whispered simultaneous or simultaneous interpreting using portable equipment is ideal. Or is it a meeting with a small group to discuss subsidized housing with many questions and answers? Then consecutive is the better choice.

How are the working conditions?

Is there adequate sound? Can you hear the case manager at the head of the table? Can you sit near or next to the service provider? Will you be standing to one side? What are the time pressures? Does the session require simultaneous because there is not enough time for consecutive? Similarly, if you have been given a document to sight translate, is there time to sight translate the entire document before the appointment ends, or should you ask the provider to explain or summarize it?

Is this an emergency?

You might be at a crime scene or in a hospital emergency department. The scene could be chaotic, with multiple responders dealing with a recent robbery, a car crash due to drunk driving or a domestic violence incident. If time is of the essence, consecutive may not be an option. If you are trained in simultaneous interpreting, use that mode. If not, you might have to resort to summarizing. Focus on the content that is most important for the service user's safety, stabilization and well-being, especially after a crime or other trauma.

Examples of mode switching: parties present

Interpreting for children and adolescents

Children and adolescents might have never interacted with interpreters, or even doctors, police, social workers or school administrators. They may be confused when they listen to the provider in English and hear you interpret. If any kind of trauma is involved, they may have a harder time understanding what is being communicated. For these reasons, simultaneous and sight translation are not recommended when interpreting for children. Information should ideally be interpreted consecutively, and you should monitor for signs of misunderstanding or confusion. In addition, you may interpret in third person to avoid confusing very young children. For extremely sensitive interviews relating to child sexual or physical abuse, follow the protocols of the interviewer and remember *it is critical that you interpret the precise way that questions are asked and answered.*

Interpreting for the elderly

If an aging person has difficulty with abstract concepts, such as interpreting in first person or speaking to the provider instead of you, interpret in indirect speech. Similarly, older service users might have difficulty tracking two people speaking at once. Consecutive will be the mode of choice. If you are in a setting with multiple people and have to track their side conversations, you might choose to summarize rather than try to interpret the back-and-forth conversation simultaneously, which can be difficult for an aging listener to follow. You may also need to slow your delivery: any traumatized person may have difficulty tracking rapid information, and the aging even more so.

Interpreting for the disoriented and/or emotionally disturbed

Service users might be disoriented or emotionally disturbed. Perhaps the session starts calmly, but the service user becomes agitated or distraught. You might have to switch from consecutive to simultaneous or even summarization. If the service user speaks rapidly and/or incoherently, and you cannot manage turn taking, switch to simultaneous or summarization (as a last resort). Interpret as completely as possible what the service user says, whether or not it makes sense. It is the provider or official's job to handle disorientation or incoherence and make diagnostic or evaluation decisions. If you attempt to "correct" or make understandable what a service user says, you could cause a serious problem. Also, sight translation is not usually feasible for service users who are deeply upset or disturbed.

Interpreting in relay situations

The need for relay interpreting

Interpreters for languages of lesser diffusion, especially indigenous languages, are hard to find. Sometimes the only interpreter available may be bilingual in the indigenous language and a common societal language (e.g., Spanish in Latin America) but does not speak the service provider's language. In those cases, relay interpreting may be required where two interpreters are necessary: one relays the service user's words from the indigenous language into a shared primary language, like Spanish, while the second interpreter relays the message from that primary language into the service provider's language.

Relay interpreting is growing common for some signed languages. For example, American Sign Language (ASL) interpreters often work in relay with a Certified Deaf Interpreter who (unlike the ASL interpreter) was raised as a Deaf person and signs with a deeper cultural and linguistic knowledge of Deaf consumers. For Deaf persons who are less fluent in ASL, the Deaf interpreter interprets into standard ASL, while the ASL interpreter orally interprets those messages to the service provider. An ASL interpreter might also work in relay with an interpreter who is Deaf but knows ASL and an indigenous signed language.

Accuracy and simultaneous mode relay interpreting

For relay interpreting, preserving accuracy is critical. With consecutive, you risk degradation or distortion of the original message because it is being filtered through an additional person and another language. If simultaneous were attempted, three people would be speaking (or signing) at the same time, making it almost impossible for the parties to choose who to focus on. In addition, the chance of serious errors in accuracy and understanding are multiplied many times. It's also less likely that the indigenous language interpreter will have had access to formal interpreter training, and simultaneous is an advanced skill that is difficult to master without formal training.

Sight translation in relay interpreting

Avoid sight translation in relay interpreting. Speakers of less common and indigenous spoken and signed languages often come from cultures that are profoundly different. Their cultures and languages may not have equivalent terminology and concepts to explain how a country's legal, nonprofit or healthcare systems work. Discussing the content of a written document might be the best choice for relay interpreting.

Interpreting for the Deaf or hard of hearing

Signed language interpreting has its own special requirements regarding interpreting modes, which this chapter will not address. For many reasons, including the lack of oral distractions for Deaf consumers (service users), the default mode in sign language interpreting is simultaneous. However, there are many variations, including finger spelling, transliteration, contact signing, tactile interpreting, low vision interpreting, working with another interpreter who is a Certified Deaf Interpreter, trilingual interpreting between ASL, Spanish and English (an activity that it has become its own specialization) and of course, video relay interpreting. However, the discussion of modes for signed language interpreting falls outside the scope of this textbook.

The need to practice all three modes—and summarization

A number of professional interpreters strongly believe that interpreters should practice for one hour every day in all three modes:

CONSECUTIVE:	20 minutes
SIMULTANEOUS:	20 minutes
SIGHT TRANSLATION:	20 minutes

This recommendation shows how important each mode is in community and legal interpreting. It also illustrates the way few specialists pay attention to the importance of practicing summarization, since summarization is not considered a mode. Do not underestimate the importance of summarization. Practice it. Summarization can be *more* important than the other three modes when they are impossible to use. Imagine a situation of life and death with the police, in a hospital or at an accident. At such times, you will want to have the finest summarization skills possible. Find time to practice summarization.

Let's Practice

Learning Activity 2.5 (a): Practice in Consecutive Interpreting
Learning Activity 2.5 (b): "I Need Another Interpreter": Educating the Requester
Learning Activity 2.5 (c): Practice in Simultaneous Interpreting
Learning Activity 2.5 (d): Practice in Whisper Interpreting (Chuchotage)
Learning Activity 2.5 (e): Practice in Sight Translation
Learning Activity 2.5 (f): Practice in Summarization
Learning Activity 2.5 (g) Practice in Mode Switching
Learning Activity 2.5 (h): Practice in All Modes

In *The Community Interpreter®: An International Workbook of Activities and Role Plays*

REVIEW OF SECTION 2.5

In this section, you studied three modes of interpreting: consecutive, simultaneous and sight translation; understood the rationale, skills and requirements for summarization; and defined, described and practiced the ability to switch modes. Here are a few key points to keep in mind:

- There are three standard, accepted modes in community interpreting:
- When you interpret in community settings, you will use consecutive, simultaneous or sight translation modes—or summarization as a last resort.
- Community interpreters work primarily in consecutive mode because it is the most practical mode to support direct communication.
- Simultaneous interpreting is the preferred mode in sessions that involve public speaking, because it saves time and is less tiring for an audience.
- Summarization functions as a de facto mode and is a critical technique for emergencies and out-of-control situations.

Important information about modes

- It is essential to master all three modes and summarization.
- You need to master the two languages at a high level and engage in a great deal of study and practice to perform accurate simultaneous interpreting.
- Whisper interpreting, or *chuchotage,* is simultaneous interpreting that does not require the use of equipment and does not involve whispering.

Sight translation

- Community interpreters should be able to sight translate short (one to two pages) and simple documents.
- Use the CALL model to decide whether or not to sight translate a document: consider declining to sight translate documents that are complex, advanced, legal or long.
- To decline a request for sight translation, use the **SAY NO** model from Chapter 1.
- Use summarization as a last resort in emergencies and other crises, or cases when consecutive, simultaneous or *chuchotage* are not effective. You should not summarize a document.
- Because any encounter can change pace and direction, often without warning, be prepared and able to switch modes at any time.

2.6 Note Taking for Consecutive Interpreting

Overview

This section will introduce you to the last skill required to master consecutive interpreting: note-taking. It is a unifying skill and yet a basic skill (though it can seem challenging). It is also a "bedrock" skill: without it, you might never master consecutive interpreting.

The main goal of this section is to show you that note-taking is *exciting and rewarding,* because it will make you a more skilled and more professional interpreter. It is worth every minute of the effort you invest into learning it.

The authors of this textbook take the firm position that note-taking is a fundamental and indispensable skill for community interpreters. By studying and practicing note-taking, you will put yourself "ahead of the curve" for community interpreters. When service users and providers see how much more smoothly and accurately you interpret longer messages than your peers, *they will value you*—and want you back.

This section provides a general introduction to note-taking skills for consecutive interpreting for community interpreters. First, it describes the basic technique, so you will understand both its purpose and how the note-taking process is structured. Then you will explore strategies to acquire and practice the skills to take good notes while you interpret.

Learning Objective 2.6

After completing this section, you will be able to:

Objective 2.6 (a)

- Understand the rationale, skills and requirements for consecutive note taking.

Objective 2.6 (b)

- Practice three effective techniques for note taking: apply a simplified Rozan technique; develop symbol and abbreviation systems; and make skills automatic through repetitive practice materials.

What is consecutive note-taking?

Origins: how note-taking for interpreters began

A formal note-taking system for consecutive interpreting was adopted when Rozan (1956) published *Note-taking in Consecutive Interpreting*. This book outlined a seven-step method that is still used today by most conference (and many legal) interpreters.

Note-taking must be efficient and quick. Interpreters need to capture core ideas with the fewest pen strokes possible. Rozan's method relies on developing a system of symbols and abbreviations that minimizes how much writing is required. It uses the physical space on paper to maximum effect: this method helps you to capture meaning *visually*. That "map" functions as a trigger to meaning stored in short-term memory.

The note-taking method taught in this textbook is a simplified version of the full Rozan technique. It is a method more appropriate to the dialogic and story-telling nature of most community interpreting.

The Importance of consecutive note-taking in community interpreting

"Just do it": Note-taking as a necessary skill

Note-taking for consecutive interpreting is not a throw-away skill. It is not an "add on," an option or a choice. It is a *necessity*. It is a key skill for mastering the technical requirements of consecutive interpreting, because you cannot be as accurate without it. To perform at a professional level, you will need to master basic note-taking skills. In addition, *note-taking helps you to promote direct communication* with much more skill.

Note-taking as a unifying skill for consecutive interpreting

To perform consecutive interpreting, first master four key skills:

- Listen actively; focusing on the speaker's intended meaning.
- Analyze the meaning.
- Convert that meaning into the target language.
- Deliver smoothly the entire original message in the target language.

Each of these tasks can be learned in a targeted way. Note-taking is no different. It is a skill. Note-taking may be part of a larger set of skills for mastering consecutive interpreting, but unlike other component skills, it also represents a *unifying* skill. In other words, note-taking helps you to *reinforce and integrate all the other component skills of consecutive interpreting*.

How Note-taking Reinforces Skills for Consecutive Interpreting

Note-taking reinforces the key component skills of consecutive interpreting in these ways:

Active listening

Active listening requires you to focus on the speaker's intentions, both within and beyond the message. For example, if a speaker says, "Oh, right…", his body language, facial expressions, the social norms and contextual information could give you one impression. But a certain tone of voice could change the meaning to its opposite—like a sarcastic tone. When we first start listening as interpreters, it is easy for our minds to wander and miss important content or lose track of what is said and meant. *Note-taking forces you to stay focused because you are channeling that message onto the page, in writing.*

Analyzing the meaning

Analyzing the meaning has to be done almost instantaneously as you listen. Learning how to separate the individual words from the broader meaning is one of the hardest tasks in interpreting. Often, as interpreters, we focus too much on words (and may panic if we don't understand them well). Note-taking helps us to analyze *meaning,* because in order to take notes you *must first have analyzed the meaning*. Already, the moment your pen touches paper, your mind has come up with meaning.

If you take notes by focusing on words, you probably won't be able to successfully interpret the message from your notes, because words alone never entirely capture what is meant. When you focus on and analyze meaning, however, *note-taking reinforces meaning extraction* because you learn how to represent the meaning both in symbols and in the visual layout of those symbols on the page. Your mind strips the words away; you reinforce the word-free meaning by writing down symbols that attach to that meaning. In essence, note-taking *allows you to process for meaning twice,* at high speed.

Converting meaning

Once you *understand* the message, you can transfer the meaning into the target language and find the right string of words and phrases to accurately convey what was said in the source language. Note-taking again reinforces this stage because *the very fact of extracting meaning and writing it in symbols frees your mind to find new words in the target language to express that meaning*. Symbols tend to be "language neutral." In other words, they can be understood the same way (at least in your mind) in either of your working languages. They show you the meaning of the source message *but with the original words filtered out*. (This is why many excellent note takers use almost no words in their notes.)

In short, the act of writing the meaning in language-neutral symbols takes you straight to the step where you can more easily convert that meaning into the target language.

Delivering the message

Note-taking supports delivery in two key ways. First, while you are listening and taking notes, the act of putting the extracted meaning onto the page frees up your short-term memory. Because you have written this information down, you can temporarily leave it out of your short-term memory, knowing you'll recapture that meaning when you look at your notes. Second, when you start your delivery, your notes act as a bullet-point outline, allowing you to go back and repeat everything said in the correct order without omissions. Much less effort is required during delivery because you aren't trying to hold on to everything you heard in your mind. It is on the page.

Make it automatic!

Note-taking, at first, seems hard, awkward and slow. But then it becomes smooth. It is just a learning process. Our interpreting might often deteriorate when we *first* take notes, before the skill has become automatic. With practice, that discomfort and distraction fade away. At some point, note-taking starts to become a habit. We realize how much it supports our consecutive interpreting and makes us better interpreters.

> *According to Gile's effort model for consecutive interpretation, the most dangerous component that might threat[en] the balance of mental energy distribution is note-taking. (Zhang, 2012)*

Note-taking supports direct communication between the speakers

Note-taking improves our ability to listen longer, understand more and interpret the message more efficiently and smoothly. It also helps the parties to communicate directly with each other in the following ways:

- *Complete thought.* You can let the speaker speak longer.
- *Fewer interruptions.* You have to interrupt to ask someone to pause.
- *Easier to understand.* You are interpreting ideas that are more complete.
- *Less tiring.* It gives your short-term memory a rest![30]
- *Better accuracy.*
- *Less frustration.* The parties can grow irritated when interpreters interrupt too often.

Challenging the myth that dialogue consecutive is easier than long consecutive

There is a general myth or idea that community or dialogue interpreting is easier than performing long consecutive. Many assume that "dialogue interpreting" involves short statements and simple content. Nothing could be further from the truth. Dialogue consecutive is often more complex because it is *unpredictable* and *bidirectional.* Dialogue interpreting can be short or long. In community settings, you routinely need to switch from simple statements, such as direct questions, to longer statements that are more complex.

When they come, be ready to capture them. By taking notes, you can allow the speaker to communicate the full set of ideas.

[30] If you ask skilled professional interpreters why almost all of them prefer simultaneous over consecutive interpreting, they tend to say, "Because it's easier." They find that consecutive interpreting taxes their memory. The effort to remember what was said is hard work for the brain.

The Rozan method

Now that you understand *why* note-taking for consecutive interpreting is important, let's examine the *what* and the *how: what* note-taking is—the method—and *how* to take notes.

Rozan's note-taking method

Consecutive interpreting note-taking, based on Rozan's basic technique, is a language-neutral, symbols-based, visual and spatial method to capture meaning using the minimum number of pen strokes possible. Rozan laid out seven core elements for note-taking during consecutive interpreting:

1. Noting the idea, rather than the words
2. The rules of abbreviation
3. Links
4. Negation
5. Emphasis
6. Verticality
7. Shift (using the space on the page to represent meaning)

Let's take a closer look at each step. Keep in mind, however, that the technique recommended for community interpreters is a *simplified adaptation* of Rozan's method, not the full-blown technique.

Note the idea, not the words

This first element of note-taking is both the hardest and most important. You listen to what is being said and work to chunk, or identify, the basic meaning units. For each unit, the goal is to find a single word (or two) or a picture or symbol that represents that unit of meaning. Sometimes it can be as simple as drawing a stick figure to represent a person or using a well-known symbol for concepts such as more (>), happiness (☺), or a car, plane or train. At other times, the core idea expresses something more abstract, such as "fighting for his rights for services" or "too much force." Learning how to transfer more complicated meaning units into a brief note is at the heart of this method.

Learn the rules of abbreviation

Learning how to use abbreviations effectively takes practice. In general, try to delete the vowels (depending on the language), then keep the beginning and end of a word. This approach works better than just using the first three letters of a word. Many words share common prefixes and roots. If you put down "com" for "community," when you interpret from your notes, you may not remember if it meant "community." "communication" or "comment." "Cmty" is a better way to capture "community" than "comm."

Create links

"Links" are symbols (such as arrows and lines) or abbreviations that show relationships (like cause and effect, before and after, or a condition and its consequence). Links are critical if you are note-taking for long consecutive, in conference settings or a courtroom.

Unfortunately, links can also be one of the hardest elements of communication to capture When a complicated cause and effect is expressed in multiple clauses or abstract ideas, the use of links can lead to capturing what was said—or missing it.

In community interpreting, conversations often develop in a question-and-answer format that lead to concrete answers for the purpose of sharing information. The speakers' primary goal is to understand each other. Service users typically are telling some kind of story that is more or less linear (how someone got injured or why a person needs food assistance). Service provider answers often address a "story" too, or a process: for example, how to become eligible for a service or what is needed for treatment. Stories usually have a beginning, middle and end. They tend to be linear. Links are needed less when people tell stories, because you can jot down the story points in order.

Express negation

Learning how to show negation (like "He refused to eat") in your notes is *very important*. There is an easy way to do so. Note the information being negated; then draw a line through it to indicate its opposite. For example, "He refused to eat" could be expressed as "~~eat~~."

Show emphasis

Like negation, emphasis is easy to capture. Assign a symbol that expresses emphasis. Many interpreters use double exclamation points—"!!" for emphasis or multiple lines underneath a word to show "many." For example, "interpreter" can mean *two interpreters*. The word "interpreter" with three or four lines underneath can mean "many interpreters."

Write vertically

As you will see in the examples below, your notes should go vertically down the page, not across the page the way most of us write text (whether right to left or left to right—but of course, a number of languages can be written vertically). Vertical text is much easier to scan and absorb with your eyes. Horizontal notes make it difficult to see where one note stops and the other starts. In addition, it is easier to use the entire note page vertically rather than across the page. Leaving more "white space" makes the notes easier to read and interpret from.

Shift

Like verticality, "shift" is another way to use the space on the page to show meaning. You use the blank page to create visual mind maps of what was said. Conference interpreters are trained to capture the subject (S), verb (V) and object (O) by writing diagonally from left to right at a downward slant. In many community settings, you can take that same idea but capture multiple sentences or meaning units. For example, "this morning the two children walked to school instead of taking their bikes the way they usually did" could be expressed as:

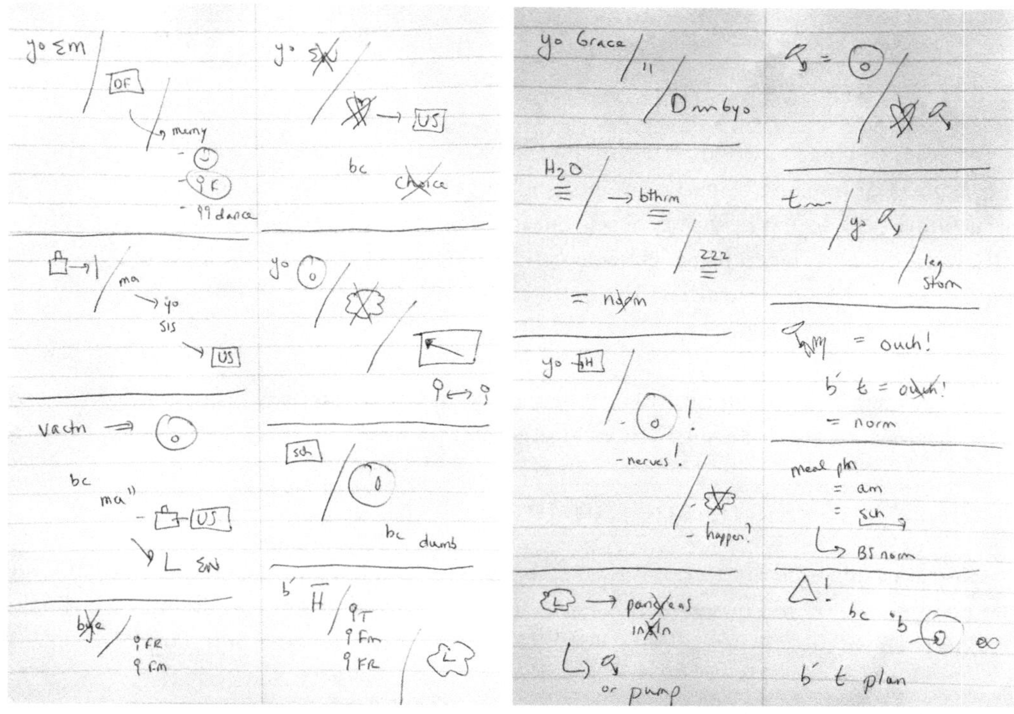

Often it is unnecessary to capture every element, such as "walk" and "usually" in writing. You have just heard what the speaker said. When you go back to read your notes, you will *remember* the context and fill in what you did not write down.

The graphics below are examples of real notes taken by interpreters working in consecutive mode.

Adapting Rozan

The challenge

> *Note-taking is a notoriously difficult skill to master for any interpreter and almost impossible to acquire in community interpreting settings. Yet it is a key unifying skill for attaining a high degree of proficiency in consecutive interpreting. It helps cement memory, analysis and rendering skills when properly learned. Furthermore, how and when to use it can change depending on the interpreting setting. Unfortunately, very few interpreter trainers in community settings have mastered the skill themselves and know how to teach it.* (Gile, 2009)

All over the world, interpreters are taught to capture meaning using a notepad and pen and Rozan's technique. This is one of key reason why learning note-taking has been hard for community interpreters. The good news is that this technique can be adapted to community settings as an effective tool. Here's why.

Everything is a story

Stories and structure

Most communication in community interpreting is a story. Stories make it easy to simplify note-taking because they have a linear structure, with a beginning, middle and end. This structure makes it easy to listen and understand a story. The human brain evolved over millennia to understand information communicated in story form. We intuitively follow the arc of storytelling. Our minds know the beginning will lead to a middle section and later to a closing statement.

Stories are concrete

Everything is a story in community interpreting, because community services focus on concrete situations. Someone needs food or housing. A patient is ill. A house is on fire. Someone's service dog is dying and the owner, who is blind, will need a new dog. Service users usually seek help from agencies that address their concerns. They tell their stories to providers who can help them get the benefits they need. Service providers tell stories too, about how a disease affects the body, the way the disciplinary hearing will unfold or what might happen the next day in court.

What is communicated in a community setting may be complex. It can be expressed in formal register or slang. Yet it still refers to concrete events with start and end points.

Storytelling chunks are shorter than a speech

Even long passages in dialogue interpreting tend to be shorter and less complex than a speech. Since two or more people are engaged in a give-and-take exchange, they tend to naturally manage the flow of communication to move the conversation forward. Otherwise it turns into a monologue.

Storytelling is easy to follow

The concrete, story-telling nature of communication requires fewer linkages and symbols that indicate cause and effect, time and location. You will still need to capture these elements but for shorter periods of speech they can be captured using simple lists, verticality and notepaper space.

Practicing note-taking

Key words, verticality and simple symbols

Practicing the steps

Find the right notepad

Now it's time to start practicing! (Note: practice these steps *outside* interpreting assignments, NOT while you are interpreting.) Start with a notepad and a pen that is easy to write with. Ideally the notepad should be the size of a stenographer's pad with a line running down the middle, separating the page into two equal sections.

Of course, many kinds of notepads are adequate, but when you first practice note-taking, try using a notepad or a piece of paper folded approximately 6 by 9 inches (15 by 23 centimeters). Many interpreters prefer a spiral notepad of this size with pages that are easy to flip. If there is no line down the middle, draw one yourself.

When you take notes, go down the page and don't let your writing extend past the middle line. When you get to the bottom, go to the top and start over on the right side of the page.

Listen first: Don't start taking notes right away

When you listen to the speaker, wait until you have understood at least the first idea before you write anything. Try to capture the main ideas, first in words and using abbreviations if symbols don't come naturally to you. (We will help you with symbols shortly.) Keep this in mind: just as simultaneous requires a lag time, or décalage, so does note-taking. You can't start interpreting if you don't understand the first idea. The same holds true for note-taking. Don't write down the first words you hear. Wait for the first *idea.*

Example: The speaker starts by saying, "I want to give everyone here a warm greeting. I'm incredibly honored to be here for your baby's birth." *Don't* start writing at the words "I want to." The speaker, in essence, is saying "Hello," which can be rendered with a simple "Hi" and a smiley face to capture the idea of warmth. You can wait until the end of the first sentence before making the first note, which will then capture a larger chunk of what the speaker said. When it's time to interpret it back, trust your memory: if you were actively listening, you'll remember how the speaker greeted the family.

Use outline forms to show relationships

As you take notes, try to use outline forms to indicate how things are connected or related. Here is an example.

> The doctor tells the patient, "I want you to change how you eat by cutting out salt, avoiding red meat, eating lots of fruits and vegetables and, most important, stopping all alcohol consumption. The alcohol is stressing your liver too much."

In this example, the foods to be avoided can be put in one list with "no" at the top or with lines drawn through the prohibited items. The approved foods can be in a list with a checkmark or smiley face next to them. An abbreviation for *alcohol*, or a bottle, can be noted with exclamation points next to it to indicate that this item was the most important one on the list.

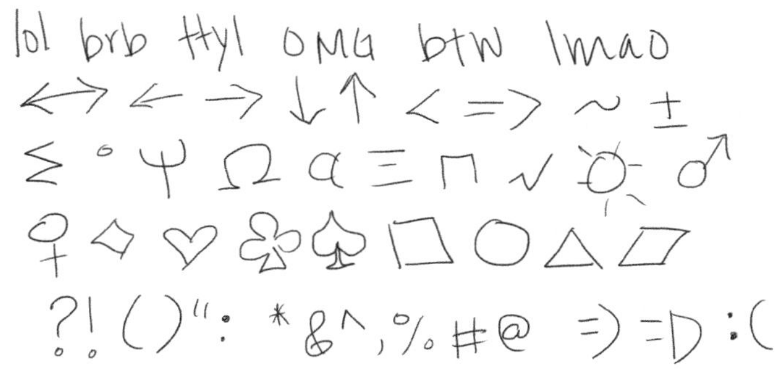

The word *liver* (or a symbol for it) can be paired with a sad face to show that the liver is not in good shape. You could also use an arrow pointing back to the word *alcohol* to indicate that drinking is the cause of harm.

Rely on symbols and abbreviations

As much as possible, practice using symbols and abbreviations instead of writing words (symbols are discussed below). Lines and arrows are symbols we all know. They can be used to indicate concepts such as moving forward, back, up, down, across or diagonally. Lines and arrows can show causation when the line is an arrow pointing between notes, and increase or decrease of any kind.

Don't write too much!

Keep it simple. Trust your memory. Perhaps the most common mistake you will make as a beginning note taker is writing too much. Don't worry: this is normal. Because your brain is struggling to add a new step, and using new tools—pen and paper—at the same time, you forget to trust your memory. Yet most of the time, with just a few key symbols, you will remember what you heard and accurately deliver it, especially if the content is familiar.

Make it automatic

How do you make a complex skill automatic? Practice. The only way to get good at note-taking is to practice it until it becomes second nature. Practice with anything, for example:

- A brief excerpt from a television show you recorded.
- Videos on the Internet.
- Podcasts.
- Radio shows.
- A friend telling a story.

Start with something spoken at moderate speed. Then practice taking notes to the same audio file several times. Don't go to a different recording yet, because each time you practice with the same recording, *you are progressively solving the note-taking challenges for the content of that recording.* By the fifth or sixth time you take notes for the same recording, you start to figure out which symbols, abbreviations and links work for *you.*

It can be very helpful to compare your symbols with other people's symbols to get ideas. But in the end, your own system will evolve into symbols that make sense to *you.*

Developing symbols

Symbols matters

When they start note-taking, many interpreters get concerned by symbols. They are often eager to get the perfect list of symbols and hope to memorize and use that list. That approach is unproductive. If you fixate on learning a hundred symbols right away, it can have a harmful impact on your learning. Symbols *are* important. First, however, you will need understand the role of symbols in note-taking and then learn techniques for developing your own symbols. Otherwise, symbols may do you more harm than good.

Fundamentally, they should represent the meaning you extracted from the message. The symbol sits on the page, ready to jog your memory when you interpret from your notes.

How to develop your own symbols

Borrowing from other sources

There are two primary ways to develop symbols. The first approach involves collecting as many examples as you can from a diversity of sources, including:

- Mathematic symbols, such signs for more than, less than, plus, minus, etc.
- Scientific symbols from chemistry, biology, and other sciences.
- Social media abbreviations for texting, Twitter, and other posts, OMG, BFF, LOL, BTW, TMI, B4, etc.
- Medical symbols, such as Rx for medications, sx for symptoms, prn for as needed..
- Symbols developed by other interpreters.

Build a glossary of symbols

Creating a symbol glossary is a useful way to capture symbols and their intended meaning. However, your glossary will not help you when you interpret unless you *practice writing* the symbols. For example, if you choose a triangle to represent "change" in your notes, practice writing that symbol over and over as you say "change" out loud in all your working languages. This is a simple, yet effective, way to attach the meaning of "change" to that symbol in your mind and in your muscle memory. By writing a symbol while you look at it and utter the word or concept it stands for, you are creating neural pathways in your brain that will make the symbol available to you when you need it.

Create symbols on the spot

Another way to create symbols is during the actual encounter. This approach may not make sense to you at first, but it is an effective technique—especially when mixed with other symbols you have identified and practiced ahead of time. For example, let's say you interpret for a mediation session between a couple who is divorcing. Before the session, you may not know the names of their family members, where they live, what the main issues are in their case, whether there has been violence, etc. But while you are interpreting, certain ideas, names, and issues will be repeated. You will naturally assign temporary symbols that work for this session, for example:

- A capital letter can be used to represent the first name of each of the main people involved.
- If the couple is fighting about where their children will spend the night, a simple box with a roof image for a house with a "Z"[31] inside might indicate "house where the kids will sleep."

Adding to your symbols glossary

If an idea for a symbol comes to you while you interpret, you can use it for the rest of the session. When you are done, scan your notes. If you have come up with any particularly good solutions, add them to your existing glossary of symbols.

[31] Zzzzz is a symbol often used in American comics to indicate that someone is asleep.

Creating root symbols

What are root symbols?

Our brains can only hold so many elements at a time. The most effective note-taking systems include "root symbols" that capture the most frequently repeated ideas that you interpret. You can also use them to capture similar meanings. A root symbol is a symbol that represents a broad idea that is often expressed in many different ways.

If you work in a medical setting, for example, you will naturally develop symbols to address symptoms, illnesses, treatment options and other healthcare related processes. If you work in a school setting, you will do the same with acronyms and symbols for that setting.

One way to keep the number of symbols you use to a minimum, making them easier to remember, is to create root symbols.

Examples of root symbols

For example, take the concept of time. Most of us (depending on our culture) tend to talk about time in the past, present, and future in terms of days, weeks, months, years, decades and centuries. Or we may speak about seconds, minutes and hours. If you were to choose the lower case to represent "t," you can add numbers and arrows to that "t" to represent the kind of time referred to.

Thus , a "t" with a dot to the left could mean "yesterday," a dot on top could mean "today" and to the right means "the future." The same process could be applied to "yr" to indicate "last year," "this year" and "next year." An arrow pointing to the left with a "2" at the end of the arrow could mean "2 years ago," and a "t" with an arrow pointing to the right ending in a "2" could mean "in two years," and so forth.

•t	ṫ	t•
yesterday	today	future
•yr	ẏr	yr•
last year	this year	next year
⬅2	t➡2	
2 years ago	in 2 years	

The value of root symbols

Root symbols, such as these, can help train your mind to quickly extract meaning and convert it into a language-neutral form captured by the symbol. It improves your mental flexibility. Practice often enough and you'll find your mind inventing symbols when people are talking—even when you are not interpreting!

Turning abbreviations into symbols

Symbols vs. abbreviations

Some of us are more naturally comfortable with symbols and drawing simple pictures than others. You may feel sure you cannot think in symbols and that your note-taking has to be in words. Don't worry. Many interpreters develop effective note-taking skills that are primarily letter-, abbreviation- and word-based. Remember to keep the consonants and drop the vowels to reduce the number of pen strokes.

Abbreviations as symbols

If you struggle with abstract symbols, you can still convert letter and abbreviations or acronyms into a form where they function more as symbols that capture broader concepts than a single word. For example, let's say you have assigned the word "work" to a capital "W." From now on, any time someone says or signs "work," you can just jot down a single letter that represents an entire concept in a few pen strokes.

Next, take your base "W" to capture tense. You can use the same dot system described above to indicate "past employment," "current employment" and "future employment." By adding a small "ing," "s" or "ed" to the top right corner, you can capture the tense used by the speaker. Finally, you can put a stick figure before the "W" to indicate "worker." If you underline that several times you can indicate "many workers."

You can apply a similar process to various kinds of words that represent root words for many related ideas, such as "govern." If you assign "G" to govern, then you can capture the verb "governing," as well as the nouns and adjectives related to "government," such as "government worker," "government policies," "government," "governor" and so forth.

Brainstorming ahead of time

Another technique that can help both your listening and comprehension, as well your note-taking, is to brainstorm about what kinds of words and ideas will come up during the assignment. This is the same technique as "anticipation" covered earlier in this chapter. Then you can consider what symbols might be helpful.

For example, if you are headed to a town council community workshop on a proposed downtown redevelopment project, you prepare for the session by looking up relevant terminology. Take that process a step further. Work out symbols time that you think will be needed. Next, brainstorm the different kinds of content that might come up at the meeting. Will the participants want to talk about parking, the impact of more noise or the need for affordable housing? Practice using symbols that will help you handle those topics.

A simple square box with a capital A inside could mean "affordable housing." Parking could be represented by a capital P with wheels on the bottom. Downtown could be a square or circle with a D inside, and so on. Even doing this type of exercise right before the session can link a symbol to the concept, so that when the idea is addressed at the meeting, you are one step ahead: you have a symbol for it.

Putting it all together

Focused practice

You have been introduced to a simplified Rozan's seven-step method for capturing meaning-based notes (not word-for-word notes). You now have a sense of how this type of note-taking can support your consecutive interpreting and make it more accurate, complete and smooth and let you interpret longer messages without interrupting. You've been given step-by-step techniques for how to take notes and looked at strategies for developing symbols and abbreviations.

Now it's time to pull all these elements together and practice them. Whether note-taking is a brand-new skill or something you have already tried to master, the best way to help make the skill automatic is by practicing with materials that cover similar topics or themes—and even the same materials. Yes, the same recordings. Interpreters often seem to resist using the same recordings for practice more than once. Perhaps you think that if you've already heard it before and taken notes, then it's not real practice to do again. It feels like cheating.

The truth is just the opposite. We often hear that "context" is everything for interpreters. The more context we have, the better we can deduce the intended meaning of a message. Interpreting familiar speech means we have probably mastered the terminology we need to know, which helps us to make our interpreting smoother and faster. Through focused practice with the same materials, we will be able to more fully absorb and understand the message so we can convert the meaning at the highest levels of accuracy. When we accept assignments that are familiar, any repeated content makes it easier to interpret. The more it repeats, the more accurate, complete and precise our interpreting becomes.

Practice in context

Work with similar topics

We need to create the "context" in note-taking practice too. One way to do that is to find audio files on similar topics. For example, if you need to get better at note-taking for developmental disabilities, search online video sites, such as YouTube, podcasts and other sites that host free content and find people speaking about that topic. Now practice taking notes on each file multiple times. As you come up with solutions, review them and try to apply them to the next recording with similar elements.

Target one skill at a time

While you practice, target each one of Rozan's steps individually. During one practice, focus on how you are taking notes vertically. Are you still going straight across the page horizontally? Then practice a few times with "verticality" as your primary focus. Don't worry about missed content for the moment. Force yourself to write your notes more diagonally down the page until that one element of Rozan's method becomes easier and more automatic for you.

Identify your weaknesses and work to build strengths

If you are having a hard time integrating symbols into your words, practice several times inserting simple symbols, such as arrows, circles and math symbols where you can. Next, review your notes each time you finish a note-taking exercise to figure out where the arrows would be most effective. If you are writing too much, practice with the same recording several times and force yourself to listen actively without writing so much. Trust your short-term memory to fill in the rest.

Put all seven techniques together with your consecutive skills

Finally, after practicing each of these seven techniques *separately*, put them all together and practice with an audio or video file where you attempt to balance all the core consecutive skills: active listening, meaning analysis, converting the message, delivery, and note-taking. Work on balancing these tasks until you find a natural rhythm to your interpreting.

It takes effort, but your time and focus will have big payoffs. Note-taking helps real people navigate already complicated situations with less hassle and effort.

We are firmly convinced that note-taking is, like a lot of things, a skill whereby the more effort you put into it, the more you will get out of it. We are also convinced that it is worth all the effort you can afford to give it.... To this day, we still get a thrill every time one of our students exclaims, "It really works. I never thought I'd say it but it really works." (Heimerl-Moggan & John, 2007, p. 7)

Let's Practice

Learning Activity 2.6 (a): Note-Taking Practice: Taking a Baseline
Learning Activity 2.6 (b): Note-Taking Practice: Basic Symbols
Learning Activity 2.6 (c): Note-Taking Practice: Repetition
Learning Activity 2.6 (d): Note-Taking Practice: Putting It All Together

In *The Community Interpreter®: An International Workbook of Activities and Role Plays*

REVIEW OF SECTION 2.6

Congratulations! After studying this section and practicing note-taking exercises, you now have a basic strategy for learning effective note-taking techniques for consecutive mode for community interpreting.

Here are the seven core elements of the Rozan method of note taking during consecutive mode that you learned to apply to community interpreting:

1. Noting the idea, rather than the words
2. The rules of abbreviation
3. Links
4. Negation
5. Emphasis
6. Verticality
7. Shift (using the space on the page to represent meaning)

You also learned why note taking matters, how to create your own symbols and why to focus on hearing the "story" when you perform note taking in community interpreting. You learned not to write too much down, to listen before you write and to avoid using words as much as possible and focus instead on using symbols. Finally, you were taught techniques for practicing each of the seven core elements of Rozan's method *separately* before putting them together.

By applying a simplified Rozan technique to targeted practice strategies, you have the opportunity to develop a skill that is much needed but hard to find. This skill could bring you more employment, because you will now be able to accept assignments that were previously too difficult. Those who note your advanced note-taking skills and smoothness of delivery may want to give you more assignments. Good luck!

CHAPTER 2 SUMMARY

Chapter 2 focused on the most important interpreting protocols and skills a community interpreter needs to master to perform at a high level of accuracy and professionalism. These are the protocols and skills needed to successfully transfer messages from a source language into a target language in community settings.

In Section 2.1, **Stages of the Encounter**, you looked at the "big picture" and noted the three different stages a typical community interpreting assignment can be subdivided into: the pre-encounter, the encounter and the post-encounter.

In Section 2.2, **Four Protocols for Community Interpreting**, you studied the main protocols that community interpreters should be familiar with: positioning, professional introduction, use of direct speech and turn-taking management.

In Section 2.3, **Memory Skills**, you studied the three memory processes of encoding, storage and retrieval and the three cognitive strategies to develop memory capacity: mnemonics, chunking and imagery.

In Section 2.4, **Message Transfer Skills**, you explored three critical cognitive processes: anticipating, multitasking and message analysis. You also examined two interpreting skills-building strategies: parroting (shadowing) and paraphrasing

In Section 2.5, **Modes, Summarization and Mode Switching**, you studied three modes of interpreting: consecutive, sight translation and simultaneous. You also examined the rationale, skills and requirements for summarization and explored mode switching.

In Section 2.6, **Note Taking for Community Interpreting**, you focused on the rationale, skills and requirements for consecutive note taking. You practiced three effective techniques for note taking: applying a simplified Rozan technique, developing symbol and abbreviation systems and making your note-taking skills automatic through repetition and targeted practice.

Now you have laid a solid foundation for your interpreting skills. The rest of this textbook will introduce you to some of the more complex aspects of community interpreting. Always come back to the basic skills in Chapter 2, however, for they are critical. When you master them, you will be a more accurate, professional interpreter.

In community interpreting, accuracy is not everything—but without it, you have nothing. If your goal is to become a *professional* community interpreter, be sure to revisit the protocols and message transfer skills explored in Chapter 2 until you master them. You will be very glad you did.

STRATEGIC MEDIATION

by Marjory A. Bancroft

CHAPTER 3

LEARNING OBJECTIVES

After completing this chapter and its corresponding exercises, the learner will be able to:

OBJECTIVE 3.1	**Unconscious Bias** Show awareness of bias while interpreting.
OBJECTIVE 3.2	**Deciding When to Intervene** Apply four decision-making criteria to assess whether or not to mediate based on potential consequences for end users.
OBJECTIVE 3.3	**Scripts for Mediation** Develop basic scripts for performing mediation in common situations in community interpreting.
OBJECTIVE 3.4	**The Strategic Mediation Model** Practice five steps to perform strategic mediation.
OBJECTIVE 3.5	**Cultural Competence and Strategic Mediation** Define cultural competence and demonstrate three strategies for performing strategic cultural mediation.
OBJECTIVE 3.6	**Culturally Responsive Mediation** Develop techniques to perform effective, culturally responsive mediation.

Community interpreting is supposed to facilitate access to community services (Zimányi, 2009, pp.19-20). Yet effective access may not be possible if you restrict your professional activities to interpreting alone. If a service user applies for food assistance and due to a cultural misunderstanding does not understand the follow-up steps, this individual's whole family might go hungry. If you as the interpreter note the misunderstanding and step in to alert the provider, who then addresses it, perhaps that family will get food.

This chapter offers you a model—the Strategic Mediation Model—that will help you understand what to do when you face a communication barrier. By the end of this chapter, you will have a better understanding of:

- Strategies to become aware of your own internal biases to help you make decisions.
- How to decide whether or not you should intervene.
- What to say and do if you intervene.
- Five steps to perform strategic mediation.
- Techniques for cultural mediation.

A special disclaimer for this chapter

As mentioned in the introduction, the authors of this textbook come from Canada, Cuba, Italy, Spain and the United States. We have a western education, and our perspectives are skewed "westward."

We have made every effort to consider the cultural beliefs, social contexts and intercultural complexity in all nations for this textbook and this chapter. Nonetheless, our world views reflect who we are as authors, as interpreters and as human beings.

3.1 Unconscious Bias

Overview

That decision about whether or not to intervene is important—yet it is influenced by processes in our mind that are not conscious. In this section, you explore how to examine your own thoughts to help you make effective decisions about whether or not to mediate. You will learn how you, the interpreter, can become aware of your unconscious feelings, beliefs and reactions, so that you can make more informed decisions about if, when and how to intervene.

Interpreting is your job. Intervening is a risky activity. Sometimes you will *have* to intervene, for example, when you are interpreting accurately and the parties still don't understand each other and the consequences of that misunderstanding are potentially grave. However, if you intervene when it is inappropriate or unwise to do so, you may cause more problems than you fix.

In general, as you will see in Chapter 5, the issue of whether and how community interpreters should address misunderstandings has led to heated debate around the world. This section recommends that you intervene only *if the probable consequences of not intervening exceed the risks of intervening.* In short, you evaluate the risks: "If I do not intervene, then X could happen—X is the probable consequence of not intervening. If I *do* intervene and say such-and-such, Y could happen—Y is the consequence of intervening in this way." Focusing on the probable risks and consequences of intervening helps you to make practical decisions on the spot about whether or not to do so.

The problem is that your motivations for making these assessments are usually largely unconscious. So your first step should ideally be to examine your own reasons for intervening. Whether a communication barrier is an ambiguous term, a racist remark or a cultural misunderstanding, the question is what (if anything) you should do about it. In this section and the next one, we will give you a few practical tools to help you make an informed decision about whether or not to intervene.

Learning Objective 3.1

After completing this section, you will be able to:

- Show awareness of bias while interpreting.

Cultural Barriers

A True Story by the Author of This Chapter

I was asked to interpret for a French refugee near Washington, DC. The social worker (an investigator) met me outside a red brick townhouse and informed me that she was looking into a school complaint about a teenage girl. The girl, who had developmental delays, had been showing up at school several days in a row wearing the same clothes. She often smelled as if she hadn't bathed.

I had been trained as a medical interpreter. I was told during the training that "culture brokering" was part of my job, and I should be the "cultural expert." As a white Canadian, I didn't feel I was a cultural expert on French-speaking African refugees—or even other Canadians.

But here I was. The social worker told me the interview was with the father. We knocked. The door opened. A tall, handsome man welcomed us. His house was bare yet impeccable, with shiny wood floors. The social worker sat in an armchair facing the father; I sat on a sofa between them, nervous.

When the investigator/social worker explained she was there to find out why the teenage daughter was coming to school in the same clothes day after day, with hygiene problems, the father shut down. His face grew blank. He remained polite but distant, answering almost in monosyllables. The social worker's eyebrows knitted. Her voice grew stern. I knew how such investigations worked in the United States: there might be serious consequences for the family. The stakes were high. My "gut feeling" (intuition) told me that there was a serious cultural barrier but I had no idea if I was right or what to do.

Finally I felt I had to act. To do something, in case the family was at risk. So I interrupted the session and told the father that, as the interpreter, I sensed a "possible cultural misunderstanding" and asked him if this was the case. He looked at me in astonishment. "Why, yes," he said. "There is."

"Is that something you would feel comfortable sharing with the social worker?" I asked.

His face lit up. "You mean—I can?" I assured him that he could and immediately interpreted what we had said for the social worker. The father then explained his situation. The girl's birth mother was in Africa. Her stepmother resented the girl and would have nothing to do with her, so the father had to care for his daughter by himself. But after she reached puberty, for cultural reasons he couldn't have anything to do with bathing or dressing his daughter. Because of her developmental delays, she couldn't do it herself. The social worker asked, "If we brought in a home health aide every morning to help your daughter bathe and dress, would that be acceptable?"

The father's face brightened into a smile. "You can do that?"

"Yes, let me explain." The problem was soon resolved. Yet I hadn't explained anything about the father's culture. I hadn't solved his problem. Instead, I gave him a voice and an opportunity to share his story. He and the social worker found the solution.

Special Note

How We Use the Terms ***Intervention*** and ***Strategic Mediation*** in This Textbook

In this chapter, we focus on two key terms used in many countries: *intervening (or intervention)* and *mediation.* Because the term *mediation* has many different meanings, as discussed in Chapter 5, this chapter will refer instead to a more targeted term: *strategic mediation.* (This usage may help to prevent confusion with other meanings of the broader term *mediation.*)

In this textbook, *intervention* refers to the act of intervening: i.e., interrupting the session. *Strategic mediation* refers to any act or utterance of the interpreter that goes beyond interpreting and is intended to remove a barrier to communication or facilitate a service user's access to the service. In other words, intervening means *interrupting* the session (for example, by leaning forward, raising your hand and saying, "Excuse me…") whereas strategic mediation refers to *what you say and do when you intervene.*

By using the term *strategic mediation* to refer to the mediation model taught in this textbook, the authors hope to avoid confusion with other types of mediation, including the work of professional cultural mediators, which are discussed in Chapter 5, Section 5.1.

The community interpreter's dilemma

Healthcare: prenatal appointment

Imagine that you are the interpreter for an appointment for a pregnant patient and that you are aware it is not usually culturally appropriate (in the patient's religion) for a male doctor to shake the patient's hand. You can also tell from the patient's dress that she appears to be religiously conservative.

Nurse: Your blood pressure looks great. The doctor will be here in just a minute to see how you're doing. And congratulations, I see you put on a bit of weight!
Patient: Yes, the vomiting stopped, thank God. It was terrible. I wondered if my baby hated me!
Nurse: No, no, it's perfectly normal to feel sick in the first trimester. In fact, some studies suggest that getting nauseated may mean your hormones are working well.
Patient: So my sickness might be a good sign?
Nurse: Exactly. Listen, I had a question before the doctor comes in. I was reviewing your chart, and it says here you're taking Coumadin. Is that correct?
Patient: I'm sorry. Yes, I forgot to tell you about it last time.
Nurse: Oh, dear. Well, the doctor will want to talk to you about that and get you off it. But why are you taking it? Do you have a bleeding disorder or a blood disease? I don't see anything in your chart.
Patient: I don't know why I'm taking it. My other doctor just gives it to me.
Doctor: (*comes in*) Well, hello Mrs. Mwabe, how are you?
Patient: Thanks be to God, I'm very well. How are you, doctor?
Doctor: Great, thanks. Just let me wash my hands before I shake yours. (*to nurse*) Nancy, is it culturally okay for me to shake her hand?
Nurse: Yes, yes. No problem.
Doctor: (*shaking hands*) Well, it's a pleasure to meet you, Mrs. Mwabe. Now let's see. (*The patient flinches, closes her eyes and looks away; the doctor looks down at the chart or tablet.*) This is your first prenatal visit with me. Last time you saw Dr. Higgins. So tell me, how many children do you have?
Patient: I had nine, doctor. But we are refugees. Two of my children were killed in the war.

Doctor: (*to nurse*) Nine? Can you believe it, that's my third patient in two days with so many kids. The other two have five and seven and. But nine! This lady's African, but my Hispanics? I swear to God they're pushing out babies like rabbits.

Questions

Would you, the interpreter:

- Tell the nurse and doctor that it might not be culturally or religiously appropriate for the doctor to shake hands with the patient?
- Tell the doctor that he has upset the patient by shaking hands with her?
- Interpret the doctor's last remarks? Omit them? Soften them?
- Remind the doctor that you are required to interpret everything (in other words, give the doctor a chance to rephrase his rude remarks)?
- Interpret the remarks and *then* intervene to remind the doctor that you must interpret everything?
- Do something else?

This situation is just one example of the decisions that face community interpreters every day. Take a moment to briefly note your answers (either in the textbook or somewhere else like a notebook or tablet where you can find your notes later). We will come back to this dialogue at the end of this section.

Internal bias

The impact of bias on communication

Bias is a personal attitude or perspective that is not impartial and tends to prefer one viewpoint or one social group to another.

Bias is often unconscious. Whether it is conscious or unconscious, bias may lead to prejudice and acts of discrimination against an individual or group.

Why issues of bias matter for interpreters

Before you can make good decisions about whether or not to intervene, you will need to become aware of your conscious and unconscious reasons for doing so. Otherwise, you may intervene when you shouldn't—or fail to intervene when you need to. You may also say or do something harmful instead of helpful.

It may help you to realize this decision really isn't about you, yet often your feelings motivate your decision—whether or not you realize it. Here is an example. The patient is speaking in a slow and confused way. You interpret exactly what the patient says, replicating the tone and style of speech. Then the doctor bursts out, "What's wrong with you, can't you interpret? Why don't you just tell me what she's saying?" In other words, the doctor thinks you're not interpreting well because *you* seem to be hesitating and speaking in confused language, when in fact you're accurately reflecting the patient's speech.

Your first instinct will be to answer the doctor instead of interpreting the remark. You will want to explain that you are acting as a professional interpreter and accurately reflecting the way the patient speaks. The reason for responding this way is because your professional identify has been attacked. Also, you might not really want the patient to know what the doctor said.

But really, your first job is to *interpret* the doctor's remarks, not to defend yourself. So what you should ideally do in this situation is interpret those remarks as said and see if the patient speaks up to explain that *she* is feeling confused. If not, you can intervene to state politely to both parties that you are interpreting exactly what is stated just as it is expressed—without defending yourself, getting emotional or engaging in a side conversation.

The risks of intervening

Intervening is a risky activity. Interrupting the session for any reason can take up valuable time, distract the speakers from what they meant to say, lead them to focus on you or cause other problems. For example, you could get caught up in a side conversation, give information that is incorrect or even offend someone.

So your first instinct should always be *to wait and see if interpreting by itself will allow the problem to sort itself out without your interrupting.* Then you, if you do intervene, you can be more certain that your reasons for doing so are about the needs of the *session*, not your personal feelings.

Decision making and bias

What is implicit bias?

One important aspect of this decision-making process about whether or not to intervene is our own implicit, or unconscious, biases. As interpreters, we are human beings. Decades of research show that all human beings have implicit bias—but just what is implicit bias?

Bias, on a simple level, is a personal attitude or perspective. It is neither fair nor impartial. It is a viewpoint that you take consciously or unconsciously. If you do not examine your possible unconscious biases, they can affect your decision making without your knowledge. Let's take a common example. No matter where you practice, service providers probably expect you to do non-interpreting tasks such as fill out forms for service users, explain procedures or paperwork or help service users understand and navigate the service system. ("Just go over this financial qualification form with him." "Tell him the paperwork that he needs to come back with." "Can you walk her down the hall to see the social worker?")

Many community interpreters do whatever the service provider asks—even if they know that perhaps they shouldn't and even if they were trained not to. Often the interpreter's reasons for complying are unconscious.

Your scope of practice

Unconscious bias and figures of authority

Think of it this way. You were probably raised to respect authority. Now, let's say a doctor, lawyer, teacher or social worker—any figure of authority (or even someone like a receptionist who represents figures of authority) asks you to do something, such as helping the service user fill out a form. During interpreter training, your instructor might have told you *not* to help services users fill out forms. Yet how easy do you find it to say, "No," to a figure of authority? Unconsciously, you may have a bias to respect and obey figures of authority, even if what they ask you to do is misguided, risky or inappropriate for a professional interpreter to do.

Implicit bias and register

One of the most common acts of community interpreters is to lower register. In other words, a service provider says something that you feel sure the service user didn't understand. So instead of interpreting the provider's message, you simplify it. After all, the service user needs to understand the provider, right? And isn't simplifying the message the best way to make that happen?

The answer is no. As you saw in Chapter 1, changing register is a violation of your ethical duty to be accurate. Simplifying or lowering register is also risky, because you are not the service provider. You could make a critical mistake with dangerous consequences. For example, the patient could overdose on the medication, the legal client could fail to understand the lawyer's intent and do something to destroy his case or the family could lose their food assistance, dental benefits or subsidized transportation card.

Also, the same provider is unaware that he or she is not communicating clearly. So you haven't even fixed the problem. *The service provider who speaks in a way that is incomprehensible to the service user probably needs to improve his or her communication skills.* Your real job in a case like this, as you will see later in this chapter, is to alert the service provider to the need to communicate more clearly.

How changing register reveals implicit bias

Changing register yourself as you interpret is also an example of your own unconscious, or implicit, bias. *You* assume the best thing to do is simplify the provider's message because *you* know better than the service provider and the people who wrote your code of ethics. *You* think you know what the service provider means and that you can safely decide how to rephrase important parts of the message. Yet your assumption may not only be wrong but dangerous.

Changing register to simplify a service provider's message is only one example of how community interpreters act on their implicit biases, but it is a very common one that reflects paternalism: a term used here to mean taking the attitude and responsibility of a parent with adults who need to make their own decisions. The idea that the interpreter knows best how to help the service user isn't only misguided. It deprives the service user of autonomy and could also mean that the interpreter is taking over the service provider's role—whether anyone realizes it or not.

Interpreter ethics and scope of practice

Many professional codes of ethics for community interpreters state, in one way or another, that you should not perform tasks that lie outside your professional scope or exceed your skill level. Some codes go further and require you to restrict your activities to interpreting (see, for example, HIN, 2007) while others might allow you to make limited interventions but set boundaries on what you do when you intervene (e.g., CIOL, 2007; NCIHC, 2004; and the *Ethics and Standards* document at the beginning of this textbook).

Even if you think you understand the code of ethics that you have chosen to follow, you will surely face challenges when you apply those ethics to real life. Every interpreter does. This chapter can help you to respect your ethics, but in a different way from Chapter 1. We will start by asking you to explore your own mind.

Scope of practice: The pragmatic reality

For example, after a prenatal interpreting assignment, if the pregnant patient begs you to give her a lift home because of snowy winter weather, and you are both refugees from the same war—how will you say "No" to her? *Why* should you say no? Are you a bad person if you refuse to take her home in your car? If your code of ethics or standards of practice clearly suggests that you should not give that patient a lift (for example, NCIHC, 2004), what will you do instead? Or should you make an exception in this case?

In fact, service users will often ask you for assistance during or outside the session ("Where can I get help with this huge bill?" "Should I trust this provider? "What did the doctor say about how the MRI works?") Do you want to help out? Why? Perhaps your parents and community raised you to be a "good person." Perhaps you have religious or cultural beliefs about the importance of helping others. Perhaps the elders in your community expect you to "give back" and help out recent arrivals. Perhaps you simply can't bear to see someone suffer, or it would feel incredibly rude or even cruel to deny this patient a lift.

The desire to help out

Why did you become a community interpreter in the first place? Many community interpreters say they want to "help out," "to make a difference" or "to give back to my community." You want to help too,—but then a code of ethics, or a trainer, or someone in a professional association tells you, in effect, "No, don't help—just *interpret*." Is that right? Should you "just interpret" and not help out service users?

To complicate your decision, the expectation to "help service users" or perform extra services for service users and providers may actually be written into your job description, especially if you are a bilingual employee. But the expectations may also be *un*written. You may be asked or *expected* to translate documents, accompany service users to their next appointment or sign documents as a witness. If you say that you shouldn't, the provider may tell you, "Well, my *last* interpreter filled out that form for the patient! Why won't you?" In other words, *you* may want to "help out," and *service users and providers may also want you to "help out."* Your code of ethics, interpreter training program or a professional association may say, "*Don't* help the service user—just interpret." With so much confusion: what's an interpreter to do?

Intervening Can Be Risky

Role conflicts, discussed in Chapter 5, lead to much confusion for the community interpreter about which types of interventions are risky, wrong or dangerous. Many interventions *are* dangerous, particularly in court, medical and mental health interpreting. That's why the first two sections of this chapter show you how to make the decision to say "Yes" or "No" to such requests or decide on your own the best course of action.

Examine your assumptions

"The interpreter knows best"

We are all human

All humans are biased. Interpreters are human. Therefore, interpreters are biased. We are biased *because* we are human. Unconscious human bias is nearly universal, yet we don't often examine our own bias. Usually, we just don't notice it is there. Because it is unconscious, implicit bias has an impact on all parts of our lives, and yet we don't see that impact (Dovidio & Fiske, 2012).

Both as interpreters and as human beings we are affected *in every decision we make by unconscious assumptions, bias and social filters* (Ambady, Shih, Kim, & Pittinsky, 2001; Contreras, Banaji, & Mitchell, 2011). Whenever you are expected to "help out" and solve problems during or after an encounter, the operative assumption is usually that you, as the interpreter, know better than all parties present what the communication problem is and how to fix it. This could be *your* conscious or your unconscious assumption. It could be the service user's assumption—the service provider's assumption—or the assumption of everyone else in the encounter and the service system.

Question the assumption that the interpreter knows best

This assumption that the interpreter knows best could be present even if a problem clearly lies outside your expertise, such as being able to tell if the service user is lying or telling the truth or trusts the service provider. (These are common questions that service users or providers ask interpreters.) You may also come to assume that you are the solver of the service user's problems because your beliefs over time can come to mirror and reflect those of the service users and providers. In other words, you, too, might feel that you know what is best for the service user, when in fact you do not know best.

The assumption that the interpreter is an expert decision maker on matters of service delivery and cultural misunderstandings must be questioned. Research does not support it. Interpreters are not psychologists, mind readers, cultural experts or conflict mediation specialists. They are simply human beings. As human beings, we filter our decisions through our unconscious assumptions (e.g., Dovidio & Gaertner, 2004).

So our first job, when we face a communication barrier involving a service user and provider, is learning *how to become conscious about our unconscious assumptions.*

How bias works

Ingroup vs. outgroup

In its simplest terms, we tend to see people in one of two ways: they appear to belong to our own social group (ingroup) or they do not (outgroup). If we consider other individuals as "ingroup," we tend to regard them in more positive ways, and see them as safer, than those we perceive as "outgroup" (Mahajan, Martinez, Gutierrez, Diesendruck, Banaji, & Santos, 2011).

In addition, from the time we are infants and small children, we tend to perceive people in terms of such groups, and those who raise us define these groups for us (consciously or unconsciously) based on various social categories, such as race, attractiveness, education and native language spoken. Ingroup vs. outgroup perceptions and the emotional sense of safety we tend to feel with ingroup members can also be found in other species, such as macaque monkeys (Mahajan et al., 2011).

How we perceive others

In short, we are biased *for* the people whom we perceive to be most similar to us, and biased *against* those we feel are different from us—but we are not usually conscious of this fact. There is no shame in being biased: however, as interpreters we have a professional responsibility and duty to develop awareness of our biases, wherever possible, so that we can see the impact of our subjectivity on our decision making. In this way, we can make wiser and more informed decisions when we interpret.

Example #1: The interpreter who explains

Let's look at two examples of situations that call for wise decision making where bias might be involved. First, patients often wait until the doctor is gone and then turn to the interpreter to ask follow-up questions about how to prepare for a test, procedure or surgery. Clearly, the doctor did not explain things in a way that the patient understood. As the interpreter, you may feel that *you* know a better and clearer way to explain it—one that the patient will actually understand. Yet that is a dangerous assumption. You are not a doctor. If you explain anything to the patient, you could make an error with potentially serious clinical consequences. For example, if the patient eats or drinks something at a certain time and this consumption interferes with surgery, the costs and consequences could be your fault. Resist the temptation to explain the test or surgery. Instead, you could find another healthcare provider to explain it, then interpret for that provider.

Example #2: Service providers who say awkward things

Here is another sadly common example. A service provider may ask you about the service user during the session, "Do you think she has some kind of mental problem?" First, service providers who ask these questions (yes, really: even during the session) are *consulting* you for an opinion—they never imagine that you will interpret the question! Yet you are ethically required to interpret everything. Well, in this case, that would be rather awkward! Second, service providers, in general, often assume that interpreters can see inside the service user's mind to know if a service user is honest, mentally competent, credible, to be trusted and so on. As we will see, that assumption is not correct. You are not a mind reader.

Furthermore, the field of community interpreting is actually quite divided about whether or not you should interpret such a question from a service provider (it is interesting that they tend to agree you should always interpret the questions and remarks of service *users*—perhaps because service providers need to know everything that service users say in order to provide an effective service). If you ask people—even researchers, interpreters, service providers and specialists—whether a service provider's well-meaning, but insensitive and offensive, remarks should be interpreted, you will get different answers such as, "Yes," "No," or "Maybe—it depends on the situation." There is no consensus.

Examining our unconscious motivations

In order to make wise decisions, then, we all need to look at our unconscious motivations as well as our conscious ones. Take the last example regarding the question about a mental problem. Your first instinct in real life (for most, but not for all, interpreters), will probably be *not* to interpret remarks like, "Does she have some kind of mental problem?" After all, you know this remark is so offensive that it doesn't reflect what the service provider would ever intentionally say to the service user (in your opinion). Also, the provider was speaking to *you*, not the patient. Yet this question reveals the provider's bias. If you were the patient—would you want to know what the provider really said about you? Probably. But you, as the interpreter, are probably too shocked even to think about what the service user wants to know. You are probably absorbed in your own embarrassment and your desire to protect a figure of authority—perhaps one whom you enjoy working with—from the consequences of her entirely inappropriate remark.

What Research in Psychology Shows Us About Bias

The idea that interpreters are less biased than other human beings has no support in the research literature. Here are a few examples of what the research literature has to say about unexamined bias:

- Unconscious bias begins in childhood and has a measureable impact on our performance. (Ambady et al., 2001)
- Prejudice is a part of typical, everyday life and activity. The assumption that bias, prejudice and discrimination are caused only by overt bigots blinds us to the reality that prejudice is part of the human condition. (Banaji, Bazerman, & Chugh, 2003)
- "The operation of prejudice and stereotyping in social judgment and behavior does not require personal animus, hostility or even awareness." (Hardin & Banaji, 2012, p. 13)
- Prejudice is very often implicit: it lies outside our awareness and control. As a result, it can go against our best intentions, even those of us who get upset about racism and bigotry. (Dovidio & Gaertner, 2004)

Unconscious bias in our own words

If you do not become aware of your unconscious feelings and motivations, they will tend to come out anyway—in your words and actions—especially in situations that might call for mediation. As human beings, we are simply unaware at times how our conscious or unconscious biases surface in our work.
Take the case of an interpreter who interrupts the session to mediate a linguistic barrier. Instead of being transparent (an ethical requirement), the interpreter who mediates often says one thing to the provider and something quite different to the service user.

An example of bias in the interpreter's own words

For example, the interpreter might tell the caseworker:

I'm sorry, that's too much jargon for the client. He comes from a small village, and I don't think he's literate. If you could use shorter words and simple language, that would help a lot.

But to the service user, he might say, *I just asked the provider to explain some terms she's using.*

Why doesn't the interpreter tell the service user everything that he told the provider? Imagine how that would sound: *I just told the caseworker that I'm sorry, but she's using too much jargon for you. I said you come from a small village, and I don't think you're literate. I asked if she could use shorter words and simple language because that would help a lot.*

The reason that a community interpreter may say one thing to a service provider and something quite different to a service user is that internal bias has revealed attitudes that the interpreter doesn't mind sharing with one party but unconsciously knows would offend, hurt or demean the other party.

Interpreter's Tip

Here is a simple rule for transparency: always say to one party *only what you would want the other party to know and understand.*

Balance of power

Who has the most power? Who has the least? Who is in the middle?

Service users and prejudice

Service users, whether they are immigrants, indigenous residents or Deaf, may be more vulnerable members of society than service providers. Research shows that beyond a doubt we tend to behave with more respect to those we see as more powerful and less respect to those we find less powerful. In one study built on decades of research on unconscious bias, Dovidio and Fiske (2012) reported that low-income black, undocumented (immigrant), Latino and low-income white individuals were seen as low in both warmth and competence, adding:

> *Groups perceived as low warmth, low competence elicit more contempt and disgust than do other groups. These are particularly dehumanizing emotions, and neuroimaging data on responses to other groups in this quadrant (homeless people and drug addicts) fit the pattern of disgusted, dehumanizing responses...*
>
> *In health care research, indicators of contemptuous prejudices could appear in inferior treatment, passive neglect, and even unnecessarily active-aggressive last-ditch treatments (e.g., limb amputations in patients with diabetes). Health-related policies have been proposed that exclude undocumented immigrants from receiving support for basic inoculations against prevalent childhood diseases.* (Dovidio & Fiske, 2012, p. 947)

The desire to "fix" the balance of power

The difficulty for interpreters is that often they may perceive this imbalance of power and want to fix it by helping out the service user. When they do so, interpreters may be unaware that actions of this kind reveal other forms of bias such as pity and paternalism. *These types of bias can also be harmful for service users.* Interpreters, like all of us, need to recognize and address what the research shows us. That is, in order to engage effectively in decision making in community services:

> *people have to be aware of the complex nature of bias, understand that various emotions (e.g., pity) and orientations (e.g., paternalism) are forms of bias, and recognize that they may have implicit biases that may be manifested subtly. Awareness of these elements is not sufficient, however; efforts simply to suppress bias can ironically activate stereotypical thoughts and interfere with effective communication across social boundaries.* (Dovidio & Fiske, 2012, p. 949)

The risk: doing more harm than good

In other words, intervening, even with very good intentions, could do more harm than good if the interpreter is being unconsciously paternalistic or filled with pity. For example, when an interpreter does not interpret everything he or she says while mediating for both parties and violates transparency, it could be a sign of paternalism or pity because the interpreter is, at least subliminally, aware that what was said to one party could offend the other. (In Section 3.3 of this chapter, you will develop basic phrases that you can safely say to *both* parties when you intervene without offending or insulting anyone.)

Service users and interpreters from the same country

Here is another common example of the interpreter's bias and also the service provider's. A service provider often thinks that if you come from the same country or region as the service user, then you understand the user's feelings, thoughts, beliefs and intentions. Perhaps you think so too. You respond to that opinion of the service provider. So when the provider compliments the parent's baby, you say, "Oh, please don't say nice things about the baby, that could bring on the evil eye, and she's going to think you cursed the baby!"

Now let's say you interpret your mediation. "I just told the social worker not to say nice things about your baby, because that could bring on the evil eye, and you're going to think she cursed the baby." But the mother, although a refugee in poor clothing, doesn't believe in the evil eye at all. Perhaps she was raised to believe the "evil eye" is superstitious nonsense. How will she feel after what you have just said?

Same country: many differences

Be careful. Do all New Zealanders think the same way? No. Do all South Africans make the same decisions? Certainly not. Do all Chinese have the same health practices? Of course not. There is complexity in all these cultures. You, the interpreter, cannot know for certain what another human being thinks or feels. To form cultural opinions about that individual and share your opinions with service users and providers is at best inaccurate (remember that accuracy is an ethical requirement that goes beyond message transfer) and may also be harmful to the service user, the encounter and the service outcome.

Instead, use your voice to help all parties communicate their questions, concerns and cultural perceptions with each other. Sections 3.3 to 3.6 of this chapter will show you how.

A Story About Discrimination

One Spanish-speaking bilingual employee, a receptionist at an information and referral center for immigrants who often interpreted for clients there, was fired for showing bias. She was Mexican. Complaints came in from clients that she was rude, condescending and unkind. To whom? To Mexicans.

Why was she biased against Mexicans? We do not know, but she was middle class and educated; the clients that she was rude to were often less educated than she was. The perception among some of her colleagues was that the receptionist was acting on her own class bias. That perception might be accurate—or also biased.

Each human is personally, socially and culturally unique. Just because someone comes from the same country as another person does not mean the two understand or even respect each other.

How to make effective decisions

Four steps to undermine bias

Here is a simple rule that we will repeat often in this chapter: "When in doubt—stay out." Simply interpret. Do not mediate—or at least, not yet. By waiting to see what happens and if the problem resolves itself, you can monitor the situation and then intervene later if you have to.

If you *do* intervene, think carefully about *why* you are intervening and whether you really know the best thing to do. How do you become aware of your own motivations? How can you decide if you are acting for the best or on the basis of unconscious bias? Here are four steps to help you prevent the negative impact of implicit (unconscious) bias on decision making about whether or not to intervene. The steps are:

Step 1: Explore your own bias.
Step 2: Plan ahead.
Step 3: Monitor the situation. ("When in doubt—stay out.")
Step 4: Assess potential consequences.

Let's go over each of these steps and examine what they involve.

Step 1. Explore your own bias.

Our mind plays tricks

Look at these two images and compare the two tables. Which table looks longer to you? Which one looks wider? (Shepard, 1990)

Now take a ruler and measure them. If you were wrong, do not be sad: almost everyone who examines this image is wrong. But there is no difference in length between the images of these two tables. What does it mean that the two table pictures seem to have different lengths and widths? It simply means that our perceptions can be tricked. What we think is true is often incorrect.

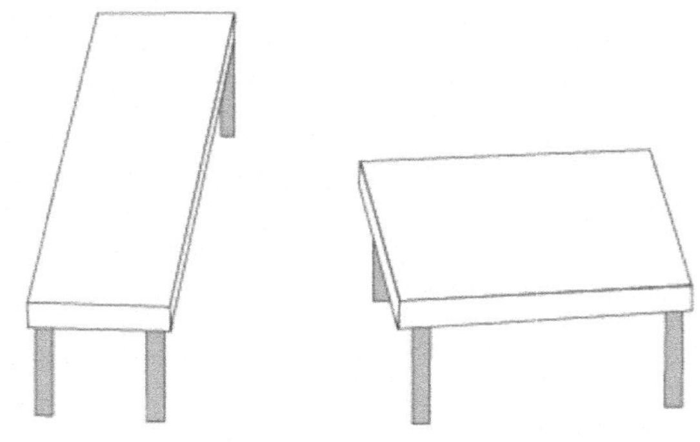

Figure 3-A
Shepard's Rotated Tables (Shepard, 1990)

The tables look different, because the angle you look at them from is different. In other words, when the perspective is different, reality looks different to us as well. Hence, our perception tricks us.

Exploring our own bias

Research supports this idea that perspective shapes our sense of what is real—for all of us. In fact, those of us fortunate enough to have a good education, a life rich in experience and some "cognitive sophistication" (which certainly applies to many or most community interpreters) are not less biased: at least one study suggests such individuals may be *more*, not less, biased than others (West, Meserve, & Stankovich, 2012). Perhaps further research can shed light on the reasons why. It might be that those of us blessed with an education and a rich life experience assume that we know better than others.

How can we explore our own bias? One of the easiest ways is to go to a world-famous website called Project Implicit, managed by researchers, and take online tests there that will assess our own implicit bias. That website address is https://implicit.harvard.edu/implicit/. Run through Harvard University and based on extensive research about implicit bias, the tests on this website are sophisticated and well-validated with a low margin for error.

Testing ourselves

Choose a test. There are many tests to choose from. You can check out your implicit attitudes toward people of different skin color, religion, age, sexual orientation, level of disability as well as gender and other categories. You may take several tests, if you wish. Each test will take only a few minutes. Please try at least one. After you do, reflect on the results of each test you take. If you are like the majority of those who take these tests, you will be surprised by the results. Those results will reveal attitudes that you were not aware of.

After taking at least one of the tests at the Harvard Project Implicit website, it will be helpful if you can make a conscious effort to observe yourself while you interpret. For example, do you:

- Introduce yourself to service providers in a different way than you do to service users?
- Treat service providers with more respect than service users?
- Treat service users with higher levels of education with the same tone, posture, attitude and deference that you treat less-educated service users?
- Dress in a professional way that shows respect for all, even in settings like homeless shelters, nursing homes for elderly patients and domestic violence centers?
- Simplify a message for less-educated service users more often than you do with service users who have higher education levels? (Remember that you shouldn't simplify the message at all.)
- Say one thing to a service provider when you intervene and something different to a service user?
- Soften rude, coarse or obscene language to avoid offending anyone?

Bias and Body Language

Observe your tone, phrasing and body language. They should mirror each other whether you speak up as the interpreter with service providers or users.

In other words, if you notice that your tone, phrasing and body language display more respect for the service provider than for the service user (which is very common), be aware that you are sending a message about your respect, or lack of respect, to everyone present. Your unconscious bias is showing—even if you are not aware that it shows.

A "Yes" answer to any of the questions above shows that internal bias seems to affect your interpreting performance. Try to make a conscious effort to become aware if you are engaging in any of the activities above. If so, ask yourself, "Why am I doing this? What does it say about me and my beliefs? What can I learn from observing myself act this way?" Armed with this information, please go to the next step.

Step 2. Plan ahead.

Type 1 and Type 2 thinking

Researchers in cognitive neuroscience and psychology make a distinction between two types of thinking called "Type 1 and Type 2" thinking (West, Meserve, & Stankovich, 2012). Type 1 refers to the kind of thinking you do on your feet. It's fast, intuitive and efficient. It gets the job done. But it isn't subtle or deep. It doesn't allow you much time to reflect, plan or capture the complexity of the situation you're in. As community interpreters, we do Type 1 thinking all the time when we interpret: we have no choice.

Type 2 thinking is just the opposite. It's slow, analytic and deeper. It takes time and effort. It requires a lot of reflection. To engage in Type 2 thinking, you have to slow down and think in a very conscious way. In other words, Type 2 thinking must be done *outside* the interpreted encounter, because you have no time for it during the session.

When to use Type 2 thinking

As an interpreter, you can use Type 2 thinking *before and after* the encounter to help you plan for the types of challenges you face often. Use Type 2 thinking outside the session to sharpen your Type 1 thinking during the session. Don't be caught by surprise: instead, plan for the types of concerns you know or suspect you will encounter.

For example, it may be common for you that service providers don't take enough time to explain things in a way that service users understand clearly. This problem often frustrates and worries interpreters. Is there anything helpful and professional you can do about that problem? (Often there is, and we will discuss such strategies in Sections 3.3 and 3.4.)

The value of Type 2 thinking

In this way, by using Type 2 thinking before you go to an encounter, when you interpret, you won't so often be caught by surprise. You will have a mental plan about what to do in the more common difficult situations. Here is how you can plan:

- Make a list of the most common communication challenges or barriers that you encounter while interpreting (e.g., providers who leave you alone to explain forms to services users; or service users who ask for your opinion about service providers), that other interpreters you know encounter, or that you have read about in textbooks and training manuals. (If you have never interpreted before or studied interpreting until now, try to consult some practicing community interpreters and ask them about the common challenges they encounter.)
- *Write these challenges down.* ***Please keep this list somewhere where you can find it again.***
- Decide which of these challenges you *should* or *should not* address by intervening. (Section 3.2 will help you decide.)
- Assess whether some of these issues are better to address *outside* the encounter.
- Develop a plan about how to address them. (The rest of this chapter will help you with that plan.)

An example from healthcare

Let's take an example. You are interpreting in a healthcare clinic, and you notice:

- Many patients don't understand a certain doctor (but they do not say so) and the doctor doesn't notice this common problem.
- Patients often seem confused by the healthcare system where you work (let us say it is a very complex healthcare system).
- A number of doctors speak in too high a register.
- Certain doctors don't check to see if patients that you interpret for understand their diagnoses—and you think this is a problem.
- Many patients leave the appointment without knowing how to correctly take their prescribed medications.
- Some cultural misunderstandings arise, because patients expect the doctors to make the decisions and don't ask questions.
- Families of patients with terminal illness believe that doctors should never tell the patient he or she is going to die. Instead, only family members should be informed.

Plan Ahead

Depending on the country where you live, the code of ethics you follow or whether you interpret primarily in schools, courts or for domestic violence and so forth, you will have a unique list of challenges. You can make your own list and your own decisions about which situations in your list are your responsibility and which ones you should ignore. We will talk more about how you make these decisions in Section 3.2. For now, be aware that by *planning ahead* how to address challenges, you will be much more mentally prepared when a problem arises that forces you to make a decision on the spot about whether or not to intervene.

Step 3. Monitor the situation. ("When in doubt—stay out.")

The importance of being careful

If a problem arises, don't jump in right away. Monitor the situation. Maybe the problem will go away. Maybe the service provider will address it. Maybe the service user will ask a question and get an answer that resolves the situation. Try to be patient. If you just wait a little, a lot of things that you think you should jump in to "fix" will take care of themselves without you.

Remember that during the encounter, it's hard to engage in Type 2 thinking. Type 2 thinking helps you make decisions in peace and quiet. But when you are interpreting, you have time only for Type 1 thinking. That's why your first reflex should be *not* to intervene but to wait and see if any problem you observe resolves itself without the need for you to jump in.

But don't wait too long

But don't wait too long either. If the end of the appointment is coming, and the doctor is about to leave, and you are fairly sure a mother will put oral antibiotic in her child's ear; or the parent is going to walk away not understanding the urgent steps to ensure his child's graduation; or the police officer is about to arrest the victim and not the abuser; or the patient is going to break the fast after midnight before a scheduled surgery, then you have a problem. Assess whether that problem could be serious.

The costs of waiting

For example, what if the scheduled surgery is so expensive it will cost a community interpreter's yearly earnings but the patient arrives having broken the required fast, meaning that the expensive surgery must be canceled. That would be a serious event for the patient, the hospital and the hospital staff. Yet all you, the interpreter, had to do was intervene during the preoperative appointment to say to all parties, "Excuse me, as the interpreter, I'm concerned there may be a misunderstanding about the pre-surgery fasting requirement." In short:

- Assess the situation carefully for mutual understanding among all parties.
- "Wait it out"—don't jump in too soon.
- Decide if the problem is serious.
- Make the decision to intervene *only if the problem seems serious.*

Step 4. Assess potential consequences.

Imagine what might happen if you don't intervene

How do you know if the problem you see is a serious one? Here is a simple answer. Think, "What will the consequences be if I decide *not* to intervene?"

If you are afraid that the consequences of *not* intervening are very serious and could result in harm for the service user, the service system, the service delivery or the service outcome (or perhaps even the service provider), then intervene. Remember that you are the communication specialist. It is your job to facilitate meaningful communication. If communication breaks down and that breakdown could cause harm, you may need to take appropriate steps to address the communication barrier.

Revisiting the doctor-patient story

Let's return to the scenario at the beginning of this section, where the doctor shook hands with an apparently religiously conservative patient who seemed upset by his action. Then he unintentionally insulted her (in a friendly way) in a side conversation with the nurse. Clearly, that doctor didn't think the interpreter was supposed to interpret his remarks. We asked you the following questions:

Questions

Would you, the interpreter:

- Tell the nurse and doctor that it might not be culturally or religiously appropriate for the doctor to shake hands with the patient?
- Tell the doctor that he upset the patient by shaking hands with her?
- Interpret the doctor's last remarks? Omit them? Soften them?
- Remind the doctor that you are required to interpret everything (in other words, give the doctor a chance to rephrase his rude remarks)?
- Interpret the remarks and *then* intervene to remind the doctor that you must interpret everything?
- Do something else?

Now write your answers down again. Then find the answers you wrote before studying this section. Are your answers the same as what you wrote at the beginning of the chapter? We will not give you our own answers yet. Instead, we will return to the scenario one more time at the end of this chapter. Please put your answers away, but remember where you put them.

Let's Practice

Learning Activity 3.1 (a): "The Interpreter's Dilemma" Role Plays
Learning Activity 3.1 (b): Implicit Bias

In *The Community Interpreter®: An International Workbook of Activities and Role Plays*

REVIEW OF SECTION 3.1

All of us are biased, because we are human. However, as interpreters we have a duty to examine our own bias to see if it has a negative impact on our conduct and decision making. In particular, when we make decisions about whether or not to intervene, we need to assess why we want to do so. Instead of letting implicit attitudes affect your decisions in negative or inappropriate ways, if you face communication barriers or obstacles to service delivery, follow these steps:

Step 1: **Explore your own bias.** Consider taking some of tests through the Harvard University Project Implicit website (https://implicit.harvard.edu/implicit/). Then observe your own interpreting and see if you can catch your biases affecting your observations and decisions. Use some of the questions in this section to guide your self-observation.

Step 2: **Plan ahead.** Practice "Type 2" (deeper, reflective) thinking when you are *not* interpreting, so that you are mentally prepared to make effective decisions when forced to do "Type 1" (quick, on the spot, spur-of-the-moment) thinking while you interpret.

Step 3: **Monitor the situation. ("When in doubt—stay out.")** Give the communication problem a chance to resolve itself before you jump in. Always stay alert to watch for possible misunderstandings, but avoid acting on your assumptions.

Step 4: **Assess potential consequences.** Only intervene if the consequences of *not* doing so are potentially serious and could harm the service user or damage the intended outcome of the service.

3.2 Deciding When to Intervene

Overview

Once you have made an effort to become more aware of your own internal bias and your unconscious filters, you will need to have a plan in place *before* the session about how to make a decision that is as unbiased as possible. Having decision-making criteria can help you do so. This section offers you four clear, simple criteria for making decisions about whether or not to intervene based on the potential *impact* and *consequences* of the act of intervening—beneficial or harmful—for service users and providers.

Learning Objective 3.2

After completing this section, you will be able to:

- Apply four decision-making criteria to assess whether or not to mediate based on potential consequences for end users.

The role of the interpreter: to mediate or not to mediate?

The big decision

Here is perhaps the biggest, most burning question in the field of community interpreting: should you, the community interpreter:

- Restrict your activities to interpreting; or
- Help the service user or provider when you observe a misunderstanding?

This question goes to the heart of community interpreting. It is, without a doubt, the deepest debate in the field today. In fact, the role of the interpreter is perhaps the most hotly discussed issue in the history of community interpreting (Avery, 2001): you can read about that discussion at the beginning of Chapter 5.

To be brief: many researchers, educators and interpreters believe that you should focus on interpreting and let the provider and user address their own misunderstandings, while others think that it is your responsibility to take action to help the parties understand each other. Still others sit somewhere in the middle of this spectrum (see, for example, the discussion in Rudvin, 2006). This debate goes back to the beginning of the profession (Avery, 2001; Llewelyn & Jones, 2009), and there is still no universal agreement on it (Toledano Buendía, 2010).

Guidance from ethics, standards and best practices

Before practicing anything recommended in this chapter, first (as suggested in Chapter 1) try to find out what is expected of community interpreters in the country and region where you practice. Sometimes national or local standards where you work will give you a clear answer about your role. For example, the standards for community interpreting in some countries, such as Canada (HIN, 2007), guide you to focus on interpreting rather than reacting to a cultural problem or advocating for the service user. In other countries, such as Belgium or Switzerland, you may be told that you have more leeway to use your judgment, especially in medical interpreting.

In other countries that take a middle path, like the United States (NCIHC, 2004 and 2005), you may be guided to restrict your activities in most cases to interpreting, but you are still permitted to intervene if a serious communication barrier arises that could have a negative impact on health outcomes or service delivery.

In countries where no group or association may have made any decision at all, you will have to decide on the best practices to follow. In such cases, you can study other countries' ethics, standards and best practices. You will find that the *Ethics and Standards* document at the beginning of this textbook and the guidance in this chapter and in Chapters 4 and 5 will help you understand your role.

Why interpreters need decision-making criteria for strategic mediation

As a community interpreter, you often need clarity on your role—and specifically, whether or not to perform strategic mediation. For example, intervening too often or mediating too long may be problematic. When interpreters get too involved, they often create other problems, such as long, side conversations and giving opinions to service users (Merlini, 2009). Service providers, such as doctors, can feel excluded and frustrated by interpreters who intervene often or take too much control (Leanza, 2005, p. 176).

On the other hand, if you do not take control of the communicative aspect of the encounter, others may decide your role for you, such as asking *you* to give bad news or fatal diagnoses to patients (rather than interpreting them), as happened to this interpreter: "The whole family was in this car accident and the grandfather had died. They made me tell the news to the family alone" (Norris et al., 2005, p. 1021). This is not the kind of mediation you should ever perform—or be asked to perform.

We will now examine two decision-making tools to help guide you through that decision-making process of whether or not to intervene: four decision-making criteria, and the ethical decision-making guidelines produced by California Healthcare Interpreting Association (CHIA) that you saw in Chapter 1.

Four criteria for intervening

The four criteria

You will recognize the four criteria listed below from Chapter 1, where they were first introduced. In that chapter they were discussed from the perspective of helping you to *identify* communication barriers and to consider which ethical principles might apply when you work to overcome those barriers. Here, we are using the same criteria to help you make a decision about whether or not to intervene. This section will help you make decisions in common situations that may challenge you.

In general, you would intervene to perform strategic mediation only if you perceive a barrier to communication or meaningful access to the service. Four basic criteria or causes that can trigger such an intervention are:

1. Linguistic challenges
2. Role confusion
3. Cultural misunderstandings
4. Service system barriers

If any one of these problems arises, it *might* justify intervening. Let's look at each of the four.

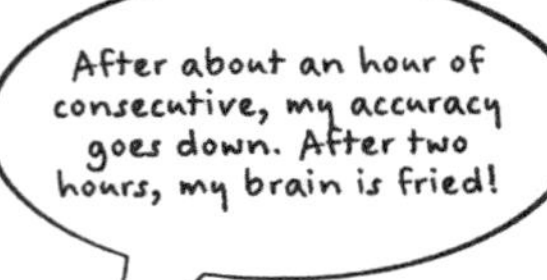

1. Linguistic challenges

Problems related to the "linguistic envelope"

As you saw in Chapter 1, linguistic challenges refer to any misunderstanding or confusion related to the language of the message, that is, its "linguistic envelope" (Gile, 2009, p. 94). Confusion can also relate to the listening conditions (or visual sightlines for signed language interpreters). After all, you cannot interpret something if you cannot hear it (or see it, as the case may be). If you, the interpreter, or the service user or provider, observe any linguistic confusion, you might have to perform mediation.

Detailed examples

In cases like these, you may and probably should intervene:

- A baby is crying next door and distracts you. (If possible, ask to move to another room.)
- Someone speaks too fast or too long. (Ask the person to speak more slowly.)
- One speaker overlaps with another, or two or more people speak at once. (Alert them to the fact you cannot interpret unless they take turns speaking.)
- The service provider uses a term or phrase, such as "occupational therapist," that you do not know. (Request a clarification.)
- A teacher speaks in high-register terms or acronyms such as TIMSS (Trends in International Mathematics and Science Study—a term used in Australia) that the parent does not appear to understand. (Perhaps ask the teacher to clarify such terms so that you can interpret them more clearly for the parent.)
- You lose the thread of the conversation. (Request a repetition.)
- You realize that you made a mistake a few sentences back. (Notify everyone and correct it).
- You need a break because your accuracy is impaired by fatigue. (If possible, wait for an appropriate moment and request a break.)
- The service user uses an idiom or phrase that is unclear or confusing to the service provider, even though you interpreted it accurately. (Intervene not to explain the idiom or phrase: ask the service user to explain it.)

2. Role confusion

General examples

Role confusion arises when you are asked to do something that exceeds your scope as an interpreter. You could be asked by providers, service users or administrators to do things that you know you shouldn't do. Here are a few common situations where you might need to interrupt the session to clarify your role as an interpreter, unless simply interpreting what is said resolves the concern:

- The provider or service user asks you for an opinion. ("Is this doctor any good?" "Can I trust the social worker?" "Is my client telling me the truth?")
- The provider or service user asks you for cultural guidance. ("How do men and women interact in her culture?" "Can you explain that whole thing about the amulets?")
- The provider or service user requests you to do something that could violate your professional ethics or best practices. ("Please explain this form to her. I'll be back in a moment." "Can you translate this consent form into her language?")
- Outside the session, the service user wants your help with a bill or to sight translate some correspondence he received. ("Can you just take a look at this and tell me what it says?")

Challenges for bilingual staff who interpret

For bilingual employees, here are some common misunderstandings about your role:

- "Other duties as assigned": For example, the provider might ask you to drive or accompany the patient/service user to various appointments. That is not an appropriate task for an interpreter. It *may* be appropriate for your other job as a bilingual employee or even for a staff interpreter—*if it is written into your job description and/or is a formal part of your duties.* (If you are a bilingual employee who sometimes interprets, it often helps to ask yourself the question: "Would I be expected to do this for other service users who need interpreters?")
- "The interpreter as a substitute provider": For example, the service provider may want you to explain something to the service user or otherwise take over some simple duties to save time for the service provider. But if you lack the training and qualifications of the service provider, and doing that job is not part of your job description and pay grade, you probably should not perform it.

Avoid Doing Two Jobs at Once!

You may also have to make clear that *while you interpret, you cannot perform any other role.* This restriction relates to the ethical issues about role boundaries and impartiality discussed in Chapter 1 and will be discussed later in this chapter and also in Chapter 5. Whatever your job requirements are, always bear in mind that you cannot wear the interpreter "hat," if you are doing something else. Even if your main task is to be a nurse, a teacher or a social worker, when you are interpreting, you need to (1) wear *only* the interpreter hat; and (2) let everyone "see that hat."

In other words, everyone involved should know that when you act as an interpreter you cannot perform your other job.

But remember: if you are a bilingual employee or even a cultural mediator (see Chapter 5 for a discussion of professional cultural mediators), *when you interpret you should follow the ethics and standards of practice for community interpreters in your geographic area until the session has ended,* or, if none exists, you can refer to the *Ethics and Standards* document listed at the beginning of this textbook.

After the session, if you are asked as a bilingual employee to do anything else on your own to help the service user in any way, ask yourself these questions:

- Are these additional tasks part of my job description?
- Does my boss/supervisor know that I am performing these tasks?
- Do I feel comfortable or uncomfortable performing them?
- Are there different expectations about what I do for service users who need interpreters and service users who do not—and if so, is there a possible pattern of discrimination?

Depending on your own answers to these questions, take action as you see fit.

Specific examples

Here are a few specific examples of situations where you may need to clarify your role as the interpreter.

The patient keeps asking you to explain what the therapist just said. You always interpret whatever the patient says and let the therapist handle the situation. But after the third request by the patient for you to explain something to her, you intervene to clarify your role: you tell the therapist and then the patient you are permitted only to interpret and not to explain what the therapist says.[32]

The patient turns and tells you he makes too much money to qualify for the service this therapist provides and adds, "But don't interpret that." Ethically, you are required to interpret what the patient says (even though he told you not to). But interpreting that message might disturb you, because the patient has a serious mental illness. Also your language community is small, and the patient could be angry with you and cause trouble by telling other people you are a bad interpreter. On the other hand, the therapist may need to know this information to assess the mental status of the patient. In a case like this one, interpret what is said and intervene to clarify your role and ask the patient to direct all his comments to the therapist. Be aware the therapist wants to know everything the patient says.

[32] In most cases, when you intervene to perform mediation, in legal and mental health interpreting you should address the service provider first.

The therapist asks you to help the service user fill out a form. You intervene to follow the SAY-NO model from Chapter 1: you suggest that she explain the form and help the patient fill it out or send in another provider to do so and then you will be happy to interpret the explanation.

The session goes beyond its scheduled time. You intervene to explain that, as you notified both parties at the beginning, you will have to leave now for another assignment.

After another session, the therapist asks you if you think the patient has a cultural belief related to what happens after death and whether people in his culture believe in ghosts. You explain that you are not a cultural expert and that beliefs about life after death vary so widely in the patient's country (as they do everywhere) that you would be happy to interpret these questions for the patient at the next session.

At the next session the therapist, before the session begins, asks you to sit with the patient to watch a health-related video and interpret what the video says. Instead you respectfully suggest that the therapist remain in the room or reschedule the session for a time when she or another health professional can be there with you and the patient. You clarify that the patient may have questions for the therapist, and also mention that you are not competent to perform accurate simultaneous interpretation of video. (If you are able to do so, explain that you will need time to view the video first and prepare to interpret it.)

3. Cultural misunderstandings

General examples

Cultural misunderstandings are among the most common challenges that face community interpreters in the field. Typical examples include:

- A cultural concept is unclear.
- The service user or patient's naming system is different (e.g., last name first, or including the maternal and paternal last names), but the provider is unaware of this difference.
- For cultural reasons, the service user does not ask questions, even when he or she doesn't understand the service provider.
- The service user does not understand how the service system works.
- The service user and provider are working with unidentified cultural assumptions, e.g., different understandings of what constitutes violence or acceptable child discipline, or what a spouse is (for example, the legal vs. common-law "living together" definition of *spouse*).

Specific examples

In every country where there are interpreters, there are cultural misunderstandings. For example, in healthcare settings:

- Providers may be unfamiliar with the patient's health remedies.
- Immigrants to western countries often don't understand the culture of biomedicine.
- Patients may want the doctor to tell them what to do—or may not want the doctor to tell them what to do.
- Providers do not ask what the patient believes caused the illness or problem.
- Patients may know nothing about basic services, like dentistry or preventive care.

Interpreters have their own set of cultural concerns. For example:

- Providers and service users often expect the interpreter to be a cultural expert.
- Both parties may want the interpreter to "explain" cultural issues.
- Certain cultural concepts have no equivalent in the target language.
- Many cultural terms (like the evil eye) mean different things in different places.
- Often, cultural misunderstandings are hidden: interpreters don't notice them until too late.
- Interpreters have to monitor all the cultures in the room for potential misunderstandings, and especially be aware of their own cultural biases—while interpreting!

Finally, providers often lack skill or adequate training in working with service users or patients from other cultures and do not realize it is *their responsibility to explore cultural concerns* rather than relying on interpreters to solve the "cultural issues." We will return to the topic of cultural mediation later in this chapter in much more detail.

4. Service system barriers

General examples

Common examples of system barriers in community interpreting include:

- Providers who are not trained to work with interpreters. As a result they may:
    - Ask the interpreter to perform certain provider tasks, such as making assessments or conveying a diagnosis.
    - Try to leave the interpreter alone with the service user/patient, who then asks the interpreter for guidance or explanations.
- Providers who discriminate only against service users needing interpreters (in other words, they treat service users who do *not* need interpreters quite differently and with more respect than the service users who need interpreters).
- Service users who:
    - Don't understand how the service system works.
    - Are confused about their next steps to obtain benefits.
    - Come to see the interpreter alone, after the session, to complain about the provider, ask the interpreter to explain what the provider said or learn how the service system works.

A specific example: advocacy

For community interpreters, service delivery barriers often raise the question of advocacy: whether or not to advocate. This is a very difficult decision and standards in some countries, such as Canada, keep the answer simple: they say that community interpreters should not advocate (HIN, 2007: whether or not everyone in the field in Canada *agrees* with those standards is an open question). In other countries, such as the United States, community interpreters are generally permitted to advocate but cautioned against doing so unless it is truly necessary, while *legal* interpreters are not permitted to advocate.

The topic of advocacy is so important one that is addressed in detail in Chapter 5, Section 5.3. Meantime, one important strategy to keep in mind is a simple one. If you find that someone who needs a service and has a right to access it, but finds the process difficult due to a service system barrier that you can't or shouldn't address yourself, you could:

a) Take that person to an appropriate provider and interpret for that provider so that the problem can be solved—but not by you.
b) If permissible and appropriate, refer the service user to the relevant service or individual who can assist, but *only* if this is an established policy in the institution where you interpret as an employee and *not* (in most cases) if you are a freelance interpreter (the reasons why freelance interpreters shouldn't do so are discussed in Chapter 4); or
c) Report the problem to the appropriate supervisor as a critical incident.

Remember that by addressing or reporting such problems, you are not only helping that service user, but also, perhaps, other people who face or could face the same problem in the future. You also protect the institution from legal liability, potentially help it to comply with relevant antidiscrimination laws or policies and help that organization provide quality services with beneficial outcomes.

The CHIA ethical decision-making process

Consider the consequences!

Before you tackle the question, "Should I intervene or not?" during an interpreted encounter, here are two steps to consider:

1. Does this situation meet any one or more of the four criteria above?
2. If so, what will happen if I do *not* intervene? What are the consequences?

If one or more of the criteria are met *and* you feel that the consequences of *not* intervening could be serious, especially for the service user's safety, well-being or ability to access the service effectively, then intervene. However, there is another tool that can help you to refine your decision-making process. It comes from California. That tool is the CHIA ethical decision-making process discussed in Chapter 1.

CHIA ethical decision-making process

The six CHIA questions

Practical guidance

The California Healthcare Interpreting Association (CHIA) is one of the most influential interpreting associations in the United States. In 2002, it published a seminal document that included ethics and standards of practice for healthcare interpreters (CHIA, 2002). Part of that document, as you saw in Chapter 1, is a set of guidelines that offer six easy steps for making ethical decisions. The guideline is valuable for interpreters who must also decide whether or not to mediate and can help them make that decision on both ethical and compassionate grounds. (This ethical decision-making process is available at www.chiaonline.org.)

You will have to make many decisions quickly, both during and outside the encounter. But the decisions you have to make *while* you interpret are usually the hardest because (a) there is so little time to think; and (b) interpreting is such a higher-level cognitive skill that it takes up a great deal of your thinking capacity. Such quick decisions will test you. Your unconscious bias could make the decision for you if you don't have a plan. This situation isn't ideal.

Reviewing the steps

To help yourself, try using the CHIA guidelines. They come in the form of these six points you saw in Chapter 1 (CHIA, 2002, pp. 55–60). To review, the steps are:

1. *Ask questions to determine whether there is a problem.* [We strongly recommend that you ask these questions silently, in the privacy of your own mind.]
2. *Identify and clearly state the problem, considering the ethical principles that may apply and ranking them in applicability.*
3. *Clarify personal values as they relate to the problem.*
4. *Consider alternative actions, including benefits and risks.*
5. *Decide to carry out the action chosen.*
6. *Evaluate the outcome and consider what might be done differently next time.*

You already have these skills!

Six steps—that's too much?

These six points may seem like a lot to think about *while* you are interpreting. Yet you already have these skills. You use them in your daily life. We are all presented with in-the-moment challenges on a regular basis and have to decide what to do. Let's look at an example. If you are a parent, this example will be familiar to you: "The kids are arguing. Not again! Now I have to do something. What should I try? Yell at them? No. Put them in their room to think about their behavior (a 'time-out')? I'm not sure. Take away the toy they're fighting about until they calm down? Or sit them together and have them try to solve the problem?"

Parents usually make this kind of decision according to their own personal values. "Well. I've yelled before, but I don't want to yell unless the kids are in danger—I feel bad when I do. Anyway I want *them* to figure it out and develop some problem-solving strategies on their own." So perhaps as parents we decide to remove the toy and have the children talk out a solution before giving it back. If they don't fight any more, great; if they do fight, well, that strategy didn't work! Either way, we know the outcome and if the strategy was successful, we remember it for next time. If it didn't work out well, we think about what could work better.

The six steps and Type 2 thinking

We can practice this type of thinking about common interpreting problems ahead of time. Remember Type 2 thinking? That is the kind you do *before* or *after* the session. And remember that list we asked you to write in Section 3.1, under "Step 2, Plan ahead"? It was a list of common communication barriers you might encounter as an interpreter, and we asked you to keep it somewhere you could find it again.

Take that list out now. Look at it. See if you can apply the six CHIA points to some situations on that list. Try to do so at a time and place where it's quiet and you can think the steps through in peace. Also consider Learning Activity 3.2(c) in the companion workbook for this textbook.

Let's Practice

Learning Activity 3.2 (a): "Should I Mediate?"
Learning Activity 3.2 (b): Decision-Making Criteria
Learning Activity 3.2 (c): Case Study for Decision Making

In *The Community Interpreter®: An International Workbook of Activities and Role Plays*

REVIEW OF SECTION 3.2

Intervening is not an act to be taken lightly. Interrupting the interpreted session can derail it. Ideally, you will do so only in situations where the consequences of *not* intervening can compromise effective service delivery or create a risk for anyone's safety, well-being or human dignity.

It is not always easy to assess consequences, but in this section we reviewed four criteria that can help you decide whether or not to mediate:

a) Linguistic challenges
b) Role confusion
c) Cultural misunderstandings
d) Service system barriers

We also examined how the CHIA guidelines for ethical decision making discussed in Chapter 1 can be useful to help you decide think carefully about whether or not to mediate. Being mentally prepared can help prevent many potential problems and contribute to making sensible decisions about mediation.

3.3 Scripts for Mediation

Overview

In this section, you will examine and practice a few simple strategies to decide what to say when you intervene. This is the first step in learning how to perform effective strategic mediation. We will use the term "mediation scripts" to refer to written formulas that you can develop for common scenarios. You can then memorize, practice and adapt these "scripts" to different situations.

As a general rule, plan ahead of time about what to say when you intervene. Otherwise, when you have to intervene you may have no idea what to say. Instead, you may:

- "Freeze like a deer in the headlights" (an expression that means your mind goes blank and empty).
- Feel nervous.
- Say something long or complicated.
- Get into a side conversation.

If you *do* prepare "mental scripts" for strategic mediation ahead of time, you will it much easier to:

- Be brief and clear.
- Identify the basis of the miscommunication.
- Avoid interfering.
- Sound professional, polished and smooth.
- Feel confident and in control.

In this section, we will give you a few basic formulas or "scripts" to help you prepare mentally. These basic scripts will offer you a plan about what to say when you intervene. However, as you will see in this section, you must also write your own scripts and memorize them to make them automatic. Practice, practice, practice the scripts.

Learning Objective 3.3

After completing this section, you will be able to:

- Develop basic scripts for performing mediation in common situations in community interpreting.

Guidelines for strategic mediation scripts

General guidelines

Here are a few guidelines for creating basic scripts for strategic mediation that you can memorize and adapt to various communication barriers and cultural misunderstandings that take place during or outside the session. They should be realistic scripts tailored to *your* country, *your* speaking style and the types of situations that *you* encounter. To be prepared, you should:

1. Develop about six basic mediation scripts in your own words that cover common misunderstandings and communications barriers that you see often.[33]
2. Make sure to have at least one or two scripts that address each of the four criteria for intervening discussed in Section 3.2.
3. Keep your scripts short and simple.
4. When you mediate in real life, tailor each script to the situation.

A Trainer's Story About Strategic Mediation

By the Author of This Chapter

I can still remember going out after basic medical interpreter training to interpret in real life. I was told to perform clarification, culture brokering or advocacy when needed—but I was never shown *how* to do so. These problems caused me stress until I developed a plan that worked. That plan was to have a mental script—a specific idea about what to *say* and *do* if I had to intervene.

Then I became a trainer of community interpreters who interpreted in nearly any community service that one can imagine. Now the problem grew even more serious, because interpreters would give me many real-life examples of the common challenges they faced and ask me, "So what would *you* do?" Often I had no idea! In fact, I had few good answers until I started developing *general* scripts for strategic mediation that could be adapted to nearly any situation in the field.

Common communication barriers

Revisiting the four criteria for intervening

Throughout this book, we come back often to four common communication barriers. Mediation scripts are one essential tool to help you navigate those issues. Before you plan what to say in your scripts, first identify the *common communication barriers* we discussed in the previous section and use them to help you to develop your scripts out loud, so that you can write down the kinds of things you would actually say in real life. Let's start with examples of the most common triggers for strategic mediation in community interpreting.

[33] If you have not yet interpreted in real life, you can choose examples from this textbook. You can also speak to fellow students or consult working interpreters for their examples.

Linguistic challenges

- You don't understand a medical or legal term that the service provider used.
- The service user doesn't understand common terms used in that service system.
- The provider speaks in too high a register for easy understanding.

Role confusion

- The service user wants you to explain the service.
- The provider speaks to you instead of the service user.
- The service provider or user asks you to do something (such as perform sight translation without a provider present) that violates your ethics or professional requirements.

Cultural misunderstandings

- There is a cultural-linguistic confusion (e.g., Chinese New Year does not fall on the same dates as western New Year's Day, but the service user and provider do not realize they are talking about two different new year dates).
- A term or concept lacks a cultural equivalent in the target language (e.g., "flashback" is not a term or a concept that exists in the target language).
- A cultural miscommunication occurs (e.g., the patient refuses to remove a sacred object or piece of jewelry prior to surgery, which delays the scheduled surgery).

Service system barriers

- The service provider denies assistance to the service user (e.g., an immigrant in detention is ill, and the provider does not request medical assistance).
- The service user does not understand the service system (e.g., the parent does not understand the child's graduation requirements).

Examples of scripts

General guidelines to develop your scripts

For each situation below, first you'll see a mediation performed by an *untrained* interpreter. Notice the problem with what that interpreter says. Then we'll show you what a professional, trained interpreter, could say instead. Then you can practice repeating the sample scripts. Then we'll show you some other common scripts used by community interpreters in the field. They are simple and easy. You can use them, or adapt them or write your own.

Linguistic challenges example (a)

The Untrained Interpreter

Do you see how the untrained interpreter in this situation mediated without transparency? She said one thing to the doctor and something quite different to the patient. Also, the untrained interpreter:

- *Assumed* the patient didn't understand.
- *Assumed* the patient wasn't literate.
- May have insulted the patient.
- Said something to the doctor that the patient might have understood and been offended by.

The last point is important: many service users have some proficiency in the language of service, although they still need an interpreter. Never assume that service users cannot understand the other language.

Linguistic challenges example (b)

The *Trained* Interpreter

Notice the difference. The trained interpreter was *transparent.* She reported to the patient what she told the doctor. She didn't hide anything. In addition, during her strategic mediation, she:

- Didn't blame the doctor for not being clear.
- Didn't blame the patient for not understanding.
- Didn't blame herself for poor interpreting.

Instead, the interpreter said she was concerned that what she was *interpreting* wasn't clear. If you try this approach, no one is likely to be offended by your mediation.

Transparency

Special concerns when you write scripts

Transparency

The ethical requirement of transparency appears in many ethics and standards of practice for interpreters around the world (Bancroft, 2005), including in the *Ethics and Standards* document at the beginning of this textbook. Remember that transparency does not apply only to what you interpret: *it also applies to what you say when you intervene.*. In other words, in your scripts be sure to interpret or report whatever you mediate to one party *faithfully and accurately* to the other party.

Transparency

Transparency shows respect. In general, those who need interpreters to access a community service have experienced discrimination. Community interpreters have a professional obligation to show respect to all, including service users. Being transparent by reporting faithfully everything you say to one party for the other party, each and every time you mediate, means that you are not only following your interpreting ethics; you are also showing respect.

Avoid unconscious bias in your scripts

Avoid unconscious bias in your scripts

Have one script—not two different scripts

Remember how we pointed out in Section 3.1 that interpreters often say one thing to a service provider and something quite different to the service user? For example, the interpreter might say to the advocate: "Could you explain more about domestic violence to her? In her culture they think it's okay for the husband to beat up the wife…" and then tell the victim, "I just asked the counselor to explain something."

Sometimes differences in the way that you address service providers vs. service users have to do with your own comfort levels and how familiar one person feels to you compared to the other. For example, if and the provider are from the same country, perhaps you feel more comfortable with the provider and his or her worldview. On the other hand, if your native language is that of the service user, but you have been living in the new country longer than the service user has, you might still feel more comfortable with the service provider than the service user. Similarly, if you grew up as a second-generation immigrant, speaking your parents' language at home and the official or national language(s) everywhere else, you may still feel more comfortable with the provider and his or her personal and professional cultures.

Scripts and respect

You may show more deference and politeness to the service provider than the service user, not only out of respect for authority or unconscious class bias: sometimes you feel discomfort with service users due to their "otherness" and cultural differences. This is not strange or wrong. Your feelings are your feelings. However, in your behavior, ideally you will become aware of these biases, so that you can show respect for all. What you say when you mediate is a very important part of your behavior as an interpreter.

Mediation and Respect

When you mediate, show equal respect for all. *Every time you start a mediation, think how it will sound when you interpret or report it to the other party.* Only say what you would want *everyone* present to understand if they spoke both languages.

Writing sample scripts

The value—and limitations—of sample scripts

Here is a secret for effective mediation:

- Learn a few basic mediation scripts.
- Adapt them to each situation.

When you interpret in real life, the scripts you use probably should not be the ones in this textbook. To fit your needs and your local context and services, the scripts will have to come from you. The scripts should sound like you and reflect who you are: as an interpreter and a human being. In this section, we will give examples of mediation scripts, but they are just that: examples. Only you can speak for yourself in a way that sounds smooth, professional and convincing. Only you know the context and nuances of your own speech patterns. Still, the examples below can help you to develop your own scripts. For practical purposes you will need:

- At least two basic scripts for common cases of linguistic challenges.
- A few basic scripts for other common situations that involve role confusion, cultural misunderstandings and service system barriers.

With a few basic scripts, you can adapt them to each situation. Let's look at examples.

Scripts for linguistic challenges (high register)

One common problem in the field is the provider who speaks in very educated language that many service users do not understand. Here is an example of a poor way to handle the situation:

> *The lawyer in a domestic violence center is explaining what a protection order is. The service user doesn't seem to understand the lawyer's legal, formal language. The interpreter interrupts and says, "Excuse me, madam lawyer, could you please simplify what you're saying? Oh, and just let me ask the service user if she understands you." Then the interpreter asks the service user, "Do you understand what the lawyer is saying about the protection order?"*

Here is an example of a more effective way to mediate:

> (to the lawyer) *"Excuse me, the interpreter wants to state that what she interpreted about the protection order may not be clear."*
> (to the client) *"Excuse me, the interpreter just informed the lawyer that what she interpreted about the protection order may not be clear."*[34]

[34] Remember that in legal interpreting, when you intervene you should ideally refer to yourself as "the interpreter," in indirect speech. The reason is that if you also interpret in courts, in many countries you will be required, when you intervene, to refer to yourself as "the interpreter" for clarity in the written record. Therefore, if you interpret in courts, to develop good habits always refer to yourself in the third person as "the interpreter" when you intervene.

Customizing your script

If you are worried that the lawyer still won't truly understand your intention, you could tailor your mediation script even more by adding other elements. For example, here is a more "customized" script:

> (to the lawyer) *"Excuse me, the interpreter has concerns that what she interpreted about the protection order might not be clear. If you explain it in different words, it may be easier to interpret it more clearly."* (Report this mediation to the client.)

Script doesn't work? Try again!

Even *that* level of detail *might* not be enough. Perhaps protection orders don't exist in the country of the client. They are culturally a foreign concept. In legal interpreting, you cannot usually perform cultural mediation (depending on the country where you practice), but you can and should address linguistic misunderstandings *even if they have a cultural foundation*. Here is one simple way to do so:

> (to the lawyer) *"Excuse me, what the interpreter has just interpreted about the protection order might not be clear because there seems to be no exact equivalent for 'protection order' in Twi [the target language]."* (Then report this mediation to the client.)

In the last example, you are communicating to the lawyer that she needs to rephrase her communication to help the client understand the meaning of "protection order"—and every competent lawyer wants his or her client to understand basic legal concepts that are relevant to the case.

Scripts for linguistic challenges (unfamiliar terms)

Here are possible scripts for situations where *you* do not understand a term or phrase:

> Example #1
> "Excuse me, as the interpreter could I ask you to clarify [the term or phrase]?"
>
> Example #2:
> "The interpreter requests clarification of [the term or phrase]."
>
> Example #3
> "Excuse me, as the interpreter I need clarification of [the term or phrase]."

Of course, you must *interpret or report each mediation* to the other party. For example, "The interpreter just asked the service user to clarify a regionalism she used—*patojito*."

Scripts for role confusion

It is very common that the provider or service user, instead of speaking to each other, starts talking to you instead and even asks you questions (like, "Do you think she follows what I'm saying?" "Is this case manager any good?"). Here are examples of what you might say in that situation:

> Example #1
> "Excuse me, as the interpreter could I remind you to speak to [the provider or patient/service user], not to me?"

Example #2:
"As the interpreter could I remind you that I can't offer my personal opinions?"

Example #3
"Excuse me, the interpreter is not permitted to give advice or recommendations."

Example #4
"Excuse me, the interpreter is required to interpret everything said during the session."

Again, always interpret or report each mediation to the other party (or parties) accurately, e.g., *"The interpreter just reminded the provider that I'm not allowed to give advice or recommendations."* If someone will not pause, you could say something like, *"Excuse me, as the interpreter could I remind you to slow down and pause more often? I need to interpret accurately."*

Scripts for cultural misunderstandings

Some of the greatest challenges arise when you encounter cultural misunderstandings. These cases are often complex and hard to articulate when you intervene. Here are two examples:

Mediation script: *"The interpreter is concerned there may be a break in communication about a traditional healing practice called cupping. You may wish to ask the patient about it."*
Alternative version: *"The interpreter is concerned about a possible cultural misunderstanding about the practice of 'cupping.' You may wish to explore this issue with the patient."*

However, cultural mediation is so complex that we will address it in more detail in Sections 3.5 and 3.6.

Scripts for service system barriers

Many obstacles to service delivery or access to services are caused by the complexities or constraints of the service system itself. Prepare for the most common ones that you will encounter. Here are a few general examples:

- The provider did not give the service user a clear explanation of the service, and you are worried about the consequences.
- The service user is treated differently from those who speak the provider's language.
- The service user comes up to you after the session to ask what the provider said, because the system is so complex that the service user relies on you to explain it.

While there is no "one-size-fits-all" script for all the system barrier challenges that you could encounter, because there are so many, here is one useful strategy: if mediation during the session does not solve a problem related to the service user's ability to effectively receive the service, and the consequences seem serious but the service provider has left, offer to take the service user to speak to another provider. Then interpret the problem (as you perceive it) for the service user and the new provider.

A helpful tip

Write your own scripts for the most common type of communication barriers you might encounter in real life. Practice saying your scripts out loud. If they sound right, write them on little cards. Memorize them. Next, if you can, try out your scripts in real-life sessions or role-play practice. If the scripts don't feel quite right or natural for you, or don't adapt easily to the new situations, adapt them or write new ones. Memorize the revised scripts and try again. Always try to think what you might really say (in both languages). Soon you will find that even in unusual situations, your brain finds the right words. Having scripts for basic situations relaxes your mind. It makes mediating easier.

Practice

Practice is important. The recommended exercises in your workbook will give you a chance to practice your mediation scripts. You can also practice with a friend or a "study buddy": another community interpreter, or perhaps someone in your class. First, share your scripts with your partner. Ask for your partner's opinion about your scripts. Then practice role plays with each other, so that you say your own scripts out loud during a simulated session.

How to Practice Your Scripts

Make small cards with your basic scripts, or put them into your smartphone or tablet. As you sit in a waiting room, practice your scripts until they feel natural. Nothing prepares your mind for what you will say like practice, practice and more practice.

Through practice, you can embed your scripts into your mind so that they become automatic. When you go out in real life interpreting and have to mediate, you won't have to think about the wording, the scripts or the steps, because it will all feel automatic and second nature. You will be *very* glad you practiced: you will feel in control. Your strategic mediations will feel smooth, polished and professional. To watch a communication problem resolved before your eyes is a rewarding feeling. The effort will all be worth it!

Let's Practice

Learning Activity 3.3 (a): Record a Sample Mediation Script
Learning Activity 3.3 (b): Write Basic Mediation Scripts
Learning Activity 3.3 (c): Mediation Script Role Play

In *The Community Interpreter®: An International Workbook of Activities and Role Plays*

REVIEW OF SECTION 3.3

Mediation is a challenging skill. It is also complex, because it is usually a response to something "going wrong." The fact that you wonder if you need to mediate already means that you face a challenge. You therefore need mediation scripts to prepare yourself, so that you don't "freeze" or say something inappropriate. So, remember:

- Prepare basic mediation scripts for common scenarios.
- Write scripts that sound natural to you.
- Practice your scripts in front of a mirror, into a recording device or with a friend.
- Adapt those basic scripts to each situation.

Remember: mediation can be a challenge, but by having short scripts ready in advance, you will make mediation an easier skill to practice. Having these scripts will help you build your confidence, boost your professionalism and show service providers and users how competent and skilled you are. Be prepared: practice your mediation scripts!

3.4 The Strategic Mediation Model

Overview

Mediation involves more than words. Knowing what to say when you mediate is not enough: you will also need to know the steps for performing strategic mediation. In fact, strategic mediation may be the single most complex skill that any interpreter will ever learn.

Message transfer is cognitively, culturally and emotionally complex. So is strategic mediation. However, mediation also involves complex social and interpersonal skills, direct interaction with all parties and the ability to think at high speed to assess many possible outcomes so you can make informed decisions. Message transfer is difficult precisely *because* it involves so many cognitive and linguistic skill sets. Mediation is therefore difficult in great part *because it interrupts the complex process of message transfer.*

You cannot be interpreting and mediating at the same time. You are doing one or the other: not both.

Mediation is a distraction. When you mediate, you must suspend your real job—interpreting—to resolve some sort of problem. The goal in this section is to offer you a few simple, basic procedures for conducting mediation to make it as simple as possible to execute your mediation cleanly, briefly and efficiently, to avoid disrupting the session. That goal of targeted efficiency is why we call this the *Strategic Mediation Model.*

Think of mediation as a "lightning strike": you want to get in and out without becoming involved or derailed. Remember. You are the communication specialist in the room. You are *not* there to solve problems. Remove that burden from your shoulders. You are there to help everyone present communicate clearly.

Learning Objective 3.4

After completing this section, you will be able to:

- Practice five steps to perform strategic mediation.

The five steps for the Strategic Mediation Model

If you need to mediate during the session, follow these five steps:

- Interpret what was just said or signed.
- Identify yourself as the interpreter.
- Mediate briefly.
- Report your mediation to the other party.
- Resume interpreting.

To show you how to perform an effective mediation, let's look at a common real-life situation. You are in a session and focused on interpreting when, for the third time, the service user turns to you and says: "Why is this provider asking me all these questions?" Here is what we recommend:

- In most cases, simply interpret the question—let the service provider handle the situation, if at all possible. ("When in doubt, stay out.")
- However, if the same problem keeps coming back (as it does here), clarify your role.

Now let's walk through the basic steps for mediation. Keep this in mind: the five steps look simple. They are. However, when you interpret, they can be hard to remember at first. Study them closely.

Analyzing the steps for mediation

Step 1: Interpret what was just said.

The first step for mediation looks simple. It *is* simple. It is basic, fundamental for accuracy and transparency, and very important. Yet it is surprisingly hard to remember this step in real life! The probable reason for forgetting it is that whenever you see the need to mediate, you become so distracted by what you are about to say and do that you forget to interpret. However, *unless you are taking excellent notes and will remember to interpret the statement after your mediation from your notes,* you must interpret on the spot (even if you don't fully understand) because otherwise you will forget later.

Caution for Medical Interpreters

If you don't interpret the last thing said or signed *before* you mediate, you will forget to interpret it *after* you mediate. While this is true for all community interpreters, for medical interpreters, the risk of omitting interpreting an important statement from a health professional might have an impact on the health outcome. Unless you are taking excellent notes, ***always interpret what was last stated <u>before</u> you mediate.***

How Can I Interpret Something I Don't Understand?

Question: What if the speaker says or signs something that you don't understand right before you have to mediate? How are you supposed to interpret a term or phrase you don't understand?
Answer: Leave the word or phrase that you don't understand in the source language when you interpret the message into the target language, then immediately intervene to request clarification of that term or phrase.
(Note: in some countries this strategy may not be advisable for court or legal interpreters. Inform yourself carefully about legal interpreting requirements and whether or not you may leave a term in the source language.)

It is critical to interpret *every* message. Interpreting everything said or signed is both an ethical requirement and a practical necessity: if the interpreter does not interpret everything stated, the principle of communicative autonomy is violated. Someone who did not get a message interpreted might not be able to make informed decisions, which is both unfair and inappropriate. This failure means that the interpreter is not facilitating direct communication. Again, to emphasize the point, this step of interpreting whatever was just said or signed needs to be performed *before* you intervene, unless you have a superb memory or advanced note-taking skills).

Of course, if you are mediating because you didn't hear or understand part of the message, simply interpret what you reasonably can.

Step 2: Identify yourself as the interpreter.

When you intervene to perform a mediation, it is an ethical requirement under accuracy to be transparent. Show that you are speaking as the *interpreter*. Depending on the language and context, different formulas are possible. You can intervene in direct speech, also known as first person (e.g., "As the interpreter could I request a clarification of…") or by referring to yourself in the third person (e.g., "The interpreter requests a clarification of…").

Legal interpreters who practice in courts are typically required to refer to themselves as "the interpreter" to clarify for the written record that the interpreter is speaking for him- or herself. Outside the court it is not usually required or necessary for interpreters to refer to themselves in the third person, but many interpreters prefer to do so. Choose to use the approach that feels right for you, unless you perform court interpreting, in which case you will need to develop the habit of referring to yourself as "the interpreter."

Two Ways to Identify Yourself as the Interpreter

Excuse me, as the interpreter could I ask you to clarify what macular degeneration means?

or

The interpreter requests a clarification of the meaning of macular degeneration.

In almost any language, the expression *Excuse me* acts as a break in communication. It gets attention. When you follow up with the expression, "as the interpreter," you make it clear that you are no longer engaging the voice of the service user or provider. We recommend that you make a habit of intervening with the words *Excuse me* to help clarify that you are speaking up as the interpreter—then follow up by saying, "As the interpreter…" or, "The interpreter requests…"

Whom to Address First?

In community interpreting, broadly speaking there is no rule about whom to address first when you intervene. Use your best judgment. However, if you perform legal interpreting, in courtrooms you might typically be required to address the judge: find out the rules for intervening for the courts in your jurisdiction.

For out-of-court legal interpreting, whether for law enforcement, lawyer-client interviews, interviews in detention or any other legal situation, it is generally preferable to *address the legal service provider first.* Lawyers and other legal service providers are (a) responsible for the legal outcome of the interview, (b) legally liable for your conduct, (c) well-informed about correct legal protocols for the situation and the setting where you interpret. In addition, the legal service provider may become suspicious if you speak first to the service user or may change legal strategy based on what you say.

In mental health interpreting, for the safety of the patient and to avoid re-traumatizing a trauma survivor, address the mental health provider first when you intervene.

Step 3: Mediate briefly with one party.

Mediating briefly and effectively is a challenge. Having scripts for mediation, as discussed in Section 3.3, will help you mediate quickly and well. The rest of this chapter will also help you understand how to perform brief, yet effective, mediations targeted to real-life situations.

Step 4: Interpret or report your mediation.

Always report your mediation for the other party or parties, for the following reasons:

- Your interpreting ethics require you to be accurate and complete.
- Transparency is also a requirement.
- Whatever you say to one party, the other party also needs to know, or effective service delivery will be compromised.

Be Transparent—Every Time You Mediate

If you do not interpret or report whatever you mediate to the other party (or parties) present, you will violate your ethical requirements of accuracy and transparency. You might also:

- Start a side conversation.
- Arouse suspicion.
- Lose trust.
- Trigger a service complaint.

Remember too, as you saw earlier, that the service user or service provider might understand more than they speak. If you choose to omit part of the message and anyone present notices the omission, that person may judge you negatively for it.

Step 5: Resume interpreting.

Avoid getting stuck in the middle. If you mediate, and one party answers *you* instead of speaking to the other party—pretend the person is speaking to the other party anyway. Cut off eye contact. Look at your notes, or pretend to take notes. Let the service provider and user *re-establish direct communication.*

Remember: it is easy to get trapped in a side conversation. Don't let this happen. After all, mediation isn't about you. It's about helping the end users communicate more directly with each other. In summary, as we said earlier, try to think of mediation as a "lightning strike." In an ideal situation:

- You notice a communication barrier.
- You make a decision about whether to intervene.
- You choose to intervene.
- You keep your mediation brief.
- You identify to all parties what the communication barrier is.
- You do not explain the problem, discuss it, fix it or "take care" of it yourself.
- Instead, *you let the service provider and user fix the problem.*

In simple terms, mediate quickly and get out. Get back to interpreting. Now let's focus on ways to keep your mediations brief so that service user and provider can communicate with each other as directly as possible. You will help to identify the communication problem, but they solve the problem themselves.

Mediation and body language

Mediation as performance

Mediation isn't only what you say: it's an act. The Strategic Mediation Model addresses and gives guidance on how to behave. Think about and monitor your behavior when you mediate—including your own body language. When you begin to practice the steps, use your body language to make it clear that you are no longer interpreting. For example, if you were interpreting in an unobtrusive position and avoiding eye contact, when you intervene you could:

- Lift your head.
- Lean or step forward.
- Make eye contact.
- Speak more loudly or firmly.
- Use hand gestures.
- Draw attention to yourself.

The end of the performance

But the *moment you have completed your strategic mediation,* use your body language in a different way to signal that change. For example, after mediating you could:

- Move back to an unobtrusive position.
- Cut eye contact.
- Look down at your notes.
- Let your voice adopt the tone of the speaker as you interpret.
-

In general, when you interpret you want to draw attention *away* from yourself. When you mediate, you want to draw attention *to* yourself (to show that you are speaking as the interpreter)—but only briefly. When you go back to interpreting, try to deflect attention.

Eye contact and mediation

Eye contact and mediation

As discussed in Chapter 2, there is no international consensus on whether or not to avoid eye contact in community interpreting. Individual circumstances will affect your decision. However, in general, we argue the following. Eye contact with the interpreter can:

- Interfere with the ability of service providers and users to develop a relationship with each other.
- Disrupt the complex cognitive demands and neural processing that interpreting requires of you.

However, making eye contact might still be appropriate when you are *not* interpreting—for example, before the encounter, during introductions or while mediating. The reason for making eye contact when you perform strategic mediation is that you are no longer speaking as the voice of the service user or provider but as yourself: as the interpreter. It can be appropriate to make eye contact (depending on the culture and the situation). And doing so may help you communicate your mediation more clearly. The cost is that making eye contact can encourage the service user and provider to continue eye contact with you after you go back to interpreting.

The Danger of Eye Contact After Mediating

The longer you mediate and make eye contact, the more difficult it is for you to resume a background position. Eye contact reminds the user and provider that you are present. It brings you into their conversation. To avoid this problem, cut eye contact right after performing your mediation. Doing so acts as a signal to the service provider and user to focus on each other instead of you.

Practice the steps

Practice the steps

Start with easy mediation: clarification

When you first start to practice the five steps of the Strategic Mediation Model, begin with simple types of mediation. One of the easiest to practice is a form of mediation often referred to as "clarification." A clarification is a request by the interpreter for one of the parties present to clarify a particular term or phrase. Here is an example. For purposes of this example, let us assume that you, the interpreter, do not understand the meaning of "fine needle biopsy."

Doctor: "I think we'll need to do a fine needle biopsy."

Interpreter: (interprets the doctor's statement but keeps "fine needle biopsy" in the source language)
(*to doctor*) Excuse me, as the interpreter could I ask you to clarify "fine needle biopsy?"
(*to patient*) Excuse me, as the interpreter I just asked the doctor to clarify "fine needle biopsy."

Patient (*speaking another language*): Oh, okay.

Interpreter: (*interprets the patient's response.*)

Doctor: Sure, no problem, I'd be happy to explain. It's a medical test where we insert a thin, hollow needle into a lump or mass to take a sampling of cells, typically to check for cancer.

Develop your own scripts for clarification

Each interpreter will have his or her own formula for clarification. Here are a few examples:

- The interpreter needs a clarification of…"
- "As the interpreter could I request a clarification of…"
- "Could the interpreter ask you to clarify…"
- "Excuse me, as the interpreter I need a clarification of…"
- "The interpreter requests you to clarify the meaning of…"

Clarification: an example from educational interpreting

The phrasing does not matter, as long as what you say is professional, clear and to the point. Find the formula that works best for you in each working language and learn it by heart. Here is another example of clarification taken from the U.S. education system.

Assistant Principal: It looks like your child's IAP school is going to be Forest Heights Middle School.

Interpreter: (*interprets the statement but keeps IAP in English*).
(*to the assistant principal*) Excuse me, the interpreter needs to know what "IAP" means.
(*to the parent*) Excuse me, the interpreter just asked the assistant principal to clarify the meaning of "IAP."

Assistant Principal: Oh, sure. Sorry—I meant to explain. IAP stands for Interim Alternative Placement. Because your child was expelled from our school, by law we have to give her an immediate placement in another school. The problem is that we don't have a final school for her yet. So Forest Heights Middle will take her in, at least for now, until we find a permanent school for her. That means that Forest Heights is her IAP—her Interim Alternative Placement school. Is that clearer?

Interpreter: (*interprets this message.*)

It is critical to prepare mental scripts for common mediation scenarios like clarification.

Let's Practice

Learning Activity 3.4 (a): Unscramble the Steps for Mediation
Learning Activity 3.4 (b): Practice the Steps for Strategic Mediation
Learning Activity 3.4 (c): Body Language and Mediation: Video Recording
In *The Community Interpreter®: An International Workbook of Activities and Role Plays*

REVIEW OF SECTION 3.4

When you work as a community interpreter, you have two key responsibilities: interpreting and mediation. Interpreting involves message transfer. Mediation takes place only when a significant barrier to communication or service delivery takes place. Mediation is complex, because it involves human relationships, social complexity and often tension. The Strategic Mediation Model was created to help you perform effective mediation that supports communicative autonomy.

If mediation is necessary, it is helpful to follow the five steps of the Strategic Mediation Model to help you perform brief, safe and effective mediation. The five steps can be used in almost any setting. Following them helps to make intervening easy and structured and gives you a mental map of what to do.

The five steps of the Strategic Mediation Model are:

1. Interpret what was just said or signed.
2. Identify yourself as the interpreter.
3. Mediate briefly.
4. Report your mediation to the other party.
5. Resume interpreting.

Remember that if you perform legal interpreting, when you intervene always:

- Speak to the legal service provider first (in court, typically you would address the judicial authority: the judge or bench).
- Refer to yourself as "the interpreter" (e.g., "The interpreter requests the defendant to speak more loudly.").

For mental health interpreting, also address the provider first when you intervene.

3.5 Cultural Competence and Strategic Mediation

Overview

If strategic mediation is a complex skill, perhaps the most challenging form it takes is cultural mediation. Questions that surround the controversy of cultural mediation include:

1. Whether or not the community interpreter is a "cultural expert."
2. If community interpreters can or should perform cultural mediation.
3. How community interpreters can safely address cultural misunderstandings.
4. What to call cultural mediation: other terms, for example, that appear to refer to the same activity include culture brokering, cultural interpreting and cultural clarification.

Cultural mediation is practiced in various countries in different ways and also differs widely within each country.

This section explores practical strategies to perform effective cultural mediation. However, each interpreter must first find out what his or her national ethics and standards for community interpreters require or permit regarding cultural mediation.

Learning Objective 3.5

After completing this section, you will be able to:

- Define cultural competence and demonstrate three strategies for performing strategic cultural mediation.

Why we must be a faithful voice

Inform Yourself About Cultural Mediation

Inform yourself. Cultural mediation is one of the most important concerns in community interpreting. You cannot be a professional community interpreter without thinking deeply about issues of intercultural communication, cultural responsiveness and cultural mediation, because you will need to make conscious, informed decisions about how to address these issues.

Culture and cultural competence

Defining culture

Culture is complex. Anthropologists, the professional experts about this topic, have developed hundreds of definitions for culture. If they cannot agree on a single definition, this lack of consensus shows something about the complexity of culture. But what is culture?

Definitions of culture

What is culture?

Here are just a few definitions of culture, to give you a sense what some western researchers and writers in the field think about it. In their view, culture is:

- *The ways of a people.* —Robert Lado
- *Integrated system of learned behavior patterns which are characteristic of the members of a society and which are not a result of biological inheritance.* —E. Adamson Hoebel
- *The ideas and the standards [we] have in common.* —Ruth Benedict
- *The whole complex of traditional behavior which has been developed by the human race and is successively learned by each generation.* —Margaret Mead
- *The shared patterns of behaviors and interactions, cognitive constructs, and affective understanding that are learned through a process of socialization.* —University of Minnesota Center for Advanced Research on Language Acquisition

What is cultural competence?

The responsibility for addressing cultural misunderstandings does not fall on your shoulders alone. A recent field of study, research, education and practice in healthcare and human services called "cultural competence," although it can have other names, has emerged. It suggests service providers and institution, not you alone, are responsible for addressing cultural differences in the provision of community services.

The field of cultural competence is most highly developed in the United States, Canada and Europe but is developing in many nations around the world. "Cultural competence" refers to the knowledge, skills, abilities, attitudes and understanding needed to provide effective services across cultural differences. The goal of cultural competence is to support equal access to quality services that promote positive outcomes.

Definitions of cultural competence

Like culture itself, cultural competence has many definitions. Here are examples from the United States.

> A set of attitudes, skills, behaviors, and policies that enable organizations and staff to work effectively in cross-cultural situations.
>
> —Cross, Bazron, Dennis, & Isaacs (1989)

The ability by health care providers and health care organizations to understand and respond effectively to the cultural and linguistic needs brought by patients to the health care encounter.

—U.S. Department of Health and Human Services
Office of Minority Health[35]

Cultural competence refers to a set of academic and interpersonal skills that allow individuals to increase their understanding and appreciation of cultural differences and similarities within, among, and between groups. This requires a willingness and ability to draw on community-based values, traditions, and customs and to work with knowledgeable persons of and from the community in developing targeted interventions, communications, and other supports.

—U.S. Substance Abuse and Mental Health Services Administration[36]

The knowledge and interpersonal skills that allow providers to understand, appreciate, and work with individuals from cultures other than their own. It involves an awareness and acceptance of cultural differences; self-awareness; knowledge of the patient's culture; and adaptation of skills.

—American Medical Association
Delivering Culturally Effective Care to Adolescents[37]

The ability of individuals and systems to respond respectfully and effectively to people of all cultures, classes, races, ethnic backgrounds, sexual orientations and faiths or religions in a manner that recognizes, affirms, and values the worth of individuals, families, tribes, and communities, and protects and preserves the dignity of each.

—Child Welfare League of America[38]

Disparities in access, disparities in outcomes

In the United States, scores if not hundreds of studies demonstrate that limited proficiency in English limits meaningful access to healthcare and mental health services (e.g., Graham, Jacobs, Kwan-Gett, & Cover, 2007; Sentell, Shumway, & Snowden, 2007; Dang et al., 2010). The common well-documented use of family members, friends and helpful bystanders to interpret simply adds to the problem. These disparities persist in the United States—the wealthiest country in the world—despite federal, state and local laws intended to ensure equal access to publicly funded services.

Comparable research in a growing number of countries around the world shows not only disparities in health outcomes and access to healthcare but also in access to education and human services. Whether in Canada (Gulati et al., 2012), Israel (Seidelman & Bachner, 2010), Australia (Butow et al., 2011, Butow et al., 2012) or Ireland (MacFarlane et al., 2009), the discussions and research on minority language patients sound eerily familiar. The countries are different. The social contexts are distinct. Yet the impact of language barriers on health and welfare is often the same.

[35] http://minorityhealth.hhs.gov/assets/pdf/checked/finalreport.pdf
[36] https://www.ctclearinghouse.org/topics/topic.asp?TopicID=28
[37] http://www.healthequityks.org/cultural_competency.html
[38] http://66.227.70.18/programs/culturalcompetence/culturalabout.htm

Who is responsible for cultural competence?

A common practice: leave cultural problems to the interpreter

Interpreters, themselves, often want to fix cultural problems. Here are a few examples of things that community interpreters really do that are not appropriate:

- Explain to a patient how the healthcare system works.
- Tell a parent why his son can't stay home from school to work for the family business.
- Advise an employee, who is about to lose his job, how to speak to the boss.
- Make dietary recommendations: for example, if the patient complains to the interpreter about the foods that don't taste good in her diabetic dietary recommendations, the interpreter might make suggestions about which "traditional" foods to substitute.

Often, the interpreters won't report what a service provider tells a service user, or they will soften or change the message, or even cover up a fatal diagnosis. The very title of one UK research paper is revealing: " 'You have to cover up the words of the doctor': the mediation of trust in interpreted consultations in primary care" (Robb & Greenhalgh, 2006).

Is managing cultural differences part of your job?

If you are a community interpreter, you already know that service users and providers often expect you to "take care" of cultural problems in the encounter. But should you? In general, culture competence experts say no, you should not. But you may be able to help the parties *identify* those misunderstandings. Cultural competence is a collective responsibility. Management, frontline staff, service providers, support staff and interpreters all share that responsibility, but interpreters are in a more delicate position because typically the interpreter either comes from the same culture as the service user or is more familiar with it than service providers and other staff.

As the interpreter, try to remind yourself that the *service provider is in charge of the encounter,* and he or she is responsible for providing culturally responsive services. That said, you will likely have to watch for cultural differences and help everyone to address them. Cultural competence only works well if everyone in community services works together to provide services effectively across cultures.

"Deep culture"

Culture as an iceberg

Culture is often compared to an iceberg. Icebergs, like culture, are only partly visible. What lies beneath the surface is often much greater—and more significant—than what is seen above. Those elements of culture that are visible when a service user arrives are the elements that are obvious, like dress, body language, religious ornaments or apparel, language and visible behavior. Elements of culture, such as values, beliefs, worldviews, life experience, spiritual views and more are largely invisible. Yet these "invisible" aspects of culture often have the greatest impact on the interpreted session.

Culture: the garden

Icebergs are cold and appear static. Perhaps culture is more like a garden. The word *culture* itself comes from a French word, *cultiver,* which means to cultivate or grow, and the Latin word *cultura*, refers to growing, tilling or cultivating. (Think of the words agriculture and horticulture, which include "culture.")

Culture, like a garden, is alive. It grows, changes and evolves. It is not static. Cultures, like gardens, are complex, beautiful and rich. Both gardens and cultures can nourish us spiritually: they give us joy and peace. On the other hand, both may include elements we do not always appreciate, such as bees and worms in gardens, or certain cultural beliefs and practices.

Cultures, like gardens, offer astonishing variety. They may appear exotic or familiar and require dedicated cultivation to remain healthy. What lies below the ground is the "deep culture" that we do not see, and we must nourish and protect deep culture. If we do not treasure our national parks and gardens, many of them wither. So too with cultures: many languages and cultures are disappearing from the planet. About half the world's roughly 7,000 languages may disappear by the year 2100—and with them, many cultures will vanish too.[39]

No culture is monolithic: we are many and one

In short, the complexity of culture means that none of us is culturally static or monolithic. The author of this chapter went from Canada to Egypt at the age of 28 to study Arabic. One of the first things she discovered was that she felt she had more culturally in common with educated middle-class Muslim Egyptians than she did with many Canadians she knew. The author has lived in eight countries, traveled through others and has resided in the United States for more years than she did in Canada. In many ways, she now feels more "American" than Canadian. Her cultures include (among others):

- Islamic, Christian and Quaker religious and spiritual cultures.
- The culture of motherhood/parenthood.
- U.S. middle-class professional cultures.
- The cultures of her British father (born in India) and Scottish mother.
- Grassroots nonprofit cultures.
- The cultures of interpreting, professional writing, training and education.
- The professional culture of U.S. small-business owners.
- The cultures of classical music and world literature.

Not one of these cultures defines her. All of them have shaped her life and worldviews. What the author is not, and has never been, is a cultural expert on anyone that she ever interpreted for. This would be true even if she had interpreted for Canadians. In fact, as a French interpreter in the United States she has interpreted primarily for Africans and Haitians. She has never lived sub-Saharan Africa or Haiti.

[39] For an interactive map showing the "language hotspots" with many languages near extinction, see the National Geographic "Enduring Voices" project at http://travel.nationalgeographic.com/travel/enduring-voices/

The Interpreter as "Cultural Expert"

By the Author of This Chapter

Many years ago, I took a famous 40-hour medical interpreter training in the United States so that I could attend its training-of-trainers program. By then, I was already not only an interpreter but an interpreter trainer. A few people in this class were past students of mine from shorter programs. The trainer for this program also knew me. She knew I was a trainer too.

On the third day, we were told that we had to be cultural experts on our service users. I was astonished. I hardly considered myself an expert on the sophisticated, complex cultures and sub-cultures of French-speaking service users. I raised my hand and asked the trainer what I, a white Canadian, could do about this dilemma. "I don't think I will ever be a cultural expert on French-speaking Africans or Haitians," I said. "So what should I do?"

The trainer looked me coldly in the eye. In a clear voice she said, *"Don't interpret."* I learned in that moment that I shouldn't interpret because I was not a "cultural expert." Yet as a cultural competence trainer, I knew that this viewpoint was culturally inappropriate, so I continued to interpret.

Arguments for and against cultural mediation

Why you should not "fix" a cultural misunderstanding

For decades, in Canada, researchers and interpreters noted the confusion caused by role conflicts and expectations for the community interpreter. In Kaufert and Koolage (1984, p. 283), "sources of role conflict were found to be associated with cross-pressures in their roles as language interpreters, culture-brokers and patient advocates." Observations such as these culminated in the 2007 publication of Canada's national standards for community interpreting services that explicitly prohibit community interpreters from performing culture brokering or advocacy (HIN, 2007).

As we discussed earlier, the problems that you might cause when you try to explain or fix a cultural misunderstanding include the following. You might:

- Be wrong.
- Take away the service user's voice.
- Undermine the service provider's responsibility and role.
- Cause practical problems (e.g., side conversations, offending someone, poor service outcomes, etc.).

Why you should address a cultural misunderstanding

> *En milieu social, les deux partenaires en présence ne sont pas généralement sur un pied d'égalité. D'un côté, un professionnel (fonctionnaire, médecin, assistant social...) qui détient l'information, le savoir, l'autorité, le pouvoir, et de l'autre, une personne en situation de demande qui, non seulement ne maîtrise pas la langue ou les particularités du pays, mais, qui plus est, peut se trouver fragilisée par la maladie, l'absence de statut, le manque de ressources.* (Sauvêtre, 2002, p. 51)[40]

If you, as the interpreter, simply ignore a serious cultural misunderstanding that leads to confused communication and misunderstandings, you are failing to facilitate direct communication. Community interpreters are quite sensitive to these dilemmas. As a result, many interpreters who were trained *not* to perform cultural mediation go ahead and do so anyway—and then feel guilty about it. The goal is honorable, yet the results can be problematic. Performing cultural mediation intrusively, without helpful training, may do more harm than good.

However, if you do not address the cultural misunderstanding at all, that decision could also cause lead to problems. For example:

- The outcome could be poor.
- The end users might feel frustrated.
- The service provider might see the same problem come up again, or often, and still have no idea how to address it.
- If the outcome is poor, you might feel guilty or unhappy.

The three strategies

The need for cultural mediation strategies

The expectation that the community interpreter is there to solve all cultural problems is a heavy one. It is also impossible. Please remove this burden from your shoulders.

If you sense a cultural misunderstanding, breathe deeply and remember these next three strategies. Practice them in this order if, and *only if,* the possible consequences of not performing cultural mediation justify the risks. (See Section 3.1 and 3.2 to help you make that decision.)

Here are the three strategies:

- Decline to act as a cultural expert.
- Identify the cultural misunderstanding.
- Mediate to describe that misunderstanding—*do not explain it.*

Remember the five steps

When you mediate, make sure to follow all five steps of the Strategic Mediation Model. However, you will want to have a special type of mediation script for cultural mediation.

[40] In community settings, the two parties present are not usually on an equal footing. On the one hand [we have] a professional (be it a civil servant, doctor or social worker) who has information, knowledge, authority, power, and on the other, a person in need who not only does not master the language or the distinctive features of the country but is also vulnerable due to sickness, lack of status, [and] lack of resources. (An informal translation by the author of this chapter.)

Strategy 1. Decline to act as a cultural expert.

Outside the session

Usually, by "declining" to act as a cultural expert, we mean that you will do so in your own mind. You will only need to declare you are not a cultural expert out loud if someone asks you for cultural explanations or opinions.

If you are asked to explain a cultural question *outside* the session, you can always use the SAY-NO model from Chapter 1 and say (for example): "That's a wonderful question. I'd be glad to interpret it for the service user at the next appointment, or interpret it for you by phone. I'm afraid I don't know the answer to your question, and I'm not qualified as a cultural expert. I'm also not permitted on ethical grounds to act as a cultural specialist."

During the session

If you are asked for cultural explanations *during* the encounter, you can of course simply interpret the question, let the other party respond and hope that doing so prevents any need to declare you are not a cultural expert. If the problem persists, you may have to make clear, even during the session, why you cannot act as a cultural expert.

Resist the temptation to act as an expert

The question is, if you feel sure you *know* the issue that is causing the misunderstanding, wouldn't it be faster and more efficient if you explain it yourself? Yet consider this: culture is complex. It is always changing and alive. As we saw earlier, no person is part of just one culture, and therefore no one, including you, can be a cultural expert on the service user. The person you interpret for is culturally unique—as we all are.

Thus, *the only cultural expert on the service user is the service user. The only cultural expert on the service provider is the service provider.*

Interpreters who explain cultural issues are therefore exposing service users to adverse outcomes and themselves to legal liability, because their assumptions may be wrong.

A Tragic Outcome

A 15-year-old girl from a Latin American country was raped and brutally beaten by her domestic partner many times. The case went to court, but the certified interpreter provided cultural "information" to the defense stating that it was typical for Latin American males to beat the women they lived with. That information was taken to the prosecutor, who found the "certified" interpreter credible by virtue of his certification. The charges were reduced to domestic violence and led to probation for the accused.

—Framer et al., 2010, p. 60

Strategy 2. Identify the cultural misunderstanding.

Examples of misunderstandings

We often assume that culture is the service user's "problem." In fact, cultural misunderstandings in community interpreting often stem from the culture(s) of the service provider, the service system, or the regional or national culture in which the service is embedded. Here are a few examples.

General examples

- In many countries, the idea of questioning authority or even asking service providers questions may feel culturally uncomfortable or simply new for service users. As a result, the service provider may assume that the service user *understands* the service because no questions are asked when, in fact, it is clear to the interpreter that the service user is confused.
- In other countries, service providers may see themselves as the decision makers. They may not welcome or expect a service user's questions, and the interpreter may sense the service user's frustration and feel caught in the middle.

Health care

- Western biomedical culture may appear culturally odd (and even bizarre) to many patients.
- Patient autonomy may be a foreign concept to many.
- The idea that only the patient should receive his or her medical information (especially for end-of-life diagnoses and treatment) rather than the patient's family may be culturally upsetting.
- Questions from healthcare providers about a patient's past sexual partners or activities may appear culturally shocking and offensive.
- Some service users may never have heard of dental services.

Social services

- The concept that certain types of social service benefits or programs (such as unemployment insurance or preventive health screenings) are a legal obligation, a legal right or a free benefit may be new to many service users.
- The concept of confidentiality in government-funded services might seem dubious to service users from certain countries.

Legal services

- Legal systems differ from country to country and are often culturally confusing.
- Many countries have complex layers or tiers of judicial systems, each with their own professional cultures.
- Indigenous individuals may have local clans, villages or tribal legal systems that differ from more formal legal systems in urban centers of the same countries or in other countries.
- Legal terms and concepts may have no equivalents in other countries due to differing legal systems and culturally non-equivalent legal concepts.

Causes of misunderstandings

When you are trying to understand the cultural misunderstanding that is taking place, ask yourself:

- Why don't the parties understand each other?
- Which particular issue might be causing the misunderstanding right now?
- How does each person in the interaction view the issue?
- Could this misunderstanding and what is causing it affect the outcome of the service?

Identifying the causes

For any specific situation that you are trying to understand, identify the most concrete concepts and ideas that may be causing the misunderstanding (as opposed to generally different worldviews), for example, the case of a Muslim patient being prescribed a medication:

- The doctor tells the patient to take the antibiotic being prescribed on a full stomach four times a day and clearly assumes that the patient will follow these instructions.
- As a Muslim interpreter (let us assume), you are aware that this patient, based on her dress and behavior, might not take medication in daylight hours during the lunar month of Ramadan but she hasn't said so.
- You are aware that if the patient does *not* take this antibiotic on the prescribed schedule, her infection may not be completely treated.
- The cause of the misunderstanding appears to be the doctor's lack of knowledge about the patient's religious-cultural fasting practices.

This is an example of how focusing on a specific, concrete concern related to a matter of religious culture, rather than general cultural issues, can help you. This approach is much more helpful then telling yourself, "The patient and the doctor don't understand each other, because she is not very educated and he is not very culturally sensitive," or, "This doctor has a bias against Muslims." The more specific you can be in your own mind about the *cause* of the misunderstanding, the easier you will find it to perform effective cultural medication. Also, remember to focus on consequences. If the medication schedule isn't that important ("Take one pill twice a day"), it really doesn't matter if the doctor understands the fasting practices or not.

Strategy 3. Mediate to describe that misunderstanding—do not explain it.

How to "describe" without explaining

When you face a cultural misunderstanding, the temptation will be for you, the community interpreter, to explain it. *Avoid that temptation.* First, if you give a cultural explanation, you may be wrong. Second, you are "training" the parties to look at you as the cultural expert. Third, the service provider needs to exercise his or her responsibility to engage in the cultural dialogue.

Let's look at the example above. Imagine that you're a Muslim interpreter from the patient's country. You say, "I don't think this patient will take the medication on the schedule you said, because it's the Muslim fasting month of Ramadan and she isn't supposed to eat or drink between dawn and dusk." The doctor assumes that what you say is true.

But perhaps this patient is aware that common Islamic traditions allow her to break her fast during Ramadan when she is sick or during travel: so, in fact, she was planning to take the medication just as the doctor prescribed. How do you know what she will do? Just because you come from a country where many or most people prefer to avoid taking medicine during the daylight hours of Ramadan does not make you a cultural expert for that whole country or for every patient from that country (far less for all patients from all Muslim countries). You face similar risks if you say things like:

- In her country, they don't know what a school progress report is.
- He didn't mean to alarm you, officer—in our country, when you see a police officer you just throw your hands up that way–it's a cultural thing, not a threat.
- They don't have retirement plans where she comes from. It's not something they even understand.
- Almost every woman in that country uses abortion as birth control. She's probably had several abortions.

Risks of explaining culture

In addition, if you start to *explain* a cultural misunderstanding you may:

- Take up valuable time.
- Get into a side conversation.
- Trigger a delicate situation.
- Offend someone.
- Make mistakes that result in a poor outcome for the service.
- Plant stereotypes in the provider's mind (e.g., "Hispanics aren't very educated." "Russian women have had abortions.")
- Create new misunderstandings.

Identifying the basis of the misunderstanding

Instead of explaining a cultural misunderstanding, describe the *basis* for that misunderstanding (as you see it) in a brief, clear way. In other words, develop cultural mediation scripts, like the ones you developed in Section 3.3. For example, you could tell the doctor:

- Excuse me, as the interpreter I sense a possible misunderstanding about when to take medication during the fasting month of Ramadan.
- The interpreter would like to point out that a current fasting period may affect a patient's decisions about when to take the medication.
- The interpreter suggests asking the patient if Ramadan will affect her taking the medication on the prescribed schedule.

Then, of course, for transparency, report to the patient exactly what you told the doctor.

Alerting the service provider

The goal of cultural mediation in this example is to alert the doctor to a possible misunderstanding. Now the doctor knows what questions to ask the patient. The doctor can make sure the patient either takes the medication as prescribed or can prescribe a different antibiotic to be taken before dawn and after sunset. The patient—not you—will answer the doctor's questions. Then the doctor will know exactly what to do.

If *you* explain the cultural issue yourself, you are closing a door to understanding. The provider thinks, "Oh, okay, now I see what's going on," and may make decisions without checking with the service user to see if your information is correct. Instead of closing the door to cultural dialogue, try to open it.

Using cultural skills in mediation

The interpreter as cultural treasure

Try to think of the community interpreter not as a cultural expert but as a *cultural treasure*. You are a "gem" because, more than anyone in the room, you have developed sensitivity to cultural issues and misunderstandings. If there is a cultural barrier present, almost no one detects it better than a community interpreter. Interpreters often learn to trust their "gut feelings" about the presence of cultural barriers.

In fact, a growing body of research shows that our intuitions are based on sensory impressions and other information that we are process at an unconscious level. Such research is sometimes addressed in discussions about expert practice in medicine (e.g., Lyneham, Parkinson, & Denholm, 2008).

Respect for all

There are many different aspects of culture to consider while interpreting, as we've just discussed. In addition, remember to:

- Respect the knowledge of all parties present.
- Resist seeing the service user in "deficit" terms (what the service user *lacks*, in every sense) and the provider in "asset" terms (what the service provider *has*).
- Remember that no one culture is "better" than another, though we often tend to prefer cultures similar to our own.
- Treat the service user with exactly the same deference and courtesy that you show the service provider.
- *Do not explain any aspect of culture, if the service user or provider can explain it.*

The right to self-determination and autonomy

➡ Instead of influencing a service user or provider's decision, use your cultural knowledge to enhance *clear communication.*

➡ Let mediation be a tool to promote communicative autonomy, not service-user dependency.

➡ Help mediation support *direct communication* without influencing the decisions of the parties present.

Let's Practice

Learning Activity 3.5 (a): Introduction to Cultural Mediation: A Role Play
Learning Activity 3.5 (b): Defining Culture
Learning Activity 3.5 (c): Defining Cultural Competence

In The Community Interpreter®: An International Workbook of Activities and Role Plays

REVIEW OF SECTION 3.5

The key lesson of this objective is that responsibility for engaging in direct communication across cultures rests with the service user and provider. Your task when you face a cultural misunderstanding during the session is to help facilitate direct communication across cultural and social differences. To do so, you will need to:

- Understand what cultural competence is.
- Monitor the situation.
- Examine your own bias.
- Be alert to the complexity of culture.
- Avoid explaining or discussing cultural issues with any party.
- Use your cultural knowledge to open a cultural dialogue between the service user and provider that can bridge the misunderstanding.

To help you remove the burden from your shoulders of being seen as a "cultural expert," here are three strategies discussed in this objective; practice all of them in the order given.

1. Decline to act as a cultural expert.
2. Identify the cultural misunderstanding.
3. Mediate to describe that misunderstanding—*do not explain it.*

3.6 Culturally Responsive Mediation

Overview

In community interpreting, there is no practical way to avoid cultural differences and misunderstandings. Because you are often expected to address and solve them, you will need to know how to perform cultural mediation in ways that are strategic, effective—and not intrusive.

This section builds on the previous one. It helps you explore further practical techniques to perform culturally responsive *non-intrusive* mediation. In other words, you will address culture without explaining it or taking on roles that are inappropriate. (See Section 3.5 for the reasons not to explain or discuss cultural issues when you perform cultural mediation.)

Learning Objective 3.6

After completing this section, you will be able to:

- Develop techniques to perform effective, culturally responsive mediation.

Non-intrusive cultural mediation

The goal of cultural mediation

The goal of cultural mediation

The goal of cultural mediation is simple. Instead of intervening to explain a cultural difference, help service users and providers communicate their cultural differences to each other. For example, let's say that an interpreter for an indigenous language of Mexico is asked to interpret for a hospital social worker who wants to bring in a chaplain for a patient who is dying. For cultural reasons, the interpreter is certain the patient would not want a chaplain present. However, the patient is not voicing that belief or informing the social worker about it. What is the best way for the interpreter to handle a situation like this? Let's examine a technique that may be helpful: non-intrusive mediation.

Non-intrusive mediation

The Strategic Mediation Model, as defined and explored in this chapter, helps you to be non-intrusive. Non-intrusive mediation means that you do not get in the way of communicative autonomy: you enhance it. You support clear, direct communication.

The way to engage in mediation without being intrusive is to alert all parties to the misunderstanding without giving advice or opinions regarding what to do about that misunderstanding—and then get back to interpreting. In the previous section, we gave you three general strategies that should help you perform non-intrusive mediation. In this section, we will go into deeper detail.

Non-intrusive mediation is an important technique for mediation in general. It is a fundamental concept in the creation of the Strategic Mediation Model. However, it is particularly important to practice non-intrusive mediation when you address a cultural misunderstanding.

An example of non-intrusive mediation

Going back to the example of the indigenous interpreter, instead of intervening to inform the hospital social worker that the hospital should *not* send in the chaplain, the interpreter could say something like this: "Excuse me, the interpreter is concerned there may be a cultural misunderstanding about whether a chaplain would be welcome." If this information isn't quite clear enough, you might even add, "You may wish to ask the patient if she is happy to see a chaplain." The interpreter would then report this mediation to the patient. At that point, the social worker would probably ask the patient if she wants the chaplain to come, opening up a discussion between the social worker and the patient.

Fostering direct communication across cultures

Enabling direct communication about cultural concerns between service user and provider is the aim of cultural mediation. Ideally, the interpreter will facilitate and foster direct cultural communication between them. To do so, it is critical for the interpreter to intervene as *rarely* as possible and as *briefly* as possible while still addressing any important cultural barriers to communication.

How to perform non-intrusive cultural mediation

Techniques for performing non-intrusive cultural mediation

It is easy to say "the community interpreter should *point out* a cultural concern and not *explain* it." But how can you make that happen? In addition to the three strategies outlined in the previous section, here are four techniques to practice when you perform non-intrusive cultural mediation:

1. If a serious cultural barrier emerges, follow the five steps of the Strategic Mediation Model.
2. When you mediate, identify the cultural misunderstanding for all parties *briefly and clearly.*
3. Do not speak about what the service user or provider believes or thinks.
4. Avoid overgeneralizations or cultural stereotypes.

Technique 1. If a serious cultural barrier emerges, follow the five steps of the Strategic Mediation Model.

For cultural mediation—or any other kind—first monitor the situation for understanding as you always do when you interpret. Then, if you sense possible cultural gaps of understanding, send up your "cultural antennae" to be alert and prepare yourself for a possible cultural mediation. (You may wish to go back and review the CHIA ethical decision-making guidelines discussed in Section 3. 2. These guidelines are particularly helpful for the delicate decisions that arise related to cultural misunderstandings.)

If and when a serious cultural misunderstanding arises, it is important to remember the five steps of the Strategic Mediation Model, because the cultural issues will distract you. Cultural issues are often so complex that you are likely to forget one or more of the five steps. Do you remember all five? Can you repeat them? Learn them now—before you practice cultural mediation. To review, the five steps of the Strategic Mediation Model are:

1. Interpret what was just said or signed.
2. Identify yourself as the interpreter.
3. Mediate briefly.
4. Report your mediation to the other party.
5. Resume interpreting.

Technique 2. When you mediate, identify the cultural misunderstanding for all parties briefly and clearly.

The challenge with Technique 2

Identifying for the service user and provider what the cultural barrier is should really just be a part of the Strategic Mediation Model. However, for cultural mediation, we break it out as a special technique because cultural issues are complex. As a result, most community interpreters tend to make their cultural mediations too long, which often leads to side conversations and other problems.

The goal is to give just enough information to let the service user and provider explore it. For example, avoid telling an investigator or lawyer, "The client doesn't understand that child abuse is illegal in this country, because he grew up in a rural village with a completely different legal system, so you need to explain what child abuse means." Instead, say something like: "The interpreter senses a misunderstanding about the legal definition of child abuse."

If necessary, it may be permissible to add something like, "You may wish to explain the difference between spanking and child abuse so that I can interpret the difference more clearly." (However, always consult with the legal interpreting experts of your country to see if this approach is permissible.)

Thinking it through

Here is an example of non-intrusive cultural mediation. It takes place in a public library.

Librarian. Here's your new library card. You're good to go. Any questions?

Interpreter: (*interprets*)

Library Patron: No, thank you.

Interpreter: (*Interprets and turns to the librarian*) Excuse me, as the interpreter I'm afraid the information about library fines may not be clear, especially fines for overdue DVDs. (*Reports this mediation to the library patron.*)

Librarian: Oh, that's actually important, thanks. So let me review how overdue fines work for our media section… (*Interpreter interprets.*)

Note how this interpreter handled the situation:

- She knew the library system had confused many of the service users that she had interpreted for.
- She was aware that many immigrants ran up large library fines for late returns of DVDs due to a lack of understanding of the cost, and that sometimes those bills went to debt-collection agencies.
- Certain bills had even damaged the credit rating of some service users (making it harder for them to rent an apartment or buy a car, for example).
- When the librarian asked, "Do you have any questions?" and the father answered no, the interpreter knew that the father, for cultural reasons, was probably being polite and showing respect, but his answer did not mean he had understood the librarian.
- The interpreter also knew from this conversation that the family had little money.
- She did not say, "This library patron doesn't understand" (which would have been condescending and perhaps offensive). Instead she reported the potential misunderstanding in a way that was unlikely to offend anyone.

Technique 3. Do not speak about what the service user or provider believes or thinks.

You are not a mind reader. Speak in *general* terms. Avoid saying "he" or "she" when describing a cultural misunderstanding: do not speak for or about the service user (or provider). Here is valuable guidance on this topic: in 1995, the Massachusetts Medical Interpreters Association (MMIA, now the International Medical Interpreters Association, IMIA) published a seminal document called *Medical Interpreting Standards of Practice* (MMIA/IMIA, 1995) available at www.imiaweb.org, that includes the following information about cultural assumptions:

> Interpreters, therefore, have the task of identifying those occasions when unshared cultural *assumptions create barriers to understanding or message equivalence. Their role in such situations is not to "give the answer" but rather to help both provider and patient to investigate the intercultural interface that may be creating the communication problem.*
>
> *Interpreters must keep in mind that no matter how much "factual" information they have about the beliefs, values, norms, and customs of a particular culture, they have no way of knowing where the individual facing them in that specific situation stands along a continuum from close adherence to the norms of a culture to acculturation into a new culture.* (MMIA/IMIA, 1995, pp. 15-16)

Technique 4. Avoid overgeneralizations or cultural stereotypes.

Coming back to bias

And now we have come full circle. At the beginning of this chapter, we talked about the need to identify our internal biases so that our biases would not have a negative impact on the interpreted session. Now we return to that topic because when interpreters perform cultural mediation, it is tempting for them to make statements like these:

1. *She won't make a big decision like this without her husband present.* (How do we know that's true? This particular service user may have quite a different opinion.)
2. *The dad doesn't understand you, because in his country, kids don't have reading disability programs.* (But perhaps they do: if you left that country 10 years ago, things might have changed.)
3. *Where she's from, they don't know anything about social workers.* (Really? Not a single person in the service user's country has ever heard about social workers? Unlikely...)
4. *They don't have words in her language for concepts like advance parole.* (Perhaps they do.)
5. *The women over there don't believe in birth control.* (Perhaps many women there do not like birth control, but perhaps a growing number do.)

Make conscious decisions

There are many ways to get around this type of problem, but the first one is to make a conscious decision to avoid overgeneralizations when you perform any kind of mediation. In others words, avoid discussing a cultural issue. Instead, focus on the *basis for the misunderstanding*. Going back to the examples above, you could try approaches to cultural mediation like these ones:

1. *You may want to explore whether members of her family expect medical information to be shared with them.* (If the patient wants to discuss the issue with her husband before making a decision, she may be willing to say so.)
2. *The interpreter senses a possible misunderstanding about what a program for a reading disability is.* (The teacher or reading specialist can then explain these programs.)
3. *The interpreter is concerned there may be a misunderstanding about what social workers do.* (Let the social worker clarify his or her job and what s/he's there for.)
4. *The interpreter is unaware of a linguistic or cultural equivalent for "advance parole."* (Perhaps an equivalent exists and you just don't know it. Either way, the immigration representative can now explain this term.)
5. *The interpreter suggests inquiring about common ways that women in her country avoid having more babies.* (By mediating in this way, and using this language, a door is opened for the healthcare provider to find out what this particular patient thinks or feels about birth control.)

Bias, stereotypes and discrimination

Ingroup vs. outgroup

Now that you have an overview of the techniques for cultural mediation, it's important to step back and look at the larger picture again. Why is it important to follow the Strategic Mediation Model and the techniques recommended in this chapter for cultural mediation? They are not universally practiced: in fact, they are innovative.

The first and most important reason for adopting the approach in this chapter to cultural mediation is that otherwise it is often very hard to prevent our personal biases from intruding when we mediate. As you saw in the first section of this chapter, we tend to see people in one of two ways: they appear to belong to our own social group (ingroup) or they do not (outgroup). Those we perceive as being like us, or ingroup, we tend to regard in more positive ways than those we perceive as being different from us, outgroup (Mahajan et al., 2011).

In short, we tend to see the world in terms of "us vs. them." We cannot escape our own perceptions, but there is evidence that we can change them—if we become aware of our internal biases.

Stereotyping and personalization

How to avoid three common errors

As any interpreter trainer who teaches cultural mediation has observed, interpreters make three common errors when they interpret. Often they:

- Speak on behalf of others (when the person can speak for him- or herself)
- Overgeneralize (speak of the person as if most people in that social group are the same)
- Personalize (speak about the person as if the interpreter can read his or her mind or culturally understand this person)

These are three big challenges to avoid when you interpret, in particular when you perform cultural mediation. We will examine them one by one and give you strategies that, instead, will help you to:

- Support communicative autonomy
- See each individual as unique
- Mediate in general, not personal, terms

Support communicative autonomy

Describing what you think is the service user's cultural problem means that you are speaking *on behalf of* that service user. Doing so is not necessarily advocacy (discussed in Chapter 5) but rather intrusive cultural mediation. To support communicative autonomy, you would instead focus on assessing what gets in the way of mutual understanding, so that each person states his or her own cultural beliefs and the parties you interpret for are responsible for addressing those beliefs—not with you but with each other.

This approach may seem simple but it takes practice before it feels natural and second nature. It is much easier to say, "She isn't asking questions because in her country everybody treats lawyers/doctors like God" than to say, "There may be a misunderstanding about who should make the legal decisions: the client or the lawyer."

See each individual as unique

Overgeneralizations are statements that are too broad and do not allow for many exceptions. For example, "In Vietnam, they use coining if someone gets sick." This statement implies that all Vietnamese practice coining (a practice of rubbing oneself or another person with a coin as a health remedy). Conversely, the statement fails to mention that a number of individuals in other parts of Southeast Asia also practice coining as part of traditional Chinese medicine.

How stereotypes work

Stereotyping goes one step beyond overgeneralizing. Most stereotypes fail to allow for exceptions and tend to be negative in their content and their impact. Stereotypes are often crude social simplifications with derogatory content, though not always. For example, to say, "Nobody in China ever says, 'No,' because that's too rude," is inaccurate and a stereotype: it could imply Chinese are afraid to say no. A number of Chinese people can and do say, "No." Sometimes interpreters make broad assumptions, such as, "Oh, you know how those people are," or, "She thinks it's okay if her husband beats her up, that's just her culture." These are examples of stereotypes.

Remember: each service user is a unique individual with a unique history. Avoid making statements about anyone present, and instead focus on what seems to be causing their misunderstanding. This way you will also avoid allowing the service provider to think that everyone from a certain country believes the same things or behaves in the same way—which is never true.

Mediate in general, not personal, terms

Personalizing means you are speaking *about* the service user or provider. For example, you may say, "These parents would never agree to organ harvesting of their child." (*Organ harvesting* refers to removing the organs of a dead person to donate them to a living person.) Yes, it is true that in certain cultures the idea of having a loved one's body mutilated by organ harvesting might be unthinkable or even devastating; however, these particular parents might feel differently.

Try not to make assumptions or speak on behalf of the family, even if a service provider asks you to. For example, a nurse might say, "You're from the same culture—how do you think this family feels about organ harvesting?" To take another example of a service provider who asks many intake questions, some of which appear intrusive, you might want to tell a service user, "The provider asks everyone these questions. She has to. It's not because you're an immigrant [or Deaf, or from a different tribe], it's just a requirement." By speaking in this way, you are taking over the service provider's role. Instead, you could say to both parties, "The interpreter wants to mention that some of these questions might cause offense in certain cultures."

When you mediate in general terms instead of speaking about the service user, you are leaving open the possibility that what you think might be wrong, while allowing the service provider to verify the facts of the situation—by asking the service user, not you.

Culturally non-equivalent concepts

The Little Turd

By the Author of Chapter 2

A Dutch friend of mine was calling her newborn boy something like *mijn pupa doucha.* I didn't understand and, of course, asked what it meant. My friend said it's a very common expression there (in Utrecht, the Netherlands). Literally, it means something like "my little turd."

What a surprise, because he, the baby, was indeed black and all covered with black hair. I still don't know how to put it into Spanish. "*Mi mierdita, mi cagarrutica, mi mojoncito*"?

Culturally untranslatable terms

Let us close this section with a common cultural concern. Some terms or phrases may catch you off guard because there is no exact cultural equivalent in the target language. Often cultural nuances and connotations that make it hard to capture meaning in a brief, clear way. For example, *Ho'oponopono* is a Hawaiian term for which a number of explanations in English exist that are somewhat contradictory, such as: an ancient practice of seeking forgiveness; trying to correct wrongs in one's life; a ceremony to an ancestor; and solving a problem by talking it out. How do you interpret a concept like *ho'oponopono* on the spot? Terms, like these, with cultural underpinnings can come at you with no warning.

If a challenge like this happens to you, you have a few options:

- Give a *brief* paraphrase of the term or phrase (a half-sentence or shorter—avoid giving longer paraphrases, because mediation is preferable to a long paraphrase). Note that not all legal interpreters are permitted to paraphrase: verify whether or not you may do so in legal settings.
- Mediate to state that you are not aware of an equivalent concept in the target language.
- Mediate to request that the party who used the term or phrase to clarify it.

Keep in mind that time is limited. As Chapter 2 showed you, please don't spend much time or mental effort on difficult words or concepts that pop up—even cultural ones. Remember that you are *not interpreting words.* You interpret meaning. If you know the meaning of the term—interpret it. Mediate only if a misunderstanding arises.

Full circle: returning to the cultural dialogue

The questions

Do you remember that doctor-patient dialogue at the very beginning of this chapter? The doctor shook hands with a woman who might have been offended by his action. He also uttered some culturally insensitive remarks. We asked you a few questions about the situation, as you may recall. The questions were as follows.

Would you, the interpreter:

- Tell the nurse and doctor that it might not be culturally or religiously appropriate for the doctor to shake hands with the patient?
- Tell the doctor that he upset the patient by shaking hands with her?
- Interpret the doctor's last remarks? Omit them? Soften them?
- Remind the doctor that you are required to interpret everything (in other words, give the doctor a chance to rephrase his rude remarks)?
- Interpret the remarks and *then* intervene to remind the doctor that you must interpret everything?
- Do something else?

Review both sets of your answers. Do you agree with them now? Would your answers be different after studying this chapter? Write any revisions that you want to include, then read our answers.

Our answers

Would you, the interpreter:

- Tell the nurse and doctor that it might not be culturally or religiously appropriate for the doctor to shake hands with the patient? *No. We recommend you perform strategic and non-intrusive cultural mediation instead. For example, you could say, "Excuse me, the interpreter suggests you verify how the patient feels about shaking hands," and then report your mediation to the patient.*
- Tell the doctor that he upset the patient by shaking hands with her? *No. Remember not to speak about what the service user or provider believes or feels. We are not mind readers!*
- Interpret the doctor's last remarks? Omit them? Soften them? *In general, interpret them—but not everyone agrees with us. Also, if you think that interpreting them would irreparably damage an otherwise good relationship between the service user and provider—then you may wish to alert the service provider that you are obligated to interpret everything and give him or her a chance to rephrase, because this message "is difficult to interpret."Report this mediation to the patient. Remember, though, this is one of the most controversial issues in the field and we ourselves (the five authors of this textbook) are conflicted about it.*
- Remind the doctor that you are required to interpret everything (in other words, give the doctor a chance to rephrase his rude remarks)? *If the relationship with a provider might be broken, we MIGHT give the doctor that reminder. This is a tough call. But remember: the patient might understand what the doctor said and see that you are "covering up" those words—service users often understand much more than they can speak of the service language. Finally, if you are "in the flow" of interpreting, you might render those rude remarks before you even realize how insensitive they are.*

- Interpret the remarks and *then* intervene to remind the doctor that you must interpret everything? *This is certainly considered one "best practice," but in situations like this, some of us will follow our conscience. After all, no one else has to live with our conscience for the rest of our lives except us!*

Your answers

- Would do something else? *We are open to hearing your creative solutions. Email us here: clp@cultureandlanguage.net. We'd love to hear from you!*

Let's Practice

Learning Activity 3.6 (a): Role Play—The Evil Eye
Learning Activity 3.6 (b): What Went Wrong? Cultural Bias and Mediation

In *The Community Interpreter®: An International Workbook of Activities and Role Plays*

REVIEW OF SECTION 3.6

Cultural mediation is a complex, yet rewarding skill. It empowers you to facilitate a deep level of understanding. However, it is also an act that exposes you to the temptation to explain cultural concepts instead of allowing the service user and provider to explain them to each other.

Try to remember that your job is to *identify* (first to yourself and then out loud) the basis for the cultural misunderstanding, instead of offering cultural explanations. To help you perform effective, non-intrusive cultural mediation, try to remember these four techniques:

1. If a serious cultural barrier emerges, follow the five steps of the Strategic Mediation Model.
2. When you mediate, identify the cultural barrier for all parties *briefly and clearly*.
3. Do not speak about what the service user or provider believes or thinks.
4. Avoid overgeneralizations or cultural stereotypes.

Remember that Technique 2 is really just a part of the Strategic Mediation Model. However, cultural issues are complex, and they tend to lead to much longer mediations than is necessary or helpful. Be brief.

As you gain experience and follow the guidelines in this chapter, you may find that you feel calmer and less stressed by cultural misunderstandings. This confidence, in turn, will give you poise and add to your credibility as an interpreter. It will inspire the trust of both service providers and users and enhance your reputation as a professional interpreter.

Most of all, by performing effective cultural mediation you will help the service user and provider to communicate effectively. You will help them work toward a beneficial outcome—even across cultural differences. In doing so, you support communicative autonomy.

CHAPTER 3 SUMMARY

Chapter 3 explored some of the most challenging concepts in all of community interpreting: how to handle communication barriers and cultural misunderstandings. It offered you concrete, practical methods to address them. It also defined *intervention* as the act of interrupting the session and *strategic mediation* as any act or utterance of the interpreter that goes beyond interpreting and is intended to remove a barrier to communication or facilitate a service user's access to the service.

In **Section 3.1, Unconscious Bias,** the chapter began with an exploration of our own implicit biases to clarify that as interpreters we bring our beliefs and values to each encounter, even without our awareness. As a result, intervening during a session imposes risks: what we say and do could have a negative impact on direct communication. This section also offered four steps to help undermine your unconscious (implicit) biases when you interpret or intervene:

- Step 1: Explore your own bias.
- Step 2: Plan ahead.
- Step 3: Monitor the situation. ("When in doubt—stay out.")
- Step 4: Assess potential consequences.

In **Section 3.2, Deciding When to Intervene,** you examined how to make sound decisions about whether or not to mediate, given the risks. You looked at the same four criteria for intervening explored in Chapter 1 when you studied ethics but applied here as four criteria that might trigger a decision about whether or not to mediate, *if the consequences of not mediating seem very serious.* Those four criteria are:

1. Linguistic challenges
2. Role confusion
3. Cultural misunderstandings
4. Service system barriers

Then you revisited the CHIA ethical decision-making guidelines addressed in Chapter 1 to help you decide whether or not to mediate on ethical grounds.

In **Section 3.3, Scripts for Mediation,** you learned how to develop your own basic scripts for mediation that you could tailor to each situation. The guidelines given here include writing about six basic mediation scripts in your own words that cover common misunderstandings and communications barriers, with at least one or two scripts that address each of the four criteria for intervening discussed in Section 3.2. This section recommended keep your basic scripts short and simple so that when you mediate in real life, you can tailor each script to the situation.

You also looked at the importance of transparency in your scripts.

In **Section 3.4, The Strategic Mediation Model,** you examined the five steps for the Strategic Mediation Model, to use whenever you intervene:

1. **Interpret what was just said or signed.**
2. **Identify yourself as the interpreter.**
3. **Mediate briefly.**
4. **Report your mediation to the other party.**
5. **Resume interpreting.**

In **Section 3.5, Cultural Competence and Strategic Mediation,** you addressed the implications of a field called cultural competence for performing cultural mediation. You explored why you should, or shouldn't, perform cultural mediation, and how to perform it effectively. The goal is not to explain culture but, instead, to describe what seems to be causing a cultural misunderstanding to facilitate a dialogue about culture between the service user and provider. This approach to cultural mediation supports direct communication, communicative autonomy and cultural competence in health and human services.

In **Section 3.6, Culturally Responsive Mediation,** you returned to the basic concepts in Section 3.5 and explored them in more depth to show how to use your cultural knowledge to enhance *clear communication* and as a tool to promote communicative autonomy, not service-user dependency without influencing the decisions of the parties. To perform effective, non-intrusive cultural mediation while interpreting:

1. If a serious cultural barrier emerges, follow the five steps of the Strategic Mediation Model.
2. When you mediate, identify the cultural misunderstanding for all parties *briefly and clearly.*
3. *Do not speak about what the service user or provider believes or thinks.*
4. Avoid overgeneralizations or cultural stereotypes.

Some of the underlying issues developed in this chapter are explored in more depth in Chapter 5. Meantime, this chapter provided you with practical guidance. May it serve you well. Success in resolving a communication barrier or cultural misunderstanding brings special rewards and satisfaction for the community interpreter. It may trigger a feeling that many of you know well: "interpreter's high": that is, the feeling of happiness when you walk out of a session knowing that you have made a real difference.

PROFESSIONAL IDENTITY

by Giovanna Carriero-Contreras
with the special contribution of Katharine Allen (Section 4.6)

CHAPTER 4

LEARNING OBJECTIVES

After completing this chapter and its corresponding exercises, the learner will be able to:

OBJECTIVE 4.1	**Professional Identity and the Community Interpreter** Explore professional identity for interpreters as individuals and as representatives of the profession.
OBJECTIVE 4.2	**Professional Practice** Understand the business practices and legal obligations of community interpreters.
OBJECTIVE 4.3	**Legal Interpreting** Explore how community interpreters can perform effective legal interpreting in community settings.
OBJECTIVE 4.4	**Emerging Specializations** Identify and explore common areas of specialization within community interpreting.
OBJECTIVE 4.5	**Preparing Terminology** Develop strategies and techniques to acquire specialized subject matter knowledge and terminology in community interpreting.
OBJECTIVE 4.6	**Remote Interpreting** Discuss the history and challenges of remote interpreting.

Introduction

The purpose of this chapter is to prepare community interpreters for what lies ahead in the field: it explores the daily realities of a community interpreter. Most important, it will frame the concept of professional identity and how you, as a professional interpreter, fit into the larger picture of the interpreting profession.

So far, everything in this textbook has applied to community interpreting in *general*. Chapter 1 gave you an overview of the profession with a special focus on ethics, which are the foundation of any true profession. Chapter 2 showed you the basic skills and protocols you need to master. Chapter 3 explored practical techniques to address communication barriers and cultural misunderstandings.

Chapter 4 will help you clarify how you can successfully navigate various settings and apply what you have learned in the different areas of specialization within community interpreting. It will address the challenges of certain specializations and will guide you on finding possible solutions. Some of these challenges arise among services users and providers who do not know how to work with professional interpreters.

Around the world, community interpreters often work in isolation. Untrained community interpreters may be unaware of, or do not feel part of, a larger interpreting community: a community that in principle should support them and that they in turn should support.

The goal of this chapter is to help community interpreters understand who they are and how they fit into the profession. It will also show how a better understanding of a strong professional identity can improve their decision-making skills and help to strengthen the profession as a whole.

4.1 Professional Identity and the Community Interpreter

Overview

Identity "represents the process by which the person seeks to integrate his (*sic*) various statuses and roles, as well as his diverse experiences, into a coherent image of self" (Epstein, 1978, p. 101). In a nutshell, the process of integration of different aspects of yourself and your experiences forms your **personal identity**. During that process, consciously or unconsciously, you perpetually manage how you are perceived by family, friends and the general public. As a result, creating a sense of identity involves a constant balancing of "who I am," "who I want to be," "who they think I am" and "who they want me to be," where *they* means everyone but *me*.

As we build a personal identity, our own values, beliefs and behaviors are challenged each time we interact with others and *their* personal identities. Perception plays an important role in the interaction. For example, the more you tend to be positive in your interactions with others, the more positively others tend to perceive you, leading to a generally positive tone in your social relations.

When you, as an individual, engage with others not only at a social level, but also in a work-related context, your identity crosses over into a different dimension: a defined public sphere. In this new dimension, the integration process is specific to your professional identity. It relates to how you engage with other professionals as peers; with stakeholders;[41] and with the profession itself. Taken together, all these elements constitute your **professional identity**.

Thus, **professional identity** frames this process of building up a sense of self in a work-related context.

Learning Objective 4.1

After completing this section, you will be able to:

- Explore professional identity for interpreters as individuals and as representatives of the profession.

[41] Stakeholders are any parties who have a vested interest in a human activity.

The journey to professional identity

Who are you?

Who are you as an interpreter? Where do you fit into the social fabric of this young profession of community interpreting?

When other entry-level professionals become lawyers, doctors or teachers, they develop a set of beliefs and attitudes about the profession that they belong to, including how it relates to other professions and to the professional world at large. They develop a deeper understanding of their role. They learn how to conduct themselves and what "professional boundaries" mean. Their understanding of their role helps them to forge their professional identity.

In other words, your professional identity is the result of who you are, what you do, how you do it and why you do it within your *work* environment (in the broadest sense).

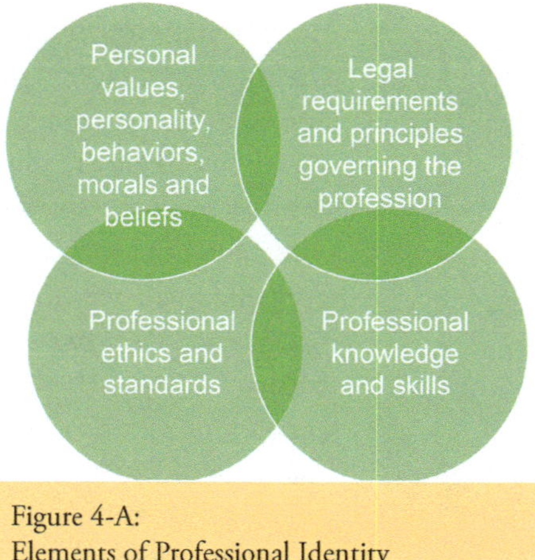

Figure 4-A:
Elements of Professional Identity

Your journey to professional identity

This textbook has helped you to build a foundation for your professional identity as a community interpreter since the first page. Now your journey continues through Chapter 4, where you will gain an awareness of the elements that shape your professional identity from both an individual and a social perspective. As you continue your journey toward a professional identity, you will grow in understanding. Your growth contributes to the professionalization of the field. Community interpreting is in rapid evolution, and interpreters are still struggling for recognition. The more you forge a professional identity, the more you will help the profession grow as well. This journey will come full circle in Chapter 5 when you explore the role of the community interpreter.

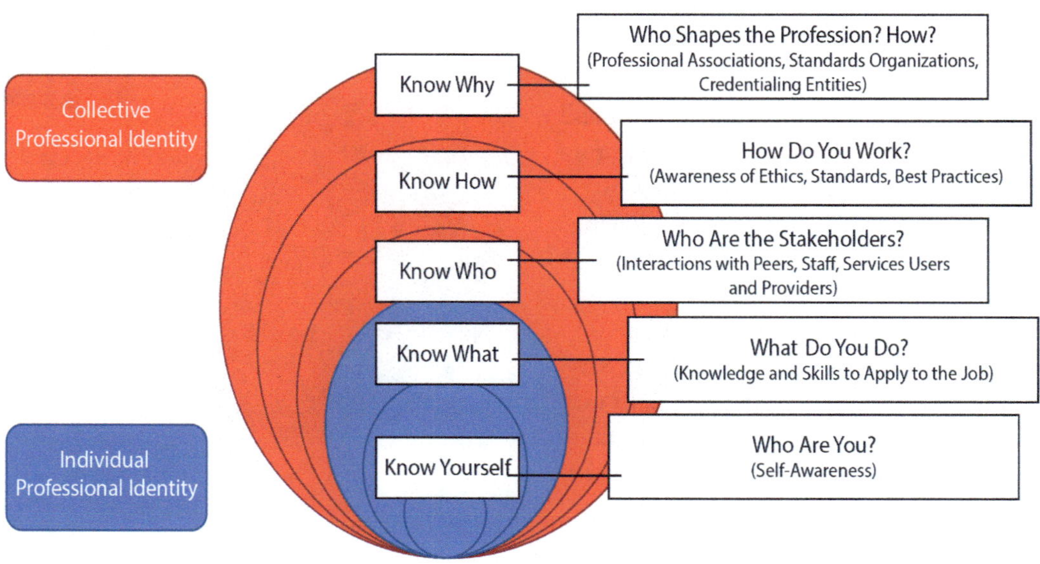

Figure 4-B:
Individual and Collective Professional Identity

Professional identity: the individual perspective

Looking for My Identity

By the Author of This Chapter

"Oh hi, this is Tanya from the New Life Transitional Housing Program. Can you send a Spanish translator right away? We have no clue what this person is telling us. Maybe you can help us over the phone?"

This has been the story of my life. I have often been called the *translator*. And I always felt compelled to correct that by saying "*You mean interpreter? I am your interpreter*!" For some reason, I always felt that others were defining who I was before I could even explain my role.

I have spent most of my professional life educating others about who I am and what I do. I have spent most of my professional life building my professional identity and projecting my professional self to others before others define me. Today, after years of dedicated work, I feel I can say: *Here I am: Ms. Interpreter!*

For many and perhaps most of us, our professional identity is at the core of who we are. As interpreters, the journey to one's professional identity starts from the individual level (the interpreter) and moves up to the collective level (the professional body as a whole). We will have fully understood who we are as community interpreters once we see where we fit within the profession.

Individual professional identity: know yourself

Who Are You?
(Self-Awareness)

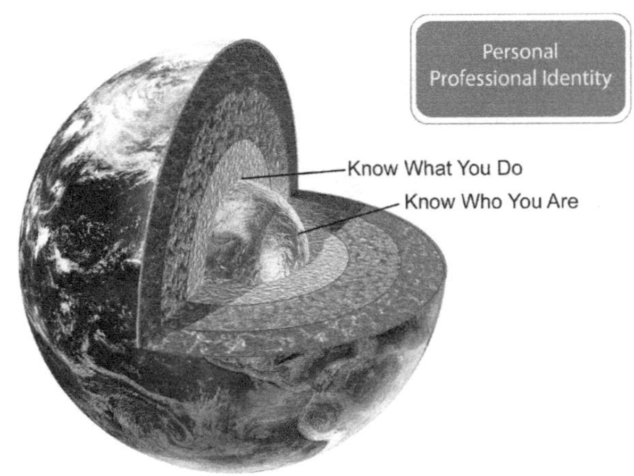

Professionalism is not just about wearing a suit and showing up on time. It's a mindset that permeates every action we take that helps us build up a professional image of ourselves instead of allowing others to define who we are.

Developing a professional identity starts with building or developing a set of core skills necessary to perform professionally. Learning these skills may involve attending a training or education program as well as adhering to a code of ethics, as discussed in Chapter 1.

Professional identity and social skills

Beside the ethics, protocols and skills proper to your profession, there are a number of other skill sets that also contribute to your professional image. They may be somewhat less tangible but are nonetheless important. Here are some of the *professional* social skills that will set you apart as a professional:

- **Values:** The ability to choose and consciously practice your core values and convey them to others is essential. They represent the fundamental principles of conduct that govern your actions, such as "honesty," "compassion" or "integrity." The more positive your values are and the more you live up to them, the more you are likely to be respected.
- **Attitude**: A positive disposition certainly contributes to higher chances of success in this field. Showing a cheerful, warm attitude in a profession that is still struggling for recognition helps to convey a positive image for that profession.
- **Personal appearance and dress code**: Despite our best intentions not to judge others, appearance matters. It may take as little as one-tenth of a second to form a first impression of someone. *Cleanliness, grooming and appropriate clothing are important factors that many people use to make decisions about whether or not to do business with you*, Also, they could have a negative impact on the organization where you interpret, leading to complaints, violations of health codes or hospital requirements, or negative feedback in the community about that organization. Some of the most common complaints about community interpreters by service users and providers include:
  - Cigarette odors.
  - Strong scents of cologne or perfumes.
  - Tight or see-through clothing.
  - Casual, sloppy or inappropriate dress.
  - Open-toed shoes in professional environments and hospitals.
  - Lack of personal grooming and hygiene.

  It is also important to consider the setting where you will interpret (e.g., a funeral home vs. a dental surgeon's office) and the professional cultures involved.
- **Courtesy**: Good manners matter. Courteous behavior in all circumstances (even when people around you are angry, upset or crying) is a sign of self-control, respect and consideration for others. Your behavior manifests itself through body language and vocabulary that you might not be aware of and that contributes to your professional image. You do not want to be an interpreter who gets reported for rolling your eyes or giggling during a sensitive session.
- **Communication skills**: The ability to use the right words at the right time matters in many professions today—and perhaps none more than the interpreting professions. Use the appropriate terminology and register. Consider how your communication skills affect your image. Be self-critical and accept feedback. You may not realize that some words or expressions are too colloquial, or not professionally appropriate, or just inaccurate. Positive and constructive feedback and your ability to give and receive it contribute to your personal and professional growth.
- **Professional solidarity:** The way you relate to others to accomplish a common goal speaks highly about your self-confidence and willingness to share. Teamwork relates to the way you interact with others in a team. Consider the profession as a larger team: share your knowledge with peers, refer colleagues to a client or guide fellow interpreters in difficult situations. It is hard to fully engage and thrive in your profession if you work in isolation. Support helps us all to rise above our challenges.

Your individual professional identity is also affected by your employment status. In Chapter 1, we identified several types of interpreters: self-employed interpreters (independent contractors, also known as freelancers); staff interpreters; bilingual staff; and volunteers. To learn more about how professional identity affects each of these types of interpreters, refer to Section 4.2 under the heading "Employed vs. self-employed."

Individual professional identity: know what

What Do You Do?
(Knowledge and Skills to Apply to the Job)

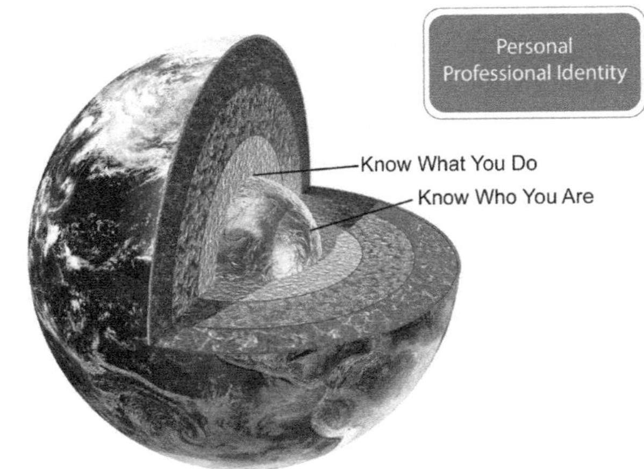

As an interpreter, what you do goes back to the skills you use when on duty, and the application of the code of ethics and standards of practice in any of your professional endeavors. You have learnt this all in Chapters 1, 2 and 3. And there is more to it that is less tangible.

Developing a professional identity involves assessing who you are and what you have to offer. Your identity is a work in progress. The goal is to improve yourself as a professional and make a difference to the field at large, and perhaps to the world. Whether you are at the beginning or the apex of your career, you will continually need to improve your skills and abilities and polish your professional image. Opportunities open up when others see you as a true professional. (See Chapter 5 for ideas on professional development.)

Be the best you can be. Keep learning. Keep striving for better and more. Most people value and enjoy working with professionals. Careless actions can harm the reputations of even the most experienced interpreters. Those who consciously identify themselves as "professional" actually convey that image. Thinking of yourself as professional impacts the clothes you choose to wear, the posture you hold and your body language, the way you greet people and other aspects of your conduct that go beyond interpreting. Satisfied customers ask for that professional interpreter to come back. Contracts multiply. Your image is enhanced. You feel happy. You earn a respectable living. You also help other people understand the work you do.

There is a number of strategies to boost your professional identity.
Here is a basic list:

Strive for excellence

Aim to provide the highest quality of service in everything you do: regardless of whom you serve, the setting where you interpret or how much you are paid, give your best. *Always* arrive on time, which means planning to arrive at your appointment at least 10–15 minutes earlier. If you are a self-employed interpreter, usually these 10-15 minutes are not paid unless you have an early arrival or set-up time specified in your contract, or previously agreed upon. It is your investment in your professional image. But your image will benefit greatly. Give yourself time to meet with the service provider, if appropriate. Educate the organization about how to work with a professional interpreter. Remain impartial. Don't find yourself alone with the service user. Refrain from gossiping with peers, clients or providers. Ignore hearsay: act on your values and your code of ethics.

Note: If early arrival is necessary for other reasons, this time may be part of your contracting agreement. For example, if you are working on a simultaneous assignment, you may need to arrive early to set up equipment, check the surroundings, etc. if so, you may want to negotiate this as part of your time commitment and be remunerated for it.

Focus on professional development

Separate yourself from your peers through the quality of your continuing education (see Chapter 5, Section 5.6), which is a critical aspect of developing a professional identity. Additional training, education, attending conferences and further skills practice will enhance your reputation, advance your career and lead to additional work. If you decide to pursue certification, continuing education is usually a requirement to maintain your certification or license.

Create or enhance your business toolkit

Every profession has a specific toolkit: every tool fulfills a specific purpose and together these professional tools help you to enhance your skills and hone the image of a professional. Look at the list below and cross check the tools you have. Which tools do you need to enhance your image?

- Résumé
- Portfolio of credentials
- Trade name
- Business cards
- Professional email
- Mobile phone with professional voice message
- Business forms
- Website or social media presence
- Branding statement
- Consistency in marketing materials

Additional ways to enhance your professional image are discussed in the next section.

A Beautiful Gift

By the Author of This Chapter

In 2010, I co-trained a 40-hour session of **The Community Interpreter**® to a class of 23 participants. They all considered themselves veterans in the field. Some had been interpreting for three years, some for five, and some even longer. Some had only interpreted for workers' compensation appointments, while some had also worked in education and social service settings. They clearly thought they were going to waste a week of their time in my training program.

Within hours, their attitude had changed. They saw they knew much less than they thought. By the end of the first day, they were questioning a lot of their own interpreting practices and felt upset because their managers were not there to listen. By the end of the week, I was paid the most beautiful compliment I think an interpreter trainer can receive. A participant said: *"I have learned that I am not alone out there. And that we interpreters are a community."*

Eagles vs. geese

Flying alone

It is striking to realize that your roadmap to a career as an interpreter might have been paved by words like these: *"Oh, you speak Swahili? Great! I need a Swahili interpreter tomorrow. Can you go?"* Many people believe that all you need to interpret is to speak two (or more) languages. Community interpreting is still fighting for recognition *as* a profession. You can help.

Think of an eagle. Eagles are powerful predators that fly from a great height with fine vision and vitality. They are known for their beauty, strength, and freedom, but they do not "hang out" with other eagles. They are loners. They do not live or fly in flocks.

Now think of geese. We hardly ever see a goose alone. These are beautiful large birds known for flying in a V-shape formation, often for great distances. They even honk to encourage the geese up front. They are never alone, care for one another and work for the same goal: to support one another and the flock, for their own survival.

Our flock: the profession

Now, think of *community interpreters*. Our flock is our profession. Too often we have been eagles, but most of us are happier in a flock. Together we support one another. In collaboration, we can move forward faster and be stronger. We need our professional networks and associations to foster professional development. We need educational institutions and training organizations to help us get formal qualifications. We need exams, credentials and regulatory bodies with the power to assess, admit and discipline members. We need support and colleagues, feedback and in-services.

Let's embark on a journey to explore the profession itself. What is the common denominator that defines community interpreters? Who are the stakeholders in our professional world? What role do standards play? What are the components of our *professional* identity at the collective level?
Ready to fly? Let's take off!

Collective professional identity: know who else is involved

Who Are the Stakeholders?
(Interactions with Peers, Staff, Services Users and Providers)

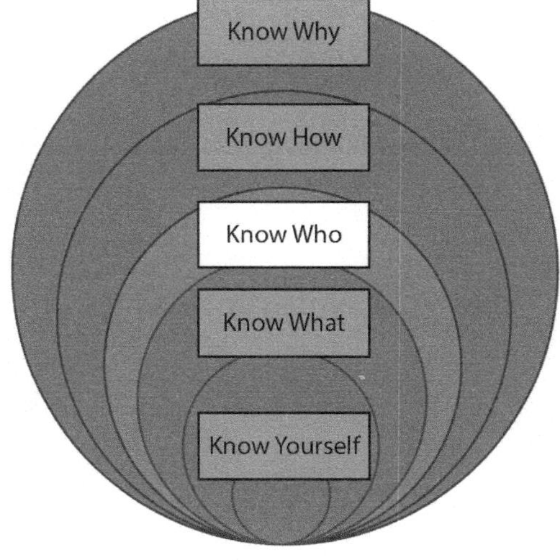

Be aware of all stakeholders

As a community interpreter, you are not alone. Think about it. You are called for an assignment, accept the job, show up, do the work, leave and go home, or on to the next job. How many people have you interacted with during that time? What about other community interpreters: how many people have *they* interacted with at work? Let's identify those players. They include:

- You: the community interpreter.
- A supervisor (in your workplace) or a scheduler who contacts you to perform an assignment.
- A receptionist, assistant or some other staff member(s) in the department where you will interpret.
- One or more service provider(s).
- One or more service user(s) and perhaps family members.
- Other interpreters: perhaps you are part of a team of interpreters or meet other interpreters engaged in other assignments.
- The person you have to report to after the assignment in your workplace or the language service that sent you.

In this simple scenario, we have identified five or more players who interact with you on a regular basis. We will refer to each one of them as a stakeholder.

How stakeholders interact

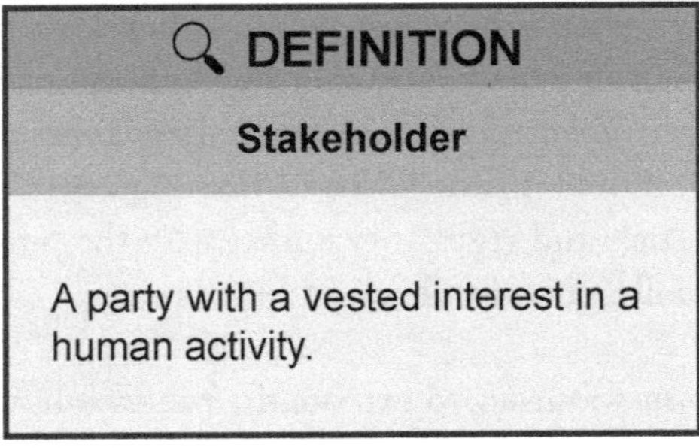

The interrelationships of these players form a system whose success is based on how well the parts interrelate with one another. For the sake of a successful outcome, no one part can be viewed as an isolated entity. The healthy relationship among the key players and the quality of their communication is the foundation for an effective service delivery. Among these players you are an entity interacting with other parties whose work is key to the success of the service being delivered, just as your own work is essential. As you build healthy professional relationships, you watch everything come together. When that work goes well, thanks to you, your contribution helps create respect for community interpreting as a profession.

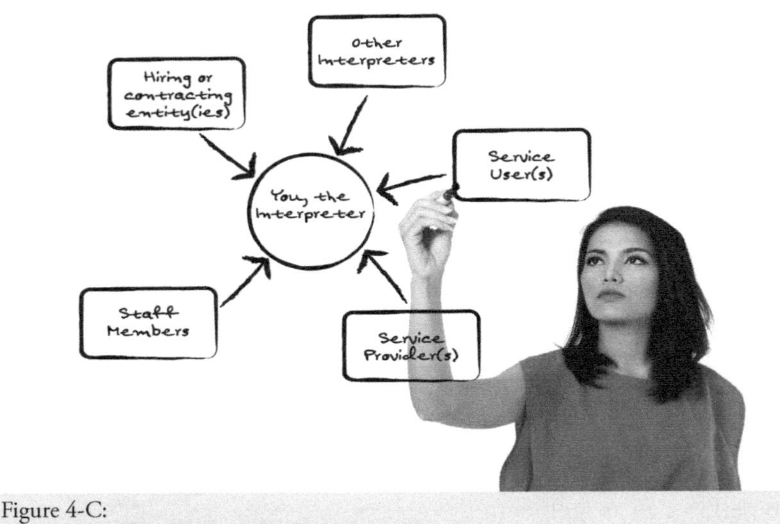

Figure 4-C:
Community Interpreting Stakeholders

Who sends you on assignment?

A stakeholder is a party with a legitimate interest in a situation, project or organization. Community interpreting stakeholders include those who hire or engage you, frontline and other support staff at the service agency, service users and services providers as well as other interpreters. Each of them, for different reasons, holds legitimate interests in the successful outcome of the interpreted session. Let's look at the first category of stakeholders: those who employ you or contract your services. They are (a) your employer; (b) a language service provider (LSP); or (c) your direct clients.

Employers

First, if you have an employer, you are an employee. You will uphold the code of ethics and standards of practice of the profession that is your primary job as well as interpreting ethics and standards (if your primary job is not interpreting) and workplace policies and procedures.

LSPs and ISPs

If you are a freelance interpreter, then probably a number of language service providers (LSPs) send you out on assignment. An LSP is a person or entity that provides translation, interpreting, localization, language and/or any other language-related services. An interpreting service provider (ISP) is a person or entity that provides interpreting services, whether or not it provides other language services. In other words, ISPs are a subcategory of LSPs. All ISPs are LSPs, but not all LSPs are ISPs.

It is important to understand that if you are a freelance interpreter, ***you are also an ISP***. A small one, yes: but still, you are an ISP. You are a business. And as such you receive requests and may accept or refuse assignments from larger ISPs. As a freelance interpreter, you will need to have a good understanding of the organizations that engage you to interpret and how they work but also to understand that you are, in effect, an organization yourself. For details, refer to Section 4.2.

Direct clients

A direct client is a person or entity for whom you provide interpreting services for and/or to, *without* being contracted through another ISP. It is the entity that ultimately pays you directly for the services rendered. In working directly with your client, you have better freedom to establish your own "rules."

Service providers

In community interpreting, you work regularly with another category of stakeholders: service providers. In your interaction with service providers, here are a few points to keep in mind. The service provider has received specialized training, education and/or formal guidance and has formally acquired the experience and qualifications to perform that job. There will be times where you might handle things differently than the service provider. You might even deeply disagree with him or her. However, they are responsible for knowing their area of competence and you are not. Even if you did know more, you are the *interpreter* and not the *provider* for that encounter.

You are, however, the person responsible for managing the communication flow. This is your area of expertise and responsibility. You do not control the people: you manage the communication, but only to support communicative autonomy. The interpreting protocols you observe and skills you practice will help build your credibility with service providers.

Service users

In community interpreting, you work regularly with service users. Here are a few points to keep in mind. Many community interpreters are individuals with a desire to help. However, often, your personal idea of "helping" defeats the mission of impartially delivering the message. Besides, often the service user looks at you as a possible ally. In situations where parties do not share a language or hold the same authority, interesting dynamics take place. Usually the party who does not speak the language of service feels outweighed and unconsciously looks to you to fix the imbalance of power. Service users might ask for your phone number, invite you to their child's birthday party or request a ride home and you may feel uncomfortable refusing these requests. If you are one of them, there are many attitudes toward this problem, such as:

- OPTION #1: Tough it up! Respect your boundaries. "Just say no." Get out. But culturally that approach may not work for you.
- OPTION #2: Do whatever the service user asks, within reason. This is generally misguided at best, dangerous at worst (especially for legal and mental health interpreting).
- OPTION #3: The middle way: show compassion, use your three-step SAY NO model and your best decision-making skills to get out of the situation as gracefully and quickly as possible without causing cultural offense or deep personal distress.

The Special Case of Bilingual Staff

If you are a bilingual staff with interpreting duties, helping the service user with some tasks before or after the assignment may be part of your job description.

Especially refrain from making any personal comments while you are on duty. Some well-meaning or apparently innocuous suggestions can have serious consequences. One interpreter suggested that a service user take her child to the doctor's office for a cold. That simple comment had such serious consequences that the interpreter was no longer allowed to interpret for that organization.

Interaction with peers

My Peers

By the Lead Author of This Chapter

You can call your fellow interpreters colleagues, coworkers, associates… I call them "peers." There is a noble flavor to it. I have the highest regard for my profession and my identity, as I do for colleagues who share my vision and practices alongside with the vision and practices of the profession. The term *peer* was once used to indicate a nobleman: a member of the nobility in Great Britain and Ireland. Then it evolved to indicate a person equal to another in abilities, qualifications, status, achievement or value.

When I interact with fellow interpreters, I treat them like peers. I offer to share my knowledge and resources with anyone who puts in the effort to become a professional interpreter.

Did you know that when they fly in formation, geese fly about 70 percent faster than if each goose flew alone? There is truth to the old Italian saying, "*L'unione fa la forza*" (united we are strong, or "strength in unity"). In any profession, you have the option to be a solo or team player. But especially in community interpreting, that decision will have significant impact. We need every bit of wing flap wind that you can generate to advance the profession.

> *Coming together is a beginning. Keeping together is progress. Working together is success."*
> – Henry Ford

Think of your profession as a huge team. Every interpreter counts on everyone else to help advance our professional status. Every interpreter is dependent on other interpreters to work together for the greater good of the profession.

Around the world, community interpreters cry out for higher pay, better work conditions and more recognition. So do interpreters in many other specializations. No one interpreter can support the whole profession alone but we can all work together—across any and all specializations. In fact, the more we all identify as *interpreters*, the stronger we will all be. The way geese work together can show us how to be better team players and collaborate for the greater good. In this way we can forge our collective professional identity.

Collective professional identity: know how

How Do You Work?
(Awareness of Ethics, Standards, Best Practices)

Consider the flock

Now let's move to the collective level, from the individual interpreter's professional identity to the identity of the "flock" as a whole: in short, we will examine the professional identity of the *profession*.

Professional identity at the collective level is of paramount importance for *you*. Wherever you live and work, how people look at your profession shapes how people see you. It has an impact on your own recognition. A strong identity for the profession helps you to be seen as a professional by all members of society. Without that collective identity, it is difficult for stakeholders to have a coherent image of you as a professional.

Know Why
Know How
Know Who
Know What
Know Yourself

The solo player vs. the team player

If you act like an eagle, you are a solo player. You lack support. If you are a team player, you will support the flock—and they will support you.

Your reputation gets you work and recognition. That reputation will be different in the mind of everyone who knows you, but it is often based not on your work alone but on public opinion about you. If that opinion is positive, then you enjoy a good reputation; if that opinion is negative, you suffer the effects of a poor reputation. What happens to your reputation if the opinion that others have of you is different from the image you want to project? Take a moment to answer the following questions:

- What is the image *you* want to project?
- What do you want others to know about you?
- How do you want the impact of your work to be perceived?

How people look at community interpreters

Now think of the larger profession. The image of that profession also affects how people see you. Let's ask the same questions at the macro level:

- What is the image you want the *profession* to project?
- What do you want others to know about community interpreting?
- How do you want the benefits of this profession to be perceived?

Your reputation is influenced by both individual and collective identity. This is one reason to join a professional association, attend conferences and support your colleagues and new interpreters entering the field. The more you help to strengthen the profession, the more you yourself will be perceived as a professional.

Collective professional identity: know where the profession is going

Know Why
Who Shapes the Profession? How?

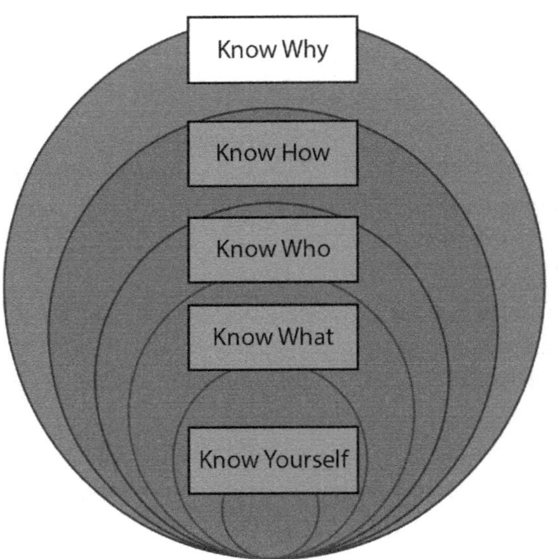

We launched this journey to professional identify with the definition of your identity: your personal identity. We focused on the two primary elements of the personal identity at the micro level by creating awareness about who you are in your growth as a professional interpreter, and what you should know to perform as one.
Then we transitioned into the collective professional identity, where these elements play into a macro sphere as you grow in your role and interact with stakeholders. We are about to complete this journey by learning about the associations and entities that shape the landscape of our profession.

Professional associations

In short, community interpreting is working hard to establish our collective professional identity. In the landscape of any established profession, there are professional organizations that support it. Professional organizations are usually nonprofit organizations that serve the needs of a specific occupation. Their purpose is to keep members connected with one another and informed about developments in the industry. They may provide additional benefits, such as trainings, workshops, group discounts on insurances, resources and continuing education. To be part of the association, members pay dues at registration and renew their membership, usually annually.
It is generally understood that when a newly credentialed professional is ready to venture into the job market, the first step is to become a member of the appropriate professional association. This

practice sends out several signals. For example, joining an association:

1. Attests to the member's commitment to the profession.
2. Affirms the member's support for professional ethics and standards.
3. Highlights the member's desire to be informed about the profession and its developments.

All these elements contribute to the shaping of collective professional identity. The fact is that while there are many local, national and international interpreting associations, the vast majority of community interpreters do not yet belong to one. It's time to change that situation. Belonging to a professional association is a declaration of professionalism. It's a powerful statement about who you are.

How to find a professional association

The quick answer is: search on the Internet! Start with words like "professional association" (in quotes), interpreters, [your country or state]." If you attend a college or university, you should be able to find help at the library or career center on your campus. Your public library might even help you.

If you do not have access to an interpreting professional association in your state or country, then you can do a wider search for other countries' associations to join. In some countries, interpreting associations are joined with translators associations. Although the two are different professions, these joint associations foster the development and the advancement of both professions. Some of the events, such as conferences or workshop days, may be intended for both professions while others may be unique to one profession or the other.

Why would I join? It's a waste of time and money

Each of us has the social and professional responsibility to join and recruit members for our professional associations. Remember, in unity is strength. There is a perception that associations are a waste of time and the yearly dues are not worth the cost. That perception is misguided.

While every organization is different, most professional associations work hard to promote and disseminate information about the profession. Also, many offer scholarships for college members and provide mentors for those joining the profession. They can also offer insight into how the industry works and how to navigate it, as well as workshops and conferences for professional development. What's more, for students and young professionals, the membership dues are often lowered substantially.

Benefits of joining a professional assocaition

Here are some important benefits to joining:

Jobs: Many professional organizations help their members find jobs, or at least post job listings.

Mentoring: A cornerstone of many professional organizations is nurturing younger members. You might get paired with a highly experienced mentor.

Professional development: Most associations offer professional development and updates on industry trends via courses, workshops, publications, and information on their website shared only with members. Some also offer online webinars.

Networking: Most associations have an annual conference. This is an opportunity to mix and mingle with others in your field. There is also a job fair where you can meet the people who want you.

"Fringe" benefits: from discount insurance policies to help with unexpected personal expenses, or no-fee credits or discounts at local business, your association might have other benefits for you. Find out!

What if there is no association in your country?

If there is no professional organization where you live, start one! Keep in mind that a professional association is usually a nonprofit organization supported by membership dues and other fundraising (including events like training and conferences). Depending on local legal requirements, starting a professional association might be challenging, but also rewarding.

Community interpreting, as a young profession, needs you to forge a strong sense of professional identity, and to contribute to the professionalization and recognition of the field. Community interpreting is still fighting for recognition—and you play a role in advancing the field. An important role: cherish and honor it, and the profession will honor you.

Let's Practice

Learning Activity 4.1 (a): Professional or Unprofessional
Learning Activity 4.1 (b): The Elements of Your Image

In *The Community Interpreter®: An International Workbook of Activities and Role Plays*

REVIEW OF SECTION 4.1

Since the early 1970s when the profession was first established, the work of community interpreters has evolved. Progress is swift and exciting. Academics, practitioners and associations have taken note. Conversations about community interpreting at local, national and international levels testify to a growing community of professionals who advocate strongly for the recognition of the profession.

The professionalization of community interpreting is a work in progress, however. It cannot be accomplished without the buy-in of the most important stakeholder: YOU. To forge a strong sense of personal professional identity, focus on learning more about the profession and strive for continuing education through professional development. You will also need to build your own professional toolkit to reinforce your reputation.

To develop a strong sense of collective professional identity you will need to act as a dignified representative of the profession, whether you are an employee or a freelance interpreter. Always maintain professional interactions with service users, providers and your peers; weigh the impact of your conduct on the profession as a whole. Most important, understand how you fit into the larger work of the profession as a whole.

As a community interpreter, your commitment to the profession and your pledge at the beginning of this book are based on accepted ethical principles, standards and best practices for the profession. Yet you, the community interpreter, are a great strength and a precious resource—the treasure of our profession. You hold the power to make communication happen. The keys to communicative autonomy lie in your hands. Dress in your best business attire, stand up tall when you walk and enter a room—chest out, chin up!—and gain the respect that any professional is due. Take pride in this profession, so that it can take pride in you.

4.2 Professional Practice

Overview

In the previous section, you identified a number of elements that contribute to the development of professional identity at the individual and collective level. A number of these elements are deeply rooted in the way we conduct business, which deeply influences the way we are perceived by the public.

This section explores how professional interpreters should conduct themselves through the lens of their business practices. It begins by addressing the types of interpreters based on their employment or labor status, then looks at how professionals within each of those categories should ideally conduct themselves in the field.

Learning Objective 4.2

After completing this section, you will be able to:

- Understand the business practices and legal obligations of community interpreters.

Employed vs. self-employed

Employed vs. self-employed

From a fiscal or legal perspective, professional interpreters usually fall into one of two categories: self-employed (independent contractors or freelancers) or employed.

Interpreters who are employees could be fulltime staff interpreters (though some are hired both to interpret and translate), or they could be employees who interpret as only one part of their professional duties. Interpreters who are self-employed are in business for themselves. However, each country has specific employment classifications, and some may also vary by locality. Therefore, to understand more about your legal status, consult a local lawyer or an accountant, especially if you are self-employed. The following paragraphs provide only very general information that is true in most countries. Nothing here, or elsewhere in this textbook, is intended as legal information or advice.

Employees

Generally speaking, in most countries an *employee* is a person who works in the service of another person or entity under a written or oral *contract of hire*. In such cases the employer typically has the right to control and manage the work performance. This means that the organization has control over how and when the job is executed. Such employees can be salaried or paid on an hourly, weekly or other basis.

As a staff interpreter or bilingual employee who interprets as one part of your job (whether you do so often or rarely), you work within the hierarchy of a specific organization. You must abide by the organization's internal policies and procedures, requirements, schedules and shifts. As a salaried employee, your compensation is usually set at a specific salary amount per year, although you might also be entitled to various benefits, bonuses or commissions.

Self-employed

In most countries, a self-employed interpreter is considered a one-person business.[42] In this capacity, the freelance interpreter is an independent contractor, which means any individual or business that provides services to another individual or business. The independent contractor is usually a separate business entity. In most parts of the world, an independent contractor can provide services to a number of individuals and businesses and is not considered an employee. Such an interpreter is called an interpreting service provider (ISP)—the most common international term—even though ISP can also refer to organizations that provide interpreting services. (For additional information on ISPs, see Section 4.1.)

Freelance? Think of yourself as a business!

As a freelance interpreter, you are a *business*. You are free to accept or turn down assignments based on your availability, your specialization or any other reason. You set your own work schedule and hours. You decide which tools to use to deliver your services, and you issue your own invoices unless you engage someone else to do so. You are responsible for filing your business or self-employment taxes and pay for your own professional insurances. You run your own business: you are your only *boss*.

[42]Be careful, however. In some countries, the legal picture can be more nuanced. For details, consult a business lawyer in your geographical area of practice.

Employed vs. Self-Employed: a side-by-side comparison

The following table gives you an overview of the differences between an employee and a self-employed contractor. While it applies to the United States in particular, similar distinctions exist in many and perhaps most countries.

EMPLOYEE	SELF-EMPLOYED
Submits timesheets or other form of regular reporting	Submits an invoice (weekly, per project, etc)
Qualifies for benefit coverage (such as paid leave, dental care, retirement plans or other benefits, depending on the country and business)	Does not qualify for benefits
Has taxes deducted from paychecks	Is usually responsible for own tax payments, including self-employment taxes (where applicable)
Follows instructions about when, where and how to work	Is free to work when and for whom she wants
Receives a salary or wages	Is paid by the job based on invoice
Often has steady, secure income	Carries the risk of profit or loss
Works only for one company	Usually works for several organizations
May be trained by the employer to perform services in a particular manner	Should be knowledgeable about the professional protocols and best practices
Renders services personally (cannot subcontract work to someone else)	Renders services and can subcontract work
May be reimbursed for expenses (e.g., for continuing education, an interpreter badge or a bilingual dictionary)	Might or might not be compensated for direct expenses (e.g., travel or parking) but is not typically compensated for business or educational expenses (e.g., training, business cards)
Furnishes tools, equipment and materials	Is responsible for providing own material and equipment
Can be terminated or can resign	Cannot be terminated except for breach of contract, but might lose a contract renewal (i.e., might never be asked back to interpret).

Table 4-A
Employed vs. Self-Employed: a Business Perspective

As a professional interpreter, it is your obligation to be informed about your legal obligations as an employee or, if you are a freelance interpreter, as a small business in your locality. Your employment status has specific legal implications that you must be fully aware of, such as a possible requirement to file quarterly self-employment taxes for freelancers.

Decide on the career you want to build for yourself

Beside the tangible differences that exist between self-employed or an employee, you should consider several factors before making an informed decision about which type of interpreter you want to be. Table 4-B lists some common (not universal) characteristics about each category:

Self-Employed vs. Employed Interpreters		
	Self-Employed	**Employee**
Business mindset	I need to be self-disciplined and organized. I must track my assignments and related expenses (mileage, travel time, highway tolls, etc.) and consult a qualified accountant. I need to invoice clients regularly and remind them to pay me as needed. I set my own financial goals to earn a living. I must consider getting liability and/or other insurance (e.g., errors and omissions).	I prefer the security of a fixed salary without constantly pursuing work or payment. I enjoy employee status rather than running a business. I do not want to worry about professional insurance or deal with paperwork. I am not detail oriented and prefer not to track all my expenses.
Marketing mindset	I need to promote myself to several clients. To do that, I will develop materials like a résumé, bio and a social media or website presence to show the credentials that highlight me and my services. I will distribute these materials to acquire more clients to help me get a steady income. Paying for these materials is an investment in my business and career.	I enjoy a collegiate atmosphere. I don't want to talk about myself or insert marketing into my conversations. I prefer to invest my free time and discretionary money in fun activities, not marketing materials. I can get free training, continuing education and paid career opportunities.
Flexibility and adaptability	I like to have full control of my time and decide when to work—or not. I like the idea of being my own boss. I want to turn down work that I do not like or that makes me uncomfortable. I don't like a predictable routine: I enjoy the fact that each day can be different—it's an adventure!	I like a set schedule so that I have full freedom outside my working hours. I like being able to plan ahead and enjoy a lot of activities that I can arrange around my schedule. It is fun to climb up the employment ladder and achieve success and recognition.
Open to freedom, new experiences and irregular schedule	I enjoy the ability to decide who to work for and to look for the clients who fit my goals and values. I don't feel isolated working for myself: in fact, I enjoy meeting new people all the time.	I prefer to work with only one organization where I have close ties and a sense of working with colleagues and friends. The structured work environment sets up clear expectations for me.
Vision, Mission and Values – a statement of professional culture	I am clear about who I am, what I do and my purpose as an interpreter. I send out a clear message to clients and users and develop a clear vision for my career path. I may do business research to understand what "vision," "mission" and "values" mean in business. My professional image revolves around the sum of these elements, which make up my professional culture and are reflected in my professional identity.	I prefer associating myself with a company that has made choices about professional culture. The company I work for has a clear vision, mission and core values. It walks its talk. When something contradicts these statements I feel comfortable bringing it up. It is important for me to work with a company whose vision, mission and values align with mine.

Table 4-B
Costs and Benefits of Being Self-employed (Freelance) vs. Employed Interpreters

Your business toolbox

To conduct yourself as a professional, consider these practices as your "business tools." These tools are standard in many professions. They can be slightly different depending on whether you are an employee or an independent contractor.

The Interpreter's Business "Toolbox"		
	Self-Employed	Employee
Résumé	√	√
Portfolio of credentials	√	√
Trade name	√	*
Business cards	√	(depends)
Professional email	√	√
Mobile phone with professional voice mail	√	(perhaps)
Business forms (i.e., invoice template, mileage and/or travel time log, expense report for tax purposes)	√	*
Website or social-media presence	√	*
Branding statement	√	*
Consistency in marketing materials	√	*

Table 4-C
Elements of a Professional Interpreter's Business "Toolkit"

Résumé

A résumé is a summary of your career and education. In some countries, it is called curriculum vitae (CV), although a curriculum vitae tends to be longer and more detailed. The résumé, often only a page or two, lists your main skills, your education, your work experience, your professional credentials and may include highlights of your career.

Portfolio of credentials

Include supporting documentation to add credibility to your résumé (or CV). In the interpreting world, examples of relevant credentials could include:

- An attestation or transcript for translation or interpreting programs or degrees.
- Certificates of attendance or completion of training courses.
- Language proficiency test results.
- Proof of certifications.
- Membership in relevant professional associations.

Consider adding letters of recommendation or names of references who will speak well of your professional experience and skills. (Always ask permission before putting someone's name down as a reference.) Do not misrepresent yourself by addition of titles or qualifications you do not have.

Trade name

If you are a self-employed, you are a business. You are your own "boss." Go a step further: give your business a professional name. In countries such as the United States, you can register as a business with a trade name. Find out if there are fees or taxes associated with a trade name. You might even want to pay a designer to create a logo for you (a visual imprint) to identify your business and make it stand out. If so, make sure it is a professional logo that fits your trade name.

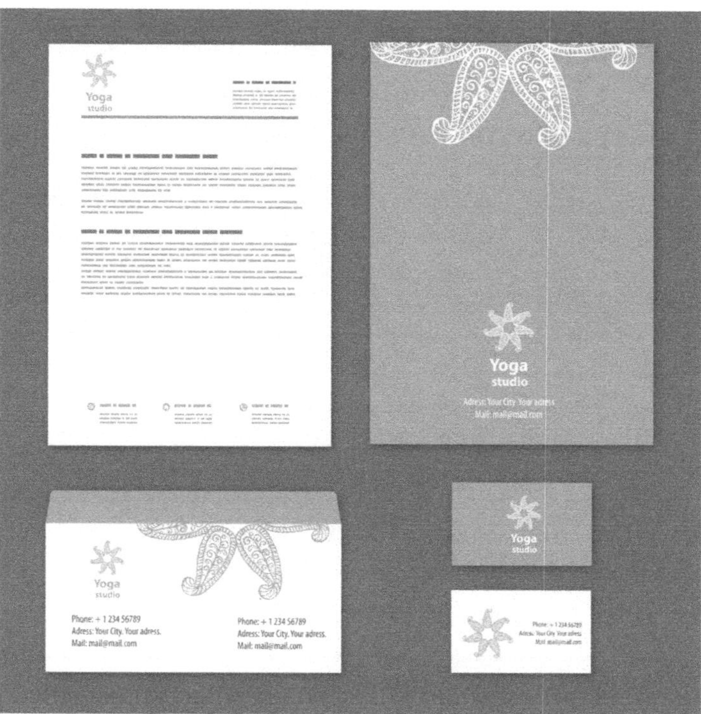

Business cards

Business cards are usually a standard size of card, printed or engraved, that should carry information about the business or individual, such as your name, your business name (and logo), the service or products you supply, and contact information including a website. They should be consistent with all your other marketing material and carry the same logo and colors.

If you are an employee, you could have a company business card; if you are a self-employed, your business cards carry your own contact information and trade name. However, when working on behalf of an ISP, it is good practice (depending where you work) to hand the service provider and service user *only the business card of the company you represent for that assignment.*

Professional email

Email is the most common form of written communication in the business world today. Some interpreters resist it. Using it well and wisely helps to build the image of a professional.

However, too often, we do not take the time to think, reread and polish our email messages before sending them. When that happens, misunderstandings can takes place or we can look sloppy and unprofessional. Your written communications can open the door to problems. Repairing damage is much harder than preventing it. *Always* reread your electronic message before you hit "send." Also, avoid personal email addresses used for work-related reasons. Addresses like guapo[43]@xxx.com or loveforyou@xxx.com look unprofessional at best. You will stand out—in the wrong way. (For an employee, your email address is usually determined by the organization you work for.)

> **Wise Words**
>
> *Verba volant, scripta manent.*
> *Words fly away. What's written stays...*
> – Latin proverb
>
> **In short:** Be careful what you write—especially in emails!

In email, for the sake of a good business relationship, try to take nothing personally. Every individual has a personality. Always respond *professionally.*

[43] Guapo is Spanish for "good looking."

Emoticons, Texting and Abbreviations

Emoticons are text or images that convey emotions such as :) or ☺ to convey amusement or happiness. They are appropriate in an email to a colleague or a long-term client you know very well but may not be appropriate when you write formally to a new ISP client. The same is true about writing with too many exclamation marks: avoid it!!!!!! (☺) Remember, too, that the language of texting is not the same as the language in emails. Professional emails should have full sentences, capitalization and correct punctuation. Avoid texting abbreviations in email.

Mobile phone with professional voice message

If you use the same number for both personal and business use, decide which image you want to project first. You may want to set up a professional greeting in your voicemail, not a casual recording like, "Hi, it's Maria, leave a message." The way you answer the phone also sets the tone for a business conversation. Answering by saying, "Who's that?" or "Who are you?" does not sound professional when a potential client calls.

Are You a Go-Getter or a Go-Giver?

By the Author of This Chapter

I discovered the hard way that brutal competition exists among many interpreters. Then I met a few generous and successful colleagues who were not afraid to share their knowledge and even referred me to clients for assignments.

Soon I learned that the confidence you gain from giving and sharing is far more valuable than envy, jealousy and worry that someone could take your assignments. I started doing the same: giving and sharing. Today I consider myself a consummate professional and delight in empowering interpreters who aspire to the highest levels of professionalism.

Business forms

If you are self-employed, you have fiscal and legal obligations. You must bill the client for work performed, track your expenses such as travel time and mileage, decide which interpreting equipment to use for your work, file taxes and pay for your business-related insurances.

Website or social-media presence

In order to stand out in the marketplace, more and more professional interpreters choose to build an online presence. Being online means more than just listing your work history and education. You can create an interesting profile that offers a memorable and concise way to sum up who you are and what you have to offer.

Online, you can post your professional identity to the world. Some interpreters use their online presence to share resources, publish blogs and share news. You can use social media sites such as Facebook, LinkedIn, Twitter, Renren, Pinterest, Orkut and more. However, it's important to be careful and easy to misstep. Often, employers check your social-media sites before hiring new employees or engaging contractors and what they see can be the deciding factor between hiring you or not.

Branding statement

A branding statement, often called a tagline, is a message of one or two sentences that tells who you are, what you are best at, who you serve and how you do it in a (possibly) unique way. It is your promise to your customers and clients. It summarizes what makes you a consummate professional.

For example, instead of saying: "I am an Arabic interpreter" you could say on your business card or your website, under your name, "The only court- and medical-certified Arabic interpreter in [list your city, state or province]." Or you could write, "Providing the highest quality medical and educational interpreting across Delaware since 1995, in Spanish, Portuguese and French." Perhaps you might write something like, "Your local specialist in Lingala and French for business and legal interpreting and translation."

Although a branding statement comes with experience and exposure to business, it should really be the foundation of your image, even before you create a business card, a website or your profile in social media. Insert your branding statement at the beginning of your bio and your "elevator pitch." (An elevator pitch is the 20- or 30-second description of yourself you can give anywhere, any time to any client—even in an elevator!) You can also use your branding statement in any other text about you, your services and your business, such as brochures and website text.

Consistency in marketing materials

The more you brand your image in all your marketing materials and even paperwork, the more your brand will be *recognized* by clients and customers. That consistency creates an image of you as a professional. Even in small, rural areas, many professionals brand themselves and get work because of it. We live in a digital age. Tiny villages in remote areas have cell phones. Visual elements contribute hugely to the recognition of a professional identity.

Working with an interpreting service provider (ISP)

What is an ISP?

An interpreting service provider (ISP) is a person or entity who provides interpreting services, whether or not it provides other language services. Examples of ISPs include:

- A language company that offers interpreting services.
- A nonprofit interpreter service.
- A provider of over-the-phone interpreting (OPI).
- A hospital interpreting department.
- A school language bank of paid community (freelance) interpreters.
- A community-wide language bank of paid community (freelance) interpreters.

That said, larger ISPs actively recruit dozens, hundreds or even thousands of interpreters. They may offer interpreting services in one or several specializations. This means that one ISP (say, a language company) can give an assignment to many small ISPs (like you). These larger ISPs should recruit and assign only qualified interpreters. In real life, that does not always happen. The burden is on you to accept only assignments you are qualified for.

ISP requirements

ISPs should have their own set of paperwork for you to sign. If not, it could be a red flag (a bad sign). ISPs should ideally require proof of your credentials and other documents depending on the professional requirements or their contractual agreements with their customers. Some of the documents they may ask you to provide include (but are not limited to):

- A résumé (or curriculum vitae).
- Proof of general education.
- Proof of interpreting qualifications and credentials.
- References.
- Proof that you have professional insurance policies.
- Documentation of continuing education (especially if you are certified or licensed).
- Information for a background check.
- Proof of vaccinations.

Look at ISPs as your clients

ISPs are your clients, which means you may reach out to ask for work, or they may reach out to you. Gather information about the ISP's reputation before you meet with them, and try to meet them before you decide to work with them. Although one interpreter's experience may not reflect another's with an ISP, here are some factors to consider when you interview with an ISP:

- Assess the mission, vision and core values of the ISP. Do not apply to "just any" ISP: interview the ISP first by phone, ask questions, check out the answers and decide if the company culture fits yours. Associate if possible with like-minded ISPs that give you the ability to grow in your profession: ISPs that you feel proud to represent.
- Beware of entities that do not require any, or very little, sort of documentation from the interpreter. Note that an independent contractor is an extension of the ISP: a reputable entity should not risk its reputation by routinely engaging unqualified interpreters. It takes time and work to gain a customer's trust and just one mistake to lose it.
- Beware of companies that do not follow relevant legal business requirements. Such requirements vary from country to country, and perhaps state to state or city to city. If you are an independent contractor, be aware of relevant local requirements.

Ethical concerns with ISPs

When you work on behalf of an ISP, you represent that ISP during the assignment. It is considered unethical to promote your own services and give out your contact information to get more business when working on the ISP's behalf. Giving out your own business card when on assignment for an ISP is a common, easy-to-make mistake that can damage your reputation.

Another common mistake is thinking one has to follow ISP procedures that contradict professional standards and best practices for fear of losing work opportunities. That might happen to you in the short term, but not over the longer term in most cases. ISPs need quality *professional* interpreters. If you work only for quality ISPs, you enhance your own reputation. Remember: the strength of ISPs is not in the work they do but in the interpreters they send out on assignment. If you refuse to contract with unprofessional ISPs, and your peers do the same, soon these ISPs will have no viable way to fulfill that work and will get the reputation of sending unqualified interpreters. You, meanwhile, will get assignments with quality ISPs who recognize your professionalism. Remember the geese. Strength in unity—and strength in numbers!

From a language company perspective

A word from this chapter's author

The author of this chapter is the owner of a U.S. language company and would like to focus briefly on the ISP's perspective. When you work on behalf of a contracting organization, you engage in complex professional relationships. Interpreting is not the world of one. These relationships work as a system. The imbalance in one professional relationship can disrupt the balance of the whole system and compromise outcomes. If your conduct at a given hospital is, or is perceived as, unprofessional, the ISP you represent may face serious consequences and even the risk of losing the contract.

Please show respect for ISPs

It is important to show utmost respect for ISPs, whether or not you agree with how they conduct business. Showing respect is part of professionalism and the professional image we convey. Your willingness to accept an assignment should be based upon a professional understanding of what is asked, what is appropriate and what you can deliver—not thoughts like, *I don't think this is fair because it's too much work and I don't get paid for that!*

Keep in mind that as an independent contractor, you have obligations as well as rights. If you do not know what they are, go back to the beginning of this section, or sign up for a business workshop. Remember, too, that you have the freedom to choose your clients and customers. Likewise, ISPs that contract your services have obligations toward *their* clients. Try to build a sense of "good business practices" and strong working relationships with your client ISPs.

Do Not Compromise Your Standards or Values

An interpreter should never compromise the ethics or standards of the profession just to get an assignment from an ISP. The ISP should not dictate a practice that is against the requirements of the profession or your values. If that happens to you, rethink that assignment—and your relationship with that ISP. You are a free agent. You get the final decision about the ISPs you want to work with.

The ISP's expectations

As a language company owner, I run a business: I have rights *and* obligations. The relationship between ISPs and contract interpreters is above all a professional relationship where the obligations of each party must be clearly stated and honored. An important aspect to remember is that an ISP that contracts your services is required to uphold its own contractual agreements with its clients, such as hospitals and school systems, and some of those requirements trickle down to you as an extension of that ISP when you accept the assignment, like vaccinations or criminal background checks. Larger ISPs must accommodate the different contractual requirements of many clients. Likewise, you as a "one-person ISP," a freelancer, might have to accommodate to a number of different specific processes and procedures.

A reputable ISP with good management and ethical practices would expect the conversation with professional interpreters to revolve around the following, at a minimum:

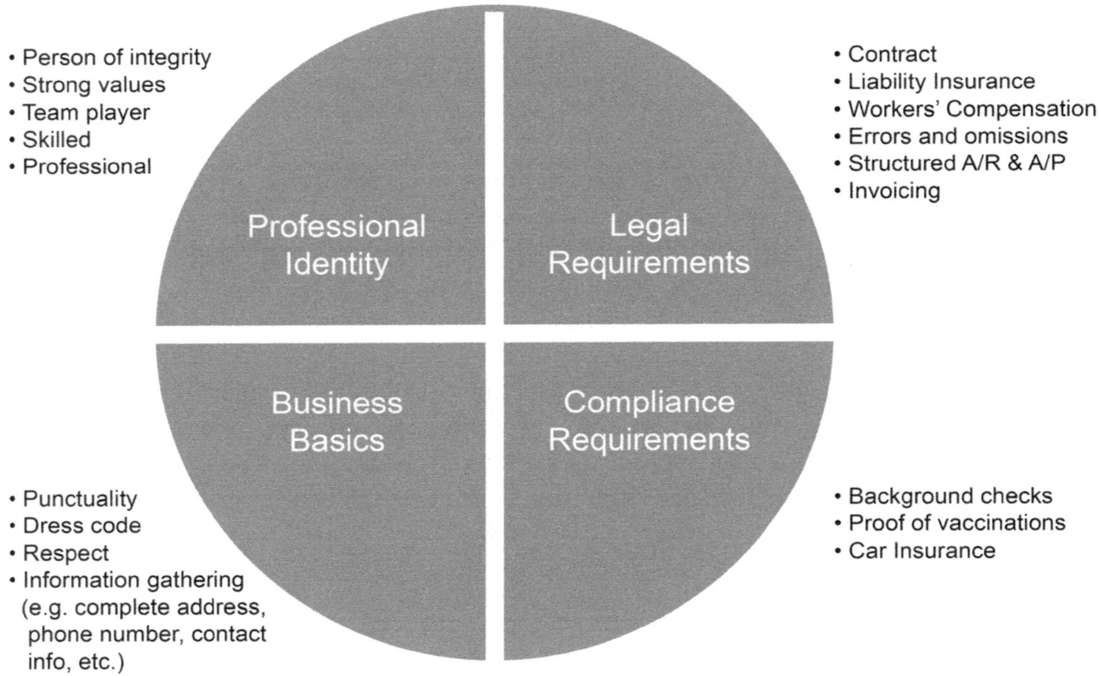

Figure 4-D
Professional identity and Freelance Interpreters

The elements illustrated here are *minimum* expectations and reflect the perspective of a language company in the United States. However, they could apply to many countries. As we have already discussed the professional identity and legal requirements aspects of the graphic above, let's examine compliance requirements and a few business basics.

Compliance requirements

What ISPs have to do

Organizational ISPs (and LSPs) have their own business, legal and financial obligations. It is advisable for an ISP/LSP to keep updated documentation on file about their interpreting resources, both employees and contractors. Failure to comply with legal requirements may result in expensive fines for the ISP if violations are found during fiscal audits.

Cost of Doing Business (CODB)

The expense or costs incurred when a business tries to make money. Liability insurance for interpreters and ISPs is an example of CODB.

To maintain compliance contractual agreements, ISPs must often require documentation from interpreters to keep on file if the ISP signed a contract to this effect or if they have certain kinds of organizational certification. Usually, for an employee interpreter the ISP would gather your needed documentation, such as vaccinations and tuberculosis testing for hospital interpreters. For freelance interpreters, it is usually their own responsibility to gather their documentation, part of what is defined as "cost of doing business." If you want assignments with a particular ISP, you might first have to submit proof of vaccination sand certification. Without it—no assignments.

"That's too much paperwork—what a headache!"

Many freelance interpreters complain about all the different requirements of ISPs, which can create a headache for the interpreter. But think about the larger ISPs: they also have many different customers—just like you. ISPs have a legal obligation to keep track of all their contractual requirements—and you are legally responsible for meeting yours. As a freelancer, you *are* an ISP—a small business.

ISPs that sign agreements can be audited at any time by any major customer. The advantage for you is that no one is likely to audit *you*—except, perhaps, a federal tax agency. Will you have all your paperwork well-organized to pass the audit with success? Some audits can add up to thousands of dollars in fines and penalties if you are not in compliance. As an independent contractor, know how to run your business. Here are some expectations that can cause frustration:

Self-Employed vs. Employed Interpreters: Legal Considerations		
	Self-Employed	Employee
Documentation: complaints about "too much paperwork!" A reputable ISP is diligent about meeting its legal and fiscal requirements.	It is your job to collect and submit all required paperwork. Refuse to submit required paperwork only if it is in conflict with your professional ethics or local laws. (e.g., the ISP should not demand that you document details of the encounter that violate confidentiality.)	Employees are mandated to comply with the employer's documentation requirements, which are usually straightforward and often the employer helps you take care of it. If you object to any of it, keep a written record of your communication.
Paperwork: complaints about "I have to submit the same document again!" Keeping interpreter files updated is a sign of a healthy organization. Updates are a snapshot of the agency's status quo.	It is your responsibility and in your best interest to keep all your records up to date, such as training or workshops, new credentials like certification, yearly tests or other required documents (e.g., vaccinations, criminal record background checks) and proof of insurances.	The employer will usually require new documentation when a document on file is due to expire. You will not have to remember it yourself but must usually comply with the request.
Lack of compliance with procedures: complaints about "Why do I have to do all this!" Each ISP is legally bound to honor its signed contractual agreements. They are not doing this to you for fun!	It is your obligation to fulfill the requirements you accepted in your contract, such as: Fulfilling administrative tasks related to the assignment. Presenting appropriate invoices with all necessary information. Reporting critical incidents or concerns that the ISP should know. Declining to perform services other than those you were engaged for.	Employers should have procedures and workflows in place to ensure compliance. They should also have a policy in place for employees who violate compliance requirements.

Table 4-D
Legal Considerations for Self-Employed (Freelance) vs. Employed interpreters

Let's Practice

Learning Activity 4.2(a): Comparing Employed vs. Self-Employed Interpreters

Learning Activity 4.2(b): What's In Your Business Toolbox?

In The Community Interpreter®: An International Workbook of Activities and Role Plays

REVIEW OF SECTION 4.2

Interpreting is not just about speaking two languages and showing up for the session. It involves a complex set of activities that relate both to professional standards and business practices. This section has highlighted the difference between the occupational status of employee versus self-employed interpreters and the characteristics of each. It also covered a number of business tools and strategies that community interpreters should have available to create a strong professional identity.

This section also covered the perspective of ISPs and their expectations of interpreters, and has warned against some of the most common pitfalls for freelance interpreters. All these business practices reinforce the image of a consistent professional identity at the individual and at the collective level that strengthens the interpreting community as a whole.

4.3 Legal Interpreting

Overview

In a number of countries, legal interpreting will have ethics and standards specific to legal settings. They may differ from those for community interpreting. However, in real life, community services and legal situations overlap more often than interpreters might realize, resulting in to what we will refer to as *hybrid situations*.

While "legal interpreting" is often referred to as "court interpreting," the two are not synonymous. Court interpreting is part of the broader field of legal interpreting. Legal interpreting takes place in courts but also in police stations, lawyer offices, depositions and detention, for example. Yet you may also interpret for sessions with legal implication that take place in hospitals, social services, schools and crisis services: these are hybrid situations.

When community interpreters who have not been trained in legal interpreting perform hybrid legal-community interpreting, the risk for legal errors is high. This section will guide you through such situations. It will also help you:

- Recognize the differences between legal and community interpreting.
- Assess whether you should, or should not, perform legal interpreting.
- Understand how to perform effective legal interpreting in community settings.
- Adopt community interpreting protocols for legal interpreting.

However, to be clear, this section is *not intended to provide specialized training for legal interpreters.*

Learning Objective 4.3

After completing this section, you will be able to:

- Explore how community interpreters can perform effective legal interpreting in community settings.

Legal and court interpreting

What is the difference?

Community interpreting is defined in this textbook as: *Interpreting that facilitates access to community services for individuals who do not speak the language of service.*

Legal Interpreting

Interpreting related to legal processes and proceedings, including but not limited to lawyer-client representation, prosecutor-victim/witness interviews, and law enforcement communications. (Framer, Bancroft, Feuerle, & Bruggeman, 2010, p. xi)

In legal interpreting, you support due process and equal access to justice

Legal interpreting typically involves interpreting for any legal process or proceeding and includes, but is not limited to, court interpreting. It is an umbrella term often mistakenly used as a synonym for court interpreting. Court interpreting is an important part of legal interpreting and relates to the provision of interpreting services in court settings out of a concern for due process and equal access to justice. However, most legal services take place *outside* courtrooms.

Some legal interpreting thus involves the delivery of a community service, such as nonprofit legal services. Others take place within the community but are not truly a "community service," such as police interrogations or interviews with witnesses. Examples of common locations where legal interpreting occurs in out-of-court settings include:

- Police stations
- Immigration offices
- Prisons and detention centers
- Mediation and arbitration offices
- Offices of human rights
- Lawyer's offices

Yet in a broader sense, legal interpreting occurs every day in healthcare settings, such as hospitals, government social services, nonprofit human services and schools. This section will show you examples from all these settings.

Is legal interpreting part of community interpreting?

A hotly debated question around the world is whether legal interpreting is part of community interpreting. The topic is so controversial that there is no international agreement. Thus, when ISO created the first international interpreting standard for community interpreting (ISO, 2014), the standard could neither include nor exclude legal interpreting.

In some countries, such as Canada or Sweden, legal interpreting is formally considered to be part of community interpreting, at least in national standards for community interpreting services (HIN, 2007). Yet even in such countries, court interpreting is a true specialization that requires specific training and accreditation, and whose protocols and code of ethics are rooted in law. In other countries, such as the United States, legal interpreters, especially those in courts, are formally obligated to follow a set of ethics, standards, protocols (like taking an oath) and requirements different from community interpreters. Despite these differences, whenever legal and community interpreting intersect they create *hybrid situations*. The next sections will help explain how to adapt our behavior as community interpreters to such situations.

Ethics in legal and community interpreting

An overview of ethical concerns

Many ethical concerns in legal and community interpreting are the same. Both specializations share a concern for accuracy, confidentiality and impartiality. Yet, some differences can be noted.

- Legal interpreting, including its ethics and protocols, supports due process and equal access to justice, leaving little to no room for intervention—a cause for concern by many in the field who find that this rigidity can lead to serious communication problems that can jeopardize due process (Moeketsi, 1999; Ra & Napier, 2013).
- Court interpreters work within an adversarial framework while community interpreters work in a more collaborative one. Hence, the systemic relationships within each session create different dynamics. In a legal process, typically there is a winner and a loser, or a victim and a perpetrator. In a collaborative session, such as a medical encounter, the team works together and the focus is on a successful communication.

However, much of non-courtroom legal interpreting is *collaborative,* for example, lawyer-client interviews, immigration services, and nonprofit legal services and clinics.

Legal interpreting codes of ethics:

- European Union Legal Interpreters and Translators (EULITA), *Eulita Code of Professional Ethics.*[44]
- National Association of Judiciary Interpreters & Translators, *Code of Ethics and Professional Responsibilities.*[45]

Community or medical interpreting codes of ethics:

- National Council on Interpreting in Health Care (NCIHC, USA), *National Code of Ethics for Interpreters in Health Care.*[46]
- International Medical Interpreters Association (IMIA), *IMIA Code of Ethics.*[47]

---

[44] Available at http://www.eulita.org
[45] Available at http://www.najit.org
[46] Available at http://www.ncihc.org
[47] For the code itself see the IMIA website, www.imiaweb.org; for the guidance, see http://www.imiaweb.org/uploads/pages/380_4.pdf

Differences Between Ethical Codes for Legal and Medical Interpreters	
Legal Interpreter Ethical Requirements in EULITA and NCSC Codes	Community Interpreter Ethical Requirements in IMIA and NCIHC Codes
Confidentiality Strict requirement to respect confidentiality	**Confidentiality** Do not disclose information unless required by law. Can share confidential information with other members of the treating team (NCIHC). When disclosing internally, consider what is best for patient (NCIHC). Obligated to keep confidentiality regarding crimes except if required by law (e.g., for imminent danger or child abuse, depending on the relevant laws).
Accuracy Message to be rendered faithfully, maintaining the register, tone and style as well as repetitions, errors and hesitations.	**Accuracy** Message to be rendered completely, conveying content, spirit and cultural context (NCIHC). Interpreter obligated to alert parties to existence of possible cultural barrier (NCIHC). Select the mode that best supports accuracy (IMIA). Interpreters to use skillful unobtrusive interventions so as not to interfere with the flow of communication in a triadic medical setting (IMIA).
Impartiality Impartality and neutrality to be maintained in all proceedings, avoiding unnecessary contact with the parties. Conflict of interest should be disclosed immediately (NAJIT).	**Impartiality** Not permitted to give advice or opinions or interpret. Should not interpret for family members or friends (IMIA). Should still show caring (NCIHC).
Cultural competence Not stated in the codes; intervention not typically permitted for cultural barriers to communication.	**Cultural competence** There is an ethical requirement to consider cultural barriers to communication.
Protocol and demeanor Interpreters to conduct themselves in a manner consistent with standards and protocols of the Court.	**Professional conduct** The community interpreter's conduct should reflect the highest standards of the profession by showing adherence to professional ethics and best practices.
Representation of qualifications Requirement to accurately represent interpreter credentials.	**Representation of qualifications** No such standard exists in either code.
Limitations of practice Interpreters not to give advice to the parties or engage in activities other than interpreting within the scope of the case.	**Professional boundaries** Medical interpreters often provide services outside encounter, although parameters are not clearly specified. Interpreters should ideally not perform another work-related task or role while interpreting. (NCIHC).
Duty to report ethical violations Requirement to report ethical violations.	**Duty to report ethical violations** No comparable requirement in the medical codes.
Professional development Interpreters required to stay abreast of relevant statutes, rules and policies of the judiciary.	**Professional development** No strict requirement to know laws and legal policies.
Advocacy Not permitted.	**Advocacy** Intervene only when truly necessary (e.g., if the patient's safety, health or dignity are at risk)."Interpreters have a responsibility to use patient advocacy and cultural interface to ensure effective cross-cultural communication" (IMIA).

Table 4-E
A Comparison of Medical vs. Legal Codes of Ethics

In many countries, perhaps most, the community and legal interpreting professions have distinct professional cultures and different perspectives on how interpreters should conduct themselves. Community interpreters follow ethics, protocols and requirements that allow them to work together with the treatment or client support team collaboratively. They often see the legal professional code as too strict (for example, court interpreters are usually told not to address cultural barriers). Conversely, when court interpreters interpret in community settings, they tend to conduct themselves as if in court and are sometimes perceived as rigid, distant or cold.

> **DEFINITION**
>
> **Community interpreting**
>
> Interpreting that facilitates access to community services.

Community–legal interpreting

Examples from the "gray zone"

Community, Legal and "Community-Legal" Interpreting

How Do You Tell the Difference?

Even when an appointment takes place in a community setting it can involve legal interpreting!

1. If the appointment is legally adversarial (arbitration, for example, in an employer-employee dispute), or involves legal representatives providing a legal service, the encounter is clearly an example of legal interpreting. It might be best to regard the appointment as ***legal interpreting***.
2. If the appointment is only about providing a community service and no direct legal process or legal paperwork is involved, then this would be a case of ***community interpreting***.
3. If the purpose of the appointment is both to provide a community (non-legal) service *and* address legal paperwork, provide a legal service or conduct an interview as part of a legal process, then the appointment could well be an example of ***community and legal interpreting***.

Let's examine the "gray zone" of *hybrid situations* where community and legal interpreting intersect. Imagine that, as a community interpreter, you are called to interpret at:

- A hospital
- A social service agency
- A school

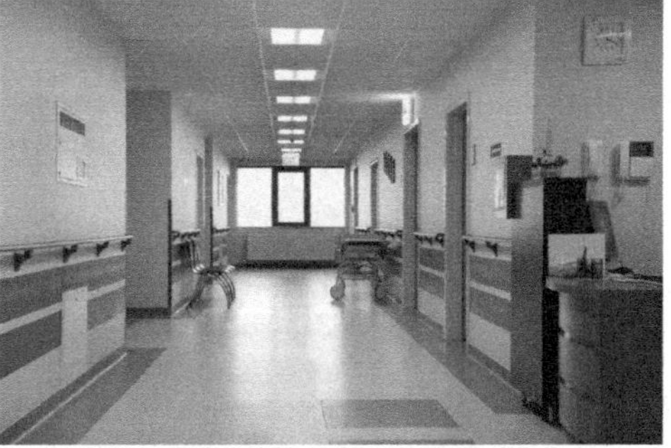

These look like classic examples of community interpreting. But some of them, when you arrive, could be community interpreting, legal interpreting, or both.

At a hospital

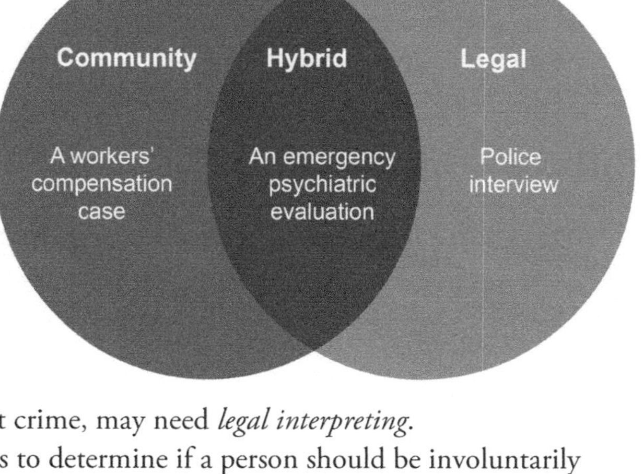

- *A workers' compensation case*: A workers' compensation case involves an injury caused by a work-related accident. When the "workers' comp" exam or visit is about the patient's health, it involves *community interpreting* because the goal is providing care. If the encounter is to determine whether or not the patient was injured on the job, then it is *legal interpreting* and part of a legal process that can be adversarial.
- *Police interview*: Police officers or detectives who come to hospitals to question a victim of a gunshot, domestic violence or other violent crime, may need *legal interpreting.*
- *An emergency psychiatric evaluation*: If the goal is to determine if a person should be involuntarily admitted to an institution, but care is still being provided to the patient: this process could involve both *legal and community interpreting.*

At a social service agency

Community
Hybrid
Legal
A child neglect investigation
Sight translation of a legal form

- *Sight translation of a legal form*: A service user is asked to sign a legal form, whether a consent form, a financial qualification document or an agreement to pay involving *legal interpreting.* However, a service may be provided at the same time (e.g., a service user signing a legal form also receives information about the service): this would be *community and legal interpreting* at the same time.
- *A child neglect investigation*: An investigator's interview with a parent could lead to legal charges or a custody court case, involving *legal interpreting.* However, the same person is a social worker and might also offer services to assist the parent (such as family counseling, a home health aide or early childhood intervention services), involving *community interpreting.*
- *Domestic violence*: Interpreting for a counselor and a domestic violence victim is *community interpreting.* Going down the hall to speak to a lawyer or immigration representative to explore the victim's legal status could shift into *legal interpreting.*

At a school

- *Services for students with disabilities* ("special education"): Such services in schools could involve request for consent (a legal process) and the discussion of services such as speech therapy: these could be *legal and community interpreting* at the same time.
- *Police interviews*: Police interviews a student who spray-painted lockers in the school bathroom: This is *legal interpreting.*
- *School board hearing about a student expulsion*: Such a hearing could involve a legal process with a lawyer present. If the student's well-being and a placement in another school is discussed, this might well involve both *legal and community interpreting.*

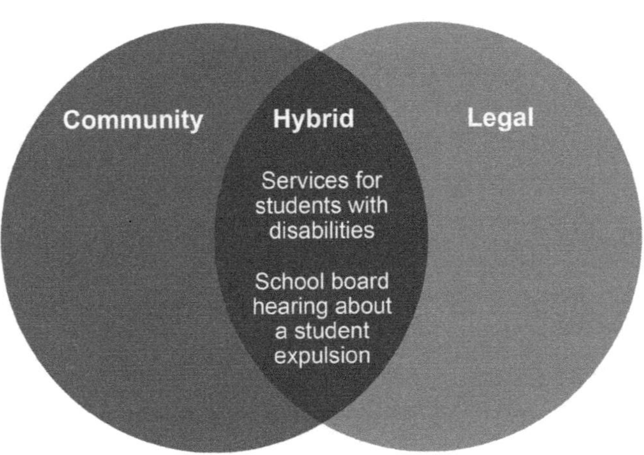

Who works in the "gray zone"?

Community interpreters perform much (and perhaps most) of non-courtroom legal interpreting—whether or not they are trained in legal interpreting. Community interpreters also perform most of the interpreting in hybrid situations. Most service providers are unaware of the distinction between legal and community interpreting. Likewise, untrained interpreters and requesters of interpreting services, associate the *setting* with the type of interpreting. Hence, community interpreters get called for many legal interviews. In addition, in many, and likely most, countries court interpreters tend to earn more than community interpreters. Therefore, community interpreters may be called to even transparently legal appointments (such as lawyer-client interviews, immigration hearings and police interviews) simply because they cost less.

The consequences of a lack of "legal-community" training

The consequences of having community interpreters perform legal and court interpreting without adequate training in legal terminology, protocols and skills may have a devastating impact on both the legal process and the outcome. Errors caused by community and otherwise unqualified interpreters in legal services have led to:

- Cases being overturned or thrown out of court.
- Individuals going free who should be found guilty and vice versa.
- Misunderstandings that lead to poor decision making by clients.
- A failure to access needed benefits, or getting undeserved access to such benefits (e.g., asylum, government disability payments or workers' compensation benefits).

Before accepting a legal interpreting assignment you, the interpreter, should carefully consider whether you have the qualifications to perform it effectively.

What community interpreters should do in hybrid cases

Should you accept legal interpreting assignments?

Often interpreters may not know beforehand if the assignment involves legal and/or community interpreting. So, if you arrive at an appointment and realize it involves legal interpreting—should you remain? And if you did know beforehand, should you accept? These are not easy questions to answer. There is no international agreement about them. In general, there is some growing consensus about the following points.

First, *all* interpreters should refrain from accepting assignments for which they are not qualified. That is an ethical requirement. Likewise, you should attempt to recuse yourself or withdraw from the encounter if it exceeds your competence. (Remember that three-step SAY NO model from Chapter 1). Often, interpreters underestimate the scope of a legal or quasi-legal meeting or the potential impact, for example, when benefits are removed, financial assistance is denied, child custody is lost or a restraining order against an abusive spouse is not filed in a case of domestic violence.

"Lack of Credentials"

Interpreters who do not hold the appropriate accreditations, or have not received at least the appropriate training, are not considered qualified to interpret at that session.

Caught by surprise: three real-life examples

Before we answer the question, "Should you accept a legal interpreting assignment?" let's look at three true stories from the field. They take place in community settings: a hospital, a social services office and an office for human rights. All three interpreters, for different reasons, assess their inadequacy to execute the assignments and withdraw or recuse themselves.

Story #1: "I Don't Know This Terminology"

In the first case, an untrained interpreter recognized her inadequacy to deal with legal implications resulting from misinterpreting the forms. She acknowledged, at first only to herself, her lack of legal terminology for sight translating forms through which the patient was giving consent or waiving rights. The interpreter's "common sense" made her feel responsible for potentially tragic outcomes resulting from the patient not understanding what she was either agreeing to or giving up. Had she interpreted, the risk of liability would have fallen on the interpreter and also the language company that sent her—and perhaps the hospital as well.

In this case, the interpreter could not live with the potentially drastic consequences of her incompetence. She used her common sense to withdraw, even though she did not know that:

a) She was in violation of several ethical principles.
b) She was exposing herself, her contracting agency, and the hospital to huge liability.
c) She was actually involved in legal interpreting.

Story #2: "I'm Sorry, I'm Not Qualified"

The Social and Human Services Department of a large county scheduled a community interpreter for a monthly meeting where all parties in a case gathered to discuss the development of the case and the treatment plan. Depending on the nature of such cases, up to 8-10 people can participate in such meetings. The decisions are binding and have legal consequences.

That specific meeting was a crowded one. As it started, the interpreter noticed not only a guardian ad litem (a lawyer who represents a child's best interests), but also another lawyer accompanied by two paralegals and a court-certified interpreter. Within minutes, the first interpreter realized that the scope of the terminology and legal processes involved were well beyond his abilities. Ten minutes in, the interpreter asked to be recused. He disclosed that the topics at stake were beyond his scope of competence and he did not feel qualified to continue. The interpreter was a professional interpreter, holding a 40-hour medical interpreter training certificate. He had no training in legal interpreting.

In the second case, the interpreter was concerned that incompetent interpreting could have hurt several members in the family. Furthermore, a court-certified interpreter was present who would have noted his errors. The interpreter fully understood his predicament and disclosed his limitations. He did exactly what a professional interpreter should do.

Story #3: "I've Never Had Training in Legal Interpreting."

By the Author of Chapter 3

I was called to interpret at a local office of human rights for a discrimination complaint. I had done so before, not knowing it was, in fact, legal interpreting. I did not have formal qualifications in legal interpreting.

I knew in advance that the case was about discrimination against a gay employee fired by a bakery. I carefully researched and memorized all the terminology available online that might be relevant to this appointment. But when I arrived, I found three clients (not one, as I had understood) as well as two lawyers (no one had mentioned lawyers) and a human-rights investigator. Furthermore, the interview would be recorded for use in a court case if it did not go to settlement!

I immediately disclosed the truth: that I wasn't a legal interpreter, had no training or credentials in that field, did not know legal terminology well and could make mistakes that put the case at risk. I recommended the office call either the nonprofit interpreter service that sent me or, to save time, one of the large national phone interpreting companies, and request a court-certified French interpreter. They chose the latter option. Fortunately all went well, and no one was upset: not even the interpreting service. I was even paid. I was lucky: but it was a huge lesson for me.

In this last case, all went smoothly. The interpreter disclosed her inadequacies, offered alternatives and the clients understood. Her conduct was professional and appropriate. These three examples show that community interpreters need to be able to assess whether they are qualified for a legal interpreting assignment. This is one reason for getting detailed information before an assignment: to help you determine whether you are competent to perform it. That said, often we find ourselves facing an assignment that takes a legal turn as it evolves. Below is a simple six-step process to address your decision making about whether or not to perform legal interpreting.

How to decide whether to perform legal interpreting

A decision-making protocol

1. Identify if the assignment is, or could be, legal interpreting.
2. When in doubt, consider the appointment legal interpreting.
3. If it is (or could be) legal interpreting, assess your competence to perform it.
4. If your competence is in doubt, try to decline or withdraw.
5. If it is not feasible to withdraw, disclose your limitations.
6. If you stay, conduct yourself as a legal interpreter.

Step 1: Identify if the assignment is, or could be, legal interpreting

In situations where interpreting is not merely related to access to services, be aware that you may be walking on legal ground. In the following examples, you can safely assume you will perform legal interpreting for at least part of the appointment:

- Lawyer-client meetings
- Meetings with paralegals, arbitrators, legal mediators and immigration representatives
- Police interviews and interrogations
- Hearings (administrative hearings) conducted under the authority of a government agency
- Adversarial meetings
- Appeals for denial of benefits
- Encounters where the purpose is to assess a legal situation and/or collect evidence

In addition, consider the following criteria:

- The meeting is part of any legal process or could turn into one.
- The meeting involves providing any kind of legal service.
- The meeting includes paperwork to be signed and/or with extensive legal terminology.
- Legal consequences could clearly come out of the meeting.
- You feel worried that this *might* be legal interpreting, even if you are not sure.

Step 2: When in doubt, consider the appointment legal interpreting.

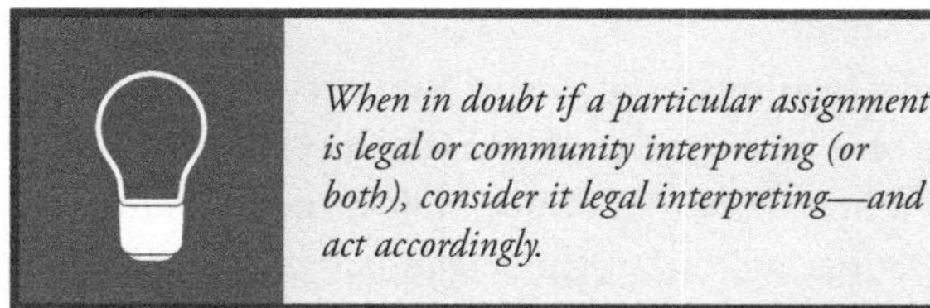
When in doubt if a particular assignment is legal or community interpreting (or both), consider it legal interpreting—and act accordingly.

There is often no way to anticipate whether a specific appointment in a community setting may turn into a session with legal implications. But you can identify certain signs such as (a) legal terminology; (b) a form that has to be signed; (c) the involvement of a legal service provider; or (d) a situation that has the potential for a legal case. If there is the slightest question in your mind, keep the decision simple: *assume* it is legal interpreting and act accordingly. You will always be safer this way, because the relevant local legal interpreting ethics and standards are almost always more limiting and restrictive than those for community interpreting.

Step 3: If it is (or could be) legal interpreting, assess your competence to perform it.

If it is clear that an encounter is, or might be, legal in nature, assess your competence to perform it. Have you had training in legal interpreting? Have you studied locally relevant legal interpreting ethics and standards? (See Step 6 for details.) Do you know this particular service setting well? Are you likely to know all the legal terminology? Will you be able to handle requests to sight translate legal documents? If you are trained in legal interpreting and feel confident you can successfully execute the assignment, accept it. However, when in doubt, assume your competence is lacking. You will almost certainly be correct.

Step 4: If your competence is in doubt, try to decline or withdraw.

If the demands of the encounter exceed your skills, decline the assignment or, if you are already there, ask to withdraw. You can do so in a professional manner by following the three-step SAY NO model taught in Chapter 1. For example, emphasize the importance of the meeting, thank them for inviting you but offer at least two ways they could find another interpreter who is more qualified, then share with the service provider why you are not competent to perform the assignment and the possible consequences if you remain.

Step 5: If it is not feasible to withdraw, disclose your limitations.

Perhaps you are the only interpreter available for a less common language. Perhaps all other interpreters for your language are busy, or none of them is trained in legal interpreting. Perhaps you are the best person for the job and the appointment is time sensitive. If, in your best judgment, you feel it is better to interpret than to decline, perhaps you should stay. In this case, it is your duty to disclose your limitations. Inform the service provider if you are not familiar with the protocols or terminology required but you are willing to help with the immediate need, or interpret while waiting for a replacement to arrive. If you take on the assignment, warn all parties that you may need to interrupt to request clarifications. A good practice is to ask service providers to speak clearly, keep the vocabulary simple and speak in short segments.

Step 6: If you stay, conduct yourself as a legal interpreter.

Follow a legal code of ethics!

Both community and legal interpreting ethics seem to apply because (a) the appointment could involve both legal *and* community interpreting; and/or (b) the interpreter is not sure which one to follow. When in doubt, follow the relevant *legal* code of ethics: you will always be legally safer by adhering to the ethics, standards and protocols for legal interpreting.

Which legal code of ethics to follow?

As you shift into a legal scenario, be aware of the more limiting rules that apply. *Know and study the relevant legal interpreting ethics in the geographic area where you practice.* If your country or region has none, and you do not belong to a professional association, consider following an established code such as the *EULITA Code of Professional Ethics* from the European Union (http://www.eulita.eu/sites/default/files/EULITA-code-London-e.pdf) or the *NAJIT Code of Ethics and Professional Responsibilities* from the United States (http://www.najit.org/about/NAJITCodeofEthicsFINAL.pdf). These are two regions of the world where the profession of legal interpreting is well established and both codes offer generally accepted principles.

Be careful when you intervene

Restrict your activities to interpreting. If you intervene at all, do so only to ask for the meaning of terms, phrases or expressions that you do not understand (or, of course, to request a break or a glass of water—use your common sense). *Avoid cultural mediation and advocacy.* Community interpreters might be uncomfortable if they are not permitted to identify potential cultural barriers to communication or engage in advocacy. But in legal interpreting, the only permissible advocate is a lawyer or other legal representative.

Is it professional or unprofessional to withdraw?

Many interpreters, especially those untrained or new to the profession, are reluctant to decline or withdraw from legal assignments because they fear they will lose business or be looked at as less competent. On the contrary: declining an assignment on the grounds that it lies outside one's scope of expertise or interpreting specialization is an excellent way to demonstrate:

- Your confidence in your area(s) of expertise.
- Your awareness of professional roles and responsibilities.
- Your adherence to the code of ethics and standards of practice of your profession.

It should also motivate you to pursue additional training in legal interpreting and general skills (such as simultaneous interpreting, sight translation, note-taking and terminology) to be able to accept a broader array of assignments. Remind yourself that it is unethical to accept assignments for which you are not qualified, and that repairing the damage from doing so is more harmful to those you serve and your reputation than declining the assignment.

Workers' compensation: a detailed study

Disclaimer

Workers' compensation insurances and legislation may exist in your country of residence under other names, using different criteria and offering different services. Interpreting in this field may or may not exist. The goal of this section is to give a clear example of a common hybrid community/legal setting and its implications for community interpreters.

This section focuses on the United States in order to provide a concrete, specific example of a certain type of hybrid legal/community interpreting usually performed by community interpreters—often with grave consequences. Workers' compensation is a particularly widespread form of such hybrid interpreting in the United States. Even if this specific field does not exist—or is not commonly interpreted—in your country, this section will help you identify similar types of situations and show you how to conduct yourself in them.

Definition of workers' compensation

Workers' compensation (WC) refers to a mandatory form of business insurance required by U.S. law, typically from employers, to cover compensation for workers who are injured at work or who contract an occupational disease. This type of insurance covers the costs of medical expenses, income replacement or both. It might also help protect companies from being sued by employees for the workplace conditions that caused such an injury or illness.

Workers' compensation and interpreting

An overview of the system

In the United States, interpreting for workers' compensation is common. Most interpreters confuse it with medical interpreting because the encounters often take place in a hospital, outpatient setting or occupational facilities that serve injured employees. Such appointments do not address general medicine but workplace injuries.

The process

When an injury happens, the U.S. employer has the legal obligation to enter a claim. The injured employee then becomes a claimant. Depending on the seriousness of the injury, the claimant may either return to work at full capacity or make changes to his/her daily duties to accommodate the restriction(s) the occupational doctor has specified. When treatment begins, the WC insurance starts an investigation to verify the injury happened at work and was work-related. If the outcome of the investigation is positive, the claimant continues with treatment. If it is determined that the injury is not work-related, the claim is denied and treatment is interrupted or does not begin. The insurance no longer covers expenses for medical visits.

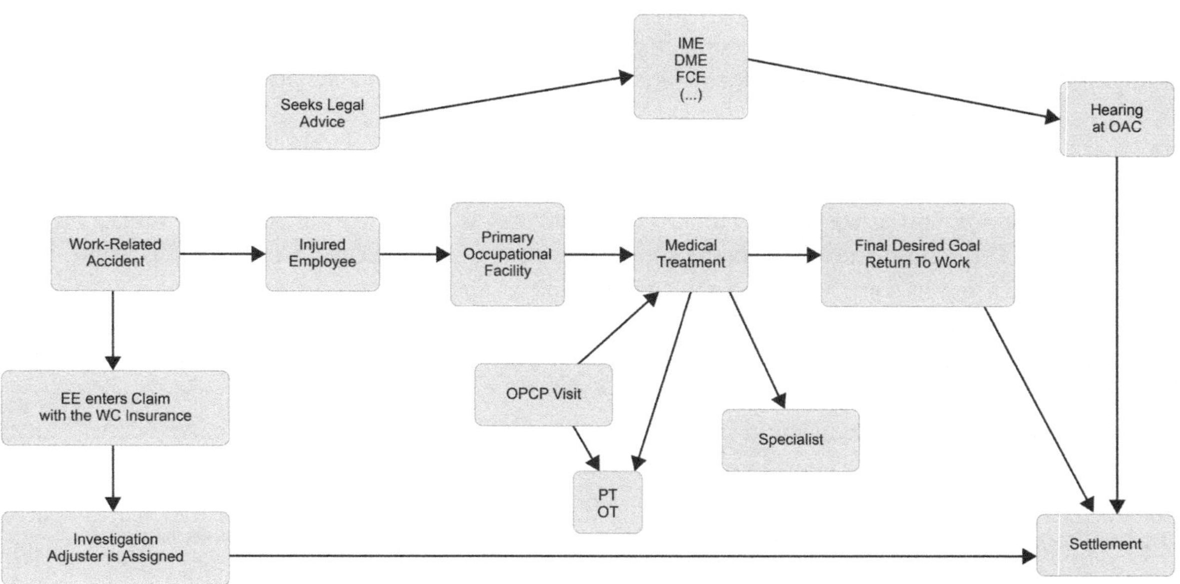

Figure 4-E
The Anatomy of a Worker's Compensation Claim

Key:
OPCP – Occupational Primary Care Physician
PT – Physical Therapy
OT – Occupational Therapy
EE – Employee
OAC – Office of Administrative Courts
IME – Independent Medical Evaluation
DIME – Division Independent Medical Evaluation
FCE – Functional Capacity Evaluation

In some instances, injured claimants hire a lawyer. A claim always ends with a settlement, when an injured worker and the WC insurance company reach an agreement on the extent, amount and type of compensation to be paid to the employee for damages caused by the work-related injury or illness.

Treatment plan vs. legal assessment

The goal of medical treatment is distinct from the legal process of assessing an injury. In general practice, doctors focus on the health and well-being of the patient. Occupational doctors focus on the specific injury and its consequences for the employee. Their goal is to restore the physical condition of the employee to what it was immediately before the accident. In legal assessment, however, their goal may be rather to *determine* the extent of the injury and make formal recommendations about services the injured worker is eligible for. Lastly, one appointment might involve both the provision of care *and* a forensic legal evaluation regarding the injuries and required services.

The workers' compensation interpreter

An interpreter might be needed to help ensure that the injured claimant understands the implications of the treatment or the legalities of the claim. Due to the interests at stake, WC interpreting could involve legal interpreting, community (medical and social services) interpreting or both. Even when the injury is treated at the medical level, the implications and the consequences of any injury-related medical appointment could contribute to a legal determination of the outcome. Often, the case is litigated in hearings at the Office of Administrative Courts, which is the equivalent of the court system of occupational claims. The hearings are overseen by a judge, and interpreting takes place as if everyone were in court. Simply put, U.S. workers' compensation interpreting is a legal type of interpreting that takes place in a mix of legal and medical settings. Interpreter services may be provided at a deposition, at appeals board hearings, at a medical-legal examination, and at a medical-treatment appointment.

Interpreting protocols for WC appointments

In medical offices, the interpreting mode used is consecutive as in most medical and community settings at large. If the claimant contracts the services of a lawyer, the interpreter will abide by legal interpreting ethics and in court settings, consecutive mode will be used if the claimant speaks, but simultaneous will be used when the judge, the lawyers or a witness speaks and the interpreter interprets for the claimant.

Interpreters working in this field should treat each session as if it was legal, abstain from advocacy or cultural mediation (typically considered to be prohibited in legal interpreting in the United States) and from making public comments about what is interpreted—which means they are not permitted to respond to requests from contracting agencies to provide reports about what took place during the session. Interpreters should familiarize themselves with both medical and legal terminology, and accept the legal or the medical assignment depending on their qualifications.

Interpreting challenges for WC appointments

Special challenges for interpreters in this field the specialized acronyms and terminology, conflicting cultural concepts of pain, and the sight translation of detailed questionnaires and consent forms. The state of California (a large U.S. state with a population surpassing that of Canada) passed a bill in August 2013 that regulates the credentialing of interpreters who work in the workers' compensation field in California. California's new DWC (Division of Workers' Compensation) regulations require that interpreters for medical appointments be nationally certified and show knowledge of legal terminology, while interpreters for the occupational hearings and depositions, or medical-legal appointments be court-certified and show evidence of knowing medical terminology.

As this in-depth example of workers' compensation interpreting in the United States makes clear, interpreting for hybrid community-legal services can be far more complex than most stakeholders realize—including interpreters.

Let's Practice

Learning Activity 4.3 (a): Quiz: Legal Interpreting in Community Settings
Learning Activity 4.3 (b): Legal vs. Medical Interpreting
Learning Activity 4.3 (c): Settlement Paperwork

In *The Community Interpreter®: An International Workbook of Activities and Role Plays*

REVIEW OF SECTION 4.3

Legal interpreting is often confused with court interpreting when in fact much legal interpreting takes place outside the courtroom. When legal or quasi-legal encounters take place in community settings, such as schools, hospitals, nonprofit organizations or government social services offices, court interpreters are rarely involved. Yet these encounters are often no less "legal" or important than court cases. Usually, legal or quasi-legal encounters set the stage for situations that ultimately could end up in court, and inappropriate interpreting may lead to poor outcomes. Service users, providers and interpreters might all be unaware of the risks of having community interpreters who lack legal interpreter training execute assignments that involve legal interpreting.

In this section you have explored ways to make decisions about whether or not to perform legal interpreting in community settings following a six-step decision-making tool. You have also examined many of the implications of performing legal interpreting when you have not received formal training in that field.

As you get more exposed to and invested in the profession, look for ways to develop your education and participate in training opportunities that help you fill the gap. Seek out interpreting- or terminology-related trainings that can prepare you for legal interpreting.

4.4 Emerging Specializations

Overview

An interpreter is, first and foremost, an interpreter. All interpreters should share a core set of skills and then layer on additional skills as needed according to their specific career path. In other words, one set of basic qualifications, skills and protocols should be the foundation for our professional practice. But we often get caught up in labels. Are we community interpreters? Medical interpreters? Legal interpreters?

This section does not provide a prescriptive view of how community interpreting specializations work in your country. Rather, it offers you an opportunity to personally define your role within and among these specializations.

If your country has prescriptive practices different from the recommendations presented here, such practices should take precedence in your day-to-day professional conduct within each specialization. Finally, because legal interpreting was discussed at length in the previous section, it is not addressed here.

Learning Objective 4.4

After completing this section, you will be able to:

- Identify and explore common areas of specialization within community interpreting.

A Medical Interpreting Tragedy

It was a normal day in the life of the hospital. Patients at the front desk were checking in while others left. Some nurses sat chatting in the coffee shop for a quick break. In the waiting area a nurse called a name, and a husband and wife stood. A third person approached the group: a medical interpreter.

The couple's son was very sick and being treated at the hospital. Accompanied by the interpreter, they walked to a doctor's office and stayed half an hour. After the family left the doctor's office they stayed ten more minutes talking with the interpreter and left. A nurse asked the interpreter if the family had had any questions; the interpreter said yes, but she had addressed their questions.

The next day, another ordinary day at the hospital. Patients at the front desk were checking in, while others left. Then came the sound of an ambulance. A child was rushed in on a stretcher and taken straight to the operating room. The parents rushed in, devastated: the mother was crying, and the dad held her tight. An interpreter arrived seven minutes later. Here was the same family from the day before—but a different interpreter. After few hours, a doctor came out with a nurse and announced something to the parents in a grave voice.

The interpreter paused, then interpreted: the child had died from complications caused by an overdose of one of the medicines prescribed for treatment. Now the doctors asked the parents urgent questions regarding the dosage given. They uncovered that the family did not remember exactly what the doctor had said about the dosage at the last visit, so they had asked the interpreter. When the interpreter stated the dosage, the parents wrote that information down and followed it. And now their child was dead.

A panoramic view of community interpreting

Community interpreting may be unique among the interpreting specializations for its panorama of sub-specializations and settings, its emotional depth and logistic complexity, as well as the personal and even intimate human connections it tends to foster.

> **DEFINITION**
>
> **Community interpreting**
>
> Interpreting that facilitates access to community services for linguistically diverse clients who do not speak the language of service.

Community interpreting touches on basic human services, from giving birth to facing end-of-life decisions, and has complex variables that impact the quality of services. Furthermore, "the role and organization of interpreters in healthcare, in education, in the legal and social settings, vary greatly precisely because they reflect the host country's perception of the phenomenon of migration and of the direct and indirect experience of living with these new communities" (Rudvin & Tomassini, 2011).

In order to address different aspects of community interpreting, this section will identify the main areas of specialization (horizontal labeling), specific settings in each (vertical labeling) with examples of where different specializations and settings may overlap.

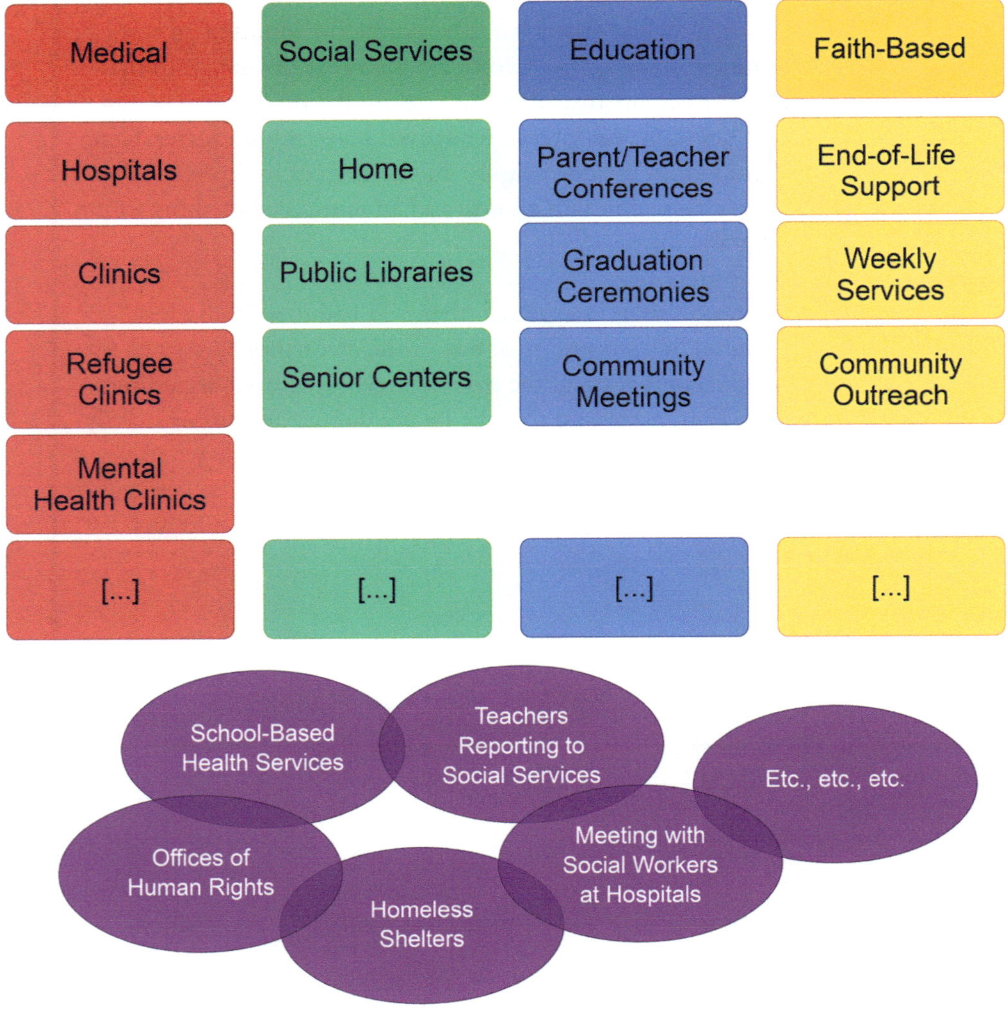

Medical interpreting

An overview of medical interpreting

Medical interpreting, also referred to as healthcare interpreting, is one of the most highly professionalized sub-specializations of community interpreting. It has evolved almost separately from community interpreting in countries such as Qatar, parts of Africa, Japan, some European nations, Canada and the United States and is an emerging specialization in other countries such as Mexico.

Medical interpreting involves interpreting for patients, their families and healthcare staff. It takes place in an array of medical and health-related settings and situations, from routine doctor's visits to medical tests and procedures, prenatal classes, and the operating room. Encounters can involve complex terminology and situations that feel emotionally overwhelming for interpreters (like interpreting for fatal diagnoses, prayers for the dying or bad news after surgery or childbirth). Encounters that take place in intense, high-stakes settings, such as emergency departments, oncology wards, children's hospitals, forensic examinations and psychiatric facilities can be taxing and stressful for interpreters. (Chapter 5 discusses interpreter self care and vicarious trauma.)

Due to this array of services and settings, healthcare organizations may use several types of interpreters (trained bilingual staff, staff interpreters or freelance interpreters) or untrained language assistants (family, friends, volunteers and bilingual staff not trained to interpret). Unfortunately, even children are still asked to interpret in medical services.

What interpreters need to know about medical interpreting

Finding out how the healthcare system works

If you work as a medical interpreter, study and understand how the healthcare system works in your country. Each country is different. In most parts of the world, the healthcare system is filled with cultural complexity. In a number of countries, the culture of the biomedical system itself and professional cultures of the institution and its providers can be at odds with the beliefs and practices of the patients it serves. You, the interpreter, may be the only person who truly understands the complexity of these conflicts of worldviews and beliefs.

Understanding how the healthcare system works will help you navigate that system and understand the intricacies of its processes and treatment plans. It is equally important to be informed about the policies of the specific facilities where you render your services. Different hospitals or medical offices may have policies in place that they expect everyone to comply with, interpreters included, such as the need for updated vaccinations. As a medical interpreter you may witness acts that violate acceptable standards for interpreting, including children and family members being asked to interpret: a dangerous practice discussed in Chapter 1. In addition, medical interpreting has seen a growing trend in some countries to use technology resources, such as telephone and video interpreting (which can be appropriate if the interpreters themselves are qualified), and even online translation software (such as GoogleTranslate) with voiced "interpreting" through speech synthesis, which is dangerous. Anecdotal evidence shows this kind of automated translation or interpreting in healthcare can be risky and even life-threatening in scope, yet substantive research on the topic is still lacking.

As an interpreter, you may be requested to answer questions outside the session. Doing so is risky with providers and dangerous with patients. While you should not, in fact, answer a service user's questions or otherwise "help" a service user during or outside the session—or even be left alone with service users—in *any* area of community interpreting, the risks in medical and legal interpreting are higher due to the risk of providing incorrect information with dangerous results.

Also, make sure that the policies in place for the healthcare institution are not in conflict with interpreting best practices and standards. If you perceive a conflict, report it to your supervisor or medical staff and explore solutions that make sense in your local context.

Training and credentials for medical interpreters

Specialized training in medical interpreting is emerging in quite a number of countries around the world. It may be part of university programs in community interpreting or shorter, private training programs dedicated to medical interpreting. Increasingly, some programs are available online, and a number of them can be found on the website of IMIA.[48]

Preparing for Specialization: Medical Interpreter Training

Interpreting in medical settings has become reasonably well-developed in some countries, to the point that it is now the norm for interpreters working in this field to undergo at least some training. Practitioners in the medical field typically undergo extensive and lengthy years of study and preparation, and in the end often specialize in a specific medical discipline.

As interpreters, we are called to interpret for the full spectrum of possible specializations. Therefore, at the bare minimum, medical interpreters are expected to have a robust knowledge of anatomy, physiology and common medical procedures. Some of this training is available online.

Often, good training in these medical fields and medical terminology is available to interpreters by taking classes at local universities or colleges. Such classes are designed not necessarily for interpreters but for healthcare or allied health professionals (such as medical lab technicians or medical assistants). The classes are not bilingual but still helpful.

In addition, there is an increasing amount of online training available for medical interpreting.

In the United States, market demand for medical interpreter credentials led in large part by hospitals, language companies and interpreter associations opened the road to certification. Today, the United States appears to be the only nation in the world with not only one but *two* national certifications available for medical interpreters: The National Board of Certification for Medical Interpreters (NBCMI, http://www.certifiedmedicalinterpreters.org) and the Certification Commission for Healthcare Interpreters (CCHI, http://www.cchicertification.org). These two bodies offer different but somewhat comparable accreditations based on language, experience and professional development. (See Chapter 1 for details). For information on how to develop specialization-specific terminology, see Section 4.5 of this chapter.

---

[48] Go to www.imiaweb.org. Currently, the online searchable database of education and training programs, which also identify online programs, is available at http://www.imiaweb.org/education/trainingnotices.asp

Ethics and standards in medical interpreting

In some countries, such as Canada, ethics and standards exist for community interpreting, including medical interpreting (HIN, 2007), while in others, such as the United States, specific ethics and standards may exist for medical interpreting, whether or not they end up being applied to other areas of community interpreting (NCIHC, 2004 and 2005).

In countries, such as Australia, the national code of ethics applies to *all* interpreters and specializations, including community interpreting and medical interpreters. In general, sign language interpreting often has national codes of ethics for general interpreting that apply to any specialization. One example is the Swedish National Association of Sign Language Interpreters *Code of Professional Conduct*[49] and other examples include Australia, Canada, Ireland, Kenya, the Philippines, Turkey and the United States.[50]

The International Medical Interpreting Association (IMIA) has published its IMIA International Code of Ethics.[51] In addition, its *Medical Interpreting Standards of Practice* (IMIA/MMIA, 1995), published when IMIA was still the Massachusetts Medical Interpreters Association, was a seminal work. These standards had a tremendous influence on the emerging field of medical interpreting and have now been translated into Portuguese, Hebrew, Spanish, Italian and Korean and have influenced other countries.

Modes in medical interpreting

Consecutive interpreting is the preferred mode in medical interpreting as it fosters direct communication. However, other modes are used as needed. Simultaneous interpreting is common in health-education programs and may be critical in situations where speakers cannot or should not be interrupted (for example, mental health emergencies or interpreting for a drunk or psychotic patient). Sight translation is requested on a daily basis in medical interpreting to assist patients with paperwork. Summarizing may be critical for emergency services.

In addition, mode-switching is very common in medical interpreting. Interpreters will need to refine their skills to assess which mode to use at any given time and be able to switch effectively as needed, because in medical interpreting a situation can change quickly and without warning—and the consequences can be serious.

---

49 Available at http://w3.sttf.nu/etiska-riktlinjer/code-of-professional-conduct
50 Available at http://wasli.org/your-wasli/code-of-ethics
51 Available at http://www.imiaweb.org/code/default.asp

Educational interpreting

An overview of educational interpreting

United Nations, *The Universal Declaration of Human Rights*

Article 26

(1) Everyone has the right to education. Education shall be free, at least in the elementary and fundamental stages. Elementary education shall be compulsory. Technical and professional education shall be made generally available and higher education shall be equally accessible to all on the basis of merit.

(2) Education shall be directed to the full development of the human personality and to the strengthening of respect for human rights and fundamental freedoms. It shall promote understanding, tolerance and friendship among all nations, racial or religious groups, and shall further the activities of the United Nations for the maintenance of peace.

(3) Parents have a prior right to choose the kind of education that shall be given to their children.

http://www.un.org/en/documents/udhr/

In almost every country around the world, access to education is considered an international human right. The obligation of a civilized country is to provide a quality education free of charge, at least in childhood. In some countries, even higher education is offered at no cost. Although different education systems around the world can be hard to compare, it is generally agreed that education is a primary service that immigrant children should have a right to experience and to which Deaf and indigenous residents also have a right.

What interpreters need to know about educational interpreting

Finding out how the educational system works

Because educational systems are so different in each country, it can be a challenging field for interpreters. Many concepts, terms and ways of tracking a student's progress can seem almost "untranslatable." Even how and why children are disciplined varies dramatically. Interpreters familiar with the educational systems of both the country and region where they interpret and in the countries where the families they interpret for are from will find that they can:

- Interpret more accurately.
- Interpret more quickly.
- Interrupt less often to ask for clarifications.
- Know when to paraphrase and when to ask a speaker to explain a term or concept.
- Feel more confident.
- Facilitate the session more smoothly.

The state of the profession

The educational interpreter may be a bilingual employee who holds another role or be contracted by the school district through interpreting agencies. Often, schools may turn to volunteers, family members or friends. In countries like the United States, an emerging practice is for school systems to create their own "community language banks" of interpreters: after a brief orientation by the school system, these interpreters are placed on a list and then any school may call on their services, for which the interpreters receive a modest payment.

From a professional standpoint, only in recent years has educational interpreting emerged as a specialization in its own right and come to the attention of researchers (Rudvin & Tomassini, 2011). Signed language interpreters in particular, in many countries, are becoming increasingly involved in educational interpreting. In addition, at international conferences that address community interpreting (including those hosted by Critical Link International, the International Association of Translation and Intercultural Studies and the University of Alcalá Public Service Interpreting and Translation), educational interpreting is now a common topic.

In an effort to bring together the views of interpreters and researchers, more research has examined what happens. What has emerged in recent years is that whether an educational system brings in trained, professional interpreters or informal language assistants who lack interpreting skills or credentials (including untrained bilingual staff, volunteers, friends, family members—and even the students themselves) is a *choice*. That choice seems to depend on a number of factors. In anecdotal observation, those factors usually include:

1. The level of understanding within the school system of the critical importance of being able to fully communicate with migrant, Deaf and indigenous children and families.
2. The impact of lack of such communication on academic achievement, parental involvement and student well-being.
3. How prepared the education system is to meet the needs of families who do not speak the societal language(s).
4. Whether localities have the resources (both human and financial) to address the need.
5. The availability of needed language resources to fulfill the need.

Furthermore, in countries where no language policy or law exists to support, mandate or provide funding for interpreters in education, the choice of interpreter is even more likely to shift to family members, friends or volunteers. Sometimes it depends on the personal initiative of teachers who find other ways to bridge the linguistic and cultural gap (Buri, 2012). A persistent problem is the use of children to interpret for their own parent-teacher meetings, despite the obvious conflicts of interest.

What educational interpreters do

Interpreters engaged in educational settings are often asked to interpret for:

- School registration.
- Parent/teachers meetings.
- Classroom teaching.
- Programs for students with disabilities (such as physical, cognitive or learning disabilities or major mental health diagnoses).
- Conflict resolutions and disciplinary hearings.
- Athletic programs or events.
- Field trips and excursions.
- Public school events.

Training and education for educational interpreters

It is unfortunate that few programs in the world are devoted to training for educational interpreting. (Anecdotally, most of the programs that do exist appear to be for signed language, not spoken language.) Given the complexity of techniques involved, the advanced terminology, the often demanding forms and documents to sight translate and some of the emotional intensity (from angry parents and upset teachers to children who engage on school property in drugs, vandalism and even sexual assault), educational interpreting needs specialized programs. Even online programs in educational interpreting are not widely available.

Ethics and standards for educational interpreters

Professional Codes of Conduct
(RID, 2010, p. 2)

Interpreters/transliterators, like many other professionals, adhere to a professional code of conduct. K-12 interpreters are to comply with the professional practices outlined by individual school districts. The EIPA Code of Professional Guidelines is another recommended resource for the K-12 setting. Furthermore, K-12 interpreters should read and be familiar with the NAD-RID Code of Professional Conduct. Fundamental professional practices for the K-12 interpreter are:

- Follow the student's IEP or Section 504 Plan [special plans in U.S. schools that address how to deliver educational and support services to students with disabilities]
- Maintain confidentiality – information is only shared within the educational team
- Maintain professional boundaries, respect privacy of students and foster independent student learning
- Provide an interpretation that meets the linguistic needs of the student
- Conduct oneself appropriate to the academic setting
- Demonstrate respect for students and colleagues
- Engage in professional development activities
- Prepare for classroom academic content, including previewing text books, teacher's lesson plans or electronic presentation slides
- Research technical educational vocabulary, as necessary
- Preview educational films, as necessary
- Provide information to teachers on how to access and utilize captioned media

Whether they are professionally qualified or not, individuals who interpret in education should follow professional interpreting ethics and standards. Unfortunately, because educational interpreting is still an emerging specialization, nearly no specialized standards exist.[52] Educational interpreters who lack a specific ethics or standards to follow can refer to the *Ethics and Standards* document at the beginning of this textbook.

Modes in educational interpreting

The primary mode of interpreting in educational settings is usually consecutive, although circumstances may require switching into simultaneous in meetings or for public events and presentations. In countries where school districts have reached out to their diverse communities, simultaneous interpreting is more common. Often these public outreach events reflect a concern by the school district for involving diverse communities and parents. If so, here is an opportunity to help educate those schools about the role of a professional interpreter and the impact of professional interpreting on the quality of communication.

Social services interpreting

An overview of social services interpreting

This section defines human and social services interpreting as interpreting that supports the delivery of benefits or services provided by a government, nonprofit or for-profit agency to improve the welfare of residents in need. Such residents must typically meet certain requirements (which vary by country or locality) in order to be eligible to receive these services. Social services interpreting is often confused with community interpreting, when in fact it is just one specialized area of community interpreting.

The sheer array of services available within this specialization of interpreting is daunting. Consider the following examples:

- Food assistance programs
- Homeless shelters
- Disaster relief services
- Crisis intervention (including hotlines)
- Domestic violence centers
- Sexual assault services
- Libraries
- Senior centers
- Employee benefit programs
- Job training
- Services to persons with disabilities
- Government welfare programs
- Subsidized housing
- Transportation services

Eligible individuals who need these services but do not speak the language of the service usually need and may require the assistance of an interpreter. As discussed in Section 4.1, there may even be laws in place to mandate that an interpreter be provided for these services.

[52] For an overview of educational interpreting in one country, the website of Registry of Interpreters for the Deaf (www.rid.org) offers significant resources and information for signed language educational interpreters on this webpage: http://www.rid.org/aboutRID/initiatives/index.cfm/AID/131

This area of community interpreting may utilize qualified interpreters yet often relies on untrained language assistants. Interpreting sessions can involve from three people (including the interpreter) to a large number of participants, including, but not limited to, other family members involved in the decision, other social services providers or administrators and other agencies' representatives involved in the provision of the services.

What interpreters need to know about social services interpreting

Finding out how the social system works

Imagine the wealth of service-specific terms, the complexity and the service system cultures at play. Here is a rich and fascinating field—and one that requires intensive preparation. Interpreters working in this field should familiarize themselves with how such services are provided in the countries where they work.

These services are provided to individuals in need, usually to address either an acute crisis or to provide longer-term support that may support the individual or family's journey to self-sufficiency. They are designed to help individuals navigate crises or chronic situations where they need external help or guidance to move forward with their lives. The ultimate goal is to help them rediscover their personal power, build on their strengths and regain autonomy.

At this point in time, it does not appear that formalized training programs, ethics or standards for social services interpreters have developed independently from those for community interpreting.

Modes in social services interpreting

The primary mode of interpreting in social service interpreting is consecutive. While simultaneous skills may be needed less often here than in either medical or educational interpreting, they can still be necessary. For example, you may be interpreting either partly or completely in simultaneous during meetings where:

- Elected officials hold meetings with their constituents.
- Persons in crisis intervention, disaster relief or homeless services speak rapidly or are out of control due to substance abuse or mental health problems.
- Emotional or contentious meetings where parties present forget to pause.
- Meetings where one individual is making a presentation to a group.

Sight translation requests are common due to the broad array of documents in some countries, many of which must be signed for an applicant to receive services. Other common documents that may be sight translated in social service settings include consent forms, brochures for services, financial qualification forms, appeals for denials of benefits and official letters about the service.

Faith-based interpreting

An overview of faith-based interpreting

Faith-based interpreting means interpreting for programs, services and events that are religious or spiritual in nature. It may involve interpreting for:

- A sermon, ceremony or a worship service in a house of faith, such as a church, mosque or temple, where communication is primarily between a speaker and the congregation
- Religious education
- Visiting religious figures, such as pastors, leaders or speakers
- Retreats
- Confessions
- Prayers, whether in houses of faith, private homes, hospices or healthcare settings, such as hospitals
- Weddings
- Funerals
- Counseling
- Youth activities
- Tours and pilgrimages

What interpreters need to know about faith-based interpreting

The faith in question

In order to be effective in the most respectful way, interpreters in religious settings need a deep knowledge of the religion or spiritual path in question, as well as the terminology specific to that faith. Linguistic knowledge is not enough to understand and accurately render a religious message. Interpreters need to familiarize themselves with the sacred text specific to the setting (i.e., the Quran, Bible, Torah, etc.) in both the source language and the target language, as well as the ceremonial prayers so often learned by heart and recited in a fixed order. In faith-based interpreting, it can be common to interpret hymns and recitations that require almost a poetic or artistic sensibility to render them effectively—or as effectively as possible. It is fair to say that faith-based interpreting is a highly underrated emerging specialization that requires immense knowledge, skill and targeted practice.

"Frozen register"

"Frozen register" refers to speech or text that has become a formal part of a ritual and acts like a script. Consider taking an oath in a court of law to speak the truth: each person who speaks that oath says the same words. Interpreters must interpret the oath with a high degree of accuracy—which is usually easy, because the court interpreter often interprets the same oath.

In faith-based interpreting, unless you interpret the same rituals often, frozen register may catch you off guard and you may have simply no idea how to interpret them, even if you understand them. They may include words that you have never heard and complex meanings tied to that faith. They may sound more like poetry than prose (and poetry, of course, is a huge challenge to interpret).

Combine this challenge with the delicacy of interpreting at a funeral or by the bedside of a dying patient surrounded by relatives. Is a group prayer for a dying child really the moment when you want to interrupt every sentence or two to request clarification? The only way to avoid the problem is to ask in advance, if possible, what ritual text, hymns or prayers might be recited or sung and if the text is available you can prepare in advance. Frozen register of this kind can sometimes be almost impossible to interpret on the spot, especially if it is unfamiliar to you.

Training in faith-based interpreting

Trainings specific to faith-based interpreting are rare. To study the topic, find a religious or spiritual mentor to guide you in what to prepare and practice, including the spiritual context, common rituals and prayers, the structure of the worship service (if relevant) and the most important terminology. Attending services and spiritual education programs in advance and exploring standard scripture for that faith may be valuable as well.

Ethics and impartiality in faith-based interpreting

It is important to assess your personal religious beliefs or biases before accepting faith-based interpreting assignments or those that may involve faith-based content. Sometimes the interpreter may have a different belief that could potentially conflict with the beliefs of those involved. Since there do not appear to be ethics and standards for faith-based interpreting, adhere to the same code of ethics and standards you use for community interpreting in general. Specifically, make every effort to interpret faithfully and impartially or withdraw if you cannot do so.

This specialization is perhaps the most sensitive of the interpreting specializations. Sometimes you may be required to share the faith you interpret for—or asked to join the prayers. It may feel awkward to refuse and might even, in some cases, be inappropriate. (Faith-based and military interpreting are two specializations where ethics and standards specific to their practice are urgently needed.)

Listeners will not appreciate interpreters unfamiliar with basic ritual text and recitations.
Furthermore, interpreters must keep confidentiality here too, given the intense privacy of conversations such as confessions, end-of-life support, spiritual mentoring and counseling.

Prior communication is recommended to make sure that the logistics are well planned to accommodate the presence of an interpreter. It is also important that everybody be informed of the presence and the role of the interpreter.

Dress code is also important: the interpreter must be sensitive to the place, the event and the people present. The interpreter should not to be an obstacle to the liturgy or ritual taking place, and should be respectful of the protocol required. The interpreter should be aware of where and how to stand or move, the places considered sacred, the acoustics, the importance of hierarchy and gender roles, and whether the service is recorded (RID, 2000).

Faith-Based interpreting often occurs in healthcare settings. Be prepared. You may interpret visits between a patient and a chaplain, visiting elder, pastor or minister. In some countries, spiritual care may be considered part of the care provided by medical staff. You, too, may be considered an integral part of the healing process. If your personal beliefs impede delivery, disclose that you are not familiar with the context or terminology and request to withdraw, or, if there is no viable replacement, ask for guidance along the way.

Modes in faith-based interpreting

The primary mode in faith-based interpreting is simultaneous, particularly for worship services. If you have not yet built up adequate skills in simultaneous, decline assignments for faith-based interpreting unless they involve consecutive.

Depending on the place and nature of the encounter, consecutive and simultaneous may be both needed. During a confession or end-of-life visit (even the administration of final rites), consecutive may help foster a bond between the individual and his religious guide. However, events could spiral quickly and require switching to simultaneous or even summarizing. Sight translation may be needed, particularly for passages from sacred texts written prayers and hymns.

A Word About Faith-Based Interpreting

Faith-based interpreting requires as much diligence as any other specialization in community interpreting, if not more. Healthcare, education, and human services have their own systems and terminology. Religion and spirituality do too. Interpreters are expected to deliver at the highest level of accuracy and impartiality, all the more so because of the depth of feeling that faith often invokes, the common inclusion of frozen register and the risk of damaging an event through interpreting that offends the sensibilities or beliefs of the participants or congregation.

Mental health interpreting

An overview of mental health interpreting

What is mental health?

The World Health Organization (WHO) defines mental health *as a state of well-being in which every individual realizes his or her own potential, can cope with the normal stresses of life, can work productively and fruitfully, and is able to make a contribution to her or his community.*[53]
This positive definition means *having and maintaining a balanced mental activity*" (Shah & Zaman, 2012). However, most societies around the world have long associated the field of mental health with negative images and feelings.

The presence of the interpreter has a considerable impact on service delivery. Consumers of mental health services in most countries often have difficulty speaking out loud about their conditions. For cultural and social reasons, such matters may be kept so private that they are rarely discussed. Many interpreters know little about mental disorders and mental illness, and may have conscious and unconscious biases about these issues that affect their ability to remain impartial. Sometimes, interpreters have likely either had a personal experience with a mental health or disorder or know a loved one with such experience, which can have a deep impact on the interpreter in these settings.

Interpreters in mental health can work with a number of different types of clinicians. Common settings include hospitals (regular or psychiatric hospitals), outpatient clinics and offices, gender-based violence services (sexual assault and domestic violence) and services offered by an array of government and nonprofit organizations, such as homeless shelters, substance abuse services and military.

[53] See http://www.who.int/features/factfiles/mental_health/en/

The impact of language and cultural barriers

When help is needed, in psychiatry and psychology, "language is the principle investigative tool and without good communication, an assessment can be ineffective" (Shah & Zaman, 2012). If the patient[54] and provider do not share a language, a qualified interpreter is usually needed. The difference in language and culture between providers and patients creates an additional obstacle, adds a layer of complexity and raises barriers to understanding that can lead to misdiagnoses. It may also increase the risk of mistrust, which can delay or prevent a successful outcome.

Furthermore, patients may belong to ethnic communities that rarely seek mental health help due to stigma, or who may seek help from spiritual healers within their cultural communities. Some patients' families may also believe that those affected by mental health problems are possessed by spirits or a spell. Patients might lack a support system that can aid recovery, a common problem with migrants and refugees.

Potential resistance from clinicians to interpreters

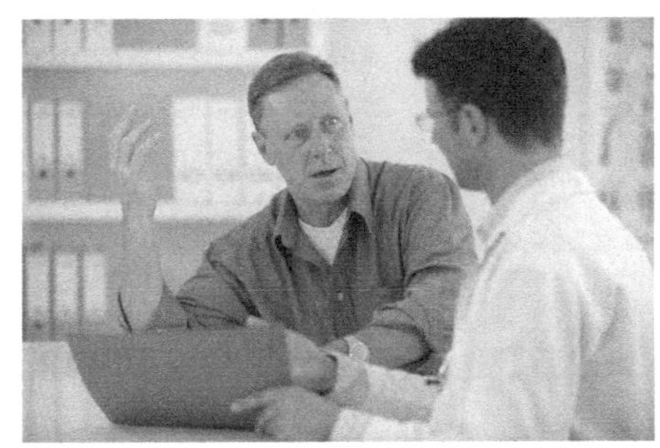

Although the presence of an interpreter can improve the quality of communication (see, e.g., Crossman, Wiener, Roosevelt, Bajaj, & Hampers, 2010) associated with better outcomes, both clinicians and patients have mixed feelings about using the services of an interpreter in counseling and therapy (Shah & Zaman, 2012). Clinicians are sometimes reluctant to work with interpreters for several reasons, often lack of trust as well as concerns about introducing a third party into an already delicate situation. Also, patients may be skeptical, hesitant and suspicious toward this stranger listening to their private conversations, not to mention the common fear of patients that this "stranger" who is a member of the same cultural community might share the private information with the community. This fear is especially common when the interpreter is from a minority group or working in rural areas.

What interpreters need to know about mental health interpreting

General considerations

Mental health services are not always a formal part of healthcare services. For example, a judge might order a defendant to undergo a psychiatric evaluation to determine if he or she is "mentally competent" to understand the legal proceedings. Decisions that providers make based on these assessments can impact the life of the individual from a legal standpoint, such as an emergency petition to have an individual forcibly committed to an inpatient psychiatric facility due to the risk of suicide or homicide. Interpreters must be aware of the legal implications often involved in mental health interpreting (see Section 4.3).

Mental health interpreting can impact the interpreter's well-being, leading to job stress, burnout or vicarious trauma: see Section 5.5 for the development of a self care plan.

[54] While in some countries the word "client" is preferred when speaking about consumers of mental health services, in most countries the word "patient" seems the more common term.

Training, ethics and standards for mental health interpreting

There are no well-established ethics and standards for mental health interpreting. Ethical challenges in this field are often discussed, especially in signed language interpreting (see, e.g., Cornes & Napier, 2005). A few short relevant programs appear to be emerging for spoken language interpreting[55] but are not readily available online.

Interpreters who work in mental health should not underestimate the complexity of its ethical challenges. Accuracy, for example, is of paramount importance, yet the content can be dense at both the verbal and nonverbal levels. It is often discussed among interpreters that special ethics and standards are needed for mental health interpreting, yet to date it does not appear that such ethics and standards are emerging.

The importance of pre-briefing and debriefing

Pre-briefings and debriefings are particularly important in mental health interpreting. Knowing in advance the situation, the sensitive issues, how not to disturb or re-traumatize the patient and other important information can prepare you both logistically and psychologically to interpret well. You can also ask about terms that will be used in advance, since it may be intrusive or counterproductive to ask for clarifications or repetitions during the session.

Debriefing after the session is critical: it may help you learn what went well and what you might have done better, and it is a valuable chance to share your feelings after an intense or traumatic session. However, the therapist is not *your* therapist. See Section 5.5 for details.

The challenge of culture

Mental health clinicians working with culturally diverse populations should ideally be trained in a field often called cultural competence. The goal in providing culturally responsive care is not for clinicians (or interpreters) to learn specific facts about many cultures but to develop universal communication skills that facilitate quality service provision, regardless of culture.

Cultural mediation is particularly risky in mental health interpreting because of the paramount need for the patient to remain in control of his or her communication. As discussed in Chapter 3, you *may* intervene to identify the cause of a cultural misunderstanding, which could involve giving a little information but always general and never about the patient. The goal is to give *just* enough information to identify the cultural barrier without explaining it. However in mental health you might need to provide a little more of that cultural context than in other areas of community interpreting.

Always refer the clinician back to the patient. The cultural dimension adds an extra layer of complexity to the assessment, diagnosis and treatment of the patient. Intervention and mediation become even more of a sensitive issue because if poorly managed they can lead to misdiagnoses or inappropriate treatment plans—but if well managed can contribute to correct diagnoses and the best possible care.

---

[55] One of the authors was involved in the creation of "Healing Voices: Interpreting for Survivors of Torture, War Trauma and Sexual Violence," a weeklong training program that involved the participation of a psychiatrist, a PhD psychologist, a PhD licensed clinical social worker who teaches a university program for mental health clinicians, a licensed professional counselor and a former therapist who is an interpreter and interpreter trainer (see www.voice-of-love.org for details).

Modes in mental health interpreting

The primary mode of interpreting is consecutive due to the potential for distraction in simultaneous (although some clinicians might prefer simultaneous). Because note-taking can be a sensitive topic in mental health interpreting, yet is urgently needed by the interpreter to keep interruptions to a minimum, clarify at the start that you are taking notes *only* to help your memory and be accurate. Make clear the notes will be destroyed as soon as the session ends. It may be a good practice to destroy your notes in front of the patient.

Simultaneous is commonly needed for patients who are disturbed, psychotic or recounting a traumatic event. You may also need to perform occasional summarizing but only as a last resort: avoid summarizing especially in therapy. However, be aware that anecdotal evidence suggests that patients do not appreciate the interpreter's interruptions. Mental health interpreting can also require sight translation but perhaps less often than in other areas of community interpreting.

Special strategies

Your voice is always an instrument. In mental health interpreting, work hard to allow it to reflect the emotions of the speaker while keeping it unobtrusive. For example, if the speaker shouts, never shout, and raise your voice less than you might for legal or general community interpreting. When interpreting the clinician's messages, be especially sure to adopt the same soft, sad or harsh tones exactly as the clinician is conveying them because there is an important strategy behind the choice of tone. In situations that affect your own emotional stability, such as when a survivor of childhood abuse, sexual assault, torture, war or other trauma becomes very graphic, you might need to switch to interpreting in indirect speech/third person and use a less emotional tone of voice to distance yourself from the content. As soon as you are able, resume your normal interpreting patterns. For other techniques to protect yourself from vicarious trauma when you interpret, including deep breathing, boundary setting and imagery, see Section 5.5.

Finally, it will be critical to learn either the exact terms in your other working language(s) or at least conceptual equivalents for common psychiatric terms, including symptoms and diagnoses.
Frequent errors in mental health interpreting such as distortion, omission and mental blocking often arise from lack of preparation in this difficult terminology, which so often lacks conceptual equivalents in the target language.

Refugee interpreting

An overview of refugee interpreting

The refugee population is now a considerable percentage of migrants worldwide. Data from United Nations High Commission on Refugees (UNHCR) show that there were about 16.7 million refugees at the end of 2013, including about half-a-million torture survivors.

Refugee interpreting has so many special concerns that it is emerging as its own specialization. It includes interpreting for asylum seekers and asylees, who are in fact identical to refugees in most regards.

DEFINITION

Refugee

"[A]ny person who: owing to a well-founded fear of being persecuted for reasons of race, religion, nationality, membership of a particular social group, or political opinion, is outside the country of his nationality, and is unable to or, owing to such fear, is unwilling to avail himself of the protection of that country."

1951 United Nations Convention Relating to the Status of Refugees

Many refugees and asylees need community interpreting for medical screenings, school registration, food assistance, job training and mental health services. (To avoid repetition, for the remainder of this book the authors use the term "refugees" to apply also to asylees and asylum seekers, including use of the term "refugee interpreting.")

A number of refugee resettlement organizations have bilingual employees but also need interpreters. The interpreters may need to be qualified to interpret highly uncommon languages. As a result, a refugee who is one of the first of a wave of refugees from a particular country might soon be called on to interpret for other refugees.

What interpreters need to know about refugee interpreting

General considerations

Interpreting for refugees often takes place in refugee resettlement centers, hospitals and community health centers, schools, refugees' homes, social and human service offices and mental health facilities. This type of interpreting has extra layers of complexity. Because so many refugee interpreters are refugees themselves, they might find themselves reliving scenarios and stories they know firsthand. If they don't, what they hear may prove unimaginably shocking. This type of interpreting requires a high level of resilience, strong boundaries and special training to perform impartially and without suffering vicarious trauma.

Because of their intense history of trauma, refugees are often referred to mental health providers and a host of other services. They may be survivors of war, torture and other abuse, and may have watched loved ones die or disappear.

Specific challenges and concerns

Much of what was mentioned about mental health interpreting applies to refugee interpreting. However, additional variables come into play, for example:

- *The dangers of active listening and visualization*—During the interpreting process, the trained interpreter focuses on active listening and visualization as techniques to enhance memory. Refugee interpreters who so do when the refugee is telling a traumatic story (especially if the interpreter had similar experiences) can be traumatized by focusing on such content and even more by visualizing it.
- *The risk of over-identification*—The risks in refugee interpreting of over-identifying with the service user are great, particularly when the interpreter is also a refugee. Doing so can lead to over-involvement of the interpreter, erosion of role boundaries, problems with impartiality and even vicarious trauma.
- *Advocacy: the great temptation*—When working with individuals whose dignity and rights have been trampled on, our own dignity and sense of justice is hurt, and some of us hear a "call to action." Interpreters can run the risk of overstepping boundaries without realizing they are doing so—taking sides and making impassioned pleas on the refugee's behalf. See Section 5.3 for a detailed discussion of advocacy.
- *Higher incidence of vicarious trauma*—Vicarious trauma (VT) is a form of secondary trauma that stems from exposure to the trauma of others. Interpreters often bear witness to pain, horrors and terror endured by trauma survivors. VT affects many service providers as well and is associated with the "cost of caring" for others (Figley, 1995). VT can impact your professional performance and lead to errors of performance and judgment. VT can also have a long-lasting effect on your well-being unless you take steps to prevent it. For additional information, see Section 5.5.

- *Too close to home*—Refugee interpreters who are themselves refugees may live at close quarters to the clients they serve. This proximity erodes boundaries. It is not uncommon for burnout to occur because refugees knock at the door or phone the interpreter at all hours, expecting assistance (often free) as the interpreter's duty to the community.
- *Pressure from elders or other community leaders*—Refugee interpreters who are from the same country or cultural community may be pressured to engage in "helping behaviors" that violate interpreting ethics or erode boundaries. Leaders or elders may ask and expect interpreters to counsel victims of domestic violence to remain with their abusive spouses, engage in unpaid interpreting, advocate for refugees and in general behave as unpaid intercultural mediators rather than interpreters.

Finally, refugee interpreting may run into challenges when the interpreter comes from a different tribe, religion or cultural community than the refugee. The interpreter may be from a country that colonized and oppressed the refugee, or from a social group that inflicted war or genocide on the refugee's social group. In such a case, it is of utmost importance that the interpreter both uphold the highest ethical and professional standards and state his or her commitment to impartiality and confidentiality but also offer to withdraw if the refugee feels discomfort with that interpreter. It is difficult to create trust when fear, betrayal and human cruelty have inflicted so much damage. Providers and interpreters may need to work together to establish trust.

Let's Practice

Learning Activity 4.4: Areas of Specialization in Community Interpreting

In *The Community Interpreter®: An International Workbook of Activities and Role Plays*

REVIEW OF SECTION 4.4

This section looked at several established and emerging interpreting specializations that fall under the umbrella of community interpreting. They included:

- Medical interpreting.
- Educational interpreting.
- Social services interpreting.
- Faith-based interpreting.
- Mental health interpreting.
- Refugee interpreting.

In addition to providing an overview for interpreters of each of these sub-specializations, this section addressed specific concerns and practical information that can help community interpreters better understand and prepare themselves for interpreting in each of these important specializations.

4.5 Preparing Terminology

Overview

Community interpreters often have little time to prepare for assignments. They are not usually subject matter experts in community services yet interpret in many areas. Poor preparation leads to many surprises, including unfamiliar terms. Excellent preparation may not prevent that problem but will reduce it. Preparing for the session and its terminology will also:

- Enhance your competence.
- Make your performance smoother.
- Reduce your stress.
- Make the work easier.
- Give a stronger impression of your professionalism and skill.

This section will focus on how interpreters can acquire the necessary skill to build their subject matter knowledge and terminology.

Learning Objective 4.5

After completing this section, you will be able to:

- Develop strategies to acquire the specialized subject matter knowledge and terminology needed to interpret in a broad array of community settings.

Knowledge vs. terminology

DEFINITION

Knowledge

Information, understanding or skill that one acquires through education and experience.

Why terminology matters

In a perfect world, before each assignment you would know the topic and nature of the meeting, gather all possible information, research and study the topic thoroughly, prepare your dictionaries and expand your glossaries, including specialized terminology. You might even learn and memorize new terms.

DEFINITION

Terminology

- Vocabulary (words and phrases) used in a particular field
- Technical or special terms used in a special subject or any field of human endeavor.

Welcome to reality: we are often deprived of the luxury of preparation time. We find ourselves working reactively to new situations. Community interpreting is notorious for last-minute and emergency assignments, and telephone and video interpreting (see Section 4.6) can involve moving all day from topic to topic, call to call, with no advance preparation time. Even when you are notified well in advance of the assignment, here is what you might know: as little as the information in example 1, as much as the information in example 5—or anything in between:

1. You will be interpreting "at a hospital."
2. You will be interpreting in the OB-GYN department of the hospital.
3. You will be interpreting in the prenatal clinic.
4. You will be interpreting there for an older female for her first pregnancy.
5. You will be interpreting for health professionals who consider this patient high risk and want her to agree to amniocentesis.

Five techniques for preparing terminology

The following five steps should help you mentally assess the situation and prepare your terminology:

- Assess the service area.
- Identify the parties.
- Narrow your focus.
- Activate and expand your terminology.
- Refine your skills.

Step 1: Assess the service area – Will you be in a new office, or with a provider and service you have already interpreted for? Where is it located? Who are your contacts there, and can they provide you with any details about the encounter? Will there be content that is new to you? A new focus? New documents or terms? Sensitive issues?

Step 2: Identify the parties – Who is going to be part of the appointment? Can you introduce yourself by phone and ask a few pre-briefing questions?

Step 3: Narrow your focus – Activate your general knowledge of the topic and look for holes (lacunae); read up on the topic but be selective in finding the pertinent material.

Step 4: Activate and expand your terminology – Are specialized glossaries available? Which terms should you be sure to know? Will you need to create your own service-specific glossary? Do your colleagues have suggestions and resources?

Step 5: Refine your skills – If no conceptual equivalents exist for certain terms, plan to paraphrase them, request clarifications or perform cultural mediations as needed—and have "mental scripts" ready (see Chapter 3).

How to research an assignment

Subject matter knowledge

What to target

All community interpreters need to develop the basic skills to research an assignment and compile the needed terminology. Here are some basic strategies:

- List the type of service providers involved.
- Identify their areas of expertise.
- Find the resources that describe their services.
- Identify both familiar and new terminology for the service area.
- Purchase or create your own glossaries as needed.
- Review and practice terms.

Whether you work as a staff interpreter, an independent contractor or a volunteer, know the providers you work with and organize them by fields and by specialties. For example, if you work mainly in a hospital, you can organize the providers you work with by listing them by department, such as cardiology, oncology, rheumatology, etc. If you work mainly in an education setting, you can list the services that schools provide, such as parent-teacher conferences, disciplinary hearings, school board meetings, etc.

How to research the service

Now proceed with your own subject and terminology research. Before each assignment, ask as many questions as possible about the encounter: the type of appointment, the service provided, the language and regional variation of the service user, if known, any specific terminology, documents that give background information, documents to be sight translated, sensitive issues to know and so forth. (See Chapter 2 for details.) There are a number of ways to learn about the subject and the terminology. Here are just a few examples:

- **Look up the provider's organization online** – Are you scheduled to interpret for a child abuse investigation conducted by a government agency? Or for a workers' compensation injury initial evaluation? Nowadays, almost all organizations have a more-or-less structured online presence, if not in your country, then for another country where you might learn some basic common features.
- **Research the topic** – Nowadays, a lot of information is available at the click of a fingertip. Once we identify a topic, it is of paramount importance to read about it. Don't limit your focus to a search on individual terms: instead, read about the subject to capture the big picture. Doing so enhances our ability to detach from individual words and catch the meaning of what is discussed. Reading about the subject in context also enhances our ability to paraphrase, helping us to find meaningful synonyms and equivalents in context.
- **Research in both languages** – Listening to and understanding the information in the source language is as important as delivering the message with clarity in the target language. Therefore, the subject knowledge must be acquired in both languages. Hence the importance of reading about the topic in both (or all) your working languages.
- **Ask peers** – Colleagues, teachers and trainers are a great resource for hard-to-find terms and meaningful equivalents.

How to organize the information

As you prepare, you can organize these fields and topics in separate computer folders and subfolders to build your knowledge about the subject matter and terminology. You may have a folder you call "Healthcare" and subfolders for each specialty, then within each subfolder even more specializations. For example:

DENTISTRY			
	ENDONTICS		
		TREATMENTS and PROCEDURES	
			Root canals **Endodontic retreatment** **Crown lengthening** **Traumatic dental injuries** **Dental implants**

While you are waiting for an assignment to begin, you might have time to review those files on your computer, tablet or even on your phone. This type of preparation becomes a lifelong journey. Nobody starts off knowing the thousands of facts or terms needed to interpret in the vast array of settings where community interpreting takes place.

Other strategies to expand subject matter knowledge

Many community interpreters use some or several of the following strategies to enhance their subject matter knowledge:

- Watch TV shows (e.g., medical shows), news and general talk shows in all your working languages, writing down new terms as you listen so that you can look them up later.
- Collect brochures and other written materials from the waiting rooms of relevant services (many are also available online).
- Join listservs of interpreter associations where many challenges, issues in the field and subject matter topics are discussed.
- Ask for any documents you will sight translate and study those documents.
- Explore the service in online encyclopedias such as Wikipedia, now available in 288 languages.
- Call another interpreter who knows that service and ask about lessons learned.
- Ask the interpreter service that sends you for any in-house resources about that service.

Developing your terminology

Dictionaries vs. glossaries

A dictionary is like a concise encyclopedia of words. Listed in alphabetical order, the words usually each have a key to pronunciation, a definition, some context and usage information, examples, and sometimes an explanation to help you understand the term. A glossary is like a short dictionary devoted to a specific topic, often with more information about each term than a dictionary offers. For instance, you could purchase glossaries like these:

- A Burmese-English medical glossary.
- A Russian-French glossary of coarse and foul language.
- A Spanish-Italian public services glossary.
- A bilingual glossary of educational terms used in a specific country.

A bilingual glossary will usually have terms in both languages (although monolingual glossaries can be helpful, for example, an English medical glossary if you can't find a bilingual glossary for your language pair). It should include, for each entry, a definition and contextual information, examples or explanations to help you understand the term and how to use it correctly. In general, you should consider purchasing any or all of the following (print or electronic format):

- A comprehensive monolingual dictionary for each of your working languages; it should more extensive than a typical "collegiate" dictionary.
- A bilingual dictionary.
- Bilingual dictionaries or glossaries in specializations where you interpret often.
- Electronic applications (apps) for dictionaries and glossaries that may be useful to you (these are typically less expensive than either print or electronic dictionaries and can be used more easily while you are on assignment).

If you conduct a search for "dictionary apps," depending on your language pair, you may find scores of bilingual, multilingual and specialized (e.g., medical) dictionaries. If you speak a less common or rare language pair, even one bilingual glossary app can be precious.

Building glossaries

As you read and learn about the topic, narrow the terminology specific to the topic and build your own glossary. First, be aware that some common words become specific terminology when used in a professional setting. In dentistry, for example, "'pulp' is not the stuff that comes in orange juice, and 'calculus' is not [...] what you studied in math class; 'plaque' isn't something you hang on your wall and 'recession' isn't what's happening to the economy" (Roat, 2010, p. 207).

There are many ways to organize your terminology, from a simple word-processing document or a spreadsheet to more sophisticated tools that can be found online.[56] Once you reach a certain number of terms and categories, you may find it harder to work with simple files and spreadsheets or even a database and may want to switch to a glossary software program. Join an interpreting association or online forum for suggestions about favorite tools.

---

[56] Conference interpreters in particular use software tools and programs such as Glossary Pro, interplex, LookUp, TermDB and InterpretBank (last access in May 2015).

Until you are ready to try out a sophisticated tool, a table in a word-processing document, spreadsheet or database entry may serve the purpose. It will keep all your terminology in one place and provide the basic features of sorting, filtering and searching functions. If you keep a simple table structure, you may be able to import it later into a terminology management system.

Sharing glossaries

If you work in a team, you can share your glossary using a cloud-based platform such as Dropbox or Google Drive. These systems help to keep the glossaries updated for all team members and can also save time and build consistency. However, remember to avoid entering confidential information if these glossaries are shared with several or many individuals.

Software tools for building glossaries

In most cases, online terminology management tools created and used by conference interpreters are intended specifically for interpreting and may be valuable for you as well. Here are a few examples of what is available (conduct an Internet search to explore these and others). For information about cost and to see a free demo of each program, check the websites.

- **Interplex** http://www.fourwillows.com/interplex.html, created by Peter Sand, Geneva –Intuitive and user friendly, this tool allows the importing of thematic glossaries initially created in Word or Excel documents. You can run a global search, or search a term per glossary, and it bypasses special characters and accents.
- **InterpretBank** http://www.interpretbank.com, created by Claudio Fantinuoli, Germersheim – Very user friendly, with a number of functions that facilitate term search; terms can be organized by subject, customer, project, and it has a very nice flashcard-like memorizing function.
- **LookUp** http://lookup-web.de, created by Christoph Stoll, Heidelberg. This tool is sophisticated; its search function will list the terms as soon as you type the first few letters, before you even hit the "enter" button. The program is limited to four languages, and only three can be displayed at a time. The search functionality does not bypass accents or special characters.
- **Terminus** http://www.wintringham.ch/cgi/ayawp.pl?T=terminus, created by Nils Wintringham, Zürich. This tool has a quick-search function and allows for terms classification by glossaries and data field. Currently available for Windows.

Other strategies to expand terminology

Many community interpreters use some or several of the following strategies to enhance their knowledge of relevant terminology:

- Memorize two, five or more new terms each day, in both or all your working languages.
- Carry a small notebook or electronic device to note terms you learn "on the job."
- Use self-study resources, print or online.
- Practice simultaneous interpreting while listening to shows or to the radio with relevant specialized terminology to master the new terms in context.
- Ask other interpreters to share their glossaries and offer yours.
- Use websites such as www.wordreference.com to find words that are not available in your dictionary and be sure to focus on the forum discussions about how to use specialized terms.
- Join a translators forum such as www.proz.com and post questions.
- Join listservs of interpreter associations to ask questions about specific terms or how to find specialization-specific glossaries in your language pair.

Above all, be sure to self-test. Before the assignment, take out your mini-glossary for that service, print a copy if you prefer to test yourself in print and cover the column that has the terms in your weaker language. Check to see which terms you already know well in both languages. Cross out those terms. Now try again those terms you did not know how to interpret. After you master them, strike them out too, one by one. Continue until you have crossed out all the terms for that glossary and feel confident you know them. Then have a friend or colleague test you by asking you to interpret terms taken at random from any of your glossaries.

Maintain your languages!

To be strong in terminology you will need to maintain your working languages. Often interpreters are "tripped up" not by technical terms but everyday vocabulary, for example, about symptoms, feelings or children's activities. Television and radio programs in hundreds of languages are widely available through satellite dish services and Internet sites. Local libraries often carry books, magazines and movies in other languages. Countless books can be ordered via the Internet, in print or ebook format. You can find classes, for example in healthcare, social work or education, offered by colleges and universities: these can strengthen your vocabulary in either language. Some interpreters enjoy playing word games to hone their general vocabulary skills.

Terminology is vital. Find the strategies to build it that work for you. Make them a habit. No community interpreter today can become truly professional without making special efforts to master specialized terminology and also the general vocabulary used every day in the field.

Let's Practice

Learning Activity 4.5 (a): Techniques to Prepare Terminology
Learning Activity 4.5 (b): Strategies to Expand Terminology

In *The Community Interpreter®: An International Workbook of Activities and Role Plays*

REVIEW OF SECTION 4.5

Not even a four-year degree program in a specialized program for community interpreting could prepare community interpreters for the diverse settings, subject matter and terms they will encounter in the field. This diversity of situations and settings makes terminology difficult to anticipate and prepare—assuming there is time to prepare at all, often not the case. Making efforts to understand the service setting and learn new terms pays off. You will become a more confident and professional interpreter.

Every language also has its challenges: some have more developed resources for professional development than others. If your language does not provide good bilingual dictionaries and glossaries for your language pair—a common problem—you might need to devote more time to developing your subject matter knowledge and terminology. Preparation and study will enhance your accuracy and speed. In short, subject matter knowledge and terminology development are a lifelong journey, not a final destination. Enjoy the journey.

4.6 Remote Interpreting

Overview

Remote interpreting involves the delivery of interpreting services over a technological platform instead of face to face. In recent years, this field has grown at a dizzying pace. Over the phone (OPI) and video remote interpreting (VRI) have transformed themselves from slow-growth industries relegated to niche markets to rapidly expanding services penetrating all areas of the interpreting market.

These trends have produced mixed reactions. Concerns around the use of new technology include varying levels of quality, consumer expectations for "in person" face-to-face interpreters, cost, the lack of developed protocols and the growing impact on interpreter work conditions.

There is little new research in the field to report since the publication of Nataly Kelly's seminal *Telephone Interpreting: A Comprehensive Guide to the Profession* (Kelly, 2008b). Section 4.6 highlights the skills necessary to perform remote interpreting as well as challenges in this new field. It also offers a perspective on the current state of the field, with special thanks for contributions by Professor Barry Olsen and Jonathan Levy during their interviews with the two authors for this chapter. Neither Mr. Olsen nor Mr. Levy are responsible for any views expressed here or errors in this text.

Learning Objective 4.6

After completing this section, you will be able to:

- Discuss the history and challenges of remote interpreting.

What is remote interpreting?

Remote interpreting does not yet have a single accepted definition: it can mean different things depending who employs the term and where it is used. In this textbook, *remote interpreting* is defined as *interpreting that involves at least one interpreter who is not physically present with other parties to the session and who is interpreting using a remote platform*. Remote interpreting involves two central questions: Who is remote? And what kind of remote platform is in use?

DEFINITION

Remote interpreting

Interpreting that involves at least one interpreter who is not physically present with other parties to the session and who is interpreting using a remote platform.

Note: Remote interpreting usually involves interpreting via phone or video. Sometimes all participants to the encounter are located in different places.

Who is remote?

Scenario 1: Only the interpreter is not present

In remote interpreting, three basic scenarios come into play. In one, the interpreter or interpreters are the only individuals in the encounter who participate remotely, while all other parties are physically present in the same place. This scenario is very common in community settings. Hospitals regularly contract with telephonic and, increasingly, with video remote interpreters for providers and patients who share the same location. Lawyers and courts rely on off-site interpreters to communicate with defendants. Refugee and other nonprofits often have to rely on remote connections to find interpreters who speak languages of lesser diffusion.

Scenario 2: All participants are in different locations

In the second scenario, every participant attends the meeting or encounter virtually. The interpreter and all the other parties communicate with the aid of a technological platform. This kind of encounter is often called a "virtual meeting" and is an increasingly common way for multiple parties located in different geographic areas to communicate and conduct business. Interpreting for virtual meetings can be as simple as a social worker calling a service user via a telephonic interpreter to something as high profile and complex as a "virtual summit" involving heads of state.

Scenario 3: The interpreter is with one of the parties

In the third scenario, the interpreter is either with the service user *or* the service provider.

Whether the meeting is partially or fully remote impacts what you have to consider when you prepare for the session and while you interpret. The specific skill set needed is addressed later in this section.

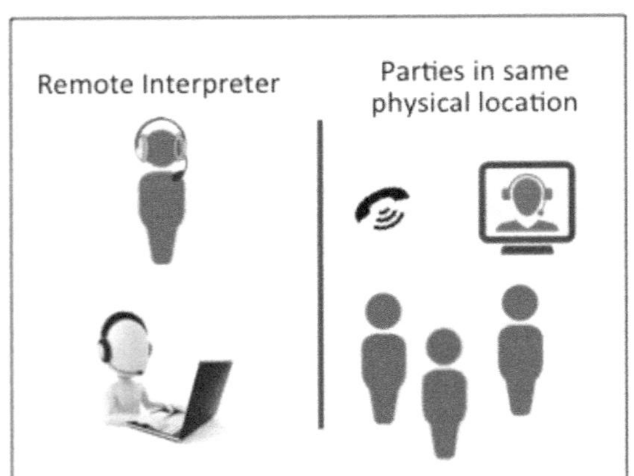

What kind of remote platform Is being used?

Interpreting can be delivered over the phone, via video, using mobile apps, computer software program or any combination of them. Delivery platforms are evolving as rapidly as the technology they are based on, making this one of the most challenging areas of the profession for interpreters to stay up to date with.

Telephonic interpreting platforms

Telephonic interpreting, often referred to as over-the-phone interpreting or OPI, is the oldest kind of remote interpreting technology. First introduced in Australia in 1973 and in the United States in 1981, this technology is growing familiar in many community services. The interpreter is on the phone at one end and is connected to the service user and provider who listen to the phone either through a dual handset or on speaker phone if they are physically together, or on their own phone if they are at separate locations from each other. In general, telephonic platforms allow for consecutive interpreting only. If the interpreter is also connected to a shared computer screen, some sight translation services may be feasible.

Video remote interpreting

Video remote interpreting (VRI) was first developed to provide signed language interpreting services to the Deaf and hard of hearing.[57] In VRI, often two or more parties are physically present at one location with a video connection to the interpreter (on a smart phone, tablet or laptop computer). The interpreter sits in front of a video camera at another location, whether an office, call center or home-based office. The equipment provides both audio and video (visual) connection on both ends. The interpreter can see and hear all parties present. VRI platforms are in increasing use in healthcare, legal and other community services. Major factors to consider include the strength of connectivity, sound conditions and privacy concerns.

Remote simultaneous interpreting

Most remote interpreting platforms, whether telephonic or VRI, are limited to consecutive interpreting because there is usually only one audio channel. Most of these technologies do not yet have multiple, separate audio tracks that would allow the interpreter to listen to what is being said and channel interpreting via a separate audio track to a single listener. For that reason, meetings that require the use of simultaneous interpreting used to be somewhat rare for telephonic and video platforms. That situation is changing. Several kinds of interpreting platforms have emerged that allow simultaneous interpreting of remote and virtual meetings. They include:

- *Conference call platforms* with simultaneous interpreting capabilities. The interpreter accesses a remote booth via a software application on his or her computer and can provide interpreting via a phone connection or over the audio in the computer.
- *Videoconference call platforms*. These are typically hybrid platforms. The interpreter is provided a video feed of the participants to receive both audio and visual information and interprets over a phone connection directly to the service user. Multiple interpreters can access the same video feed to provide simultaneous interpreting in different languages.
- *Webinar platforms*. One company[58] has developed an app-based platform that allows for webinar participants to listen to a webinar presentation in real-time in multiple languages. Both the interpreter and participants access video and audio feeds separately. The interpreters cannot facilitate a dialogue between the webinar attendees and the presenter.

Demand for remote simultaneous interpreting is growing swiftly. As these technologies mature, new work opportunities will open up for interpreters willing to adapt to them.

---

[57] Video remote interpreting (VRI) should not be confused with video relay services (VRS), "a form of Telecommunications Relay Service (TRS) that enables persons with hearing disabilities who use American Sign Language (ASL) to communicate with voice telephone users through video equipment, rather than through typed text." http://www.fcc.gov/guides/video-relay-services

[58] See http://www.voiceboxer.com/

Apps, software, and agnostic platforms

Many traditional OPI companies have created multiple pathways to connect to their services, such as phone numbers, mobile applications, and website interfaces. VRI services are beginning to adopt "platform-agnostic" models, which means their services work across different devices and operating systems. These advancements make it more likely we will see rapid integration of remote interpreting platforms in community interpreting. As the cost of providing services remotely drops below the cost of providing onsite interpreters, more healthcare providers, courts, schools, businesses and nonprofit organizations will consider requesting remote interpreting.

Hybrid remote interpreting/translation

Interpreters are increasingly asked to provide brief written translations for short, essentially verbal communications in *writing*. Schools communicate with parents via emails, prerecorded phone messages and apps. Emergency dispatch services in the United States can now accept text messages that interpreters often have to translate. When our primary places of work change the way they communicate with clients, interpreters must adapt. How our job descriptions will change because of these developments is still unclear, yet it is of vital importance to our field.[59]

Why remote interpreting has exploded

A growing number of interpreting service providers (ISPs), some larger than others, offer OPI as an alternative to onsite interpreters. South Africa, with its community interpreter phone service called Telephone Interpreting Service of South Africa (TISSA: established in 2002 though later embroiled in controversy[60]) emulated Australia's TIS, the national Telephone Interpreting Service. Later video remote interpreting (VRI), initially used for signed language interpreters, evolved for spoken languages as well. VRI was at first popular in medical interpreting in the United States and is now used extensively in certain U.S. court settings and in EU courts, where it seems poised thanks to 2010 EU policies and directives to become perhaps far more widely used (Braun, 2013a).

Five main factors influence these developments:

- Immigration trends.
- Language policy.
- On-call accessibility.
- Cost reduction (when used efficiently).
- Advanced technology.

[59] For a discussion, see, for example, http://www.interpretamerica.com/interpret-america-blog/have-we-reached-the-tipping-point-change-has-arrived

[60] See http://www.powershow.com/view/14e4fd-ZDlmZ/BRIEFING_NOTES_ON_THE_TELEPHONE_INTERPRETING_SERVICE_FOR_SOUTH_AFRICA_TISSA_PROJECT_TO_THE_PORTFOLIO_powerpoint_ppt_presentation

Immigration trends

Rising and sustained global migration increases the demand for competent community interpreters. As more and more hospitals, clinics, nonprofits, schools and community services struggle to provide interpreters, remote interpreting will become more prevalent.

Language policy

Nations around the world have passed legislation and policies that explicitly address the need to provide interpreting and translation services for immigrant populations (as discussed in Chapter 1). When such laws pass, two things typically happen: organizations are more likely to add interpreting services to their policies and procedures, and those who need interpreting services learn to ask for them as their legal right. Thus, language policy serves as a driver in the expansion of all interpreter services, both onsite and remote.

On-call accessibility

Remote interpreting can be available day or night, all days of the year for fires, earthquakes, accidents, emergencies and other short-notice assignments. Geography, scarce resources and a timely response often justify the use of remote interpreters, whether OPI or VRI.

Cost reduction

Both OPI and VRI costs have been going down. While OPI and VRI are typically billed by the minute, at a cost usually greater than the hourly rates of community interpreters, OPI or VRI interpreted short appointments, follow-up phone calls, scheduling appointments and other short services can result in reduced costs. Remote interpreting can be one way to contain costs yet continue to provide needed services around the clock, anywhere that Internet and/or phone service is available, in virtually any language. OPI/VRI providers are finding ways to cut costs (such as expanding call centers with staff interpreters), expand their geographical coverage and offer 100 to 300 languages at lower costs than for many or most face-to-face assignments.

Advanced technology

Over-the-phone interpreting (OPI)

Remote interpreting technology has expanded at a feverish pace. Over the phone interpreting is available almost everywhere, though the bulk of the market is currently in the United States, the United Kingdom and Australia. According to the research firm Common Sense Advisory, the OPI interpreting market in 2014 was valued at US $2.03 billion.[61] The need for special terminals or equipment is giving way to interpreting delivered via smart phones, tablets or computers.

Video remote interpreting (VRI)

VRI has overcome some of the initial disadvantages of earlier versions, such as unreliable connections and pixelating images. It offers advantages over OPI: the visual element allows interpreters to see all parties and pick up critical nonverbal cues. For sign language interpreting, VRI is clearly an essential service. Furthermore, the introduction of tablet devices and improved technology are making quality VRI more affordable and accessible.

[61] "The State of the Interpreting Market," by Hélène Pielmeier and Donald DePalma, Common Sense Advisory, January 2015, http://www.commonsenseadvisory.com/AbstractView.aspx?ArticleID=24088

Videoconferencing

VRI is not confined to dialogue settings. It can offer multiple languages for a single meeting. The videoconference and Web conference industries are poised to explode.
The web conferencing market is expected to reach US $2.88 billion by 2017, with a compound annual growth rate (CAGR) of just under 10 percent, according to the independent research firm Future Market Insights.[62] While Global Industry Analysts, Inc. projects that the cloud-based videoconferencing market is expected to grow to US $2.9 billion by 2020.[63]
VRI seems an increasingly attractive option in community interpreting—initially in industrialized nations, but perhaps soon around the world.

The remote interpreting workplace

Every working environment has its peculiarities, required skills and protocols. As a result, a very good community interpreter may not be the best OPI or VRI interpreter or vice versa. In general, the workplace for remote interpreting will usually be at the interpreter's home, with the provider or at an OPI or VRI call center.

Home office for remote interpreting

If you work as a contract interpreter remotely, a mobile phone, headset and note-pad are not enough. There are increasingly strict requirements. Your remote office is likely to need at least some of the following:

Possible requirements	• Landline phone equipped with headset (not a mobile phone) • Notebook/steno pad/pens/pencils (or an erasable marker board) • Shredder • Computer with adequate specifications • Virus protection software • High-speed Internet connection and router • Locked document filing cabinet (in some cases) • Dedicated quiet room to conduct interpreting (without background noise from babies, children, animals, running water, etc.)

[62] "Web Conferencing Market to Witness Fastest Growth Between 2015 and 2020, Driven by Globalization http://www.futuremarketinsights.com/reports/details/web-conferencing-market#src=whatech

[63] The Global Video Conferencing Services Market: Trends, Drivers and Projections. http://www.strategyr.com/MarketResearch/Video_Conferencing_Services_Market_Trends.asp

Working remotely from an onsite location

It is increasingly common for large institutions, such as hospitals and courts, to provide both face-to-face and remote interpreting. Several large hospital systems in the United States now have call centers located on their premises. Their staff interpreters may work solely in the call center or provide a mix of face-to-face and remote interpreting. In courthouses, sometimes the interpreter might be at one station providing remote services for that location, or providing interpreting for cases both there and in other courthouses across the state. In this scenario, the interpreter may be in a small office or a larger call center.

Call center

In this scenario you are likely to have a cubicle with some sound protection. You are surrounded by other interpreters taking calls in many languages. Your cubicle will come equipped with a computer, monitor, headset and other tools for receiving calls.

Remote interpreting skills

The skill set required to perform on remote platforms is arguably more advanced than that required in many face-to-face encounters. At the very least, remote interpreting requires learning additional and distinct skills, which include:

1. Adapting interpreting modes over remote platforms.
2. Obtaining, learning and using technology platform(s).
3. Applying ethics and standards and protocols over remote platforms.

Table 4-F will help you understand the ways that interpreting over remote platforms requires adapting your existing skills and acquiring new ones.

On-Site Interpreters vs. Remote Interpreters		
	On-site Interpreter	**Remote Interpreter**
Listening Skills	The interpreter needs active listening skills to extract meaning with access to quality sound and nonverbal cues.	OPI: The interpreter needs active listening skills to extract meaning even with inferior sound without nonverbal cues. VRI: Active listening skills to extract meaning with inferior sound and limited visibility.
Consecutive Interpreting and Note-taking	Ideally the interpreter has note-taking skills but can rely more on short-term memory because it is easier to manage turn-taking and ask for repetition face to face.	The interpreter must have adequate note-taking skills to capture longer statements, numbers, medications, instructions, etc. It is harder to manage turn-taking and interventions.
Intervention and Mediation Skills	Interpreters can use their full range of verbal and nonverbal cues to indicate the parties' needs to pause or for an intervention.	OPI: The interpreter must be assertive and ask for pauses. The timing of interventions is a nuanced skill.. VRI: Gestures to request a pause might not be noticed. The interpreter will need to find a viable technique for intervening.
Delivery Skills	Onsite interpreters can monitor nonverbal cues to capture, understand and convey meaning.	With reduced or no access to context and visualization, remote interpreters more fully rely on voice, breathing, inflection, pronunciation and volume to communicate clearly. They must make the best use of voice pitch, tone and volume to effectively convey meaning in the absence of visual cues.
Accents and Language Variations	Onsite interpreters are typically exposed to a limited amount of variability of accents and language variations, as they are interpreting in a limited geographic area for a finite number of immigrant communities.	Remote interpreters are exposed to a variety of accents, language variations and regionalisms, often more than onsite interpreters. Remote interpreters are virtually connected with everybody from anywhere.
Context	Onsite interpreters typically know the settings where they interpret often, including local geographic, social, cultural, legal and societal knowledge. They are aware of how local immigrant, Deaf or indigenous communities use language and are familiar with the locally represented regional variations.	Remote interpreters may lack knowledge of a service system because it is located in another country or locality. They may miss references, cues and meaning or make errors due to lack of relevant knowledge. They may need to request more clarifications and explanations.
Professional Contact	Onsite interpreters have more direct interaction with colleagues and other professionals. They may have greater opportunity for networking, debriefing difficult sessions and socializing.	The remote interpreter may work extensively from home, in call centers or in another environment where stress is high and opportunities to socialize with colleagues may be limited.
Self care	Onsite interpreters may have better access to resources for managing job stress and for implementing a self care plan.	The remote interpreter may need to develop specialized strategies for self care tailored to the job to avoid stress, burnout and vicarious trauma (see Chapter 5).
Technology	Onsite interpreters have fewer technologies to interact with to interpret. They should use every available tool to support their interpreting, including smart phone dictionaries and language apps.	Remote interpreters have to learn to manage multiple technological platforms, possibly including video, OPI, dedicated WiFi connections, headsets, scheduling software and website interfaces. They typically have better access to digital resources during their interpreting.

Table 4-F
On-Site Interpreters vs. Remote Interpreters: A Comparison of Skill Sets

Training

Training in remote interpreting is underdeveloped and not widely available. It is not yet generally included in standard curricula. Most training appears to be provided by OPI and VRI service providers. Yet in some countries, it may be illegal for the ISP to provide training for contract interpreters. Some ISPs providing OPI and VRI therefore work with employees (full and part-time), while some work with freelancers and others work with a combination of the two. The need to provide remote interpreters with quality, effective training is hard to achieve, in part because the work itself might involve a combination of community, legal, business and technical interpreting—every day.

Code of ethics and standards of practice

Currently there is no code of ethics or standards specific to remote interpreting. Such a code might not differ in the core ethics and standards for community interpreters but could include concrete guidance for how to apply interpreter ethics over remote platforms, as many of the current strategies and protocols are difficult or impossible to use remotely. Kelly (2008b), like a number of ISPs that have created or adapted existing codes to support remote interpreters, published a code of ethics for phone interpreters (Model Code of Ethics for Telephone Interpreters (Kelly, 2008b, pp. 95-114). Its purpose is to provide general guiding ethical principles for professional telephone interpreters. She cautions that all interpreters employed by a telephone interpreting company are held accountable for adhering to its principles.

Working conditions on remote platforms

The costs of rapid change

Change has come so quickly that attention to quality, the experience of end users and interpreter working conditions can be lost in the shuffle. Professional associations and interpreter groups are just beginning to determine best practices for employers, ISPs and interpreters themselves. Research into how remote interpreting impacts interpreters, service providers and users is scarce. Much more is needed. Some basic standards exist for conference and court interpreters through their leading international interpreting associations, AIIC[64] and NAJIT.[65]

[64] See http://aiic.net/page/143/guidelines-for-remote-conferencing/lang/1
[65] See http://www.najit.org/publications/Telephone%20Interpreting.pdf

The Human Costs of Remote Interpreting

"It has become clear that interpreter complaints were not only due to the inferior technological conditions, but also the result of a number of physiological (sore eyes, back and neck pain, headaches, nausea) and psychological complaints (loss of concentration and motivation, feeling of alienation) stemming from the remote interpreting conditions. These complaints resurfaced in subsequent experiments, conducted in a variety of technical conditions and by a number of multilingual organisations." (Mouzourakis, 2006, p. 52)

The toll on the interpreter

Fatigue in remote interpreting

Anecdotally, it has emerged that remote interpreting (RI) takes a toll by increasing workload and fatigue. Some studies show more encouraging trends. The mixed results include:

- Errors caused by higher levels of RI fatigue (Moser-Mercer, 2003).
- Stress, fatigue and demotivation of interpreters (Mouzourakis, 2006; Moser-Mercer, 2005).
- Interpreter feelings of isolation (Roziner & Shlesinger, 2010).
- Relatively high quality for RI yet poor interpreter perception of quality (Roziner & Schlesinger, 2010).
- Cognitive processing problems more common in RI in legal interpreting (Braun, 2013).
- Difficulties managing the flow and turn-taking (Braun, 2013).
- Challenges successfully faced over time in business remote interpreting (Braun & Taylor, 2012).
- Interpreters for refugee hearings held remotely reported poor interpreter rapport with refugees; difficulties managing turn-taking and sight translation; concern by interpreters that body language and emotions might be missed; while researchers had grave concerns about accuracy and cases involving physical and sexual abuse and torture (Ellis, MacDonald, Lincoln, & Cabral, 2008).
- Studies on RI in medical settings are more encouraging, but were mainly conducted from a "client" as opposed to an interpreter's perspective(Azarmina & Wallace, 2005).
- A study in business settings reveals problems arising from the technology but also the adaptability of interpreters to the conditions (Braun, 2004, 2007).

Other negative impacts for the interpreter

Problems that can plague remote interpreters who perform the work regularly include:

- Fatigue (leading to errors, omissions and other declines in performance).
- Increases an interpreter's mental workload.
- Greater effort for problem-solving strategies.
- More than the usual physiological and psychological strain.
- Feelings of lack of control.
- Technical difficulties that can cause intense frustration and stress.

Let's Practice

Learning Activity 4.6 (a): An Analysis of Remote Interpreting
Learning Activity 4.6 (b): Comparing Face-to-Face, Over the Phone and Video Remote Interpreting

In *The Community Interpreter®: An International Workbook of Activities and Role Plays*

REVIEW OF SECTION 4.6

Remote interpreting represents a swiftly growing field. Whether over the phone, or via video, it offers solutions and platforms to clients focused on reducing costs, increasing access, finding more languages and shortening response time for emergencies. While there is still much to be done to establish protocols, ethics and training in the field, remote interpreting is here to stay and a critical, growing part of the community interpreting market.

This section provided an overview of remote interpreting, including the technology involved, workplace requirements and conditions, and needed skills. While this new trend for the profession represents benefits and costs, one of the greatest benefits is its rapid growth and increasing work opportunities for all community interpreters, including those who interpret in languages of limited diffusion.

CHAPTER 4 SUMMARY

In Chapter 4 you explored your professional identity: who you are as an interpreter and how you fit into the larger profession. This chapter is a journey through several areas of specialization in community interpreting and new methods of delivery of interpreting services.

In Section 4.1, **Professional Identity and the Community Interpreter**, you looked at what professional identity is, and how it contributes to the perception that the public has of interpreters individually (you, the interpreter) and collectively (we interpreters, the profession.)

In Section 4.2, **Professional Practice**, you saw how interpreting involves a complex set of activities that relate both to professional standards and business practices. This section highlighted the difference between employed versus self-employed interpreters as well as the perspective of ISPs and their expectations of interpreters. It also covered a number of business tools and strategies for community interpreters to enhance their professional practice.

Section 4.3, **Legal Interpreting**, examined the differences between legal and non-legal community interpreting and also identified hybrid situations where both legal and community services were involved in the same sessions. You learned the implications of performing legal interpreting and the importance of specific training in the field. Finally you explored ways to make decisions about whether or not to perform legal interpreting in community settings following a 6-step decision-making tool.

In Section 4.4, **Emerging Specializations**, you looked at several established and emerging interpreting specializations that fall under the umbrella of community interpreting. In addition to providing an overview for interpreters of each of these "sub-specializations," this section offered practical information to help community interpreters better understand and prepare themselves for interpreting in these specializations.

In Section 4.5, **Preparing Terminology**, you recognized how challenging yet rewarding is to research and enhance terminology to competently prepare for assignments. Making efforts to understand the service setting and learn new terminology is a critical skill for interpreters.

In Section 4.6, **Remote Interpreting**, you learned about the history of the field, the skills required for remote interpreting and some of the challenges of over the phone or video remote interpreting. As in all new areas, this field is full of challenges but also exciting opportunities. It has become clear that this is a critical new trend for our profession, one that every interpreter today should study closely.

THE ROLE OF THE COMMUNITY INTERPRETER

by Sofía García-Beyaert

CHAPTER 5

LEARNING OBJECTIVES

After completing this chapter and its corresponding exercises, the learner will be able to:

OBJECTIVE 5.1	**Communicative Autonomy and the Role of the Community Interpreter** Discuss how the role of the community interpreter supports communicative autonomy.
OBJECTIVE 5.2	**Interpreting and Mediation** Discuss the complex relationship between interpreting and mediation.
OBJECTIVE 5.3	**Advocacy and the Community Interpreter** Define advocacy and use a decision-making protocol to determine whether and how to advocate as a community interpreter.
OBJECTIVE 5.4	**Standards of Practice** Identify general best practices for interpreters that support the Ethics and Standards document provided in this textbook.
OBJECTIVE 5.5	**Self Care and Personal Wellness** Identify work-related risks for community interpreters and develop a wellness-and-safety plan.
OBJECTIVE 5.6	**Professional Development** Create a professional development plan that supports high standards for community interpreting.

Introduction

Your journey through this textbook has taken you to many exciting places. Chapter 1 discussed the profession; Chapter 2 introduced technical and cognitive skills and interpreting protocols; Chapter 3 showed you how to deal with communication barriers and introduced the Strategic Mediation Model; and Chapter 4 described your professional identity and explored a variety of settings where you may work. Chapter 5, the final chapter, offers you a look at critical concepts and considerations for professional practice gathered under the overarching concept of the community interpreter's role.

If there is one notion that has generated heated debate among professionals, researchers and trainers in the field since its inception, it is that of the interpreter's role. This chapter, in alignment with the textbook as a whole, supports the idea of a non-intrusive role for the community interpreter with the goal of supporting communicative autonomy. It recognizes, however that human interaction is complex and that the interpreter's active intervention is sometimes needed.

Professional practice is characterized on the one hand by a command of professional techniques, and on the other by an ability to apply insightful criteria to situations that require decision making. "*How* should I do this?" and "*Why* should I do it?" are the two questions for which a professional interpreter needs to have thoughtful answers. This final chapter, then, is concerned both with reviewing the *why* and facilitating the *how*. That means you will find two kinds of content here:

1. Conceptual content, which is related to explaining the why.
2. Practical suggestions, which clarify the how.

The chapter starts out in Section 5.1 by exploring the contribution of community interpreting to society at different levels. This way of looking at community interpreting allows us to distinguish between the micro context of community interpreting (the interpreted encounter) and its macro level (the social fabric). Section 5.2 addresses the relationship between community interpreting and mediation. How are they similar? How are they different? Most important, how should the community interpreter approach mediation? Section 5.3 tackles the difficult topic of advocacy with two chief goals: to bring clarity to the concept of advocacy in the context of community interpreting; and to offer guidelines for decision making and action when you encounter situations that call for advocacy.

The second half of the chapter offers, in Section 5.4, a review of every standard of the Ethics and Standards document. Section 5.5 identifies possible risks and hazards that the interpreter might be exposed to and provides specific guidelines on how to prevent them. To close the book, Chapter 5 ends with a discussion of professional development: Section 5.6 covers aspects of life-long learning and continuing education for the community interpreter, including tips that you should be able to apply no matter where you live.

5.1 Communicative Autonomy and the Role of the Community Interpreter

Overview

Like every other profession, community interpreting exists *as a profession* to offer a unique contribution to society. What do community interpreters offer that is unique, that no other professional can offer? How do community interpreters contribute "special value" to society? The goal of this first section of Chapter 5 is to put actual words to the value that community interpreters bring to their communities and to society as a whole.

The unique *contribution* of community interpreters and the *role* adopted by community interpreters to support their contribution are the two big discussions you will explore in Section 5.1. The *role* of practicing professionals refers to the patterns of behavior they engage in to effectively conduct their work. A clear professional role, often influenced by professional ethics and standards, allows those who practice a profession to do so appropriately and with reasonable consistency.

Central to this textbook is the idea that the special *contribution* of community interpreters is enabling communicative autonomy in the provision of community services across language barriers. To explore this special contribution, this section will offer a fictional example (the story of a patient and domestic violence victim named Monica) to highlight the concept of communicative autonomy. Communicative autonomy goes to the heart of community interpreting: why the profession exists, what it is meant to accomplish and how it can be most effective. Monica's case will show how communicative autonomy is the main impact of the community interpreter at the *micro level*—for the parties in the interpreted encounter—and also at the *macro level*, as a contribution to society as a whole.

Keeping that larger picture in mind helps to understand and accept reasonable limitations on the interpreter's role. The last part of this section addresses both the constraints and sophistication of that role.

Learning Objective 5.1

After completing this section, you will be able to:

- Discuss how the role of the community interpreter supports communicative autonomy.

Communicative autonomy

The *Ethics and Standards* document that begins this textbook is based on the idea that *communicative autonomy is a fundamental value of the profession.* In fact, enabling direct and autonomous communication across language differences is the unique contribution that community interpreting offers to society. Yet what, exactly, does making communicative autonomy possible involve?

A Unique Contribution to Society

The unique contribution that community interpreting has to offer to society is to enable the **communicative autonomy** of two or more individuals who need to interact for the well-being of at least one of the parties, despite the fact that they do not share a common language.

In a situation where the lack of a common language prevents service users and providers from communicating with each other, a third party is needed to assist. Community interpreters have specific techniques to support cross-linguistic and cross-cultural communication. Ideally, they aim to facilitate communication in a way that is the least intrusive possible. The goal is for service users and service providers to achieve autonomous communication despite their language barriers.

DEFINITION

Communicative autonomy

The capacity of each party in an encounter to be responsible for and in control of his or her own communication.

From this textbook's *Ethics and Standards* document

Through the interpreter the parties can communicate directly with each other despite their language differences and own their decision-making processes. The interpreter is not acting as a filter. He or she strives to be a faithful reporter of each message. Each party is then able to make decisions about what to say (or not to say) and what to do. The service providers and users make these decisions based on what the other party is sharing or asking and also based on each party's communication style. That decision-making process could be called the service user and provider's "power of self-government" in the communicative process. They have the power, the ability and the authority to make their own decisions despite the language barrier. They are enjoying communicative autonomy.

Autonomy is usually understood [...] as self-government or self-direction: being autonomous is acting on motives, reasons, or values that are one's own.

Stoljar, 2013

Monica's story below is just one example of how community interpreting can play a crucial role in people's lives. Her story will illustrate what communicative autonomy means and why it matters.

Case study: Monica's communicative autonomy as a life-changing gateway

Monica's story is inspired by several real-life stories. In fact, the types of situations described are common. The story is presented in three parts that offer three types of reflection and takeaways. In this story, Monica's journey takes her from the life-threatening danger that isolated her to a situation of safety and a sense of human dignity. Throughout this life-changing process, professional community interpreting has a deep impact not only on Monica's safety and dignity but also on her sense of empowerment.
As you read her story, keep in mind the following question: what would have happened to Monica if she lived in a place where community interpreting was not an established profession?

Part 1: The way out of isolation

Monica went to the local hospital for a check-up after she detected a lump in one of her breasts. Monica had recently arrived in the country, so an interpreter was booked. The nurse was going through her standard procedures, communicating through the interpreter. She ended her "patient history" with a last question: "Are you being forced by anyone to do things you don't want to do?" After a hesitation, Monica said, "Yes."

For the first time she began to share the story of how her husband was beating her and forcing her to engage in sex. Since this new hospital policy was introduced, the nurse had been surprised more than once by how it helped her detect cases of abuse. Monica was one of those cases. The interpreter's professionalism helped create a climate of trust, and Monica and the nurse felt a sense of connection, which was critical for Monica's disclosure.

Consider this: Without access to a professional interpreter, Monica would probably have brought along a family member to help, or a friend, or maybe even her abuser. The nurse would probably have asked the same question, but would Monica have answered the same way? Would she have confided her troubles? Without a professional interpreter, the nurse might never have found out that Monica was in danger. Monica might have remained in isolation in her terrible situation, risking her health, her well-being—and perhaps her life.

Part 2: Multiple contexts, one reliable service

After the nurse suggested several resources, Monica looked into them and made the difficult decision to leave her abuser and enter a shelter for female survivors of domestic violence. A long journey began with that decision. Along the way, Monica engaged with many professionals: therapists, police officers, lawyers, health professionals and social workers, among others.

Consider this: All of those services require interpreting. Will the same interpreter always be available for Monica? Should that matter? In some cases, such as therapy, it may be advisable to have the same interpreter each time to give Monica a sense of continuity and flow and to foster feelings of trust, safety and well-being. But expecting the same interpreter for other services would be unrealistic and perhaps inadvisable. However, it is important for all service users and providers to be able to expect *consistent, professional* conduct from *any* professional community interpreter. Knowing that "community interpreting" exists as a profession and what to expect from it eases the process both for Monica and for the professionals who work with her.

Part 3: Owning communicative autonomy

After leaving her husband, Monica became close to Mara, a shelter volunteer who came from the same country as Monica. Their common nationality and life experiences helped them bond: Mara was also a survivor. But Mara had lived in their new country much longer and taken language classes to become fluent, so Mara offered to accompany Monica to her various appointments to help with the language barrier. After discussing this offer with her therapist, Monica decided instead to continue having a professional interpreter attend. Occasionally she did ask Mara to come with her for support—for example, to court—but not to interpret.

Consider this: What motivated Monica to turn down her friend's offer? What did a professional interpreter have to offer over a trusted friend's help? Monica was grateful to be able to count on Mara's emotional support but turned down Mara's offer to interpret precisely *because* they had become so close. With Mara as her interpreter, Monica might feel uncomfortable in some situations, as if she had to justify her decisions to Mara. Mara would become a witness of the process instead of a supportive friend. If Mara accompanied Monica to all her appointments, their relationship might have changed. Monica wanted Mara as a friend—not an interpreter. She also valued the sense of empowerment she had started to feel by being able to go to different appointments by herself.

The micro-level and the macro-level contributions

Monica's case makes clear that the contributions of community interpreters happen at many different levels. Many health professionals looked after Monica: a lawyer defended her when she had to go to court and a team of social workers, caseworkers and advocates supported her throughout the process. A whole system of professions contributed—each with its own specialization—to the process allowing Monica to regain control over her own life.

Within that system, the community interpreting profession offered Monica and her service providers the ability to communicate *autonomously* despite the fact that they did not share a common language. *Autonomously* here means that the parties could speak in their own voice, as themselves. They could control their communication. They made their own informed decisions during the communication process. Without the existence of the community interpreting *profession*, not only the interpreters themselves, the rest of the service system would not be able to work effectively in Monica's case. Community interpreting is a crucial part of the service delivery system that connects all its components.

For the system to run smoothly, clear communication is vital. In cases where a language barrier can interfere with service provision, community interpreting allows parties to communicate. We are going to spell out the contributions of community interpreting both at the micro level and at the macro level.

The **micro level** refers to the communicative event (the encounter). This is the situation in which the parties communicate with each other through the interpreter.

The **macro level** is a more abstract concept, but just as important. It refers to the big picture. When we look at the macro level, it's as if we changed the lenses in our observation device and zoomed-out from the encounter so that we can see what's around it. We can then observe how each interpreter's decisions, behaviors and actions and the sum of all of them impact not only the encounter itself but also the social context that informs the encounter.

The micro level: the interpreter supports communicative autonomy

MACRO LEVEL

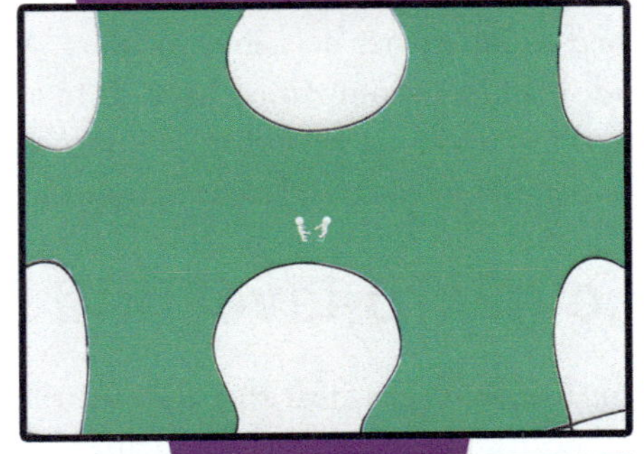

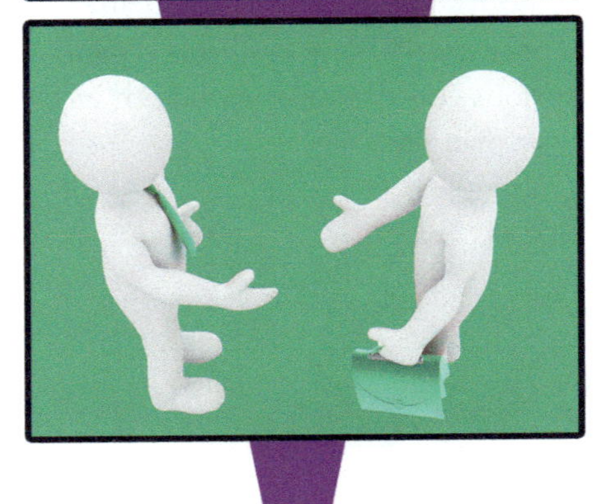

MICRO LEVEL

Throughout this textbook, you studied various protocols and techniques that help you to enable and support communicative autonomy. They include decision-making protocols, strategic positioning techniques, how to perform a professional introduction, the importance of using direct speech, managing the flow and strategic mediation. Ideally, to offer quality services in any encounter, professional community interpreters are fluent in their working languages, sensitive to the cultures and cultural complexity at play and aware of divergent worldviews. They can assess whether the goal of the encounter is being met or not, and whether communication is flowing well. They are committed to honoring the voices, feelings and intentions of all participants to the encounter as a matter of professional integrity. Above all, community interpreters need to be aware of the complexities of intercultural communication and how the presence of an interpreter can impact the situation.

In Monica's case, all these factors had a critical impact on Monica's willingness to disclose the abuse and seek help. She felt empowered thanks to the fact that she could trust not only the nurse, but also the interpreter. The interpreter gave Monica the gift of her own voice and the freedom to make her own decisions.

The macro level: the profession supports communicative autonomy

Effective communicative autonomy relies on you, the interpreter, and your ability to apply your professional skills in often challenging situations. Now let us explore how you and your actions are embedded in a broader structure.

A broader structure

When we look at community interpreting from a distance, with a zoomed-out device, or from "high in the sky," so to speak, we can see and discover interrelationships. Here, *interrelationship* refers to the fact that connections exist beyond the one-on-one relationships you observe during the interpreted encounter. What happens during the interpreted encounter and how it happens has an impact on outside events and connections. These, in turn, have an impact on what happens during interpreted encounters and the way they unfold.

Let's look at a concrete example. A caseworker initially had a biased perception of Monica's national group and her local community of immigrants. She thought they were lazy and did not want to learn the local language or help themselves. After working with Monica and a professional interpreter, this same caseworker saw Monica first and foremost as a human being—which allowed her to see other members of that immigrant group in a different, more understanding way, which affected her interactions both with them and with her colleagues who worked with immigrants as well. As a result, the interpreter's professional behavior led to positive change that had an impact beyond the interpreted encounter.

Here is another example: when the Pediatrics Department of a hospital heard about the Obstetrics and Gynecology Department's satisfaction with the new interpreting service and the level of professionalism of its interpreters, they decided to start using that service more often. They ended up becoming strong advocates for hospital policies that addressed cultural diversity in general and requesting qualified interpreters in particular. A couple of interrelationships are clear in this example: (1) The quality of interpreting services generated new demand for those same services throughout the hospital; and (2) Better communication between the hospital staff and local cultural communities generated increased sensitivity towards issues of cultural diversity and resulted in new hospital policies.

An important connection between the micro level (quality, reliable interpreting services for each encounter) and the macro level (the impact on society at large) is the way community interpreting enables communication among members of society who would not otherwise understand each other. That mere *option* is the starting point for communicative autonomy. Without that option, there is no reliable chance for autonomy.

It is important to look at the profession as a whole (instead of the interpreter only as an individual) to understand the special contribution of community interpreting and how it impacts and relates to society. The next few paragraphs highlight how the profession as a whole offers true value to people like Monica.

The profession

In Monica's story, we can identify three concrete ways in which communicative autonomy is supported by the profession through "big picture" aspects; that is, through macro-level interrelationships:

1. From Monica's story, Part 1: By existing as a profession, community interpreting opens doors that would otherwise remain closed: it makes community services accessible to those who do not speak the language of service, which in turn has an enormous, positive impact on the basic human rights of millions of individuals around the world.
2. From Monica's story, Part 2: Because community interpreters belong to a profession, there is typically more than one qualified person who can do a reliable job following a consistent approach. Where professional community interpreters are available, service users and service providers know what to expect. They know they can count on the existence of a professional service. One particular interpreter is not "irreplaceable."
3. From Monica's story, Part 3: What is irreplaceable, however, is the service that a professional interpreter can offer vs. an improvised solution such as the assistance of a friend or a family member. Professional interpreters are crucial to support autonomy. A service user does not depend

on someone's goodwill or on personal favors for which the service user should feel indebted, meaning that the service user is better positioned to make independent and autonomous decisions.

As a community interpreter and a member of a professional body, not only do you have an impact on every interpreted encounter (the micro level): you also have a broader social impact (the macro level) by contributing to effective and meaningful service delivery and its beneficial social consequences.

Individual autonomy and the system in place

The general public often fails to see why we need a *profession* to overcome language barriers. Many regions of the world do not have professional community interpreting. Also, some cultures attribute less importance to the concept of service user autonomy than others, which might contribute to the lack of a community interpreting profession in some places. Wherever autonomy is a goal, however, the need for a professionalized service system arises. That system is critical to provide an effective response to individual needs. Overcoming language barriers is only one of many such needs.

Let's use the example of public transportation to explain this idea of autonomy supported by professional service delivery. The distance between point A and point B in the images to the right is big enough that walking between the two every day would not be realistic. Let's say that Monica lives at point A and works at point B. She cannot walk to B and back every day, and she also does not have a car.

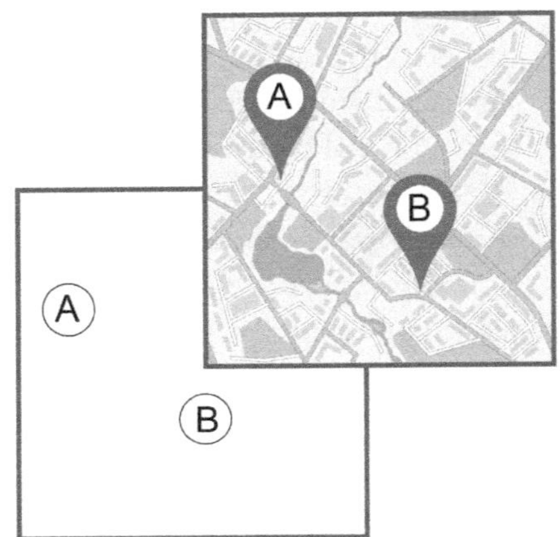

Thanks to the public transportation system in her city, Monica can go to work without having to ask for help. If the transportation grid did not exist, Monica would either not have the option to work at B, or would have to depend on the help of someone to go to work every day. This is what public transportation offers to Monica: an external service that is reliable and consistent. Thanks to those features, Monica can count on the system in place to go to work by herself (autonomously).

The system in place is a grid of means of transportation that includes many different lines: bus, train and subway, for example. These services operate throughout the day (every few minutes a bus, train or subway departs) and they respect their routes and schedules. That system is represented by the multi-colored grid. What every individual bus, train or subway operator does (micro) is important for the correct functioning of the overall system (macro).

The role of the community interpreter

So far, this section has explored the special contribution of community interpreting from both a micro-level and a macro-level perspective. Now let's turn to the patterns of behavior expected from community interpreters. In other words, we are going to focus on the community interpreter's *role*. The main ideas are: (1) Establishing clear limits around the interpreter's role strengthens the profession as a whole. (2) Setting limits is a delicate task, which makes the community interpreter's role a highly sophisticated one.

A limited role

Without the broader picture in mind, it is easy to forget that some of the strengths of the community interpreter's contribution are precisely the limitations of role. If the bus driver who takes Monica to work every morning at 8:15 decided, instead, to help out every passenger by taking detours to drop them off at their exact destination, Monica would not be able to arrive at work every day on time. The purpose of public transportation is defeated if Monica cannot rely on it.

Role Limitation Is a Strength

Only if you respect professional boundaries and role limitation can you offer your unique contribution to society. Remember that:

- Your responsibilities are shaped by the fact that you belong to a wider system.
- Your contribution is concrete, unique and crucial.
- You are only responsible for what is under your control.

The same is true for community interpreting. If you, as a community interpreter, stray from your professional role without a deeper understanding of the benefits and costs, there are high chances that your contribution (and that of your profession) will be undermined. Whether or not you can see those detrimental effects with "the naked eye" and on the spot doesn't mean the problems don't exist. If you can step back and look at the big picture, you may see the ripple effects: they do exist.

This perspective might conflict with cultural values in some cases. In some countries, for example, patient autonomy is not a high value: doctors may tend to make decisions for their patients. This textbook however supports the argument that most human beings in most circumstances are better off if they remain in control of their own communication.

System-related restrictions can generate frustration. Very often, community interpreters want to help service users in every possible way. It is important to remember that your specific contribution is to help the service user and provider achieve communicative autonomy. No other professional than the community interpreter can offer this valuable contribution to society.

Many professionals are restricted in their scope of action. The social worker's testimonial on the right is a good reminder that any professional who wants to "help out" faces limitations. Community interpreters are no exception.

I think that what we have to realize, and that sometimes is a struggle, is that you may want to do more for that person, but because of the mental capacity you realize you can't—they have the right to make poor decisions, they have the right to make bad judgment calls, they have the right to live in filth if they want too [sic]... you learn that it's ok. It truly is ok, as long as you have done what you could for that person, that's all that matters... Yes, some people see it as failing, but I don't. We have done what we can do.

Testimonial from a social worker.
In Bergel, 2007, p. 105

A sophisticated role

Any idea that putting limits on the interpreter's role will make that role easier to adopt is wrong. It is a misconception. In fact, one could argue that the sophistication of the interpreter's role can rival that of nurses, attorneys or therapists.

Limitations on one's role are, in and of themselves, a source of complexity. Role boundaries are challenging for interpreters in any area of community interpreting. They are also challenging for social workers, nurses, case managers and other professionals. Role boundaries are the source of many ethical dilemmas, and a source of stress and strain.

The role of the community interpreter requires particular sophistication because the interpreter is in a special and unique position among professions: not only do you provide a service (interpreting); in doing so, you become an integral part of another service delivery, even though you are most often not trained in how that service is provided. You have to adapt to varying circumstances across a broad spectrum of services.

There is no magic wand; no single answer about how to manage your role. Every cultural and professional context is unique; every encounter is unique; each individual is unique. While the methods, techniques and protocols for professional interpreting guide your choices, you still have to adapt them to each and every situation. To be a competent community interpreter is a high calling. By learning your role well, you can have a deep and important impact not only on the encounter but also on our precious social fabric.

Let's Practice

Learning Activity 5.1 (a): The Interpreter's Role
Learning Activity 5.1 (b): "Role" Plays

In *The Community Interpreter®: An International Workbook of Activities and Role Plays*

REVIEW OF SECTION 5.1

Through the example of Monica's story, we explored how community interpreting is a service profession. It plays a critical part, as one piece among others, in a wider system that supports the well-being of individuals and society as a whole.

Enabling direct and effective communication (communicative autonomy) across languages is the unique contribution of community interpreting. This social contribution takes place at both the micro level (the communicative event) and the macro level (society at large). The micro level refers to the encounter and your ability to help all parties present to communicate autonomously. The macro level refers to the conditions necessary for members of society to have access to communicative autonomy when they face language barriers. The existence of a professional body of community interpreters, not only supports communicative autonomy: it enables it.

For community interpreters to offer their special contribution at both micro and macro levels, their role needs to be clear in scope and limited, like other "helping and healing" professions. Yet a clear, limited role does not make the job simple or easy. The role of the community interpreter involves a high level of sophistication: many skills, techniques and considerations are involved in the provision of interpreting that facilitates autonomous communication.

5.2 Interpreting and Mediation

Overview

The interpreter sometimes needs to mediate. In Chapter 3 you examined specific methods to perform mediation in a way that supports direct communication and does not undermine communicative autonomy. In this section, you will explore how the term *mediation* is used in our field to signify different things. Some of the distinctions could strike you at first as details or nuances, yet they have a critical impact on whether mediation should be considered a *part* of interpreting, the *same thing* as interpreting or diametrically *opposed* to interpreting.

Every community interpreter needs to have a clear understanding of the relationship between interpreting and mediation. Understanding that relationship is not always easy. One big problem is the conceptual fuzziness around "mediation." To help you see the difference between interpreting and mediation, the first part of this section explores three different uses of the term and their relationships to interpreting. The second part examines why both the interpreter and all other parties to the encounter must make a clear distinction between acts of interpreting and acts of mediation.

Learning Objective 5.2

After completing this section, you will be able to:

- Discuss the complex relationship between interpreting and mediation.

Many uses of the term mediation

In this textbook, mediation has been formally defined as "any act or utterance of the interpreter that goes beyond interpreting and is intended to address barriers to communication between parties who do not share a common language." However, the term *mediation* is used in many different ways around the world. For example, in legal settings it is often used in the context of conflict resolution. Here, we will focus exclusively on the meaning of the term in the context of interpreting and intercultural communication.

DEFINITION

To mediate in a general sense

Mediate

Occupying a middle position.
Acting through an intervening agency.

Merriam-Webster's dictionary

False Synonyms

The term 'cultural mediation' is sometimes used as a blanket term to cover both translation and interpreting and the terms interpreter and cultural mediator can appear synonymous.

Martín and Phelan, 2010, p. 2

Mediation can refer to at least three different concepts or practices in community interpreting and in the broader fields of interpreting studies and intercultural communication. Because these fields are rather young (both as fields of scholarly inquiry and professional practice), and because "to mediate" is such an encompassing concept, it is only natural to find multiple uses of the term.

Multiple uses, however, bring an important downside: conceptual fuzziness. Martín and Phelan (2010) point out that the terms *interpreter* and *cultural mediator* can appear synonymous. Are they interchangeable? The answer depends on what is meant by mediation. We will see that in most cases the two terms do not, in fact, have the same meaning and they should not be interchangeable, although many people do get them mixed up.

Conceptual fuzziness is a particular problem in this case because depending on the meaning attributed to mediation, how community interpreters do or should relate to it can change dramatically. Looking at three different uses of the term mediation will encourage you to think of each of them as separate categories of behavior. Exploring them may help bring clarity to the fuzziness. Be aware that phrases involving the term *mediation* vary internationally even in community interpreting, which adds to the confusion.

The three uses of the term *mediation* identified here are:

- "Mediation" as a formal task or responsibility of the community interpreter or CI (the inner circle in Figure 5-A). For clarity, we refer to this usage as "strategic mediation."
- "Mediation" as a formal profession, usually referred to as "cultural mediation" or "intercultural mediation" (the middle circle).
- "Mediation" as any action taken by an intermediary, an all-encompassing concept (the outer circle).

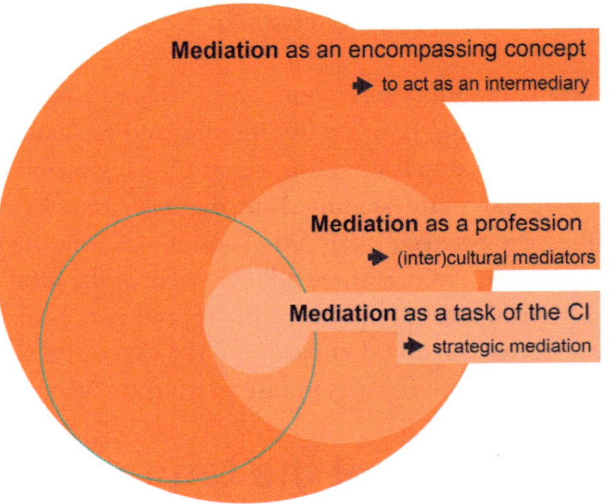

Figure 5-A
Three Different Uses of the Term Mediation

Without clarification, these three types of mediation might appear to be the same or have the same meaning, especially when only the word "mediation" is used without specifying the type of mediation involved. These three usages are *not* the same. In fact you will see that their relationship to interpreting as a profession is very different in each case.

Mediation as a task of the community interpreter

In this textbook, the term *mediation* refers to a task of the community interpreter. It is "shorthand" for the full phrase "strategic mediation." The Strategic Mediation Model presented in Chapter 3 as a practical tool helps interpreters to address communication barriers while interfering as little as possible with direct communication.

What strategic mediation involves

You explored basic protocols and techniques for performing strategic mediation in Chapters 1 and 3. The Strategic Mediation Model is designed to address two competing demands:

- The need for the parties to communicate with each other directly despite language barriers, while the interpreter intrudes as little as possible and focuses on faithfully transferring messages.
- The need for the interpreter, who is in a unique and insightful position, to help parties overcome barriers to communication that may arise despite accurate interpreting.

If a therapist fails to catch a reference to a refugee who is suicidal because a cultural idiom was too opaque, can the interpreter simply let the session end and walk away without finding a way to alert the therapist that "There is no bird left on the horizon" could mean that the refugee plans to kill himself? Very often, barriers to communication arise because of cultural differences (differences of worldview) between the parties. Assumptions by either of the parties based on their worldviews can dramatically impede communication, even if the interpreter is highly qualified and performing well.

Cultural differences are not the only potential barriers to communication that justify the interpreter's mediation during an interpreted encounter. In some cases, the interpreter needs to intervene to request clarifications or make corrections. In fact, even in countries such as Canada or the United Kingdom where interpreters may be discouraged from performing *cultural* mediation, they are permitted to intervene for clarifications or corrections.

The Strategic Mediation Model is based on the assumption that the interpreter needs to briefly step out of the interpreting role to proactively address a communication barrier. The model offers decision-making tools to decide whether or not to intervene, and protocols and techniques to manage what to say when the interpreter intervenes. Strategic mediation, then, involves an active role of the interpreter who adds his or her own messages to help remove a communication barrier, but does so as *briefly* and *unobtrusively* as possible.

How strategic mediation relates to community interpreting

The relationship between strategic mediation and interpreting seems straightforward: strategic mediation is simply one of the tasks of the community interpreter.

Look at the position of the strategic mediation circle in Figure 5-B: it falls inside the larger circle of community interpreting. Strategic mediation helps the community interpreter address sources of miscommunication in a way that interferes as little as possible with direct communication. Strategic mediation, then, is a very specific kind of mediation that is specifically intended for the interpreted encounter.

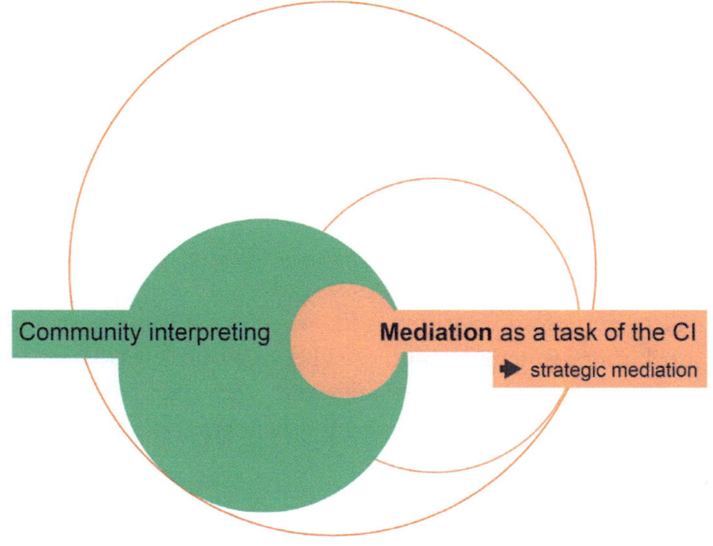

Figure 5-B
Strategic Mediation As a Task of the Community Interpreter

Mediation as a distinct profession

Mediation, as in the phrases "cultural mediation," or "intercultural mediation," can refer to a specific professional field that has emerged in certain countries where societies have become increasingly multicultural, primarily in Europe. Cultural mediation and intercultural mediation are both common expressions used to refer to this profession and they are often interchangeable in the field of intercultural communication.

What intercultural/cultural mediation involves

The goal of cultural or intercultural mediators (we will refer to them as "intercultural mediators") is to help people with different cultural backgrounds reach a better understanding of each other's perspectives. The focus is often to improve access to services, enhance service delivery quality and promote beneficial outcomes for service users, or simply to promote harmony among groups of a different cultural background.

When people from different backgrounds come into contact, they may or may not share common worldviews. Intercultural mediators help find common ground. Their own intercultural experiences and knowledge at play are assets that help them identify and address the sources of misunderstanding or cultural conflict. Through a variety of tasks they take on a middle-party role to bring those of different cultures closer to a common understanding. These tasks often involve providing cultural explanations intended to help one party understand the other party's point of view.

Here is an example: a pregnant patient from a conservative Muslim background learns that all the obstetrician-gynecologists in that practice are male and refuses prenatal care on religious grounds. Concerned, the intercultural mediator finds an older woman well-respected in the local Muslim community who has had male doctors. The mediator brings the patient to the older woman, who offers her a religious rationale for accepting care from male doctors. The younger woman changes her mind and accepts prenatal care. Intercultural mediators also can help design preventive health campaigns, accompany refugees to service appointments, help immigrant families adapt to their new school system, etc.

How intercultural/cultural mediation relates to community interpreting

The relationship between interpreting and intercultural mediation is complex. Community interpreting and intercultural mediation are two different professions (Figure 5-C). It is also true that intercultural mediators' job descriptions often include interpreting (Figure 5-D).

Interpreting and intercultural/cultural mediation as distinct professions

As distinct professions, community interpreting and intercultural mediation make important but different contributions to society. Both exist because of (increased) multiculturalism in society and the need for members of society to interact efficiently regardless of their cultural background. They also tend to work in the arena of community services. Yet their specific contributions are distinct.

Intercultural mediators bring their own understanding to the encounter and share it strategically to find common ground. For example, an intercultural mediator can explain to a new immigrant student how his new school works by comparing it with how schools work in the student's former country. Or an intercultural mediator can tell the designers of a health-outreach campaign about how diabetes is culturally perceived (including beliefs about what causes diabetes) in the group targeted to effectively reach their audience.

Community interpreters, on the contrary, would ideally avoid to the extent possible bringing their own understanding of culture to the encounter because their goal is to allow people to communicate directly and remain in full control of their exchange. If interpreters articulated their own perception of the parties' cultures and worldviews during an encounter, they would become a third active party in the interaction. Instead, community interpreters should use their cultural knowledge to detect breaches in communication and alert the parties; not to provide explanations themselves. If they do so, they are taking on another task—that of the intercultural mediator—without having been assigned, trained or qualified for that role. They are also contributing to the confusion about who a community interpreter is and what a community interpreter should be allowed to do (see Sections 5.1 and 5.3).

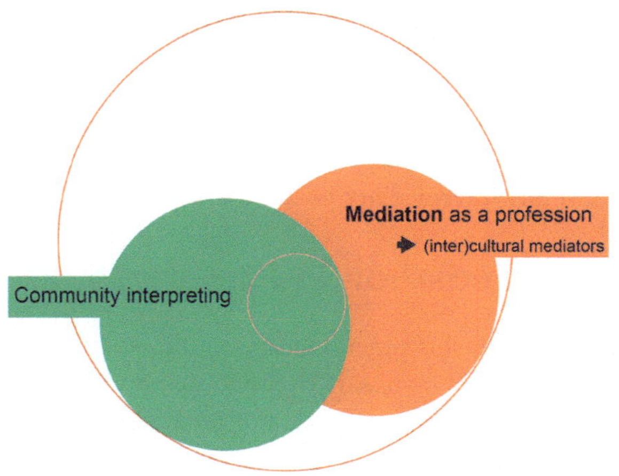

Figure 5-C
Community Interpreting and (Inter)cultural Mediation As Two Distinct Professions

Using "interpreter" and "cultural mediator" as synonyms shows a misunderstanding about these two professions. We can be sensitive to the shared context of the two professions, yet there are essential differences in their contributions to society. It is true that one person could take on the work of a community interpreter on some occasions and of an intercultural mediator on others. One person could, in principle, be trained and qualified for both jobs. Yet just as you saw in Chapter 1, a nurse should not practice nursing and professional interpreting at the same time, even if she is trained and qualified to do both. The same applies here: one person can be both a cultural mediator *and* a community interpreter as long as the two jobs are not confused and carried out at the same time. For these reasons and others soon to be discussed, Figure 5-C represents the two as distinct from each other.

Interpreting as a task of the intercultural/cultural mediator

In most cases, a deep understanding of more than one culture comes with the knowledge of more than one language. That, and the fact that intercultural mediation deals with intercultural communication, are probably the main reasons why one of the common tasks of intercultural mediators is to interpret. In fact, job descriptions of intercultural mediators often include interpreting and translation duties in addition to their primary workload. For example, Switzerland, Belgium, Italy and Spain are among the countries where some public institutions have chosen intercultural mediators as the default professional to overcome language and cultural barriers in public services and community settings.

In some countries, then, community interpreting is one task of the intercultural mediator, as represented in Figure 5-D. It seems clear that specific training in interpreting techniques, ethics and standards should then be a prerequisite for intercultural mediators if they are expected to interpret. Whether or not they receive such training depends on the region.

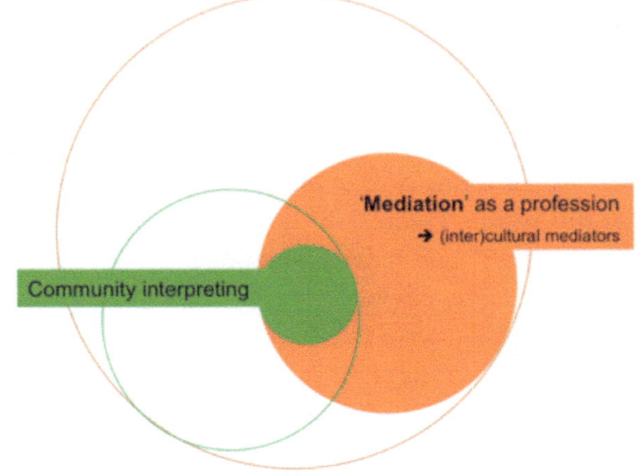

Figure 5-D
Interpreting As a Task of Intercultural Mediation

Mediation as a broad and encompassing concept

The root *med-* in Latin means to be in the middle. In its broadest sense, mediation can mean very different things. Nowadays, in everyday language, mediation is often—but not always—associated with resolving conflicts where a third party is needed to help bring agreement. In the field of intercultural communication, almost any intermediary position can be referred to as fulfilling a mediating role.

What mediation (as an encompassing concept) involves

Mediation, in this general sense, simply involves a process that goes through a middle party. Sometimes not even a person is involved. The process itself can be the mediating element. For example, translating a text is sometimes referred to as an act of mediation. The idea here is that *translation itself* serves as an intermediary between readers and cultures. Two different cultures come in contact through the intermediary of translation. The same could be said of interpreting. It enables individuals to communicate despite language and cultural barriers and exposes them to other worldviews. Thus, interpreters act as *intermediaries* between individuals and cultures.

Other professions also play intermediary roles and are emerging to address the increasing need for intercultural communication. They include not only intercultural mediators but also patient navigators (who accompany and guide patients and their families through the healthcare system in the United States), health promoters or community agents (outreach specialists from a targeted community), bilingual or multicultural parent-teacher liaisons and classroom assistants for Deaf students.

How mediation (in its broad sense) relates to community interpreting

Because interpreters act as intermediaries, their work is sometimes referred to as an act of mediation. This usage does *not* necessarily imply strategic mediation or intercultural mediation: it can simply refer to the idea that the interpreter occupies a middle position in a process between two parties or cultures.

In Germany, the community interpreter is often called *sprachmittler*, i.e., "language intermediary." In Italy, the term *mediazione linguistica* (linguistic mediation) designates undergraduate programs for interpreting and translation. Looking at this general sense of *mediation*, interpreting can be considered one type of mediation. For this reason, Figure 5-E shows interpreting as one activity contained within the larger circle of mediation as an "umbrella" term (a broad, encompassing concept.)

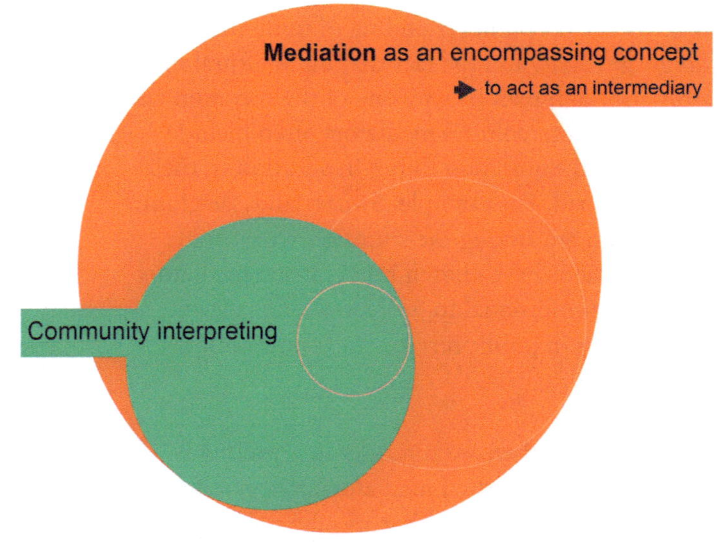

Figure 5-E
Mediation As a Concept Encompassing Interpreting

Community interpreters and their mediation tasks

We saw above that mediation can mean at least three different things. Very often we don't stop to think about which meaning is attributed to the term when we hear it or read it. Yet depending on the meaning, the way the interpreter should look at mediation changes completely.

In the first meaning that we covered (strategic mediation), the interpreter's job clearly encompasses mediation tasks. In the second meaning (intercultural or cultural mediation), mediation and interpreting are two distinct professions: a community interpreter could consider becoming an intercultural mediator, instead of or in addition to working as an interpreter, but should not practice both professions within the same assignment. In the third meaning we explored (the umbrella concept), mediation actually encompasses interpreting because interpreting is an act of intermediation.

These distinctions could seem unimportant, but we are going to see how without clarity about them, interpreters in the field may have a hard time supporting communicative autonomy.

The actions are different

Mediation in the first and second meanings discussed involves actions different from interpreting. Mediation involves *generative acts*, whereas interpreting involves *message transfer acts*.

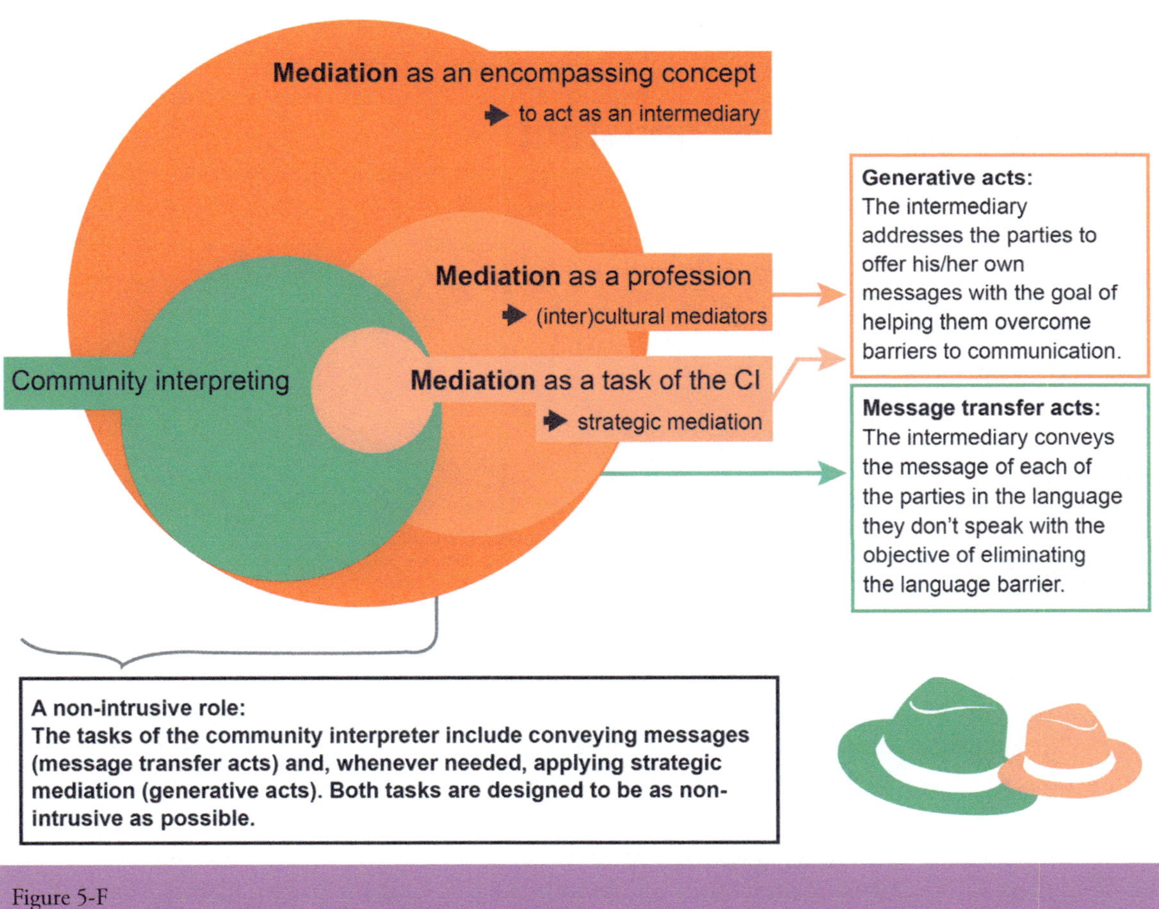

Figure 5-F
Mediation vs. interpreting: Generative Versus Conveying Acts

Generative acts: Both intercultural mediation and strategic mediation involve generative acts from the person who is acting as an intermediary. What is a "generative act"? Here it means that the intermediary is offering his or her own messages to help parties communicate by generating content and change. He or she is offering in words and actions something of his or her own, such as explanations or advice (for intercultural mediators) or pointing out a possible source of misunderstanding (for interpreters). Pointing out a source of misunderstanding, even without explanations, still constitutes a message that comes from the interpreter (when he or she is engaged in strategic mediation), so, both intercultural mediators and interpreters create new content whenever they mediate.

Message transfer acts: The act of interpreting is by definition an act of transferring messages from one language into another. Interpreters convey meaning from one language into a different language and refrain from altering the messages in any way. The act of interpreting, unlike mediation, is therefore not generative, and indeed almost the opposite of generative.

A non-intrusive role: As is clear in Figure 5-F, the role of the community interpreter, as the authors of this textbook understand it, encompasses both transferring acts (interpreting) and generative acts (strategic mediation). Most of the time, the interpreter should engage in the first kind (interpreting), but in some instances the interpreter does intervene to help overcome barriers to communication (strategic mediation). Whether the interpreter is interpreting or intervening to perform strategic mediation, the interpreter strives to remain as non-intrusive as possible. As for acts of mediation during the interpreted encounter, Chapter 3 teaches you how to mediate strategically so that your intervention helps the parties avoid misunderstandings while ensuring that the focus of the exchange remains among the parties and not with the interpreter. Your role is to assist the parties in a way that lets them remain in control of their communicative process, whether you are interpreting or performing strategic mediation.

The difference should be apparent

Whether the intercultural mediator is interpreting or the community interpreter is performing strategic mediation, the distinction between the two functions needs to be clear and apparent. The intermediary must understand the difference so that he or she only carries out one of the two tasks at a time.

COMMUNITY INTERPRETING

Interpreting	Strategic mediation
Message transfer acts: The intermediary conveys the messages of each of the parties in the language they don't speak with the objective of eliminating the language barrier.	**Generative acts:** The intermediary addresses the parties to offer his/her own messages with the goal of helping them overcome barriers to communication.

It is equally important for all parties to know what the intermediary is doing: is the intermediary speaking for him/herself? Or is he or she delivering the original messages? If the intermediary mixes up two roles without warning, how will anyone know what exactly was said by whom and what was omitted, added or changed? The intermediary should at all times wear only *one* of two hats: either the mediator's or the interpreter's. Wearing one hat means that you are taking on one of the two functions *exclusively*; it also means that everyone present knows *which* of them you are carrying out.

As a community interpreter, you wear the green interpreter hat by default. See Figure 5-G. But you may have to briefly abandon your message-transferor role (interpreting) to help the parties address a break in communication. When you stop interpreting and intervene to perform strategic mediation, you are changing hats. The five steps of the Strategic Mediation Model taught in Chapter 3 (Section 3.3) include letting the parties know when you are transferring messages and when you are using your own voice to intervene. They show everyone which hat you wear.

Let's Practice

Learning Activity 5.2: The Meaning of Mediation

In *The Community Interpreter®: An International Workbook of Activities and Role Plays*

REVIEW OF SECTION 5.2

This section reviewed three different uses of the term *mediation*. It explored how each of the meanings applies to you and how you, as a community interpreter, can use that knowledge in the field.

In a general sense, interpreting itself is an act of mediation, because mediation in this sense can simply refer to the act of being in the middle of a communication process. In two other uses of the term, however, the difference between mediation and interpreting is clear. They are, in those cases, different (although complementary) acts. Strategic mediation is simply a set of tasks of the community interpreter; intercultural mediation is a distinct profession with some characteristics that overlap with the work of community interpreters, but with distinct goals. That overlap often leads to confusion.

Remember that mediation involves acts incompatible with interpreting in the sense that you cannot perform both at once effectively. Mediation includes generative acts, whereas interpreting itself does not. The former involves using your voice to express your own messages, whereas the latter involves using your voice to convey only the messages of the parties you interpret for.

The distinction between the two kinds of functions is sometimes overlooked, and yet that distinction is crucial to be able to provide effective assistance as an interpreter. Not only is it important for you, as a community interpreter, to understand and respect the difference. It is equally important for the service user and provider to know what you are doing at any given time: are you interpreting or are you offering your own comments?

We have used the image of hats to reflect the ideas that: (1) Only one function can be carried out at a time (interpreting or strategic mediation). (2) The parties in the encounter should know at all times which hat you are wearing; that is, whether you are interpreting or intervening to help bridge communications gaps.

5.3 Advocacy and the Community Interpreter

Overview

Whether or not to advocate as a community interpreter is a conundrum. It is a question you will face often in the field. Coming up with clear and helpful guidelines about advocacy for community interpreters has proved a challenge for researchers, trainers and managers of interpreting services, who do not always agree about what advocacy is or whether community interpreters should engage in it. There is difficulty in understanding how community interpreting and advocacy are related, in part because some conceptual fuzziness exists around the term *advocacy*. The other difficulty is that even if the field came to a universal agreement about what advocacy means and whether or not it is part of the community interpreter's role, you will almost certainly encounter ethical dilemmas related to advocacy while doing your job.

The goal of this section is to bring clarity to the concept of advocacy and to help you apply grounded decision making when you face a situation that seems to call for advocacy. First, we will establish an operational definition of advocacy. Next, we will examine the implications involved in making a decision about advocacy, then you are invited to consider some of the actions that a community interpreter should (or should not) take in the name of advocacy. The fourth and last part of this section will offer some final tips and considerations that could help you feel more at peace with the competing demands that surround advocacy.

Learning Objective 5.3

After completing this section, you will be able to:

- Define advocacy and use a decision-making protocol to determine whether and how to advocate as a community interpreter.

Defining advocacy

Conceptual fuzziness around the term *advocacy*, just like the term *mediation*, is probably due to the fact that "to advocate" is a broad term. It can be applied to an endless number of situations. We will narrow the definition to help make it relevant and clear in this context. The following paragraphs will: (1) Explore multiple perspectives of what advocacy means. (2) Establish an operational definition of advocacy for community interpreters.

Just what is advocacy?

Just what is advocacy?

A *general* definition of advocacy is provided in the box to the side. It is very broad: "the act or process of supporting a cause or proposal" is a definition that leaves room for all sorts of understandings—and misunderstandings. Think of all the causes to be supported, and how many ways there are to provide support! It is only fair to wonder: What does advocacy mean in the context of community interpreting?

> **DEFINITION**
>
> Advocacy in a general sense
>
> **Advocacy**
>
> the act or process of supporting a cause or proposal.
>
> Merriam-Webster's dictionary

Ask a few interpreters what advocacy means to them. You will get different answers that vary from making sure everything gets interpreted to suggesting alternative courses of action that lead to better outcomes for the service user, or even urging the service user to report a critical incident. If only one thing is clear about advocacy and community interpreters, it is that interpreters tend to associate it with the idea of supporting the service user, either directly or indirectly—generally not the service provider. The underlying assumption is that socioeconomic, racial and cultural differences generate power imbalances in the user-provider relationship, and that those imbalances can have a negative impact on the service-user's well-being. The big question is whether it is part of your role as the interpreter to redress those power imbalances to support the service user's well-being.

As it turns out, codes of ethics published by professional interpreting associations show different approaches to advocacy. Some professional groups, like NCIHC and CHIA, both U.S.-based and in the field of healthcare interpreting, include advocacy among their ethical principles and standards of practice for interpreters. Others, like the AUSIT code from Australia or the HIN National Standard Guide for Community Interpreting Services from Canada, explicitly rule out advocacy under the ethical principle of role boundaries.

In reality, the issue of advocacy is tightly tied up with the difficult question of role definition for the community interpreter. The term advocacy is a very Anglo-Saxon term that is difficult to translate into other languages, especially in this context. Yet the issues that underlie the term are internationally relevant (and have been explored in other sections of this textbook). They center on the question of where the role of the interpreter begins and ends when it comes to the service user's well-being.

Operational definition

Operational definition

To address the conundrums around advocacy, first we need a working definition of advocacy for community interpreters. It needs to be relevant and clear. If advocacy can mean a variety of things, it is hard to explore clear guidelines for interpreters about whether or how to advocate. In other words: only if we are clear about concepts can we be specific about actions. We need to set boundaries around the concept to be able to use it effectively.

> **DEFINITION**
>
> **Advocacy in community interpreting**
>
> Taking action or speaking up on behalf of a service user whose safety, health, well-being or human dignity is at risk, with the purpose of preventing such harm.

For this textbook, we will use the operational definition of advocacy provided in the box. It reflects a widespread (though not universal) understanding of what advocacy has come to mean in our field. Under this definition, advocacy is intended as direct support to the service user.

Implications of advocacy

Using this operational definition of advocacy, we can now tackle the choices available to community interpreters. The case study below offers an example of a situation that would tempt many interpreters to advocate. We will use this example to explore the basic implications of advocacy and some of its complexities.

Maria's story

Maria had never been a successful student, but it was her behavior at school—which was becoming more and more problematic—that had caused her to be suspended from class for three days. Now she faced a disciplinary hearing and might be expelled.

Maria, her mother and the principal of her high school all gathered to discuss the situation. The interpreter could not believe what she heard when the principal asked Maria: "Do you want to become a no-one like your mum? Or do you want to be able to get a real job and go somewhere in life? If you want a job and a good life, you'd better try hard. We're here to help, but you have to do your part."

What would you do if you were the interpreter in the session? Would you:

a) Avoid interpreting the insult to Maria's mother (simply omit it)?
b) Inform the principal his comments are racist or bigoted?
c) Tell the mother, after the session, that the principal was a bigot?
d) Simply interpret everything said and avoid any further involvement?

(the response to this question is found on page 384)

Each situation you encounter while you interpret is unique and you might come up with other solutions. In this case, not only basic ethical requirements but also real-world consequences help us justify why option d) is the only viable one in this case. If you omit the disrespectful comment, you deprive the mother of her right to take action against the principal. If you speak alone with the mother and take sides with her, will she perceive you and your fellow professionals as impartial in future encounters? Likely not. Ultimately, breaching the code of ethics on one occasion can not only have immediate consequences; it can also impact the mother's communicative autonomy in future encounters.

The reality is that your role leaves little "wiggle" room for you to take actions that go beyond transferring messages, performing strategic mediation or clarifying your professional role because any other actions open the door to risk: the risk that you will undermine communicative autonomy and provoke other unwelcome consequences. Here are just three examples of other ethical principles and standards of practice that also limit your scope of intervention:

- To promote the ethical principle of direct communication, you should refrain from becoming an active participant in the communication.
- Under transparency, you are not supposed to share with one party information that you are not sharing with the other.
- Role boundaries set limits on activities that go beyond facilitating communication.

The "Proper Response" of an Interpreter (from a Deaf Consumer)

"[S]ocial justice should be a concern for everyone. I would hope that any of us, witnessing social injustice, act to change it. In doing so smartly/well, context matters. In the context of an interpreting job, I believe the proper response of an interpreter is to facilitate communication, period. Doing so promotes social justice by setting an environment where language and communication presumably free parties to engage in higher level interactions. I prefer interpreters to NOT step outside that role—no matter what. Doing so robs me of my own expression and reinforces a picture to hearing parties that I have little/no power of my own. I feel interpreters do have a place for expression—just not on the job, except to make communication clear and complete. This may be different for other deaf folks, but I think it's generally good policy and practice for all. Surprised to see myself say that, as I am usually a strong believer that people should speak up. However, interpreting is not that same kind of situation as direct communication between individuals is."

Commentary by Julianne Bonta in StreetLeverage Blog, 2014

The essence of these ethics and standards can be found in one form or another in almost all ethics and standards documents that apply to community interpreters. They also respond to the central goal of helping to ensure that you, the community interpreter, support the parties' ability to communicate effectively with each other (communicative autonomy).

Look at the comment in the box that a Deaf commentator posted online. As a user of interpreting services, she argues in favor of a restricted scope of action for the interpreter. On many occasions, the community interpreter may be tempted to defend service users like Maria and her mother or get personally involved with their processes in other ways. But if you and every other interpreter did that, who would fulfill the role of the interpreter? Who could create "an environment where language and communication presumably free parties to engage in higher-level interactions" (Bonta, 2014)? Who, in other words, would empower the parties in their right to effective and autonomous communication?

Balancing Out Priorities

When feeling the human and compassionate instinct of correcting a situation that seems wrong while on an interpreting assignment, take a second to breathe in and reflect on the compassionate and social role of community interpreting. Which is most important? In most cases, respecting your interpreter role is more important.

The interpreter (response to Maria's story found on page 382)

The only answer that the authors of this textbook unequivocally support for the case study above is option d: "Simply interpret everything said and avoid any further involvement." Options a, b and c undermine the principles that support communicative autonomy. For example:

- Omitting information (option a) violates the ethical principle of accuracy.
- Intervening to say that the principal is being racist or bigoted (option b) violates the ethical principle of impartiality and direct communication.
- Providing an opinion after the session is over (option c) violates the principles of impartiality and professional boundaries.

As we saw in Section 5.2, you can only wear one hat at a time. Always remember that your unique contribution as a community interpreter is often more valuable than the help you could provide by stepping out of your interpreting role. This leads us to spell out a key insight about advocacy: *taking action or speaking up on behalf of a service user whose safety, health, well-being or human dignity is at risk is not part of the interpreter's professional role.* When acting as an interpreter, avoid taking on an advocacy role.

While there is no consensus about advocacy, and many around the world might disagree with the statement above, this section explains why the authors of this textbook support it. This section also offers guidelines for extreme cases where you might feel that, as a compassionate human being who is also an interpreter, you need to consider ways of advocating for a service user.

Advocacy as an ethical dilemma

It is worth repeating: when acting as an interpreter, avoid taking on an advocacy role. The word "avoid" is intentionally chosen. It implies that there are cases when it might be unreasonable not to advocate. The obvious question is: how do you determine when it is reasonable or unreasonable to advocate?

The answer depends in part on how serious the risk appears to be to the safety, health, well-being or human dignity of the service user. When the risk is or seems serious, you may feel you have no other choice than to take action or speak up. It might be inhumane to stand by and do nothing. When the circumstances are extreme, your sense of professionalism is challenged by your sense of morality. For example: you would not let someone starve or allow physical aggression against a service user based on your ethical requirements: after all, you also have a simple, moral duty to assist someone in life-threatening or extreme circumstances.

Your human condition and morality will most likely override your professional ethics. And rightly so. No professional code of any profession should ever ban anyone from acting morally. For example, a legal interpreter who swore she would never advocate on the grounds that it violated her professional role *did* advocate one time. She interpreted for a teenage pregnant immigrant being detained by police. The teenager was bleeding, and no one took care of her. The interpreter reported the incident to a higher official at the police station to make sure the girl received appropriate medical care. This interpreter had a strong sense that advocacy was prohibited to legal interpreters in her country and she cared about respecting her professional ethical duties. In this case, however, she made an exception; she felt she had no choice.

What an Ethical Dilemma Is

A situation is considered an ethical dilemma when, whichever action you take, some ethical or moral requirement will be transgressed.

Facing an ethical dilemma means the interpreter needs to make a choice between two or more competing solutions, but none of the solutions is perfect. If you are faced with an ethical dilemma, you will have to settle with the less potentially harmful option.

Starvation, physical aggression or health emergencies are black-and-white examples. They clearly point to critical circumstances that call for action. Note, however, that in cases like these at least two different demands have entered into conflict: one is the demand of observing professional ethics and standards (such as impartiality or confidentiality); the other is the demand of responding to the moral requirement of assisting someone in need. The existence of competing ethical or moral demands that cannot be reconciled is called an ethical dilemma. Situations that call for advocacy in community interpreting are, without exception, ethical dilemmas for the interpreter.

Ethical dilemmas about advocacy can be explained using the concept of *identity*. The ethical dilemma sets up a conflict between two identities: your professional identity as an interpreter and your identity as a member of society, a human being who becomes a witness of an unfair or dangerous situation. Should you look away and pretend that the unfair or the dangerous circumstance does not exist under the pretext that you are an interpreter and your code of ethics tells you to respect role boundaries and remain impartial? Should you, on the contrary, disregard your professional code of ethics and go ahead and act as you choose, without concerns? Neither of these two choices is appropriate because they show no effort to weigh the pros and cons and understand where the lesser evil lies.

Whichever action you decide to take when you face an ethical dilemma, you will need to apply *conscious, critical and responsible decision making*. You will need to weigh out the circumstances and take things into thorough consideration before and while you carry out the action chosen. Such courses of action are discussed below.

Why community interpreters are likely to face ethical dilemmas related to advocacy

One could think of several reasons why community interpreters are often exposed to circumstances that call for advocacy. For example:

- They witness a broad array of situations that involve crucial aspects of people's dignity or well-being. If something goes wrong, the stakes could be high and the interpreter might feel an urge to do something about the situation.
- Big differences in power and resources between service users and providers are often present and they increase the chances for unfair circumstances if and when something goes wrong.
- If an interpreter works with the same service user in different services, the interpreter ends up knowing many of that person's life circumstances. The more privileged knowledge an interpreter has, the more chances to realize that a situation can be critical.

- Community interpreters tend to be socially conscious individuals interested in serving others. Often, that "desire to help" or "give back to my community" is what draws them to the field.
- For all these reasons, interpreters might feel the urge to speak or take action on behalf of the service user. However, professional boundaries limit the scope of action of the interpreter. This tension leads to ethical dilemmas.

Recap on the implications of advocacy

- Advocating involves taking the side of a service user in need to correct an unfair or risky situation. Advocating, then, involves helping someone out.
- However, by its very nature, advocating requires you to step out of your professional role. Whenever you advocate, you tend to breach ethical requirements, like impartiality and professional boundaries. (Your profession evolved in a strategic way to empower people to communicate clearly with each other so that they can make informed decisions.)
- A situation in which you feel the urge to advocate is a dilemma that involves two competing demands: you will need to choose the less potentially harmful of two (or more) possible courses of action.
- In the majority of cases, the best option (the lesser evil) is to stay close to your professional role and avoid advocacy. The safest attitude is to stay out of it by default (just as you saw for mediation in Chapter 3.)
- Advocacy should be reserved for extreme circumstances in which stepping out of the role of the interpreter is really a no-choice. "No-choice" situations are those in which a moral requirement to help a service user outweighs professional ethical requirements. Those exceptional situations include life-threatening circumstances or serious irreversible consequences to someone's life.
- Advocating should always be treated as an ethical dilemma. It requires conscious, thorough and analytical decision making. Ethical dilemmas involve having to make a choice among different options of which none is ideal.
- The more experienced you are as a community interpreter, the more prepared you will be to judge difficult situations and make appropriate decisions. Making them soundly requires a deep understanding of your scope of practice and a command of relevant ethics and standards. In other words, appropriate advocacy requires sophisticated skills. Remember the mantra from Chapter 3: When in doubt, stay out!

Courses of action

Given the high stakes involved, the first consideration is whether you should advocate or not. Often, interpreters are tempted to advocate under a somewhat unconscious premise that they know better than the parties involved. That is absolutely not a good reason to advocate. To avoid unconscious motivations, you should develop an awareness-based, decision-making mechanism to help you decide whether or not to advocate and decide exactly what to do. The first question is, "Should I step out of my role?" If the answer is *yes*, the next question is, "How should I advocate?"

Should I?

Should I?

As we have seen so far, only a *serious* risk to the safety, health, well-being or human dignity of the service user justifies advocacy. Determining whether the risk is serious relies on subjective considerations. It is ultimately a personal call. You decide what to do on a case-by-case basis. Such a decision-making process, however, can follow consistent steps to help you make sound decisions. Since time is often short, that mechanism should be simple, clear and easy to use on the spot. However, as covered in Chapter 3, it is best if it can also be used after a real-life situation to help develop "Type 2" thinking—the long-term, deeper kind of thinking that you have time for only outside the session but that can help inform your decisions while you interpret.

A roadmap for advocacy

The "roadmap" below (Figure 5-H) can guide that decision-making process. It shows you the *steps* you are encouraged to take to determine what action is desirable. These steps are presented in the form of questions. You will have to decide the answer to each question before you move on to the next step.

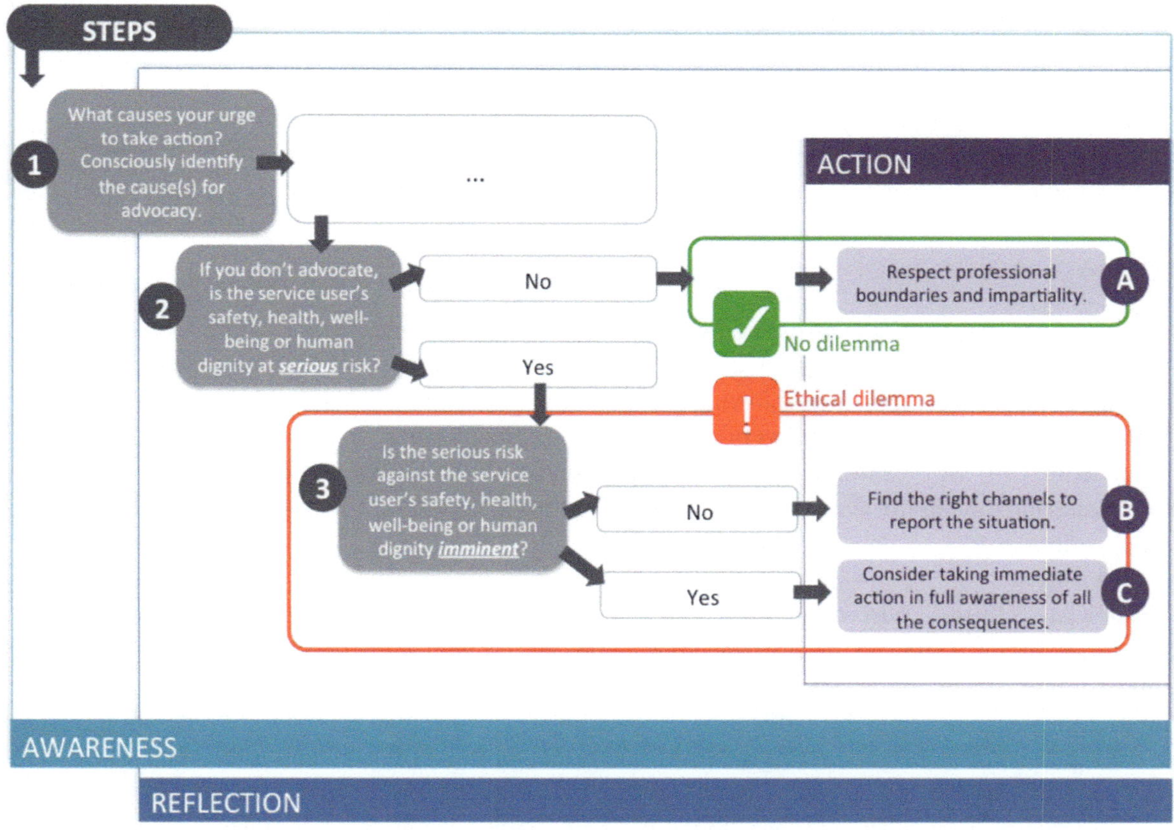

Figure 5-H
A Roadmap for Advocacy

The most important prerequisite for effective advocacy is *awareness*. From the outset, it is important to detect problems to act on them effectively. But the need for awareness goes beyond detection. Effective advocates also maintain awareness of the implications of their involvement. Only then can you make sound decisions at each stage of the unfolding situation. Awareness underlies every aspect of your decision-making roadmap. Yet once you detect an impulse to take action, awareness is not enough. You have to engage in active reflection and conscious analysis to answer the following questions: What causes me to feel I need to advocate for the service user? (Step 1); If I didn't advocate, would the service user's safety, health, well-being or human dignity be at *serious* risk? (Step 2); If the service user is at serious risk, how *imminent* is that risk? (Step 3).

A positive answer to questions 2 or 3 takes you to a situation where you face an ethical dilemma. If the risk is serious *and* imminent (action C) and you have exhausted all possibilities within your scope of practice (through strategic mediation, most likely), then advocating means you will undermine one or more of your ethical principles: impartiality and professional boundaries are the two most obvious.

If the risk to the service user is serious but not imminent (action B), you can at least remain impartial and respect professional boundaries during the interpreted encounter, but you may have to consider sharing information about the encounter if you decide to report the situation to the appropriate authority. Let's say that during an interpreted encounter it becomes clear that a woman is being abused by her boss, but it is also clear that the social worker has no interest in addressing the situation (though doing so is part of her job). You used strategic mediation techniques to address any possible misunderstanding. They didn't work. The circumstances are serious. The ethical dilemma is then between reporting the social worker (and risk breaking confidentiality) vs. respecting all your ethical principles (and doing nothing to prevent or correct the serious risk that the service user faces).

Decision making for ethical dilemmas

The community interpreter may be especially exposed to ethical dilemmas, but ethical dilemmas are not unique to community interpreting. Many professions share a roughly common approach to tackling an ethical dilemma. The following guidance (or versions of it) is typical: (1) Identify the problem. (2) Consider potential courses of action. (3) Consider good and bad consequences of the different actions. (4) Opt for the course of action that you consider the least harmful. (5) Evaluate afterward the outcome of the action chosen in a reflective way that can inform your decisions in future situations.

Chapters 1 and 3 introduced you to the CHIA model for ethical decision making guidelines. The CHIA model responds to the basic structure above. You can certainly apply that model here.

Because of the very nature of ethical dilemmas, there is no such thing as a single correct answer on what the right actions are. When facing an ethical dilemma, your critical thinking skills are called into action more than in any other situation. It is your call. Whichever strategy you apply, always include the following questions addressed to yourself: How sure can I be that my understanding of the situation is complete? Am I ready to face professional consequences (and even to lose my job or contract work) for carrying out this course of action?

How do I advocate?

The next few paragraphs are devoted to the "Action" section of the roadmap. Answering the different questions for Steps 1, 2 and 3 will take you to Actions A, B or C. Let's explore each of them.

Action A

If the risk for the service user is not serious, like the case of Maria, you should not take any other action than what your professional role entails. Just follow the ethics and standards that govern your basic decisions and conduct and the protocols that help you do so. The value of keeping to your professional role cannot be overemphasized. The case of Monica in Section 5.1 showed how maintaining role boundaries is important both at the micro and the macro levels of your work.

Action B

If the risk for the service user is serious, you will need to consider taking actions that go beyond your "official" role. Unless the risk is imminent, work within the system in place, that is, do not take it upon yourself alone to correct the situation. For example, imagine the interpreter for Maria's mother learned that the principal at that high school was not only discriminatory against the mother but also against Maria herself. The principal is bluntly racist. As an interpreter, you are concerned about the well-being of Maria and other students in her school. Rule number one is to *engage the service system.* In other words, continue interpreting; then, *after* the session, consider reporting the situation to an appropriate authority.

There are several important considerations you need to be aware of to know how to report. Some have to do with your employment status. Others have to do with finding the right person to report to.

What are the system reporting requirements?

The answer to the question "Whom do I report to?" will be different depending on your employment status. If you are a *staff interpreter*, you are an employee hired by an institution to interpret there. You should have a job title and a job description. In that case, you should *report the situation within the institution as a critical incident* to a supervisor or following established protocols for reporting critical incidents, as any other employee might do.

If you are *self-employed* (a freelance interpreter or contract interpreter), perhaps you were contracted by an agency for the encounter. In that case, *report to the agency.* Do not report to the institution where you interpreted (e.g., a school or hospital) because the agency that sent you assumes legal liability for your conduct. The agency will need to decide what to do about the situation you report.

If you are a *self-employed interpreter who was engaged directly by the institution* where you interpret, you may wish to find someone within that institution to report to, as the institution assumes legal liability both for the critical incident and your conduct. You may have to make inquiries to find out the right person to receive your report, which you may also make in writing.

Who is the appropriate person to report to?

Before you report to anyone and reveal any details about the situation, find out the *proper channels* to report those types of circumstances. It could be your supervisor at the institution, the head of the department where the encounter took place, or the interpreting services coordinator at the agency that contracted you. There is not one single type of "right person" to report to, so the quest to find that person might involve some research. Remember that even an inquiry about where to report should honor confidentiality. Do not offer details of the encounter of those involved unless you are sure you are addressing the appropriate person (and think hard about what details you may or may not disclose).

What if the person you report to doesn't care?

You have taken the right action: you have found the appropriate person and reported the incident. Then it becomes clear to you that this person doesn't care or won't take action, or has no idea what action to take. Let's say you report the incident to the interpreting service that sent you, but they don't want to upset their hospital client, so they do nothing about your report. Now your ethical dilemma takes a new turn because new layers of complexity are added to the situation. You will have to go through the roadmap again to decide if you need to report the incident to the institution where you interpreted. Doing so is your choice: but it could result in legal liability for all parties and the loss of your interpreting work.

These are not easy decisions. In cases like these, before taking further action and without violating confidentiality you may wish to consult a fellow interpreter, a professional interpreters association or group, an interpreter listserv, a trusted family member, a lawyer (to guide you through the legal ramifications) or a therapist (to help you navigate the decision-making process).

Action C

If the risk for the service user is not only serious but also imminent, and resorting to the system would make it too late to correct a terrible situation, then, and only then, consider taking proactive action: that is, action that goes beyond your professional duties and that you take upon yourself not as an interpreter, but as a human being. If you choose to do so, you need to be aware of this: not only are you taking the actions upon yourself; the consequences will also be your sole responsibility. Yet the legal liability for your actions could affect multiple parties.

Here is an example that would justify imminent action: a misleading lawyer or administrator is making a mother sign an agreement to give her infant daughter up for adoption, and the interpreter has a very strong feeling that the mother does not understand that giving her daughter up for adoption is an irreversible act and that she might never see her daughter again. Given the legislation in that country, once the document is signed, nothing can be done to correct the situation. Another example could be a case where a nurse is about to administer a drug to which the interpreter knows the patient is allergic.

Even in cases for which imminent action is needed, always exhaust the possibilities within your job description *before* you step out of your role as a last resort. In the examples above, the interpreter should follow the protocol for strategic mediation before attempting anything else.

Final tips and considerations

Restricting your role to interpreting when you witness situations that deeply move you can be frustrating. The next paragraphs offer you some tips and considerations to help you find peace with these guidelines.

Consult with peers

Advocacy invariably involves active decision making and awareness. It is always helpful to consider different opinions and perspectives. After facing, or while you face, an ethical dilemma, consulting with experienced professionals, your professional association or peers within your organization can be helpful. Keep in mind as you explore these situations that confidentiality is usually violated only if you share identifying details. There are exceptions with stricter rules for court or medical interpreters in specific countries or regions. Be sure to know how local confidentiality requirements affect what you may disclose.

In coming to this decision—to advocate or not—[interpreters] may want to seek the advice of supervisors and colleagues in the field, remembering, however, to preserve the anonymity of the parties involved when seeking such advice.

NCIHC "A National Code of Ethics for Interpreters in Healthcare," 2004

If there is no one to consult, when you face an ethical dilemma a common recommendation is to ask yourself: "If I had to share my reasoning and my decision in a public interview, what would people think?"

Consider the advantages of addressing the service system

The advantage for you of reporting within the system rather than taking action on your own is that you can share the burden with other professionals or stakeholders. When you engage the system, you are not alone in making decisions and not the only person responsible for the outcome. Furthermore, you are likely to learn things that help you understand the situation much better. (For example, you might learn that a particular service provider is known to be abusive, or that other service providers have found a solution to the bureaucratic hurdle that has left some service users homeless.)

For others, the advantage of your taking a system-oriented approach is that it contributes to the autonomy of everyone involved. If you advocate unilaterally, you run the risk of undermining autonomy and showing a paternalistic attitude ("the interpreter knows best"). If others are involved, the chances of the interpreter undermining autonomy decrease. This is not to say that the structures or the system might not be paternalistic themselves, but at least when you leverage the service system, more than one person is assessing the situation. You may have blind spots. Sharing the situation with other professionals brings perspective and may help you to avoid the temptation of taking on a "hero role."

The advantage of a system-oriented approach for society as a whole is that when you engage the system, the outcomes can benefit more than one individual. An interpreter who reports Maria's principal can have a wider impact than an interpreter who reprimands the principal or privately empathizes with the mother. If you advocate within the system's structures, over time, more users will benefit from your advocacy.

Find outlets

Putting limitations on your professional role if you witness human suffering can lead to work-related stress (see Section 5.5). This is true for other professionals, such as nurses, teachers, social workers and advocates. Here are a few tips to avoid frustration:

- Remember that your profession is part of a social justice system. Doing your job means working for a cause: by supporting communicative autonomy, you are supporting basic human rights.
- If the restrictions on your scope of action frustrate you, find other advocacy causes in which you are more involved with solving problems first-hand. For example: volunteer with the local shelter for the homeless or be a volunteer crisis counselor on a domestic violence hotline.
- Advocate for your profession to the world at large: tell people what you do and why it matters.

Let's Practice

Learning Activity 5.3 (a): Maria's Mom
Learning Activity 5.3 (b): Follow the Road Map
Learning Activity 5.3 (c): Consider the Consequences: Advocacy Role Plays

In *The Community Interpreter®: An International Workbook of Activities and Role Plays*

REVIEW OF SECTION 5.3

This section is based on the following definition of advocacy for community interpreters: "taking action or speaking up on behalf of a service user whose safety, health, well-being or human dignity is at risk, with the purpose of preventing such harm." It argues that the issue of advocacy cannot be taken lightly. "Taking action or speaking up on behalf of a service user" inherently goes against the ethical requirements of impartiality and professional boundaries. For that reason, when a community interpreter witnesses a situation that places the service user at risk, that interpreter faces an ethical dilemma.

Ethical dilemmas involve making a decision between at least two solutions, neither of which is perfect. Ethical dilemmas arise when two or more ethical and/or moral demands cannot be reconciled. In community interpreting, situations that call for advocacy are ethical dilemmas. The interpreter needs to thoroughly assess and weigh different options before he or she can make a decision.

The general roadmap offered in this section provided a visual tool for a three-step process to guide decision making about advocacy. In situations in which the risk for the service user is serious enough, you may find it necessary to give priority to moral demands (helping out the service user) over professional ethics (observing ethics and standards). In those situations, you can report the situation. Avoid breaching confidentiality when you do so, and share the situation only with the appropriate authority.

The last part of this section offered you a few tips and suggestions to help soothe some of the frustration you may feel if you decide not to advocate—or even if you do advocate. Doing the right thing is not always easy or intuitive! Be kind to yourself. Your experience on the job will teach you a lot over time. Meanwhile, try to remember that you are making an enormous contribution to the well-being of individuals and society by working as a community interpreter.

5.4 Standards of Practice

Overview

This section will help you review and gain a better understanding of the standards of practice included in the *Ethics and Standards* document at the beginning of this textbook. It will show how they relate to your professional practice and how you can implement them even in challenging circumstances. This section is also intended as a review of the different professional practice tips covered throughout this textbook.

It starts with a brief discussion of different types of professional guidelines for interpreters, which is followed by a review of the 41 standards in the *Ethics and Standards* document discussed by category. Those categories are presented here as 13 general best practices. Under each of these 13 categories, you will find lists of statements (with checkmarks), potential challenges (noted by bell signs) and recommended actions to help support implementation (with arrow signs). For concrete examples of each standard, please refer to the original *Ethics and Standards* document.

Learning Objective 5.4

After completing this section, you will be able to:

- Identify general best practices for interpreters that support the Ethics and Standards document provided in this textbook.

Professional guidelines for interpreters

Professional guidelines for interpreters come in many forms and formats issued by different kinds of organizations. Yet they all have a common goal: to provide guidance about how to conduct yourself professionally. The types of organizations that typically issue written guidelines for professionals include interpreter associations, government bodies (ministries, government agencies, etc.), interpreting departments within service institutions (e.g., a hospital or a social services agency) and interpreting service providers.

Depending on the body that issued them, these standards can apply to the profession as a whole in a particular country or region, or to a small group, such as the employees of a local government agency or the interpreters for a language company. Such documents can be short or long. They can be issued as mandatory regulations or helpful advice. Their structure varies. They have many different names. The regulatory kind are often called "code of ethics," "code of conduct," "deontological guidelines" or "code of professional responsibility." Documents that tend to be less rigid might be called “guidelines for practice,” “standards of conduct” or “standards of practice,” among other names. For an international overview of professional guideline documents for interpreters, see Bancroft, 2004.

Some guidelines for interpreters include both types of contents: ethical principles and standards of practice. The structure of this textbook’s *Ethics and Standards* document is inspired by this approach and offers several standards to support each of its eight ethical principles.

It is your professional responsibility to find, understand and act on the codes that apply to you. Which guidelines are available in your region? Who issued them? Pay particular attention to those issued by professional interpreter associations and/or national or regional government bodies. There are countries with no guidelines for community interpreters. In that case especially, you may find the contents of this textbook’s *Ethics and Standards* document helpful.

Standards of practice

You saw in Chapter 1 that ethical principles are the canons or directives that help you make decisions about your conduct in the field. Ethical principles show you the general direction to take: they tell you where the “true North” of your profession is by guiding you in basic principles of right and wrong as they apply to community interpreting. In this sense, ethics are the ultimate guide for your professional behavior. Whenever you are in doubt, try to remember and act on the relevant ethics.

Standards of practice, on the other hand, are usually more detailed than ethics. They tend to offer more concrete strategies that help you understand what to do to support your ethical duties. If ethical principles are the arrow on your compass, standards of practice are the steps you take to move in the right direction. The destination is communicative autonomy. Ethics help you map out the destination; standards describe behaviors that help you get there. They also help you achieve consistent quality in your performance.

Overview of the *Ethics and Standards* document

This section covers the standards of practice in the *Ethics and Standards* document. It presents 13 different categories of standards that could be considered general best practices. Organizing the standards into these categories can help you see the connections between standards and makes it easier for you to remember and absorb them. These 13 categories are based on the type of action or attitude they involve, whereas in the *Ethics and Standards* document, standards of practice are gathered according to the ethical principle they support. These thirteen general best practices are as follows:

- Interpret faithfully.
- Be aware of the impact of your presence.
- Avoid interfering.
- Intervene cautiously and only when needed.
- Wear only one “hat” at a time.
- Avoid personal involvement.
- Do not take sides.
- Show fairness and earn trust.
- Act with integrity.
- Prepare for assignments.
- Show professionalism.
- Keep business interests to one side while on assignment.
- Educate others about professional interpreting as needed.

General best practice #1: Interpret faithfully

The four standards gathered here all address one common idea: when you transfer messages from one language to another, make every effort to render them faithfully. Do not change messages, omit parts of them or add anything to them. While these are clear instructions, the application may be a little challenging. It is worth exploring the most common challenges to overcome them.

To strive for ACCURACY

7. The community interpreter should make every effort to maintain the style, tone and register of the speaker.

To strive for ACCURACY

6. The community interpreter should interpret everything, including vulgar language and nonsensical statements.

To display IMPARTIALITY

12. The community interpreter should, when interpreting, let his or her tone of voice, body language and demeanor reflect the speaker's feelings, not the interpreter's.

To strive for ACCURACY

9. The community interpreter should interpret in the mode that enables the greatest clarity and accuracy with the least direction.

Interpreting in direct speech is often considered a sign of professionalism and it certainly helps you strive for faithful interpretation. It was covered as an interpreting skill in Section 2.2. Using direct speech supports accuracy and completeness because it:

- ✓ Makes it easier for you to focus on the parties' messages.
- ✓ Enables you to remain closer to the original message.
- ✓ Helps you emulate the style, tone and register of the speaker (Standard 7).
- ✓ Supports the back-and-forth rhythm that naturally happens in dialogue interaction (when an interpreter is not present).
- ✓ Makes it easier to transfer seemingly irrelevant bits of information like fillers, casual or offhand remarks, rambling speech or offensive language.

What Can Hide Behind Offensive Messages

If a service provider is offensive because she is prejudiced against the service user, the service user needs to know that to be able to decide if he wants to choose a different provider or make a complaint. Similarly, if a service user is consistently rude or contemptuous of the service provider, that information is important for the provider, who may decide the service user is at high risk for not complying with their treatment protocol or service requirements.

Interpreting offensive language (Standard 6) can be challenging for many interpreters because:

- Interpreting coarse language or insults in direct speech can make you feel uncomfortable, as if you were the one being offensive.
- You might not be totally proficient in such vocabulary.
- You may fear a bad reaction.
- Your cultural background or religious beliefs could make it difficult for you to interpret coarse terms.

You can overcome each of these challenges:

- Make sure you expand your language skills to include curses, coarse language or other offensive phrases in all your working languages.
- Practice interpreting such words and phrases until it becomes easy, in front of a mirror or with an interpreting partner. Practice desensitizes you.

- ➲ Remind yourself that the offensive message is not your own. You are the speaker's voice. Let the speaker be heard as intended. It is the right of all present to own their communication.

Standard 12 instructs you to not show your feelings, emotions or opinions while you interpret. If you frown, mutter, stiffen or roll your eyes, you are communicating something different than the original message. You are adding to the message, and by doing so, you are changing it.

- ➲ Be aware of your emotions and consciously try to hide them, so as to appear as neutral as possible.

What about body language? Body language is part of communication. It can sometimes be just as important for meaning as words. Should you imitate or adapt body language when you interpret? Here are some considerations:

- Interpreters take the speakers' body language into account when they process or analyze a message for meaning.
- Repeating gestures and reenacting messages would likely distract the service user and the provider.
- Not every aspect of body language is culturally universal. Many gestures are "culturally loaded." Misunderstandings could arise because of body language.
- In many countries legal interpreters, especially in court, are prohibited from interpreting or noting body language.

Interaction Also Happens Through Body Language

Eye contact has different meanings in different cultures. A service user who avoids eye contact to show respect might be misinterpreted by a service provider who feels it shows shame, guilt or dishonesty. Distress or alarm is also shown differently in different cultures.

Consider the following example: a service user in North America who comes from Jordan is asked a yes–no question. She nods sharply (with a tiny click of the tongue). The interpreter knows that the service user means "no," but that a nod in North America typically means "yes." In court, most court interpreters would simply say nothing. However, in a community setting such as healthcare or social services, the interpreter might be permitted to interpret, "No," for clarity. When dealing with body language, we recommend that you:

- ➲ In most cases, do not address body language directly, except as it informs meaning.
- ➲ Remain attentive however to any source of potential misunderstanding caused by body language cues and use your cultural knowledge to assess whether it interferes with accurate understanding.
- ➲ If the misunderstanding is potentially serious, perform strategic mediation to handle it (see Chapter 3) except in legal interpreting.

Sometimes certain expressions have no true equivalent in the target language: it is hard to accurately interpret them without adding explanations. In such cases:

- ➲ Try hard to find equivalents.
- ➲ If the equivalent takes more than a few words, perform strategic mediation instead. Inform the parties you are aware of no equivalent and suggest that the speaker explain or re-express the concept.

- ➲ Do not omit anything difficult to interpret.
- ➲ Do not give explanations. Remember that the interpreter should only *point out* cultural differences (if needed) during the session; explanations should be provided by the speakers (see Chapter 3).

To support accurate interpreting, you may need to manage the flow and address turn-taking.

- ➲ Ask the speaker to slow down or pause whenever you exceed your "memory load." Accuracy comes first. (But work hard on your memory and note-taking skills to improve them over time.)
- ➲ Interrupt to ask for clarification as needed. It is your right and duty.
- ➲ If you find yourself often asking for clarification, you may need to withdraw or reconsider this type of assignment until your skills and terminology have improved.
- ➲ If you have the skills, you can switch to simultaneous when a speaker starts talking fast (Standard 9).

To progressively acquire the skills you need for accuracy, make sure to:

- ➲ Participate in skills-based continuing education programs (see Section 5.5).
- ➲ Monitor your own performance.
- ➲ Engage in reflective practice (see Section 1.6).

General best practice #2: Be aware of the impact of your presence

To promote DIRECT COMMUNICATION

22. The community interpreter should remain attentive to possible misunderstandings, including his or her own potential misunderstanding arising from misconceptions, biases or prejudices.

To ensure TRANSPARENCY

16. The community interpreter should interpret everything that is stated during the interpreted session wherever possible, including his or her own utterances.

Interpreters have often been told, "you should be invisible." That advice is misleading: interpreters cannot avoid the impact of their presence. It is actually important that you acknowledge your presence and ask yourself how it could interfere with direct communication. Still, the *ideal* of invisibility could be pursued. As a goal, it helps you remember several things:

- ✓ The conversation is not with *you* but between the other parties.
- ✓ Your own opinion about the service or situation is not usually relevant (even if someone asks for it).
- ✓ Not having any impact at all is impossible, but having as little impact as possible should be your goal.

There are times when you cause misunderstandings. It is a common interpreter mistake to assume that misunderstandings always originate with the parties. It is healthy to remember that:

- ✓ As the interpreter, you are an added "input channel": you could misunderstand when processing the message.
- ✓ As an interpreter, you are an added "output channel": you could be misunderstood when uttering the message in the target language. In other words, you too can be misunderstood by the parties.

Here are a few examples of sources of misunderstanding by the interpreter:

- 🔔 You may make wrong assumptions.
- 🔔 You may not know that a certain expression is used with a different regional meaning.
- 🔔 You may have simply misread someone's intentions and the essence of their message.
- 🔔 You may be interpreting for the first time for parties who have had multiple interactions and you lack sufficient contextual information to understand their dialogue.

Imagine you are interpreting for a parent with only an elementary-school level of education. You may assume he cannot possibly understand details of chemotherapy. That parent may in reality know much more about it than you do from his extensive experience since his child was diagnosed.

Here are a few tips for how to apply Standard 22 on remaining attentive to possible misunderstandings, including the interpreter's own misunderstandings:

- ➲ Keep an open mind and constantly reassess and question your own assumptions.
- ➲ Try to become aware of your own cultural bias.
- ➲ Be aware of your own process of cultural assimilation and acculturation.
- ➲ Remember that every individual is different regardless of his or her cultural background.
- ➲ When watching out for communication gaps, keep in mind your own potential misunderstandings.

"Interpret everything" is one of the interpreter's mantras. "Everything" includes your own utterances (Standard 16). Sometimes you have to intervene and use your own voice when you need to ask for clarification, choose to address a misunderstanding or you have to clarify your role. Transitioning from being another person's voice to using your own voice is a break in the rhythm of interpreting. Be careful:

- 🔔 Many interpreters forget to interpret their own words, and someone in the encounter is left wondering what you just said.
- 🔔 Even if your message is addressed only to one person, everyone should know what is going on: report everything you say.

To ensure transparency be sure to interpret or report immediately whatever you say when you intervene:

- ➲ Whenever you say "the interpreter requests a clarification of…." or "as the interpreter, could I ask you to clarify…." etc., immediately follow up in your other working language by saying "as the interpreter, I asked X to clarify…." without allowing anyone else to say anything else until you have completed your mediation in *both* languages.

General best practice #3: Avoid interfering

To promote DIRECT COMMUNICATION
21. The community interpreter should make every effort to ensure that all parties communicate directly with each other and not the interpreter.

To display IMPARTIALITY
11. The community interpreter should avoid offering opinions or advice, even when requested to do so.

To support INTERCULTURAL COMMUNICATION
30. The community interpreter should never make statements about the service user or the service provider's cultural beliefs or intentions.

To support INTERCULTURAL COMMUNICATION
28. The community interpreter should refrain from providing cultural explanations and instead direct parties to seek relevant cultural information from each other.

Offering your own input is not the reason you are there. The prospect might be tempting, but the consequence is much too often that you end up interfering in the communicative process. This is not to say you should never intervene, but there are sound reasons for avoiding direct interaction. Here are a few:

- ✓ You are present so that the service user and provider can communicate with each other. If they are communicating with you, you may become an added barrier to their communication.
- ✓ Every interaction with you is a missed opportunity for the service provider and the service user to better understand each other's needs, concerns or interests and points of view.
- ✓ You may interfere with the service user's ability to develop a relationship of trust with the provider.
- ✓ You may make vulnerable parties feel you are taking control, leading them to shut down.
- ✓ By breaking your rhythm and flow, you may interfere with your own accuracy and performance.
- ✓ If you provide information on the service or the service user, you can find yourself giving advice for which you can be held legally liable.

Standard 21 tells you to be proactive in preventing these situations. There are a few techniques for redirecting parties to each other when they keep looking at you, talking to you, or asking you questions.

- ➲ Be strategic about positioning. Choose positions that support direct communication.
- ➲ Limit eye contact. Observe the parties for your understanding but avert eye contact to visually disengage from them.
- ➲ Use your notes as a symbolic professional role marker. Looking down at your pad or taking notes (whether you need to or not) avoids eye contact without your appearing cold or rude. Instead you appear professional and focused.
- ➲ Use hand gestures, if needed, to redirect the parties to speak directly to each other.
- ➲ Intervene, as needed, to explicitly remind the parties about your role.

Both service user and service provider are likely to ask you questions, especially when the other party is not present. Standard 11, however, reminds you that it's better to avoid offering personal opinions or advice even when requested to do so. Be aware of the temptations:

- 🔔 Service users and service providers both tend to see you as closer to them because you speak their language and often prefer to speak to you rather than the other party.
- 🔔 You often know "how things work" (whether in the service user's culture or the service system) and might feel tempted to "explain" things.

Answering Questions?

The interpreter will often be prompted to answer questions with service users and providers before or after the interpreted encounter. Conversation before or after the session is generally to be avoided but sometimes necessary.

It's generally ok when:

- ✓ You are educating the parties about your profession and the best circumstances for an effective interpreted encounter.
- ✓ You are debriefing with the service provider in a way that helps both of you gain insight for future sessions and always using extreme caution to avoid making generalizations or absolute statements especially regarding cultural differences!

It's generally not ok if:

- ✗ You are offering one of the parties information that they could be obtaining from the other party.
- ✗ You are offering advice or services that another professional could/should be offering

You should generally avoid answering questions regarding the service being provided or the situation of the service user even if you know the answer and or have a strong opinion. Consider these tips:

- ➲ If you are alone with the person asking the question, invite him to ask the other party: "That's a great question for the social worker. Let's go find her and I'll be happy to interpret for you!"
- ➲ If someone asks you a question during the encounter, simply interpret it.
- ➲ If you feel that interpreting the question might feel like a betrayal or could compromise trust, then intervene transparently to clarify your role: "As the interpreter, I cannot answer this type of question. You might want to ask the doctor directly" and then immediately report your intervention.

There are advantages to simply interpreting a question addressed to you (if it is not about your interpreting):

- ✓ You stay within your interpreting role.
- ✓ Someone else can answer the question.
- ✓ You avoid entering a side conversation with the party that posed the question.
- ✓ Both parties get the message that you are there to interpret, not to answer questions.

There are also advantages to the option of not interpreting the question and instead intervening transparently in a neutral way to avoid answering questions during the interpreted session.

- ✓ If the question was very personal and private, you are preserving confidentiality by intervening instead of interpreting.
- ✓ If the question is from a provider who does not mean to be insensitive and is speaking only to you (e.g., by asking, "Do you think she's mentally capable of following what I say?") you avoid a potential rupture of the service-provider/service-user relationship.
- ✓ Referring to the question without interpreting it still offers an opportunity for the parties to address concerns.
- ✓ Intervening transparently is an opportunity to explicitly remind everyone of your role.

This last option also has disadvantages. You will have to decide on a case-by-case basis. Here are some arguments against it.

- By not interpreting a problematic question or remark, you violate the ethical principle of accuracy.
- Your assumptions may be wrong: perhaps everyone has the right to know exactly what was said.
- Many service users understand some of the service provider's language: if they realize you intentionally avoided interpreting an insensitive remark, you may lose the service user's trust.

Standards 30 and 28 advise you against making statements about the parties' cultural beliefs or intentions. It is a common habit that the authors of this book strongly discourage for the following reasons:

- Absolute cultural expertise is impossible (by the interpreter or anyone else).
- Statements or generalizations about a cultural group may not apply to a particular individual.
- Overgeneralizations about culture contribute to bias and misconceptions.

Letting the parties discuss their cultural differences supports intercultural communication. The following tips can help that happen:

- Apply the Strategic Mediation Model (see Chapter 3) to point out cultural differences causing miscommunication in the least intrusive way.
- Let the parties explore their own way of looking at the world and interpret for them as they do so. Intervene only to help them ask each other the right questions; try not to give them answers.
- Remember that your cross-cultural insights are extremely valuable to help you detect possible sources of misunderstanding or breaches in communication and to alert the parties to them (not to provide explanations of your own).

General best practice #4: Intervene cautiously and only when needed

To promote DIRECT COMMUNICATION

20. The community interpreter should refrain from becoming an active participant in the communication and should intervene only when a major barrier to communication emerges.

To support INTERCULTURAL COMMUNICATION

27. The community interpreter should point out cultural differences that service users or service providers have not identified themselves when they appear to be barriers to meaningful communication.

To support INTERCULTURAL COMMUNICATION

31. The community interpreter should provide his or her explanation of a cultural difference or cultural misunderstanding only when such misunderstanding does not appear to be resolvable by the parties themselves and is likely to jeopardize a service user's health or safety, or to jeopardize public safety.

Avoid interfering at all costs: your goal is to facilitate communication, not impede it. However, some circumstances justify your active intervention *in order to* facilitate communication. Chapter 3 (Section 3.2) offers criteria on how to determine whether a situation justifies mediation: see Standard 20. Cultural differences are often the source of barriers to communication: see Standards 27 and 31. Interpreters are in a privileged position to detect misunderstandings because they have been exposed to different cultures and are careful observers of communication. Their input is often needed. However, each of these three standards includes caveats. Intervene with caution.

To apply a cautious approach to intervention, remember to:

- Give everyone present a chance to clear up an apparent misunderstanding on their own.
- Only intervene when a major barrier to communication with possible adverse consequences arises.
- Alert everyone to the source of a major cultural misunderstanding but avoid providing cultural explanations. Let the parties explore their differences.
- Provide your own plausible reasoning about the possible source of misunderstanding only after attempting strategic mediation and only if the situation generates real risk.

- ➲ Whenever you have to provide your own cultural reasoning, avoid making statements about any person's beliefs or customs and instead suggest asking relevant questions.

Here is an example of providing cultural reasoning without making general statements: if the nurse doesn't see that the Chinese mother of a newborn isn't drinking any liquids (and is growing dehydrated) because no one offered her hot liquids instead of cold ones, and your attempt at strategic mediation didn't work, you may respectfully suggest that the nurse ask the mother if she has cultural reasons for preferring hot liquids over cold ones after childbirth. See Chapter 3 for details.

General best practice #5: Wear only one "hat" at a time

To respect PROFESSIONAL BOUNDARIES
24. The community interpreter should limit his or her assistance to facilitating communication and refrain from engaging in other types of assistance or support, even when requested to do so by the service user or provider.

To respect PROFESSIONAL BOUNDARIES
25. The community interpreter, who simultaneously holds other professional or voluntary responsibilities should, during the interpreted session, limit his or her role to interpreting even when requested to perform additional duties.

To ensure TRANSPARENCY
19. The community interpreter, when intervening, should inform all parties that he or she is speaking as the interpreter.

Getting involved with the service user or provider in tasks other than the interpreting responsibilities is not impossible, but also not recommended. It carries risks, for example:

- ✓ Carrying out more than one task at a time can compromise your impartiality and accuracy.
- ✓ Taking on tasks that go beyond interpreting can undermine the service user/service provider relationship.
- ✓ Adopting more than one role at once can be confusing for all and compromise transparency.

Standard 24 recommends you avoid providing any other assistance than facilitating communication. Standard 25 establishes that even professionals who hold responsibilities other than interpreting should limit their role during the encounter to message transfer, yet many circumstances can make it difficult for the interpreter to respect the general rule of wearing only one hat at a time:

- 🔔 It is common to find bilingual staff who provide bilingual services and also interpret for colleagues. Dual-role staff can find it particularly challenging to wear only one hat at a time.
- 🔔 Whether you are a staff member who has also been assigned interpreting tasks or an intercultural mediator who also interprets, attempting to perform both jobs at once is counterproductive.

To respect professional role boundaries, you can follow these recommendations:

- ➲ Establish a friendly professional rapport that is not personal: use your position, posture, other professional body language, notepad and demeanor to signal both warmth and distance.
- ➲ Avoid executing tasks that are not part of your job description. Exceptions foster expectations.
- ➲ Use the SAY NO model to decline requests that undermine professional boundaries (Section 1.5).
- ➲ Refer service users who ask you for extra services to organizations that offer them, if appropriate.

For bilingual staff who interpret, the following tips can help you wear only one hat during the session:

- ➲ If you are asked to provide another service while interpreting, apply the SAY NO model and ask if the requester would like you to assist as the interpreter or as a provider.
- ➲ Refrain from taking over another provider's role during an interpreted session.
- ➲ If the provider leaves, you are encouraged to leave (and return) with the provider.
- ➲ Avoid consulting with another provider while the service user is present; if you absolutely need to do so, always report what is said and respect transparency.

In order to make your different "hats" more visible:

- Adopt a different demeanor when you interpret than when you carry out other responsibilities and carry note-taking materials.
- Use your professional introduction (Section 2.2) to mark the spatial and temporal boundary between the interpreted session and your other duties.
- Whenever you intervene, let the parties know both by identifying yourself as the interpreter and in your body language, for example, by looking up and making eye contact, leaning forward, etc. (Standard 19).

General best practice #6: Avoid personal involvement

To respect PROFESSIONAL BOUNDARIES
26. The community interpreter should, wherever feasible, avoid personal, business or romantic engagements with the service user.

To maintain PROFESSIONAL CONDUCT
38. The community interpreter should typically refrain from accepting gifts from service users or providers.

It is important to set clear boundaries around your role. "Helping out," giving advice, doing favors, attending social events with service users or giving out your personal phone number are all ways to get personally involved that can erode professional boundaries. Standard 26 stresses the importance of avoiding nonprofessional engagements with the client and Standard 38 tells you to not accept gifts.

Role Boundaries Are Also Important For Your Well-being

In a study about the experience of interpreters in mental health settings, Lor (2012, p. 23) found the following:

"All the participants except one [...] continually emphasized the need to maintain clear boundaries between themselves and the clients in the work setting and in session. The three aforementioned participants identified different sitting positions; constant transparency; continuous reminders to clients before, during, and after sessions; being emotionally neutral or impartial; and staying away from advocacy roles as all strategies to avoid dual relationships and set clear limits on their sphere of influence and role responsibility."

While both standards can seem straightforward, in practice they pose challenges for many interpreters:

- The very nature of a "community" can come in the way of avoiding personal involvement. You may encounter the service user in your daily personal life in nonprofessional settings.
- Many service users are so relieved and grateful they want to show you their deep gratitude.

Respecting professional boundaries and avoiding personal involvement (at least to the extent possible) is usually better for everyone, including the service user. In some cases, this distance of the interpreter might seem counterintuitive or downright culturally rude and inappropriate. The interpreter's professional boundaries help to focus attention away from the interpreter and more on the building of trust between the service user and provider, which is important for these reasons:

- ✓ Trusting a professional as part of a wider system is more beneficial for service users and society than the goodwill of one "nice" interpreter who may not be there in the future (see Section 5.1).
- ✓ A professional relationship makes the service user less dependent on you and more autonomous.
- ✓ Understanding and respecting clear role boundaries can protect you from burnout and vicarious trauma (see Section 5.5). The interconnection between role boundaries and healthy practice is clear.

Leave the Room with the Provider

Having the interpreter leave when the service provider leaves is becoming an institutional policy in a number of U.S. hospitals and other organizations. Would it help to suggest such a policy in the institutions where you interpret?

Here are a few tips that can help you avoid getting personally involved with the service user:

- Avoid, to the extent possible, staying alone with the service user.
- Show a clear understanding of your professional responsibilities and avoid taking on a rescuer role.
- Do not disclose personal or contact information to the service user.
- Do not give the impression that you are special or irreplaceable. Let service users come to trust that other interpreters are caring and competent.
- Refrain, if possible, from post-session contact with the service user unless it is part of your other job.
- Avoid socializing with service users if possible.

We once had a survivor of domestic violence that came to us very upset. An interpreter from a non-profit had promised her that she would find her a shelter but then she never heard back from the interpreter. The interpreter disappeared and this lady was put in a very difficult situation.

A social worker from a nonprofit legal service

Accepting gifts from service users carries its own risks:

- Accepting a gift can create an expectation in the service user that interpreters should receive gifts.
- After accepting a gift, your impartiality might be compromised.
- The perception that service users should bring gifts for interpreters may spread by word of mouth. (Service user might not truly be able to afford such gifts.)
- Once you accept one gift, how will you say no to the next?

Here are a couple of ideas on how to handle this situation:

- Apply the three-step SAY NO model to graciously decline, for example: "Thanks so much for thinking of me! You're very kind, but I'm already being paid for interpreting and that's why I'm not allowed to accept gifts. It makes me happy to see that you are well served. My agency will be delighted if you want to send them a thank-you note. You can also take this gift to the Red Cross and tell others how helpful it was for you to have an interpreter."
- If your employer or interpreting service has no rule about accepting gifts, discuss this problem and let them know that many interpreting ethics documents strongly discourage accepting gifts.

General best practice #7: Do not take sides

Saying "do not take sides" is another way to say "display impartiality." Yet impartiality is not entirely under our control. We all have opinions. We all are biased. Without making certain kinds of judgment, we could not make sense of the situations we interpret in and the messages we interpret.

To display IMPARTIALITY

10. The community interpreter should refrain from taking sides during the interpreted session.

To display IMPARTIALITY

13. The community interpreter should consider declining or withdrawing from an assignment if her or his faith, ethnic group, tribal, political or other affiliation may be perceived as unduly influencing her or his impartiality.

To display IMPARTIALITY

15. The community interpreter, while avoiding taking sides during the interpreted session, may consider reporting a service provider who is breaking the law or violating his or her professional ethics to an appropriate supervisor or an institution of justice.

Interpreters are not expected to avoid the kind of judgment that helps them to assess situations; they are however expected to make every effort to be aware of their own biases so that they can *display* an impartial behavior and strive for impartial decision making. Without your conscious effort, taking sides during the interpreted session (see Standard 10) could happen at two different levels:

- The way you deliver messages can be affected by your opinions and show in your demeanor (e.g., coughing, rolling eyes, shuffling feet or more subtle signs).
- Your decision-making process can also be affected by your judgments. You make decisions constantly about the choice of words to transfer messages, the best way to support direct communication and whether it is necessary to intervene or not.

Here are some key points to bear in mind:

- ✓ It is important for everyone present to see you as trustworthy.
- ✓ Striving for impartiality helps you to remain detached and focus on the messages.
- ✓ Whether ideas, atittudes or beliefs seem right or wrong to you, equally value everyone's opinions.

To show impartiality while you interpret, consider these guidelines:

- Try to become aware of your own biases and remind yourself that everyone's opinions and perceptions are equally valid and important.
- Remember that your own judgments about a situation could change as you gain more insights. Whenever you form an opinion, leave room for doubt.
- Don't let it be perceptible to anyone what you think of a situation.
- Avoid allowing your personal feelings to be visible in your attitude, body language or tone.

Standard 13 revolves around perception. It is based on the importance for parties to the session to be able to trust that you will not take sides. If you sense or see that your group affiliations could be impacting service-user trust, you should:

- Inform the parties.
- Let them decide whether your affiliations interfere with their ability to trust your impartiality.
- Withdraw if you sense one of the parties is uncomfortable but does not dare to say so.

In some cases, interpreters encounter situations that seem unfair or morally wrong. It is tempting to take action. Standard 15 mentions situations in which the service provider breaks the law or violates his or her professional ethics. Should the interpreter remain impartial? The answer is: show impartial behavior during the encounter and consider taking action by reporting the situation afterward. Consider this:

- 🔔 Unless the service providers' actions result in immediate irreparable damage, you should support communicative autonomy and not interfere.
- 🔔 There is always a risk that your understanding of the situation could be mistaken.
- 🔔 If the situation seems unfair or morally wrong, you could face an ethical dilemma and decide to advocate. See Section 5.3 for details.

Here are some tips to help you respect the general best practice of not taking sides during an interpreted encounter, even when a service user is breaking the law or his or her professional ethics:

- ➲ Do not consider yourelf responsible for a service provision breakdown: remember all the good reasons for your professional limitations.
- ➲ Before disclosing information about the session, make sure you are reporting to the right authority.
- ➲ If you have any doubts about how to proceed or whether to report a service provider, consider discussing the case with peers or supervisors (but remember to observe confidentiality).
- ➲ If you think you might be facing an ethical dilemma because whichever action you take compromises at least one moral value, use the roadmap for advocacy provided in Section 5.3 and apply the CHIA ethical decision-making process (see Sections 1.5 and 3.2).

While it might be morally tempting to intervene during the session to defend a service user, remember that Standard 15 (about considering reporting) offers advantages, some of them with ethical and moral values:

- ✓ Both parties need to be able to trust that interpreters are impartial facilitators, and both parties have a right to communicate autonomously, even in difficult circumstances.
- ✓ Your professional duty and boundaries are comparable to those of other professionals.
- ✓ It is not always moral, practical, effective or judicious to try to correct an unfortunate situation on your own. Engage the system: this is often the most ethical and effective way to make a difference.

General best practice #8: Show fairness and earn trust

Several aspects of your professional conduct can help all parties present develop and maintain trust in you. Keep in mind:

- ✓ To earn trust from both parties, show fairness toward both parties.
- ✓ Given the often-personal information shared, parties (especially the service user) need to know their confidentiality is safe.

To ensure TRANSPARENCY

17. The community interpreter should make sure all parties know that everything that is stated will be interpreted.

To support INTERCULTURAL COMMUNICATION

29. The community interpreter should show respect for all parties while interpreting and when identifying and pointing out cultural differences and misunderstandings.

To maintain PROFESSIONAL CONDUCT

34. The community interpreter should display a respectfuldemeanor that balances professionalism and warmth for all parties present.

To observe CONFIDENTIALITY

1. The community interpreter should use professional discretion to avoid sharing personal information disclosed by participants, even when that information was disclosed at a public event.

To observe CONFIDENTIALITY

4. The community interpreter should not disclose private information unless one of three conditions pertain:
   (a) The service user has given explicit permission (preferably in writing) for disclosure of that information;
   (b) A law, statute, legal requirement or workplace requirement compels the interpreter to disclose otherwise confidential information;
   (c) The interpreter has signed an agency or inter-agency confidentiality agreement permitting the interpreter and a group of service providers to communicate information with each other about the service user; and/or
   (d) The information disclosed is relevant for the service being provided and/or the service user's health, well being or safety; it follows institutional regulations for the service being provided; and the interpreter discloses it only to a member of the treatment team or service team working with the same service user.

Because so many see you as an ally or confidant, there is always a risk that you might have to interpret a statement intended only for you, perhaps making you seem a betrayer. Standard 17 reminds you to make sure that everyone knows that you will interpret everything. Do as follows:

- ➲ Start your introduction (after stating who you are and why you're there) by saying you will interpret everything said.
- ➲ If you cannot perform a full introduction, make sure you clearly state at least this part; emphasize it by saying it plainly and making eye contact with both parties, for example.
- ➲ If you find that people talking to you "on the side" is a recurring problem, add toward the end of your introduction the following reminder: "Please don't say anything you don't want me to interpret, because I'm ethically obligated to interpret everything."
- ➲ You might need to remind parties during the session that you are there to interpret.

For the service user to feel comfortable with the service, he or she needs to feel comfortable with and respected by you too. Standards 29 and 34 stress the need for you to show a respectful human demeanor.

- 🔔 Professional role boundaries do not oblige you to appear cold.
- 🔔 Showing a friendly demeanor does not mean becoming friends. Conversely, avoiding personal involvement does not mean being cold. The happy balance is in between.
- 🔔 Cultural differences between service users and providers are a common reason why interpreters might show a different attitude toward different parties present often without realizing it.
- 🔔 Many interpreters show more respect in their tone of voice, style of address, body language and behavior for service providers than for service users. Unconscious bias is the typical cause.

To show equal respect toward all parties, here are a few tips:

- ➲ Become aware of your own beliefs and biases to avoid displaying them (as mentioned earlier).
- ➲ Whenever you have to intervene using your own voice, avoid using language that is acceptable for one party but not the other. Remember that the principle of transparency requires you to interpret everything, including your own utterances.

➲ Develop scripts for typical intervention needs (as seen in Chapter 3), and perfect them overtime.
➲ Think of the difference between showing your humanity and taking on a hero role. Being friendly does not mean being friends with the service user or service provider.

Standards 1 and 4 deal with confidentiality. Especially in small communities, confidentiality has effects both at the micro and macro levels (see Section 5.1). Word of mouth is powerful and can have damaging consequences.

➲ Remember that confidentiality is a key part of your professional role.
➲ If you ever need to disclose information under one of the four conditions listed under Standard 4, make sure you would be able to present a clear argument about which specific circumstances justified the disclosure.
➲ If you ever disclose confidential information, keep written records of the decision and circumstances, including date, time and persons involved (make sure to protect that information).

General best practice #9: Act with integrity

Embracing integrity means being honest and honoring basic values. As an interpreter, you often find yourself in the position of being the only one who can scrutinize your actions: you may be the only one who knows more than one language, and you typically have no interpreting supervisors during the encounter. You could easily skip taking actions that may feel uncomfortable (such as informing the parties that you made a mistake). However, your lack of action will have consequences. You work on the honor system.

To observe CONFIDENTIALITY

2. The community interpreter should honor confidentiality indefinitely.

To observe CONFIDENTIALITY

3. The community interpreter should take additional steps to maintain confidentiality when information pertaining to an interpreted session is shared with other parties through the use of computers, electronic mail, facsimile machines, telephones, voicemail and other electronic technology.

To display IMPARTIALITY

14. The community interpreter should declare all actual and potential conflicts of interest.

To strive for ACCURACY

8. The community interpreter should correct interpreting errors during or after the interpreted session, whether orally or in writing.

To maintain PROFESSIONAL CONDUCT

37. The community interpreter should accept only assignments for which he or she is qualified and should disclose all professional limitations when appropriate.

To ensure TRANSPARENCY

18. The community interpreter should inform the parties whenever he or she has had to summarize or omit part of the session.

Standards 2, 3 and 14 deal with aspects of confidentiality and impartiality. These standards are easy to forget or overlook. You might think that disclosing information about a case after years have gone by represents no harm; that disclosing a potential conflict of interest is not necessary because no one would notice anyway; or no one will ever have an interest in accessing the information stored in your computer, so why bother with passwords?

By taking pride in your professional responsibilities you can come to realize that all these aspects are important because:

✓ Your conduct and decisions have an impact on the profession as a whole (Section 4.1) and your professionalism plays a role both at the micro and macro level (Section 5.1). For example: disclosing information, even after a long time has gone by, taints the reputation of all interpreters and can affect trust in the profession.
✓ Abiding by such key principles as confidentiality and impartiality in all their complexity and detail is part of your professional responsibilities. It is also important for your dignity, your well-being and your legal safety.

Standards 8, 37 and 18 deal with accuracy, transparency and professional conduct. What they have in common is that they go a step further in requiring integrity compared to 2, 3 and 14: they require you to take action when it's easier not to, and they also involve putting you in the spotlight.

- It can feel uncomfortable to correct an error.
- Accepting limitations can be hard, especially because it is sometimes misconceived as a lack of professionalism.

Correcting errors, being transparent or declaring a conflict of interest are all clear signs of professionalism. They show that you care about the quality of your service. Therefore:

- Treat all these standards (and any relevant ethics or standards you are required to follow locally) as a matter of integrity and professionalism.
- Be professional and assertive whenever you take uncomfortable actions that show integrity.
- If anyone is surprised, explain your professional motivations. Refer to professional codes of ethics if applicable.

General best practice #10: Prepare for assignments

While community interpreting happens in diverse circumstances and often with surprises (even for the most experienced interpreter), preparing for the foreseeable is your ethical responsibility. You have learned techniques to prepare for an interpreted assignment given its specific characteristics.

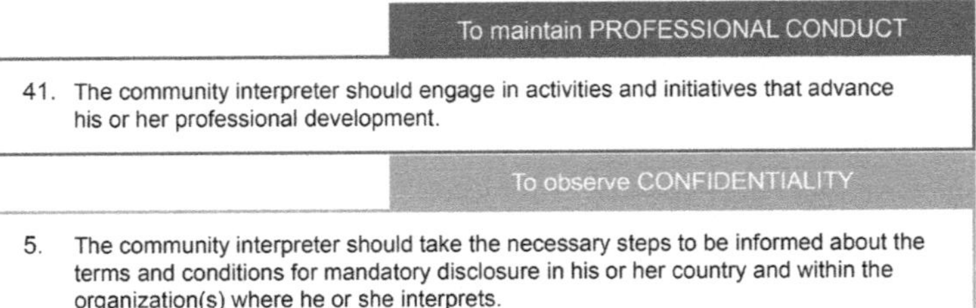

To maintain PROFESSIONAL CONDUCT

41. The community interpreter should engage in activities and initiatives that advance his or her professional development.

To observe CONFIDENTIALITY

5. The community interpreter should take the necessary steps to be informed about the terms and conditions for mandatory disclosure in his or her country and within the organization(s) where he or she interprets.

You can also take proactive steps to be prepared in general. It requires more discipline and commitment because there is no particular deadline. Following Standard 41 about professional development could entail a variety of initiatives (many of which are discussed in detail in Sections 4.6 and 5.6):

- Maintain your working languages.
- Become familiar with the services you typically interpret for: know the terminology, and also the culture of the service.
- Keep updated on the latest developments of the profession.
- Attend conferences and training events.
- Set up study groups to help you structure your practice, be accountable and exchange feedback.

Different countries' services or institutions have different laws and policies regarding confidentiality. An agency might tell you that it is acceptable to share information about a patient with members of the treatment team. Another agency may have a policy that prohibits such practice. It is your responsibility to know what rules apply in which circumstances (Standard 5). For these reasons:

- Contact relevant professional associations to inquire about applicable policies and laws related to interpreter confidentiality.
- Make sure you understand the policies of the institutions you work for
- Research or seek advice about what the law says in your region
- Be ready to cite such policies and laws when needed. Not only is it important to know how to act, but also to be able to explain why you acted that way.

General best practice #11: Show professionalism

Many aspects of professional interpreting are invisible to the outsider. Others are very apparent. The difference between an improvised solution and a service provided by a professional interpreter is clear in the way the interpreted session develops, whether professionalism is clearly apparent or invisible.

Arriving at the assignment prepared and on time (Standard 32) is a basic sign of professionalism.

- ✓ If you arrive late and service is delayed, or you lack the needed skills and terminology, you discredit the profession (many service providers have yet to be convinced why a professional interpreter is even needed).
- ✓ It takes a great deal of planning and coordination to set up an interpreted encounter. Once you have accepted an assignment, the appointment depends on you.

Making sure you can be prepared and on time starts the moment you are offered the assignment:

- ➲ Before accepting an assignment ask yourself: Do I have enough information to decide whether this assignment is a good fit? Do I have enough information to know how to prepare? Do I know where the encounter will take place and if it's feasible for me to get there on time?
- ➲ Plan to arrive 15 minutes early.
- ➲ Show reliability. Give proper notice if, for a very good reason, you need to cancel your commitment.

As for every other professional activity, what you wear is important. Standard 33 requires you not only to wear professional clothes, but also that your professional outfit be appropriate for the specific setting where the interpreted session takes place. For example:

- ✓ Some hospitals have implemented policies that require staff interpreters to wear clothing similar to that of other members of the healthcare team. They are then perceived as part of the professional team and their intervention is more valued and effective.
- ✓ In any setting, if you overdress or underdress, you might draw undue attention.

Practical considerations include the following:

- ➲ If you expect to have to stand for a long time, look for comfortable, yet professional, shoes.
- ➲ To match the level of formality, study the service providers. Social workers often wear more casual clothes than lawyers in court, for example.

Standard 36 reminds you to leave personal matters on one side while you interpret. Accuracy and sound decision making require no distractions. But also both the service user and the service provider need to trust your full commitment to the service. Therefore:

- ➲ Remember to turn off your cell phone and any other communication devices.
- ➲ Address any personal matters before or after the session.
- ➲ Be mentally prepared to detach from the emotional content of the interpreted session (see the section on impartiality above).

General best practice #12: Keep business interests to one side while on assignment

To maintain PROFESSIONAL CONDUCT

39. The community interpreter should not seek new business opportunities for his or her own benefit while on assignment.

To maintain PROFESSIONAL CONDUCT

40. The community interpreter may accept a new business opportunity offered during an assignment only with formal approval from the first assigning organization.

Seeking business is an important part of your professional life. You need to make a living. However, time and place matter. Assignments are not the time or place to recruit clients. Here are a few reasons why:

- ✓ Seeking your own interests while you are on assignment challenges your ability to be, and be perceived as, impartial.
- ✓ Marketing your services while on assignment is a source of distraction for everyone.
- ✓ You can make those you approach uncomfortable and give a poor impression of the profession.
- ✓ If you are working for an ISP (interpreting service provider) seeking business while on an assignment is unfair competition and unethical conduct (sometimes even illegal.)

To respect Standards 39 and 40, here are a couple of tips:

- ➲ Do not hand out business cards while on assignment (unless asked and only if you are not there on behalf of another ISP.)
- ➲ Refer clients to the ISP that sent you if they ask for an interpreter for a new assignment.
- ➲ If the parties present insist that they want you (and not another interpreter) to come back, tell them to place such a request with the assigning ISP (or the requesting department).
- ➲ Find other channels for your business development (e.g., networking events, human resources departments, professional associations, etc.)

General best practice #13: Educate others about professional interpreting as needed

In your field of expertise, you have professional authority. You are the expert responsible for enabling intercultural communication across languages. Not only are you entitled to use your professional voice; it can be important to do so, especially when your input is needed to ensure good working circumstances.

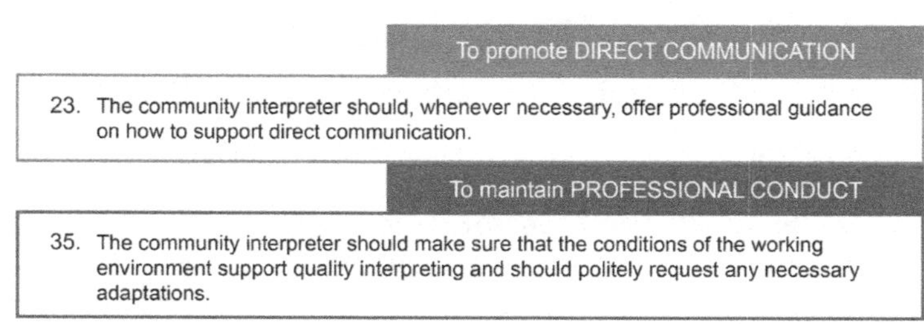

To promote DIRECT COMMUNICATION

23. The community interpreter should, whenever necessary, offer professional guidance on how to support direct communication.

To maintain PROFESSIONAL CONDUCT

35. The community interpreter should make sure that the conditions of the working environment support quality interpreting and should politely request any necessary adaptations.

Standard 23 encourages you to give explicit guidance on how to support clear communication. Standard 35 refers to the conditions of the working environment. Through that standard, you are entitled and encouraged to use your professional criteria to request the best circumstances for efficient and professional interpreting. Here are examples of situations where you might request adaptations:

- If the seating arrangements are not optimal (as discussed in Section 2.1). For example, if you find the service user is clinging to you and turning to you too often, you might need to request a change of position.
- If the acoustic conditions are not adequate. For example, if someone is talking too softly, or loud noise prevents you from hearing the speakers, you will need to request accommodations.
- If the session is longer than expected. Fatigue could compromise the quality of your interpretation.

Sometimes it can be difficult to get what you need. Sometimes providers are not familiar with professional interpreting. For example, they might not understand why you need a break because they do not realize that interpreting is a highly demanding activity that involves both multitasking and high concentration (with complex decision making and high cognitive skills involved). Advocating for decent working conditions is not always simple, yet doing so is important. It is your right and duty to ensure adequate working conditions. In addition:

- You can share with providers and supervisors relevant interpreting ethics documents to raise awareness. Formal written considerations and procedures with the backing of an institution help spread the awareness that community interpreting is emerging as a formal profession.
- Try to hold regular conversations with your supervisors about interpreting services: what is working and what can be improved. Such conversation with the teams you work with can help to make change.
- Suggest policies and procedures about working with interpreters, such as having breaks for the interpreter every two hours maximum and having a private space for the interpreter to go during breaks. Another good example is a policy where the interpreter is obliged to walk out of a session each time the provider leaves the room.

Fostering quality working conditions for community interpreters is a shared responsibility: some of it falls on the individual interpreter, and some of it falls on other stakeholders and the profession itself, including our professional associations. But all of us have the responsibility to educate the public about our work and what we need to do it well.

Let's Practice

Learning Activity 5.4 (a): Always, Sometimes, Rarely
Learning Activity 5.4 (b): Traffic Lights: Applying Standards
Learning Activity 5.4 (c): The Standards of Practice Role Play Game

In *The Community Interpreter®: An International Workbook of Activities and Role Plays*

REVIEW OF SECTION 5.4

The beginning of this section briefly reviewed some differences between ethical principles and standards of practice. Ethical principles show you the general direction and help you tell right conduct from wrong conduct as laid down by the profession. Standards of practice tend to be more concrete actions that guide the professional interpreter on how to support ethical conduct and requirements.

This section then explored each of the standards of practice included in the *Ethics and Standards* document laid out at the beginning of this textbook, as a way to review much of this curriculum. It covered each of the standards by aggregating them into a discussion of "general best practices." Thirteen such general best practices were addressed:

- Interpret faithfully.
- Be aware of the impact of your presence.
- Avoid interfering.
- Intervene cautiously and only when needed.
- Wear only one "hat" at a time.
- Avoid personal involvement.
- Do not take sides.
- Show fairness and earn trust.
- Act with integrity.
- Prepare for assignments.
- Show professionalism.
- Keep business interests to one side while on assignment.
- Educate others about professional interpreting as needed.

5.5 Self Care and Personal Wellness

Overview

Your health comes first, and it is also important for your professional practice. Finding a balance between the search for the highest professional standards and paying careful attention to your physical and mental health is critical. If you let yourself get overinvolved with your job without setting boundaries to protect yourself, you can pay a heavy price. Your physical and mental health can suffer, and so can your professional practice. A highly professional interpreter is a *healthy* professional.

The first goal of this section is to draw attention to different sources of potential harm that you can be exposed to in your work. The second goal is to help you identify good habits that can help you avoid different kinds of occupational hazards. Finally, you will develop a self care plan to guide your self care activities.

As you learn more about stress-related professional risks that are common in the helping professions, and physical hazards related to specific settings, you'll see how to plan different strategies to address each type of risk. This section will also provide practical tips on wellness that can help you stay healthy in mind and body.

Learning Objective 5.5

After completing this section, you will be able to:

- Identify work-related risks for community interpreters and develop a wellness-and-safety plan.

Interpreter's safety and well-being

As a community interpreter, you will insert yourself into other people's communication in an astounding variety of settings. As a result, you can be exposed to any of the sources of stress and physical risk that face service providers and other professionals in the field. Most service providers in the "helping and healing professions" are trained to understand the hazards they face and learn how to prevent them. Do you know how to keep yourself healthy and safe as an interpreter?

The following pages will raise your awareness and help you prevent health problems. If you think you may be suffering from an illness, see your doctor. This chapter does not provide medical advice: it offers suggestions for self care.

Risks, hazards and harm

Risks, hazards and harm

We will explore different kinds of *hazards* and *risks* that expose you to *harm*. Let's be clear about the difference between these three concepts.

- **Harm** refers to an injury or to damage. It is the *consequence* of being exposed to circumstances that affect your health or well-being. Harm can be physical or mental.
- A **hazard** is a *source* of potential harm. It refers to something that can become dangerous. For example, if you interpret in an operating room or a kindergarten, bacteria are a hazard there. If you are infected and get sick as a result, the sickness is not the hazard: the bacteria that caused the infection are the hazard. Being exposed to a hazard does not mean that you will be harmed. It means there is a risk you could be harmed.
- A **risk** is the *chance* that you might encounter harm. If you are interpreting in detention for a violent offender and a detective, or in a psychiatric facility for a patient and a clinician, there is a risk that the offender or the patient might get violent. Then you might be hurt. The risk could be low—but it is real.
- "**Occupational hazards**" is a common expression that refers to the variety of circumstances and factors that can negatively affect a professional's physical or mental well-being. This is the term that we will use to refer both to the sources and the chances of harm when you work as an interpreter.

Types of occupational hazards for interpreters

Types of occupational hazards for interpreters

Many of the occupational hazards you will face are stress-related. Some are specific to the helping professions (such as nursing, social work or counseling), and affect interpreters too: compassion, fatigue and vicarious trauma are real sources of mental harm for many community interpreters. Other hazards are related to the physical strain you might feel as a result of repetitive actions. Finally, because you might work in such a variety of settings, it is important to look for other sources of hazard that could come from the setting (like a construction site or a police raid). We will refer to those hazards as environmental dangers.

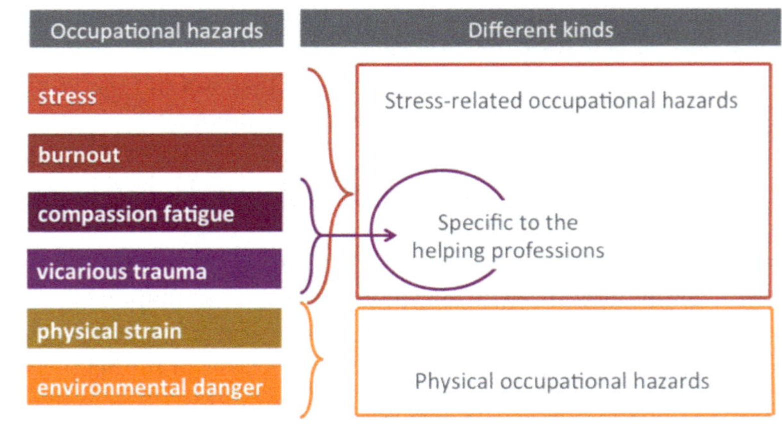

Figure 5-I
Types and Kinds of Occupational Hazards

Let's explore the two main categories of hazards identified in the right column of Figure 5-I: Stress-related and physical occupational hazards.

Stress-related occupational hazards

You are a community interpreter: You transfer messages from one language to another as accurately as you can. You monitor the situation to make sure no one is left out and that no major misunderstanding is taking place. You process messages, information and emotions while showing an impartial attitude. You are on time and courteous. You display professional conduct. As if all that were not challenging enough, your work requires you to jump from one situation to another. You dive right into each of these situations as part of your daily routine. No matter how skillful you are, community interpreting *is* a demanding job.

Stress by itself does not always become an occupational hazard, but it can become one if the sources of stress are not handled appropriately. Managing stress effectively is partly your responsibility, partly an organizational responsibility. Most community services do not seem to look out for (or even be aware of) interpreter work stress.

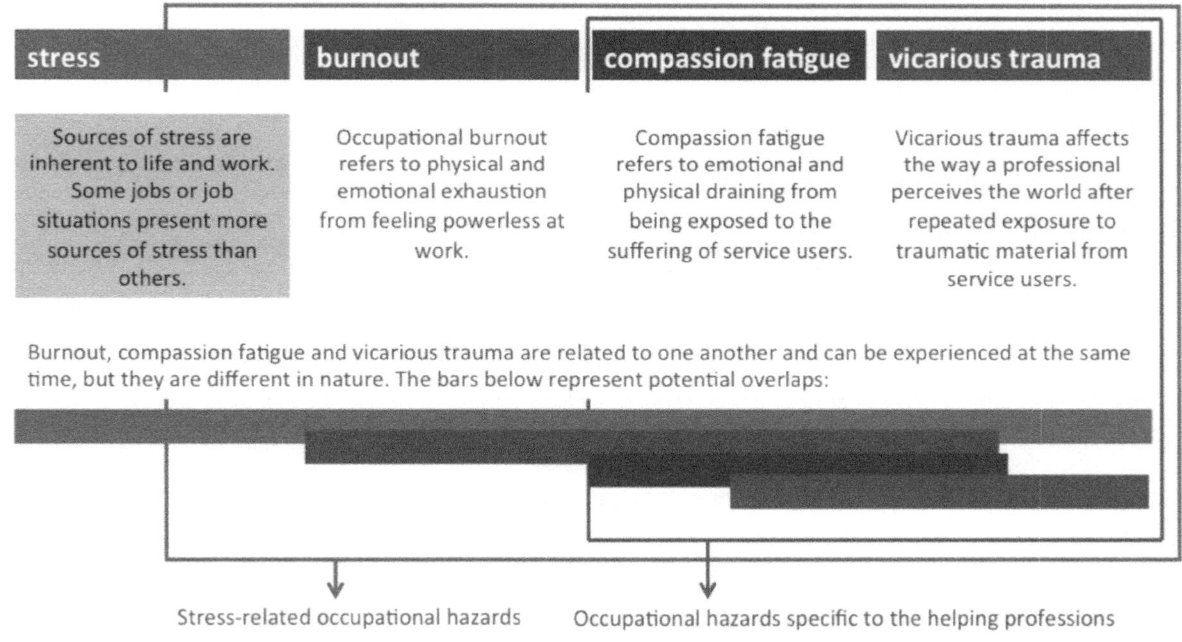

Figure 5-J
Stress-Related Occupational Hazards

The chart above (Figure 5-J) shows different types of stress-related illnesses. This section will discuss each of them. Even if each category refers to a different condition, they are actually related to each other and you can suffer from more than one at the same time. Often their names are used interchangeably in different settings and not everyone agrees on the definitions. However, understanding the difference among the categories can be useful for your self care. If you understand each condition well, you are more likely to identify what can contribute to making you feel drained, depleted or upset.

Stress

A popular definition of stress is "a condition or feeling experienced when a person perceives that demands exceed the personal and social resources the individual is able to mobilize" (The American Institute of Stress, n.d.). Did you notice in the definition the choice of the verb *to perceive*? Research on stress suggests that our beliefs about stress and our attitudes when we experience stress can have a critical impact on whether its consequences are good or bad for us.

The impact of stress

One dimension of stress is the physiological response: your heart pounds, you breathe faster or your muscles get tense. These are common manifestations of stress. Such reactions in your body are natural, unavoidable and necessary. It is how your body lets you cope with threatening situations.

Stress becomes problematic when it turns into part of your routine instead of something occasional. If stress isn't handled appropriately, it can over time damage your physical and mental health. An increased risk of cardiovascular disease might be the most striking physical damage, but it is not the only one. Higher social vulnerability, decreased problem-solving skills and depression are some of the stress-related harms to mental health. Stress can trigger negative *psychological responses*. But we do have some ability to exert control over it.

Balancing stress

> *"How you think about stress matters."*
>
> McGonigal, 2015

Research suggests that in moments of stress, if we focus on the positive value of stress, we can be less anxious and more confident, and the negative effects on our health are reduced by this simple thought process (Jamieson, Nock, & Mendes, 2013). A good attitude could be as follows, then: Whenever you feel your body reacting to stress, be thankful. Think to yourself: "My body is doing this to help me rise to the challenge, to help me perform better" (McGonigal, 2015). With a positive attitude toward stress, you can destroy an important vicious circle. For many of us, worrying leads to more worry. Anxiety feeds on anxiety. So making a decision to look at stress from a positive angle can make all the difference in your response.

Also, individuals who have a good life/work balance find it easier to put a stressful event into perspective and see it as just one small part of a larger picture. If you keep a good balance and find life interesting beyond your work, you cope better with work stress, compared to someone whose life centers on work alone. Those of us with a life rich in interests (like hobbies and volunteer activities) and strong social support from family, friends or acquaintances, tend to respond to stress in a healthier and more constructive way than someone with a poor life/work balance or few social supports.

The demand-control model

Another dimension of stress worth exploring is the degree to which we feel *empowered* to address challenges. Karasek (1979) developed the demand/control model of occupational stress (on which Dean and Pollard (2001, 2013) have worked in the field of sign language interpreting) to explain that workers experience most strain when the demands of their job are high, and yet their ability to make decisions to respond to those demands is low.

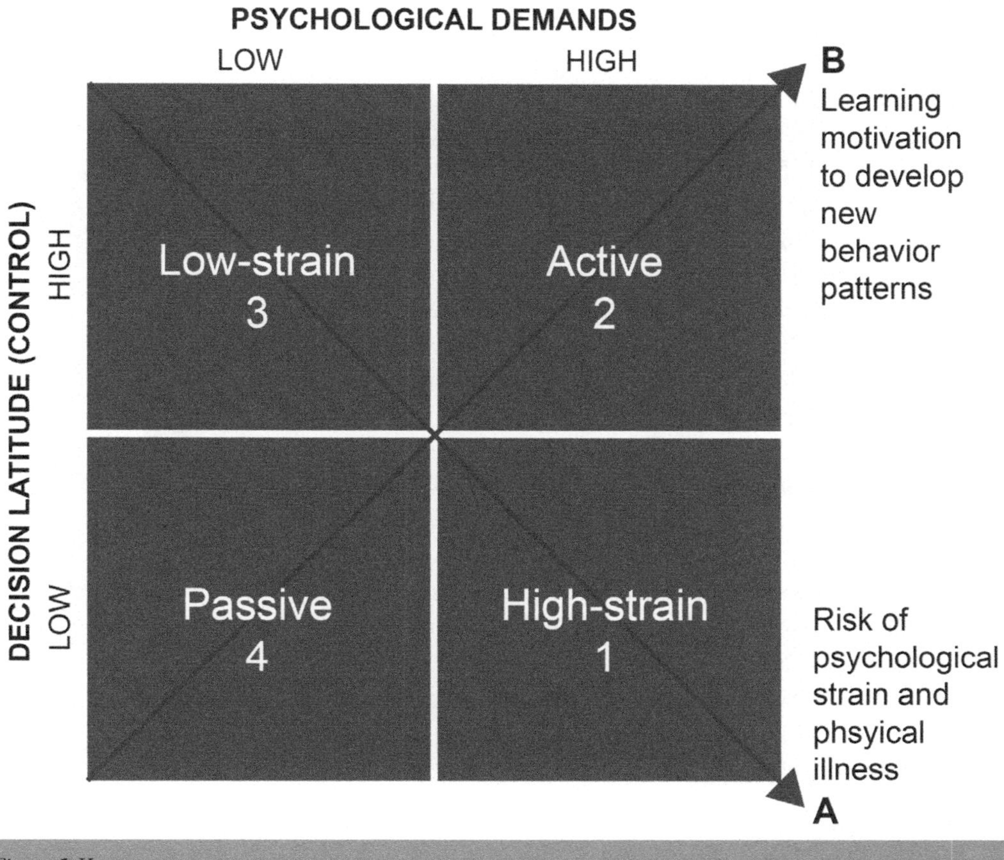

Figure 5-K
Karasek's Demand/Control Model

Low ability to make decisions can be related to the workers' personal skills, but it can also be related to the way their job tasks are defined, or to the way the organization they work for functions. For example, you could be very skilled and capable of making excellent decisions, but if your boss does not want to leave any room for you to implement them, you can face a high demand/low control situation that increases your levels of stress (lower right corner of Figure 5-K). However, if you work in an environment where you can use your skills and implement your own decisions about how to carry out your tasks, you are likely to be motivated and feel more capable of managing stressful situations (upper right corner of Figure 5-K).

As an interpreter, your professional skills often give you control over some aspects of the encounter, such as the flow of communication, but you have little control over many others. For example, your professional ethics don't allow you to insert your thoughts or opinions during the encounter. You are there to facilitate the communication of others, leaving you little time or mental energy to take care of your own needs. You have to make constant decisions considering many factors all at once. This combination of high demand and little control exposes you to the risk of stress-related illness (Karasek, 1979; Dean, Pollard, & Samar, 2010, p. 42).

You can take for granted that you will be exposed to demanding situations (with high levels of stressors). Here are a few questions worth asking yourself: How well does your work environment let you rise to the challenge? How ready are *you* to rise to the challenge? A good work environment, a good life-work balance, and a positive attitude toward challenges are key to good stress management. They are not enough. We will explore some practical suggestions for stress management in the second part of this section.

Burnout

Occupational burnout is the consequence of long-term exposure to stress. The opposite of burnout could be engagement (Maslach, Schaufeli, & Leiter, 2001). Engaged professionals feel like their contributions matter. Their work is important. It lives up to the required standards, and these professionals sense that what they are doing is appreciated. Their interest in the job is high. Professionals who burn out, on the contrary, lose that motivation. Nothing seems to make a difference anymore. These professionals often feel that the quality of their work is irrelevant because they cannot have a positive impact no matter what they do. Exhaustion takes over. This level of tiredness goes beyond the physical fatigue caused by overwork. It leads to emotional draining.

Occupational burnout is most common in jobs with high levels of stressors. The awareness that the well-being of others partly depends on a service you provide can be a major stressor. Those in the helping professions are particularly exposed to burnout for that reason (although they are not the only professionals affected by it.) They want to support the well-being of their clients, but they feel like they are never doing enough. The need always exceeds what the professional can provide. Over time, that feeling of inadequacy drains their motivation.

Causes of occupational burnout

The following list identifies several causes of burnout for public education professionals in the United States (Cedoline, 1982):

- *Lack of occupational feedback and communication*: Knowing what is expected and what to expect (values, aspirations, objectives) is crucial to maintain motivation.
- *Work overload or underload*: Too much responsibility with unpredictable hours can cause distress and burnout. Tedious jobs with no variety can be equally distressful.
- *Contact overload*: Frequent encounters can be draining. They also leave few opportunities for communication with other employees and for peer support.
- *Role conflict or role ambiguity*: Role conflict happens when two or more opposing demands are made of one professional, where complying with one makes it impossible to comply with the other. Role ambiguity describes a situation where expectations are not clear.
- *Training deficits*: Lack of preparation can reduce confidence. Lack of training on organizational culture and on how to communicate with supervisors is a common source of distress.

Call Centers

There is a rapid rise of call centers where community interpreters work all day long—or even all night—via telephone or video. Such call centers now exist in many countries. It would be necessary to explore the work conditions of call-center interpreters in detail to determine the impact of prolonged stress. Jumping from call to call with almost no time to recover, debrief or rest seems like a perfect recipe for burnout. Many calls involve conflicts, crises and emergencies. There is an urgent need for research in this field that can inform effective preventive measures. Bower (2015) provides one the first empirical studies on this topic in the field of sign language interpreting.

As a community interpreter, can you relate to any of these circumstances? Burnout occurs most often, but not only, among those who interpret traumatic material, often in therapy and court hearings for refugees and survivors of torture, war trauma or sexual violence (Bambáren-Call et al., 2012).

The impact of occupational burnout

Burnout affects your mental health. It is also usually accompanied by professional underperformance: in most cases you cannot do a good job if you are physically and emotionally drained. Sadly, burnout often leads to community interpreters abandoning the profession. This problem is true even for individuals that entered the profession with a strong commitment to doing good things.

Stress management on your part is critical. On the part of the system in which you work, are the role expectations clear? Do your values align with those of the profession? Do you feel you have some control over your work conditions?

Occupational hazards specific to the helping professions: the role of empathy

Many community interpreters prefer interpreting to translation because each day brings new challenges that require quick decision making. When stressors are known and you are prepared to deal with them, stress does not necessarily become a problem. Professionals in the helping professions, however, face the added risk of feeling too much empathy for service users. "Overtaxing your empathy" means you might put your own mental health at risk by becoming too involved with the well-being of others, which can generate high stress levels. It has been called "the cost of caring" (Figley, 1982).

Unknown Empathy Is an Added Risk

Dean and Pollard (2001) and Anderson (2012) have noted that interpreters may not always be aware of their sense of empathy or compassion toward the service user. Their professional identity is not defined around empathic engagement; they rigorously make an effort to show a neutral position; also, their mental process in the task of interpreting may capture all their attention and not let them realize they are feeling empathy. These circumstances can constitute an important risk: "Rothschild (2006) cautioned that a sense of empathy that remains *unknown*, or *unconscious*, to the helper may result in increased vulnerability to compassion fatigue." (Anderson, 2012)

Community interpreting is often incredibly rewarding, but it also involves witnessing difficult situations. Community interpreters interpret for happy events like cultural festivals and births, and routine situations like pediatric appointments or parent-teacher meetings. On average, however, their exposure to human hardship can be high. The service users you interpret for tend to be underserved and often live on the margins of society. Some interpreters also interpret for survivors of major trauma (e.g., interpreters for refugees, sexual violence and torture survivors) or can even witness traumatic events firsthand (e.g., interpreters in emergency situations where people die in hospitals, conflict zones or disaster relief.)

> *The most insidious aspect of compassion fatigue is that it attacks the very core of what brought us into this work: our empathy and compassion for others.*
> Mathieu, 2007

Practicing community interpreters can use empathy to help them understand and accurately render messages. But they also need to show impartiality and respect role boundaries that should, in principle, give some protection from getting personally involved. Be careful: interpreters are particularly exposed to the risk of emotional burnout precisely *because* of the way their role is defined (see research box). The more you understand this risk, the more easily you can prevent it.

Compassion fatigue

Compassion fatigue is a type of burnout. It often affects those in the helping professions: because of their exposure to difficulty and human pain, the helper's empathy and compassion drain away. The "helping professional" usually has a strong commitment to make a positive difference in society and in people's lives. Yet, with extensive exposure to hardship and suffering on the job the motivation is lost. The professional burns out and stops feeling compassion. "I just don't care," is a common feeling.

Causes of compassion fatigue

What causes burnout is feeling powerless in the face of other people's suffering. Your scope of action is restricted: you have to remain as unobtrusive as possible. That may leave you with a feeling of little accomplishment. You might even feel powerless. Researchers have found that focusing on a sense of accomplishment even when you witness hardship that you can't "fix" can help to prevent compassion fatigue and negativity (Adams, Matto, & Harrington, 2001).

The impact of compassion fatigue

Professionals whose compassion is overwhelmed can lose the ability to feel empathy, not only for service users but also for colleagues, friends and loved ones. They can also lose trust in their colleagues and the work. They lose interest in their career as well and show disengagement from daily tasks.

Compassion fatigue is the result of a progressive process of exhaustion. Recovering from its effects is also progressive. Preventive measures involve developing a balanced life and being realistic about what you can and cannot do. Set boundaries for yourself. Think about your profession as a contribution to society (see Section 5.1). Remembering everything that community interpreting gives to the community can give you many reasons to feel like a proud and skilled professional. Interpreting for a service user who is in distress may be hard and painful. Try to cultivate pride in the quality of your work not only for *this* service user but *all* those who would lack access to basic services without professionals like you.

Vicarious trauma

Vicarious trauma is secondary trauma caused by repeated exposure to the trauma of others and is a common concern among nurses, therapists, social workers, refugee resettlement case managers and interpreters. Vicarious trauma can happen if you often hear stories about other people's trauma in the workplace. Victims of vicarious trauma perceive and interact with their surrounding world in a different way than they used to. Unlike other professionals, most interpreters don't have much access to training on how to avoid vicarious trauma.

Causes of vicarious trauma

sVicarious trauma is developed through repeated exposure to details of painful events, such as abuse, assault, war trauma or torture. Listening to one difficult story may be heartbreaking, but does not typically trigger vicarious trauma. Like burnout and compassion fatigue, vicarious traumatization tends to develop over time. This gives you time to notice and prevent it.

Just as burnout and compassion fatigue are closely related, so too are compassion fatigue and vicarious trauma. They are often experienced at the same time. It can be hard to tell one condition from the other. Some of the symptoms for compassion fatigue are common for vicarious trauma.

The impact of vicarious trauma

Vicarious trauma affects the way you experience aspects of your daily life. It can manifest itself in many ways. For example, if you are exposed to trauma interpreting at a children's hospital, you might become more fearful for the safety for your children. If you interpret for emergency services, you might have trouble watching some news shows on television. Other symptoms of suffering vicarious trauma are intrusive thoughts and dreams about the traumatic stories you were exposed to. It can feel like having the service user's nightmares.

If you have a history of trauma, you may be at higher risk of vicarious trauma. Even more so if your trauma mirrors the story of someone you interpret for, which is a particular challenge for interpreters who are refugees and interpret for other refugees. It is also especially common for survivors of sexual assault or domestic violence who have not fully processed their own trauma.

> *You have to visualize you know, when you do the interpreting, the interpreting process is not just about words. When you're telling a story it's complex, it's set in a place and you have to process all that. So you're hearing the story but you're also saying the story and imagin[ing] what it was like for the person. You know the emotions, they can never be as strong as what the client feels, but you get a sense of the way they might have felt.*
>
> Interpreter testimony in Splevins et al., 2010

Interpreters are particularly vulnerable to vicarious trauma because of the kind of service they provide. When interpreters are exposed to traumatic material, their involvement with such material is active. Service providers process the traumatic information to provide their services; interpreters process that information in a special way. They not only hear it and act on the traumatic content: in a way, they reenact it by retelling the traumatic accounts in the target language. You saw in Chapter 2 that interpreting involves at least four distinct stages of processing, which means that the degree of cognitive processing of traumatic content is complex and deep.

Community interpreters should have access to specialized training on how to interpret traumatic content. Some specialized programs are now emerging to help interpreters protect themselves when interpreting for survivors of major trauma. (See Bancroft, Allen, Green, & Feuerle, in press, and Bancroft et al., in press).

You might have a friend, family member, or neighbor who has just seen the same thing. You don't want to remember that and yet somebody else is [...] taking you back to the incident and you have to interpret and be actively involved in the vocal part and talk. So, it's not easy.

Interpreter testimony in Lor, 2012, p. 19

Physical occupational hazards

Not all the occupational hazards that you are exposed to as an interpreter are stress-related. What could seem to be the most obvious hazards—physical hazards—are very often overlooked. Some relate to the way you use your body to do your job, while others derive from external danger that you can be exposed to while you are doing your job. We will start with how you use your body. See Figure 5.L.

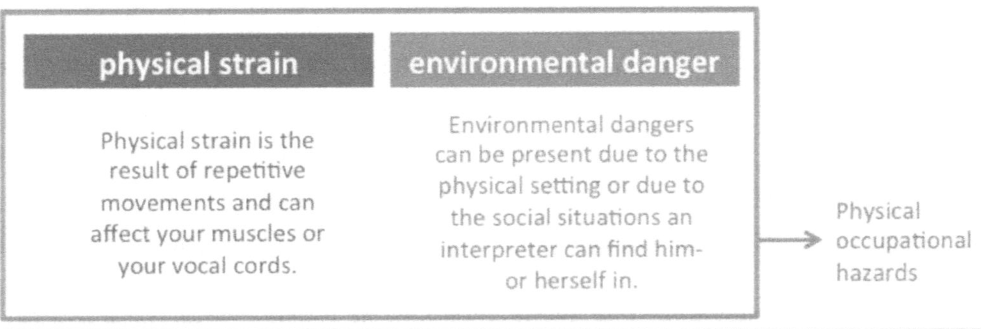

Figure 5-L
Physical Occupational Hazards

Physical strain

Physical strain

You may not think of your professional activity as a highly physical one. After all, interpreting is nothing like the work of a dancer or a construction worker. Yet your body is fully involved in your daily tasks. Awareness of your body is important for your long-term health as well as your short-term comfort.

Causes and impact of strain injury

Strain injury is caused by constant repetitive movements that can damage your tendons and your ligaments over time. The most obvious strain risk for the interpreter is on the voice. For sign language interpreters, neck, arms and hands are also at risk. There is no reason to be alarmed. But it makes good sense to learn and apply preventive measures.

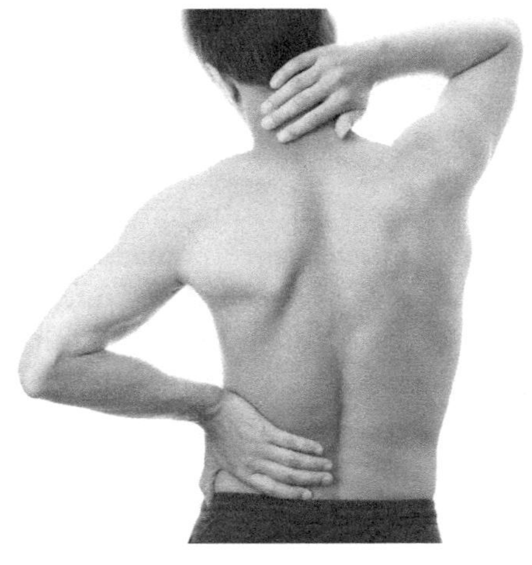

Strain injury in your vocal cords can take different forms: nodules, polyps or contact ulcers or laryngitis (an inflammation of your larynx and vocal cords that can cause you to lose your voice for a time). Information on cumulative strain injury in your hands, arms or neck can be found under the umbrella term repetitive strain injury (RSI).

Good preventive habits

Gain awareness. Both stress management and an adequate posture are important to prevent strain injuries. Are your muscles tense when you interpret? What is your general posture like when you interpret? Depending on the settings you interpret in most often, you may be mostly seated (for lawyer-client interviews), mostly standing (for public events or hearings), or a combination of both (such as interpreting for job training). If you are mostly seated when you interpret, how are you sitting? Erect, with a straight back? (Recommended.) Or are your shoulders curved forward and hunched? If you are mostly standing, are you aware of how you stand? Your head, shoulders, hips and feet should be lined up, your shoulders down and pulled back. What about your feet? Also, does your overall posture help you project your voice? Are you able to breathe deeply from the abdomen, and not your throat?
Strain injury is caused by overuse. Taking breaks, throughout the day and throughout the year is perhaps the best thing you can do to prevent strain injuries. Both for sign language and spoken language interpreters, keeping your face and neck relaxed is important. Do gentle stretches and warm-up exercises for your neck, arms and hands (if you are using them a lot) before you start your day or at the end of the day. Make yourself yawn to expand your throat. Become aware of any tension in your jaws and try to relax them.

Keeping well-hydrated is also very important to prevent general strain injuries. Vocal cords will function better if you drink water often. Carry a bottle with you (if permitted—some settings, such as hospitals, prohibit it). A common reflex is to clear your voice when it feels hoarse. That might clear the sound of your voice, but it actually can contribute to irritating your vocal cords. Try to drink water instead.

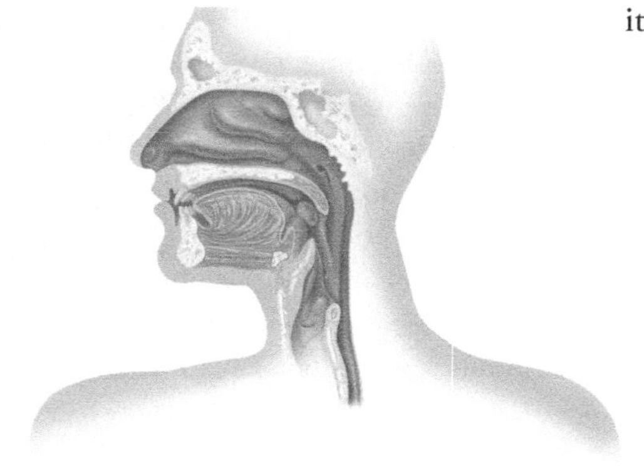

Take care of your voice. It's a precious instrument for interpreters. If you have already used your voice a lot from interpreting all day, avoid loud environments that require you to strain your voice further, like loud bars or sports events. Also, as you saw in Chapter 2, avoid whispering. If you must perform whisper interpreting (chuchotage), speak in a low voice instead of whispering to avoid damaging your vocal cords.

See a doctor and/or a specialized coach if you find clear symptoms of strain injury like hoarseness in your voice, pain while talking or pain in your arms and or hands that doesn't go away or that is recurrent. Strain injuries are developed over time, not overnight. It is very important to address their causes before the injury becomes chronic. Prevention is key.

Environmental danger

Transferring messages from one language to another is not typically a dangerous activity. But you may find yourself in dangerous *situations*, for example, when you interpret:

- For police at the scene of an incident;
- In psychiatric institutions;
- For violent offenders who have been detained;
- In conflict zones, including urban-street conflicts;
- In emotionally charged sessions where one or more parties become hostile and belligerent;
- In disaster relief settings where flooding, fire, volcanic smoke, nuclear radiation, earthquake after-shocks or other dangers are still active, etc.

They Can Forget About Your safety

Police officers typically do not remain alone with a detainee. Yet there have been instances where police have left the interpreter alone in a closed room with the detainee. The interpreter is often not explicitly mentioned in safety protocols for law enforcement. Many service providers forget the interpreter's safety is at risk as well.

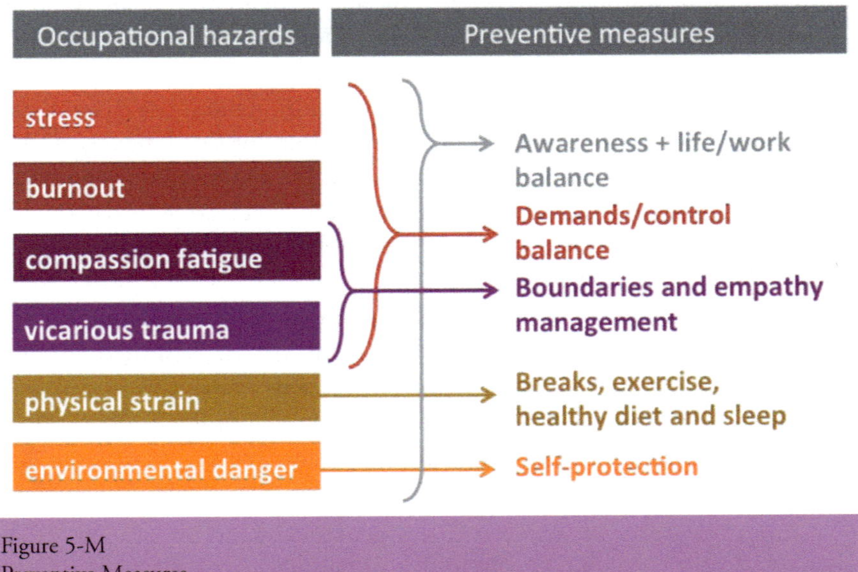

Figure 5-M
Preventive Measures

Your active attention is needed at so many levels to be able to do a good job as an interpreter that your usual sensitivity to danger may be dulled. You may not pay attention to your instincts. Yet, not all service providers you work with may alert you of potential hazards. It is your responsibility to be vigilant. Apply the same safety measures as service providers. Are they wearing a mask? Ask for a mask. Are they wearing a helmet? Request a helmet too. If you notice service providers following safety protocols, ask to be informed about those protocols yourself. Remember to watch out for your own safety. Always remember that you have the right to set boundaries for yourself and make firm requests to protect your safety.

Your self care plan

Here is an ethical issue: should you keep interpreting if you are not in full command of your skills? If you feel exhausted near the end of a busy day or after a few draining weeks or months, can you still offer a high-quality service? Here is another point to consider. Interpreters who burn out or suffer vicarious trauma often end up quitting. We lose their experience and work—and all their potential contributions to the community. Not only do you have the *right* to be healthy and safe: you also have a professional *duty* to take care of yourself.

Types of preventive measures

Let's review some of the general attitudes that can help prevent hazards, and then talk about specific actions that you can take on a daily basis to stay healthy, both mentally and physically. See Figure 5-M.

- Awareness of occupational hazards is probably the most important of all preventive measures. So far in this section, you have explored areas of risk in your professional life. Congratulations! By taking the time to read these pages, you helped to reduce your occupational hazards.
- Life/work balance is the other overarching preventive measure. The reason it matters is simple: stress underlies or exacerbates other hazards we are exposed to, whether those hazards are at work or in our life in general. The importance of spending time with family and friends, of having a variety of interests and activities outside work, the importance of a healthy diet, adequate sleep and regular exercise cannot be overemphasized.
- We also saw that the way we think about stress is critical. If you understand stress as a natural response from your body, the negative effects on your health are reduced. And if your work environment allows you to feel in control when you face demanding situations, your experience of stress will be less harmful.
- When your empathy is engaged (which happens constantly in community interpreting) you are at risk of suffering from compassion fatigue or vicarious trauma. Find the right balance between remaining empathic enough to interpret accurately and to make appropriate decisions, while at the same time keeping enough emotional distance as to not be affected by the situation that is interpreted. Also, find your comfort zone in community interpreting: perhaps interpreting for therapy or police is not for you. Know your limits and respect them.
- If you want to avoid injuries from physical strain, besides building a general healthy lifestyle, try to incorporate good daily habits for interpreters. Warm up, stretch, take breaks and rest well. Yes, your voice can also be warmed up. A simple Internet search will access videos on how to do so.
- Finally, pay attention to your surroundings: avoid danger and reduce potential hazards. Never hesitate to ask for protection or to decline assignments that feel unsafe. Your safety comes first!

Set up goals

It makes sense to develop a personal list of good habits that will help prevent or reduce occupational risks and hazards. These habits should become professional goals. Remember that you have a professional duty to take care of yourself. As you brainstorm, it might help to list habits in three separate categories.

A first category could be made of habits that help you stay healthy in the long term. They are *preventive habits*. They do not address a specific problem that you have detected: they help you maintain the overarching goal of life/work balance and a healthy lifestyle.

A second type of habits could fall under the category of *coping techniques*. Those would be actions you could resort to *during* an interpreted encounter that is particularly stressful due to its content (traumatic material) or to the way the exchange is taking place (fast speakers, a dispute between the parties, etc.). They help you to provide an effective, professional service desp ite the challenging circumstances. They also help reduce stress over time.

A third category is the habits that can help you recover from and gain strength *after* a particular challenging assignment or set of assignments. We could call those *post-challenge routines*. They can help you build resilience for future situations of a similar kind. They can, for example, be targeted toward gaining awareness. They can help you feel better right away. They can lead to reflection about how to protect yourself during your next stressful or traumatic encounter.

The three lists offered in these boxes represent only a sample of ideas to inspire you. They are not exhaustive or specific to you. When you come up with your own list, set the three sample lists here aside. What works for *you*? What would help *you* the most? How exactly would *you* do it? When? How often? How could you measure the effectiveness or the result? Be specific and revisit your list often. Consider incorporating some of the elements of the list into your calendar and keeping the rest of them on a list that you can carry with you.

Self Care Plan Checklist

DEVELOPING PREVENTIVE HABITS

- ❑ Incorporate exercise in your routine.
- ❑ Eat healthy.
- ❑ Make sure to rest well and enough.
- ❑ Exercise regularly.
- ❑ Sleep enough.
- ❑ Develop awareness/mindfulness.
- ❑ Assess your workload.
- ❑ Find sources to improve job skills.
- ❑ Warm up/stretch.
- ❑ Leave time for hobbies, leisure activities, family and friends..
- ❑ Drink a lot of water.

COPING WITH A DIFFICULT SITUATION

- ❑ Apply deep breathing exercises in moments of stress.
- ❑ Apply mindfulness (internal check).
- ❑ Take a small break (use the restroom, drink some water).
- ❑ Stretch between assignments.
- ❑ Develop boundary-setting mechanisms (like using indirect speech as an exemption measure).

RECOVERING FROM A DIFFICULT SITUATION

- ❑ Ask for a debrief session with the service provider.
- ❑ Find social support.
- ❑ Write about the event that caused stress.
- ❑ Connect with colleagues for peer consulta-tion/vent feelings
- ❑ Do not hesitate to contact a professional counselor!

Find Support

Find support

There are many ways in which organizational support is important for interpreter health and well-being. They are often not yet common practice. You may need to advocate for yourself and the profession. Here are some examples:

> *I too had similar esperience [sic] after interpreting in a highly charge [sic] atmosphere for a patient suffering with terminal cancer. After the interpretation I felt taken over by a range of emotional states and as the assignment was over a certain period of time I felt I was not able to cope and nearly quit but then slowly I adjusted to the situation.*
>
> *However everytime [sic] at the end of the session I felt very abandoned with my strong feeling going all over the place and once at the Hospital I asked if they have a councelor [sic] I could talk to. They hadn't. [...] a debrief of any kind should take place after the session is over.*
>
> Commentary by Ravagni (2012)

- Your employer should give you information about the encounter ahead of time. You saw in Chapter 2 that this information is crucial to help you do research, look up terminology and prepare for the encounter. It is also crucial to prepare yourself emotionally, especially if you expect the session to be a difficult one. You also have the right—even the duty—to decline an assignment if it could be traumatic or too stressful, or if you will be too tired, or the assignment exceeds your skill level or goes outside your scope of practice.
- Debriefing difficult cases can be an especially effective measure to prevent compassion fatigue and vicarious trauma. The institutions or language services you work with/for should take that into account and ideally provide opportunities for a debrief with the interpreter.
- The organizations providing services for end users, the agencies that contract interpreters, and professional interpreter associations should ideally offer, publicize, financially support or make available training opportunities for interpreters. Research shows that offering professional development opportunities is a protective factor against stress-related work illnesses (Mathieu, 2007). If you interpret often in contexts that expose you to traumatic material, it is important to have specialized training about how to interpret for trauma survivors. If you interpret often for children, programs in pediatric interpreting would be valuable. Continuing education can help you learn specialized techniques and expand your terminology; it will also help to keep you feeling motivated and connected to your work and to the profession.

In a young profession like community interpreting, support can be hard to find. Many interpreters feel isolated and alone. Connect with interpreters from other geographical areas over the Internet; or set up your own professional association with your peers. Think about it this way: taking any initiative like these gives you a sense of control. Just feeling in control helps you overcome work stress (see the demand/control model).

Peer Support

Anderson (2012, p. 12) noted that the use of peer support (individually or in groups) is not a widespread practice. Anderson also reminds us that Dean and Pollard (2009) are right to recommend that "talking about one's work for the express purpose of professional development and work improvement clearly is consistent with the highest ethical standards" (p. 28).

Vicarious healing can happen too!

The flipside of vicarious trauma is vicarious healing. The official name for this effect is "vicarious post-traumatic growth." A study based on the experience of eight interpreters who had been working in mental health settings for three to eight years suggests that the typical approach to vicarious trauma may be incomplete because it does not account for the beneficial aspects of witnessing healing from trauma (Splevins, Cohen, Joseph, Murray, & Bowley, 2010).

> *I feel like I know more about this world. I know how people are feeling. It's very helpful. I feel it's very good. It helps me, it helps my feelings, and it helps my community...What I love the most is to help people open their feelings. When I translate for people who are experiencing hardship, I feel like I learn about that. It helps me understand how I can be better, how I can help my family, how to talk to my family. I don't think, as I used to, that 'these people are out of their minds'. I have new skills and I am a better person.*
>
> Interpreter testimony adapted from Lor, 2012, p. 22

While some suffering is unavoidable for those who witness trauma, the authors say, when the necessary coping mechanisms are in place, exposure to other people's healing processes can result in the interpreter's personal growth. Here are some of the study results that emerged from interviewing the interpreters:

1. Seeing the progression of service users over time is rewarding.
2. Witnessing other people's therapeutic sessions is therapeutic for the interpreter, who learns new approaches to life, and who also witnesses the revitalization that can happen among those who have endured extreme suffering (one interpreter said it felt like "free therapy").
3. Feeling distress is perceived by some interpreters as a necessary process both to be empathetic enough to do a good job as an interpreter and to vicariously feel the transformative process and its benefits as an individual.

According to the authors of this study, overall "there was a sense of feeling 'wiser,' 'richer,' or 'deeper.' These are all qualities that the interpreters felt made them 'better' people." (Splevins et al., 2010, p. 1711).

Interpreter's high

Vicarious healing is not the only good news. A related feeling could be called "interpreter's high." It refers to the feeling of accomplishment that many interpreters feel when they sense the difference they make in the lives of real people.

Watching and recognizing the positive impact you have is extremely important for your health. Be aware when service users and service providers thank you. Listen when they compliment your work and tell you things like, "I don't know what I would have done without you." Take the time to appreciate when something positive happens. Perhaps death is averted by a timely diagnosis. Someone's house is saved from burning down. A family gets reunited because of a successful asylum application. At times like that your contributions are very clear. Community interpreting can be an extremely rewarding profession.

Let's Practice

Learning Activity 5.5 (a): Delivering Rough News: A Role Play
Learning Activity 5.5 (b): The Interpreter's Self Care Quiz
Learning Activity 5.5 (c): Your Self-Care Plan

In *The Community Interpreter®: An International Workbook of Activities and Role Plays*

REVIEW OF SECTION 5.5

In this section you explored many of the occupational risks and hazards for community interpreters. Some of these are related to stress alone. Others arise because it can be hard to maintain professional boundaries and not feel too much empathy (which is typical in the helping professions). Still others affect your body or are related to a particular service setting. In some other cases (hopefully rare), you could face danger. These are the kinds of occupational hazards that we looked into in this section: stress; burnout; compassion fatigue; vicarious trauma; physical strain and environmental dangers.

Whichever the type of risks or hazards, being aware of them is the most important strategy for protecting yourself. Another important aspect is having a good life-work balance. Remember: it is a professional responsibility to maintain health. A highly professional interpreter is a healthy professional.

This section ended with some suggestions on how to establish a self care plan for yourself and with some ideas about the importance of systemic support and the secondary (positive!) effects of being exposed to other people's recovery and healing. With the right system in place, and a good self care plan, community interpreting can be a wonderful profession!

5.6 Professional Development and Continuing Education

Overview

Whether you are new to the profession or an experienced interpreter, your professional skills constantly evolve. There is always room for new knowledge. In community interpreting the unexpected is the routine. That unexpectedness is a source of motivation: you can always encounter new terms you didn't expect, a crisis you've never seen, a rare setting or a conflict. Without motivation and enthusiasm, it is hard to do a good job, so if you ever feel like nothing can be improved and your tasks are routine, easy or boring, it is time to revisit what you do. Interpreters can always set up new challenges for themselves! Lifelong learning is actually a key part of interpreting.

The reason why lifelong learning is a key part of interpreting is twofold. First, being exposed to a variety of new situations with every assignment gives you the chance to always keep learning new things. Learning is inherent to interpreting. But, second, as a professional interpreter you also need to be proactive about learning outside of interpreted encounters. You need to make sure you are well prepared for each particular assignment and you need to make sure you have the skills to address different situations.

This last section of the textbook is devoted to different aspects of lifelong professional development. It is an aspect of your career that has no "expiration date." First, you will explore reasons to take professional development seriously. Then you will examine different strategies to pursue professional development. Broadly speaking, you can either look for professional programs for continuing education or find ways to continue learning on your own. Ideally, you will do both. They are complementary approaches to lifelong learning. This section examines some of the differences between the two and the benefits of each. It closes with some tips and tools, including suggestions on how to create a personal plan for professional development.

Learning Objective 5.6

After completing this section, you will be able to:

- Create a professional development plan that supports high professional standards for community interpreting.

Why you should be proactive about your professional development

Professional development is a requirement in nearly any profession. It addresses your ability to keep learning and improving through practice, study and continuing education. Many community interpreters fail to see why they should invest time and money in professional development. It is a professional responsibility of the community interpreter because it is the only way to achieve the highest performance levels.

Of course, lifelong learning in the interpreting profession is bound to happen: the more you interpret, the better you get at it. Yes. But professional development is also something to strive for. Most community interpreters need to improve the following skills urgently: memory skills, note-taking techniques, simultaneous interpreting, sight translation, technology-related skills and specialized knowledge of key areas (such as advanced medical interpreting or interpreting for call centers, trauma survivors, children, community conferences or law enforcement, coping skills, etc.).

When you encounter a new word in pediatrics, you can either be content with learning something new or take action: once you are home, you could enter the word into a glossary you keep for that medical specialty, look up its official definitions, find out what synonyms exist and study related terminology and equivalents in your working languages. The difference between the first approach and the second is that the first approach is *passive* and the other is *proactive.* Proactive professional development makes sense for obvious reasons and for reasons that are less obvious.

Here is the obvious reason: the more you learn and practice, the more you know and the better you are at your job. It's that simple. The not-so-obvious reasons for engaging in professional development relate to the demand-control model discussed in Section 5.5. If you know that your professional "toolbox" is full of resources, you feel more prepared to face difficult circumstances. To use Karasek's terminology (1979), in a situation of "high demand" you are more capable of "high control." As a result, stress and burnout decrease. You are more likely to experience job satisfaction. As a satisfied and proud professional you are in a much better position to honor this important profession.

Some experienced professional interpreters think they have been around long enough that they don't have anything else to learn. That is a sad situation, and it calls for red flags! First, the performance standards of an unmotivated interpreter tend to be rather low. Also, unmotivated interpreters run the risk of finding themselves in the perception of a low-demand situation, which leads to job dissatisfaction.

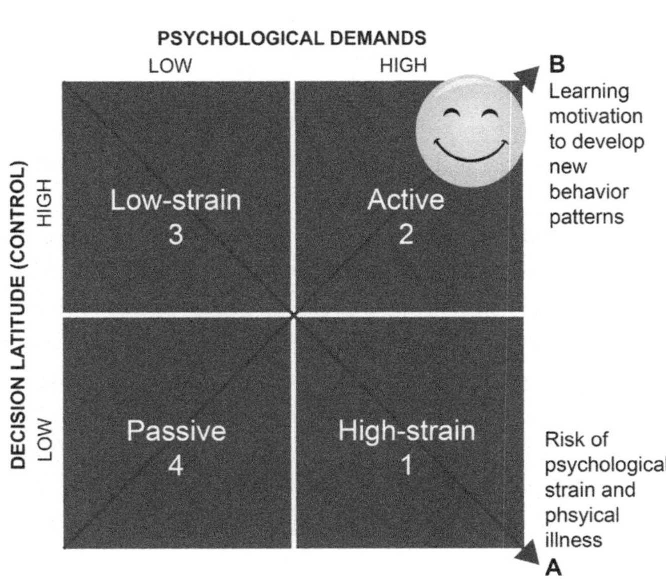

Professional development keeps you engaged, alert and alive. It also helps you remember how much your work matters. The well-being of service users is actually at stake. A motivated, focused interpreter will be a better professional than someone who is disengaged (or over-challenged).

> *No matter how good we are as interpreters, we can always learn something more: vocabulary, interpreting skills, a new way of looking at our role, trends in the field, new technologies.*
>
> Roat, 2010, p. 163

Areas of professional development

There are many areas of your professional life on which you can focus for lifelong learning. Let's brainstorm about some of them.

- **Command of working languages:** Being bilingual is considered a prerequisite for becoming an interpreter. Is full and perfect bilingualism ever possible? Some people claim it's not. They might be right. No matter how much you practice all the languages you speak, you generally have a stronger language. Also, languages are not static and they don't live in compartments. Because languages are alive, they influence each other, vary by region and evolve constantly. If you don't live in your country of origin, chances are, over time, that your proficiency of your own native language gets affected by your new language. How about regional variants? If you are a Spanish, Mandarin, Arabic or French interpreter, for example, you may face important challenges when you interpret regional variations. You cannot possibly know them all. This is to say that you cannot ever claim you know everything about all your working languages—not even your native language. Keep looking for chances to improve your proficiency in *all* your working languages.

- **Interpreting modes and techniques:** Consecutive interpreting, simultaneous interpreting and sight translation all require regular practice. If your job rarely requires you to do sight translation, it would be wise to practice at home so that you are ready and smooth when the need arises during an assignment. If you are a novice interpreter and can only interpret consecutively very short pieces of information, train your memory and your note-taking skills to be able to interpret longer and longer segments with ease. The sooner you can interpret longer messages smoothly, the less you will interrupt or annoy speakers and the more people will respect the professional quality of your services. Also, although in most circumstances, consecutive interpreting is recommended over simultaneous, simultaneous is sometimes the best option as you saw in Chapter 2. Like other modes, simultaneous requires intense training and practice. Many community interpreters lack skills in simultaneous.

- **Trends in the profession:** Community interpreting is a young profession in rapid growth. Its international relevance is growing too. This is an exciting time in history for the profession. As a member of this profession, it is important for you to know its most recent trends and innovations. An example of innovation is the role of technology in interpreting services. Some attention was devoted to that topic in Chapters 1 and 4. Following newsletters, blogs and listservs and attending professional conferences and continuing education programs (in person or online) are some of the best ways to keep knowledgeable about the current trends in the profession.

Complementary approaches to professional development

Two complementary approaches are available to community interpreters to continue learning after basic training and education, and throughout their careers. One approach is supported by external structures—continuing education programs—and the other relies on your own resources and willpower to keep learning—independent professional development.

Continuing education programs

In many countries, several professional fields offer or require continuing education. Some organizations, professional associations and government agencies make it a requirement for their employees, members or licensed professionals to take a minimum number of continuing education credits per year. As a result, "professional development" often requires taking courses to maintain a certain professional or legal status.

If you are licensed by a government or by a professional board, and you fail to meet its continuing education requirements, you may lose (depending on the country and on local requirements) your legal ability to practice that profession, e.g., medicine or law. Similarly, if you obtain certification as an interpreter and you fail to maintain your continuing education requirement, you could lose your certification. (For a discussion of the differences between certification, licensing and other professional credentials, see Chapter 1.)

Independent professional development

Independent professional development does not depend on formal programs. One could argue that independent development is actually more important than attending formal courses. In a young profession like community interpreting, you might have few opportunities to study all aspects of your fields of specialization. You will need to identify your own needs for learning and make them happen. In other words, you need to be proactive.

Researching and creating your own specialized glossaries is just one example. Identifying an area, such as domestic violence, that you want more knowledge about and finding a book, documentary, e-learning course or local conference on that topic is another example. You will need to make a commitment to monitor your own professional practice. Chapter 1 showed you how to assess your own performance. It gave you concrete guidelines to identify areas where you need to improve. You can use that knowledge to find resources to help you. Observing other interpreters can also be inspiring. How did they become so expert? What do they do to maintain their skills? Ask them. Perhaps what works for them may work for you. Try it and find out.

Types of continuing education programs

Continuing education programs take different forms. They can be online or face-to-face. They can last from one hour to several weeks or more. They can be practical and hands on, or theory lectures. They all have in common the intent to help you develop your specialized skills, gain new knowledge and stay up-to-date on developments in your field. They usually track participant attendance and issue credits, a letter or a certificate of attendance upon completion. In some cases a test might follow the program.

Face-to-face programs

In face-to-face programs you are in a classroom with the instructor and the other participants. They may last a few hours, a few days or several weeks. Professional associations and private training agencies are the two major providers of face-to-face programs. Government agencies sometimes provide them too. Sometimes, professional conferences offer pre-conference or other workshops with continuing education credits.

Online programs

A new emerging option is online training accessible to community interpreters around the world. If the course is offered in a different language than your native language, you get extra benefits for enhancing one of your working languages while you attend the program! There are three broad categories of online programs, which we shall label here as e-learning (asynchronous), distance learning (synchronous) or a hybrid.

MOOCs

MOOCs are courses available on the Internet, typically through established universities, which offer education online for an unlimited number of people. They address a multitude of subjects.

Community interpreting requires knowledge of so many different fields that it is a good idea to consider courses that may not relate directly to interpreting but that offer you a structured way to learn about a new field of knowledge.

Coursera, Udacity, and edX are only some of the organizations that make university programs available online for free.

- **E-learning** (asynchronous) simply means the program involves a participant and a computer, usually with an Internet connection. There is no live instructor and no class where people meet online. You open the program and you work with the materials on your own. You may hear a lecture, see a video or watch a series of slides. Perhaps you will have a quiz, engaging activities and a test. You might get to watch role plays or even act them out. The program may give you assignments to complete and submit. You do all this on your own time.
- **Distance learning** (synchronous) means the session is live. It is scheduled at a certain time and there is usually a live instructor. There could be one instructor displayed to several different groups or one instructor could be speaking to any number of single participants in separate locations. This type of learning is very tiring for participants (and trainers). As a result, it tends not to last more than an hour or two at a time, unlike face-to-face training, which can last all day or many days in a row without the same level of exhaustion.
- **Hybrid programs** typically involve some e-learning (on the participant's schedule) with distance learning (on the instructor's schedule). A growing number of colleges and universities offer these hybrid programs for interpreters. Some academic programs of these kinds, particularly master's level programs, might require some face-to-face attendance in addition to the synchronous and asynchronous parts of the program.

Tips and tools for independent professional development

Independent professional development takes commitment and discipline. Here we will cover some tips for a successful lifelong learning plan. The act of writing down goals and objectives increases the likelihood they will happen. As with self care in Section 5.5, you are encouraged in this section to plan your professional development. Each year, set up goals for yourself and write down concrete ways to achieve those goals.

Set up goals

Take some time to reflect on the areas you need to prioritize. It is helpful to break your list into separate topics or areas. For example, consider a category called "events" and list those you would like to attend in the next year. Have you checked out the websites of professional associations? Keep their main events and deadlines for registration on your calendar.

You could also look at peer-support activities. You don't need to work in isolation. Peer-support activities help you feel connected to your profession and give you perspective. It is fun to learn from each other!

Some activities, however, are better achieved on your own. Personal tasks include personal study sessions and routines that can trigger reflection and self-evaluation. Remember that much of your work happens outside the assignment when you are preparing for an encounter, debriefing a recent session or building your skills for the long term.

When you put together a professional development plan, remember to: (1) Be concrete in the goals you set for yourself. (2) Break your goals into measurable and realistic objectives.

Professional development checklist

EVENTS

- ❑ Attend interpreter conferences, workshops or seminars.
- ❑ Sign up for online webinars.
- ❑ Take training course online or in person

PEER-SUPPORT ACTIVITIES

- ❑ Set up "study buddy" sessions.
- ❑ Join interpreter groups in social media.
- ❑ Subscribe to interpreter blogs and listservs.

PERSONAL TASKS

- ❑ Create specialized glossaries.
- ❑ Study the glossaries.
- ❑ Record myself and do a written self-assessment.
- ❑ Keep a journal of my professional evolution.
- ❑ Listen to the radio and read online newspapers in my different languages.

The three lists included here suggest sample items as examples to inspire you. Decide on your own lists and develop your own measurable and realistic objectives. The act of creating such personal lists to improve your performance and increase your knowledge shows you are acting as a professional.

Establish a routine

Establish a routine

It would be easy to let professional development fall through the cracks. With no deadlines for personal tasks that require a lot of self-discipline and that often provide rewards that are not immediate, it is only natural to forget these activities unless you have a clear plan and a commitment to make them part of your routine. For example, how many times a week are you going to practice your modes of interpreting? For how long each time? How many new words are you going to learn every day? Make up your mind, set realistic goals and stick to your decision! Professional development doesn't happen in a day. It yields results over time.

The 20-20-20 Routine

If you have one hour you can devote to practicing interpreting modes a couple of days a week, for example, you could practice one day and do self-assessment the second day. Split the hour in three and devote approximately 20 minutes to consecutive, 20 minutes to simultaneous interpreting and 20 minutes to sight translation. Make records of your progress as you do your self-assessment.

It is much more important to be consistent than ambitious. Put short professional development sessions in your calendar, but then stick to them. If you set yourself too high a goal and can't achieve it, you might get discouraged. Rather than aspiring to do too much, be realistic from the start. Small steps and changes of habit will take you far in the long run.

Finally, keep self care in mind (Section 5.5) when you are planning your calendar and activities: for example, you could try to add a pleasant, relaxing activity, like seeing a friend as a reward for having achieved your weekly goal of sight translation. Combining professional development with self care is the secret to success for the professional interpreter.

Find support

Find support

As you saw in Chapter 4, it is incredibly important for community interpreters to feel connected to their professional community. A community of professionals offers you a framework that makes expectations clear. Shared values and clear expectations help you avoid burnout. It is important to find ways to stay connected to other members of the profession. Let's explore what professional associations can offer (where they exist) and what other opportunities for networking and collaboration you might find.

Professional associations

Professional associations are usually nonprofit organizations that work to support the interests of the profession and the interests of the general public regarding professional services. They promote professional ethics and legitimate practice. They are made up of an elected governing body and their members. Members generally pay an annual membership fee that contributes to the running expenses of the association. The professional association offers a variety of services to members, such as access to listservs and newsletters, conferences and seminars, legal advice, business-related information, conflict arbitration with clients, networking opportunities and online directories that connect professionals with clients.

Joining a professional association is one of the best ways to continue professional development. You have access to timely information and a wealth of resources. You gain a sense of belonging. If you are lucky enough to have a relevant professional association in your region, join it! You are not only helping yourself. You are strengthening the profession—and giving the profession a chance to strengthen you.

Other networking and collaborative opportunities

If outside support is not easily available where you live, you'll need to be proactive about finding ways to connect to other community interpreters. Watch what other associations are doing (either in other fields of interpreting, or in other regions): they can inspire you. You might want to found an association for community interpreters yourself.

Connect with other community interpreters in your region and make sure to get together once in a while. Practice interpreting together. Give each other feedback on your performances. Exchange opinions on ethical challenges you face. Discuss challenging aspects of your daily work. In other words, support each other. Make sure to connect with interpreters who have just joined the profession as well. Mentor them, offer them advice and ideas. They can benefit from the framework of a professional community, and you will feel more connected too.
It is also important for you to find connections with potential clients. Having an active Web presence (e.g. a good social media profile) is an excellent way to make yourself visible to people who might potentially hire you. See Section 4.1 for details.

Build your personal collection of resources

Your personal resources can include a variety of elements. Some are tangible (actual objects, like books) and some are in electronic format. Here are a few examples: monolingual and bilingual dictionaries for all your working languages, specialized dictionaries (e.g., medical, social services, mental health), specialized glossaries, vocabulary flashcards, bookmarked Internet pages (e.g., professional associations, interpreter blogs you like to follow, online glossaries, helpful videos on how to warm up your voice) and mobile applications (e.g., anatomy apps, dictionary apps), etc.

Let's Practice

Learning Activity 5.6 (a): Elements of a Plan for Professional Development
Learning Activity 5.6 (b): My Top Three Goals

In *The Community Interpreter®: An International Workbook of Activities and Role Plays*

REVIEW OF SECTION 5.6

Every time you learn a new word, interact with an unfamiliar service or assess a professional decision you have made, you are learning and progressing. Professional development is integral to your profession. You will always keep learning… if you are up to the challenge! You can and should look for in-person or online programs to help you develop your professional skills. You will need to carefully evaluate those options. However, professional development also involves creating learning opportunities for yourself.

To engage in professional development in any meaningful way, it helps to set goals and objectives and write them down. This section has discussed some important areas of professional development for community interpreters and offered you suggestions on how to incorporate different aspects of professional development into your daily work.

Remember too that professional development is rewarding and often fun. It energizes and excites you. It reminds you what you love most about this profession. Most of all, it can help you feel connected to the larger world of the profession, so that you can see where you belong and what you bring to it. Take pride in your professional development, so that the profession can take pride in you.

CHAPTER 5 SUMMARY

Chapter 5 has addressed the question of the role of the community interpreter. The role of the community interpreter is probably the most debated issue in the field. What part should you play as a community interpreter? What part does your profession play in society? These two questions are closely related.

A clear understanding of your role as a community interpreter is fundamental. It affects almost every aspect of your work. For that reason, even if this issue is mainly addressed in-depth in Chapter 5, every previous chapter in this textbook has taught you skills, strategies, protocols and models that support one consistent vision of the role of the community interpreter. That vision is also captured in the *Ethics and Standards* document found at the beginning of this volume.

The goal of this closing chapter, then, has been to provide a rationale on *why* your role is shaped the way it is throughout the textbook (starting with the *Ethics and Standards* document) and to offer you concrete guidelines on *how* you can best act in a consistent role as a community interpreter. Chapter 5 closes the textbook leaving you with concrete elements to help answer the questions "How should I do this?" and "Why should I do it?"

You have learned that the concept of communicative autonomy is central to the *why*. As community interpreters, our special contribution to the communities we serve is to offer service users and providers the ability to be in control of, and responsible for, their own communication (regardless of language barriers). This textbook, then, has taught you patterns of professional behavior that can help you support the communicative autonomy of users and providers at every stage of the interpreted encounter.

Section 5.1, **Communicative Autonomy and the Role of the Community Interpreter**, uses the story of Monica (a fictional character) to show that although your restricted scope of intervention may feel frustrating and even counterintuitive at times, such a restricted role truly supports the goal of communicative autonomy. This section also showed how doing so is, after all, the unique contribution of your profession to society as a whole. You considered your role as a professional both at the micro level (during the interpreted encounter) and also at the macro level (the interrelationships between you, your professional body and the wider community).

Section 5.2, **Interpreting and Mediation**, helps to draw a clear picture of the profession by analyzing the differences and similarities between interpreting and mediation. Mediation is a term that can be used to mean different things. Different Venn diagrams show you that, depending on the meaning attributed to the term, mediation can be considered a part of interpreting, interpreting can be considered a part of mediation or they can be diametrically opposed types of actions. Two key takeaways from this section are that (1) mediation and interpreting often complement each other as a way to support cross-cultural communication; and (2) the difference between the two should be understood and apparent to all parties involved (the professional, interpreter or mediator, the service user and the service provider).

Section 5.3, **Advocacy and the Community Interpreter**, addressed the difficult decision that community interpreters sometimes face in their professional careers: "Should I advocate for the service user in these unfair circumstances or not?" The concrete guidelines offered to answer that question on a case-by-case basis rely strongly on the reasons why your role is restricted the way it is. A decision-making roadmap points you toward a couple of decisive questions: how serious is the risk you identified? And how imminent is that risk? If the risk is neither serious nor imminent, you should refrain from advocating. If the risk is either serious or imminent, there are thorough considerations for you to process (discussed in detail in Section 5.3) before you take any action.

Section 5.4, **Standards of Practice**, reviews the main strategies that this textbook offers you by going over each of the standards of practice in the *Ethics and Standards* document. It classifies the 41 standards into 13 general best practices. It also offers explanations of the implications of the different standards and tips on how to apply them even in adverse circumstances.

Section 5.5, **Self Care and Personal Wellness**, explores professional safety. Being aware of potential occupational hazards is critical to help you prevent them. Both stress-related and physical hazards specific to interpreting are addressed. This section also offers tips on how to develop a self care plan. Identify healthy habits that work for you and put them on your schedule. A highly professional interpreter is a healthy professional!

Section 5.6, **Professional Development and Continuing Education**, ends the chapter (and the textbook)! Every community interpreter can always keep learning. The section identifies different ways to do so and offers tips on how to develop a professional-development plan. Small but consistent tasks can make all the difference. Learning more about community interpreting is a lifelong process, and the profession itself needs you to learn more. Support the profession: support yourself. The rewards of professional development go beyond a successful career: they can bring you job satisfaction, fulfillment and a deeper sense of purpose and meaning. Enjoy the gift of professional development!

BIBLIOGRAPHY

Adams, K.B., Matto, H.C., & Harrington, D. (2001). The Traumatic Stress Institute belief scale as a measure of vicarious trauma in a national sample of clinical social workers. *Families in Society, 82*(4), 363.

AHRQ. (2012). *2012 national healthcare quality report.* Washington, District of Columbia: U.S. Department of Health and Human Services, Agency for Healthcare Research and Quality.

Ambady, N., Shih, M., Kim, A., & Pittinsky, T. (2001). Stereotype susceptibility in children: Effects of identity activation on quantitative performance. *Psychological Science, 12*(5), 385-390.

The American Institute of Stress. (n.d.). Daily Life. Retrieved from http://www.stress.org/daily-life/#sthash.Ij0dxyQd.dpuf

Anderson, A. (2012). Peer support and consultation project for interpreters: A model for supporting the well-being of interpreters who practice in mental health settings. *Journal of Interpretation, 21*(1).

Anderson, G.F., & Hussey, P.S. (2000). Population aging: A comparison among industrialized countries. *Health Affairs 19*(3), 191-203.

ASTM International. (2015). Standard practice for language interpreting.

AUSIT. (2012). *Code of ethics and code of conduct.* Melbourne: The Australian Institute of Interpreters and Translators. Retrieved from http://ausit.org/AUSIT/Documents/Code_Of_Ethics_Full.pdf

Avery, M.P.B. (2001). *The role of the healthcare interpreter: An evolving dialogue.* Washington, District of Columbia: National Council on Interpreting in Health Care.

Awh, E., Vogel, E.K., & Oh, S.-H. (2006). Interactions between attention and working memory. *Neuroscience, 139*(1), 201-208.

Azarmina, P., & Wallace, P. (2005). Remote interpretation in medical encounters: A systematic review. *Journal of Telemedicine and Telecare, 11*(3), 140-145.

Baddeley, A. (2012). Working memory: Theories, models, and controversies. *Annual Review of Psychology, 63*, 1-29.

Bambarén-Call, A., Bancroft, M.A., Goodfriend-Koven, N., Hanscom, K., Kelly, N., Lewis, V., Roat, C., Robinson, L., & Rubio-Fitzpatrick, L. (2012). *Interpreting compassion: A needs assessment report on interpreting for survivors of torture, war trauma and sexual violence.* Columbia, Maryland: The Voice of Love.

Banaji, M.R., Bazerman, M., & Chugh, D. (2003). How (Un)Ethical Are You? *Harvard Business Review, 81*, 56-64.

Bancroft, M.A. (2005). *The interpreter's world tour: An environmental scan of standards of practice for interpreters.* Menlo Park, California: The California Endowment.

Bancroft, M.A. (2013). *Cultural competence: A trainer's guide.* Columbia, Maryland: Culture & Language Press.

Bancroft, M.A. (2014). *Cultural competence in health and human services: A trainer's guide.* Columbia, Maryland:

Culture & Language Press.

Bancroft, M.A. (2015). Community interpreting: A profession rooted in social justice. In H. Mikkelson, & R. Jourdenais (Eds.). *A handbook of interpreting.* London: Routledge, 217-235.

Bancroft, M.A., & Like, R.C. (2006). *Caring with CLAS: Cultural competence in healthcare. A trainer's manual.* Thousand Oaks, California: NetworkOmni.

Bancroft, M.A., & Rubio-Fitzpatrick, L. (2011). *The community interpreter: A comprehensive training manual.* (5th ed.) Columbia, Maryland: Culture & Language Press.

Bancroft, M.A., Allen, K., Green, C., & Feuerle, L. (in press). *Breaking silence: Interpreting for victim services.* Washington, District of Columbia: Ayuda.

Bancroft, M.A., Bambarén-Call, A., Berthold, S.M., Chevalier, A., Goodfriend-Koven, N., Green, C., Hanscom, K., Kelly, N., Lewis, V., Piwowarczyk, L., Roat, C., Robinson, L., & Rubio-Fitzpatrick, L. (in press). *Healing voices: Interpreting for survivors of torture, war trauma and sexual violence.* Columbia, Maryland: The Voice of Love.

Bancroft, M.A., Olsen, B.S., & Allen, K. (2011). *Interpreting—Full speed ahead: Interpreters propel the profession toward national unity.* Monterey, California: InterpretAmerica.

Bergel, D.P. (2007). *Compassion fatigue among adult protective services social workers.* PhD dissertation. University of Maryland.

Bonta, J. (2014). No Title. StreetLeverage. Retrieved from http://www.streetleverage.com/2014/05/social-justice-an-obligation-for-sign-language-interpreters/

Bower, G.H. (1970a). Analysis of a mnemonic device: Modern psychology uncovers the powerful components of an ancient system for improving memory. *American Scientist, 58*(5), 496-510.

Bower, G.H. (1970b). Educational applications of mnemonic devices. In M. Foley, R. Lockhart, & D. Messeck (Eds.). *Contemporary Reading in Psychology.* New York: Harper & Sons.

Bower, K. (2015). Stress and burnout in Video Relay Service (VRS) interpreting. *Journal of Interpretation, 24*(1).

Braun, S. (2004). *Kommunikation unter widrigen Umständen? Fallstudien zu einsprachigen und gedolmetschten Videokonferenzen.* Tübingen: Narr.

Braun, S. (2007). Interpreting in small-group bilingual videoconferences: Challenges and adaptation processes. *Interpreting, 9*(1).

Braun, S. (2013). Keep your distance? Remote interpreting in legal proceedings: A critical assessment of a growing practice. *Interpreting, 15*(2), 200-228.

Braun, S., & Taylor, J. (Eds.). (2012). *Videoconference and remote interpreting in criminal proceedings.* Antwerp: Intersentia.

Buri, M.R. (2012). *La Comunicazione Interculturale, il ruolo dell'interprete per i servizi pubblici.* San Cesario di Lecce: Manni.

Butow, P.N., Lobb, E., Jefford, M., Goldstein, D., Eisenbruch, M., Girgis, A., King, M., Sze, M., Aldridge, L., & Schofield, P. (2012). A bridge between cultures: interpreters' perspectives of consultations with migrant oncology patients. *Support Care Cancer, 20*(2), 235-244.

Butow, P., Bell, M., Goldstein, D., Sze, M., Aldridge, L., Abdo, S., Mihaeil, M., Dong, S., Iedema, R., Ashgari, R., Hui, R., & Eisenbruch, M. (2011). Grappling with cultural differences; communication between oncologists and immigrant cancer patients with and without interpreters. *Patient Education and Counseling, 84*(3), 398-405.

Carrier, L.M., Cheever, N.A., Rosen, L.D., Benitez, S., & Chang, J. (2009). Multitasking across generations: Multitasking choices and difficulty ratings in three generations of Americans. *Computers in Human Behavior, 25*, 483-489.

Cass, A., Lowell, A., Christie, M., Snelling, P.L., Flack, M., Marrnganyin, B., & Brown, I. (2002). Sharing the true stories: Improving communication between Aboriginal patients and healthcare workers. *Medical Journal of Australia, 176,* 466-470.

Cedoline, A.J. (1982). *Job burnout in public education: Symptoms, causes, and survival skills.* New York: Teachers College Press.

Chassin, M.R., & O'Kane, M.E. (2010). The history of the quality improvement movement. *Toward improving the outcome of pregnancy III.* March of Dimes. Retrieved from http://www.marchofdimes.org/materials/toward-improving-the-outcome-of-pregnancy-iii.pdf

CHIA. (2002). *California standards for healthcare interpreters.* Sacramento, California: California Healthcare Interpreting Association. Retrieved from www.chiaonline.org/

Christoffels, I.K., & De Groot, A.M.B. (2004). Components of simultaneous interpreting: Comparing interpreting with shadowing and paraphrasing. *Bilingualism: Language and Cognition 7*(3), 227-240.

CIOL. (2007). *Code of professional conduct.* London: Chartered Institute of Linguists.

Contreras, J.M., Banaji, M.R., & Mitchell, J.M. (2011). Dissociable neural correlates of stereotypes and other forms of semantic knowledge. *Social Cognitive and Affective Neuroscience. 7*(7), 764-770.

Cornes, A., & Napier, J. (2005). Challenges of mental health interpreting when working with deaf patients. *Australasian Psychiatry, 13*(4), 403-407.

Cross, T., Bazron, B., Dennis, K., & Isaacs, M. (1989). *Towards a culturally competent system of care, Volume I.* Washington, District of Columbia: Georgetown University Child Development Center, CASSP (Child and Adolescent Service System Program) Technical Assistance Center.

Crossman, K.L., Wiener, E., Roosevelt, G., Bajaj, L., & Hampers, L.C. (2010). Interpreters: Telephonic, in-person interpretation and bilingual providers. *Pediatrics, 125*(3), 631-638.

Curlik, D.M., & Shors, T.J. (2013). Training your brain: Do mental and physical (MAP) training enhance cognition through the process of neurogenesis in the hippocampus? *Neuropharmacology, 64*, 506-514.

Dang, J., Lee, J., Tran, J.H., Kagawa-Singer, M., Foo, M.A., Nguyen, T.U., Valdez-Dadia, A., Thomson, J., & Tanjasiri, S.P. (2010). The role of medical interpretation on breast and cervical cancer screening among Asian American and Pacific Islander women. *Journal of Cancer Education, 25*(2), 253-62.

Dean, R.K., & Pollard, R.Q. (2001). Application of demand-control theory to sign language interpreting: implications for stress and interpreter training. *Journal of Deaf Studies and Deaf Education, 6*(1), 1-14.

Dean, R.K., & Pollard, R.Q. (2009). Effectiveness of observation-supervision training in community mental health interpreting settings. *Redit: Revista Electrónica de Didáctica de La Traducción Y La Interpretación*, 1-17.

Dean, R.K., & Pollard, R.Q. (2013). *The demand control schema: Interpreting as a practice profession.* CreateSpace Independent Publishing Platform.

Dean, R.K., Pollard, R.Q., & Samar, V.J. (2010). RID research grant underscores occupational health risks : VRS and K-12 settings most concerning. *VIEWS*, *27*(1), 41-43.

A declaration on the promotion of patients' rights in Europe. (1994). Retrieved from http://www.who.int/genomics/public/eu_declaration1994.pdf

Dovidio, J.F., & Fiske, S.T. (2012). Under the radar: how unexamined biases in decision-making processes in clinical interactions can contribute to health care disparities. *American Journal of Public Health*, *102*(5), 945-952.

Dovidio, J.F., & Gaertner, S.L. (2004). Aversive racism. In M.P. Zanna (Ed.). *Advances in experimental social psychology* (Vol. 36, 1-51). San Diego, California: Academic Press.

Du Plessis, T. (2012). A language act for South Africa? The role of sociolinguistic principles in the analysis of language legislation. In C. Brohy, T. du Plessis, J.-G. Turi, & J. Woehrling (Eds.). *Law, language and the multilingual state: Proceedings of the 12th international conference of the International Academy of Linguistic Law.* Bloemfontein, South Africa: University of the Free State, 195-214.

Du Plessis, T., & Verhoef, M. (Eds.). (2008). *Multilingualism and educational interpreting: Innovation and delivery.* Hatfield, South Africa: Van Shaik Publishers.

Dysart-Gale, D. (2007). Clinicians and medical interpreters: Negotiating culturally appropriate care for patients with limited English ability. *Family and Community Health*, *30*(3), 237-246.

Elderkin-Thompson, V., Cohen Silver, R., & Waitzkin, H. (2001). When nurses double as interpreters: A study of Spanish-speaking patients in a US primary care setting. *Social Science & Medicine, 52*, 1343-1358.

Ellis, B., MacDonald, H., Lincoln, A., & Cabral, H. (2008). Mental health of Somali adolescent refugees: The role of trauma, stress, and perceived discrimination. *Journal of Consulting and Clinical Psychology*, *76*(2), 184-193.

ENPSIT. (n.d.). *Constitution.* Brussels: European Network for Public Service Interpreting and Translation.

Epstein, A. (1978). *Ethos and identity: Three studies in ethnicity.* London: Tavistock Publications.

Erasmus, M. (2000). "Community interpreting" in South Africa. Current trends and future prospects. In R. P Roberts, S. Carr, D. Abraham, & E. Dufour (Eds.). *The Critical Link 2: Interpreters in the Community. Selected papers from the Second International Conference on interpreting in legal, health, and social service settings, Vancouver, British Columbia, Canada, 19-23 May, 1998* (191-206). Philadelphia, Pennsylvania: John Benjamins.

Ertl, A., & Pöllabauer, S. (2010). Training (medical) interpreters—The key to good practice. *The Journal of Specialised Translation, 14*, 165-193.

Figley, C.R. (Ed.). (1995). *Compassion fatigue: Coping with secondary traumatic stress disorder in those who treat the traumatized.* New York: Routledge.

Flores, G. (2005). The impact of medical interpreter services on the quality of health care: A systematic review. *Medical Care Research and Review, 62*(3), 255-299.

Fougnie, D., & Marois, R. (2009). Dual-task interference in visual working memory: A limitation in storage capacity but not in encoding or retrieval. *Attention, Perception & Psychophysics, 71*(8), 1831-1841.

Framer, I., Bancroft, M.A., Feuerle, L., & Bruggeman, J. (2010). *The language of justice: Interpreting for legal services.* Washington, District of Columbia: Ayuda.

García-Beyaert, S., Bancroft, M.A., Allen, K., Carriero-Contreras, G., & Socarrás-Estrada, D. (2015). Ethics and Standards for *The Community Interpreter®:* An International Training Tool. Columbia, Maryland: Culture & Language Press.

Gile, D. (1999). Testing the effort models' tightrope hypothesis in SI—A contribution. *Hermes Journal of Linguistics, 23*, 153.

Gile, D. (2009). *Basic concepts and models for interpreters and translators training.* (Rev. ed.). Philadelphia, Pennsylvania: John Benjamins.

Golash-Boza, T., & Menjivar, C. (2012). Causes and consequences of international migration: Sociological evidence for the right to mobility. *The International Journal of Human Rights, 16*(8), 1213-1227.

Gonzalez, R.D., Vasquez, V.F., & Mikkelson, H. (2012). *Fundamentals of court interpretation: Theory, policy and practice, 2nd ed.* Durham, North Carolina: Carolina Academic Press.

Graham, A.M. (2012). *Training provision for public service interpreting and translation in England.* Southampton, United Kingdom: Routes into Languages.

Graham, E., Jacobs, T.A., Kwan-Gett, T.S., & Cover, J. (2007). Health services utilization by low-income limited English proficient adults. *Journal of Immigrant Minority Health, 10*(3), 207-217.

Greenhalgh, T., Robb, N., & Scambler, G. (2006). Communicative and strategic action in interpreted consultations in primary health care: A Habermasian perspective. *Social Science & Medicine, 63*(5), 1170-1187.

Gulati, S., Watt, L., Shaw, N., Sung, L., Poureslami, I.M., Klaasen, R., Dix, D., & Klassen, A.F. (2012). Communication and language challenges experienced by Chinese and South Asian immigrant parents of children with cancer in Canada: Implications for health services delivery. *Pediatric Blood & Cancer, 58*(4), 572-578.

Gupta, R., Koscik, T.R., Bechara, A., & Tranel, D. (2011). The amygdala and decision-making. *Neuropsychologia, 49*(4), 760-766.

Hadziabdic, E., Albin, B., & Hjelm, K. (2014). Arabic-speaking migrants' attitudes, opinions, preferences and past experiences concerning the use of interpreters in healthcare: A postal cross-sectional survey. *BMC* [BioMedCentral] *Research Notes, 7,* 71.

Hale, S.B. (2007). *Community Interpreting.* Basingstoke: Palgrave Macmillan.

Hall, C.J., Smith, P.H., & Wicaksono, R. (2011). *Mapping applied linguistics: A guide for students and practitioners.* New York: Routledge.

Hardin, C.D. & Banaji, M.R. (2012). The nature of implicit prejudice: Implications for personal and public policy. In E. Shafir (Ed.). *The Behavioral Foundations of Public Policy*. Princeton, New Jersey: Princeton University Press, 13-31.

Harris, B. (2010). Unprofessional translation: Earliest depiction of an interpreter. Retrieved from http://unprofessionaltranslation.blogspot.com/2010/07/earliest-depiction-of-interpreter.html

Heimerl-Moggan, K., & John, V.I. (2007). *Note-taking for public service interpreters*. Timperley: Interp-Right Training Consultancy.

Hein, A. (2009). Interpreter education in Sweden: A uniform approach to spoken and signed language interpreting. In J. Napier (Ed.). *International perspectives on sign language interpreter education*. Washington, District of Columbia: Gallaudet University Press, 124-145.

HIN. (2007). *National standards guide for community interpreting services*. Toronto: Healthcare Interpretation Network.

Hoffrage, U., & Reimer, T. (2004). Models of bounded rationality: The approach of fast and frugal heuristics. *Management Review*, *15*(4), 437-459.

Hudelson, P. (2005). Improving patient–provider communication: insights from interpreters. *Family Practice, 22*(3), 311-316.

ISO. (2014). ISO 13611 *Interpreting: Guidelines for community interpreting*. Geneva: International Organization for Standardization.

ISO/IEC. (2004). ISO/IEC 17000 *Conformity assessment—Vocabulary and general principles*. Geneva: International Organization for Standardization.

ITI. (2013). *Code of professional conduct*. Milton Keynes, United Kingdom: Institute of Translation and Interpreting.

Jamieson, J.P., Mendes, W.B., & Nock, M.K. (2013). Improving acute stress responses: The power of reappraisal. *Current Directions in Psychological Science*, *22*(1), 51-56.

Jiahong, Y., Liberman, M., & Cieri, C. (2006). Towards an integrated understanding of speaking rate in conversation. In *INTERSPEECH 2006 and 9th International Conference on Spoken Language Processing* (Vol. 2, 541-544). Red Hook, New York: International Speech Communication Association (ISCA).

Jones, G. (2012). Why chunking should be considered as an explanation for developmental change before short-term memory capacity and processing speed. *Frontiers in Psychology*, *3*, 167.

Karasek, R.R.A. (1979). Job demands, job decision latitude, and mental strain: Implications for job redesign. *Administrative Science Quarterly*, *24*(2), 285-308.

Karliner, L.S., Jacobs, E.A., Chen, A.H., & Mutha, S. (2007). Do professional interpreters improve clinical care for patients with limited English proficiency? A systematic review of the literature. *Health Services Research*, *42*, 727-753.

Kaufert, J.M., & Koolage, W.W. (1984). Role conflict among "culture brokers": The experience of native Canadian medical interpreters. *Social Science & Medicine*, *18*(3), 283-286.

Kelly, N. (2008a). A license to interpret. *ATA Chronicle, 37*, 24-32.

Kelly, N. (2008b). *Telephone interpreting: A comprehensive guide to the profession.* Victoria, British Columbia: Trafford.

Laws, M.B., Heckscher, R., Mayo, S.J., Li, W., & Wilson, I.B. (2004). A new method for evaluating the quality of medical interpretation. *Medical Care, 42*(1), 71-80.

Leanza, Y. (2005). Roles of community interpreters in pediatrics as seen by interpreters, physicians and researchers. *Interpreting, 7*(2), 167-192.

Lindenberger, U., Kliegl, R., & Baltes, P.B. (1992). Professional expertise does not eliminate age differences in imagery-based memory performance during adulthood. *Psychology and Aging, 7*(4), 585-593.

Llewellyn-Jones, P., & Lee, R.G. (2009). The "role" of the community/public service interpreter. Supporting Deaf people, online conference. Retrieved from http://core.kmi.open.ac.uk/download/pdf/9632182

Llewellyn-Jones, P., & Lee, R.G. (2012). Deconstructing and reconstructing role: Towards a new paradigm. European Students of Sign Language Interpreting Conference University of Applied Sciences, Zwickau, Germany, 18 May 2012. Retrieved from http://whz-cms-10.zw.fh-zwickau.de/els100oh/Keynote_speakers.pdf

Lor, M. (2012). *Effects of client trauma on interpreters: An exploratory study of vicarious trauma.* Master of social work clinical research paper. St. Catherine University, University of St. Thomas.

Lyneham, J., Parkinson, C., & Denholm, C. (2008). Explicating Benner's concept of expert practice: Intuition in emergency nursing. *Journal of Advanced Nursing, 64*, 380-387.

MacFarlane, A., Dzebisova, Z., Karapish, D., Kovacevic, B., Ogbebor, F., Okonkwo, E. (2009). Arranging and negotiating the use of informal interpreters in general practice consultations: Experiences of refugees and asylum seekers in the west of Ireland. *Social Science & Medicine, 69*(2), 210-214.

Mahajan, N., Martinez, M.A., Gutierrez, N.L., Diesendruck, G., Banaji, M.R., & Santos, L.R. (2011). The evolution of intergroup bias: Perceptions and attitudes in rhesus macaques. *Journal of Personality and Social Psychology, 100,* 387-405.

Martín, M.C., & Phelan, M. (2009). Interpreters and cultural mediations—Different but complementary roles. *Translocations: Migration and Social Change.* Retrieved from http://www.academia.edu/250428/Interpreters_and_Cultural_Mediators_-_different_but_complementary_roles

Maslach, C., Schaufeli, W.B., & Leiter, M.P. (2001). Job burnout. *Annual Review of Physiology*, 52, 397-422.

Mathieu, F. (2007). Running on empty: Compassion fatigue in health professionals. *Rehab & Community Care Medicine*, 8-10.

McGonigal, K. (2015). *The upside of stress: Why stress is good for you, and how to get good at it.* New York: Penguin Random House.

Merlini, R. (2009). Seeking asylum and seeking identity in a mediated encounter: The projection of selves through discursive practices. *Interpreting, 11*(1), 57-92.

Meyer, B. (1998). Interpreter-mediated doctor-patient communication: The performance of non-trained community interpreters. Paper presented at The Critical Link 2: Interpreters in the Community, Vancouver, Canada. Retrieved from http://criticallink.org/conferences/conference-papers/critical-link-2

Mikkelson, H. (1996). Community interpreting: An emerging profession. *Interpreting: International Journal of Research and Practice in Interpreting, 1*(1), 125-129.

Miller, G.A. (1956). The magical number seven. *The Psychological Review, 63*, 81-97

MMIA. (1995). *Medical interpreting standards of practice.* Boston: Massachusetts Medical Interpreters Association (now the International Medical Interpreters Association).

Moeketsi, R.H. (2003). Redefining the role of the South African court interpreter. *Proteus, 8*(3-4).

Moody, B. (2011). What is faithful interpretation? *Journal of Interpretation, 21*(1), 37-51.

Morris, R. (1993). The interlingual interpreter—Cypher or intelligent participant? *International Journal for the Semiotics of Law, 6*(18), 271-291.

Moscoso del Prado, M.F. (2009). The thermodynamics of human reaction times. Retrieved from http://arxiv.org/pdf/0908.3170.pdf

Moser-Mercer, B. (2003). Remote interpreting: Assessment of human factors and performance parameters. Retrieved from http://www.aiic.net/

Moser-Mercer, B. (2005). Remote interpreting: Issues of multi-sensory integration in a multilingual task. *Meta, 50*(2), 727-738.

Moser-Mercer, B., Künzli, A., & Korac, M. (1998). Prolonged turns in interpreting: Effects on quality, physiological and psychological stress (pilot study). *Interpreting, 3*(1), 47-64.

Mouzourakis, P. (2006). Remote interpreting: A technical perspective on recent experiments. *Interpreting, 8*(1), 45-66.

NAJIT. (2005). *Summary interpreting in legal settings.* Washington, District of Columbia:. National Association of Judiciary Interpreters & Translators.

NAJIT. (2006). *Modes of interpreting.* Washington, District of Columbia: National Association of Judiciary Interpreters & Translators.

NCIHC. (2003). *Guide to interpreter positioning in healthcare settings.* The National Council on Interpreting in Health Care Working Paper Series. Washington, District of Columbia: National Council on Interpreting in Health Care.

NCIHC. (2004). *A national code of ethics for interpreters in health care.* Washington, District of Columbia: National Council on Interpreting in Health Care.

NCIHC. (2005). *National standards of practice for interpreters in health care.* Washington, District of Columbia: National Council on Interpreting in Health Care.

NCIHC. (2011). *National standards for healthcare interpreter training programs.* Washington, District of Columbia: National Council on Interpreting in Health Care.

Niska, H. (2004). *Community interpreting in Sweden.* Retrieved from http://www.docstoc.com/docs/50666212/COMMUNITY-INTERPRETING-IN-SWEDEN

Norris, W.M., Wenrich, M.D., Nielsen, E.L., Treeze, P.D., Jackson, J.C., & Curtis, J.R. (2005). Communication about end-of-life care between language-discordant patients and clinicians: Insights from medical interpreters. *Journal of Palliative Medicine, 8*(5), 1016-24.

Packard, M.G. (2009). Anxiety, cognition, and habit: A multiple memory systems perspective. *Brain Research, 1293*, 121-128.

Pandya, C., Batalova, J., & McHugh, M. (2011). *Limited English proficient individuals in the United States: Number, share, growth, and linguistic diversity.* Washington, District of Columbia: Migration Policy Institute.

Pew Forum on Religion & Public Life. (2012). *The global religious landscape: A report on the size and distribution of the world's major religious groups as of 2010.* Washington, District of Columbia: Pew Research Center.

Pielmeier, H., & DePalma, D.A. (2015). *The state of the interpreting market.* Cambridge, Massachusetts: Common Sense Advisory.

Pöchhacker, F. (1999). "Getting organized": The evolution of community interpreting. *Interpreting, 4*(1), 125-410.

Pöchhacker, F. (2004) *Introducing interpreting studies.* New York: Routledge.

Pöchhacker, F. (2004). Critical linking up: Kinship and convergence in interpreting studies. In C. Wadensjö, B.E. Dmitrova, & A-L. Nillson (Eds.). *The critical link 4: Professionalization of interpreting in the community.* Philadelphia, Pennsylvania: John Benjamins, 11-23.

Pöllabauer, S. (2012). Community interpreting. *The encyclopedia of applied linguistics*. Hoboken, New Jersey: Blackwell Publishing Ltd.

Ra, S., & Napier, J. (2013). Community interpreting: Asian language interpreters' perspectives. *The International Journal of Translation and Interpreting Research, 5*(2), 45-61.

Ratha, D. (2013). *The impact of remittances on economic growth and poverty reduction.* Washington, District of Columbia: Migration Policy Institute.

Ravagni, G. (2012). Vicarious trauma in interpreting. Retrieved from http://www.expresslanguagesolutions.com/blog/2012/07/vicarious-trauma-in-interpreting/

Rheingold, H. (2000). *They have a word for it: A light-hearted lexicon of untranslatable words and phrases.* St. Paul, Minnesota: Consortium Books.

RID. (2000). *Interpreting in religious settings*, standard practice paper. Alexandria, Virginia: The Registry of Interpreters for the Deaf.

RID. (2010). *An overview of K-12 educational interpreting*, standard practice paper. Alexandria, Virginia: The Registry of Interpreters for the Deaf.

Roat, C. (2006). *Certification of health care interpreters in the United States: A primer, a status report and consideration for national certification.* Menlo Park, California: The California Endowment.

Roat, C.E. (2010). *Healthcare interpreting in small bites.* Victoria, British Columbia: Trafford Publishing.

Robb, N., & Greenhalgh, T. (2006). "You have to cover up the words of the doctor": The mediation of trust in interpreted consultations in primary care. *Journal of Health, Organisation and Management, 20*(5), 434-55.

Robert Wood Johnson Foundation. (2013). Quality/Equality Glossary. Retrieved from http://www.rwjf.org/en/library/research/2013/04/quality-equality-glossary.html

Rozan, J.F. (1956/2005). *Note-taking in Consecutive Interpreting.* Cracow: Tertium.

Roziner, I., & Shlesinger, M. (2010). Much ado about something remote: Stress and performance in remote interpreting. *Interpreting, 12*(2), 214-247.

Rudvin, M. (2006). Issues of culture and language in the training of language mediators for public services in Bologna: Matching market needs and training. In D. Londei, D.R. Miller, & P. Puccini (Eds.). *Insegnare le lingue/culture oggi: Il contributo dell'interdisciplinarità*. Bologna: Asterisco, 57-72.

Rudvin, M., & Tomassini, E. (2011). *Interpreting in the community and workplace.* Basingstoke: Palgrave Macmillan.

Sauvêtre, M. (2002). L'interprète en milieu social en Europe. *Ecarts d'identité, 99,* 48-53.

Schlesinger, M. (1994). Intonation in the production of and perception of simultaneous interpretation. In S. Lambert, & B. Moser-Mercer (Eds.). *Bridging the gap: Empirical research in simultaneous interpretation.* Philadelphia, Pennsylvania: John Benjamins, 225-236.

Schuster, M. (2013). From chaos to cultural competence. In C. Schäffner, K. Kredens, & Y. Fowler (Eds.). *Interpreting in a changing landscape.* Selected papers from *Critical Link 6*, 61-82.

Seidelman, R.D., & Bachner, Y.G. (2010). That I won't translate! Experiences of a family medical interpreter in a multicultural environment. *Mount Sinai Journal of Medicine, 77*(4), 389-393.

Sentell, T., Shumway, M., & Snowden, L. (2007). Access to mental health treatment by English language proficiency and race/ethnicity. *Journal of General Internal Medicine*, *22*(Suppl. 2), 289-293.

Shah, M., & Zaman, W. (2012). *Introduction to mental health for community interpreters.* London: Lulu.com.

Shepard, R. (1990). *Mind sights: Original visual illusions, ambiguities, and other anomalies.* New York, New York: W.H. Freeman.

Smedley, B.D., Stith, A.Y., & Nelson, A.R. (2002). *Unequal treatment: Confronting racial and ethnic disparities in health care. Institute of Medicine Report.* Washington, District of Columbia: National Academy Press.

Splevins, K.A., Cohen, K., Joseph, S., Murray, C., & Bowley, J. (2010). Vicarious posttraumatic growth among interpreters. *Qualitative Health Research, 22,* 250-262.

Stanley, D.A., Sokol-Hessner, P., Fareri, D.S., Perino, M.T., Delgado, M.R., Banaji, M.R., & Phelps, E.A. (2012). Race and reputation: perceived racial group trustworthiness influences the neural correlates of trust decisions. *Philosophical Transactions of the Royal Society, B,* 367.

Stoljar, N. (2013). Feminist perspectives on autonomy. *The Stanford Encyclopedia of Philosophy.*

Swift, O.B. (2012). *The role of sign language interpreters in post-secondary settings in South Africa.*

Master's dissertation, University of South Africa. Retrieved from http://uir.unisa.ac.za/bitstream/handle/10500/6302/dissertation_swift_o.pdf?sequence=

Tiayon, C. (2005). Community interpreting: An African perspective. *Hermēneus. Revista de Traducción e Interpretación,* 7. Retrieved from http://www.google.com/url?sa=t&rct=j&q=&esrc=s&source=web&cd=17&ved=0CEoQFjAGOAo&url=http%3A%2F%2Fdialnet.unirioja.es%2Fdescarga%2Farticulo%2F1293379.pdf&ei=5ET1UZ-JGri64APftICoBg&usg=AFQjCNFshNNjJpt06s0uoovflN6d9ClFaA&bvm=bv.49784469,d.dm

Toledano Buendía, C. (2010). Community interpreting: Breaking with the "norm" through normalization. *Journal of Specialized Translation, 14*, 11-12.

Transkom. (n.d.). *Comparative study on language and culture mediation in different European countries.* Retrieved from http://www.saludycultura.uji.es/archivos/Transkom.pdf

Tusting, K., & Barton, D. (2003). *Models of adult learning: A literature review.* London: National Research and Development Centre for Adult Literacy and Numeracy.

Unsworth, N., & Spillers, G.J. (2010). Working memory capacity: Attention control, secondary memory, or both? A direct test of the dual-component model. *Journal of Memory and Language*, *62*(4), 392-406.

Vargas Urpi, M. (2012). State of the art in community interpreting research: Mapping the main research topics. *Babel, 58*(1) 50-72.

Wande, E. (1994). Translating machine or creator? On Finnish-Swedish community interpreting in Sweden. *Hermes, 12*, 109-126.

Weast, R.A., & Neiman, N.G. (2010). The effect of cognitive load and meaning on selective attention. In *32nd Annual meeting of the Cognitive Science Society CogSci, 2010* (Vol. 1, 1477-1482. Red Hook, New York: Curran Associates.

West, R.F., Meserve, R.J., & Stankovich, K.E. (2012). Cognitive sophistication does not attenuate the bias blind spot. *Journal of Personal Social Psychology, 103*(3), 506-19.

WHO. (1994). *Declaration on the Promotion of Patients' Rights in Europe*. Geneva: World Health Organization.

Wolf, O.T. (2009). Stress and memory in humans: Twelve years of progress? *Brain Research*, *1293*, 142-154.

Zhang, M. (2012). The study of note-taking and memory in consecutive interpretation. *Lecture Notes in Information Technology, 16-17,* 178-184.

Zimányi, K. (2009). *What's the story: A narrative overview of community interpreting in mental health care in Ireland.* PhD dissertation, Dublin City University. Retrieved from <http://doras.dcu.ie/15057/1/ZimanyiPhD.pdf>